T. S. Allen
11 Victoria Mews
Magdalen Road
Earlsfield
London SW18 3PY
(020-8879-4097)

THE SHAPING SEASON

An Author's Autobiography

Childhood and Schooldays

Norman Longmate

'This was my shaping season'
Henry Vaughan

Fairford Press
2000

© Norman Longmate 2000

The right of Norman Longmate to be identified as the author of this work has been asserted by Norman Longmate in accordance with the Copyright, Designs and Patents Act, 1988.

This edition first published in 2000 by
Fairford Press
58 Ashcroft Road,
Cirencester,
GL1 QX, UK.

Tel/Fax +44 (0) 1 451 861464
PO Box 323, Eliot ME 03903-0323, USA
Tel/Fax: (1) 207 459 5932

All the editorial work and some of the administration of the Fairford Press are carried out in the United States, the rest in the United Kingdom. Correspondence and other communications may be addressed to either office, as above or as follows:
e-mail: anharr@cybertours.com
web-site: www.fairfordpress.com
To order by e-mail, click on e-mail address shown above.

A cataloguing-in-publication record for this book is available from the British Library.

ISBN 0-9538037-0-8

Manufacture co-ordinated in UK from the publisher's crc by Book-in-Hand Ltd, London, N6 5AH

All rights reserved. No part of this book may be reproduced or transmitted in any form, electronic or mechanical, including photocopy or any information storage and retrieval system, without permission in writing from the author or publisher.

To P.McW.

In gratitude and affection

CONTENTS

Illustrations		vii
Foreword		ix
Acknowledgements		xv

PART 1: BERKSHIRE BOY

1	Proudly Longmate	1
2	An Out of the Way Place	10
3	A Bright and Flourishing Town	26
4	E.Longmate Photographer	39
5	Breeding will out	50
6	All the Longmates is daft	60
7	Sorry, Mum's Out	78
8	A Pinch of Tea	92
9	Absent 0 Late 0	109
10	The Glorious Reign	121
11	Pantomime	134
12	Very Fond of Books	142
13	To Maintain and to Clothe	155

PART II: A REMARKABLE SCHOOL

14	Lodging and Learning	165
15	A Thorough Reform	182
16	Transplanted	196
17	Downs and Woodlands Fair	214

PART III: BLUECOAT BOY

18	Old World Habit	227
19	Form Two Deep!	238
20	Straight and Square	245
21	Lock Up 4.30	256
22	Bread at the Shop	270
23	Holidays Now Ending	288
24	A Dramatic Diversion	300
25	Not Out	311
26	A Dose of Black Draught	327
27	Not Ready for War	343

28	Call the Roll, Sergeant Major!	362
29	Strange Alterations	375
30	More Boring than Glorious	383
31	Carrying On	391
32	Inspiring Sundays	402
33	A Jolly Good Whacking	418
34	For Noel's in Bed	432
35	Learning Psalms for Kappa	442
36	Are you Calling Me a Liar?	454
37	Not Worth the Candle	467
38	Sussex by the Sea	482
39	Housie versus Hitler	497
40	Efficient Service	506
41	Satisfying the Examiners	516
42	Teacher Extraordinary	532
43	Sunday Morning Soldier	548
44	Being Educated	562
45	Scholarship	578
46	Never Forget	591

PART IV: LIFE AFTER HOUSIE

47	Deemed to Have Enlisted	611
48	A Frightful Bang	615
49	A Better and a Happier Place	621
50	Author Retired	645

A Note on Sources	648
Books by Norman Longmate	660
Index	664

ILLUSTRATIONS

BETWEEN PAGES 78 AND 79
1. My mother aged twelve
2. My mother as I remember her, at the door of our home
3. The village of Holton, Somerset
4. Parade in Newbury, c.1909
5. Float advertising my father's business, c.1924
6. No 8 Newport Road, Newbury
7. Alley off Northbrook Street, Newbury
8. Parade in aid of the unemployed, 1933
9. Newbury Market Place, date unknown
10. 'Cocky', the Jack Hotel's resident cockatoo
11. The Jack Hotel, Newbury, now demolished

BETWEEN PAGES 174 AND 175
12. My mother with my elder brother and sister, c.1921
13. With my toy garage, c.1932
14. My childhood home, No 78 Camp Close
15. On holiday from school, c.1937
16. Blackberrying with my brother and sisters, c.1932
17. With my sisters, date unknown
18. The former St Nicholas school, Newbury
19. St Nicholas scholarship winners, 1936
20. In London the day I was admitted to Christ's Hospital
21. New boy at Christ's Hospital
22. Happy Newbury schoolboy, 1936
23. Unhappy Bluecoat boy, 1937

BETWEEN PAGES 334 AND 335
24. 'The Garden', Newgate Street
25. Entrance to Christ's Hospital, London
26. Dinner Parade at Newgate Street
27. A 'Ward' at Newgate Street
28. Games in progress at Newgate Street
29. Big School at Horsham
30. Quadrangle and Dining Hall at Horsham
31. Chapel interior, Horsham
32. Dining Hall interior, Horsham

BETWEEN PAGES 462 AND 463
33 Inside the Library
34 Schoolboy scientist
35 A typical dayroom, date unknown
36 Dinner Parade at Horsham
37 The band playing for Dinner Parade
38 Marching into dinner
39 Big Side
40 Ploughed up playing fields, 1941
41 Sandbagged school office, 1941
42 The Old Science School
43 The Library and Garden
44 Exterior of the former History Grecians' room

BETWEEN PAGES 558 AND 559
45 Christ's Hospital. An aerial view.
46 St John's church, Newbury, 1943
47 My brother in server's robes
48 With my father, date unknown
49 With my brother, c.1941
50 My elder sister, 1943
51 My twin sister in WRNS uniform, c.1944
52 My friends Harold and Gerald
53 With my twin sister and friend Keith, 1943
54 Peele A, c.1937
55 The Avenue seen from Peele, c.1937
56 House photograph, c.1941
57 On my eighteenth birthday, 1943
58 Still in uniform, c.1945
59 Goodbye to Peele, 1943
60 Return to Peele, 2000

IN THE TEXT
Advertising leaflet for my father's business p.40
'Tombstone' commissioned by James Tufnail p.42
Map of Camp Close p.64
Drawing of Camp Close entrance p.65
Map of Christ's Hospital p.225
The Infirmary, Christ's Hospital, photographed in 2000, p.341
School turntable ladder p.555
Coleridge B. The roof scaled during Fire Guard practice in 1943, photographed in 2000 p.555

FOREWORD

Any autobiography is a work of self-indulgence and this is more so than most. My excuse must be that it is the fruit of many years' deliberation and six years of sustained effort in the research and in the writing. I had naively supposed that writing about my family, myself and my schooldays would be easier than undertaking a normal historical work, but I rapidly realised that I had been wrong. In the end I only completed the manuscript because I wished to repay part of the debt I owe to the thousands of informants who have contributed accounts of their wartime experiences for use in some of my own books, and because enquiries about its progress became an embarrassment. Here at last, I hope, is a document of record which, even if it offends some of my contemporaries, future historians of British education may find of interest and value.

I first contemplated writing about my own life in my thirties, under the influence of Beverley Nichols's *Twenty-Five*, published in 1926, though I planned to produce my book at 35, under the title *Halfway*. In the event, *All the Way*, or conceivably *Past It* (referring to my seventieth birthday rather than my declining faculties) would now be more appropriate. What goaded me into beginning to write was the totally unexpected discovery, late in December 1992, that I required a major heart operation. I filled in the dismal, post-Christmas week before I went into hospital writing an account of my childhood for my daughter, whose early years and schooldays had been so different from mine. The operation, a quadruple bypass, was performed on 10 January 1993, and proved, contrary to my private expectations, a complete success and I have dedicated the book to the individual who kindly cared for me during my convalescence. With the reluctance, common among writers, to waste any material, I decided, having recovered, to expand this 80-page essay into a full-length book. Because reviewers of biographies so often remark that it is the opening years of any person's life which are the most interesting, I decided to end my story at the age of 18, the moment when I left school and, in a sense, though not then legally, came of age.

By a happy chance I had, as soon as I left school, written an autobiographical novel, a thinly fictionalised account of my years at boarding school. This has proved invaluable in reminding me of events I had forgotten and my response to them. Occasionally I have quoted this work, *First Bloom*, which remains unpublished, direct, and I have supplemented it with extracts from essays written at the time. None of my letters home from school and few other documents of the period seem to have survived, and, as I recall later, I was barely mentioned in the school magazine *The Blue*.

Although this is solely my story, I have sometimes quoted from the recollections of contemporaries, often written at my request, and am impressed to find how often their experiences and reactions mirrored my own. The school is currently, to its credit, engaged in a major oral history project, designed 'to record on tape for the benefit of future CH historians the memories of Old Blues and others of their time at Housie'. The reminiscences so far collected (to which I have declined to contribute until this book has appeared) bear out my account of conditions when I arrived there in 1936. 'In many ways,' acknowledged the project's organiser in December 1998, 'CH Horsham changed little between 1904 and 1939.'

> Many recall the total lack of privacy and the other often apparently pointless restrictions. Clearly life was not always a bed of roses. 'Endured rather than enjoyed' is a phrase that crops up and some of the darker sides of life at CH Horsham are not forgotten. But it is unprofitable to review times past. There is an almost universal, deep sense of appreciation of what Housie provided...for people whose lives would otherwise have been totally different.[1]

With these sentiments I would readily agree, other than the 'unprofitable' observation, which seems to me profoundly wrong. Why, one wonders, did the compiler of the collection undertake this useful task if that was his view? I believe on the contrary that the past is not merely of absorbing interest in itself but has many lessons for us, indeed I regard the historian as in a sense both prosecuting and defence counsel, simultaneously judge of first instance and court of final appeal.

A favourite Christ's Hospital principle is 'Love the brotherhood' and many Old Blues have readily interpreted this to mean helping me to tell what I believe to be the truth about it. Only one of those I approached refused to help. 'I sense...your vital concern is a critique... of Housie,' he wrote, 'and I want to have nothing to do with this, though,' he was kind enough to add, 'I expect you will do it very well.'

'The besetting sin of Old Blues,' the school's most recent historian, who is one himself, has written 'is an inordinate affection for relating reminiscences of their schooldays.'[2] Here, at least, I have proved a typical son of the foundation, indeed I do not think anyone, including Charles Lamb, as obsessed with his old school as myself, has written about his time there in comparable detail.

An enormous amount has also been written by way of formal history. 'There would appear to be no end to the making of many books about Christ's Hospital,'[3] wrote its then Clerk, another Old Blue, when adding to the total in 1937. 'Christ's Hospital boasts a literature richer than that of any other school,' agreed its next historian, quoted above, in 1984. The reasons are not hard to understand. 'Christ's Hospital,' concluded a public Commission of Inquiry as long ago as 1867, is 'a thing without parallel in the country and sui generis', ie unique.[4]

This uniqueness has presented me with by far my greatest difficulty in writing the present book. It is, I believe, impossible to understand why the school I attended took the form it did without some knowledge of its past, indeed it is only while writing the present book that I have understood the origin of many of the practices and attitudes which dominated my schooldays. I tried various solutions, including writing much of a full-scale history of the school, before finally settling on a combination of school history and personal narrative. The book now consists, therefore, of Part I, on my pre-Christ's Hospital childhood and schooldays; Part II, a concise history of Christ's Hospital from 1552 to 1936, highlighting those events which were echoed in my own day; Part III, by far the longest section, an account of my own time there, from 1936 to 1943; and Part IV, a summary of what happened at Horsham in the closing period of the war, from 1944 to 1945, with a more detailed account of the major changes which took place between 1945 and 1999, plus a brief account of my own post-school career.

I was also tempted to digress into a history of late Victorian rural Somerset, where my mother grew up, and Edwardian Newbury, where she and my father settled. Here too, I have included, I hope, enough material to capture the flavour of both time and place, without compromising the main thrust of my narrative.

I recognised from the first that to tell my story at the length and in the detail I wished must make it a non-commercial proposition, involving self-publication and a limited circulation. I am all the more grateful, therefore to the following who have assisted me in various ways:

On my recent ancestors to my daughter, Miss Jill Longmate, for her investigations on the ground in Lincolnshire and in the official records at St Catherine's House, as well as for transferring my typescript to computer disk and undertaking with exemplary patience the successive revisions I made to the supposedly final text; also to Dr Stephen Taylor, for his professional research in areas that had defeated me; and to Miss Idina Le Geyt for solving a number of problems for me, for her determined pursuit of elusive bibliographical details of books that I half-remembered from half a century earlier, and for assisting in the wearisome task of checking the hundreds of references, in the hope that my own book, whatever its other defects, will at least escape the grotesque inadequacies and inaccuracies to which, as mentioned later, Old Blue writers seem notoriously prone; on the Newbury period of my childhood to my sisters, the late Mrs Freda Lipscomb and Miss Peggy Longmate; I am grateful to Mrs Kathleen Fisher (née Andrews) and to the late Mrs Mildred Streeter (née Aldridge); to my schoolmates at St Nicholas, Mr George Giles, Mr John

Jennings-Giles and Mr John Tillett, and to the present headmistress, Mrs Tricia Whiting; to Mr Keith Allen, a mine of information on the history of the Newbury pantomime, on St Bartholomew's Grammar School, and on local matters in general; to Mrs Jennie Jackson, librarian of *The Newbury Weekly News* and Ms Penelope Stokes, who has written extensively on the town's past; to the late Miss Helen Purvis, formerly Borough Librarian; to Mrs Elaine Arthur, Group Librarian, Mrs Susan Deering-Punshon, Team Librarian, and Mrs Pauline Thomson of Newbury Library; to Mr Tony Higgott, former Curator, and Mr Paul Cannon, Assistant Curator, of the Newbury District Museum; to Ms Kate Willis, of the former Berkshire County Record Office. I also gratefully acknowledge the help of the staff of the Local History Library and the Reference Library of the London Borough of Richmond upon Thames. The Local Studies Information service of Horsham Public Library kindly enabled me to correct *The Blue*'s mis-spelling of 'Prewett', while Guildhall Library explained the significance of 'freeman of the City'. Mr Leslie Longmate, of Grand Prairie, Alberta, provided some information about the Canadian branch of the family. Mrs Margaret Bird of the Sherlock Holmes Society of London kindly traced for me a quotation relating to the great detective.

Those connected with Christ's Hospital may be reluctant to have their help acknowledged and I must emphasise that none of them have seen the manuscript or are in any way responsible for the opinions I express. This said, I owe a great debt to Mr David Young, formerly archivist of Christ's Hospital, and have also received assistance from the following: Mrs Rosie Howard, Mrs Wendy Killner, of the Christ's Hospital Club, Ms Rhona Mitchell, the present Archivist, the Rev. Mrs Nicola Mitra and Mr Nicholas Plumley, Curator of the Christ's Hospital Museum. On Wests Gifts I received much help from a fellow West Gifts Newburian, Mr Donald Willis, and a non-West Gifts Old Blue, Mr Peter Hill. Others associated with Christ's Hospital who helped me included two former members of staff, Mrs Margaret Street (née Mathew) and Mr Arthur Humphrey, and the following, mainly Old Blues, the widows of Old Blues, or members of masters' families, or others in some way associated with the school: Mr Chris Bartlett; Mr John Bennett; Mr John Burton; Mr Richard Cavendish; Mrs Alison Crowther; Mr Robert Crewdson; Mr Michael Herzig and the late Mr Christopher Herzig; Mr John Mobbs; Mr John Paine; Mrs Pat Pitman, widow of my old friend, Robert Pitman; Mr Martin Roberts and Mrs Peggy Roberts, son and widow respectively of the late David Roberts; Mr Peter Scroggs; Mr Gordon Silk; Mr Dennis Smith; Mr Leslie Stone; and Mr Rex Sweeney. Particular thanks are due to my Peele A contemporary, Mr Bryan Harris, who, apart from giving me his own memories, which bore out my own, was very helpful at the publication stage.

Among Old Blues I must make special mention of Professor FD (Robin) Hull. His autobiography, *A Schoolboy's War*, was not reviewed in *The Blue*, though extracts have appeared there since, and was intended for family circulation. I was able to read it, after my own book was finished, thanks to the kindness of the author and his half-sister, Miss Patricia Quin. Robin Hull's experience was wider than mine since it included two years in the Prep and extends to the immediate post-war period, while his half-brothers were both Old Blues and his half-sister worked for a time in the Infirmary. As his book is so scarce, and its theme so relevant to my own, I have quoted from it at a number of points, with the author's generous permission.

For helping me in a variety of ways I am grateful to Mr Tim Allen; Miss Sonia Anderson, of the Royal Commission on Historical Manuscripts; Ms Caroline Reed, Museum Curator of the Royal Pharmaceutical Society; and Mr Julian Roberts, formerly Deputy Librarian of the Bodleian Library. Mr Frank Collieson gave great assistance while I was preparing the manuscript for publication; for any inconsistencies and infelicities which remain the responsibility is mine.

This last observation is much more than the pious disclaimer customary in such circumstances. Books about Christ's Hospital are notorious for their low standards of accuracy and presentation. 'Many of us have been waiting for a CH-related book which is competently edited and proof-read,' commented one contributor despairingly in *The Blue* in 1992, complaining of the 'false constructions, eccentric punctuations and miscellaneous errors' in the history of the CH Club he was reviewing.[5] The Old Blue editor of the same, invaluable, magazine, has blamed such, almost invariable, mistakes, on 'the Housey Gremlins', defined by the dictionary as 'mischievous goblins'. I doubt if I have escaped their attention altogether, since I have not employed, for reasons of economy, a professional copy-editor or proof-reader. I have, however, tried to correct the more obvious errors in the texts I have quoted, and to adopt a standard usage in such matters as masters' names and frequently used terms, such as 'Bluecoat', the form I have adopted throughout. I have felt free to alter punctuation and capitalisation in a quoted text when they seemed wrong or inconsistent, and, in a very few cases, have changed the names, or slightly altered the details of an incident, to avoid embarrassment to the people concerned. These alterations apart, my text is as accurate as research and memory can make it.

I suspect some Old Blues, especially those of a later era, may feel I have been too hard on our old school. My response must be that of Mrs Harriet Beecher Stowe when accused of being unfair to the South in *Uncle Tom's Cabin*. She had, she replied, tried to show the good side of slavery as well as the bad. I have tried to approach Christ's Hospital in the same spirit, though I cannot, I fear, echo Mrs Beecher Stowe's claim: 'The Lord himself wrote it and I was but the humblest of instruments in his hands.'[6]

The theme of the book is set out in its title. While describing as objectively as I can what life was like for a bright child of poor parents between 1925 and

1943 I have tried to identify those events, individuals and books which have had what I now judge, 50 years later, to have had a lasting influence on me. This is not because I have had exceptional success in the world, for manifestly I have not, but simply because I possess the memories, the documents and the aptitude to recount my story. There are, I am sure, others who have lived through the last three quarters of the twentieth century, especially many Old Blues, who will disagree with my conclusions and would have told a very different story. Let them tell it. This is mine, as comprehensive and truthful as I can make it.

NRL

2000

---

[1] *The Blue* Dec 1998 p.242
[2] Morpurgo p.33
[3] Allan p.1
[4] *CH Book* Title page
[5] Dec 1992 p.236
[6] *The Little Book that Caused a War.* See list of scripts.

ACKNOWLEDGEMENTS

Grateful acknowledgement is made for the use of copyright material as follows: to Richard Adams for *The Day Gone By*; to Robin Hull for *A Schoolboy's War*; to Ian Allan Publishing for *Christ's Hospital* by GAT Allan, as revised by JE Morpurgo, and CME Seaman, *Christ's Hospital, The Last Years in London*; to JE Morpurgo for extracts from *The Christ's Hospital Book*, and for *All I Did Was This*, by Philip Youngman Carter; to Malcolm Yorke for *Keith Vaughan*. Material from *Barnes Wallis A Biography* is reproduced by permission of Penguin Books Ltd and Professor Morpurgo. The extracts from *The Blue* are reproduced by kind permission of Christ's Hospital. Every effort has been made to trace the owners of other copyright material, and amends for any inadvertent breach of copyright will gladly be made in any future edition.

ILLUSTRATIONS

Christ's Hospital Museum: 24, 25, 26, 27, 28, 29, 33, 35, 45,

Country Life: 30, 31, 32

West Berkshire Heritage Services: 4, 8, Line drawing on p.65

The map of Camp Close is taken from an Ordnance Survey original of the period. The plan of Christ's Hospital is based on the 1932 Ordnance Survey map, reproduced with the insertion of some additional names.

The copyright in all other illustrations, including those incorporated in the text, rests with the author. Many of the photographs were taken either by himself or his late father, a professional photographer, whose work is here appearing in a book for the first time.

PART I

BERKSHIRE BOY

Why is Berkshire known as the Royal County?

*Question in Berkshire County Council examination
for grammar school entry, March 1936*

1
PROUDLY LONGMATE

Deaths, February 25th. In Margaret Street, Cavendish Square, aged 68, Mr Barak Longmate, heraldic engraver.

The Annual Register, *1836*

Why my great-great-grandfather should have been given the unusual name of 'Proudly' (or 'Proudley') I have never discovered. It has a Puritan 'Praise-God Barebones' ring about it, but there is no nonconformist tradition in the family and all my other ancestors were given solid, conventional names appropriate to their social status. Whatever the reason, my knowledge of my forebears begins with Proudly, one of seven children, who lived in the then remote village of South Hykeham, five miles [8km] south-west of Lincoln. Today it has been merged with North Hykeham, a mile [1.6km] nearer the city, to form a single parish but it remains a basically agricultural area and it is in its now disused churchyard that generations of Longmates still lie. It was at St Michael's church, South Hykeham, that on Tuesday 13 September 1796 Proudly married Mary Singleton. She was probably a local girl, for his occupation is recorded as 'labourer' and he is thus unlikely to have had much contact with people living further afield.

Proudly Longmate was almost certainly illiterate, as was his son John, my great-grandfather, born at South Hykeham in 1800. There is no record of his having attended school, but he must have picked up enough education to become a tradesman, for in 1844 his occupation is listed as 'grocer'. Possibly the keeping of accounts and correspondence was the responsibility of his wife Rebecca (or Rebekah) Redhead, whom he married late in life, when he was 44. His wife was unquestionably able to write her name for she signed the wedding certificate after the ceremony, held on 12 December 1844, at Doddington parish church, about four miles [6.4km] from her husband's native village. Rebecca, born at Cainby, Lincolnshire, was, at 31, also coming to the altar late, but the partnership was successful enough for John, by the time of the 1861 census, to be described as 'grocer and baker'.

The couple had only one child, Frederick, born at Scothern, nine miles [14km] from South Hykeham, from which they had evidently moved, on 10 August 1846. Frederick, though education was not yet compulsory, was in

1861 described in the census returns as 'scholar', but instead of going into the family business he was by 1868 working as a draper in Caistor, 25 miles [40km] from his birthplace. Here on 17 February 1868, he married a local girl, Harriet Rebecca Broadgate, at Caistor Congregational chapel. The bride's family were evidently dissenters, socially a step down from the Anglican Longmates, but otherwise they were well matched in terms of class, for Harriet's father was also a draper – possibly they met while Frederick was working for him – and her paternal grandfather was an ironmonger. Harriet, 25 when she married, had clearly anticipated the ceremony, and, as was then common, it was probably her pregnancy which caused them to get married. Her first child, Elizabeth Meanwell, the latter having been her mother's maiden name, was born less than seven months later, on 5 September 1868. Two more girls, Ada and Maud, of whom I shall say more later, were born to the couple and three boys, Frederick (Fred) who died in 1895, aged 23, John Henry (Jack) born in 1863, and my father, Ernest, his parents' final child, born in 1880. A record of these events, along with marriages and deaths was, in true Victorian fashion, maintained on the pages provided for the purpose in the family Bible, now in my possession. It seems likely that it was my paternal grandmother, Harriet, who inserted these entries, but whoever was the scribe wrote a tidy, educated hand, though, sadly, they end before my father's marriage to my mother and the final ones added later are inaccurate.

At some stage the family moved from Caistor to Grimsby. A Lincolnshire directory of 1856 contains no reference to the name, though this may mean only that they were of insufficient importance to qualify to be listed, ie labourers without a trade.[1] The criterion was not pitched very high up the social scale, however, for the same directory records a John Longmate in business as a blacksmith at Aubourn, a village of 300 inhabitants seven miles [11km] from Lincoln, and a William Longmate, a farmer, at North Hykeham, a slightly larger place with a population of 443, four miles [6.4km] from the city and about the same distance from Aubourn.

Apart from having their names entered in parish registers and similar documents the only record of the Lincolnshire branch of the family is an occasional mention in *Kelly's Directory*, which lists the tradesmen and leading private citizens of every sizeable location from the later nineteenth century onwards. Others elsewhere who bore the same, even then, uncommon surname made a slightly greater mark, or had once done so. Although people of substance had begun to use a second name, not merely a Christian one, from the time of the Norman Conquest it was not until the reign of Edward II, which began in 1307, that the practice became general for humbler families. The first recorded Longmate was probably a landowner since the name is generally assumed to mean 'the dweller at the long meadow', a derivation supported by the variant sometimes encountered, 'Longmead'. I have also seen 'Longmaid', ie a woman remaining unmarried, as the name's original form, and clearly, if this happened often, it would explain why it is so infrequently encountered. The first reference I have discovered to a name resembling Longmate is to a Geoffrey de Longo Prato, who was living in Cambridgeshire in 1273, and was probably of Norman origin. Thereafter the family seem to have settled in Lincolnshire and a standard source, the *International Genealogical Index*, lists about a hundred who were baptised or married in that county between around 1550 and 1850, with a few others in Nottinghamshire. The name has remained relatively common in East Anglia but almost entirely unknown elsewhere and the current London telephone directory, as well as a Longmead has only one person of my own name.* I have never come across anyone who possesses it in any school I have attended, or job I have held, nor seen it in any newspaper report.

Curiously enough, the only members of the family to achieve any kind of public recognition were professional genealogists and heraldic engravers, an extremely rare occupation even in the status-obsessed eighteenth century. Barak Longmate, a doubly distinctive name, who died in 1793, was editor of *Lownde's and Stockdale's Peerage*, and important enough to earn a place in the *Dictionary of National Biography*. So was his son, also Barak, who by the time of his death, in 1836, was sufficiently well known to receive an obituary in the *Annual Register*:

Deaths: February.
25th. In Margaret Street, Cavendish Square, aged 68, Mr Barak Longmate, heraldic engraver, son of Mr Barak Longmate, a scientific genealogist and heraldic engraver, who died July 23, 1793. The late Mr Longmate succeeded his father as editor of *LOWNDE'S AND STOCKDALE'S PEERAGE*.

Even in those days the family seems to have been cursed with bad luck, for the entry records that 'owing to the fire at Mr Nichols's Printing Office in 1808', Barak was forced to abandon his *magnum opus*, for which he had collected numerous notes, 'the continuation of Bigland's *Historical and Monumental Collections for Gloucestershire*'. It seems likely that James Longmate, recorded as having married Elizabeth Callender at St George's Hanover Square, in 1802, was a member of the same family – perhaps Barak junior's brother – but I have no further information about them. One diligent researcher has however discovered the coat of arms appropriate to the Longmate name, perhaps originally authenticated by the Baraks themselves, though it is, I

---

* My Canadian namesake, mentioned in the Foreword, supposed, until he discovered one of my books, that the name was confined to his own family. As his father, John, born in 1887, emigrated to Canada from Aubourn in Lincolnshire, there is almost certainly a connection between the Canadian branch of the family and my own.

believe, most unlikely that my branch of the family, with its background of labourers and drapers, was ever armigerous, ie officially entitled to a coat of arms. During a visit to the College of Heralds in 1999 I confirmed that no Longmate had even applied for such a distinction since at least 1880. However, for the sake of any more eminent members of some future generation I record the designs to which we might have been entitled:

Arms: Gules a lion rampant argent on a chief wavy of the last, a leopard's face between two cinquefoils of the first.

Crest: A boar's head and neck erased gules gorged with a chaplet of oak proper.

To sum up this somewhat negative account of the family's past, no other Longmates, apart from Barak and his son, feature in any of the standard bibliographies listing books and articles on individual families and the name fails to appear in almost all lists and dictionaries of surnames. 'The Longmates must indeed,' one helpful archivist informed me, 'be a rare breed.'

To return to Lincolnshire, the one county where the name was relatively common, on 4 May 1875 my paternal grandfather Frederick Longmate, made his will. This bequeathed his whole estate 'to my dear wife, Harriett' (*sic*), the witnesses being a chemist and an accountant. Frederick himself was described as a 'grocer and provision merchant', but soon after this he changed his occupation to that of commercial traveller, dealing in surgical appliances. This was still his trade when at 4.15 am on Thursday 4 November 1880 my father was born at 100 Cleethorpes Road, New Cleethorpes, Grimsby. In the family Bible his single Christian name was entered as 'Earnest' but he always used the normal spelling.

My father never spoke to me of his childhood but, according to what he told my mother, his father was often away from home, and, as was not uncommon among commercial travellers, drank too much, a recollection borne out by the fact that my father detested 'drunk' scenes in plays. This apart, his early years seem to have been reasonably happy, though he suffered much ill-health, for reasons unknown to me, constantly missed school, and finally left it for good around the age of 13.

His lack of education was, I suspect, something of a handicap later in his life. He could write an adequate business letter and an enjoyable private one, but made some regular mistakes – 'fed up' always emerged as 'feed up'– and when speaking, occasionally, though rarely, dropped his 'h's. He was, however, always good with his hands and had a natural talent for drawing and it may have been these 'artistic' tendencies which led his parents to apprentice him, around 1894, to a photographer, an imaginative choice, for this was still a relatively new trade. He must have shown some aptitude for it, for he proved excellent on the technical side, and was much respected for his skill. I know nothing of his life at this period but it is possible, indeed likely, that he trained in Lincoln, for he always retained a great affection for that city and a deep admiration for Edward King, its famous, High Church, bishop from 1885 until 1910.

The page of the family Bible on which the births of children were recorded bore the inscription 'Happy is the man that hath his quiver full of them' and some generations at least seem to have lived up to this dubious assurance. My father was as previously mentioned, himself one of six children and the eldest of his siblings, Elizabeth Meanwell, known in the family as Lizzie, who was born on 5 September 1868, and married at the age of 25 on 30 October 1893, had a family of truly Victorian dimensions, consisting of five girls and six boys, born between 1895 and 1910. Lizzie seems to have done well for herself for her husband, Walter Martin, was the manager of a boot and shoe manufacturing firm and the Martins were clearly a much more prosperous clan than the Longmates. Although they were in fact our cousins, I never understood the relationship and was somewhat bewildered when, on a visit to Kettering, I was introduced to those still resident there.

Kettering, not Grimsby, now became the family's home town, for by 1910 my father's father Frederick, was living there, at 151 Rockingham Road, where he was to die on 31 December 1914. He had presumably moved there to be near his grandchildren. His widow, Harriet, survived only until 1918, so I never knew either of my paternal grandparents, nor indeed my maternal ones. The Longmates at least do not seem to have acquired any wealth to leave to their children. Frederick's house was rented, not owned, though this is not conclusive evidence since house ownership then was a rarity, but neither my father, in the army when his mother died, or his brothers or sisters, seem to have received any significant legacies. My father's elder sister, only three years older than him, had been living in her parents' home and continued to do so, supporting herself as a piano teacher. The house was, as I shall describe later, far more spacious than ours but even worse equipped. By the 1930s, when I visited it several times, it was already a gloomy, distinctly out-of-date property, dating back perhaps to the early years of the century, much inferior to the modern and comfortable one owned by the Martins. Kettering itself had also probably changed little since my grandparents had moved there and I remember it as an unattractive medium-sized industrial town, lacking the amenities of a large city or the charm of a market town like Newbury. Kettering was, like the county town, Northampton, a centre of the boot and shoe trade, but what interested me was that it also contained the country's major manufacturer of playground equipment like slides and roundabouts, and its products can still be seen in many a recreation ground.

In my childhood our relations, with one exception whom I shall mention later, impinged on us very little and I cannot recall that we ever received as much as a birthday card from them. None, I think, made any great mark in the world, or merited an obituary in a national newspaper. I can, however, recall being intrigued throughout my childhood by references to 'Cousin Eric'

Martin, born in 1900, whom I knew to be serving somewhere in the British Empire and vaguely imagined to be a tree-planter in Ceylon or, after I had seen *Sanders of the River,* a district officer in Africa, keeping order, clad in khaki shorts and solar topee, among tribes of naked savages. Later I discovered that he had in fact been an agricultural consultant for the British administration in Uganda, often out in the bush, just as I had pictured him. We got on extremely well and I have always regretted we never met in my childhood, when he might have caused me to modify my jaundiced view of 'relations' in general.

My father's brother Jack, by contrast, was spoken of, I suspect unjustly, as something of a black sheep, following, I believe that traditional source of family ill-feeling, a dispute over a legacy. There was a suggestion, so far as I know without foundation, that he had disposed of some pearls which should, by rights, have gone to his sister Maud. The fact, however, that he gave the same name to his own daughter hardly suggests a guilty conscience, and this canard apart, I never heard anything of the slightest interest about any of my paternal relatives.

Grandparents, a source of treats and sympathy for so many children, played no part in our lives and aunts and uncles, with the few exceptions I shall mention later, very little. I feel no great regret at this; friends, whom one chooses, have been infinitely more important to me than people with whom I share no community of interest but happen to possess some distant tie of blood. A number of relations have contacted me late in life after seeing my name in print or hearing me broadcast, and though they have been pleasant enough I feel no great sense of deprivation at not having known them better. My unspoken reaction has echoed, in humbler prose, that of Dr Johnson's response to Lord Chesterfield's offer of patronage when he was already successful.[2] 'Where,' I have wanted to ask, 'were you when we really needed you?' Here indeed is the first of the lessons I learned in my 'shaping season' that, immediate family apart, relations count for little and that friendship is infinitely thicker than blood.

Whether or not my father moved to Kettering with his parents I never discovered, indeed I know nothing of his life as a young man. The first document I have which throws any light on him at this time is a testimonial from the local dramatic society, to be mentioned later, which shows him by 1904, at the age of 23, to have been sufficiently involved in the life of the Berkshire town of Newbury to have been helping behind the scenes at an amateur play or opera. It must have been at this period that he met and married a Newbury woman, Ellen Keep, though why he was in the town and how they got to know each other remains a mystery. My father never mentioned this first match to us, perhaps with good reason, for when, in our late teens, my mother casually remarked, separately, to my sisters and myself that he had been married before, we were both shocked and upset, regarding this as in some way a slight upon our mother. As my eldest sister later remarked, 'I thought "Why couldn't he have waited till mum came along?"'

The location of this first marriage came as almost as great a shock to me when I discovered it during the research for this book, for the ceremony proved to have been held in the town where I was later to marry myself and to spend almost all of my adult life. My father had never mentioned its name to me, nor, so far as I knew, ever set foot in it before we visited it together many years later, but the evidence of the marriage certificate is unchallengeable. On Monday 29 July 1907 Ernest Longmate, bachelor, aged 26, and Ellen Keep, spinster, aged 43, were married at St Matthias church Richmond, Surrey. Her father's occupation is shown as 'Brewer's Manager', though the family were in fact well known in Newbury as successful bookmakers. My paternal grandfather was described as 'manufacturer', also a step up from the reality of commercial traveller.

According to hearsay and family tradition, Ellen's family disapproved of the match, less, perhaps, because of the groom's insecure financial position than on account of the wide gap in their ages. It may be that my father hoped that Ellen would provide the funds to enable him to set up in business on his own account, while she perhaps saw the young photographer as providing her last chance of escape from spinsterdom, but they may also, of course, have been genuinely fond of each other. Many years later my father remarked to a friend of my own age, who was going out with an older woman, that he should ignore warnings against such a relationship as an age gap was no bar to happiness.

I have striven without success to establish why my father should have chosen Richmond, then, as now, a charming riverside suburban town, for his wedding. He seems to have had no relatives there for, according to the two contemporary directories, no one called Longmate was living in Richmond, or no one, at least, of sufficient status to qualify for mention either as a 'private resident', ie a householder, or as a tradesman. Richmond already contained six photographers, but no bookmakers are listed. Two males called Keep were living in the adjoining parish of Twickenham and the name is sufficiently uncommon to suggest these were probably relations. It was perhaps this that dictated the choice of location for the wedding, which might have embarrassed the bride's immediate family if she had been married in Newbury. The certificate reveals that the couple were married after the calling of the banns, not by special licence, and describes them as being 'both of this parish'. The address shown, 54 Rosemont Road, a mere five minutes walk from St Matthias church, which stands high on Richmond Hill, must therefore have been theirs, at least officially, for the previous three weeks. The two directories, identify the owner, or occupier, as 'Miss O'Shea' in one and 'Mrs Parnell' in the other. This was presumably the legendary Kitty, or Katie, O'Shea who had in 1891 married the Irish Nationalist leader, Charles Stewart Parnell, after a notorious divorce which wrecked his career. He died only a few months later but she is known to have lived in numerous houses in Southern England before her own death in 1921.[3]

To return to my father's own marriage, that bride and groom lived under the same roof before the wedding lacks the significance it would have today; the times were strict enough to demand, and the house large enough to provide, separate rooms for an engaged couple.

St Matthias church is still in use, a large, handsome building, though much of it is devoted to other purposes, such as an art gallery. Of the wedding, and whether or not it was followed by a honeymoon, I know nothing. It is not mentioned in the gossip column or the main news pages of either of the local newspapers, which suggests that the participants were not local residents, nor was there a paid announcement in the 'Births, Marriages and Deaths' column. If any members of the Longmate and Keep families were present they chose not to serve as witnesses, for these are identified as Charles Frank Arman and Cyril Vernon Aubray-Grathan, though these names mean nothing to me and they were conceivably total strangers to the couple themselves.

The event did not, however, go wholly unremarked. It is duly chronicled in the *Richmond Parish Magazine* for August 1907, but with the groom's name given as 'Longmote', a variation I have never encountered. How typical of my father's luck, I have felt since, that even a report of his wedding should get his name wrong.

After his marriage my father settled in, or, more probably returned to, the small town of Ringwood in Hampshire. He was, according to what my mother later told me, already working there, though why he should have strayed so far from his native Lincolnshire and from his surviving family in Northamptonshire I have no idea. The likeliest explanation is that he supposed that it had sufficient potential business to support another photographer, but at all events his association with Ringwood was to be short-lived and sad, for the next document relating to him that I have discovered is the death certificate of his first wife. Ellen died on 12 May 1909, less than two years after her wedding day, at Christchurch Street, Ringwood, in her husband's presence. The cause was recorded as 'Cancer of Uterus' and 'Cachexia', the latter, which means 'wasting away', suggesting a long illness. Clearly they cannot have enjoyed a carefree married life for very long, if at all, and I have wondered whether Ellen already knew when she met my father that she was cursed with this horrible disease and seized the fleeting chance of happiness. My father, incidentally, is described on the death certificate as 'a photographer (master)', which suggests that he was already in business on his own account.

Ellen was buried three days after her death in plot V25 of Ringwood cemetery. This already contained another body, which was not uncommon, but along with the fact that no tombstone was erected, suggests that money was scarce. The Newbury Keeps would, I believe, have given her a more handsome send-off and memorial. As it is, all that survives of her, apart from these official records, is an entry in the family Bible. By a final irony, this is in my mother's hand, but records the wrong date of death.

His tragically brief, but otherwise so far as I know happy, marriage was to bring my father the one outstanding piece of luck in his life, his meeting with my mother. She was, as all fortunate enough to know her will agree, a person of outstandingly sweet disposition and, as events were to demonstrate, of remarkable endurance. They were, for most of their lives together, to know little except poverty and hardship, but the circumstances which led them to meet were romantic. My mother's background was very different from my father's. His forebears, as I have described, had only a generation or so back been not merely working class but illiterate. His own father had nudged his way, somewhat precariously, into the lower-middle class, while he himself, as a skilled tradesman, seemed set to climb a step or two higher up the social ladder. My mother's origins were more complex. Her background was rural, not urban, but she came from a long line of working farmers who, if never rich, had enjoyed a secure position, both financially and socially, for generations, living not merely in the same village but on the same small farm, which did not finally pass outside her family until around 1993. Somewhere in the background, where and how I never learned, were more monied relations, though they never benefited us.

In spite of being brought up in somewhat uncultured surroundings, though they were certainly not poverty-stricken, in the heart of the country, my mother was well-read and well-spoken, naturally well-mannered and at ease with women of all classes. She would have made an admirable wife to a schoolmaster or clergyman or, conceivably, for she always loved animals and the countryside, a prosperous farmer. Instead she chose to marry a precariously placed, poorly educated, widower of no obvious attractions, with no capital and only modest prospects in a still uncertain trade. I am not aware of any active opposition, but it seems to have been a match about which no one, except the participants, was enthusiastic.

---

[1] White's History
[2] Boswell, Vol I p.156
[3] Marlow p.293

2
AN OUT OF THE WAY PLACE

Life need never be dull in the most out of the way place in the kingdom.

George Sweetman, History of Wincanton, Somerset, *1903*

Margaret Ellen Lush Rowden, known as 'Maggie' in her native village and to her husband as 'Meg', never 'Margaret', had been born on Thursday 28 July 1887 in the small Somerset village of Holton. Her father, Harry, was a farmer and I know nothing of her mother, who died as a result of the birth; it was presumably from her side of the family that my mother's unusual third name came, but by the time of her marriage she had discarded it. My mother was, as a new-born infant, not expected to survive and it was suggested that her mother's funeral should be postponed so the two could be buried together, but she clung tenaciously to life. Her bereaved father felt unable to cope on his own and the motherless little girl was brought up by a great-uncle and his wife in the same village, until, at six, her father having remarried, she was suddenly taken back at night, as if to make the move more acceptable, to her own home. After a fortnight she settled in happily enough. Her stepmother proved kind and my mother had a very happy childhood, until her stepmother died, when my mother was aged 16, followed, when she was 19, by her father. Harry Rowden had had a frustrating life. He had not wished to be a farmer but a schoolmaster, no doubt possessing the literary interests and aptitude which he passed to his daughter, but his father, my maternal grandfather, was a domineering individual possessing private means, who had insisted his son follow this unwelcome career. It remains to me a matter of vast regret that this distant, tyrannical figure should have blighted my grandfather, Harry Rowden's, life and thus indirectly my mother's, for I am sure she would have followed her father into the profession he wished to choose. It would in the 1890s have been perfectly possible for her to have qualified as a teacher through the recognised pupil-teacher route and she would have been in her element as a village schoolmistress. As it was, her grandfather's obstinate refusal to let his son abandon the family farm cast a shadow over her childhood and relations between father and son were such that when the older man was visiting the United States, which itself demonstrates a degree of affluence and enterprise, the family openly expressed the hope that his ship would founder on the return crossing so that he would be drowned.

Holton at the time of my mother's birth in 1887 appears to have been, as it is today, a village of no particular character or attractiveness, but a pleasant enough, if excessively quiet, place in which to grow up.[1] There had been farmers there since at least the Norman Conquest and perhaps earlier. Domesday Book, in 1085, recorded: 'Humphrey holds Altone and Abric holds it of him. There is land for two ploughs.' Two ploughs was a modest enough requirement for any community but the village had grown large enough by Tudor Times, if not earlier, to support a church, for there was a parish register going back to 1558. A Baptist chapel had come later. Otherwise nothing much had happened in Holton over the centuries. It had produced no famous sons or daughters and suffered no great calamities. *Kelly's Directory of Somerset* for 1889 described it clearly and succinctly:

> A village and parish situated on the road from Wincanton to Taunton and Yeovil, 6 miles [9.6km] south from Bruton, 6 south-east from Castle Cary and 2.5 [4km] south-west from Wincanton station on the Somerset and Dorset railway....A stream flows to the south of the parish, but does not form the boundary. The church of St John is a building of stone in the Perpendicular style...The living is a rectory...The land is chiefly used for dairy purposes, the arable growing wheat and barley. The area is 1,187 acres [480 hectares]...The population in 1881 was 169.

Kelly's Directory listed 24 of the inhabitants by name, including the rector and another clergyman, two men and two women of private means, this whole group forming the local gentry, though not identified as such, and 17 inhabitants described as 'commercial'. These included a butcher, an innkeeper, a wheelwright, a miller and a shopkeeper, the rest all being farmers. The shopkeeper, who combined the job with running the post office, was William Rowden, my mother's uncle, while her father, Harry, officially known as Henry, was one of the eleven farmers. To send a telegram or money order one had to go into Wincanton but the village had a good postal service. 'Letters arrive from Bath to Wincanton and are delivered at 7.30 a.m.; dispatched at 6.10 p.m.; Sundays 10.25 a.m.' It was indeed a better service, at least at the weekends, than most rural communities have today.

The restoration of the church, completed in 1885, had been the last big event in Holton and such other changes as had occurred over the two succeeding decades were hardly of a kind to cause much excitement, though doubtless a fruitful source of discussion over the locally brewed beer at the Old Inn. This still stands directly opposite The Farm, where my mother was born and brought up, and her childhood home was to remain unmodernised until long after she had left it. But even in Holton some changes took place. The miller who in 1889 had carried on his trade exclusively by water power had, by 1894, begun to use steam as well. By 1897 one of the farmers had also diversified his output, describing himself as a 'cider grower', while a thatcher, with the Hardy-esque name of Eli Tucker, had taken up residence in Holton and become successful enough to qualify for mention in *Kelly's Directory.*. But the features of daily life which must have affected my mother most had not changed. Her father still owned The Farm; her uncle was still sub-postmaster and ran the village shop, and my mother herself, like all the other children, walked a mile [1.6km] every day to and from the nearest school, at North Cheriton, which still serves the area. In Holton indeed, although it had only recently become compulsory to do so, even the poorest families had always sent their children to school. Most were destined to end up like their parents, as farm labourers, the humblest, worst-rewarded and hardest-worked of all the Victorian working class.

In a small Somerset village in the 1890s the entertainment was still entirely self-made. There were Penny Readings in the Diamond Jubilee Room, opened in 1897 when my mother was aged ten, a handsome, somewhat church-like building in the centre of Holton, now known as the Village Hall. Such events were a great feature of Victorian life, the modest admission price being designed to ensure that everyone could attend, and numerous anthologies with titles like *Recitations for All Occasions* catered for would-be performers. There were also village concerts, at which everyone with any suitable gift was expected to perform. These were eagerly looked forward to and the threat of not being allowed to attend was frequently used to tame troublesome children. My mother regularly recited on such occasions, to great applause, and distinguished herself on one such evening by bursting into tears after the company had been noisily singing the rousing chorus of *Widdecombe Fair,* which described how one person after another, including 'Uncle Tom Cobley and all', had climbed on to the back of Tom Pearce's grey mare. When asked the reason she replied: 'I feel so sorry for the poor horse!'

The village children took it for granted that the boys would touch their forelock to the squire or anyone else from the 'Big House', as well as to the rector and his wife, while the girls would curtsy. Attendance at church was the big social event of the week. My mother recalled with what anticipation the congregation awaited the arrival at Cheriton church (not Holton, for some reason) of an elderly spinster who would arrive carrying a lantern, which had lighted her walk over the fields to evensong. She would blow heartily at the flame, but regularly failed to extinguish it, whereupon all her neighbours in the adjoining pews would also blow loudly to put it out. Once, despairing of success, she put the lantern on the ground in the pew beside her, only to find her vast encircling skirt set on fire when she knelt to pray, causing an even greater disturbance, happily without disaster. The following week she failed to bring the lantern but arrived much muddied; she had, she loudly revealed, to the amusement of the congregation, fallen over a cow on the footpath.

Politics made little impact on the village, though agricultural labourers, who made up most of the electorate of Holton, had been enfranchised as recently as 1885. My mother recalled one revealing incident, when a local landowner was expected to lose his seat as its Conservative MP. His brother toured the constituency in a horse-drawn carriage, which halted by every group of farm workers he encountered, to shout to them: 'If my brother fails today I close – – House for ever'. With unemployment a constant source of fear – there was, of course, as yet no benefit for those out of work and no social security system – this threat proved effective. The landowner's brother was safely elected. Years later I recalled and made use of this incident when writing an academic essay on the limitations of the Ballot Act, specifically designed to prevent such abuses, and in a television programme for schools on the same theme.

Another incident I used in the same series, *How We Used to Live,* also came straight from my mother's childhood. She described to me how the farmers' children, like herself, brought food to be heated up at dinner-time around the schoolroom stove. The labourers' children's lunches were more modest and poorest of all was one small boy whose meal consisted of a solitary uncooked turnip.

The kind of life enjoyed by the inhabitants of Holton cannot have been vastly different from that depicted in Thomas Hardy's novels, set in Dorset and the adjoining counties. My mother personally witnessed as a child the last 'skimmity ride' to take place in Holton, similar to the 'skimmington' described by Hardy in *The Mayor of Casterbridge,* first published in 1886. A local woman was known to have been unfaithful to her husband with another man from the locality and all the villagers turned out with saucepans and metal lids and beat them noisily together, a process known as 'making hollyhoop', as they marched through the village and then walked round and round the homes of the offending parties booing and shouting. This crude expression of public disapproval proved effective, for the couple concerned thereupon broke off the affair or at least conducted it more discreetly. Here, too, an old tradition was being invoked, for later, reading about the expulsion from the Andover workhouse around 1845 of a woman suspected of murdering her baby, I felt an instant sense of recognition, for the offending pauper was driven out by a similar demonstration, in this case orchestrated by the workhouse master's wife.*

On one occasion my mother was herself the innocent cause of another illicit liaison coming to light. After visiting a local woman she helpfully pulled back the curtain covering a downstairs window as she left, not knowing that this was a signal to warn her lover to stay away as her husband was at home. My mother had inadvertently indicated that the coast was clear and she had hardly

---

* See my *The Workhouse* p.132.

left when the woman's admirer arrived, to be greeted by an astonished and furious husband, an incident soon immortalised in village legend.

My mother also told me of almost the only genuinely psychic experience of which I have heard; the only other example involved my daughter, who had no doubt inherited this unwanted gift from her grandmother. Having been to visit a sick neighbour whom she had not seen for some time my mother went upstairs to her bedroom and chatted animatedly to her, only to learn on leaving that the woman concerned had died a day or two earlier. I would not have believed this story had I heard it from anyone else and can only imagine that my mother's innocence and simplicity made her vulnerable to this still unexplained spiritual force.

The book which comes closest to evoking life in Holton in the last two decades of the nineteenth century, as my mother described it to me, is Flora Thompson's autobiographical account of her childhood in a village on the borders of Oxfordshire and Northamptonshire, *Lark Rise to Candleford*, of which the first part was published in 1939. The author had, however, been born in December 1876, and was thus only ten years older than my mother. *Lark Rise* catches admirably the overwhelming poverty of rural life, both in the material sense and in the limited choices open to the ordinary villager, though my mother's family were higher up the social ladder than most of those in Flora Thompson's 'Juniper Hill'. Life in Holton must also have had something of the character of the fictional villages of Fairacre and Thrush Green created by 'Miss Read', ie Dora Jessie Saint, who was born in 1913 and worked as a village schoolmistress at various periods from 1933, living for a time in a village near Newbury. Miss Read's first book, *Village School,* published in 1955, like its successors, was much enjoyed by my mother in the last few years of her life. I confess I find them excessively cosy and insipid, lacking the bite and realism of Flora Thompson's autobiographical work, but it was probably these qualities that appealed to my mother. Although she had no illusions about the hardness of the life for most country dwellers she was happy at school, being exceptionally good at English. She could recall how the boys, when a poem was being read round the class, would compete to deliver the lines, 'Oh Christ, it is the Inchcape Rock', from Southey's poem, a rare opportunity to indulge in blasphemy unpunished. Similarly, in the choir, the cruder elements were convulsed with giggles when the choirmistress would innocently cry, in urging them to follow the instruction 'p' for 'pianissimo', 'Come on boys, all p together!' The teaching was clearly of a high standard for my mother acquired a love of poetry which never left her and could still late in life quote lines learned at school, like those from Tennyson's *Locksley Hall*:

> He will hold thee, when his passion shall have spent its novel force,
> Something better than his dog, a little dearer than his horse.[2]

She was fond, like others of her generation, of Charles Dickens, a taste I never shared, especially *The Pickwick Papers*, and liked to recall incidents from it, especially the slightly scandalous ones. I can remember her quoting to me in a letter, in what connection I have now forgotten, the description of Mr Pickwick's discomfiture when the unscrupulous Jingle had deceived him into a midnight visit to a 'seminary for young ladies'.[3]

My mother, here in my view showing better judgement, also greatly admired Anthony Trollope's Barsetshire novels. The first, *The Warden*, had been published in 1855, but her particular favourite was *The Last Chronicle of Barset*, which had appeared in 1867. She could quote many incidents from this and particularly identified with the proud but desperately poor Mr Crawley, perhaps remembering how often she had to put aside her own pride for the sake of her children.

The author, a very minor one, over whom we disagreed most strongly was Angela Thirkell, whose life covered the same span as my mother's: the writer had been born in 1890 and died in 1961. I am now ashamed to admit that I, too, enjoyed her novels as a schoolboy, longing to belong to the safe upper-middle class world they depicted, but as I grew up I came to regard them as not merely trivial but contemptibly snobbish, a view I could never persuade my mother to share. My own attitude has mellowed since I learned that Angela Thirkell had no great opinion of her own work but wrote what, in that class-conscious age, would sell, having undertaken the task, just like the humble but less rewarding jobs my mother had undertaken, to support her family. I now feel grateful to her, in that she provided my mother with a well-deserved escape route from the shabbiness and poverty of her daily life into a world where, its unkind excesses apart, she would have been more at home.

Salisbury, the original of Trollope's Barset, was only 33 miles [53km] from her home, but I do not think my mother ever visited it as a girl. London must have seemed impossibly remote, but could be reached by rail from Wincanton via the junction with the main line at Castle Cary, seven miles [11km] distant. 'Cary' was the limit of the world for most of the residents of Holton and they mainly kept in touch with events outside the village via the carrier's cart which regularly travelled into Wincanton, or walked the two and a half miles [4km] on foot. Holton apart, this small town was the most important place in my mother's life and she always retained a deep affection for it, which I could well understand when I finally visited it. Like Newbury, it was extraordinarily typical of its time, providing a microcosm of England's rural past.

This still sleepy small town was aptly described by the author of its most recent history, published in 1985, as the 'Pleasant Town in the Vale',[4] but unlike Newbury, it lacked an eventful past. If, as has been said of nations, a town was happy that had no history Wincanton must have been the most contented of places. The author of the classic *History of Wincanton, Somerset, from the Earliest Times to the Year 1903*, published at that date, when my mother must often have been there, explained in a foreword that he had undertaken the task after hearing a speaker at the 1871 annual meeting of the Somerset Archaeological Society observe 'Wincanton has no history.'[5] His own work, however, bore out this contention. It had, he explained, provided him with an interesting occupation – 'These pursuits and enquiries have helped to fill in my life' – and his conclusion was that 'Life never need be dull in the most out of the way place in the kingdom.' But 'out of the way' Wincanton certainly was. All the diligence of this author, George Sweetman, had failed to uncover anyone from Wincanton who had made any mark nationally. 'Wincanton's greatest son,' he concluded, was an obscure judge, born in 1512, who had become Speaker of the House of Commons, one of only two Wincanton men to have achieved an entry in the *Dictionary of National Biography*. (Even this is doubtful; I failed to find anyone of the name given by Sweetman in the invaluable *DNB*.) Since its appearance in Domesday Book, as Wincaleton – the present name only developed around 1800 as the most commonly used of 53 variants – and the granting in 1556 of the first charter authorising the holding of a market there – barely a word had been heard elsewhere of Wincanton. It has a tiny place in the history of the 'Glorious Revolution' of 1688 when almost the only blood to flow during the whole of the Prince of Orange's victorious march from Brixham to London was shed near the town, as an advance cavalry patrol looking for a crossing point over the River Stour encountered a troop of James II's Irish horsemen. In the best Wincanton tradition it proved to be a very minor skirmish which did not delay the progress of the future William III[*] and the next event of note was a disastrous fire, in 1707, when, according to the summary given in *Kelly's Directory*,[6] 'a great part of the town was consumed', amounting to 44 houses. In 1768 came more excitement when, for reasons unexplained, vandals set fire to the Old Market House. By around 1800 the former dominance of agriculture as the main source of employment had already declined,[7] with the development of the linen industry, with around 200 looms. In the very first census, held in 1801, 1064 of the inhabitants were described as engaged in 'trade and manufacture', compared to 582 in agriculture, in a total population of 1772, a figure which was to increase only very slowly during the century.

The Napoleonic wars made an unexpected impact on Wincanton, for more than 400 French prisoners of war were housed there, leaving a permanent legacy, a recreation room which later became the Baptist chapel, and a booklet, *The French in Wincanton*, recording this unprecedented intrusion of foreigners into this West Country backwater.[8]

The years following 1815 were, as elsewhere, a time of hardship and repression. Wincanton helps to give the lie to the traditional picture of idyllic

---

[*] *Kelly's Directory* wrongly places this battle on 5 November. It is correctly dated, on 3 December, and described, by Carswell, p.197.

rural life in Victorian England. In 1830 here, as in many places, there were rick-burnings and riots, put down by the yeomanry, the volunteer cavalry recruited from among the better-off gentry to resist invasion but more commonly used as an emergency police force against the English working class.* For many years even a harsh winter was sufficient to cause widespread privation. 'Wincanton has suffered severely in the past from poverty caused by general depression or severe weather conditions,' acknowledged Puffy Bowden in 1985, recording the efforts local benefactors had made to blunt their worst effects.[9] In 1836 a Wincanton Coal Charity was founded, and, he recorded, 'distributed between 60 and 70 tons [59-69 tonnes] to more than 100 families', a notably high proportion of the population, 'the price to the recipients', heavily subsidised, 'being 5d per cwt', [2p per 50kg]. In the same year work began on the new workhouse,[10] erected under the Poor Law Amendment Act of 1834, to serve a 'union' of 40 parishes, Holton among them, with a total population, by 1888, of 21,000.[11] Wincanton had hitherto managed with a small and no doubt relatively cosy workhouse of its own, although the number of occupants testified to the poverty of the area; in 1742 its 63 inmates had included only four classed as 'aged', ie aged 60 or more, and 36 'infants', under the age of 10. The workhouse, built like that at Newbury on the outskirts of the town, was soon, as there, a place of dread, as my mother could remember, and as George Sweetman's description confirms:

> When first built, the floors everywhere were of brick; the rooms were heated with a brick flue raised above the floor; the walls were bare; the windows high and barred, all of them looking upon one of the yards. The dietary was coarse and only of a few kinds, large quantities finding its way into the hogs' trough.[12]

Wednesday was Board Day, when the Guardians of the Poor, one from each parish of the union, met to decide the fate of the unfortunates who had sought the help of a Relieving Officer, or been referred by a local magistrate or clergyman. Here the major decision was made as to whether the applicant should be given a weekly allowance, 'out-relief', to enable him, or her to stay in his or her own home, or be ordered, as the price of assistance, to accept 'indoor relief' and 'enter the house', the dreaded alternative. My mother could not recall this latter happening to anyone from Holton, perhaps a sufficiently close and small community to care for its own.

Only a few years before my mother was born, however, the workhouse had, as George Sweetman recorded, to be enlarged to 'hold 150 inmates', while the workhouse infirmary, opened at the same time, 1871, had, as elsewhere, come to provide the only free, public hospital for the poor. By 1903, when

---

* See my *Island Fortress* for numerous references to the yeomanry.

Sweetman's *History of Wincanton* appeared, the whole institution had undergone significant changes:

> It has become more home-like; the classification is better; the food and clothing are better; the children do not wear the pauper's badge as formerly; they go to the Board School with other children and their moral tone is altogether raised…Instead of resembling a jail, it partakes more of the character of a hospital…It is…less a harbour for loafers and women of light character. Each half yearly statement more and more shows that it is the aged of both sexes who go there to rest to the end of their days.[13]

In 1871 the first Board Schools were opened in the towns,[14] an essential step in the process of making education universal, compulsory and free, instead of its provision being left to private charity, usually of a strictly denominational kind. Almost as important to many children, however, were the Sunday schools organised by local clergy which had sometimes provided the only regular education a child received. Whether or not my mother attended a Sunday school at Holton or Cheriton I never learned, but the Rev. Colin Grant-Dalton, Rector of Wincanton at this time, took his duties to his child flock very seriously. In 1891 when the penny a week hitherto charged to the children was abolished he wrote a letter to their parents urging that this should now 'be paid into the Sunday School Savings Bank. One penny a week,' he pointed out, 'makes 4s 4d [22p] a year; to that we will add 8d [4p] making 5s [25p]…if you allow us to open an account with it in your child's name in the Post Office Savings Bank this would form a "nest egg" to which you can add year by year.' Here were the Victorian virtues of thrift and self-help, with suitable encouragement from above, admirably illustrated and in Wincanton, as elsewhere, the annual Sunday school outing was a major event, providing for many children the only holiday of the year. Those organised for pupils attending St Peter and St Paul's church, Wincanton, sometimes involved merely a march 'to Cash's Park' for 'games and sports and a fine tea', but occasionally a trip by train, and later charabanc, to Weymouth or Bournemouth. The rector made the most of this powerful incentive, warning that 'no child will be admitted who has not made 40 per cent of the possible attendances.'[15]

For most people, of all ages, life was hard and treats rare. By mid-century, George Sweetman established, the average local wage for labourers was still only 1s 0d to 1s 7d [5-7.5p] a day, while bread cost from 10d to 1s 0d [4-5p] for a quartern [4lb or 1.8kg] loaf. Beer was 5d per quart [1.8p a litre] and generally 'considered one of the chief necessaries of life', though Sweetman himself did not share this view and in 1843 was one of the first, at the age of nine, to sign the pledge when the Wincanton Temperance Society was founded, after a lecture at the Town Hall.[16] Like other places, Wincanton claimed to have an exceptionally large number of public houses, but there seems to have been little disorder, for the town's first policeman was not appointed until 1856. Another cause which found an echo there was the campaign against slavery and Wincanton, like many larger places, acquired its own 'Uncle Tom's Cabin', presumably a shop or cafe, in 1861, following the success of Harriet Beecher Stowe's great classic, first published in 1852 but newly topical because of the American Civil War.

The great event of the century, ending the town's near isolation and opening up new markets as well as new employment opportunities and the prospect of an altogether richer life, was the arrival of the railway, in the shape of the Somerset and Dorset line, the 'S and D', letters said to stand for 'Slow and Doubtful'. This ran from Bath to Bournemouth and linked the little town, via Temple Combe, to London 115 miles [186km] away by rail; by road it was a mere 108 miles [174km].[17]

The first train passed through Wincanton station in January 1862, amid scenes recorded, in a distinctly patronising way, by the *Taunton Courier*:

> It was evident that a railway train running through the district was as great a novelty as a Chinese junk floating up Glastonbury Tor would be, for at every station there were crowds of rustics gaping with astonishment at the spectacle, and uttering exclamations of wonder and surprise. At one station the attention of the travellers was particularly attracted to a body of peasant boys, dressed in garbs which had been provided for them by necessity rather than by taste. These lads gazed with astonishment, now at the wheels, then at the engine, and then at the heads of the travellers as they emerged from the windows; and were it not that their coat sleeves were occasionally raised to wipe off the surplus moisture from their faces, there would have been some difficulty in deciding whether they were not rustic statues with moveable eyes.
>
> Wincanton was certainly more lively than its neighbours. Here the people flocked forth from their domiciles at the approach of the train – a couple of the upper class rode their nags out to witness the scene and the nags danced, pranced and curvetted in response to the snorting of the fire-horse; and a host of juveniles, apparently from some Ragged School, set up continuous cheers as the train rolled out of the town.[18]

With the start of a regular service in August 1862 the railway came to play an important part in the life of Wincanton, from the arrival of the 'Wincanton alarm clock', as it became known, at 7.10 a.m., until the departure of the 9.10 p.m. for Bath, 'the signal for many folk to drink their cocoa, fill their hot water bottle and go to bed'.[19]

With the coming of the railway, Wincanton began steadily to acquire the other amenities expected of even the smallest market town; in 1881 it still had a population of only 2,410, of whom 235, drawn from the whole Poor Law union of which it was the centre, were 'officers and inmates in the workhouse'. Social life revolved round the Anglican church and the numerous chapels, each with its associated Sunday school, but there was also a Constitutional, ie Conservative, Club, a Wincanton Liberal Association, a Cricket Club, founded in 1883, and a Football Club and Town Band, both dating from around 1890. Wincanton was not a very martially minded place. It responded only lukewarmly to the creation of the Volunteer Movement, a peacetime Home Guard, in 1859, and the unit founded then soon lapsed. It was re-formed, but by 1899 had attracted only 20 members. This was not many more than the town's great pride, its twelve man fire brigade, established in 1886, nine years after a disastrous fire had burned down the rebuilt Town Hall. The brigade's informal headquarters was the Greyhound Hotel, still happily to be seen today, and already the town's chief hostelry. *Kelly's Directory* promised in 1889 that 'An omnibus meets trains at Wincanton Station' and an advertisement offered 'Splendid accommodation for Hunting Gentlemen, LOOSE BOXES fitted up on the newest improved principle...Lock-up Coach Houses. Posting in all its branches', 'posting', whereby one hired a horse, or horse and carriage, to complete a journey, being the taxi-service of the time. For those of more modest means three carriers' carts operated, though only on market day, Wednesday, when Wincanton came to life and the people of the surrounding villages made their weekly contact with the wider world. It was dominated, according to *Kelly's* by 'the sale of corn, cattle and cheese', but no doubt every other variety of produce was sold as well.

To the farmers visiting the town on Wednesday Wincanton offered a glimpse of developments not yet known in their own localities. The town, *Kelly's* assured its readers, was 'paved, lighted with gas from works situated in Station Road and well supplied with water...conveyed through pipes...the town has also been efficiently drained.' My mother, in rural Holton, however, never saw such wonders except when visiting Wincanton, her life being one of water from the well, oil lamps and earth closets.

By the turn of the century, the time when my mother was entering her teens, the march of progress had not eradicated earlier traditions, lovingly recorded by George Sweetman. A practical joke was known locally as 'a George Turk's lark', the original holder of the name having become notorious for his much repeated remark; 'I've had such a spree this morning!...I emptied a kiddle [kettle] o' boiling water over brother Bill's legs.' 'A thing of little value,' Sweetman also noted, 'is described as "summet o' nothin' like what Tom Gough zeed at the show"', though what Tom Gough had actually seen was now forgotten. A man asked why he was idle would, for equally mysterious reasons, reply: 'I be keeping Burfitt's commandements (*sic*) to do no manner of work.' I cannot recall my mother mentioning any of these local phrases, and she was, I am sure, too kind-hearted a child to have joined in the traditional street cry raised after the town crier had ended an announcement with 'God save the queen!': 'And hang the crier.'[20]

In 1887, the year of my mother's birth, the first modest industrial development occurred in her part of Somerset, the establishing of a milk processing plant.[21] This rapidly expanded until in the 1920s it became part of the giant Cow and Gate baby food company, later absorbed into the even larger Unigate. The opening of this 'creamery', as it was known, was important both to dairy farmers, like my grandfather, for whom it provided a large, new and reliable market, and to workers on the land, offering them at last an alternative to the ill-paid drudgery of farm labour. My mother was never expected to work either in the fields or in a factory, but her life was nevertheless one of wearisome toil which made no real use of her talents. I now feel she was extraordinarily unlucky in that no one seems to have recognised them, nor set her on the path to acquiring proper qualifications. The obvious person to do so was the schoolmaster at Cheriton, where she was a star pupil, or the local vicar, who knew her well. I still have the eminently suitable book, *Something to do* by Louisa M. Alcott, of *Little Women* fame, 'Given to her by her friend and priest...', as the inscription reads, 'in grateful remembrance of her regular attendance in the choir and at the catechism services.' This was on Lady Day, 25 March 1900, when she was approaching her thirteenth birthday, by which time her intelligence and literary aptitude must have been apparent. Her father, however, having failed to stand up to *his* father over his own career, seems to have made no attempt to help his gifted daughter, and other relations, confirming my low opinion of them, seem to have seen her intelligence, good nature, willingness to work hard and trustworthiness merely as an invitation to exploitation. Around the age of 13 she left school to begin a whole series of prolonged visits to members of the family, or their friends, as an unpaid domestic and general help, a kind of native *au pair* girl. Her first hosts were the best, a schoolmaster and his sister who lived at Launceston in Cornwall; they gave her some private tuition and encouraged her to gain experience of teaching small children. She recalled with pride to me years later how, after she had taken the infant class in scripture, they received the most glowing report on their progress and knowledge in the school's history. Had she stayed there her life might well have proved very different and more fulfilling, but around the age of 15 she was shunted off elsewhere to become what was essentially an unpaid domestic servant, 'living as family' with friends of her father, a couple who let high-class apartments in Bath. The clientele consisted of retired admirals and other comfortably off people and it was here that my mother acquired the educated, though never affected, voice and naturally polished manners which cannot have been learned on The Farm at Holton. She always thought this period had been socially helpful to her and never displayed any resentment at what still seems to me her disgracefully shabby treatment.

From Bath the young Maggie Rowden went to stay with her father's sister, known as 'Aunty Tri', short for Trifena, and her husband, 'Uncle Corny', ie Cornelius, at Lane End Farm, at Ringwood in Hampshire. She was always fond of animals – her children often teased her about her affection for cows – and she had acquired a pet lamb, which she took for a walk on a long ribbon in the evenings. This unusual pet attracted the attention of my father, who was still earning his living in the town where his first wife had died a year or two before and was finding his business, as well as his personal, life hard. When he left Ringwood to work in Newbury he asked my mother to tend his first wife's grave, which, with characteristic unselfishness, she agreed to do.

My father was by no means the only suitor taking an interest in my mother. She was, as surviving photographs show, of attractive appearance, and clearly much better educated than most women at the time, while her wholly exceptional sweetness of disposition must have been evident even then. She had, while still living at Holton, caught the eye of a master at Wincanton council school, whose sister had introduced them, and, from what my mother told me of him fifty years later, he sounded admirably well suited as a husband for her. He did in fact correspond with her for some time but when, eventually, he did propose, she turned him down, for reasons she failed to explain. He later married a farmer's daughter from the Wincanton area and, in 1960, was still alive, though retired, and living in Bristol.

More romantic, and tragic, was the story of 'Billy', a Holton farmer who wrote to my mother while she was staying at Lane End Farm, explaining that he wished to discuss their future and asking her to meet him at Ringwood station at a specified time. If she failed to come, he said, he would know she did not wish to consider his proposal. But my mother never saw the letter. Billy's handwriting was recognised by the evil Aunt Tri, who having opened the letter and read it, realised that, if my mother accepted him she would move away and her services as an unpaid domestic would be lost for ever. With a wickedness that I still find hard to contemplate she destroyed the letter, leaving my mother in ignorance of it, and poor Billy to wait for hours at Ringwood station, supposing that my mother could not even be bothered to reply to his offer. The consequences again are reminiscent of a story by Hardy. Billy duly married someone else, but with such reluctance that he was discovered in tears the night before the wedding, and, when questioned, protested that he was marrying against his better judgement and that Maggie Rowden had been, and would always be, the only woman for him.

The affair had an unexpected sequel. Many years later Billy's wife happened to meet my mother who was, she told me, conscious of the other woman's violent antipathy toward her even before they had exchanged names. On Aunty Tri's death the whole sad business came to light. On her deathbed she sent for my mother's brother, Tom, and the local vicar, to confess what she had done, declaring she could not die in peace with such a sin on her conscience. Unhappily they do not seem to have thought to suggest she should make amends by leaving a legacy to my mother, trivial recompense though it would have been for such a monstrous wrong. But my mother did at last learn the truth, years after she had married my father, with all the consequences I shall shortly describe. 'Would you have married Billy, if you had met him that day and he had proposed?', I asked her. She thought not, but I was not convinced and, typically, what distressed her was not the loss of her own opportunity but the thought of the sad young man waiting at the station and looking up hopefully at each approaching step. 'I would certainly have gone to meet him', my mother said, and my strong impression is that she would have accepted him.

As it was, thanks to a selfish old woman the field was left clear for my father, who returned to Ringwood to propose and be accepted. No one else showed any enthusiasm for the match, due in part to my father's sallow complexion which led to the rumour that 'Maggie Rowden is marrying an Indian', though, as I have shown, he came from generations of impeccably Anglo-Saxon stock. The monstrous Aunty Tri, having failed to keep my mother as an unpaid servant and companion – the disappointment she must have felt at losing my mother's services after all is the one cheerful aspect of the affair – no doubt opposed the marriage and the gulf between him and his family, after his previously unpopular and short-lived marriage, seems to have remained unbridged. The wedding was, my mother told me, a very quiet affair. The witnesses were Alice Mary Moore Rowden, evidently a relation, and Albert B. Bartlett, whose connection with the family remains unexplained. Nothing survives of that day except the official certificate and a single postcard from an EE Smith of Bournemouth offering 'every good wish for your future health, wealth and happiness'; of the second of these at least the marriage was to yield remarkably little.

Why my mother should have chosen to marry my father when at least two other suitors belonging to far more promising professions and already better known to her were already in the field, remains a mystery to me, as it did to all of us. 'Why on earth did mum marry dad?' I recall my brother asking me. It must, I think, have been the very qualities in my father which I find it hardest to forgive which attracted her. She was above all a *kind* woman and my father, essentially ineffective and already, I suspect, possessing the air of a lifelong loser, must have made her feel that he needed her more than the other men who wished to marry her. This was the impression she gave me, when, in a suitably roundabout way, I raised the subject with her and it was certainly true, as she said, that he was an essentially decent man, good-natured, generous, when, rarely, he was in funds, and trusting, the reason perhaps that he was the worst businessman I have ever met. In brief, I think he aroused her protective instincts and the fact that he was practising a relatively new, even mildly glamorous, trade may have added to his appeal. No doubt, too, there were other reasons. As a young widower, so rapidly and tragically bereaved, he must have attracted some sympathy in Ringwood, while – though we never discussed such matters in the family – my mother once hinted to me that, even late in life, he remained an ardent lover. He was certainly always utterly devoted to my mother, as who could not have been?

So the 32-year old widower photographer and the 24-year old farmer's daughter were married, at the parish church of Ringwood, on Tuesday 30 April 1912. There was no honeymoon, an indication perhaps that already my father had no money to spare, merely a celebratory supper. It was hardly an encouraging beginning.

---

[1] Local History Pack, Holton Library
[2] *Poems of [Alfred Lord] Tennyson 1829-1868* p.168
[3] *Pickwick Papers* Chapter XVI
[4] Bowden title page
[5] Sweetman pp.3-4
[6] *Kelly's Directory* 1883 & 1889
[7] Bowden p.5
[8] *Kelly's Directory* 1883
[9] Bowden p.172
[10] See *The Workhouse*, though it makes no specific mention of Wincanton, for a general account of this important institution.
[11] Bowden p.5
[12] Sweetman p.111
[13] Sweetman p.111
[14] Sweetman p.264
[15] Bowden p.173
[16] Sweetman p.263
[17] Bowden p.93, *Kelly's Directory* 1889
[18] Bowden p.92 from the *Castle Cary Visitor* quoting the *Taunton Courier*
[19] Bowden p.93
[20] Sweetman p.279, Bowden p.5
[21] Bowden p.91

3

A BRIGHT AND FLOURISHING TOWN

The bright and flourishing town of Newbury is an ancient and interesting place.

Walter Money, A Popular History of Newbury, *1905*

At the beginning of the twentieth century Newbury was still similar in character to Wincanton, 54 miles [87km] away to the south-west, though much larger. Its population in 1911, the year before my father settled there with my mother, was 12,107, but, after substantial expansion during the Victorian period, it was now growing more slowly, acquiring a mere 200 extra citizens by the time of the next census, in 1921.[1] Already its time of greatest prosperity and importance, it seemed, lay in the past. There had been a settlement close by since Roman times and the name, derived from 'new bourg' or 'new borough', had been in use since at least 1079.[2] It had, however, been the wool trade which had made the town rich and well known thanks to the activities of its most famous citizen, the successful clothier, John Winchcombe, 'Jack of Newbury', who had died in 1519.[3] Subsequently the town had achieved some notoriety as a hotbed of protestantism. The three 'Newbury martyrs', who rejected Queen Mary I's attempt to re-introduce Roman Catholicism, were burned in 1556, and in the Civil War, which broke out in 1642, the citizens were, predictably, on the side of the puritans and parliament.

The two Battles of Newbury, in 1643 and 1644, also earned a place in the history books and the town was a familiar name throughout the kingdom thanks to its geographical situation, which made it a communications centre during the coaching era. At the peak of this trade, around 1800, every frequent traveller to the South of England was likely to have passed through it or changed coaches there, though with the coming of the railways – Newbury station was opened in 1847 – its significance dwindled.[4] Newbury was now a mere stop on the less important of the routes from London to the south-west and though it became a junction for the cross-country line linking Southampton and Didcot, in 1882, and the very minor branch line from Newbury to Lambourn in 1898, the glory of the coaching days had vanished.

Newbury in 1912 was a small, highly typical, market town serving a substantial area of fertile countryside, with a basic structure which had changed little since medieval times. The three main streets formed a 'Y', of which the base stood on the main Bath to London road, the former being 48 miles [68km] away to the left, i.e. due west, the latter 57 miles, if one turned right, to the east. Down one arm of the 'Y' came traffic from Southampton, 36 miles [58km] to the south, and Winchester, 22 miles [35km] away in the same direction. Via the other arm Newbury was linked to Andover, 17 miles [27km] to the south-west, and thence to Salisbury and the Dorset coast at Weymouth. Oxford lay 27 miles [42km] to the north and Reading, the 'big town' of my childhood to visit which was a great adventure, 17 miles [27km] eastwards on the road to London. The natural centre of the town was the water bridge over the Kennet and Avon Canal which bisected Newbury, and was at the middle of the 'Y' just described, with the two streams of traffic coming together there before entering the main street. Just across the bridge, going south, lay the heart of the town, still basically unchanged since my father had first seen it. Here one found the Market Place, with on one corner the somewhat functional-sounding Municipal Buildings, formerly the site of the historic Guildhall and now more romantically known as the Old Town Hall. To the left, going upstream towards Reading, on the right bank of the river, was the Wharf, another prosaic name, though formerly apt, for it had once been a thriving centre of the canal trade. By the time I knew it, it was a bus station, but this has now moved elsewhere.

On the far corner of the Market Place still stands, though now much modernised inside, the principal public building of the whole area, the Corn Exchange, opened in 1862.[5] Market Day in Newbury has always been Thursday, just as in Wincanton it had invariably been Wednesday, and on that day throughout my childhood the Corn Exchange reverted to its original purpose, with the Dickensian high desks with their sloping tops and capacious interiors being brought out of store for use by the traders. Market Day also saw two other places coming to life. One was the Cattle Market, which had been extended in 1873. 'The opening ceremony,' the town's historian, Walter Money recorded, 'was an occasion of considerable festivity, being attended by the three county Members and leading agriculturists.'[6] The guest of honour – who else indeed could it have been in that deferential, class-conscious age? – was the principal local nobleman, the Earl of Carnarvon, 'who recalled the fact that his father, thirty-two years previously, had presided over the annual dinner of the Newbury Cattle and Agricultural Association'. I shall mention later our, strictly business, contact with the Carnarvon family. For the ordinary townsman or woman, and not least for the local children, the real centre of activity on Market Day, however, was the street market, of which, too, I shall say more later.

Though much larger, Newbury, like Wincanton, provided in textbook fashion a reflection of every major trend or development in national history, from the Reformation to the arrival of the bicycle. It was neither a pioneering community, nor a particularly old-fashioned one, rather the very archetype of a borough that never took the lead, nor dragged its feet, a decent, dull place more likely to inspire in its sons, as it did in me, a mild loyalty than a passionate devotion.

My father must, for reasons I explain later, have been resident in Newbury, at least for a time, as early as 1904, and already become an active member of the community. Just about this time the first comprehensive account of the town's past was published, Walter Money's classic *History of Newbury*, which appeared in 1905, when a copy was buried beneath the foundation stone of the public library.[7] The work bore many resemblances to George Sweetman's *History of Wincanton*, issued two years before and Money described his native town in almost identical terms. 'The bright and flourishing town of Newbury is an ancient and interesting place,' he declared, going on to recount how it had been visited over the centuries by a series of famous diarists and other writers, John Evelyn, in 1654, Samuel Pepys, in 1668, Daniel Defoe, about 1724, and William Cobbett, in 1821, all of whom had written about the experience. I shall say more of Cobbett's reaction later.

Newbury was by any test a more important place than Wincanton and had exerted far more influence on English history, but in many ways the story of the two places was remarkably similar. Newbury had, in 1835, like Wincanton, become the centre of a Poor Law union and acquired its own workhouse, which I shall also mention again. It had, like so many places, including Wincanton, suffered a disastrous fire, only extinguished by setting up a chain of buckets from the river by the Town Mills to the seat of the blaze between Bartholomew Street and Cheap Street, where the two approaches to the Water Bridge come together.[8] As a result, the Newbury Volunteer Fire Brigade was founded, a part-time force manning a horse-drawn pump, later replaced by a steam engine, bought by public appeal.

I remain in the dark as to why my father moved back from Newbury, where he seems to have had an assured place at least in the dramatic and operatic societies, to Ringwood but I have my mother's recollection as to why he finally settled in Newbury. He had, she told me, developed an affection for the town and he had failed to have much success in Ringwood. The return to Newbury was intended to provide a fresh start, the new business being financed by my mother's money, presumably left to her by her father, though I never established from where it originated – The Farm, when I visited it much later, still gave no sign of prosperity and my mother had, as I have described, been sent to the village school along with the humblest labourer's children. Nor do I knew how much was involved, but it should, I believe, have been sufficient to establish him in at least a modest way. I can recall my mother telling me that, having given her husband the money to make some small purchase, she had told him to keep the change for himself, nearly £5, a large sum at that time, sufficient to feed a working class family for a month.

With hindsight it seems that the town was not the ideal place to choose for such a venture, but I have no doubt that my father's optimism, and his incurable inability to take a business-like approach, must have influenced my mother. The best prospects for a young man setting out to make his mark in this still new and essentially luxury trade surely lay in a place with no one already practising it. Newbury, by contrast, already possessed several photographers, more, it seems now, than it could really support. The best known seems to have been JW Righton, with whom my father was later to go into partnership. Righton had published as recently as 1900 a collection of photographs with accompanying text, *Newbury and Neighbourhood*.[9] It is not merely the drab sepia of the prints but the reverential quality of the captions which admirably conveys the forelock-touching atmosphere of a small market town at the turn of the century. One evocative picture shows an imposing brake, drawn by two elegant 'greys' under the direction of a top-hatted coachman, about to take a house party and their extensive luggage back to Newbury station – where, no doubt, an equally deferential reception awaited them – after a hunt ball at Arlington Manor, 'the country residence of Sir Francis and Lady Jeune'.[10] A bare-headed, black-tied butler stands at a respectful distance in the rear. The only photograph in the whole book of ordinary local residents shows schoolchildren and teachers being entertained by the Earl of Carnarvon and his household – the ladies in strikingly elegant outfits, with parasols – at Highclere Castle, the 'big house' of the Newbury area. Also featured in Righton's collection was Stargroves, 'a small but luxuriously appointed mansion, the residence of Sir FW Carden'. Although my father later shed the Conservative opinions which, like most small tradesmen, he held at the time, he always spoke warmly of 'Freddie' Carden, a popular figure locally, and indeed of the Carnarvon family and they were to remain notably loyal to him when he fell on hard times.

JW Righton's photographs, uninspired though they were, reveal what a peaceful place Newbury must have been at the turn of the century. The Broadway, which sixty years before would have been alive with coaches arriving at or departing from the cluster of inns in Speenhamland, and thirty years later would have been thronged with motor traffic, is deserted except for a solitary horse and trap, watched by a handful of idle passers-by. Another picture shows the Water Bridge end of Northbrook Street. This presents a slightly more lively picture, with several single-horse conveyances, but not a single motor car. The main signs of activity are a dog crossing the road in a leisurely way and a schoolboy sauntering across with a basket on his shoulder.

The advertisements in Righton's book also reflect a very different world from today. One tailor's announcement evokes the memory of the legendary 'Newbury coat', made, for a bet, from wool taken from a sheep's back at sunrise, one morning in 1811, and worn, fully finished and dyed, before sunset that evening. 'Equal dispatch today by Hannibal Hill', the latter, somewhat improbably, promised. 'Family and Furnishing Drapers', a 'Family Bread and Biscuit Baker' – 'Every description of bread made and delivered daily to all parts of the town, district and country, including the Bermaline Bread, as supplied to Her Majesty the Queen' – 'Corn and Cake Merchants' – 'Corn Ground and Dressed or Cracked and Split' and a Cartage Agent, 'By Horse or Steam Power', all offered their services. An echo of the past was provided by the advertisement of 'The Old Pelican Posting House', on the site of the once nationally renowned inn, now reduced to offering 'Livery and Bait Stables' and 'Good Loose Boxes for Hunters'. Only one advertiser foreshadowed the more aggressive selling methods of the new century, Newbury's best known, self-made and wholly irrepressible businessman, James Tufnail. Typically, he was the only tradesman to buy a double page spread in *Newbury and Neighbourhood* and he exploited the space to the full, with bold, slanting displays in modern type announcing the variety of services his shops offered. He was not, however, involved with what had become Newbury's most famous product at this time, the cloth trade which had created its wealth having long since declined and the industry which today dominates it, electronics, not yet having been invented. The standard bearer of the town's trade in Edwardian times was the sausage. People were said to come from miles around to buy sausages made in the town and one pork butcher, although displaying all the deference then expected of shopkeepers – 'Your Patronage and Recommendation respectfully solicited' – included in his advertisement the wholly modern element of an analyst's report, dated 1897, testifying to 'the wholesome digestive and dietetic excellence of the sausages', modestly priced at 8d per lb [3p per 450gm].[11] (A piano, by contrast, advertised in the same publication, was offered at £24.)

Although King George V was already on the throne when my father settled permanently in Newbury in 1912 the town remained, both in appearance and outlook, much as it had been in Victorian times. Peat, cut on Greenham Common, was still being sold door to door from a horse and cart.[12] Newbury possessed its own brick kilns, tanners, flour mills and, in 1901, six brewers, who, according to one new arrival who counted the inn signboards as he enjoyed his first walk round the town, supplied more than eighty public houses.[13] Ploughs and similar equipment were made by the town's own iron founders and there were numerous blacksmiths.[14] The principal saddler did a brisk business catering for farmers and 'the carriage trade', which, according to a local historian, included 'the rector, the residents of Donnington Square and Miss Myers of Sandleford Priory'.[15] The shops were largely long-established and looked it, often small, with goods set out on the steps leading down from the street. At least two of the butchers' shops had been on their existing sites since 1800[16] and still had their own abattoirs directly behind them, as in the case of one, Maggs of Northbrook Street, I was personally to discover. Two registry offices supplied domestic servants, one of the commonest categories of employment, and two taxidermists were kept busy preserving the game and fish shot or caught by local sportsmen. No leading chain stores had yet reached the town but one large shop was soon to blossom into its first department store and there were several substantial drapers, whose owners were easily identifiable by the frocktailed coats and striped trousers they wore in business hours. The assistants were also formally dressed, the women in black dresses or suits, and commonly lived in. The greatest business expansion in the town in the previous two decades had been the multiplication of bicycle shops, which numbered at least four, and stored machines while their owners were attending the market. [17] For anything except personal transport, and still, for the better-off, for that as well, the horse remained supreme. The carriers' carts which kept those villages not near the railway in touch with Newbury, and whose owners also carried out commissions for villagers, even to the extent of choosing a new hat for a village woman reluctant to travel into town, were still mainly horse-drawn. Such visits provided a weekly treat and an opportunity to visit the hairdresser in Cheap Street, where the ritual of shampooing and curling was carried on with the help of a primitive hair-dryer, a cane fan waved back and forth by the owner, to supplement her exertions with the towel.[18]

A photograph taken around 1909, just before my father set up business in Newbury, shows the shop at Number 42 Northbrook Street he was later to occupy, and above which I was later to be born. 'The building,' a recent Newbury historian has captioned the picture, 'is early Georgian in an unusual "Spanish Netherlands" style; the figure at the top left was one of four depicting the Four Seasons.'[19] Outside an open wagon is being drawn by two large carthorses in the annual Whit Monday Horse Parade, in which up to fifty entrants took part. On the pavement are two boys in sailor suits and a woman in an elaborate gown and bonnet.

Such a scene might have been captured at any date since the invention of photography, but even in Newbury there were signs that the times were changing. In 1900, when the relief of the besieged town of Mafeking in distant South Africa had produced a spontaneous outburst of national rejoicing, the news had only reached Newbury via the railway, and it was the firing of rockets from the station which alerted the rest of the town and set in motion the celebration of Mafeking Night. Around the same date, however, the first telephone was installed in Newbury and, before long, the tiny, all manual exchange was linked to others elsewhere.[20]

The opening of the public library, already mentioned, in 1905, had supplemented, and was ultimately to supplant, the small commercial lending libraries, devoted mainly to fiction, which already existed, like that operated in his shop by the ubiquitous James Tufnail.[21] The 'free library', as it was commonly described, was an important feature of the town and the first of its institutions of which I became aware. It had first established its place in the town, rather as the BBC under Sir John Reith was to do in the nation, thanks to being presided over by a notoriously censorious and dictatorial individual who refused to issue books of which he disapproved.[22] He was able to impose his tastes on the whole town because borrowers were not allowed access to the shelves but had to select the title they wanted from the printed catalogues and then apply to borrow it.[23] Happily by the time I began to use it a more liberal regime, and a more enlightened librarian – who, in retirement, answered some of my questions for the present book – had taken over. There was from the first a large reading room, much used during the first world war for consulting casualty lists in the newspapers, though I remember it as a resort, during the dismal 1930s, of sad looking, shabbily dressed, unemployed men, hopelessly combing the 'Situations Vacant' columns of the local newspapers, and occasionally of a grubby, unshaven tramp enjoying the chance to sit down, and sometimes doze off, in the warm.

Newbury had had a piped water supply since 1878[24] and a modern drainage system – something my mother's village in Somerset was not to enjoy for many decades – since 1895, it being a great source of local pride that the pumps had, since 1912, been operated by electricity.[25] This had otherwise made little progress in the town. Walter Money, boasting of its public utilities in 1905, had claimed that 'all indicate that the place is now well abreast of the times, though', he added, 'as a rule improvements have only been introduced after rather long reflection on the part of the municipal authorities. Unfortunately this *laissez-faire* has resulted in the water supply and electric lighting passing into the hands of private companies and thus sensibly affecting the future interests of the ratepayers',[26] a well-merited criticism, as my own experience was to confirm.

In 1912 the name of Newbury was familiar throughout the country thanks to a recently acquired amenity, its racecourse.[27] The area had long been used for training racehorses and occasional race meetings, on makeshift courses, had been held locally for nearly two centuries before a leading local trainer sought a licence from the Jockey Club to open a permanent, full-scale course there. He had, for no very good reason, been turned down, and smarting from the rebuff, happened to run into Edward VII, for whom he had trained horses. The king personally intervened to get the decision reversed and the new Newbury racecourse was opened in 1905 and soon acquired its own railway station and a regular schedule of meetings, of which I later became aware, thanks, as I shall describe, to the crowds of visitors it brought to the town and the casual employment race days sometimes provided for my father.

Newbury boasted of its ancient charities but I remain somewhat sceptical about them; none proved of the slightest assistance to us when we needed them, nor did we benefit, until the National Health Service made them universally available, from the town's medical facilities. As a self-supporting small tradesman my father would not have expected to make use of the free Dispensary which was still functioning in the opening decade of the twentieth century, though established as long ago as 1778 'for the purpose of relieving, with advice and medicine gratis, such persons whose poverty and indigence will not permit them to procure other medical assistance',[28] a description soon to apply to my family. The town had had its own Medical Officer of Health, partly financed by a government grant, since 1874, and Newbury District Hospital, which was to play a significant part in our lives, went back almost as far, free in-patient provision having before that been confined to the workhouse infirmary, which catered primarily for the institution's own inmates. 'The Hospital', as it was always known, owed its existence, unusually, to the railway revolution.[29] A small Nurses Home and Navvy Hospital had been set up in a group of private houses to care for labourers injured while building the Didcot, Newbury and Southampton Railway and when this establishment closed, on the completion of the line, a subscription was raised to provide a public hospital. When it opened, in 1885, it contained a mere twelve beds, but the buildings were later extended, in time to accommodate men wounded on the Western Front during the first world war, and one of my earliest memories is of attending the 'open day' which marked the addition of extensive new wards and a modern operating theatre in 1931. I was deeply impressed by the general air of light and spaciousness, in striking contrast to our dark and cramped surroundings at home.

A hospital at the beginning of the century tended to be in every sense a place of last resort, a charitable institution caring for those from humble and overcrowded homes who could not be treated under their own roofs, and a great fear remained of epidemics. The names of the most notorious infectious diseases were still being spoken of in my childhood, just as in Victorian England, with real dread. As recently as 1903 a smallpox epidemic had raged through Newbury and in 1910 an outbreak of scarlet fever, then often fatal, caused several schools to be closed.[30] In 1914 the council girls' school was similarly shut down for a time on account of another deadly scourge, diphtheria. By most tests, however, Newbury children were not badly cared for. Those classic indicators of malnourishment and overcrowding, rickets and ringworm, showed a fall in the number of cases reported each year by the Schools Medical Officer,[31] and the number of heads infected with vermin, still a great preoccupation when twenty years later I started school, was over the long term declining.

As might have been expected of a market town in an agricultural area Newbury had for many years been represented in Parliament by a Conservative landowner. It had been a great sensation when, in the famous 'landslide' election of 1906, he was defeated by a Liberal lawyer, whose election address had bravely criticised 'the power of the big house, the brewery and the parsonage, the influence of the farmer' and 'the still lingering serfdom...of the labourer'.[32] Such talk was not at all what the electors of South Berkshire were accustomed to hear; the result was recognised as a brief-lived aberration and in 1910 the town returned to its traditional, solidly Tory, allegiance.

The Liberal government which took office in 1906 undoubtedly, as is often said, laid the foundations of the welfare state, but it did not erect the main edifice, for which the credit belongs to the great Labour Ministry of 1945. The schemes of national unemployment and medical insurance which the Liberals introduced benefitted only a minority of the population and in Newbury the most obvious sign of provision for the poor remained 'the house on the hill', as the workhouse, from its location at the top of Newtown Road, was known.[33] Admission to it, regarded as the ultimate disgrace, was euphemistically referred to as 'going up the hill'. The workhouse was, as I shall describe, to remain a threatening presence throughout my childhood, but must have seemed infinitely remote to my parents when they set up house a good way from it, in the main part of the town, in 1912.

My parents no doubt assumed when they came to live in Newbury that children would arrive before long and, if they considered their education at all, presumably planned that they would, like other tradesmen's children, go initially to fee-paying private schools and to 'the Grammar School', officially St Bartholomew's Grammar School for Boys, or 'the High School', ie the Newbury Girls' School.[34] The former had a long history, variously said to go back to 1467 or 1547. Since 1885 it had been housed in impressive, custom-built buildings,[35] which had in 1912, around the time my parents arrived in Newbury, been further extended to cope with its rapid expansion. It enjoyed considerable status under a much respected headmaster, Edward Sharwood Smith,[36] later author of a minor educational classic, *The Faith of a Schoolmaster*. 'The High School', like the whole idea of secondary education for young women, was a much more recent development.[37] It had been founded only in 1904 but its initial hundred pupils had, by 1914, risen to 250, the school having moved in 1910 to splendid new premises on the Andover Road, not far from the equally handsome hospital.[38] The school's first headmistress, of whom I shall say more later, the formidable Miss Esther Luker, was a champion of women's rights as well as of education; in 1909 the first suffragette meeting, a great curiosity, had been held in the town.

At the time my parents settled there Newbury had for many years lacked a theatre but a new, and what then seemed almost miraculous, type of entertainment had recently taken its place, the Newbury Cinema, described by the *Newbury Weekly News* as an 'animated picture theatre' when it opened its doors in November 1910.[39] It was the boldest venture yet of that great self-publicist and innovator, James Tufnail, who in the best traditions of poor boy made good had arrived in the town in 1887 with his total wealth, 7d [3p] in his pocket.[40] 'Jimmy' Tufnail, also known as 'Tuffy', was soon to be at odds with the council, but at the opening of his cinema the councillors were present in force and the mayor warmly congratulated him on his enterprise. A rival establishment, the Picture Palace, was opened a month later, in a better location, in the main street, but both had closed down by the time I reached cinema-going age and been replaced by more impressive establishments, as I shall describe.

The other great innovation of the decade before the first world war was the appearance on the streets in sizeable numbers of the motor vehicle. In the early part of the period the horse remained supreme, as surviving pictures testify. One of the King's Arms Hotel, in the Market Place, dating from around 1907, shows a single horse gig standing outside, with signs over the frontage advertising 'Harness Horse and Cobs on Hire' and 'Hunters and Hacks for Sale or Hire'.[41] Six years later a photograph covering an immediately adjoining area reveals the presence of a large number of bicycles and a horse-drawn removal wagon. Photographs of the other main streets taken around the same time are equally bare of motor vehicles. But change was on the way. A photograph of an early 'rally' on the Wharf shows five brave pioneers at the wheels of a variety of vehicles and can be dated as being taken before 1904, when licence plates, not to be seen in the picture, became compulsory.[42] Another early motorist was the Superintendent of Police, who bought himself a 15hp Darracq, later acquired by the County Council for police use,[43] though ordinary 'bobbies' still went on foot or by bicycle. The fire brigade finally replaced its horse-drawn steam pump with a petrol-powered appliance in 1913 after a shaming experience in which it failed to attend a fire because no horses could be found to pull the pump. By the following year at least one rural carrier serving the Newbury area had abandoned his faithful horse and cart for a motor-van, which carried passengers as well as parcels.[44]

It was the expense of maintaining a car which was prohibitive, rather than the initial cost, which could be surprisingly modest. An advertisement in the *Newbury Weekly News* offered 'CARS FOR 1914' which included a 15/20 hp Studebaker, priced at £200, though more powerful models cost from £245 to £350. The less well off could settle for a motor-cycle, such as 'the marvellous Humberette cyclecar', available 'at £120 complete' – shown in one of the first photographs to appear in the newspaper, another sign of the changing times. In 1897 Queen Victoria's Diamond Jubilee celebrations had been recorded by the *Newbury Weekly News* not in photographs but line drawings; by 1911 it was able to mark the coronation of George V with a pictorial supplement, with photographs printed on specially coated paper.[45]

I doubt if my father's financial position at this time would have permitted his buying a car, but I do, with hindsight, regret that he failed to buy a house, a solid asset that might have enabled him to survive the financial storms ahead. Instead, like most newly married couples at the time, my parents rented a property, of which an enormous number were readily available at a modest cost. My mother recalled one landlord remarking eagerly, 'I do hope you'll take it' as they looked over one house costing 7s 6d [37.5p] a week. They finally settled on a semi-detached house in Queens Road, not far from Newbury station, a middle-class district entirely suitable to their station in life.

Looking now at the position which confronted my father when, in 1913, he set out to establish himself, in his early thirties, in a town he already knew, helped by a loyal and devoted wife, I still find it hard to discover any obvious reason why he should not have achieved a modest degree of success. Newbury had, as I have mentioned, several photographers already, but it served a wide hinterland, my father must have made many contacts through his amateur dramatic activities, and he was excellent at his job and no doubt younger than most of his more established rivals. Photography, as the opening of the two cinemas in the town had in a way confirmed, was an expanding occupation, long known in Newbury. The first 'photographic artist', as his advertisement described him, had set up in business in the town in 1854, though the profession was then often combined with another, such as picture framer or teacher of drawing. One early photographer was also a hairdresser and others sold jewellery, spectacles and even toys. Two of Newbury's earliest photographers were also artists of some reputation and by 1912 there were four others practising in the town, with several more in the larger villages.[46]

In 1913, when he first appears in a local directory, both as householder and professionally, he apparently worked from home in Queens Road, but he had hardly become known in Newbury when the first world war broke out. The big event of the year was the fete on August Bank Holiday, which in 1914 fell on Monday the 3rd and at midnight that day the British ultimatum to Germany expired.[47] The planned festivities included an obstacle race and comic football match and the weather was, for once, ideal, but everyone's thoughts, as the Territorials gathered at the Drill Hall in Craven road, were on the sudden crisis that seemed to have come out of a clear sky. My parents had vivid memories of how muted was the enjoyment of all those at the fete, though no one had the faintest inkling of the slaughter ahead and the *Newbury Weekly News* that Thursday kept a proper sense of proportion: the modest single column heading 'WAR DECLARED' shared the upper half of a page with 'DISTRESSING FATALITY. Misadventure with a gun', describing a shooting accident on Wash Common. Ten weeks later the newspaper recorded the first deaths in action of a Newbury man, then, for a time, the dead were identified in the 'Roll of Honour' of all those serving by a black line under their name, until, with the coming of conscription, they became so numerous that the list was dropped altogether.[48]

Apart from the loss, often for ever, of most of its younger men, Newbury was less affected by the war than many other places, though troops were stationed in the locality and, years later, I came across the remains of some of the trenches supposedly dug during exercises on Greenham Common while they prepared to leave for France. My mother's chief memory of this period was not of the food shortages which must have affected Newbury as they did other places, but of the sight of men drilling on the fields of the local grammar school and especially the horrifying commentaries of the NCOs in charge of bayonet practice. Newbury seems indeed to have been notably lacking in hatred of the enemy, for when several thousand German prisoners of war were housed on the racecourse there was, the *Newbury Weekly News* reported, 'no indication of hostility' and the captive enemy good-naturedly sang *It's a Long Way to Tipperary*, though, it was observed, their rendering of it 'lacked the sincerity and swing with which Tommy Atkins rolls it out'.[49]

Trade everywhere was at first depressed in spite of the official campaign for 'Business as usual' and my father's firm no doubt suffered with the rest, but demands for regimental group photographs must have gone at least some way to fill the gap. Perhaps it was none the less a decline in income which encouraged my father to volunteer for the army, as well as the general pressure on every man of military age to come forward, though at 35, with a record of childhood ill health, and as a married man with a one-man business, he might easily have found excuses to hold back. As it was, during 1915, just when my mother was expecting their first child, he became Private Longmate in the Oxfordshire and Buckinghamshire Light Infantry.

I cannot imagine that the camaraderie and coarseness of the barrack room remotely suited him, though he retained some memories of military drill and I would sometimes 'Quick March' and 'Right Wheel' to his orders when we went for walks on Greenham Common, but the suggestion always came from me and followed my initiation into these manoeuvres at school. He spoke little of his time in the army and all I remember him telling me of this period is that the unit orderly room had not bothered to pass on to him the telegram reporting that his mother was dying so that he arrived too late to see her, the only occasion on which he mentioned either of his parents to me. He did recall, however, that when the rest of his battalion of the 'Ox and Bucks' was sent to France he was held back at the depot as medically unfit for front-line service. This had, ironically, almost certainly saved his life, for most of his former comrades were killed during the bloody campaigns of 1917. Around this time it was realised he would be of more use practising his civilian trade in the Royal Flying Corps, to which he was transferred, again remaining in Great Britain, and in due course he became an Aircraftsman in the Royal Air Force, when it replaced the RFC on 1 April 1918.

With the rapid demobilization which followed the armistice he was, I assume, back in Newbury early in 1919, now the father of a son, my brother having been born on 28 October 1916. He was christened Arthur Gordon but always known by his second name, and occasionally within the family, for reasons I cannot recall, as 'Joe'. He was rapidly joined by a sister, Freda Elsie, born on 15 May 1921, in the family home in Queens Road. The transition from bachelor tradesman to family man with an established business seemed to have been painlessly accomplished and the dull but not unpleasant life of a small town small business man appeared to lie ahead.

[1] Garlick p.227
[2] Money pp.11-12
[3] Money pp.25-28
[4] Money p.108
[5] Money p.130
[6] Money p.130
[7] Money p.v
[8] Garlick pp.56-7
[9] Cannon p.7
[10] Righton p.32
[11] Righton p.59
[12] Garlick p.170
[13] Purvis p.32
[14] Garlick p.173
[15] Garlick p.171
[16] Hopson p.29
[17] Garlick p.172
[18] Garlick p.171
[19] Hopson p.29
[20] Garlick p.188
[21] Garlick p.201
[22] Hopson p.64
[23] Garlick p.193
[24] Purvis p.30
[25] Garlick p.189
[26] Money p.115
[27] Tolman p.98
[28] Garlick p.199
[29] Tolman p.58, Hopson p.76
[30] Garlick p.201
[31] Garlick p.201
[32] Garlick p.36
[33] Stokes p.62
[34] Stewart Allan p.1, Dolman p.49
[35] Hopson p.76
[36] Allan p.31
[37] Purvis pp.34-5
[38] Hopson p.75
[39] Tolman p.100
[40] Tolman p.100
[41] Hopson p.52
[42] Hopson pp.39-40
[43] Garlick p.54
[44] Tolman p.69, Hopson p.56
[45] Stokes pp.38-9
[46] Cannon pp.2-5

[47] Stokes p.55
[48] Stokes p.54
[49] Stokes p.55

4

E. LONGMATE PHOTOGRAPHER

Professional photographer's work is available to you here without extra cost.

Note on receipts given to customers, c. 1925

The years immediately following the first world war must have been the happiest of my father's life, reunited as he was with a devoted wife and with two small children of whom he was undoubtedly proud. He had a recognised, if modest, place in the community, both in his business and his hobby and he never aspired to civic office, though many shopkeepers like himself served on the council and his chief business rival became mayor. When not in his shop, or attending with his camera at weddings and other public functions, he was happily occupied as stage-manager of both the Newbury and District Amateur Dramatic Society and the Amateur Operatic Society. The latter often held the first rehearsals of new productions in the large studio above his shop and my elder sister had early memories of hearing Gilbert and Sullivan choruses floating through the upstairs rooms as she was going to bed.

My father was never a great drinker, and had no affection for pubs, but did enjoy an occasional whisky. Like other members of the 'Operatic' and 'Dramatic' he was often to be seen in the Jack Hotel[1], named after the great Jack of Newbury and situated at 22 Northbrook Street in what remained of Jack of Newbury's house, a few doors away from my father's shop. Once a centre of the coaching trade and the starting point for many local carriers, the Jack was famous for its welcoming owners, Horace Cadd and his wife, later the landlords of an even more famous hostelry, the Bear at Hungerford, and for 'Cocky', a loquacious cockatoo, who dominated the bar. A portrait of this pampered, self-assertive bird was probably the most popular photograph my father ever took.[*]

The details of my father's business at this time still remain something of a mystery to me. On his return from the war he apparently continued to live in Queens Road while working as an assistant, and junior partner – a position probably purchased with my mother's money – to JW Righton, the town's leading photographer, whose collection of local photographs I have mentioned

---

[*] See illustrations

earlier. A register of local photographers shows Righton as in business at 42 Northbrook Street until 1920, while my father is listed as occupying the same premises from 1924 to 1931. What seems to have happened, according to my mother's later recollections, is that my father increasingly did most of the work of the firm and from 1920 was effectively its owner until in 1924 JW Righton finally retired and the business continued under my father's name. During this period he moved from Queens Road to live over the shop.

A surviving piece of business stationery, almost my only souvenir of this period, issued by 'E. Longmate, Photographer', sums up what the business offered:

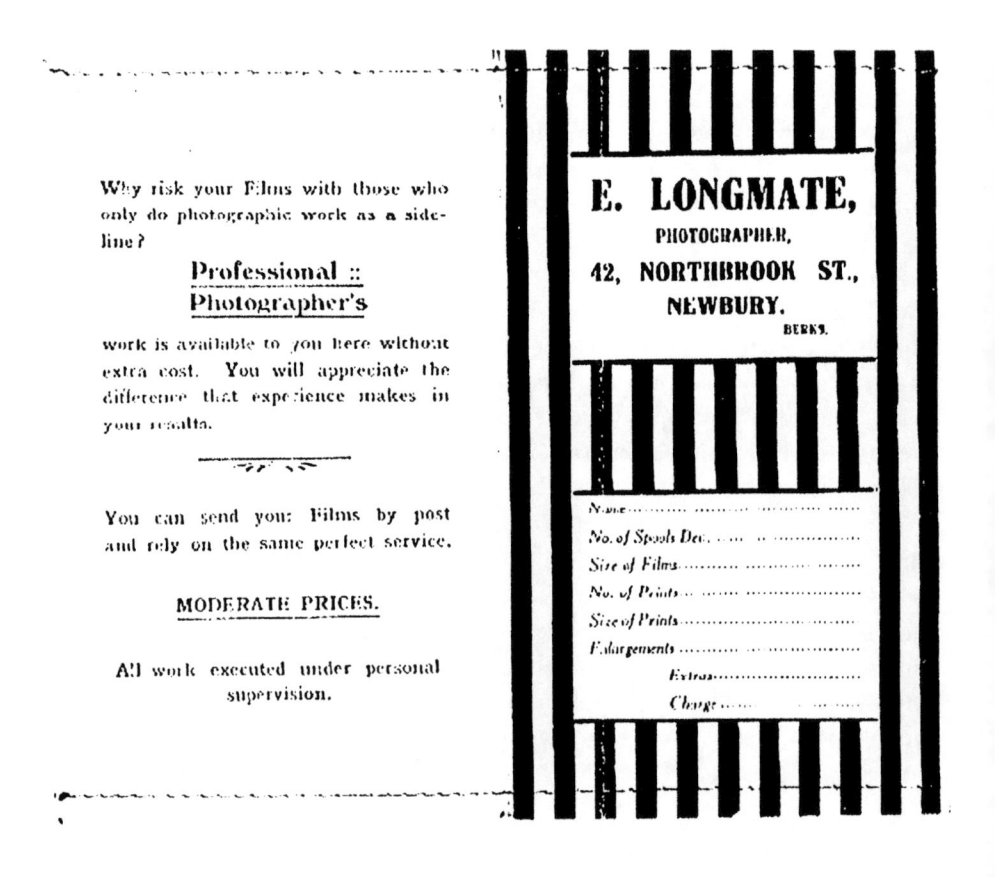

> Why risk your Films with those who only do photographic work as a sideline?
>
> **Professional Photographer's**
>
> work is available to you here without extra cost. You will appreciate the difference that experience makes in your results.
>
> You can send your Films by post and rely on the same perfect service.
>
> **MODERATE PRICES.**
>
> All work executed under personal supervision.

> **E. LONGMATE,**
> PHOTOGRAPHER,
> 42, NORTHBROOK ST.,
> NEWBURY.
> BERKS.
>
> Name............
> No. of Spools Dev............
> Size of Films............
> No. of Prints............
> Size of Prints............
> Enlargements............
> Extras............
> Charge............

Although there was one other successful photographer in Newbury, as well as others offering less serious competition, the Righton/Longmate business was the leading photographers in the town, with a substantial clientele among the local gentry and a regular trade in the 'bread and butter' of the photographic world, private portraits, family groups and, most valuable of all, weddings. There was also a regular trade in selling films and cameras and in developing and printing for their owners. Most cameras were still relatively primitive and for formal occasions no alternative to employing a professional existed while it was extremely rare for the owner of a 'Box Brownie' or similar camera to process the film himself, indeed it was a common request for the expert in the shop to insert it for him. Newbury was a sizeable town, the immediate post-war years were mildly prosperous, and, if properly run, the Righton/Longmate business should have provided a decent living.

Although adequately equipped, so far as numeracy and literacy went, to run his own business, my father was temperamentally unfitted to be self-employed, partly because he was far too trusting and even gullible. I have never seen any of the documents relating to this period, nor did my father ever speak of it, and my knowledge rests solely upon what my mother told me as an adult. According to her, in spite of his lack of financial aptitude, my father might conceivably have survived the depression had he not, as emerged too late, bought a business which, though reasonably flourishing in terms of its current turnover, was from the first loaded with bad debts, which, combined with a decline in income as the economic climate worsened, finally proved insupportable. My mother blamed herself for not insisting on having the books of the business into which my father bought his way professionally examined, but my father resisted all her urgings that he consult an accountant or solicitor, and preferred instead, to tell the vendor, all too typically – I was later to witness similar examples of the same grand, but naive, approach myself – 'I trust your word as a gentleman.'

To this initial handicap of debt were, in my mother's recollection added some other misfortunes, notably a dishonest employee who reduced still further the already dwindling takings, but I have no doubt my father's own reluctance to face reality was the principal factor in converting a poor investment into a totally disastrous one. His open-handedness and good nature made him an easy target for slow payers and the deliberately dishonest. He failed to collect money due for completed work and left unpaid those vital suppliers without whom he could not continue to operate. I came as a child to dread seeing the postmark 'Ilford' on an envelope, since this was the site of the main manufacturer of photographic plates and chemicals, and usually meant a final demand for some long overdue account or that an order had been rejected as previous bills remained unpaid.

While the name of Longmate must soon have been distrusted by such companies, professionally it remained in Newbury a valuable asset. Perhaps inheriting his partner's connections, perhaps because his manner, respectful without being servile, appealed to them, perhaps simply because he always did a thoroughly competent job – the inscription 'E. Longmate' on a photograph was, in its modest way, a proof that the customer could afford the best that was available locally – the business had a valuable clientele among the titled families living near Newbury and among the better-off middle-class citizens who followed their lead. There were regular commissions from the Earl of

Carnarvon and when King George V joined a shooting party at Highclere Castle it was my father who was called on to record the occasion. The resulting picture remained one of his proudest possessions, though I still feel irritated at the lady-in-waiting or female guest in a black 'hobble' skirt who moved during the long exposure, spoiling an otherwise perfect photograph. The king himself, my father told me, had been a model of courtesy, readily accepting the need to stand still for an uncomfortably long time. Another individual of whom my father spoke well, both as client and 'sitter', was Sir 'Freddie' Carden, a much respected baronet with a splendid house, already immortalised by JW Righton. I also remember someone I now regard as a 'temporary gentleman', 'Captain' Bradshaw, who had retained his wartime rank and felt entitled to address my father by his surname, which I found offensive. (The captain, however, later earned his rank a second time, playing a leading part in the formation of the Newbury Home Guard.)

This must have been for my father a comparatively affluent period of his life and it would have been typical of him, so long as there was money in his pocket, to put out of his mind the longer term shadows hanging over the business. He later described to me, while showing me the photographs concerned, some of the unusual commissions that had come his way. One of these was from the already legendary James Tufnail, whom I have already mentioned as opening the town's first cinema and later, ever delighted by the latest novelty, he set up its first skating rink in what would now be called a shopping and leisure centre, the Plaza, opening off the Market Place, and now demolished.[2] 'Tuffy' thought the council (on which he briefly and combatively served himself) was being unreasonable in the restrictions imposed upon him and reacted by commissioning a belated foundation stone for the building, with a provocative inscription, which my father was called on to photograph. The stone was then put on public display in the window of Tufnail's shop, close by the Municipal Buildings where the council met:

> 1925
> THIS STONE WAS LAID BY
> JAMES TUFNAIL,
> A MAN WHO COULD NEVER SUITABLY DESCRIBE
> THE ROBBERY CORPORATION,
> WITHOUT USING BAD LANGUAGE.

My father also showed me, after I was grown up, a set of photographs which would have led to the public disgrace of a prominent local citizen had they been circulated, though today they seem very tame. They depicted, somewhat oddly, a youngish woman posing in her underclothes, with her slip pulled up to her thighs, one leg outstretched to rest her foot upon a signpost pointing to a nearby village. It was a strange souvenir of a no doubt illicit relationship and, as the car in the background proved, was no mere studio reconstruction, but neither the pictures nor the story ever leaked out.

The oddest commission my father received I heard of only at second hand, via my mother. One day a stranger, who in retrospect she thought somewhat sinister-looking, had called at my father's shop and asked him to go to a local house where, to his great surprise, he was taken upstairs to a bedroom and instructed to photograph the dead man lying on the bed. He was told to deliver the prints immediately they were ready and to bring the plates with him. He duly did so and was then asked the cost and what he would expect to earn from further copies if, as was customary, he retained the negatives. The amounts he specified were paid immediately and without question, in cash, and thereupon the negatives were smashed in front of him and all but one of the prints torn up. He was then dismissed with a hint that he should say nothing about the matter, and the customer put the remaining photograph in his pocket and left without further explanation. This Hardyesque incident is still a mystery but my father, since no report ever appeared of any suspected crime or violent death, assumed the picture was required to substantiate a claim to the dead man's property.

My father's shop was well situated in the main street, not far from the Broadway, and my elder sister remembers the premises above, of which I have little recollection myself, as being reasonably spacious, and life there as moderately comfortable, an impression confirmed by two other informants who worked there or were frequent visitors. Unlike most people at their social level at that time my parents had no live-in domestic help, but someone did come in every day to do the cleaning and keep an eye on the children. The only incident I remember of this period, though even this may rest on later hearsay, resulted from its situation next to Maggs the butcher, who, as was then common, slaughtered cattle for his shop in the yard behind, which adjoined that of my father's premises. On one occasion a cow or bull, maddened with fear, broke loose and charged down the yard, possibly leaping the low fence which separated our garden from it, and facing the nursemaid in charge of my infant sister and myself with a classic dilemma: which child should she snatch up and carry to safety? It became a joke in the family that she had chosen me, but happily the animal was caught before it could do any harm.

A slaughterhouse was by no means the ideal neighbour for any business and I have distinct memories from a very early age of the revolting smell which periodically pervaded our garden and seeped in through the back windows when an animal had been recently killed. I can recall seeing the carcasses of the newly dead animals hanging outside the shop, and later, when writing about the 'nuisances' which afflicted Victorian towns, keeping, and even worse, killing, cattle and other beasts in the middle of a town struck me as a prime example of what our forebears had, on a far worse scale, to put up with.

In 1924 my father engaged as an apprentice a young girl who was paid 2s 6d [12.5p] a week. She can still remember how periodically the quiet of the studio and darkroom was shattered by the frenzied squealing of the pigs next door, as they were driven, evidently anticipating their fate, to the place of execution and, almost as upsetting, the sudden heavy thud which echoed through the building as a cow was felled by the slaughterman.

This informant, known to the family as 'Andy' – her real name was Kathleen Andrews – enjoyed her work, which involved assisting my father with developing, printing and enlarging, routine tasks which had to continue when he was in the studio or out on a job. The atmosphere seems to have been happy, and my father an undemanding employer and conscientious instructor. Two other young women worked with her, their time largely taken up with retouching negatives, ie filling in the tiny holes which appeared on the emulsified plates then in use, work often farmed out to part-timers at home. There was also, as in every self-respecting small business in the 1920s, an errand boy, Denis, complete no doubt with solid bicycle with large frame over the front wheel, who presumably delivered the completed orders, but, most unusually, he and my father fell out and he was not replaced.

The business must have appeared at this time to have been in a flourishing condition. There was a steady flow of customers to pose for portraits in the studio and my father was much in demand for weddings, a lucrative part of his business since orders tended to be large and customers were in an open-handed mood, many later returning to have their babies photographed. In addition to selling films and doing 'd and p' – developing and printing them – my father had a useful sideline, taking views of the town and selling the resulting picture postcards to local newsagents. Occasionally he was called on to do work for the council or the police and, much more frequently the *Newbury Weekly News*, in which his byline frequently appeared in these years. Sometimes he got a call from a national newspaper, being listed as a local 'stringer'. The business never, however, supported a car, though this was not at all uncommon at this period and he had, I suspect, no aptitude for driving, for I recall my mother remarking that she was almost grateful that he could not afford one. It must nevertheless have been a great inconvenience, for a photographer's equipment in those days included a heavy camera and tripod, boxes of plates and – a little later – accompanying electric lights for interior work. When he first started in Newbury a horse and gig could be hired when needed from Mr Humphries at the Monument public house, further down Northbrook Street, and this later gave way to a car. I also have memories of my father setting off on a heavily laden bicycle to some more remote villages or staggering to the station to use the little Lambourn line.

Sometimes his work took him to the homes of the rich and perhaps it was visiting such aristocratic establishments which encouraged my father's illusions of grandeur. At all events, my elder brother and sister were, absurdly, sent to private schools which were clearly in all respects, except social cachet, inferior to what was available free from the local authority. Both Gordon and Freda began their education at an establishment run by an elderly, and I suspect unqualified, woman, Miss Day, who seated all her ten pupils on a single long bench – there were no desks – and charged a modest 3s 6d [17.5p] a head each week. From here my brother was sent to a slightly superior school at Thatcham, three miles [4.8km] away, to which he cycled daily. I doubt if it did much for him, though he possessed a lively mind and was always intensely interested in changes in the world around him. He still retained when he died a framed certificate, signed personally by one of the early Children's Hour 'uncles', confirming that he had in 1929 joined the 'Radio Circle', 'consisting,' according to Asa Briggs's *History of Broadcasting*, 'of child listeners throughout the Midlands encouraged not only to take a keen interest in the programme but to do useful work for afflicted children'. [3] Gordon never mentioned his membership to me, but evidently at this time we were well enough off to own a wireless, then still a rarity, though later this was to vanish with similar luxuries, as I shall describe.

My father no doubt wished to do the best he could for his children but I would respect his memory more if his ambitions had been rooted in reality. Apart from acquiring a cricket bat, which, unlike the wireless set, somehow survived our later downfall, although Gordon was even less likely to have wielded this effectively than I was, I never saw any evidence that my brother had benefitted in the slightest from his exposure to fee-paying education or, more precisely, non-fee paying, since my father proved incapable of keeping up the small payments required. What, I have often thought, could be more absurd than sending one's child to a private school and then defaulting on the fees? My father's ludicrous pretensions merely resulted in my unfortunate brother suffering the humiliation of having to leave the school at Thatcham when it was too late for him to have the chance of a grammar school education, from which he would undoubtedly have profited. My elder sister was fortunate to escape a similar fate, for in the days of his apparent prosperity, and actual self-delusion, my father seems to have contemplated a more grandiose education for her, though she was the least academic of us. Years later when we were desperately poor I came upon what I at first assumed to be a picture book and, such luxuries being by then rare in our household, eagerly turned the pages, which showed disdainful looking girls, elegantly dressed, in locations like 'The drawing room' and 'The terrace'. There were, so far as I can recall, no pictures of classrooms or libraries. It took me a little time to realise that this was in fact the prospectus of a boarding school for young ladies, to which my father had apparently thought of sending his elder daughter.

My mother once remarked to me that she liked to believe that Gordon's cruelly-terminated venture into being privately educated had left him with a social polish he would not otherwise have acquired, but I thought this nonsense then and still do. Gordon himself was under no such illusions. He assured me once that he considered that he belonged to the working class, wherever other members of the family might place themselves. My only criticism of my mother, whose memory I still idolise, is that at this period of our lives she did not keep my father's feet more securely on the ground. 'Perhaps I should have been firmer with him,' she once remarked to me, and I could only agree.

As it was, the business must already have been revealing somewhat shaky financial foundations, when, at 6 am on Tuesday 15 December 1925, I was born in one of the upper floors of No 42 Northbrook Street, Newbury. My mother later told me that she attributed the start of labour, a week or more earlier than expected, to her having insisted on carrying my brother and sister up to bed unaided, since my father was attending the big social event of the year, the annual dinner of the Newbury Amateur Dramatic Society. He was hastily fetched, and, according to family tradition, had no sooner left than the assembled company voted that 'Longy's' child, having arrived at such a propitious time, should become an honorary life member of the society. I cannot recall ever profiting from this honour, indeed only learned of it when writing this book, and perhaps the society was taken aback to learn that it had acquired not one new infant member but two. My mother had no idea that she was carrying twins; nor, apparently, had the doctor. The arrival of my sister, 15 minutes after I had been born, seems to have astonished all concerned, including 'Nurse Snowy', the woman, probably unqualified but highly competent, who assisted at many Newbury births.

My mother's own mother had, as I have mentioned, died in childbirth, though her own two previous confinements had been uneventful. The delivery of my twin sister and myself, however, left her dangerously exhausted. By Christmas Day, ten days later, she was well enough to be carried to an upstairs room where the rest of the family had assembled, but had to be laid, visibly not yet herself, on a settee. When she had, nominally, recovered, she suffered, she later told me, from an intense and uncharacteristic depression, today recognised as a common post-natal condition, and seems to have been gripped by what would now be called an anxiety phobia. She had always, though I only learned this very late on in life, been a victim of claustrophobia. Now, for weeks after the birth of my sister and myself she found it required an enormous effort, she later told me, even to enter a shop. She was not, however, the person to let her personal difficulties interfere with her duty to her family and so successfully overcame these problems that I only learned of them a few years before her death.

I was baptised at St Mary's, Speenhamland, on Sunday 18 April 1926, presumably with my twin sister, though the certificate I have makes no mention of her. My 'sponsor', presumably godfather, was identified as 'Arthur Gray Palmer', whom I later knew as 'Brother Palmer', a family way of referring to close male friends. My parents had missed the opportunity to secure, as they had done for my brother, a godfather who was a well-off and influential local figure. *His* godfather, Alderman Burns, was a successful local jeweller and leading local figure on the council, and I was very envious when Gordon received the enormously generous tip from him of £5 when he was confirmed. I cannot recall that my godfather ever showed any awareness of his obligations to me, whether spiritual or practical. Looking back I can appreciate that he was another of nature's losers, a pleasant enough man with a limp who, I believe, earned his living as a cobbler. His real interest lay in music and he regularly joined the orchestra at the Operatic Society performances, but, though clearly part of our circle, he never played any part in my life.

I was christened Norman Richard, though what prompted this choice of names I have no idea, for neither appear in the family Bible and I never met any relation bearing either of them. In any case, I was never known in the family by either name, partly by my own choice, though I would happily have settled for 'Richard'. 'Norman' I always disliked and from an early age was known in the family as 'Jim', which was also invariably used by visitors and close friends, who assumed it was a diminutive form of James, a name I *would* have welcomed. In fact, according to my elder sister, it had its origin, like many nicknames, in irony. As a baby, I am told, I was often in tears, causing the family to refer to me as 'Sunny Jim', after the character featured on a cereal packet:

> High o'er the fence leaps Sunny Jim!
> FORCE is the food that raises him.

Being known by two names has been a minor irritant throughout my life and sometimes an embarrassment. At school, where only surnames were used, no confusion arose and later, I opted wherever possible for 'Norman', after this had been used, without reference to me, on my first newspaper byline. Today a few close friends, as well as my family, know me as 'Jim', but otherwise I have, belatedly, settled for the name my parents chose for me. My twin sister, incidentally, was more fortunate. She happily accepted her baptismal names, Peggy Ruth, when old enough to object to them, and has remained 'Peggy' or 'Peg' ever since.

Living as we did in the main street, and no doubt often to be seen in my father's shop, 'the Longmate twins' rapidly became well known in the town, particularly after we had graduated from our pram into the first twin pushchair ever seen in Newbury. I suspect that we were spoiled by the young women who worked for my father or helped my mother in the house and according to the recollections of my elder sister and one of these helpers I was a wilful, somewhat aggressive infant. My insistence on having my own way became notorious after an incident in the pram I shared with my sister, and this is the first event in my life of which I can feel entirely certain since my mother herself described it to me. I had apparently offered my sister an empty mug, containing imaginary coffee, and when she refused to join in the pretence I struck her sharply on the head with the metal mug, declaring, 'You shall drink my coshee!' the first remark of mine to be remembered.

I seem indeed to have been a somewhat quarrelsome child for, according to a school essay, *Recollections*, which I wrote at the age of 15 and shall quote again, I once engaged in 'a furious fight in my pram with my sister which ended in tears on both sides, on her part after I had bitten her finger and on mine when retribution overtook me on the parental knee'. This is the only evidence, or recollection, I have that either of my parents ever struck me, though I do recall a sudden slap aimed at me, somewhat ineffectually, by my father when I had torn up a drawing belonging to a friend with whom I had quarrelled. From my mother I cannot recall even the mildest physical punishment and I cannot imagine her ever striking anyone, least of all a small child.

The 'coffee' incident occurred, I believe, when the pram was parked in the yard behind the shop in Northbrook Street and sometime around my second birthday, in December 1927. Soon afterwards we moved to what I remember as by far the pleasantest house we ever occupied, No 8 Newport Road, about half a mile [1km] from our previous home. This, though no doubt improved since then, still stands and resembles millions of others built in the early decades of the century. There were two reception rooms on the ground floor, with three bedrooms above, a garden front and back and, what was in retrospect to seem a great luxury, a bathroom and kitchen. There was no garage then, but we did, I believe, have electric light, by no means as yet universal. We cooked, I imagine, by gas stove, although the open fire was also used to heat up water, as an incident I shall describe in a moment confirms, and it seems likely, therefore, that the house lacked a proper hot water supply.

Newport Road was not then fully made up. At one end it opened on to the main London road, but a few yards walk in the other direction brought one into open fields. Years later my mother told me that just round the corner was a house, the only one in the town, containing women who would 'oblige' men, but this was otherwise an extremely respectable residential area.

I cannot recall the move from Northbrook Street but I do recall feeling happy and – how wrong I was – secure at 8 Newport Road, to which I looked back as the epitome of luxury and spaciousness, of a kind we were never to enjoy again. In fact it was, I now realise, having re-visited the area, a very ordinary semi-detached house, inferior to many then being built and less imposing than my father, with his ideas of grandeur, might have been expected to rent. It still provides, however, my very earliest memory, recorded, in the essay already cited, when I was 15:

> I remember Christmas Eve and the warm glow of the fire but my chief memory is of gazing through the window into the drifting snow and thinking what a huge number of sugar basins must have been upset to cause all these white piles…Later I remember playing in a sandpit in the garden and also one thrilling afternoon when a neighbour discovered a wasps' nest just outside his pantry window, and how after attacking the nest itself he destroyed individual wasps with a folded newspaper, while I watched in spellbound amazement.

The 'sugar-basin' story seems altogether too cute to be true but my mother had a clear recollection of it, though I suspect that placing it on Christmas Eve is less reliable. The same essay reveals that at this period of my life money must still have been relatively plentiful:

> Round about this time I was in the throes of learning the alphabet and I remember the pennies with which correct identification of letters was rewarded.

Curiously, I have absolutely no recollection of what should have been a traumatic experience that occurred at this time and have had to rely for an account of it on my elder sister. She was, she remembers, about to go out for the evening and in the flurry of the preparation a saucepan of boiling water on the open fire was tipped up and cascaded all over my head. I was so badly scalded that I lost both hair and skin, which only returned after a long period of treatment and daily visits from the district nurse to change the dressings. My sister can remember all too vividly the ordeal for everyone in the house as I screamed in terror at the sight of the nurse coming down the road, but – making me somewhat sceptical of the influence even sub-conscious events are supposed to exercise over our lives – my own memory, like my scalp, remains unscarred.

---

[1] Hopson p.33
[2] *Newbury Weekly News* 16 Oct 1980, *Newbury Advertiser* 22 Mar 1983
[3] Briggs Vol 1 pp.208-9

5

BREEDING WILL OUT

Don't worry, my dear, breeding will out.

Sympathetic teacher to my mother, 1931

Although it was every tradesman's ambition to cease to live above the shop, the move from the main street of Newbury to a quiet residential area was, I suspect, prompted more by my father's financial problems than by social ambition. The electoral register confirms that from the first we had a lodger at Newport Road, Arthur Palmer, my godfather. Meanwhile the vacated rooms at No 42 Northbrook Street had, I believe, been let to bring in some much needed income.

My father, my mother told me later, never discussed his business troubles with her and anything he did tell her was no doubt coloured by his own ill-founded optimism. The firm of E. Longmate was undoubtedly already close to, if not actually already on, the rocks when, in October 1929, the Wall Street crash ushered in the great world-wide depression, in which luxury trades, like photography, were among the first to suffer. Even before this, however, my father's inability to pay his debts had been revealed in court. On 7 October 1927, two months before my second birthday, he was accused at the Newbury Borough Petty Sessions of being in arrears with the rates on his shop, though the results are not recorded, the relevant registers having been destroyed. On 31 January 1930 he was charged again, this time with failing to pay National Health Insurance contributions, presumably for his employees. Again what happened in court is uncertain, but on 5 October he was back again, this time being found guilty and fined £1, as well as being ordered to pay £1 3s 6d [£1.17] costs, and the £4 3s 5d [£4.17] contributions he owed. At the same time he suffered a similar fine and costs – evidently standard figures at the time – plus a slightly larger fine of £5 8s 4d [£5.42] for failing to pay Unemployment Insurance contributions – a benefit for which, like National Health treatment, he was, as a self-employed person, himself ineligible. Whether or not he managed to raise these sums is not clear, but on 28 March 1930 he was back at the Petty Sessions to answer a complaint from the Borough Rating Authority and this time a distress warrant was issued to enforce payment of the debt. On 3rd April 1930 the documents record the arrears had been paid under a distress warrant, the total, including arrears and costs, amounting to

£5 7s 9d [£5.38]. It seems to have been this modest sum, which even in 1930 amounted to no more than a labourer's wage for about three weeks and a clerk's earnings in a fortnight, which finally destroyed my father's business and came close to destroying our family. He did not, it seems, as I had always supposed, formally go bankrupt, but the distress warrant was enough, for it meant that sufficient goods could be seized to pay the debt. All I know for certain is that he suddenly told my mother that the bailiffs would be arriving next morning, even though she must have been aware that money was desperately short. My sister can recall the mother of her teenage help, Vera, who had been kept on long after such a luxury could be afforded, arriving to ask for her daughter's unpaid wages. 'It's been three weeks now!' she protested. Since Vera's pay was only 5 shillings [25p] a week the total debt was a mere 15 shillings [75p] and this I still find hard to forgive, for here was my father forcing my mother, herself a good manager, to defraud someone in an even humbler walk of life than us.

Of the day the bailiffs called I have no recollection, though my elder sister had some understanding of what was happening and remembers my mother, before they left the house, taking Freda's bicycle to the neighbours' house, commenting: 'I don't see why they should get that!' This must have been almost all that survived the shipwreck of our home and of my mother's devoted years of marriage, apart from the few essentials protected by the law – tools of the trade of the debtor, basic cooking utensils and the bare minimum of furniture, like a bed. By the time we returned to it, though I cannot recall the scene, the house must have been stripped, leaving only a few battered sticks of furniture, which we continued to use till after my mother's death, as a reminder of happier times. The house itself, with the rent no doubt badly in arrears, was surrendered soon afterwards. In a matter of days we had been reduced from being the family of a respected and apparently successful tradesman to the hungry dependents of an out-of-work failure, lacking all prospects, deprived even of a home.

This must have been for my mother the most bitter and humiliating moment of her life. No doubt some families in our situation took such events in their stride, but my mother had come from a comparatively affluent background, more likely to be applied to for help in such a situation than to be its victim, and I have always been amazed at how remarkably forgiving she was about the straits to which my father's failure, as both businessman and individual, had brought her. A small town photographer lacking any expensive or extravagant tastes and eager only to make a success of his profession should, I still feel, have been able, considering the basic skill he possessed and his reputation and friends in the community, to survive somehow even in those harsh times. The sad truth was that, having got into debt, he never seems to have faced up to the reality of his position or adopted any coherent strategy to escape from it. He could at the very least have confided in my mother, a far more intelligent person, who might well have worked out some solution before it was too late. As it was she was kept in the dark as he blundered from bad to worse – or, as she put it in her saintly, forgiving way, 'Things just got on top of him.' In fact her troubles were only just beginning. The court records reveal that my father was again charged with not having paid his rates, on 27 March 1931, when it was decided that another distress warrant should be issued. Whether the bailiffs now returned I do not know, and the result of the warrant, due to be executed in 28 days, and even the amount are not recorded. I am uncertain indeed whether it may not have been this, rather than the earlier default, which led the bailiffs to our house. But at all events the two episodes together were what finally caused my father's career as a self-employed shopkeeper, and our whole way of life, as a small tradesman's family, to founder.

A studio photographer, to give my father's occupation its official description, as finally recorded on his death certificate, needed not merely a studio itself, but a shop to take orders and sell his wares and a darkroom to practise his craft. All these had been familiar to me as long as I could remember. My pram had often been briefly placed, and the 'Longmate twins' no doubt admired, in the Northbrook Street shop, and I must, long before I understood its significance, have been taken into the studio, and been impressed by its spacious air and bright lights. My earliest memories of my father are of seeing him stooping beneath an enveloping dark cloth to focus the large box-like camera before drawing out the cover shielding the plate and whipping off the lens-cap while the sitter stayed unnaturally still, and the relief of both parties, rather like that of dentist and patient, when the operation was completed without mishap. I must, too, have been very young the first time I was taken into my father's darkroom, then a place of enormous mystery to me. It was impressed upon me even as an infant that one must on no account open the door or move the curtain to allow in the light and it was in any case dangerous to move about in the dim red glow that *was* allowed, intriguing though I found this, for fear of blundering into fragile negatives or spilling the seemingly ubiquitous dishes of 'hypo' used to 'fix' the picture before it was developed. Sometimes only total darkness would do, when my father was handling 'pan', ie panchromatic, plates and I was impressed at his skill and confidence in working in the to me impenetrable blackness. I found the darkness more exciting than frightening and my father was a kindly, indulgent parent who liked to have us around him. Letting us roam about his workplace was, I now realise, one treat that cost nothing.

After he had been forced to leave No 42 Northbrook Street and abandon both his shop and studio my father made valiant efforts to restart his business in a single room, used as a darkroom, in an alley behind Northbrook Street, two or three doors away from his former premises. The local street directory for 1932 and 1933 contains the somewhat inglorious entry in its list of occupants 'Back of 45 – Longmate, E., photographer', No 45 itself being occupied by a printer and an insurance firm, and No 45a, entered via the same alley, by a bootmaker. His own former shop, at No 42, was also occupied by a bootmaker. I have clear memories of No 45, which seemed, like our new home, to be described in a moment, a vast come-down from the one that had preceded it. I recall entering a damp, dark, depressing alleyway, before turning off through a plain, unpainted door – no shop style glass panels or doortop bell here – into a single shabby room, with almost bare benches, a flat, stained sink with, I think, a single cold tap, and none of the useful clutter I associated with a darkroom. My father, too, seemed to look greyer and shabbier than in his former shop, with no sign of the smiles with which he had once greeted us, though I was small enough to be intrigued by his new surroundings and perhaps asked embarrassing questions about the reason for the move. After a year or two even this modest toehold off, rather than in, Northbrook Street was given up, presumably because the rent, though it cannot have been more than a few shillings a week, had fallen into arrears. My father still had his cameras and his skill but nowhere to make use of them. It must, I now appreciate, have been an even more miserable and hopeless time for him than for us, especially as my mother managed to shield us, or at least Peggy and myself, from a real understanding of our desperate situation.

When, in February 1995, I revisited No 45 Northbrook Street after an interval of more than 60 years, I found that my heart still sank as I walked through the adjoining archway and though some former openings had now been bricked up I could, I believe, still identify the door which had once led into the darkroom and the original brickwork of the walls seemed unchanged. I was glad to return to No 42, occupied by my father at the time of his comparative prosperity, though after all these years no trace of his occupancy remained. The ground floor was occupied by a firm of opticians, after obvious modernisation, and, perhaps significantly I felt, the rooms above, where I had been born and spent my first few years, were empty and to let.

Along with the disastrous, and, I now recognise, symbolic move of my father's business from the main shopping street of Newbury to a back alley, went our departure from the modest luxury of No 8 Newport Road to a couple of rooms in a much inferior house at its far end, one of a group which must even then have been sub-standard properties, now long since demolished without trace. Years later, when writing about nineteenth century slums, I read a complaint by a doctor about streets so down at heel that they lacked even a name, and this seems to have been true of our new home, for a map of the time shows only an open space, linked to the built-up part of Newport Road by a footpath, and then a few houses close to the River Lambourn near Shaw bridge. A street directory for 1931 duly lists the occupant of the house we shared, but does not identify it by name or number, the sole written evidence that I did not imagine the year or so we spent there, by far the worst period of our lives.

I have still a recollection of small, overcrowded rooms, a squalid, evil-smelling kitchen, the most primitive washing facilities – the lavatory was no doubt even worse – and of a garden heaped with rubbish. We were, I imagine, glad to find it, for the owners were a working class Irish family, who must have been little better off than us, but had at least a roof over their heads and welcomed the few shillings a week we no doubt promised to pay, though I suspect it was often in arrears. The children had, I now appreciate, not been brought up, as we had been, to appreciate others' privacy and would happily barge into our two rooms without warning. One of the rooms we had rented accommodated my parents and elder sister, now aged around nine, but required to occupy a cot far too small for her since there was no money to buy a bed. The other room housed my brother, now in his early teens, my twin sister and myself, now approaching the age of five.

My recollection is that there was no bathroom and no electricity and water certainly had to be pumped by hand every day into the tank in the roof, though this was still a common arrangement even in better-off households. The kitchen was shared and preparing such meals as we had, which must have been scanty and few enough, must have been a time of misery for my mother. Cheerful as she normally was even she must have been almost overwhelmed at this time, and she indeed confessed to me many years later that she felt a great distaste for this end of the town and was reluctant to return there, because of the unhappy memories it brought back.

When, in 1995, I revisited Newport Road I was far from sorry to find that the house which witnessed our misery had disappeared without trace, being replaced by pleasant, modern properties, admirably laid out with well-planned footpaths and some even enjoying a view of the river. When, and how, our former home was demolished I have not discovered, nor what became of our landlord. By 1932 his name had vanished from the list of the occupants of his nameless address-less property, but as his children may still be alive I have omitted it from this account.

This is the period I now regard as the Dark Ages of the family history. (My time at boarding school may similarly be compared to the Middle Ages, wretched and barbarous enough, but with the prospect of something better to follow.) It was, of course, my mother, as always, who kept us going. She must have hated being a lodger in that rough household, so different, except in its poverty, from ours, but, even thirty years later, I hesitated to question her about it, so painful must the experience have been.

More fortunate in this perhaps than my mother I have no clear picture of our life at that time, only occasional 'snapshot' memories, almost all of them unhappy. My sharpest image is of fleeing in terror to seek her protection after the son of the house, an uncouth and aggressive child, not much older than me but never any kind of playmate, had attempted to thrash me with a bicycle tyre or piece of discarded garden hose. Persuading his mother, barely more articulate than her son, to admonish him, especially if, as seems likely, we owed them rent, must have taxed all my mother's eloquence and diplomatic powers, but our salvation then, as so often, must have been that she automatically commanded liking and respect and was recognised as a true 'lady', lacking all 'side' but innately a gentlewoman, by the women among whom she now found herself. I never knew anyone to show any resentment towards her, even though her accent and manners made clear enough that her background had been very different from theirs.

Almost my only cheerful recollection of this period relates to Christmas; we spent, I think, only one there. I have a clear picture of seeing a joint of beef resting in a dish on Christmas morning after being cooked in the oven of a nearby baker, a common practice then, when working-class kitchens were ill-equipped and often lacked a decent sized oven. The meat was, my sister believes, the gift of Horace Cadd, licensee of the Jack Hotel, where my father must, in happier times, have often stood his round. He was a good friend to our family and also produced the only presents we received that Christmas, for my parents had not a penny to spare for such inessentials, something that must, I am sure, have distressed them deeply. My brother received *Treasure Island*, which still has an honoured place among the thousands of books that now line my study walls, my elder sister a doll dressed in a crinoline with crackers concealed beneath the skirt, which not long before had stood on the bar of the Jack as part of its Christmas decorations. I am sure Peggy and I were not left out, though I cannot recall what we received.

Whatever else we enjoyed that Christmas was probably bought with a voucher from the Mayor's Benevolent Fund, a charity designed 'to help our less well off townsfolk enjoy Christmas' for which an annual appeal was made. This Christmas, almost certainly that of 1930, when I was just five, was not to be the last when the Mayor's Fund came to our aid and I can recall much later in life my father's enormous pleasure in giving a donation to it, telling me that he had vowed to do so long ago when he was himself a beneficiary.

Another memory of this period is of my mother's delight when my elder sister was asked to take to school some examples of grass or flowers growing in the vicinity. Here, she clearly felt, was an occasion where her family could show to advantage, and we went out as a family to pick the required plants, producing, I do not doubt, the best collection brought by any child.

My outstanding recollection of this period, the absolute nadir of the family fortunes when I felt most desolate and frightened, is of my mother, looking terrifyingly unlike her normal self, lying on a bed covered by her frayed overcoat, on top of the few thin blankets spared by the bailiffs. Her skin was bright yellow and she was, I now realise, in the grip of a high fever. Dr RG Wyllie, our family doctor in the days when we could afford such a luxury, was called and rapidly diagnosed jaundice, observing that this was the most severe case he had ever seen.

The disease, of which one form is now better known as hepatitis, was in 1930 not uncommonly fatal and conditions for treating the patient, with no money or comfort in the house, and precious little room, could hardly have been worse but Dr Wyllie, despite his reputation in the town for enjoying a drink, rallied round nobly. I suspect he never submitted a bill for his treatment, and if he did it cannot have been paid, but he remained on good terms with the family. Since chemists, unlike doctors, had to be paid in cash I imagine that whatever medicines were required he provided himself. Removing my mother to hospital – we did not pay into the 'Hospital Fund' and could not have afforded even the smallest fees – does not seem to have been contemplated and she was nursed at home by my father and elder sister. Myself and my four or five-year-old twin sister – I cannot be certain of the precise date – were merely encumbrances who had to be fed and kept, so far as possible, out of the way. This was not easy to achieve given our cramped living conditions and I caught occasional, terrifying, glimpses of the invalid, my mother's discoloured complexion and obvious weakness being in striking contrast to the calm, resourceful, ever reliable person round whom the whole household normally revolved.

Friends must, I suppose, have helped. I cannot imagine that any credit was to be had anywhere, given my father's record. His bank account had been ignominiously closed. ('It's been a long time since we had one of those in the house,' I recall my mother remarking when, before going up to university, I showed her my first cheque book.) It was, as I shall mention again, the loyalty and generosity of a few individuals which provided the few oases in the desert through which the family was now passing. Of our relatives we heard, to the best of my knowledge, not a word.

Those weeks when my mother lay ill marked the very bottom of the abyss into which we had fallen. That she might die never then occurred to me but I have often reflected since of our fate had this disaster happened. The family as a unit would, I believe, have foundered, with the children no doubt being farmed out separately to resentful and unwelcoming relations or, given their poor record in this respect, perhaps sent to one of the grim orphanages of the period. Often at disheartening moments in my life since then I have felt that nothing can ever approach, in its immediate unhappiness and potential for even greater and enduring misery, that dark and desperate time of which I was, happily, too young to appreciate the full horror.

Thanks to Dr Wyllie's generosity and professional skill my mother eventually recovered, aided, I am sure, by her own fierce resolve not to abandon her family, by dying when they needed her most. (As a devout Christian she must sometimes, I suspect, have thought longingly of the promised peace beyond the grave.) I have no doubt she was back on her feet long before she should have been and once again facing the impossible task of trying to make ends meet with no money coming in. Around this time we benefitted from another act of kindness. With the collapse of my father's business the Dramatic and Operatic Societies had ceased to rehearse in his studio and moved instead to the Jack Hotel. It was there, I suspect that a kindly plot was hatched to help us in our time of need while trying to spare my father's feelings. I still possess the illuminated scroll presented to him in March 1930, the sole document of this period of our lives to have survived:

> Presented to Ernest Longmate with the accompanying cheque by the President and Members of the Newbury and District Dramatic Society in grateful recognition of twenty-six years splendid service as honorary stage manager of this society and other societies in the past.

The reference to 26 years confirms my father's earlier association with Newbury, since it means he must have had some connection with the town as early as 1904, and the 'accompanying cheque' no doubt kept us fed for several weeks. My father was also, I believe, presented with a 'chain of office' consisting of a necklace of beer bottle caps, but this – distinctly inappropriate – gift has now vanished. The president of the Society, incidentally, who signed the testimonial, was Sir Frederick Carden and this was by no means his only act of kindness towards us. My elder sister recalls how, when she and Peggy were appearing as very young members of the chorus in one Operatic Society production and might have been left out of the last night distribution of bouquets and presents Sir 'Freddie' personally presented them with boxes of chocolates.

The kindness of friends and even mere acquaintances at this time provided the few bright moments in a generally grim time. My elder sister, now at the local church school, St Mary's, Speenhamland, had cause to be grateful to a teacher who noticed how hungry and wretched she looked and having discreetly established what she had had for dinner that day – it was bread and dripping – thereafter brought her fruit and sandwiches each day and provided her with a hot drink. My brother meanwhile had attended the same school until, on reaching the age of eleven, he moved on to the 'council school' near the station, the ordinary local authority school catering for boys up to the age of 14. Perhaps he looked less appealing than his sister, for, so far as I know, he was never given either food or clothes, but – as remained his stoical way throughout life – he never complained, either then or later about his miserable childhood.

Around this time Peggy and I reached the age of five when attendance at school became compulsory. Thanks to our poverty we were to start on a proper education, publicly provided, instead of the inferior schooling to which my father's ill-founded social pretensions and dreams of affluence had subjected my unfortunate older brother and sister. It has to be said, however, that this first school was vastly inferior to any we attended later and almost justified those parents who struggled to pay for their children to receive something better. The school nearest to us, St Mary's, Speenhamland, lacked an infant department, so we were sent to Speenhamland School, now officially a County Primary School, then a 'council elementary'. This was situated in what is now called Pelican Lane, just off the Oxford Road, a little way beyond the Broadway, and, as I realised many years later, almost on the site of the former Pelican Inn, where the so-called 'Speenhamland Act' was passed by the Berkshire magistrates in 1795.[*] The school was a Victorian foundation and looked it, while its teaching methods in the 1930s had changed little since it was opened. In the essay, already quoted, which I wrote

---

[*] The magistrates resolved to subsidise inadequate wages out of the poor rates, a policy which led ultimately to the introduction in 1834 of the New Poor Law. See *The Workhouse*, p.34 and, for the full text of the 1795 motion, Garlick, *A Newbury Scrapbook*, pp.104-5.

at the age of 15, its deficiencies were still clear in my mind and the scene I describe was one which could have been witnessed a century before:

> I recollect repeating the usual jargon, 'The cat sat on the mat,' etc...There were three classes in one large room and in the centre the headmistress sat by the fire. She was an old and fearsome lady and I can find little to say in her favour. If one was especially naughty one might be told to go to Miss Hood (the headmistress) and it was a terrifying experience to cross the rather dark and gloomy pit with many eyes upon one, only to be met by a cold welcome when the desk by the fire was eventually reached.

Twelve years later I still smarted at these same memories, as the essay, 'What have twelve years of Education done for me?', written at the age of 17, to which I shall refer again, makes clear:

> It was a bad school for the buildings were old and inadequate, as was the headmistress. She was a large lady, dressed usually in black, and as she sat at a great desk before the fire and presided over the uproar of several classes chanting different things, I was terrified of her.

Since my recollection of the premises has proved to be correct I believe I was not unjust to this disagreeable woman who, I now suspect, actively disliked small children. When I went back to Speenhamland she had long retired but the original circular building, formerly single storeyed, was still there, although the ceiling had been lowered and the interior was as bright and welcoming as any other primary school today. New buildings, of modern design, had also been added, though I could still identify the building in the playground which was the scene of one of the earliest humiliations of my life. This, although today disused, then housed the appallingly inadequate lavatories and, as an unassertive, undersized five year old, I was invariably at the end of the queue to use them. The end of one playtime came when I had still not reached the front and, far too shy to explain the situation to the teacher who mustered us into line for some form of exercise, I secretly wetted myself, to my great shame, fortunately without anyone else noticing.

'Playtime', taken up with this elemental need, was always for me a misnomer, and so, was 'playground', for though I was, like all of us, glad to escape from the claustrophobic classroom and the brooding presence of the unsmiling, even sinister, Miss Hood, an apt-sounding name that Dickens might have coined, I dreaded our principal outdoor activity, euphemistically called 'Country Dancing'. I was already demonstrating that inability to distinguish one type of tune from another, much less to make any form of rhythmic movement, which has stayed with me throughout life, and I can still remember cavorting ineffectively about the playground, shouted at for being in the wrong place and throwing out everyone else's tidy footwork. Nowadays I simply plead an inability to dance, but at five one was not allowed to be a sitter-out and, as so often later with other subjects, was unjustly accused of being deliberately obtuse.

Even more repellent than Miss Hood, if that were possible, was the school nurse, who also features in other Newburians' recollections of their childhood. She bore no resemblance at all to the spotless, kindly, smartly uniformed figure the phrase now conjures up, but was, in appearance at least – she may, for all I can judge, have done her distasteful job as sympathetically as she could – the sort of individual who must have inspired Dickens to create Sarah Gamp. I can picture her still, a grim-faced, elderly, overweight woman in a capacious dark, possibly mauve, dress, stretching from her neck to her ankles. She seemed to me enormous, resembling a predatory spider who spread in all directions, as she sat in the very centre of the large classroom, where all normal teaching was suspended, while we overawed infants formed a long line to kneel before her in turn. As we did so she parted our hair with a knitting needle in search of lice, which I assumed to be the reason for her nickname 'Nitty Norah', though some children called her 'Bluebottle'. Not surprisingly, in view of where we were living, both my sister and I were found to be infected and were sentenced to have our hair washed each night in an evil smelling liquid, an operation which, as we had so little room and no separate water supply, meant further complications in the household routine. My mother was much upset at our public humiliation, reported to her, perhaps by 'Nitty Norah' herself, or if not, no doubt with relish, by Miss Hood, when she called to collect us. She was, however, she later told my elder sister, much comforted by one of the other teachers, who knew the family history and recognised my mother for what was then commonly called 'a lady'. 'Don't worry, my dear,' this kindly woman told her. 'Breeding will out.'

6
ALL THE LONGMATES IS DAFT

Message chalked on the wall of the family home, c.1932

My first-hand experience of poverty as a child no doubt accounts for my subsequent interest in the development of the Poor Law, which preceded the coming of the welfare state. Knowing now, as a historian, what should in theory have been available to assist a family like ours, I am still puzzled that, even in the bleak and barren 1930s, we seem to have received no assistance from the agencies which should have provided it. If there had ever been an example of the 'deserving poor', decent people who had come down in the world and were doing their best to support themselves, surely it was my family. For all the help we received, however, we might as well have been feckless, drunken idlers to blame for their own misfortunes.

The early 1930s were a particularly bad time to be poor. What is still known as the Great Depression had begun in 1929, just when my father's business was foundering. The National Government was formed in a panic in August 1931 in the same atmosphere of fear that had led in 1834 to the foundation of the union workhouse, when it was believed, just as in 1931, that over-generous benefits to the unemployed were dragging the whole of society down into ruin. This belief led in September 1931, when I was five and a half, to the introduction of the hated Means Test, still remembered with bitterness.[1] This was the period when the dole was cut by ten per cent, family relationships were soured by grown-up children being required to support their parents, and, according at least to working class legend, unfeeling inspectors ordered respectable people who had struggled to build a decent home for themselves to sell prized possessions like a piano or an armchair, before they could qualify for help.

Officially the workhouse and the Poor Law it epitomised had been abolished in March 1930, the month when, as already described, our fortunes reached rock bottom and the Dramatic Society rallied round with their 'accompanying cheque'. In theory a more enlightened system of poor relief was introduced that month; in practice the workhouse was still invariably spoken of by that name and the reality of Public Assistance was no different from the 'out-relief' which had preceded it, indeed, thanks to the Means Test, help to the poor was now granted even more grudgingly than in the past.

The Minister of Health responsible for the changes made in 1930 was Neville Chamberlain, whom Lloyd George, the real pioneer of the social reforms of the twentieth century, described in a classic gibe as only equipped to be 'a good mayor of Birmingham in an off year'.[2] (Aneurin Bevan, the great architect of the National Health Service, was even more scathing. In 1929 he declared in the House of Commons: 'The worst thing I can say about democracy is that it has tolerated the Right Honourable Gentleman for four and a half years.'[3]) Chamberlain's real failure, like that of most politicians of the time, lay in his lack of knowledge of the life of the poor. Here was the great contribution the Labour Party was able to make to the national life, but in 1931, though twice in office, it had never held real power and the formation of the National Government had left it hopelessly split and in eclipse. As I now know, in those years from 1930 to 1935 when we so desperately needed it there *was* a system in place to help families like ours, however ungenerously. My father, as a self-employed tradesman, was not entitled to 'the dole', which was in practice confined to manual workers and a few low-salaried white-collar workers. For the same reason he did not qualify for free medical treatment under the 'panel' system established by Lloyd George. Looking back, I can see how almost any of the benefits introduced by the Labour government of 1945, from family allowances to supplementary benefit, from free school meals (in theory available in our day but never provided in any school I attended) to the National Health Service, would have not merely made my mother's life infinitely easier but in combination would have transformed it. The coming of the Means Test did not affect us. My father had no unemployment benefit to be cut and we had no surplus family possessions left to sell; the bailiffs had seen to that. Nevertheless some help should have been forthcoming from the state. The local Public Assistance Committee, successor to the Guardians Committee abolished by Chamberlain, and its chief instrument, the Relieving Officer, were empowered, and indeed required, to provide funds to destitute families to ensure they did not actually go hungry. My father certainly applied for Public Assistance, but years later, when he had become an enthusiastic Labour supporter, as I was from childhood, he recalled the experience with great, and for him most unusual, bitterness. Applicants like himself, he said, were treated not merely with a total lack of sympathy but with such near contempt that one would have to be starving to make a second attempt. The officials in Newbury were probably no worse than those elsewhere, but the whole tradition and philosophy of the Poor Law, since Victorian days, had been to deter applicants. At the time my father sought help there was no doubt intense pressure on everyone involved to save every possible penny. His status as a well-known local tradesman may well have told against him and I can well imagine that, lacking an impressive presence and not particularly articulate, he made the worst of a good case. At all events, having pocketed his pride, he was so crushed and defeated by his treatment that I believe he never applied again. My sister recalls that my mother, on learning that he had been humiliatingly rebuffed – though, sadly, none of the records survive and I have been unable to discover what actually happened – remarked, for once displaying despair: 'Well, there's no help to be got there!' It must have been, for her even more than my father, coming from a line of successful farmers, a bitter moment, having been forced to apply to 'go on the parish' and then been rejected.*

For the next few years there was no regular income coming into our household at all and how we stumbled through this wretched time I still cannot understand. We survived, I suppose, though always appallingly hard-up and sometimes literally hungry, on my father's rare and occasional earnings, on the gifts in money or kind given us by old acquaintances, and through the generosity of shopkeepers who had known my mother in the days of her prosperity and now let her run up bills she had little hope of paying or even slipped her essential items and 'forgot' to put them on the slate. The truth was that no one liked to see my mother suffer and her dignity and courage, which I can only now fully appreciate, must have brought us more sympathy and help than all my father's efforts to restart his business or, when this became visibly impossible, to find any kind of work. He now joined that hopeless quest for a job on which by 1931 2,630,000 previously insured men and women were already engaged, as well as many hundreds of thousands like himself who did not appear in the statistics because they had never been covered by the state scheme. The figures confirm, too, how he had come on the labour market at the worst possible moment. The official figure of those registered as out of work leapt from 1,216,000 in 1929 to 1,917,000 in 1930 and was on an ascending curve which reached its peak, 2,745,000, in 1932 and only fell below 2 million in 1936.[4] These were the very years when, with four children still at school, my parents' income was at its lowest and the demands on it at their greatest.

Now came the first improvement in our situation, though it can hardly have seemed like this to my parents at that time. One night, around the time I started school, in December 1930, our landlord in Newport Road and his family simply disappeared with their few possessions, leaving behind no forwarding address. They had taken what was then the recognised, almost respectable, way out of their financial difficulties, 'doing a moonlight flit' to some new area. This was not, with our middle-class background, a solution my parents ever contemplated, and in any case we would, I am sure, have rapidly been traced; a

---

* For a detailed study of the history of the Poor Law see *The Workhouse*. The classic description of 1930s poverty and the effect of the Means Test is in Walter Greenwood, *Love on the Dole* (1933). A fictional account of a middle-class man's application for Public Assistance, though he is treated sympathetically, can be found in Winifred Holtby, *South Riding* (1936).

photographer, especially one with an unusual name, could not, unlike a labourer, simply move away and set up elsewhere with any hope of anonymity.

The departure of our landlords must have been in some ways a relief, leaving us without their unwelcome presence and wiping out any debt for unpaid rent we owed them, but the owner of the house presumably tried to repossess it for we were forced to move again. We were now officially homeless and this perhaps encouraged the council to offer us a home on one of its estates, at the far end of the town. This meant a change of school for Peggy and myself, though my brother and sister were already, I think, attending the 'council schools' near the station, towards that end of the town, though still a mile or so [2-3 km] from our new home. It meant a long walk into Newbury for Gordon and Freda not merely to attend school but if and when they started work, and for my father as he searched for a job; there was seldom the necessary 2d [1p] – 1d [0.5p] for an under 14 – to spare for the bus.

How we paid for the move, the type of extra expenditure for which a family such as ours cannot possibly have budgeted in advance, I have no idea, but I suspect some acquaintance with a horse and cart may have helped. The day of the move, though my elder sister believes we had a similar experience on the day the bailiffs called and I may be confusing the two, I remember vividly. The two older ones no doubt being at school, my mother took Peggy and myself to spend the day in a local park, Greenham House, though the weather was grey and not very suitable for the excursion. Somehow she had collected a few coins together and led us into a cake shop. I can still picture the alluring display of eclairs and cream buns and now feel ashamed of pleading for more than I could eat and leaving half of one of my chosen purchases, since I realise how ill she can have spared even a single wasted penny.

The house to which we had moved, where I was to spend the whole of my childhood, was No 78 Camp Close, off the Newtown Road, just beyond the top of the hill out of the town on the Winchester road, and almost directly opposite the Newbury union workhouse. Opened, as already mentioned, a whole century earlier, in 1835, this remained an ever looming presence, from which everyone on the estate felt separated by only the narrowest of financial, as well as physical, margins, but, unlike the rest of Newbury, we spoke with dread of 'ending up over the road', instead of, as mentioned earlier, 'up the hill'. An ordnance survey map dated 1911 shows open country around and beyond the workhouse, the only building marked being on the main road, almost opposite the workhouse entrance. By my time the site was occupied by a large public house, the Rokeby Arms, known to us as 'The Rook', though none of us ever set foot in it, there being in Camp Close a clear line drawn between those who frequented it and those, the more prudent and financially secure, who did not. Only many year later did I discover that the place was named after an Irish peer who had owned the nearby Sandleford Priory, of which I shall say more later.

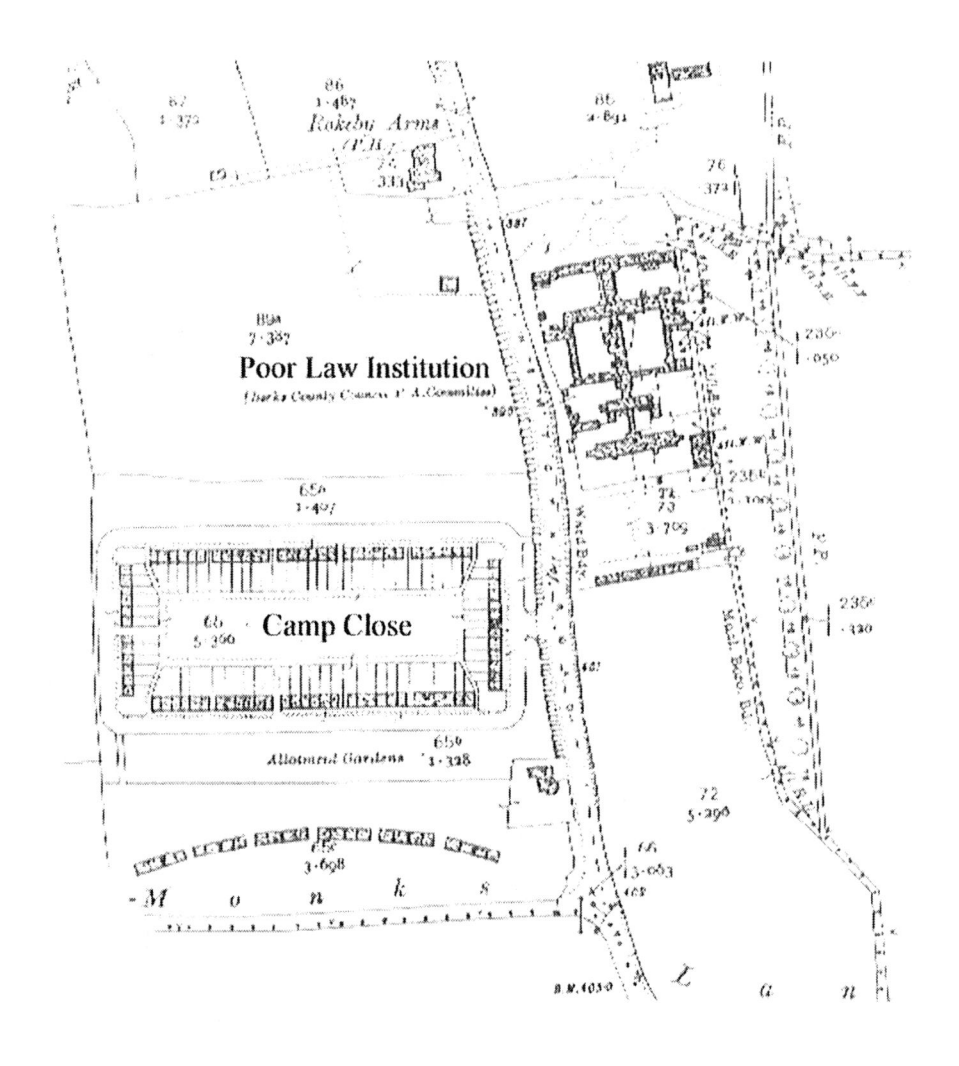

The open area facing the workhouse was soon to become valuable building land and a typical inter-war development came to occupy much of it, consisting of the archetypal middle-class houses – four bed, two recep., with electricity and a real bathroom, kitchen and hot water supply, mainly semi-detached – that I then deeply coveted. When the council bought what was then a 'green-field' site, however, a good way out of the town and with only the workhouse for company, it no doubt got it cheap and no money was wasted on the estate erected there. It could have been, and perhaps was, argued, that the less the houses cost, the lower the rent could be fixed, a fair point, though what, it might be asked, were subsidies for public housing for if not to offer the occupants something better than, by strict economic criteria, they could afford? Making all allowances, however, I still find it surprising that the standard of both accommodation and equipment was pitched so low. By now, when private developers were running up more spacious but low-cost, houses the most enlightened local authorities were already trying to provide their tenants with something more than the bare minimum of shelter and facilities. When, as an historian, I came to study the design of homes built by charities for the Victorian and Edwardian poor they seemed immediately familiar, for this was just the type of house I lived in. I had always assumed till then that Camp Close had been built before the first world war by an uninspired architect, working for an old-fashioned and highly cost-conscious, if not mean-minded, council. I now suspect that I was unjust to him and that he did the best he could, given a no doubt strict brief and minimum budget, but I still find it astonishing that such low standards should still have been acceptable when bodies like the London County Council were demonstrating what could be achieved even within the existing constraints.

A contemporary drawing, presumably commissioned by the council, gives a misleading impression of dignity and even elegance, while a snapshot of the front doorway of our house conveys a sense of comfort and cosiness.[*] Both are equally false. The houses at Camp Close were cramped, squalid and badly equipped. The best feature was the name, taken from a large field near the workhouse, which appears on a tithe map as early as 1839. Whether obvious local need or pressure from central government caused the council to erect Camp Close I have no idea, but the relevant minute records, on 16 September 1927, that 'The connection of the sewer of the 84 houses is just being completed and...it is expected that 60 houses will be ready for occupation by the end of the month.'[5] Our house must therefore have been almost new when we moved into it three years later, only the second family to live there. Long after we had left it for a better, post-1945 council house on another, new, estate, Camp Close was modernised, with the addition of electricity and better plumbing, and, as it had acquired a bad reputation, it was given a new and even more elegant name, Sandleford Rise.[6] Subsequently even the improved property

---

[*] See illustrations.

failed to measure up to modern standards and the whole estate was demolished, being replaced by attractive bungalows for the elderly.

In 1931 No 78 Camp Close was a vast step up, however, from our two horrible rented rooms in the waste land at the far end of Newport road, though I can still recall feeling that it seemed a sad come down after No 8 Newport Road, which remained in my mind as an over coloured ideal. I have no other recollections of the move, nor can I imagine how it was paid for, but I do remember how delighted my mother was to have her own kitchen again and only now did she reveal how she had hated living in sordid proximity to our previous landlords, and largely by their sufferance. My brother, who had also never complained of our former wretched surroundings, found another cause for rejoicing. The handles on the doors, he remarked, were far higher than in our rented rooms, and would have been welcome there, to prevent our landlord's ill-mannered children reaching up to them to burst in on us uninvited.

The estate consisted of 84 identical small houses, built in a rectangle round an open space of rough grass, which, so far as I can recall, was left uncared for. No 78 was on one corner of one of the longer sides, which consisted of terraces of twelve and eighteen houses respectively; the two end terraces each contained twelve, divided into two blocks. The eight end-of-terrace houses were in effect semi-detached and accordingly much prized, although four of them, including ours, had virtually no back garden, only a tiny triangular plot, known as 'the backyard', alongside the footpath which linked the road round the estate to the enclosed green behind the houses. We had at the front a tiny patch of garden where my mother struggled bravely to raise a few plants, a sad echo of the arable fields and grassland surrounding her childhood home. The whole estate was more reminiscent of a working-class road in an industrial town than of one in a rural area where space was still plentiful, but I cannot pretend I much felt the lack of a garden. There was, however, a high price to pay for having a wall directly beside a public path, for this proved a constant temptation to graffiti writers. It cannot have been long after our arrival that one child living a few doors away recorded on this side wall his verdict on these new neighbours: 'All the Longmates is daft.'

Like the 'model cottages' created by Victorian and Edwardian reformers for farm labourers, all the houses at Camp Close possessed an allotment, on the uncultivated land which encircled the estate. These gave the owners some opportunity to express their individual personality, for which there was little opportunity in their identical houses. In fact people went into each other's houses very little, partly because there was little room to spare for visitors, partly because offering even a cup of tea to a neighbour might have stretched the family budget. I believe the rent for all 84 houses was the same, 5s [25p] a week when we moved in, 7s 6d [35.5p] when we moved out 20 years later.

The interior of the houses reflected the rural tradition already mentioned. The main room downstairs was officially 'the kitchen', though we knew it as 'the sitting room'. It had a coal-burning grate on which pots could be heated and an oven beside it in which bread could, in theory, be baked, though I do not believe it ever was. The 'kitchen' was never used for cooking by us or any other family to my knowledge, this being performed in what was supposedly 'the scullery', which we more commonly knew by the grander name. This consisted of a small dingy space with, if my memory can be trusted, a stone, though not flagged, floor, a shallow flat stone sink with a cold tap, and in the far corner – though one could almost touch both simultaneously, a small gas stove. One side wall gave on to a coal store which, even in our house, with its outside wall, could not be filled from outside, and a pantry, a large cupboard, more than adequate for any stores we ever accumulated. More commonly the shelves were almost permanently bare. Beside the gas stove a door led into the bathroom, again something of a misnomer, for it was essentially a laundry room, dominated by a large copper. There was no wash basin or lighting in the bathroom, but there was a cold tap over the bath, and a pipe ran from a small, second, tap, into the copper. This was heated up by coals carried on a shovel from the grate and inserted via a small hatch. The theory was clearly that after, with some difficulty, the water in the copper had been heated up and used for the weekly clothes wash it could then be fed into the bath to clean their owners, but it was an inefficient arrangement. It was impossible to get enough hot water to cover oneself, though the bath was not very large, so the copper had invariably to be stoked up again half way through. When I reached the age of puberty I was embarrassed at my mother having to come in for this purpose and if in some families baths were a rare event they could hardly be blamed since providing them was so troublesome. For routine washing one had to boil a kettle on the gas stove and carry it upstairs to the china basin in the bedroom – an object now often seen in antique shops – or pour it into some similar container in the sink in the kitchen.

There was no lavatory in the bathroom or indeed inside the house. It had instead been fitted, presumably as an economy in both space and plumbing, in the outside corner, being reached from the garden. It was unlighted and though an obvious step up from the communal privies many families in built-up urban areas had to endure was far from ideal in cold weather or after dark. I still find it surprising that such obviously inadequate provision should have been made in a house built in the late 1920s.

My overwhelming impression, looking back, is how little space there was overall, though the architect had clearly made the best use he could of what was available. The front door opened almost directly on to the stairs, though we grandly called the few square feet of space at their foot 'the hall'. Upstairs were two rooms just about large enough to accommodate a double bed, and an even smaller single room, with little space for more than the bed itself. The main bedroom, at the front, had an open fireplace but no grate, and it was not, I think, ever used by us or any other family, since it would have been dangerously close to the bedclothes, even if anyone could have afforded the luxury of a second fire. For practical purposes, therefore, the bedrooms were unheated. There was not even the pretence of providing lighting in the two smaller upstairs rooms. The largest, at the front, did contain a gas lamp fitting, though – on grounds of both cost and convenience – we never, that I can recall, used it.

What now strikes me most, apart from the generally cramped nature of our home and the meagre degree of comfort considered suitable for its occupants, was the lack of electricity. These houses had, after all, been built by a public authority, with the help of a government subsidy and as part of a national policy of providing cheap public housing, as late as 1926. Certainly by the time we moved in, in 1931, electricity had become the normal means of lighting, if not of heating and power, in most towns, though not in the countryside. (Had Camp Close been in a remote village it would not, of course, even have been supplied with gas; coal, oil and candles were still the countryman's sources of energy and light.) The explanation, when I learned it, struck me as a powerful argument for the nationalisation of public utilities: Newbury Corporation owned the gas works but not the electricity power station, so its unfortunate tenants had, for several decades to come, to grope about with gas mantles and candles even on its newest, showpiece estate. I decided, too, a view I have never changed, that central government was a better protector of the less well-off than their own local authority, and that decent standards in housing were more likely to be imposed from the centre than be introduced by an individual council. As it is, I am grateful to the somewhat primitive conditions of my childhood, of which I was for several years barely aware, for having given some insight into how a large part of the population then lived, knowledge which has often proved useful to me since both as a writer and a historical consultant. I recall suggesting the inclusion in a script of a scene involving the ritual of lighting the gas, with the suspended chains that turned on the supply pulled down, the careful introduction of a lighted match to the fragile mantle – far more liable to damage than an electric light bulb – and the final loud pop as it burst triumphantly into life.

The move to Camp Close had left us better housed but no better off and it was now that I began to be really conscious of how poor we were, even in comparison to our new neighbours, who mostly had at least one member of the family in work, and often several. All four of the Longmate children were still at school. My brother and elder sister must, I think, have been allowed to finish out the school year at St Mary's, for from a surviving document – my brother was, happily, like myself, a hoarder, while virtually nothing survives on paper about my parents and little about my sisters – I find that he was admitted to what is here described as the Council Senior Boys' School on 8 September 1931, when he was already past the official leaving age of 14, which he had reached the previous October. Why he stayed on I cannot be sure, for we needed every penny he could earn. The likeliest explanation is that there was no job for him to go to, but it may be my parents also felt that in keeping him at school they were improving his chances in life.

It must, I feel with hindsight, have been Gordon who suffered most from our poverty. He was, unlike Peggy and myself, old enough to be aware of all the deprivations and humiliations my father's lack of income forced upon us, and if he never, then or later, complained this does not mean that the scars inflicted were any less deep and lasting. He had already a quiet, introverted temperament which made it difficult for him to make friends and form normal relationships and these characteristics remained with him throughout life. Although he would, I believe, have liked to marry, he never did so and never had a girl friend, though, I think, enjoying women's company. His life came, as I shall describe, to revolve round his church and, for almost the whole of his life, his job, with essentially the same employer; he died only a year after retiring from it, not visibly unhappy, but after, I still feel, a basically frustrated life.

Too old when the family fortunes collapsed to take the 'scholarship', which I am sure he would easily have obtained, Gordon could still, had my father been able to afford the fees, have entered the grammar school, but this was totally impossible. Conceivably had he already been attending it funds might have been found from some charitable source to keep him there. As it was, my father's idiotic venture into private education for his older son had destroyed his prospects of fulfilling his intellectual potential and effectively ruined his life – as well, of course, as creating yet another creditor who remained unpaid.

The Council School to which Gordon now moved was, I am sure, no worse than others of its type and date and was well regarded in the town, though a world apart from the Grammar School attended by brighter or wealthier boys. Discipline was strict and once Gordon was caned, no doubt unjustly, for he was naturally law-abiding and well-behaved. I remember being shocked by the sight of the weals on his hand, my first, though far from my last, confrontation with the results of corporal punishment, for which I felt then, in spite of the constant beating in my favourite reading, *The Magnet*, an instinctive disgust.

The council school was designed to turn out boys ready for the labour market at the age of 14 and at least able to read, write and do simple calculations and did so competently enough, but provided no real opportunity to shine academically. Foreign languages, for which Gordon later showed some aptitude, were not taught, but he did well in English. When, in 1931, aged 14, he joined a school excursion to Portsmouth organised by the Newbury branch of the Navy League, a patriotic organisation in favour of a strong fleet, founded earlier in the century, he won first prize in the subsequent competition. His reward was a stirring novel by TC Bridge, *With Beatty in Jutland*, intended no doubt to arouse loyal feelings and perhaps – a remote possibility in my brother's case – a desire to join the navy, in its young readers. This was probably more to my taste than to his and like the copy of *Treasure Island* mentioned earlier, now rests on my bookshelves, an honoured relic of those grim years. It may also have helped to develop my interest in the whole subject of national defence and the role of the navy as its key component.[*] My brother's essay 'A Trip to Portsmouth', neatly written on lined paper with not an inch wasted, still survives, so I know he was particularly impressed by the dry dock built to 'accomadate' (*sic*) HMS *Hood*, which was, ironically, in the second world war to demonstrate the vulnerability of even the mightiest battleship. More significant, however, than his literary success was my brother's extraordinary unselfishness. The Navy League no doubt paid for the coach to Portsmouth or he could not have joined in the outing but my mother, by what sacrifices I cannot imagine for this was at the very nadir of our fortunes, had given him sixpence [2.5p] for spending money. Knowing how desperately every penny was needed he brought it back untouched and I can still remember my mother's delight as he returned the precious coin to her.

My brother was, I am sure, sorry to leave school, but accepted his lot unprotestingly, as he did everything else that happened to him in life. I never heard him complain, even on his deathbed. What he would have liked, though not in the least mechanically minded, was to work in a public transport undertaking; he was always fascinated by bus, and to a lesser extent, train timetables, and clearly my father tried to find him a post in this field for a letter, dated 4 July 1932, when my brother was aged 15, from the Thames Valley company based in Reading still survives. Its contents, courteous but discouraging, must have been typical of thousands of such communications sent at this time:

> We thank you for your letter of the 1st instant, but have to say that we have no vacancies at all at present. As our tendency at the moment is to curtail staff rather than increase, we are afraid that it is unlikely that we shall have anything of interest to your son in the immediate future.

In the end, perhaps feeling fortunate to have found any job at all, though it was obviously a dead-end post far below his capacity, he became a petrol pump attendant in what was then the town's principal garage, Martin and Chillingworth, on the London Road near the Broadway. For a six day week, which included Saturday afternoon, he earned ten shillings [50p]. The garage was at the other end of the town from Camp Close and meant a long journey each way, as he did not yet own a bicycle. I recall one Saturday afternoon when I was perhaps seven or eight going to see him when he had been left in charge and somewhat envying him his position and his brown overall. He allowed me

---

[*] On the Navy League see my *Island Fortress*, pp. 368-9. *With Beatty in Jutland* was published by Collins in 1930. *Treasure Island* by Robert Louis Stevenson was published in 1883.

to play in one of the secondhand cars parked on the forecourt and I can still recall my horror when, on releasing the handbrake, it began to roll down a slope towards the busy main road; luckily I had the presence of mind to re-apply the brake in time.

The events which, I am sure, permanently blighted my brother's life left the next eldest child in our family less affected, for Freda, who celebrated her twelfth birthday soon after we reached Camp Close, was of a cheerful disposition, never happier than when playing in the open air and she was not concerned at having failed the vital 'scholarship', school work never having appealed to her. She was, she remembers, happy at Camp Close and enjoyed her freedom, for, confident we would come to no harm while in the company of other children, my mother left us to roam about it at will. Freda's greatest pleasure, she remembers, was to run round the road encircling Camp Close, it being believed that four circuits added up to a mile [1.5 km].

Even Freda's happy-go-lucky nature, however, could not shield her from the consequences of being miserably poor. Normally more considerate than her two younger siblings, Freda once, most untypically, remarked, 'Well, I didn't think much of that' after some particularly meagre meal and was horrified when my mother, for the only time she can recall, dissolved in tears. It must have been around this time, too, that my mother explained to Freda that she was now too old for a Christmas stocking, whatever she had scraped together being destined for Peggy and myself, four years younger. Freda was, however, so distressed at being deprived of this expected treat that my mother relented, no doubt transferring to her stocking some of the items intended for 'the twins'.

With the move to Camp Close Peggy and I also had to change schools, to our great benefit. We now attended a church school, St John's Infants, close to the church of the same name, at the foot of Newtown Hill, which was to become an important part of our lives. The school was close to what was traditionally the roughest part of Newbury, the City, once an almost self-contained community with its own traditions, including the annual appointment of a City Mayor, who more resembled a medieval Lord of Misrule than the conventional civic dignitary.[7]

At first with my mother, then alone, Peggy and I made the journey to and from school twice a day on foot every weekday, covering the same route each Sunday to attend church. A former headmistress of St John's, Miss Luckett, was still a familiar figure about the parish and I always looked on her with awe for my mother told me she had been a missionary, and I imagined her in the jungle confronting hordes of hungry cannibals, Bible in hand. She belonged, I suspect, to that breed of stern, mainly unsmiling, spinsters often found at that time in the teaching profession.

The regime at St John's school by the time I arrived there was still strict but not unkindly and infinitely superior in every respect to the dismal Speenhamland. No money was wasted on equipment, for my first memory is of being required to write on the back of scraps of wallpaper, and we were kept hard at work until Friday afternoon when the last lesson of the week, regarded as a treat, was to select cut-out words like 'sofa', 'chair' and 'lamp' and place them in the proper places on a drawing of a fully furnished room. I have two other recollections of St John's, both less comfortable. Once I heard a young woman teacher scream in agony as her fingers became trapped in the hinge of one of the folding partitions which divided the main ground floor area into classrooms. It was the first time I had heard such a sound and I was profoundly frightened by it and shocked by the realisation that grown-ups, too, were vulnerable to pain. My other recollection is of falling down in the playground and having the resulting graze painfully splashed with iodine, a process, I now suspect, intended rather to discourage trivial complaints than to promote antisepsis.

I liked St John's school and was impressed by the church to which it was attached. It was an impressive building, consecrated in 1860 to serve the newly created parish around it, and from the beginning loyal to the Anglo-Catholic movement then gaining ground throughout the Church of England. Its architect was the famous William Butterfield who had also designed All Saints, Margaret Street, in central London, a High Church shrine of which my brother spoke with the same awe as a Moslem might of Mecca. A little later Butterfield was also to be responsible for the equally High Church, but less universally admired, Keble College, Oxford, the butt of many undergraduate jokes. St John's church had been consecrated by the then Bishop of Oxford, Samuel Wilberforce, unkindly known, thanks to his smooth tongue and effusive manner, as 'Soapy Sam'.[8] His successor, by 1937, was equally 'sound' doctrinally, ie solidly Anglo-Catholic, Kenneth Kirk, who was respected rather than liked in the diocese. St John's could seat 500, though it was rarely full, and was said to be a fine example of the Victorian 'Decorated' Style, though I always found the interior gloomy rather than uplifting.[9] The same was true of the large, rambling vicarage, also by Butterfield, beside the church, to which, as I shall later describe, I had to pay occasional duty visits. Its occupant, the incumbent of St John's, was the Rev. E Stenning, 'Father Stenning' as we always knew him. He was a kindly middle-aged, somewhat unworldly bachelor, cared for by a cook and maid, and easily flustered. I recall the congregation's delight one Sunday when he began his notices 'Next Tuesday being Ash Wednesday...' He was to be, in a minor way, a private benefactor of mine, though disappointed, I now suspect, that I felt no call myself to Holy Orders and indeed, as I grew older, became only an irregular attender at his church. In these early years, however, from around 1931, St John's was central to the family's life and especially to my brother's. In his late teens, with no money to spare for a young man's normal interests, even if they had appealed to him, bored by sport and too shy to go out with girls, he found in St John's a second home. He enjoyed the discussions on doctrine it provided, as well as the ecclesiastical gossip which had always been the lifeblood of the Church of England, read the *Church Times* whenever he could afford a copy, found sympathetic companions at church functions and, above all, was able every Sunday, and often during the week as well, to escape from the deprivations and frustrations of his daily life into the splendid ritual for which St John's was famous.

Gordon rapidly became a keen server at sung mass and evensong, and in due course was appointed secretary of the St John's branch of the servers' 'trade union', the Guild of the Servants of the Sanctuary, whose minute books for this period I have still. Eventually Gordon was able to combine two of his interests in one in organising coach trips for the Guild to sing their office at other churches in the district, followed by a sociable drink. (The Anglican church, to its credit, never suffered from the foolish inhibitions about alcohol which have left their mark upon so many generations of nonconformists.)

A regular hierarchy existed among the servers, whose roles were allocated each week, and whose moves were directed by the Master of Ceremonies, or MC, a place filled in rotation from among the more experienced. Others took on the duty of crucifer, carrying the cross, or bearing banners or candles, the technical names for which escape me. The humblest roles, usually filled by the smallest and latest recruits, were those of 'cope boys', who held up the priest's robes as he stood at the altar or processed round the aisles, and 'boat boy'. The latter acted as assistant to the thurifer who swung the censer. His role was to walk beside the thurifer carrying the 'boat', a brass vessel containing incense, for the censer needed to be replenished at frequent intervals. Anticipating when more would be needed and having the lid on the boat swung back and the spoon poised ready for the thurifer to use was the whole art of being a boat boy. The respective advantages, in smell, combustibility and price, of different types of incense was the type of topic my brother loved to discuss, indeed his favourite role was that of thurifer, at which he seemed particularly adept. Once, when he had excelled himself, and billowing clouds of incense filled the church so that one could hardly see across it, Father Stenning took as his text 'Our prayers go up as the smoke to heaven' and commented 'Our thurifer must, I think, have been aware of what text I should choose this morning', a remark which passed into church legend.

Like many clergy, though the Church of England at that time was a model of conformity compared to what it has since become, Father Stenning could rarely resist improving on the generally recognised rites and loved to introduce little variations of his own. This prompted another much-quoted observation from one long suffering MC: 'Sarum' – a standard form of ritual – 'I know, and Western I know, but Stenning I know not.'

Although I quite enjoyed being boat boy – and my mother, I am sure, delighted in seeing me accompanying my brother and hearing the comments, deeply embarrassing to me, of other female members of the congregation, on my 'angelic' appearance in cassock and surplice – I never graduated into being a full-blown server. One needed, I fear, something of the actor in one's temperament, which I lacked but which my brother, who shone in amateur productions in the parish, undoubtedly possessed. I became disillusioned with serving after being paired with an incompetent small boy who failed to drop his side of the vicar's cope when he turned round at the altar, so that on stretching out my hands to pick up the hem of the garment I found myself taking hold of my 'partner' instead. Somehow he had managed to squeeze himself between the vicar's legs and the front of the altar and I was left to scurry round and take his place. I felt the other servers, if not the congregation, were blaming me for his clumsy performance and it shattered my self-confidence so that I refused to serve thereafter.

We used, when I was a little older, to joke that St John's 'had one foot in the Tiber'. As grown-ups, Gordon and I visited Rome together and amused ourselves sending a postcard to a dissenter friend with the Vatican postmark, bearing the message 'From the seat of authority'. I do not think, however, that my brother's loyalty to the Church of England ever really wavered, though he would certainly have left it had women priests been ordained in his lifetime.

Back in the early 1930s the whole family regularly attended church and my mother was punctilious about taking Peggy and myself – I have some recollection that Freda, the least pious of us, managed to stay away – to the Good Friday morning service. Here Christ's sufferings on the cross were illustrated by coloured plates and I remember my mother, deeply moved, remarking quietly to us 'How terrible!' I felt even then some distaste for such gory scenes and am now revolted by the more garish statues to be found in Roman Catholic churches, such as 'Jesus displaying his bleeding heart'. We were, very sensibly I think, never sent to Sunday school. My mother had herself been a Sunday school teacher in her youth, but she always believed children were shipped off on Sunday afternoons more from a desire for parental privacy than to promote piety in their offspring. On Sunday evenings we walked down the hill to evensong, which I found agreeable enough, especially if, as often happened at St John's, it included a procession. I remember as one of the most shaming moments of my childhood being entrusted with the family's collective offering to the collection, a halfpenny [0.25p], which I somehow mislaid and my mother's whispered explanation to the sidesman with the offertory bag, 'He's lost the collection money.'

Our attendance at St John's gave a shape to our week, just as the changing pattern of the church's calendar provided a structure for our year. Events connected with St John's provided subjects of discussion pleasantly removed from our own impoverished and restricted lives. The misdeeds of curates, who seemed to change with remarkable frequency, were a rich source of gossip. 'Soundness' in doctrine and liturgical practice were, it appeared, no guarantee of piety or even honesty. One young man was summarily dismissed after being caught helping himself to the proceeds of the collection. (He had, it appeared, foolishly stolen some of the offerings at an ill-attended early morning service when the actual number of coins collected could be calculated.) Another was said to be too fond of a drink, though church occasions could legitimately end in the pub and we despised the nonconformists for their teetotalism. A third curate, though this must have been later as I can recall hearing him offend while I was myself enjoying a drink, used to indulge in coarse stories and excremental language. This was, I think, less from a desire to be thought 'one of the boys' than because, as I have often witnessed since, the professionally pious sometimes seem to feel a compulsion to behave in this way, perhaps as a substitute for what they regard as grosser sins. I found such conduct on the part of a priest indefensible and do so still.

In those days the clergy made regular visits to their parishioners and no doubt our house, a little bastion of faith in a landscape of non-believers, was a welcome port of call. For my mother, like my brother, the church was the source of such social life as she enjoyed and she was an active member of the Mothers Union. At its regular meetings in the St John's parish hall, the so-called 'Iron Room', she excelled in tests of Bible knowledge as well as in the games and quizzes with which the meetings ended. Once, I recall her telling me, they played charades and she suggested an apt word that was universally applauded and not too easily guessed, 'Fellowship'.

A major event during 1933, so I must have been aged seven, was the consecration of the new St George's church on Wash Common, or rather, half of it, for the money had run out before the original project could be completed. This stands out in my mind, like the opening of the new wing of the hospital, already mentioned, and probably for the same reason; it provided, I suspect, the occasion for a family outing, with free refreshments. St George's was if anything even 'Higher' than its parent and its Italianate architecture, white painted walls and detached campanile were curiously reminiscent of Newbury's impressive Roman Catholic church, St Joseph's.[10]

My mother delighted in minor mishaps on formal occasions or in unexpected eccentricities in church. She remembered one clergyman, at, I think, St George's, having urged his congregation to be more generous than usual, concluding: 'And to ensure that you are, I shall myself take the collection', which he duly did, with an all-too-open plate instead of the customary bag. On another occasion a visiting preacher agreeably scandalised her by, as she put it, 'using the word b' – she never used swear words herself, even in, as it were, quotation marks – in the pulpit. He had described how another clergyman, visiting a parishioner who constantly complained of the poor condition of her house, and finally of an increase in her rent, had urged patience, commenting soothingly: 'It's the Lord's will!', until goaded beyond endurance, she retorted, 'Tain't the Lord. The Lord's all right. It's that bloody landlord!'

Like all children, I took my parents for granted at the time, but I now realise what a remarkable woman my mother was, with a saintly disposition. I cannot recall her ever saying an unkind word about anyone and it was totally typical of her that when, towards the end of her life, she should have received an unexpected legacy of £500 from some distant relative she should have kept none of it for herself. This must, when the will was drafted, have been a handsome legacy, sufficient to buy a comfortable house, and a few years earlier would have transformed our lives. Even in the 1950s it remained a significant sum, and my mother immediately shared out most of it among her children and spent the rest on presents to friends and acquaintances. In one case the recipient was a hard-up housewife on our estate who had repeatedly told my mother that she hoped for a legacy from some distant relations; my mother, having sent her some money anonymously, was absolutely delighted when the woman concerned, when they next met, boasted to her of how the long hoped for bequest had duly appeared.

My mother, although a woman of strict Christian principles herself, was remarkably tolerant of the failings of others, of which, since so many of the local women confided in her, she acquired considerable knowledge, though these confidences were never betrayed and she would sometimes interrupt herself during what sounded a purely harmless anecdote to say, 'No, I don't think I'll tell you that.' Even the phrase 'child abuse' had not then been invented, but I can recall her mentioning that she had been told of a man who had 'interfered with' his grown-up step-daughter. She barely condemned him, merely commenting that his wife had recently had an operation which made 'anything like that' impossible. Her Christian faith was unwavering, but our home was always open to a young man we knew as 'Brother T.' He professed himself a communist, which was almost like declaring oneself a mass murderer, and, what was even worse, a non-believer. On occasion Brother T happened to be in the house when the curate called and, anxious that there should be no misunderstanding, bravely informed the young cleric 'I'm an atheist.' I half expected the skies to fall in and there was a somewhat uneasy interlude until one or both men left. Brother T, true to his refusal to conform to the ordinary rules, eventually married a woman with an illegitimate child, a pretty girl whom he brought to see us. To have a child out of wedlock was, in those pre-war times, proof of almost unfathomable depravity, but my mother was notably supportive to Brother T though, I suspect, privately sharing the popular opinion that 'No good will come of it'. Rather sadly, the pessimists proved right and the woman concerned – with, it seemed to us, a notable lack of gratitude – ran off with someone else.

[1] Taylor p.352 & Mowat p.483
[2] Taylor p.256
[3] *A Dictionary of Historical Quotations* p.21
[4] Mitchell & Deane p.66
[5] Berkshire Record Office N/AC w/12/2
[6] Information from Newbury Museum
[7] Garlick pp.20-21
[8] Garlick p.76
[9] Money p.151
[10] Purvis p.36

7
SORRY, MUM'S OUT

Traditional Camp Close response to the rent collector, c. 1933.

Nineteen thirty-three was an important year for my twin sister and myself, for we moved to a new school, of which I shall say more later. For the nation, for Newbury and for the Longmate family it was a grim time. I can remember an incident which epitomises the atmosphere of that wretched year, in which Hitler came to power in Germany, and the depression continued to engulf Great Britain. One morning the headmaster came into our classroom and issued the simple instruction: 'Stand up, all those children whose fathers are unemployed!' Later I was to recall this event in my speech when seeking to become prospective Labour candidate for Newbury. What I did not tell the selection committee was that my sister and I, after exchanging a glance, stayed seated. I imagine she felt, as I did, that it would somehow be letting dad down to admit what we both knew to be true, that he *was* unemployed, though not actually drawing the dole. Our filial loyalty was a mistake. The children who had got to their feet were fitted with shoes, no doubt the result of a public appeal. The cost of children's boots features large in every account of charitable efforts to help the poor in Victorian and Edwardian times. These in fact were not boots, but mainly flimsy plimsoles. However they were a great deal better than nothing and would have saved my mother one worry. I have regretted my misplaced pride ever since.

As it was, something like half the class admitted what still seemed to me the shameful truth, a surprisingly high proportion since Newbury was nowhere near as hard hit by the depression as comparably sized towns in the north of England or South Wales. No doubt, however, there were many families like ours where the breadwinner did not appear in the statistics and was not officially unemployed at all. Nationally there was in fact a slight drop in 1933 in the total of insured individuals out of work, the beginning of a continuing trend, though it was not until 1940 that the average for the year fell below one million.[1] Newbury in 1933 had 800 'official' unemployed in a population, according to the 1931 census, of 13,340, though there must have been many

1: My mother around her twelfth birthday, already a model to others

2: My mother at the door of the house we occupied from 1931-1947

3: Holton village, date unknown. The Farm is on the left beyond the property adjoining the church

4: Easter Monday parade in Newbury, c.1909. I was born above the former Righton's shop, where my father ran his photographic business

5: A float advertising his business, c.1924. The two children in the float are my elder brother and sister

6: No.8 Newport Road, the first home I remember, photographed in 2000

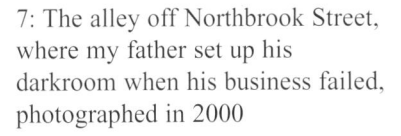

7: The alley off Northbrook Street, where my father set up his darkroom when his business failed, photographed in 2000

8: A parade in aid of the unemployed, July 1933. My father later managed Blandford's, on the right

9: Newbury Market Place, with Corn Exchange. Date unknown but probably c.1947

10: 'Cocky', my father's most successful picture, used in his advertising

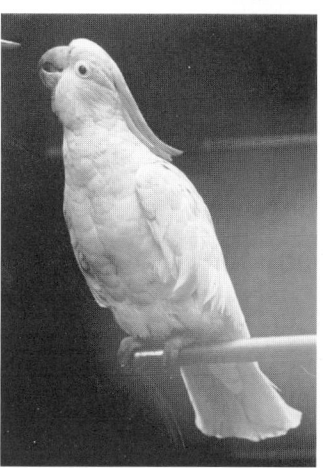

11: The Jack Hotel, Northbrook Street, Cocky's home, demolished 1935

more, like my father, who did not appear in the statistics.[2] In 1932, when unemployment nationally reached its peak, the rector of St Nicholas had been so distressed at the sight of the sad lines of men queuing for long hours outside the Labour Exchange in nearby West Mills that he had opened his parish room as a shelter for them.[3] Now the Mayor, Alderman Elsie Kimber,[*] a large, impressive, lady, always spoken of with respect, called a public meeting in the Corn Exchange to launch a Work Fund scheme, partly financed by a voluntary levy of 2d [1p] a week on all those fortunate enough to have a job. The intention was to extend the improvement works already financed by the council. These were of a traditional kind, surfacing and draining two hitherto neglected streets and extending the gas mains to the neighbouring village, today a separate town, of Thatcham. Another scheme of which the great Victorian reformers would also have approved was the levelling and draining of the former Marsh, officially Victoria Park, estimated to cost £1,700. This was to be spread as widely as possible among those in need, though not at very generous rates, the proposed wage for a married man being no more than £1.15s [£1.75] a week. Such enterprises, useful though they were, brought no benefit to white-collar or professional unemployed like my father; it was labourers who were needed, not photographers.

Since the only regular income coming into the house at this time was the 10s [50p] a week earned by my brother, how my mother fed and clothed us remains to me something of a mystery. Although my father had fitted up our inadequate bathroom with a foldaway wooden bench – he was, as I have mentioned elsewhere, always good with his hands – and converted it into a darkroom, so that I became used to knocking before I entered for fear of ruining undeveloped plates, he received very little work and for weeks at a time remained demoralisingly idle. Sometimes he sat slumped for hours, saying nothing, visibly overwhelmed by his misfortunes. Often since then, watching film of unemployed men in the 1930s, hanging about street corners surrounded by an air of desolation matching their external shabbiness, I have felt I was again glimpsing my father as he was then. In the evenings he often wandered off, without a coin in his pocket, for hours at a time. Once, after a particularly long absence, and fearing the worst, my mother send word to 'Uncle John' Stoodley at the far end of the town and he obligingly went to look for my father and found him sitting alone, the picture of misery, on a bench by the canal. He was, I have suspected since, contemplating suicide but he never, to my knowledge, attempted it and this episode perhaps cleared the air for after it my mother went to stay for a week with relations, nominally for a rest but in practice, I suspect,

---

[*] I remember this admirable, highly respected spinster for a trivial and inappropriate reason. My mother sent me the service leaflet from her funeral which had caused much amusement in the town, since the phrase "'tis immortality" in one of the hymns had emerged as "'tis immorality".

to appeal for their help. What the result was I do not know, but somehow we staggered on, going to school or in Gordon's and soon also Freda's, case, to work, desperately poor and insecure but still visibly a family.

Although he had periods of depression when he seemed inactive – 'He was afraid I thought he really wasn't trying to get a job,' my mother told me later, 'but I knew he was' – my father was throughout this period desperately searching for work. He did not, in the phrase of a later Conservative minister, 'get on his bike' because he could not afford one, but he did, for a man of his sedentary background, walk long distances in this hopeless quest. I still have a clear picture of him in my mind dusty, shabby and in broken shoes, having had nothing to eat all day, returning dejected to Camp Close. He had, he told my mother, just walked to, and back from, the village of Stockcross, a good four miles [6.4 km] from our house, but the hoped for vacancy had not materialised.

The truth was, as I now see more clearly than I did then, that my father was not really qualified for any occupation but his own. He lacked the physique for manual labour and the education to be a good clerk, while he would have been a hopeless manager of almost any business enterprise. As it was, like many another white-collar worker, he tried a variety of dead end jobs, with conspicuous lack of success. One, a classic resort of unemployed workers at this time, was to sell vacuum cleaners, a hopeless venture from the start since he was no salesman and, with no electricity in our house, he was not even able to experiment with the machine before arriving with it on some middle-class doorstep. I remember the episode because the parts provided me with an unexpected plaything until they were snatched away with the fearful warning that, if damaged, we would be expected to pay for them. Occasionally old friends – far more to be relied on than relations – found him temporary jobs, for which there was, of course, keen competition. On race days, thanks, I imagine, to a kindly recommendation from one of his Jack Hotel acquaintances, he sometimes worked as a car park attendant at Newbury Racecourse, unpaid, I believe, but offering the chance of tips from those who had struck lucky, and providing an unforeseen bonus, a gift of some of the small metal balls used by the tote, which he brought home for me to use as marbles. Unskilled, casual work was really the most he could hope for and the best such opportunity occurred at Christmas, when, as I was later to do, though under very different circumstances, he was taken on for a week or two by the post office. Less fortunate than me, however, for I was always employed indoors as a sorter and worked reasonable hours, my father was invariably assigned to parcel deliveries, no doubt visiting in this humbler capacity some of the great houses in the neighbourhood where he had once been welcomed as Mr Longmate the photographer. He had to get up appallingly early; I remember my mother telling me how she hated to have to wake him when he had at last got to sleep, in the room which I shared with them. How, lacking an alarm clock, she managed to be awake herself I never thought to ask, but I imagine that she sacrificed herself and barely slept.

In the summer the ice-cream firms took on 'Stop me and buy one' vendors, who rode up and down the streets on tricycles with a large container at the front, ringing their bells to attract attention. An obvious place to wait was outside schools at the end of the afternoon, though very few children in those days had any coins to spare and even for the best salesmen ice-cream must have provided a thin living. I can remember one sunny afternoon seeing my father, wearing a white coat and peaked cap, perched on his tricycle seat, looking absurdly out of place, and dispensing 'Snofrutes' or halfpenny cornets. Even at the age of seven or so I felt embarrassed for him, for his unhappiness was apparent, and the job lasted in any case only a few days; he was no better at selling ice-cream than vacuum cleaners.

Once beneath his black cloth, behind the camera tripod, or even when 'fixing' plates in the darkroom, my father became a different man. He had, I believe, a real dedication to photography and a natural talent for it, and, with a little capital and a competent, business-minded partner, might well have got back on his feet again. As it was, the occasions when he had cash in his pocket were red letter days for us. 'When I've got money you can have it. You know that,' he told me once, on a rare trip to buy sweets, and it was true enough, but I always regretted the lack of any regular pocket money and, I fear, made my disappointment plain. My father was in fact naturally generous and delighted in visiting the shop which served our estate and handing round cigarettes to our neighbours, which became something of a tradition; etiquette on working-class estates in the thirties did not require anyone smoking to offer a cigarette to anyone else. Cigarettes were and remained my father's great pleasure. I disliked the habit then and loathe it now, and neither my mother nor my sisters ever adopted it, but I am in retrospect glad that my father found in his basically unfulfilling life something to give him enjoyment, though for long periods even the humble Woodbine, the cheapest brand on the market, was out of his reach. His greatest luxury, only indulged in on the rarest of occasions, was a packet of some superior brand, such as Ardath.

My father's aristocratic clients remained faithful to him after the business had foundered. I recall one Christmas which was transformed by the arrival of a cheque from the Carnarvon family, delivered, I believe, though this may be a false recollection, by a footman, clad, sadly, in everyday clothes and not the fancy costume the name still evokes. The cheque proved in fact somewhat troublesome, for my father had long since ceased to have a bank account and no one else on our estate had ever possessed one; I believe 'the shop' rallied round, and no doubt the ritual distribution of cigarettes followed, indeed this may have been the year it began.

Sir 'Freddie' Carden, whose kindness to our family via the Dramatic Society, of which he was patron, I have already mentioned, also proved consistently loyal to my father, who was still, in his increasingly shabby clothes, summoned from time to time from our poky little council house to undertake commissions in the spacious surroundings of Stargroves. (Much later it became notorious, and featured in the national newspapers, as the venue for wild parties given by the 'pop' singers who ultimately acquired it.)

Grindingly poor as we were, somehow our parents managed to mark our birthdays. One year I was given what seemed a splendid toy garage, made of cardboard and complete with a ramp and inspection pit, lovingly cut out and painted after I had gone to bed to ensure surprise. My sister received a similarly made dolls-house. I remember with what delight we accepted them and I am glad to reflect now on the pleasure this must have given the donors. I have less happy memories of being taken round the toy department of a local store one Christmas for I was totally captivated by a toy tank with caterpillar tracks which was on show there and actually climbed over obstacles on the floor. The price, 3s 6d [17.5p] ruled it out, as I was already half aware when I stood entranced by it, but my mother managed to find the nearest similar item within her price range, a small armoured car which spat fire as it advanced, and cost 9d [4.5p]. I was delighted with it and am glad to feel I made this, rather than my disappointment, evident, but we were both aware it was not at all the same.

One year Peggy and I were given slippers for our birthday. This was, I think, just after the move to Camp Close when things were at their toughest for my mother and I can now realise what a sacrifice it must have been to buy them and the love with which they had been packed and handed to us, but I am ashamed to remember that I burst into tears at not receiving the 'real' present I had expected, and Peggy, ready to follow my lead in such matters, joined in. How my mother soothed us down I do not know but I suspect it may have been this incident she had in mind when she told me many years later how it had hurt 'not to give you things you needed'. Oddly enough, when we were asked at school to write down on a slip of paper what we would buy in Woolworths if suddenly given sixpence [2.5p], I opted not for a toy but for something useful, namely two torch batteries, but this was felt not to be festive enough and I received instead a flimsy dartboard and rubber darts which gave me little pleasure. One particularly bleak year I remember that the four of us in the family gave each other presents of our own possessions. I did very well out of the exchange, receiving from Freda a large money-box shaped like a clock tower, of which the dial spun round when a coin was inserted, a souvenir of more prosperous days.

I can understand fully now, and was dimly beginning to understand even then, how painful it must have been for my mother, from her secure background, to have to practise the shifts and deceptions which poverty now forced upon her. Our neighbours had long since come to terms with their way of life and had never known anything different. Now my mother had to acquire the skills which they took for granted to enable a family to survive on a miserably small, and what was worse, insecure income.

Rapidly my mother learned, like the other Camp Close housewives, to buy goods in absurdly small amounts – a quarter of a pound [110 gms] of sugar, two ounces [55 gms] of butter – for some reason we never ate margarine – a single rasher of bacon, two or three eggs. Even so, she often had to ask for her purchases to be put 'on the list' – we avoided the term 'on the slate' and I cannot recall hearing 'on tick' used by anyone – and periodically the total had to be paid off, or at least reduced. Many people on the estate were little better off than us but my mother, with her natural delicacy, made a point of looking away when some other customer was asking for credit and, not infrequently, being refused it. Almost as embarrassing as her inability to pay cash were the occasions when we had to call at the adjoining house, where the shop's owners lived, after it had closed. I sympathised with their irritation then, but now understand the reason for disturbing them. There must, literally, have been nothing in the house and my mother had just received, perhaps from one of my father's casual jobs, the cash to restock our larder. It pleases me now to reflect that my friendship with the owner's son, an only child, whose parents were constantly in the shop, may have encouraged them to be more indulgent towards her than they might otherwise have been, for Harold, bored at home, spent far more time in our house than his own.

Clothes, very rightly, came far lower down our list of priorities than food, but there was even for my mother a limit to what could be achieved by patching up and cutting down. There came a time when I simply had to have a new pair of shorts and my mother duly met me from school carrying two heavy shopping bags which clanked and clattered as we walked through the streets to a rag and bone merchant. Here she exchanged the large load of jam jars she had collected for a few coins, at the rate of threepence [1.5p], I believe, for a dozen, which yielded perhaps two or three shillings [10-15p]. Then, with money in her purse, she took me to one of the cheapest drapers in the town, Inch's, still in business today though catering for better-off customers. I should have been grateful but did not enjoy the transaction and disliked having to be measured for, and perhaps try on, the garment paid for with so much effort and sacrifice. I still detest buying clothes and can remember my mother remarking that anyone wishing to see me at my worst should accompany me on such an errand.

Lack of clothes was, of course, more evident than lack of food. Kindly 'Uncle John', who had come to the rescue when my father seemed to have disappeared, was horrified to see my sister Freda, then aged about twelve, going to school one bitterly cold day with bare legs. He must have reported what he had seen to his sister, another good friend whom we knew as 'Auntie Gertie', an elderly spinster who worked as a cashier in Newbury's only department store, Camp Hopson's, still very much part of the Northbrook Street landscape. From this prestigious shop, normally outside our price range, stockings were found by this generous, good-hearted couple for my shivering elder sister. Other clothes, for my twin sister and myself, came from a former Northbrook Street neighbour, whose daughter, Doris Lashley, had at one time, in the days of his comparative affluence, worked for my father.

What we needed most was some regular income. My brother's weekly ten shillings [50p] was handed over intact to my mother, the child supporting his parents just as the authors of the Means Test had intended. It was, however, insufficient to support six of us, however carefully husbanded, and it was a happy day for my mother when someone who had known my father in earlier days authorised a local grocer to serve her, at his expense, with five shillings' [25p's] worth of groceries each week. I am still uncertain of our benefactor's identity but he was, I believe, a local solicitor and his thoughtful generosity enormously lightened my mother's burden in keeping us fed. The credit was opened at a now vanished shop, Dean's, in Bartholomew Street, not far from St Nicholas school, and I can remember with what pleasure my mother went there after meeting us on Friday afternoon, able for once to shop like a normal housewife. Every penny was carefully spent, and she positively enjoyed, I believe, carrying her loaded basket home up Newtown Hill, thereby saving the twopence [1p] her bus fare would have cost. We now regularly enjoyed a reasonable dinner on Sunday and, except at the very worst times, a cup of cocoa at bedtime, made with milk and well sugared, drinking which became a family ritual to round off even the most dismal day.

I also feel a lasting debt to the Newbury branch of Rotary, an often-mocked organisation which in a quiet way does much good. I must have been about seven or eight, and the family fortunes at their lowest around 1932, when one night there was a knock on the door and, answering it, we found no one on the step but a large crate of food. I remember with what incredulity we brought this inside and opened it, exclaiming with delight at each new discovery. There was, I think, no message, but sugar, butter, flour and tins of meat and fruit. Although it was too early for supper, if indeed any was expected, we fell immediately on this unexpected manna from heaven, which included even such luxuries as chocolate and cake. It provided the most memorable and satisfying meal of my life and, a kindly and thoughtful touch, the crate also contained toys, indeed my twin sister still cherishes the memory of the stuffed Pekinese, instantly named Pinkie, she acquired then. Years later I was delighted to be asked to speak at a Rotary luncheon and to be able to say a belated 'thank-you' to this under-appreciated organisation.

When, after the period covered by this book, we were sufficiently prosperous to enquire about moving to a better house on a newer estate, my mother was told by one councillor that they would be sorry to see us leave Camp Close as our presence 'raised the tone of the estate', an interesting echo of the 'breeding will out' remark made to her long before. The truth is, however, that it was not Camp Close which adopted our manners and attitudes but we who, perforce, conformed to our neighbours' customs. My mother hated to be in debt, though my father by now, I suspect, regarded it as the natural state of man. In any case, with an income inadequate to cover essentials we really had no option. On our estate, as in other working class areas at that time, failing to pay the rent was hardly regarded as discreditable, much less dishonest, and my siblings and I soon learned, as our neighbours' children had always known, that one should hide as the rent collector approached. Sometimes, to try to catch out the very worst payers, he varied the time of his round and then a warning would be passed from house to house by bush telegraph. If he continued banging on the door in face of the silence from within, the recognised procedure was for the most innocent looking child to answer the door to explain, as apologetically as he or she could, 'Sorry, mum's out.'

I never heard anyone, apart from my mother, express any appreciation, or even recognition, of the benefit subsidised housing provided, though I later came to understand how much worse our situation would have been without it. The council was, on the contrary, regarded not as a benefactor or protector, but as the enemy, cheating which was more a duty than a crime. My mother did not share this view but had little option except to behave as our neighbours did. The task of putting on a convincing performance usually fell to Freda, as the older girl, and I can well imagine how much it must have distressed my mother to have to tell her to lie on her behalf. She was, I suspect, even more upset to have to leave the milkman unpaid, for we well understood that he was not so much better off than us. (The rent collector, by contrast, was regarded as having a secure, white-collar, job.) The milkman could not, in any case, simply be ignored, for milk was not left in bottles on the doorstep but had to be poured into the customer's own jug, from a dipper filled from the churns on the milkman's cart. Personal contact was thus unavoidable and if the bill remained unpaid for more than a week or two supplies simply dried up. In spite, however, of our being unreliable customers, our Camp Close milkman, 'Ratty' – ie Mr Ratcliffe – proved a good friend to our family, no doubt because my mother's situation and courtesy aroused his sympathy; I never knew anyone, acquaintance or tradesman, who did not instantly like and sympathise with her. 'Ratty' proved far from demanding over his often overdue bill and I suspect that the jug into which he poured our milk received considerably more than we were paying for. Sometimes, a great treat, he would let me travel in the passenger seat of his milk float as he made his rounds of Camp Close and once, I remember, forgot all about me. I was too shy to remind him of my presence and we must have been well on the way back to his depot when he realised I was still there.

Another regular visitor to Camp Close was the 'insurance man', premiums collected weekly on the doorstep being the only type of long-term saving most working class families could consider. He was, as a man of some education, a welcome visitor, even when a household was falling behind with its payments and risking having a policy prematurely terminated, with a loss of much of the money saved. It was to him (or after our arrival, to my mother) that women would turn to have a puzzling letter explained, or to seek help with an awkward form. We had, of course, no need of such assistance, and most of my father's policies had lapsed when his business foundered, their 'surrender value', a phrase I did not fully understand but which sounded ominous, being lost amid his debts. My mother, miraculously, managed to keep an ancient penny a week policy going, and this was to yield a few pounds, his only asset, on his death many years later.

I have little recollection of our meals at this time, apart from Sunday dinner. This was the big family occasion of the week and however short we had gone at other times my mother tried to serve the traditional joint with Yorkshire pudding and roast potatoes, followed by some substantial second course, like apple tart or occasionally, as a great treat, tinned peaches or pineapple. None of these, however, were enjoyed by my father, who – the only person I have known with this particular aversion – could not eat fruit of any kind.

In our different ways we all developed dietary peculiarities, which I would hesitate to dismiss as fads since in my case at least my stomach would simply reject the item I disliked. Equally there were foods of which I never seemed to tire, like our great indulgence when the larder was more full than usual, fresh bread and butter spread with sugar. Gordon had the oddest tastes. He subsisted primarily on Force, the cereal which had inspired my 'Lucky Jim' nickname, and brown bread; since he was literally the breadwinner my mother, whenever she could, bought his favourite brand, Hovis. He would eat bacon and, I think, fried meat like sausages, and, later in life after serving in the RAF in Italy, Bolognaise sauce, something then unknown to us, on spaghetti, but he always declined ordinary butcher's meat, like the Sunday roast, or what we saw in any case only at Christmas and after our lives had begun to improve a little, poultry. He refused all vegetables except potatoes, and those were only acceptable in the form of chips. Eggs, particularly if fried, and cheese, he enjoyed, as well as puddings of all kinds, but overall his diet would now be considered the epitome of all that is unhealthy. When I questioned him about it he assured me that it did not rest on any coherent principles but was merely a collection of his natural likes and dislikes, though I have heard since of only one other person who shared them.

Although caring for a depressed husband and four growing children my mother also managed to find ways to contribute to the family income. Work of any kind was scarce but she was always universally liked and anyone needing a respectable woman of obviously 'ladylike' background was glad to employ her, though such commissions came all too rarely. Her best paid work came from a local nursing home where she was engaged to sit at night with dangerously ill patients who needed a 'watcher' rather than medical attention. How she managed to combine being up all night with hurrying home to see us all off to work or school, including providing us with a meal at midday, I never discovered, but her earnings, 25s [£1.25] a week, made us for a time almost affluent. I enjoyed hearing her accounts of her experiences and remember her astonishment at the vocabulary of the elderly ladies with whom she sat. While asleep or delirious, she later told me, they would utter the most appalling obscenities which one would not have expected them even to know.

I also often came upon her in the streets carrying out her most regular job, acquired by personal contact and perhaps recommendation from the nursing home, pushing old ladies – I cannot recall any old men – about in their bath chairs, to the shops, to the doctor, to visit friends and, most frequently of all, to church. A two hour stint could be fitted in while we were at school and earned a princely two shillings [10p]. My mother was extremely popular with her clients, who readily identified her as belonging to that large, unfortunate but recognisable category of gentlewomen who had come down in the world. Occasionally they gave her small presents and my mother, of course, in her generous fashion, instantly passed on to her children whatever she was given. I still have a fountain pen acquired in this way and the household for a long time possessed a pair of opera glasses donated by another grateful client, though I hardly understood their purpose and they seemed somewhat out of place in our council house. Her job, I now realise, though apparently humble, gave my mother something more than the money we so badly needed, some contact with the world to which she had herself belonged. We joked about her old ladies, but they invariably treated her with respect, almost as an equal, and she continued to push some of them about even when, years later, our circumstances had improved and she was doing the job more out of kindness than necessity. She was, I now appreciate, on the same wavelength as those who employed her. Mostly they were, like her, High Anglicans – I do not think that any ever asked to be trundled along to a nonconformist service – and they enormously enjoyed gossip about the clergy and the essentially innocent but slightly risqué sounding phrases she sometimes used. I can recall one old lady beaming with delight at a reference to her 'sex appeal', which sounded very daring at the time.

Somewhat snobbishly, I feel today, I was almost as embarrassed to meet my mother while she was plying her trade as I had been when my father was engaged in his short lived spell as an ice-cream vendor on a tricycle. I did not deliberately try to avoid her but these encounters were never a success. One lady being pushed, after I had gone away to boarding school, insisted on my trying to look for some distant relation's name on the school war memorial and, when I failed to find it there, seemed to hold me responsible for the omission. Almost worse was the occasion when I must have been aged 16 or so when my mother's customer gave me a sixpence [2.5p] with an air of regal generosity, a meagre tip even then for someone of my age. I cringed inwardly and longed to refuse it but, after a glance from my mother, said a polite but insincere thank-you.

Just as my mother's good nature was transparent and uncomplicated, so her opinions were simple and straightforward. Her ideal fictional heroine, though the latter was unmarried, was Miss Marple, of the Agatha Christie stories, and the views that Miss Marple expressed were often those my mother shared. She was too kind to condemn anyone, though during the war, with good reason, she made an exception of the Germans, but she disapproved of servants marrying masters, recalling some disastrous ventures of this kind in the village society in which she had grown up, and, though never claiming to feel superior to anyone, was certainly conscious of different backgrounds. 'It's nice to find a bit of class there,' I can recall her saying of some young woman's suitor. I cannot recall that we ever saw anyone of a different colour, or indeed any foreigner of any description, but she would certainly have disliked marriage between people of different races. She rejoiced in such phrases as 'a poem in stone' as a description of Magdalen College Tower, which by my teens already tended to make me wince, and the traditionally naughty but golden-voiced choirboy was a stereotype to which she always responded. My lack of musical talent must, I think, have been a disappointment to her, and I can recall her eagerness to contribute to the collection, allegedly in aid of the boys' pocket money, when we attended a recital in the Corn Exchange given by a choir school. William, of the *Just William* stories, was the type of boy who really appealed to her and here, too, I think I must have been a sad disappointment. Although later in life a Labour voter her natural instincts were, in non-political matters, conservative. She liked, rather as a romantic concept than as a useful institution, the existence of the ancient public schools and once told me she would have liked to have had a son at Bedford School because of its school song, which ran, if her memory can be trusted:

> And wherever you go, all over the world,
> You'll find the boys of the eagle crest,
> Of Bedford by the river.

My mother's patriotism was of a simple, uncomplicated kind. Her generation had been exposed to the full horrors of the first world war and at the annual ceremony of remembrance held at the Corn Exchange no one more fervently joined in the pledge: 'We will remember them.' She showed no particular enthusiasm for the royal family and was free altogether of that nauseating sycophancy about its members which I was to find so repellent later on in my life and have lived to see replaced by a healthy scepticism. She delighted, however, in reports of such national occasions as the Aldershot Tattoo and I recall being deeply impressed on hearing her relate how people who collapsed while watching it – it was apparently a particularly hazardous event to attend – were passed back to safety over the heads of the crowd.

My mother had little time for recreation of any kind. Church-going, often in the company of her old ladies, and the Mothers' Union, provided almost her only social contacts and, uneasily located between the classes as she was, she had no particular friends. Her chief pleasure, as mentioned earlier, was reading. When, years afterwards, our circumstances had improved, she enjoyed an occasional glass of Guinness, but I only learned long after her death of another indulgence, which lack of cash prevented her from enjoying for most of her life. In her early, more prosperous, years in Newbury she had, I discovered, enjoyed an occasional flutter on the horses and one unexplained visitor to my father's shop, his presence at the time altogether mysterious to me, was a friend who called to collect her modest bets and to deliver her winnings. These can never have been substantial, for I can recall no interludes of sudden affluence – and, had she won, her family would instantly have benefitted – but she did tell me later in life, when she was a widow, of an elderly admirer who would 'do' horses, uninvited, on her behalf, giving her any winnings but generously paying for the 'also-rans' himself.

Thanks to her intelligence and educated manner, and her kindly disposition, my mother soon came to be regarded on the estate as the automatic confidante of any woman in trouble, though they knew well enough she could not provide the financial help which would have resolved the vast majority of problems. This role of universal friend became almost official when she was asked by the organisers of the Hospital Fund to become their representative and collector for Camp Close, Newbury District Hospital being at that time supported by voluntary contributions, with fees being charged to in-patients. Those who could not afford them were treated in the infirmary of what everyone still called the workhouse. To 'belong to the hospital' a family had to pay 6d [2.5p] a week, in return for which they received some useful sum, I think £1 a week, towards their treatment or to help support them while the member – often, of course, the breadwinner – was unable to work. One afternoon a week my mother toured the houses of the subscribers collecting their sixpences, which were placed in a black bag hung under the stairs in our house, but also hearing of the problems, and occasional triumphs, of the women she had visited. No one could have been better informed about the domestic secrets of the other 83 houses on the estate, nor more discreet about them. Although welcomed as a sympathetic ear my mother was to some extent inevitably regarded in much the same way as the rent collector, milkman or insurance man, for sixpence was no mean sum to set aside for a disaster that might never happen. Often someone who had got badly into arrears would turn up pleading to have them overlooked, or to pay them in a lump sum, as a member of the family required treatment. My mother acceded to such requests whenever she could, erring on the side of generosity, so that it was always an agonising time when, every quarter or so, the money collected had to be handed over and those who had run up debts had to be persuaded to pay up.

My experiences at this time made me a passionate supporter of the National Health Service, both when it was introduced and since, indeed I find it hard to understand how any rational person, least of all a doctor with any true regard for his profession, could ever have opposed it. I well remember with what dread the prospect of having to call out a doctor was regarded, though no doubt many were generous to obviously poor families or 'forgot' to send a bill at all. I remember one occasion when one of our neighbours, driven desperate by her child's toothache, did summon the doctor, who prescribed a painkilling tablet. 'It was,' as the mother remarked, 'an expensive aspirin,' for the doctor charged 3s 6d [17.5p] for the visit, probably all the money there was in the house.

Dental treatment was, in theory, available without charge to children from poor families of school age, though not to their parents, but no provision was made for emergencies. I remember one Sunday evening when my mother was at church with one of her old ladies; Sunday was never a day of rest for her. My twin sister Peggy, then aged about eight, having suffered from toothache all day – it turned out she had an enormously painful abscess – began to scream with pain and my mother had to be fetched from St John's. She hurried back up the hill to give what comfort she could to my sister, went back down it again to push her client home, then faced the steep climb up again. Next morning she took Peggy to a private dentist in Newbury's 'Harley Street', St John's Road, and to his great credit he extracted the damaged tooth without enquiring about his fee, indeed I suspect that no bill was ever submitted. I remember the aftermath: a bottle of brightly coloured Lysol antiseptic being supplied for my sister's use, for I was only just stopped from dipping my pen into this miraculously provided 'red ink'.

My life has spanned the vast revolution in dental technique which, even more than the changes in general medicine, has lessened one of the primary causes of human pain and discomfort. The school dental service, so impressive sounding on paper, was in the 1930s of a distinctly primitive kind, with treatment, or at least surgery facilities, vastly inferior to those available to private patients. Local anaesthetics were then not given for anything except extractions and 'having a filling' was a painful and protracted business. To receive more than one took a whole morning. Having a tooth pulled was as unpleasant as it sounded, involving either what, perhaps inaccurately, we described as 'having cocaine', a painful slow-acting injection followed by what seemed an almost equally painful process of extraction, or 'having gas', for total oblivion. This was almost worse, for though one felt nothing during the operation itself, it involved having a mask, smelling of rubber, applied over the whole face, a terrifying experience for a small child and one which I have often suspected may lay at the root of some otherwise unexplained phobias. The greatest contrast between private and public treatment came when one left the dentist's chair. Instead of a sink with running water and a receptionist with antiseptic tablets tidily dissolving in a glass the battered child was led into the waiting room and seated by a bucket with a mug of water, being instructed to swill this round his mouth and spit into the bucket, a procedure that cannot have changed since Victorian times.

---

[1] Mitchell & Deane p.66
[2] Hopson p.31, Garlick p.227
[3] Garlick p.106

8

A PINCH OF TEA

'Can you spare a pinch of tea, mum?'

Request of tramps approaching Newbury workhouse, c. 1934

The proximity of the workhouse to our estate was an ever present reminder of our precarious social situation. I can still recall the sight of its inmates, sitting in their striped pyjama-like garb on the ugly iron balconies or wandering pointlessly about the grounds. They had in fact only recently been relieved of the requirement to earn their keep, even in extreme old age, by hoeing potatoes and I have a vague recollection of seeing some still, as I supposed, 'gardening' in this way. We saw far more, however, of what in Poor Law jargon were officially 'casuals', more commonly known as tramps, then an everyday sight everywhere. I now realise that those we saw were aptly named, for they were probably walking from 'union' to 'union', our workhouse being a convenient twelve miles [19km] or so from its nearest neighbour to the south, Andover, immortalised in Poor Law history thanks to the great Andover Workhouse Scandal of 1846-7.[*] Our estate was the last promising stopping place for the weary wayfarer before he reached the workhouse, and even after the building of a large number of much more substantial houses on Chandos Road, as already mentioned, between us and the actual workhouse entrance, Camp Close remained the preferred port of call, to fill in time before the Casual Ward opened its doors. The men concerned – I cannot recall any women – no doubt reasoned they would get a warmer reception from working-class families than from the more obviously prosperous residents of Chandos Road, and our house, near the main road and with a path leading to the back door, for none ever came to the front, became a particularly popular halting place. Perhaps, too, word spread through the notorious tramps' grapevine that my mother was too good-natured to turn anyone away wholly empty handed. I can picture these applicants still, standing in their grubby rags, hung with clanking metal cups and bags housing their mysterious possessions, in our tiny backyard, making their modest demands, often with surprising dignity. They were invariably

---

[*] See *The Workhouse*, chapter 10.

polite and I cannot say that I ever felt threatened by any of them; the literature of the period, which depicted such unfortunates as thieves and thugs, is here misleading. The most frequent request was 'Can you spare a pinch of tea, mum?' – they seldom, I think asked for it ready brewed – and if there was no tea to spare they would settle for boiling water to make their own, producing the tea leaves from the recesses of one of their innumerable pockets.

It was not merely in their treatment of these vagrants, even worse off than themselves, that the occupants of Camp Close demonstrated the truth of that familiar cliché about the poor helping the poor. 'Casuals, without a settled way of life', as the Poor Law system of classification described them, aroused the ire of better off reformers, who felt they discredited the claims of the deserving poor and, by using the Casual Ward to provide free board and lodging, forced the whole workhouse to adopt tougher, more deterrent, standards, than it might otherwise have done. We, however, knew better, being well aware that, though the tramps we saw might by now wish for no other way of life, the poverty which had initially precipitated them into it was more commonly the result of circumstance and misfortune than idleness or viciousness. Despite the reputation, already mentioned, which Camp Close later gained, whether deserved or not, at the time we lived there our neighbours were overwhelmingly well-behaved and decent people. One was said to be a poacher and to possess a shotgun for which he can hardly have found a legitimate use, for I realised even then that he was unlikely to be invited to join a shooting party at Highclere Castle or Freddie Carden's Stargroves. I never heard of any hint of criminal activity except some childish shoplifting and the story of this was recounted with disapproval and the goods destroyed to prevent the culprits enjoying their loot. According to the mythology of the temperance movement, of which I was later to write a history,[*] it was drunkenness which prevented the poor from rising out of poverty, but this was certainly not true of Camp Close. I can recall only one notorious drinker and his family were the object of general sympathy, while we children regarded his exploits as amusing rather than threatening. I remember seeing him reel about the green behind our houses on his way home from 'The Rook' one Saturday afternoon while we laughed at his uncertain progress so loudly that he turned to reprove us. 'You should,' he told us, with drunken dignity and uplifted finger, 'get back to your slates and your spenshils,' which delighted us even more.

Death cannot have been very far distant on many occasions in those interwar years and funerals were treated with respect. One of the best features of Camp Close was how the various residents rallied together to help each other and I can recall years later, when my father died after we had moved from the estate, someone delivering to us the proceeds of a collection made to buy flowers, with a message explaining that the gift was 'from neighbours and old neighbours'.

---

[*] *The Waterdrinkers*, published 1968.

Twice death struck down boys I knew. The first, an exact contemporary, was killed while cycling in the lunch-hour near school and we were invited to go and see his body, laid out at home. I declined; exhibiting the dead has always seemed to me a barbarous idea, indicative of a somewhat primitive culture. Nor did I go to the funeral and was glad I had not done so, for my mother, who did, to support the bereaved mother, reported that she had broken down in hysterical grief and that she hoped never to see such a sad exhibition again. This tragic event had an embarrassing aftermath, for the mason carving the boy's tombstone – somehow money had been raised for a suitably imposing one – misspelt the word 'accidentally' as 'accidently'. No one, I think, noticed this except my mother, when invited to inspect it, and she wondered whether to keep quiet about the mistake but finally decided to mention it while it could still be corrected without extra expense.

The other boy who died was younger than me, around six or seven, and fell from the back of a cart on which he had been playing, being extraordinarily unlucky to suffer fatal head injuries. He had been the author of the 'daft' inscription chalked on our house soon after our arrival, for which I bore him no real ill-will, but I had been shocked on hearing him refer while playing in the street to 'My little bugger ball', a term of endearment picked up from his mother. It seemed to me in my priggish way, coming from a household where such language was unthinkable, that he had by swearing almost invited the fearful fate which had overtaken him. Our family was again affected, though indirectly, since his mother, normally no churchgoer, decided to attend communion on the Sunday morning following her son's burial and, not knowing the liturgical ropes, asked my mother to escort and guide her. This meant my mother lost her sole luxury of the week, an extra hour in bed on Sunday morning, and would have to climb Newtown Hill at least twice that day, since she would attend church again later, but she did not hesitate. 'I wouldn't be much of a Christian if I refused,' I remember her saying, but, sadly, this was, I think, the last time our bereaved neighbour set foot in St John's.

What we feared more than such unpredictable disasters, which were indeed regarded in the insurance industry's phrase, as 'acts of God' – Why, I sometimes wondered, did God never do anything nice? – was disease. I learned very early in life the names of the chief afflictions of childhood, and we hesitated even to mention the most dreaded of all, diphtheria. I always felt uneasy at dark references to 'the isolation hospital', to which the victims of infectious diseases were carried off, to die, as we believed, far from their families. I never actually saw this dread institution, but the road leading to it was pointed out to me, a sinister looking, narrow, deserted lane leading westwards from the crossroads at the foot of Sandpit Hill on the Andover Road into what appeared to be unpopulated countryside. My terror, though I did not know it then, was in the best local tradition, for at that time people still remembered 'the fever coach', a small, enclosed horse-drawn van, its windows permanently covered, which had spirited sufferers out of town to this destination, from which few returned.

Having herself come from a better-off background my mother was no doubt more conscious than other mothers on the estate of her children's deprivations. Much later in life she confessed to me how she had, by other people's standards, spoiled us, 'to make up for what you had missed'. Now a parent myself, I feel what must have been hardest to bear was being unable to give us the small treats of childhood as well as losing such experiences as shared family holidays. Other mothers on the estate, she told me, reproved her for not, as they did, taking the best of whatever was going for themselves on the ground that the children were not contributing to the family income and that it was the adults who mattered most. One mother, I remember, boasted to her that when her small son had carefully piled up a heap of bricks she would, without warning, knock them down, as a way of helping to prepare him for the future harshness of life. This toughening-up philosophy my mother utterly rejected, instead doing all she could to enable us to enjoy such occasional pleasures as our poverty allowed.

Once, and in my recollection only once, there was a children's party on our estate, given for a boy of my own age who lived a few doors away. He had been given a toy I enormously coveted, a battery-powered projector which showed strips of film, an obvious step up from the magic lantern we still possessed. I recall him announcing to a later arrival the presents he had received, including ours, 'two twopenny bars of chocolate'. It was a reasonable, even generous gift, provided, of course, by my mother, but I was embarrassed at his inadvertent bad manners in mentioning the cost, something that would never have happened in our house and well illustrated the subtle differences in behaviour which identified one's background.

I can recall another occasion when my mother was invited, probably through the Mothers Union, to help staff a stall at a fund-raising fete in the grounds of a large house in Wash Common. She was allowed to bring us with her on condition that we gave what assistance we could and we were promised 'a ripping tea' in return for good behaviour. The meal did not, I think, come up to our expectations but I can remember how well my mother fitted in among the other, solidly middle-class, helpers, though I find it hard now to imagine what cause it was to which she gave her labour that could possibly have been more in need of help than us.

I have very different, and far clearer, memories of a similar but much larger occasion, for which St Nicholas school required us to volunteer. This was held, though I cannot recall for what charity, in the grounds of the Dower House in the London Road, a large private property of which much of the gardens have now been built over. It had occurred to someone that what were no doubt described, inaccurately, as 'Board school' children, would provide a cheap and appealing sales force. I remember how I resented, at the age of seven or eight, being forced to dress up as an elf, in a tight fitting green jersey and humiliating girlish-style knickers, before being issued with a tray on a string round my neck, which I held in front of me like a cinema usherette offering chocolates and cigarettes for sale. Thus equipped, and crippled by self-consciousness – I hated my outfit and was already aware I was no salesman – I had to wander round the grounds, supposedly selling my wares to the large number of what I can now identify as upper-middle-class women whose attendance at such functions helped to fill up their empty lives and give them the illusion that, without any personal sacrifice, they were helping those worse off than themselves. I can still picture their absurdly elaborate hair styles, their coarse plump features and overweight bodies, and their loud, arrogant voices. I was far too shy to actually solicit custom, but one woman eventually beckoned me over, complaining loudly to those around her that 'he' – she spoke as though I were not there and never enquired my name – had not responded to her earlier summons. Some of the group round her also obligingly made purchases, but even so I had by the end of the afternoon only taken ninepence [4p], which can hardly have covered the cost of the cake and lemonade which were, with due condescension, handed out to us at the end of the afternoon.

That sunny afternoon made a lasting impression upon me in many ways. I was left with a feeling of disgust for the type of under-employed, over-rich, self-indulgent, self-satisfied women who feature so large in so many interwar novels. This was the other side of the life described in *The Diary of a Provincial Lady*, published in 1931, and it did not surprise me later to discover that the author, EM Delafield, having lived among the breed I have described, was herself a committed Socialist. Here was the unacceptable face of the world of comfortably off, servant-employing, idle wives depicted in *Brief Encounter*, the 1945 film which provides a classic picture of the pre-war period, when the only occupation open to most upper-middle-class women was a little charity work, not too demanding, enlivened perhaps by a little would-be adultery. If this took place on our estate, incidentally, I never heard of it. Both sexes were too exhausted by the struggle for mere survival to have time or energy left for infidelity; pre-marital fornication, as the war was to demonstrate, was another matter. There were ample open spaces nearby, to make up for the lack of privacy indoors, but for a man to have been seen disappearing in the direction of Greenham Common with someone else's wife would certainly have attracted disapproving comment and probably reprisals.

Another legacy of that afternoon as an elf was the realisation, far from obvious in our enclosed world where poverty was the universal lot, that many people had a far easier life than ours. I reflected on this again when reading John Betjeman's delightful poem ('Meet me when you've finished eating') *Indoor Games near Newbury*, first published in 1948, about a party given for children from the sort of homes my customers must have occupied. This, again, was not at all the Newbury I knew, but I was by no means surprised when reading later of civilian life during the war to discover that Newbury had a bad reputation with the billeting authorities. The better off tended to find excuses for not accepting evacuees in their large, half empty, houses, while working-class estates like ours, already overcrowded, were expected to absorb even more transferred factory workers or refugees from the cities.

I also began later, as a result of my humiliation as a conscripted charity collector, to reflect on the whole nature of such occasions. What had any charity except the Mayor's Christmas fund, where the purpose was obvious and the distribution of funds immediate, ever done for us? And was not charity all too often an excuse for people acquiring a virtuous glow of self-approval for doing something they actually enjoyed, like serving on a committee or sitting around with their friends, as in the Dower House grounds, patronising their supposed inferiors? Greater experience has merely strengthened those initial doubts. None of my contacts since with charities supposedly aiming to do good in the traditional sense – I exclude those which are only charities in the legal sense, promoting obviously useful causes, like the National Trust – have left me favourably impressed. On the contrary there seem to be many in almost every field which compete with each other or are visibly out of date, and almost all seem more eager to acquire funds than to disburse them. I particularly dislike sponsored walks and the like, where an individual feels that he or she is entitled to exert moral blackmail on their acquaintance or even total strangers, to pay them to engage in some enjoyable or, even worse, futile activity. What could be more ridiculous and further removed from a spirit of real benevolence than to risk one's life making a parachute jump in aid of some supposedly deserving cause? I realise now that had the fat women who so irritated me on that distant afternoon really wanted to help the poor they would have been urging that taxation levels on the rich should be raised to make money available for the sort of social services the nation proved well able to afford under a later government.

Although I was too young to realise it at the time this experience, trivial in itself but in its effects traumatic, was to help shape my political thinking and, as I shall describe, to make me an avowed socialist long before I entered my teens. It also had another, minor, consequence. I felt I had looked ridiculous, as well as been humiliated, and have ever afterwards had a lasting distaste for fancy dress, which should, I felt, be confined to plays and pageants. It was to be more than fifty years before I could be persuaded to put on such a costume again, to take part in a 'Tudor' occasion commemorating Henry VIII's festivities at Hampton Court. That occasion confirmed my earlier misgivings. It rained the whole evening, I shivered miserably in the ridiculous outfit, even more impractical than my later school uniform, and suffered acutely from its lack of pockets. How, I have wondered since, did the Elizabethans survive a single day, let alone a lifetime, so handicapped and unable, as I was, to be a walking anachronism, carrying my possessions about in a plastic carrier bag?

How different my life might have been had we been better off I have realised since on reading the autobiography of the novelist Richard Adams, *The Day Gone By*, published in 1990, to which I shall refer again later. Much of the book, like some of his novels, is set in and around Newbury; he was only four years older than me and lived barely a mile from Camp Close, but, these facts apart, for all his life and mine had in common we might have been growing up on different planets.

The son of a local doctor, and a fee-paying boarder at a local prep school and subsequently a public school, Richard Adams's life was probably as typical of his background as mine, in many respects, was of our council estate. Much had been said of the rigidity of the English class system and it certainly seemed real enough, as I have made clear, in the 1930s, so it is pleasant to reflect that, by our different routes, Richard Adams and I were to find ourselves following the same course in the same college at the same time and later to share the same publisher, though not for our respective autobiographies. Perhaps the doctor's house on Wash Common and No 78 Camp Close had not been so far apart after all.

Sex features so large in many biographies and autobiographies today, though *The Day Gone By* is an exception, that it seems almost a matter for apology that it played only a very small part in our lives on our council estate. Despite this being reputed to be the toughest in the town, the world we occupied was an entirely innocent one. It was not until I went away to boarding school that I ever heard the classic swear word without which no play or novel now seems complete and even the mildest coarseness was not so much discouraged as never contemplated. 'Bum', now used in the pulpit and on the political platform, was considered intensely vulgar; 'bottom' was distinctly rude and 'behind' only marginally better. I can recall one of my friends when I was aged about eight telling me that he had discovered a really dirty word and whispering it to me: 'Maternity'. Mostly, however, such 'naughty' talk as we indulged in merely involved excretion, without sexual overtones. Even this, which would probably now be considered normal and even desirable, preventing the formation of future inhibitions, was a rare event. I can remember one child, suddenly struck by the resemblance between his own anatomy and a teapot, who would shriek with laughter when pouring from it, declaring 'You can see it's a boy!' A neighbour's son once took us on a tour of his house, identical to ours, and at the end, evidently feeling there had been something lacking in his hospitality, offered us the chance to see his slightly smaller sister, aged about five or six, relieving herself. We duly crowded inside and solemnly watched, uncertain whether to blush or applaud, but settled on silence, conscious that this was very wicked behaviour which must be concealed from the grown-ups. Once we put on some form of entertainment for our parents and my older sister became almost hysterical with anxiety after, at the dress rehearsal, I had threatened to recite some lines I must have picked up at school about a London landmark none of us had ever seen:

> Around the Marble Arch,
> Around the Marble Arch,
> Oh what a glorious sight to see,
> Seated on the lavatory,
> Around the Marble Arch.

Only at the last moment, with Freda's hand clasped to her mouth in anticipatory horror, did I instead substitute the harmless, but nonsensical, 'Seated on a cup of tea', for the offending line.

Looking back on this dark period when my father's unemployment and our consequent lack of food, money and every other essential, overshadowed every day I am astonished to find how many memories are happy, a tribute to my mother's resilience and unfailing cheerfulness. ('Life is good!' she would sometimes exclaim, when manifestly it wasn't.) The golden days in our house were when the gas meter was read for invariably we were entitled to a small rebate, and I can still recapture the joy of seeing a heap of pennies piled on the table when we came in from school and my mother's pleasure in pushing some of them across to us before settling us down to a more than usually substantial tea. On one such day we even had strawberries. They cost ninepence [4p] I remember, and, served with the top of some of Mr Ratcliffe's creamiest milk, made the second most memorable meal of my childhood, Rotary, as described earlier, having provided the first.

The most gloom-laden day I can remember belongs to the same period and I was later to remember it after hearing the great Labour politician Ernest Bevin – notorious for his uneducated accent but an outstandingly successful minister in the wartime coalition – declare his desire to represent those for whom a lost ten shilling [50p] note was a major disaster. This illustrates how only those who have experienced it can have any real insight into what it means to be poor, for this is precisely what happened to us. On one occasion when such a note was the only money in the house it vanished and my mother eventually decided, after an intensive search in which I joined, well aware of the scale of the tragedy, that it must have fallen down the lavatory from the pocket of her skirt. There was no money to be expected from any other source and barely another coin in the house, so my mother conquered her pride and was, in effect, reduced to begging, telling the story to the bathchair customer for that afternoon. She, as my mother had hoped, insisted on replacing the lost cash, and so a cheerless evening was averted.

Food, very properly, dominated my mother's budget; candles, for lighting the way to bed, matches and gas mantles which seemed to burn out all too often and were easily broken, were all also essential. Batteries, to enable you to see your way to the dark lavatory, were a semi-luxury – hence their appearance on my Christmas present list at school – while some items of clothes clearly had to be replaced eventually but enjoyed a low priority. What struck me when I visited better off families, and continued to amaze me even later in life, was the contrast between the quality of the household linen and that with which we managed throughout my childhood. There was simply no money to spare to replace items like sheets and towels and they were patched and repatched until finally they must have become unusable, though I cannot recall ever seeing any new ones brought into use. Blankets, similarly, were never bought and those we had were inadequate in number and wretchedly thin. I still have a clear picture of our shabby overcoats heaped on top of the inadequate blankets on our beds. Furniture we never bought, indeed I did not realise as a child that one could simply walk into a shop and, on handing over money, emerge with a new chair or curtains. I can remember in the whole of my childhood only one new, ie secondhand but new to us, piece of furniture appearing in the house, a battered armchair bought by my mother from a neighbour for two shillings [10p], which made it a major purchase. To her disappointment we all disliked it, whereupon she immediately went out and found another potential customer and brought her in to view it and, while we watched open-mouthed in astonishment, proceeded to sell it to her for, I think, 2s 6d [12.5p]; she was clearly a far better salesman than my father.

When first at Camp Close we could not afford a wireless, but my brother, nine years older than me and even more the victim of our circumstances than I was, and I amused ourselves by creating what would now be called a soap opera. We spent hours devising, and relating to the rest of the family, the adventures of Mr Warwick, a Midlands car manufacturer who was both rich and enterprising but in whose life, otherwise highly colourful, women played no part. He was, I remember, addicted to driving fast cars, of which my brother's knowledge came, I can only suppose, from his time as a petrol pump attendant, while my contribution involved landing Mr Warwick in various scrapes reflecting no doubt a degree of wish fulfilment on my part. Once, I remember, he escaped from some unwelcome encounter by hiding in the basement of a cinema, only to be hoisted unexpectedly into view when the cinema organ, an object of which at that time I had heard but never seen, rose up from its well in front of a packed audience. At Christmas Mr Warwick, unlike us, was never handicapped by lack of funds and he was generous to his numerous domestic staff, though I now feel the pair of driving gloves with which he rewarded his long-suffering chauffeur in our scenario was on the mean side.

Our principal recreation as a family was going for walks, the splendid open space of Greenham Common being barely a mile away down a then peaceful lane, and still unsullied by the presence of aircraft and, far worse, the notorious and inappropriately named 'peace women' who later camped there in their futile campaign to leave the public defenceless. Today Pinchington Lane, which led to the common, is a busy built-up road, complete with supermarket and Hilton hotel, but in the 1930s it was still unspoiled and a vehicle was a rare sight. In autumn we spent hours blackberrying on the common and for weeks afterwards enjoyed my mother's excellent blackberry pie, for she had a marvellously light touch with pastry. She was also an expert jam-maker and throughout the winter we would enjoy blackberry jam on our teatime bread and butter, which I seem to remember for Peggy and myself was the last meal of the day.

Newtown Common, with its even less frequented paths, and the quiet country roads adjoining it, the area later made famous by Richard Adams in *Watership Down*, involved a slightly longer walk down a main, but not much busier road, now so choked with traffic that it is a frightening experience to walk along it and almost impossible to cross. Where the Winchester road crossed a bridge over a shallow, slow-flowing stream, the River Enborne, stood, as it still does, the Swan Inn, also now greatly changed. It was then a typical country pub, though I only discovered this years later when I became old enough to go inside, with a stone-flagged public bar containing upright wooden benches, usually occupied by elderly farm labourers with rustic accents. We did not, however, encroach on this, their recognised territory, our place – or rather my father's, while we were still children – being in the comfortable, carpeted lounge, the very epitome, with its cheerful flowered curtains and brassware, which in winter caught the light from the open fire, of a rural English inn. Our visits, however, were made in summer, and we would cluster round the porch – a sight which in a town might have suggested a neglected family and drunken parent – while my father went inside to buy us lemonade. While we passed around a couple of bottles between us he would, if exceptionally in funds, enjoy a small whisky. These were the only family outings, apart from the regular visits to church and, later, occasional trips to the cinema, that I can recall and they formed red-letter days in our lives.

The route to Newtown took us past the building with the most interesting history in the whole area, Donnington Castle and Shaw House not excepted. This was Sandleford Priory, a long, low, elegant, white building, easily visible from the road, which had, though I only learned this much later, a significant place in the social and literary history of the nation. Originally a monastic institution, it had been rebuilt in the late eighteenth century by the architect James Wyatt, whose life, from 1746 to 1813, covers a period rich in eminent authors and playwrights. He was at one time labelled 'Wyatt the destroyer' because of his enthusiasm for replacing older buildings with the modish and often extravagant, Gothic then in favour. Sandleford seemed to me then, however, as it still does, in impeccable taste, at once imposing and homely. The version we saw from a distance on our walks, without realising its significance, and which still remains today, was built in 1781 by Mrs Elizabeth Montagu. She was the widow of a rich aristocrat who divided her time between a famous town house in Portman Square, where she presided over a renowned literary salon, and her new home in the country, which stands just inside the border of Berkshire with Hampshire. Although the term in fact originated abroad and before her time, she is often referred to as the first 'bluestocking' and she was famous for championing the cause of educated women and of acting as hostess to the leading writers and artists of her time. Among her guests was one who was to become a particular hero of mine, Dr Samuel Johnson, at the height of his fame after 1755, when his classic *Dictionary* was published, until his death in 1784, when Boswell's equally classic *Life* of his friend, published in 1791, was to consolidate his reputation. (Unlike so many literary figures, both Johnson and his biographer proved more appealing the more I later read of them, and I was delighted to be able to pay tribute to them in a radio programme about Boswell's masterpiece.)[1]

Mrs Montagu was modest about her estate. Writing to seek advice on landscaping from the already legendary expert Lancelot 'Capability' Brown, around 1780, she apologised for troubling him about such a 'paltry' plot, far smaller than his customary assignments. 'Paltry' or not, by 1782, more than twenty unemployed weavers from Newbury were at work on carrying out his suggestions. At least one subsequent visitor, however, was not impressed, another of my heroes, William Cobbett, who belonged to a slightly later generation; his life covered the years from 1762 to 1835. The first of Cobbett's *Rural Rides* began near Newbury in 1821 and he knew the whole area well, though his experiences seem to have been more frustrating than rewarding. From his account it seems almost always to have been raining and the local farmers were distinctly unresponsive to his reforming ideas. The weather, and their hostility, perhaps account for his jaundiced judgement on Sandleford Priory and its grounds, which he dismissed as 'of all the ridiculous things I saw in my life...the most ridiculous.'

Not long after I had first seen it Sandleford Priory became at least potentially an object of even greater interest to me, for it was transformed into a girls' day and boarding-school, run, as if returning to its religious origins, by a community of Anglo-Catholic nuns, who catered for the daughters of local professional men for whom the High School was insufficiently grand. I later got to know well one of its former pupils who did not seem to have been inhibited by the strict regime enforced there, but I was impressed by Sandleford Priory even before it suffered its intriguing metamorphosis. It not merely made me conscious of how some families clearly had a way of life in every respect much richer than ours, but also made me aware of the legacy left by the past to later generations.

Railways were never a particular interest of mine, but Newbury Station was in my childhood a place of romance. As the arrival at Speenhamland of the coaches from London and Bath had once been the big event of the Newbury day, so now it was the moment, around 7.15 pm, when 'the six o'clock' drew in, the one train of the day that ran non-stop from Paddington and thereby seemed to confirm the town's importance. It was even more thrilling to see the famous Cornish Riviera express, which served the distant south-west as far as Penzance, roaring through the station at speed, its plume of steam streaming behind it. I longed to be aboard it, but this seemed an impossible dream, though Cornwall has since become for me a favourite holiday resort.

The station-master – there was no nonsense in those days about 'station managers' – was a major and much respected local figure, undoubtedly outranking in the local hierarchy all but the grandest hotel proprietors and tradesmen. When the local newspaper ran a quiz inviting readers to guess the identity of some well known local personality, few had much difficulty in identifying the individual suggested by the clue, 'he does not smoke himself but sees many who do', a reminder not merely of the ubiquity of steam trains but of the extent to which being a non-smoker was itself exceptional. (Once, to his great gratification, and marking surely his public rehabilitation, my father was the mystery celebrity and I was mentioned along with him. This was, however, after the period covered by this book.)

Among the station-master's responsibilities was despatching trains along the little Lambourn Valley line, now long since closed. It had only been opened in 1898, more than 20 years after work on it had begun, though Lambourn was a mere 13 miles [21km] away from Newbury, and had never been a great success. Lambourn was, as it still is, the centre of a productive agricultural area, but its most important product then, as now, was horseflesh. Racing stables dominated the countryside and future Derby winners and lesser animals were often to be seen being led through its quiet streets or galloping along the high downs which overlook it. The platform of the siding at Newbury, which adjoined the main 'Up' platform, from which the little two coach trains, with a 'toy' locomotive at the front and a heavily laden guard's van at the rear, set off for Lambourn was easily the most interesting place on the station. It was invariably piled high with bags of seed and feed, sacks of fertiliser, empty milk churns, pieces of brightly coloured farm machinery, with fluttering labels, and, most fascinating of all, a variety of livestock. I was never a trainspotter, and Newbury station would have provided poor pickings for anyone with such a hobby, but on the rare occasions I visited the station, I enjoyed inspecting the chickens clucking in their pens, the squealing piglets, noisily protesting against their confinement, and standing tethered on the platform, rather as if waiting to board on their own, the restless lambs and stolid, placid calves.

It was a never to be forgotten occasion when my mother, as a great treat, took my twin sister and myself for our first ever train journey, though we travelled only as far as the first stop on the Lambourn line, Speen Halt, too small even to merit a proper station, and we had the wooden platforms and footbridge to ourselves, I believe, while waiting to make the return journey. I loved every moment of this first experience of rail travel, from the yellowing pictures of seaside resorts I never expected to visit on the walls of the small non-corridor compartment, to the heavy leather strap used to hoist and lower the window, with its minatory notice warning against looking out. If one did, I instantly understood, one's head would assuredly be knocked off by a bridge or another train, though the chances of this happening on this rustic little backwater must have been very remote.

More than once, though this must have happened a little later, my father took me up to Reading on a 'cheap evening return', available from 4 pm. The cost for an adult was, I believe, a shilling [5p], for me presumably half that, and my father must have been relatively affluent for the outing at least once included a trip on a river steamer and a bar of chocolate. Typically, having decided to postpone the pleasure of enjoying it – a train ride *and* a boat journey were as much joy as one day could decently encompass – I only retrieved it from my pocket later, to find it irremediably melted. Here, perhaps, had I realised it, was a lesson for life, *Carpe diem;* to seize the real delights of the moment instead of trusting to an uncertain future to provide them.

I have never been a great enthusiast for making one's own entertainment, usually commended, I suspect, by those rarely compelled to do so, and have as an adult sometimes been accused of being unsociable because I preferred the diversion of radio or television to taking part in pen and pencil games and – a particular nightmare, charades – but in our childhood there was no option. For many years we had no wireless or gramophone and there was no money to spare for amusements outside the home. I have memories of hours spent playing games like 'I spy' – 'I spy with my little eye something beginning with "d"' – or 'Mrs Brown's Cat', in which each player in turn had to find a suitable adjective beginning with the next letter of the alphabet. This was easy enough at the start – 'Mrs Brown's cat is a', pause for thought then, triumphantly, 'an amiable cat', and so on through 'beautiful', 'cunning' and, more dubious this in our respectable circle, 'dirty' cat – until the more demanding 'k' or 'q' were reached and the altogether impossible 'x' or 'z'. To the same genre belongs 'Family Coach', where each member of the family was assigned a role, of wheel, or whip, or coachman, and had to stand up and turn round, under penalty of a forfeit, when the narrator mentioned this particular word. It was always an exciting moment when the phrase 'family coach' was used and all the participants had to leap to their feet and spin round simultaneously. We also staged improvised quizzes, like trying to list all the shops on either side of Northbrook Street in their correct order, or guessing the name of a particular company from some not too difficult clue. (Burns the jeweller was easy enough and Hawker the photographer only moderately difficult but how on earth we dealt with Timothy White's and Toomers I cannot imagine.) Charades, which involved being sent out into the unheated and unlighted scullery while the word to be performed was being selected, were less popular. Years later, while working for a tabloid newspaper at the time of the Coronation, I was asked to invent games for our readers to play on the pavement while they waited for the royal procession to arrive and, lacking a convenient reference book, found my memories of our Camp Close evenings useful, though in the event the space allocated for the feature was taken over for the unforeseen news of the conquest of Everest.

Family holidays, or even day trips away, were out of the question, and I cannot recall my mother ever having a single real break apart from two brief periods when she stayed with relations who, I imagine, paid her fare. My father never had even a day away from home. In not having holidays outside Newbury we were in no different a situation from other children on the estate, but my mother was always trying to do her best for us and, I now realise, not to have to feed any of us for even a few days must have made it easier to care for the others. My elder sister was sent to my mother's brother's farm at Holton, where she met our Aunt Minnie, wife of Uncle George, but I never encountered either of them and am still puzzled by the origin of their exotic, most un-Somerset-like surname of Fleur. Freda came back full of stories of the unusual children she had met, who had been invited in to help entertain her. Almost inconceivably in this remote rural backwater, they were of mixed race, the progeny of a Chinese mother and English father, once a diplomat in the Far East, another unlikely person to find in Holton. My sister came back quoting a mildly coarse rhyme taught her by these new friends, of whom I think we never heard again, about the consequences of 'Chin, Chin, Chinaman' taking a Beecham's pill, whispered when my mother was out of earshot.

Far less successful was another of Freda's visits, to two elderly spinsters, known as Aunt Nancy and Aunt Sissie, though the family connection, if any, must have been an extremely tenuous one, since my mother never mentioned any siblings except her brother Tom. These perhaps reluctant hosts had no idea how to entertain a teenager and Freda was left alone to spend a miserable week, bored to tears, with no occupation except to read whatever books were available.

There was one relation of whom we saw and heard a great deal, my father's sister, Maud. Like so many of her generation, and perhaps through no fault of her own, she was what was then derisively known as 'an old maid', though she was already in her thirties when the first world war began. My own impression, though her attitude may have been the consequence of her situation rather than its cause, was that she simply did not care for men, which the terms of her will seemed to bear out. Both my sisters received small bequests but neither my brother nor myself were even mentioned, while my father, far more hurtfully, especially as he had so often welcomed her into his home at vast inconvenience to all of us, was also ignored. I can hardly complain on my own account, for I always disliked her, a feeling she clearly reciprocated, but I still feel indignant that Gordon should have suffered, since he was wholly innocent of any offence and, in his non-complaining way, never even grumbled about what seemed her all too frequent visits. It was even harder on my father, who was bitterly disappointed, since they had been close as children and, according to his own account, he had been her champion against local boys who had bullied her – perhaps the start of her dislike of the male sex. What was worse, my father *had* been included as, I think, her principal beneficiary, only to be cut out in favour of other relations, certainly less in need than he was, on her deathbed. I can recall Aunt Maud speaking approvingly of only one male, her star pupil – as mentioned earlier, she supported herself as a piano teacher – who was exactly my age; no doubt she made mental comparisons between him and me. His success as a child pianist seemed the outstanding source of pleasure in her unexciting life and it must have been a disappointment to her, when, on reaching Cambridge, he chose to read science instead of taking up music professionally. I met him while he was an undergraduate and liked him, but found it astonishing to hear him refer so appreciatively to 'Miss Longmate', whose visits, as Aunt Maud, I had ten years or so before so much dreaded.

It must have been, I now suspect, a lack of other friends and relations wishing to accommodate her which led Aunt Maud to spend so many holidays with us, for she seemed to have no particular affection even then for her brother Ernest, my father, and certainly no natural rapport with children. How we squeezed her into our already overcrowded home I now find hard to understand, though I suspect that my mother slept downstairs on our battered sofa, on which it was impossible to stretch out fully and for which we had no proper bed linen.

The first sign of Aunt Maud's impending arrival was a visit to a butchers in town to buy a delicacy she favoured, pickled pork, always served in her honour at the first meal we had together. I have never heard of this, or desired it, since. During the week or so she stayed with us the whole household revolved around her, though she did introduce a little variety into our lives and was generous in providing clothes for the girls and in taking us all with her on trips into Newbury. Once she led us into a cafe and ordered ice cream and I remember feeling amazed when this arrived in individual dishes, each with its spoon and wafer, which seemed the height of luxury; ice cream, everyone knew, arrived in penny cornets, or, if one was affluent, in twopenny tubs.

Aunt Maud also enabled us to expand our horizons in other ways. Peggy and I visited Kettering several times to stay with her, by far the best part of the holiday being the coach journey there by Royal Blue coach, with a change at Northampton. Aunt Maud's gloomy old house, far more spacious than ours but hardly any more modern, was, however, full of interest for a child. She let us, with great self sacrifice, thump away on the oldest of her pianos, though I never learned to read music and have a total indifference, if not actual hostility, to all things musical. Her house also contained a surprisingly good collection of children's books and it was here I discovered the first author to give me any real pleasure, GA Henty. I can still recall one particularly exciting story – it was probably his first great success, *Out on the Pampas*, published in 1868 –

in which brave white settlers were besieged by a host of ferocious natives and beat them off by firing rockets at them. The best feature of all in Aunt Maud's house was the antique water system which involved water being pumped up into the tank each night to prevent the taps running dry. I readily undertook this chore, heaving on the heavy wooden handle in the kitchen, collecting thereby praise I hardly deserved. More often, however, I was in disgrace. Once when we were taken to a local putting-green by our relations by marriage, the Martins, I contrived to lose a ball by hitting it too hard. The cost was only a few pence and while it would have been a serious matter for my parents it can have meant little to my hosts or Aunt Maud, but I recall being upbraided as though I had ruined both families. I was also, far more unjustly, in some way treated as though I were to blame when some other children were brought in to play with us in Aunt Maud's garden and one of them ate some Deadly Nightshade berries. I had, I think, tried to dissuade him and when I was unsuccessful carried this unwelcome news to the grown-ups who greeted it with a gratifying flurry of excitement. The culprit, or victim, was forced to drink a glass of heavily salted water by cries of 'If you don't, you'll die!' and eventually taken to the doctor, who pronounced him out of danger. His parents were, not unnaturally, furious with Aunt Maud. They angrily criticised her for allowing such a dangerous plant to flourish in her permanently overgrown garden. They only apologised after it had ceremonially been torn down. My role in saving the life of our playmate went unappreciated and, far from being commended, I felt I was in some obscure way, held responsible, an early example, I now realise, of the phenomenon I was later to witness repeatedly when working for the BBC, of the messenger being blamed for bad news.

I experienced a similar undeserved reaction from Aunt Maud when, walking home with her after one of our trips into Newbury, we enlivened the slow climb up Newtown Hill by playing 'I spy'. She was carrying a newspaper, so I spied 'something beginning with "j"', ie journal, a word I had only recently learned. She failed to guess it, but instead of commending me for ingenuity admonished me for that heinous childhood offence of 'showing off'. After what was, by my choice as well as hers, my last holiday in Kettering, Aunt Maud wrote to my parents describing Peggy as a model and appreciative guest but me as wayward and spoiled. I doubt if my mother was much upset, since, as I have said, she rather hankered after a 'William' type small boy who was always in trouble, but Aunt Maud's letter was duly shown to me and I was warned I would probably never be asked to stay in Kettering again, which caused me no grief at all. Later, as I shall describe, Aunt Maud tried to have a further act of revenge on me, perhaps persuading herself in her Victorian spinster fashion that it was for my own good. Looking back, I now feel that it was enormously bad luck that the only relative with whom we still had regular contact should have taken against me and that it was perhaps partly in consequence of my alleged misdeeds and ingratitude that other members of the family were penalised.

When after Aunt Maud's death, I felt able to admit what I had felt about her, my mother, characteristically, said there was much to admire about her, especially her gallant end. When too ill to sit at the piano or stand beside it she took to her bed in an adjoining room and would shout comments and criticism through the wall to her pupils. They clearly remained loyal to her and admired her to the end, but I cannot pretend I ever felt either emotion and my principal reaction to her memory now is mild annoyance that, partly because of her courage in old age and partly for the reason which follows, I cannot remember her with single-minded dislike.

Aunt Maud's generosity on a specific occasion was to have indirectly a lasting effect on my future. In the summer of 1931, at the very pit of the family's misfortunes, when Peggy and I were aged five-and-a-half, we were taken to Bournemouth for the day by Aunt Maud, the only time I saw the sea until the age of twelve or 13, though Newbury is a mere 40 miles [64km] from the coast. I can still recall the coach trip, when, by grasping the handle in front of the seat, I tried to 'push' the vehicle up each hill, and the wonder I felt at seeing the beach and the sea with the sun shining upon them, a magical transformation from the drab confines of Camp Close. My other chief memory is of total terror at being thrust suddenly into some sit-down game which involved a whole circle of children, with rules I never began to understand, the first appearance, as it proved, of what has been a lifelong disability which has handicapped me in trying to master a whole variety of activities, from chess to croquet. I remember feeling immensely relieved to be pushed out of the group of competitors, having won nothing, with a small flag as a consolation prize. The recollection of this day, however, and particularly its more enjoyable parts, was to linger in my mind as an outstanding and stimulating experience, the more memorable in that it was unique. This was, as I shall describe, to re-emerge into my memory later with beneficial and enduring consequences.

---

[1] *The First Book in the Whole Universe.* See list of scripts in *Sources.*

9
ABSENT 0 LATE 0

Regular entry on termly report from St Nicholas Junior School, c. 1934

Outside our home, the dominant influence in my life between 1931 and 1936 was St Nicholas Junior School and its dedicated, forceful headmaster, George Frederick Pyke – 'Georgy' Pyke to disrespectful adults but emphatically 'Mr Pyke', a name to be spoken with awe, to his pupils. Although by no means a progressive town, Newbury had a relatively respectable record so far as education was concerned. This was due less to municipal initiative than to private charity, though the corporation, while not footing the bill, had usually managed to involve itself in some way. As early as 1715 a Newburian called Richard Cowslade had bequeathed funds for the education and clothing of ten poor boys, to be chosen by the corporation, though, showing a proper sense of priorities, he had also arranged for £5 to be given each year towards the incoming mayor's inaugural feast.[1] Early in the nineteenth century a county newspaper, the *Newbury Weekly News* not yet having come into existence, commented on the great number of schools in Newbury and observed that 'the great qualification was that the children must be poor', a very proper requirement. Already the so-called 'public' schools like Winchester and Harrow, founded for the benefit of deserving boys from modestly-off homes, had been taken over by the rich, a wrong still not righted and indeed now given tacit acceptance by the description of such institutions as 'charities', enjoying a privileged tax status.

Underlying most early developments in education was the fear of the spread of nonconformity through schools founded specifically to promote its teachings. In 1811 the National Society for the Education of the Poor in the Principles of the Established Church was launched. In Newbury the first 'National' school, also a misnomer since it was confined to Anglican children and, of course, local families, was opened in 1813, in Northcroft Lane just off the main street, but does not seem to have been a great success. State involvement in education did not begin until 1833 with the first Exchequer grant to the National Society and another, similar, body.

The real forerunner of the school I was to attend was opened in 1860, the motivation again being a desire to ensure that the Anglican church was not left behind in the provision for teaching children. The driving force behind it was the recently appointed Rector of Newbury, the Rev. James Randall, whose living was officially St Nicholas, but always known in the town as 'the parish church'. According to a local historian, he 'found the parish church in a deplorable state and in due course effectively changed the scene'.[2] James Randall was a man of both talent and energy. He had been a curate in the neighbouring parish of Speen but Newbury was his first benefice and he approached it with all the enthusiasm of a member of the Oxford Movement, although the real flagship of the Anglo-Catholic cause in the town was St John's church, opened, as already mentioned, in 1860. St Nicholas' church by my time was ecclesiastically 'middle of the road' if not, by our standards, somewhat 'low'.

James Randall had hardly arrived in Newbury when he called a public meeting to explain the need for a new, specifically Anglican, school, closely linked to the church. According to the school's historian he considered the existing establishment in Northcroft Lane to be 'inadequate', while another local historian claims it had closed down altogether in 1849.[3] This seems to be borne out by his speech, which brushed aside the existence and achievements of the 1813 foundation. 'It was,' he declared, 'a matter for regret that there had been no church school for children in Newbury. They had either been left to indisciplined ignorance or received their earliest instruction from nonconformists' – in Anglican eyes, almost a worse fate.

The founding of St Nicholas School was therefore a tactical move in the inter-denominational warfare which in Victorian and Edwardian times played so large a part in educational history and, to use an apt verb, has bedevilled the nation's school system for the past century. It was considered important that the new school should not merely teach sound Church of England doctrine but should be almost literally under the rector's eye, and a new rectory was erected close by. According to the school's historian, the site selected for the school was 'chosen for the benefit of the children of the humbler townspeople', close to the populous, and notoriously raffish, 'City' district, much further from the centre of the town than its predecessor in Northcroft Lane. Enborne Road, on the southern side of the town, was then almost open country and the rectory possessed its own source of milk and other produce, re-named Rectory Farm.

Though not, as one local historian asserts, by the famous William Butterfield[*], who was indeed responsible for St John's church which stood not

---

[*] Garlick p.117. Newton p.4 says the architect was 'H. Goodyear, of Grafham near Guilford' (*sic*). Accuracy has, sadly, not been a characteristic of Newbury's historians.

far away, St Nicholas School was of impressive design, Gothic in inspiration and built of stone as well as brick. The two main blocks were at right angles to each other, linked by a strikingly visible square tower, 72 feet [22m] high,[4] and looking at it since I have often thought of Sherlock Holmes's reaction to the Board schools built a little later in the slums of London. They were, he declared, 'lighthouses...beacons of the future', pointing the way out of poverty for those who attended them.[*]

The buildings cost £1,750, of which the government, by now committed to improving the nation's educational facilities, contributed £900. The rest of the money was raised locally but slowly, for, according to Bishop Wilberforce, who returned for the school's opening only two months after presiding at the consecration of St John's church, £400 was still owing.[5] There was, however, no collection. Recognising that the parents of children attending the school had, by definition, no money to spare, he urged them to pray for the school's success, while encouraging other local residents, themselves too well-off to send their children to it, to be generous with their donations.

St Nicholas was built to accommodate between 400 and 500 children, in separate but adjoining premises for boys and girls, an optimistic target in a town with a total population of 6,000.[6] Its first headmaster, an energetic 26 year old, found himself required to canvass for pupils and did so with great success. He stayed for twenty years and by the time he left St Nicholas was well established, though, as elsewhere, fees were still being paid. They were raised in 1880, for all but Standard 1, the lowest form, from 2d [1p] a week to 3d [1.5p].

The school had a tradition of helping poorer pupils. In 1895, during a period of exceptional distress, some free dinners were provided and, closer to my time, in 1921 one-and-a-half gallons [7l] of milk were donated from the mayor's unemployment fund, though this cannot have gone very far. 'Self-help', beloved of Victorian reformers, was also encouraged. A penny bank, for the pupils' savings, was established in 1892 and, as I shall mention, was still going strong 40 years later.

Discipline was in those days, as in almost all schools, strict and included corporal punishment, to such an extent that in 1895 the then Head was taken to court for allegedly overdoing things, though the case was dismissed. Curiously, there was also for a time a violent antipathy between the two 'Nats', as the St Nicholas schools were known, and the far longer established Grammar School, St Bartholomew's, further out of Newbury along the Enborne Road. Starting innocently enough in a series of snow fights in December 1894,[7] the ill-feeling, presumably prompted on both sides by class loyalty, became so serious that pitched battles occurred in which real injuries were inflicted. On one occasion

---

[*] See illustrations. Holmes's remark is from the short story *The Naval Treaty*, set in 1889.

the headmaster of the Grammar School, a militant clergyman, mustered his boys to attack the doctrinally sound but socially inferior masses of St Nicholas, leading them in a charge to disperse the St Nicholas Boys' School band. A court case followed, ending in a concordat, observed by both sides, to keep the peace. [8]

Shortly before my sister and I arrived there St Nicholas had been closed for almost a year for improvements and around the same time, in January 1933, a new headmaster GF Pyke, already mentioned, of whom more will be said later, was appointed. We thus had the benefit of modernised premises – the school's historian notes that it was 'now lit electrically throughout', which the homes of many pupils, including ours, were not – and a 'new broom' in charge, no doubt eager to make his mark.

One sign of the slowly changing times was that the original two segregated schools had now become one 'Junior Mixed', with the two sexes taught together. The only divisions were by age, with the younger forms on the ground floor and the more senior ones above, and ability. I can still picture both sets of classrooms clearly and the 'large assembly hall' installed as the school history recorded, in 1932, where every day began with prayers. My career has taken me into many such schools since, and St Nicholas still seems to me to have been excellent of its kind, well-planned, well-staffed and well-run, directed, as is by no means true of comparable schools today, to a single central purpose, that of imparting knowledge and of enabling every child to obtain the best qualifications of which he or she was capable. We were, it was made clear from the first morning, there to learn. If we could enjoy ourselves at the same time, well and good, but it was the learning which was really important. In this demanding atmosphere I blossomed. I had been positively unhappy at that gloomy monument of old-fashioned ideas, Speenhamland, and had hardly been long enough at St John's to find my feet, but at St Nicholas I felt at once at home.

It has often been remarked that it is the personality of the head teacher which more than any other factor dictates the atmosphere and quality of a school and my many later visits to schools as an adult have confirmed this. GF Pyke was admirably qualified for this, his first, and as it turned out, lifelong headship. He was himself an old boy of St Nicholas who had taken the scholarship route to both the schools to which he hoped to send his brightest male pupils, Newbury Grammar School and Christ's Hospital, and he was equally conscientious in trying to send the girls on to Newbury High School. (Some girls may have gone to the then separate female Christ's Hospital at Hertford but if so I have no recollection of it; it was the boys' school at Horsham that commanded our headmaster's loyalty.) From Christ's Hospital Mr Pyke had gone on to the Education Department of Reading University, to take a teaching diploma, before returning to teach at the 'council' school, for which those who failed to obtain a scholarship were destined. Our paths were hardly to cross again after I left his care at the age of ten, but along with another schoolmaster to be mentioned later, he had a lasting effect on my life.

St Nicholas was further away than St John's Infants School, about one-and-a-half miles [2.6km] from Camp Close, down Newtown Hill, a journey we made unescorted four times a day in all weathers, and though there must have been many cold or wet days, and we were never very warmly clad or well shod, I cannot remember them. Nothing, certainly, was ever allowed to interfere with our attendance and our regular termly reports invariably contained the entry: 'Times Absent: 0. Late 0'. Once, I remember, I was told by a teacher to wait for him after morning school but he then forgot the appointment, so that I finally left for home, twenty minutes late, sobbing at the thought of not being on time that afternoon. I ran all the way home, gulped down my dinner in tearful haste, and duly returned punctually. The long journey home at lunchtime may have implanted the habit of eating fast on which candid friends and astonished hostesses have sometimes commented since, but, unless sociability is the main purpose of a meal this seems to me a most valuable attribute, saving much time for more important activities. This tendency was to be consolidated at my next school for different reasons, as I shall describe.

Our impeccable attendance record was regarded in those days, when all children were not shipped off to the same school at eleven irrespective of their aptitude and character, as the norm, and it would certainly have been impossible, as so often happens today, for a child to miss even a single lesson without this being noted and due enquiries set in hand. Some parents did keep their children at home, for whatever purpose, but this was unusual and although the School Attendance Officer – known, I believe, as 'the truancy man from the council' – was sometimes to be seen lurking about our estate he rarely made a catch. Once he must have thought his luck had changed when he found my twin sister, still legitimately on holiday from the High School, which had longer holidays than the non-academic schools in the town, and myself, home from boarding school, playing together on the green. He was highly apologetic when we explained our situation, exclaiming 'Oh you must be the Longmate twins,' evidently well known within the Education Department.

Schools like St Nicholas were financed and managed jointly by the local authority and the church, but neither seems to have appreciated the need to provide free school meals any more than St Mary's Speenhamland, where my elder sister would, as I have described, have gone hungry but for one teacher's kindness. This still seems to me a serious reflection on both, for the legal power to feed necessitous children already existed and, heaven knows, we, and scores of our schoolmates, were in need. Today's arguments about the relative merits of healthy foods and those which the children actually want to eat seem unbelievably remote to survivors, like me, of the 'hungry thirties'. Boiled potatoes and stew, chips or crisps, salad or cabbage, steamed puddings or ice cream, we would have eaten them all with relish and looked around for more.

As it was, no child that I can recall brought his or her own food; the school certainly provided none, and everyone in my recollection went home, even when, as for us, it was a substantial uphill walk. Free milk had, however, recently been introduced and we benefitted from it, though I believe those who could afford it were charged a halfpenny [0.25p] for the small, third of a pint [0.2l] bottle we drank at playtime.

Children today, incomparably better fed whatever their home circumstances, are said sometimes to need coaxing to drink their school milk but I never saw any such reluctance among my contemporaries. We looked forward to the little ceremony of collecting our bottles and pushing in the perforated circle in the cardboard top to insert a straw, for this might produce a sudden jet of milk which struck one's neighbour. I also remember Mr Pyke publicly praising a visiting Education Officer from the council. 'Mr Swingler,' our Head told an audience of children and parents in front of this visibly embarrassed individual, 'is a young man who gets things done.' What he had got done in this case was to have metal trays fitted on the top of the radiators in the school hall so that the milk reached us warm instead of cold. It now seems to me a somewhat unnecessary expense but what struck me then was Mr Pyke's blatant flattery, evident even to his pupils. Here, we realised incredulously, was someone even more powerful than himself.

St Nicholas, in my mature judgement, looking back 60 years later, served admirably the purpose its headmaster had set himself, of giving as many children as possible the chance of a grammar school education. Many years afterwards, when attending a parents' evening at my own daughter's primary school, I was asked by one teacher – the 'eleven plus' exam was then still in existence and academic success was not yet regarded as 'elitist' if not actually discreditable – what I regarded as the aim of grammar school education. Without hesitation I replied: 'To secure open awards at Oxford and Cambridge.' This was, I now realise, somewhat insensitive, for the young woman I was addressing had herself gone to a 'redbrick' university, but something of the same spirit, if one substitutes 'grammar school' for Oxford, inspired Mr Pyke. He made plain to staff, parents and pupils alike that 'winning a scholarship', ie passing the Special Place exam to secure one of the limited number of free places reserved for bright children from the public sector at the basically fee-paying Grammar School and High School, was the great aim at St Nicholas and that failure or success on those two vital days would dictate the whole of one's life thereafter. There was no second chance and no opportunity for transfer later for so-called late-developers, a category then unidentified. Probably if my father's business had not foundered, and he had managed to curb his dreams of grandeur for his children, Peggy and myself would have ended up there anyway, like the offspring of other local tradesmen. Now, with no money to spare to pay for education, it was up to us.

In the campaign against the successor to the old 'scholarship' exam, the 'eleven-plus', much was to be heard of the danger of a child's whole future being blighted because he or she was unwell or emotionally upset on the crucial days of the great trial. I have always been sceptical of this argument. I cannot recall any such case and it is, I think, no bad thing that an examination should be a test of stamina and character as well as knowledge, as selection procedures later in life are expected to be. Who wants to be operated on by a surgeon, or for that matter have his central heating boiler repaired by a plumber, who lacks qualifications because he was off-colour when being tested for them?

I have always felt grateful that St Nicholas did not suffer from the now modish nonsense which has in recent years done so much, on the pretext of benefitting them, to deprive the under-privileged of the chance to achieve equality with those from wealthier backgrounds. Very sensibly, the brighter children were recognised as such early on and 'stretched' accordingly. The slower and less academic were taught appropriately and not made to feel inferior by finding themselves constantly outshone by their cleverer classmates. 'A' and 'B' forms were identified as such and not concealed under the initial letter of their teacher's name or some similar deception. The idiocy of 'mixed ability' classes embracing everyone from the barely literate to the potential graduate, where those unwilling or unable to learn prevent others from doing so, had not infected the educational system. Nor had the comparable lunacy which has so harmed secondary education, whereby highly qualified teachers are required to occupy rather than instruct classes of children incapable of profiting from contact with them. This has, I believe, driven many able people out of the profession and discouraged others from entering it. One of my university tutors declared on his retirement that the greatest change he had experienced in his career, roughly from 1950 to 1990, was that by the end of it hardly any of his ex-pupils went into teaching, opting instead for financial institutions.

St Nicholas was, to use a then unfamiliar phrase, 'child-centred', but in a rational and creative fashion. The staff were undoubtedly devoted to their pupils' welfare but, precisely for this reason, those lacking self-discipline had it imposed from outside. Children were required to make an effort to learn and not simply found some softer option when they found conventional methods difficult to master, nor were they allowed to talk when they felt like it or wander about the classroom disturbing those who wished to work. Self-expression was, as I was to experience, by no means discouraged, but it was within an ordered structure, the basis, I have felt since, not merely of rational education but of most worthwhile art.

The fees at the High School and Grammar School were then around £7 a term, with books and uniform involving substantial extra cost. These amounts placed them totally out of our reach, but fortunately both Peggy and I were duly assigned to the 'A' stream at St Nicholas. Our routine was no doubt tougher than that of the children thought to be incapable of winning a scholarship, but everyone was expected to work hard and reach certain minimum standards. For any child to have left St Nicholas unable to spell decently, let alone read fluently and write legibly, would have been considered a disgrace.

The emphasis on Writing and Arithmetic was unrelenting. Reading, the third of the traditional 'three Rs' which dominated elementary education, was by now taken for granted. In a junior class untidy work was penalised with bright adhesive labels stuck to the offending scrawl or blot, conveying the message: 'Where there's dirt there's danger.' Good work was rewarded with prizes, not always well chosen. I can still recall my disgust at being presented with a babyish book called *The Little One's Budget* at about the age of eight, contemptuously slamming it shut after a single disdainful glance at its contents.

Mostly we seemed to be at our desks, which suited me very well, barely venturing into the playground except at mid-morning playtime. A previous headmaster had been very keen on games and was credited with having introduced Association Football to the Town, creating the Newbury Football Club in 1887, but Mr Pyke had different priorities.[9] Only occasionally was the stern process of academic education interrupted. On Empire Day, 24 May, a parade was held in the playground which culminated in our saluting the Union Jack, hearts swelling with patriotic pride. There was, to my relief, no country dancing, but May Day had always been an important occasion in country districts and Newbury had its own tradition of celebrating it with the 'Sootybobs', a name no doubt linked to the custom that chimney sweeps treated it as a holiday. One Newbury historian, writing in 1988, quoted 'an elderly lady who had been a Sootybob',[10] so it seems likely that it was still being practised in the 1930s. The required ritual was for local children to blacken their faces with soot and to walk the street carrying bunches of flowers tied to a pole, knocking on every door they passed while chanting the rhyme:

> First of May, Sootybob Day
> Give us a penny and send us away.

According to the woman just quoted, 'Sometimes we got as much as ten shillings [50p] and then we would go home to a ham tea.' Such rewards help to explain the survival of sootybobbing, but anyone taking the day off for the purpose, keen though he was on local history, or turning up with a soot-marked face, would have got short shrift from Mr Pyke. Indulging in this local tradition outside school hours was another matter, and I have a vague recollection of actually seeing some black-faced, flower-laden children on my way home from school through the City, the part of Newbury, as mentioned earlier, where ancient customs endured the longest.

Nature has blessed me with as little aptitude for singing as for dancing, but singing lessons, in the school hall, were no ordeal for solo performances were not required. Nor were they, even for the unmusical, a waste of time, for every opportunity was taken to explain the meaning of the songs we sang. From *The Minstrel Boy* I learned what a minstrel was and *Hearts of Oak* provided an opportunity to emphasize the importance of British sea power. It was not till many years later that I realised, while writing a history of the defence of the British Isles, that the song, written in 'this wonderful year' of British victories, 1759, is almost a historical source in itself, though I was gratified to find that I could still remember the words.[*]

The provision of homework is a good test of a school's dedication to its task and from the earliest years at St Nicholas Peggy and I had, I believe, at least an hour's learning or writing set for us. Doing this, I now realise, meant a considerable sacrifice for my elder sister and brother, who had for the first part of the evening to sit silent in our overcrowded sitting room, away from the table and the gaslight, for the needs of learning automatically took precedence over any other activity. Our parents delighted in any success we had and I think my mother was almost more pleased than me – infuriatingly, as I now see, I took every academic success for granted and without obvious excitement – when one of my 'compositions' was singled out for commendation. The occasion was one of the few non-work activities at St Nicholas, a concert in which each class performed a sketch or entertained the rest of the school with a song or recitation. Even this diversion, however, was put to good use and my class was instructed to write a review of any other class's contribution, an imaginative idea for seven or eight year olds. Later, when I worked as a television and theatre critic on a national newspaper, readers often complained that I was over-critical – 'Nothing pleases Longmate', wrote one reader and another declared, even more damningly: 'You are the sort of person who enjoys Shakespeare!' My debut as a critic saw me going, however, to the other extreme. I recall describing the costumes worn by a younger form as 'very attractive' and their dancing display as 'most effective'. I had, I am sure, no thought of sycophancy when writing in such flattering terms and certainly no expectation of reward but, to my surprise, I was sent to show this tribute to the teacher of the class concerned, who, visibly gratified, read it out to the children I had praised, remarking, 'I think, don't you?, he deserves something for saying such nice things about us,' and presented me with a penny. This coin, the first ever earnings from my pen, I spent that same afternoon, probably at the little shop at the top of the Old Newtown Road, which dispensed halfpenny worth's of bullseyes. The incident left me, however, with the conviction, which has proved life-long, that praise for one's literary work is no substitute for money.

It was, all the same, pleasing in, I think, the following year, being told to show another composition to Mr Pyke; significantly, at St Nicholas being 'sent to the Head' was not a threat preceding punishment but more commonly the

---

[*] See my *Island Fortress*, p. 180.

prelude to praise. This time we had been set the subject of Market Day, a colourful weekly occasion likely to excite the imagination of even the most prosaic child. Every Thursday morning the town really came alive, to fulfil the function it had served for at least five centuries of combined meeting place and commercial centre. I can well remember seeing herds of cows lumbering through the street towards the cattle market in Market Street, now the main bus station, driven by shouting, stick-wielding men in gumboots and long brown overalls, while Market Place itself was crammed with stalls, each attended by a loud-voiced salesman. One, during the school holidays, was always surrounded by children because the vendor who presided over it sometimes gave away an orange to be tasted, the lucky recipient being invited to bite into immediately and exclaim on its juiciness. I was too shy to push myself forward for this purpose and really preferred watching another visiting huckster who sold off by Dutch auction what seemed incredibly cheap china and regularly struck the cups and plates he was offering to show how robust they were. A complete tea-service – a dinner-service was not something that featured in any of our lives – cost only a few shillings, though even so beyond our means, and there was always a big display of the china water jugs, basins and chamber pots then indispensable in a working-class home. I was even more impressed by the man selling steel wool, which I had never seen before. He would pick up and show the crowd a badly tarnished penny and then, after rubbing it for a moment, would display it again, clean and shining. The transformation always seemed to me miraculous and, though this was not the sort of inessential we contemplated buying, I still feel a sense of wonder when I use steel wool today.

Some of my sense of excitement and enjoyment at the market must have come through in my description, but what I remember best is being urged to round it off at the bottom of the page, as I had already covered two sides of exercise book paper, and while not actually forbidden to write any more, was warned not to waste another sheet by writing merely a line or two. This was not perhaps a bad discipline for a future journalist and often enough in my later life I was to be forced to shorten some supposedly un-cuttable story, but at the time I felt highly aggrieved at being forced to draft an abrupt pay-off to my piece, while I still had more to say. I remember that this took the form of a tribute to the street-cleaners who arrived after the stall-holders had gone, 'so that the streets are not left dirty', a dull and downbeat conclusion to the lively account that had gone before.

More than once I heard members of the staff at St Nicholas remark in my hearing 'That Longmate boy is very bright,' and I was sometimes, I suspect, guilty of showing off or playing up to my supposed reputation. I can recall in the next-to-top form, presided over by a Mrs Curwood, who was presumably a widow since teachers had to resign on marriage and the only teacher at St Nicholas to whom I never really took, asking how to spell the word 'ignore', which I knew perfectly well, when asked to write in our own words the story of

Pied Piper of Hamelin. (The town authorities, I related, were dismissive of his claim to be paid for ridding their town of rats and went ahead with their deliberations 'quite ignoring the fact that he had spoken'.) It was, however, Mrs Curwood who illustrated the meaning of the word 'amiable' by reference to Peggy and myself – 'The Longmate twins are an amiable pair' – and she could be unexpectedly kind. I remember once she required some pieces of glass to frame pictures for the classroom and my father, delighted to be of help, scraped clean for her a number of old photographic plates which we proudly took to school. We expected only to be thanked and were delighted to be rewarded with a large Christmas stocking each, which seemed magnificently generous.

If my father's status as one of the unemployed embarrassed us, his profession, when he was able to practise it, was a source of pride. At one school concert he was asked to come and take the commemorative photographs of each class's performance and he was entirely in his element, emerging from his black cloth to issue directions to the wriggling group of children on the stage. I was full of admiration at his mastery of the situation and felt that other children envied me for having such an accomplished parent.

However hard I tried to conceal it, and I cannot say I tried very hard, I realised early on that there was often a difference between my work in the classroom and that of most of the other children. Once we were asked, the word having just been defined for us, to write a sentence containing a simple fact. Most of the class produced mundane, though perfectly acceptable, examples such as 'The board is black'. My offering, thanks to information recently received from my brother, who having missed out on his own education, was as it were attending St Nicholas by proxy, was more interesting: 'There is a new cinema in Reading called the Granby'. On another occasion we were asked to explain how to distinguish between a florin [2s ie 10p] and a halfpenny, a now vanished coin of much the same size, in the dark. Most of us got it right, but mine was the only answer to be commended for its accurate and neat phrasing: 'The florin has a milled edge, while the halfpenny does not.'

Almost as valuable as discovering where my talent lay was realising where I totally lacked aptitude. When it was my class's turn to mount the stage at the end of term concert seven of us were given a placard bearing the name of a day of the week and each in turn had to describe its character and events. I had the plum part of Saturday but failed to make anything of it and have ever since shown a complete incapacity to play any part except that of myself, or indeed speak in any accent but my own.

I also learned early on that I had not inherited my father's facility with his hands and for this I have, I suppose, also to thank Mrs Curwood. In addition to general subjects she also taught what were then, I think, called handicrafts, which we knew as 'raffia work'. Week after week, while more talented children produced impressive looking baskets, I struggled still to construct the base of mine, which involved fastening several strands of raffia together to form what was known as 'the button'. 'You still haven't finished your button!' Mrs Curwood would declare in critical tones at the end of each lesson and on the next reappearance of this soon dreaded piece of work. She was entirely right. My 'button' regularly unravelled itself in between sessions and when the box containing our work was unpacked it had spread octopus-like through the far neater constructions of my classmates. Like many other teachers I was to encounter later Mrs Curwood seemed to assume that because I was reputed to be clever, and was exceptionally good at one subject, English, only idleness or obstinacy prevented me being outstanding at them all. To be a total failure in her particular speciality she clearly regarded as a form of deliberate insolence. I can still remember her public reproof when at last the end of term came with my craft project still not so much unfinished as not begun. 'It's no use being top of the class in English and arithmetic, Norman Longmate,' she declaimed loudly, 'if you can't do your raffia work.' This remains, for all this lady's good qualities, the silliest remark I heard in any classroom throughout my schooldays.

We remained for all the years I was at St Nicholas wretchedly poor, even by comparison with most of our schoolmates. The school had, very rightly in my view, a uniform and though I do not think we ever managed to acquire the whole outfit my mother certainly managed to obtain for us, perhaps second-hand, the official scarf, in green and gold, which I wore with great pride. There were, fortunately I now feel, no school excursions and I can only recall one occasion when there was an optional entertainment, by a conjurer who performed in the hall after school. Admission was a penny [0.5p] a head and for an agonising day or two it seemed this sum could not be found for both Peggy and myself, but once again my mother did not let us down, perhaps recounting the problem to one of her old ladies. For herself she would not beg but for us she would suffer any humiliation. It was money well spent. I enjoyed the show and we talked of it for weeks afterwards, but I felt then, as since, that 'magic' rates very low on the amusement scale.

---

[1] Money p.166 & p.168, Newton pp.2-3
[2] Newton p.3
[3] Tolman p.51, Newton p.3
[4] Newton p.4
[5] Garlick p.76, Newton p.4
[6] Newton p.4, Garlick p.227
[7] Newton p.12
[8] Garlick pp.117-8
[9] Newton p.7
[10] Purvis p.36

10

THE GLORIOUS REIGN

Phrase heard on all sides during the Silver Jubilee celebrations, 6 May 1935

Few periods in history can have been more packed with significant events than the years I spent at St Nicholas. They stretched from 1933, when Hitler came to power in Germany, to 1936 when he openly defied the Treaty of Versailles by occupying the Rhineland, the event which, thanks to Britain and France's failure to respond effectively, made a second German war inevitable.

My first totally clear memory of international affairs can be dated precisely by outside evidence, to the afternoon of Thursday 13 November 1933, a month before my eighth birthday. That afternoon my mother and I were walking past Herring's the newsagent and I can remember asking her the meaning of the single word 'Ja', which both amused and intrigued me, on a newspaper placard advertising the now defunct *Morning Post*. My mother, revealing a degree of knowledge that now surprises me, explained that 'Ja', though pronounced 'Yah', meant 'Yes', and this was what the Germans had responded when asked to support their new leader, called Hitler. What, I now know, they had in fact endorsed, by a massive majority of 92 per cent, was his decision to walk out of the Geneva disarmament conference. They had also in effect approved the Nazis' open rejection of democracy in favour of a single-party dictatorship, a fact worth remembering when it is suggested that the Germans were innocent victims, rather than responsible for all the misery that was to follow.

My mother, though not greatly interested in politics, seemed mildly concerned at the news of the Germans' support for Hitler, being a good deal more perceptive than the then government, headed by an ex-pacifist, and ex-Socialist, whose ministry had done precious little for us, Ramsay MacDonald. Even at seven, more perceptive than the misnamed National Government, I felt vaguely apprehensive, knowing that my father had had not long ago to serve in the army to fight the Germans and reasoning that if they were in the headlines again it was bad news for everyone else. Our household remained far more sceptical about the Germans' intentions than the gullible diplomats and politicians whose job it was to protect us. Appeasement never had as much appeal in Camp Close as in Downing Street.

Neither of my sisters showed much concern about what was happening in the world outside Newbury, but my brother, aged 17 and all too likely to get caught up in a future war, had a more than average interest in current affairs, though they came a poor second to the Church of England. I particularly remember my brother bringing home around this time a number of copies of a forcefully written political magazine, with a brightly illustrated cover, the *Saturday Review*, the subsidised mouthpiece of its eccentric, aristocratic owner, the immensely wealthy and fiercely patriotic Lady (Fanny Lucy) Houston. Lady Houston had a particular and, I now feel, well-merited, contempt for the prime minister and, so my brother admiringly told me, had moored her yacht off the South coast, with an uncompromising message picked out in lights along its side: TO HELL WITH MACDONALD. This beat any of Mr Warwick's fictional achievements and impressed me deeply, though, since MacDonald resigned in June 1935, I cannot have been more than nine-and-a-half at the time. Lady Houston herself died in the following year, leaving her countrymen in her debt for another of her achievements. In 1931 she had financed the winning British entry in the competition for the Schneider Trophy for the world's fastest aircraft, the forerunner of the world-saving fighter, the Spitfire.

These have since been called 'The locust years', a time eaten away by illusion and irresolution when firm diplomacy might still have preserved the peace. I cannot pretend, however, that even an alert child like myself, precociously interested in politics, was much aware of the drift towards war. For our family even more than most the great event of the summer of 1935 was King George V's Silver Jubilee, for this meant some welcome commissions for my father, as on the day itself the surviving photographers in Newbury already had all the work they could handle. The day was a public holiday and a tea party, though I have no recollection of it, was duly held on the green at Camp Close and, of course, photographed by my father. This cannot have been very lucrative for few of our neighbours had money to spare for copies, but orders for other party photographs flowed in and for days the bathroom serving, as I have described earlier, as a makeshift darkroom, was out of bounds to the family.

The Silver Jubilee also remains in my mind for a very different reason. Among the hysterically adulatory reports of the king's progress in the great royal procession through London, to and from St Paul's, was one describing, in terms of horrified disgust, the single jarring event of the day. This was the unveiling of a banner on the route which had, like all those around it, read, 'The Glorious Reign', the great catchphrase of the time, but, when a concealed seam had been cut, had unfolded further to reveal a very different message below: 'Unemployment, Hunger and War.' The Communist Party was blamed for what was described as a disgraceful outrage, but I was impressed by the ingenuity of the protestors, and, once the excitement of the Jubilee had died down, reflected that what had been said summed up our family's experience of the past 25 years all too accurately.

The big event of the year for our family was the addition to its income of another regular pay-packet, albeit a somewhat slim one. Ten days after the Silver Jubilee my elder sister, Freda, reached the age of 14. Instead, however, of leaving school at the end of the term, two months later, she was able to start work at once, for the owner of Herrings, the newsagent and tobacconist whose shop by the railway bridge in Bartholomew Street I have already mentioned, called on the headmistress of the council school to ask her if she could recommend a girl assistant. The post offered only low wages, long hours and poor prospects but any job at that time was too good to be turned down and Freda started work behind the counter that same Friday evening. Her hours were from 8 am to 1 pm, followed by a break, then, for the evening paper trade, from 5 pm to 8 pm, with a half-day, from 1 pm on Wednesday. Saturday, however, involved a full day's work from 8 am to 6 pm, with a short break for lunch. She earned 8s 6d [42.5p] a week, ie just over one penny an hour, and had to provide her own overall. We did not have such an item in the house but a Camp Close neighbour kindly lent one of hers, a typical example of the helpfulness of this community, although this woman, who worked as a cleaner, had a reputation for being 'rough'. The post, ill-paid, and with long, broken, hours, nevertheless suited Freda. Her friendly, outgoing disposition made her popular with the customers and her employer was a kind and considerate individual. I benefitted from Freda's employment that November for she brought home some fireworks from the shop as a gift, and I was proud of seeing her serving behind the counter of a shop we all knew and dispensing such desirable items as sweets.

Less satisfactory was the fact that Mr Herring's son, John, was my greatest rival at St Nicholas and that later we went away to the same boarding school together. He was not, I now appreciate, a very appealing child, being already grossly overweight, so that he made me think of Hubert Lane in the William stories. He also later on developed an unpleasant habit of repeating to me items he had picked up concerning the family thanks to his position. Once he told me how he had never had for *his* lunch merely a single boiled egg, as Freda had artlessly reported after her regular slog back up Newtown Hill for the meal, and later he quoted back to me something I had said in a letter home, which had reached his ears via Freda and his father. It gives me no satisfaction to remember that he died in early middle age, but I am pleased to think that academically I later out-distanced him and that he left school long before I did to serve in his father's shop. I remember calling in there as an adult for some small purchase and that, having failed to recognise me, he called me 'Sir', a pleasing revenge for earlier slights.

We were always well informed about world events, John Herring seeing all the papers at his father's shop and Freda bringing an occasional one home, along with even more welcome sweets. I have a clear recollection of someone remarking to me as we stood in the school hall, 'Heard the news? Italy's invaded Abyssinia' and of responding with a surge of excitement, since this seemed likely to make life more interesting. We had little idea where this odd-sounding place was, and the alternative of 'Ethiopia' we rapidly rejected as it was not half as amusing, but 'Abyssinia' rapidly became a favourite way of saying goodbye. The name of its capital, Addis Ababa, always pronounced by us 'Ah-bah-bah', we thought hilariously funny, but I am ashamed to recollect now that I privately favoured the Italians, who seemed an altogether more civilised race than the half-clad spear-bearing tribesmen they were fighting. The latter resembled the lesser citizens of the empire whose pictures appeared in our geography books, the Italians being, by contrast, altogether more like us. Mussolini himself was admittedly something of a figure of fun, his figure, it struck me, somewhat resembling that of Mr Herring.

I cannot recall that the international situation was ever mentioned at school but the reports in the press undoubtedly influenced my vocabulary. That November of 1935, when I was approaching the age of ten, we were set the subject 'Bonfire Night' for a composition and I remember describing the increasingly tense atmosphere which prevailed at Camp Close as the great day approached. As I explained, there were rival bonfires at the 'top' and 'bottom' end of the green, the former being built by the more aggressive and less scrupulous boys who occupied that part of the estate. They were not above raiding our 'bottom' end bonfire for material after dark or even setting fire to it before the famous fifth of the month. Each side, I explained, would 'try to bring off a coup' at the expense of the other, a phrase taken straight from the *Daily Express,* the newspaper then favoured in our household.

Bonfire Night that year fell in the middle of the General Election campaign, polling day itself being Thursday 14 November. This was a better than usual time for us for my father, somewhat ironically I now feel, had a temporary job, addressing envelopes at the Conservative Club of which he had once been a member. I was intrigued by the stories he told me of earlier, more bitterly fought elections, notably those of 1906 and 1923, when the Liberals had won what was normally a safe Conservative seat. During one of these campaigns a near-riot had occurred, with a mob storming the Conservative Club in Cheap Street, and the members standing shoulder to shoulder on the steps to keep them out. They had succeeded but been pelted with stones and my father had, he remembered, had his waistcoat cut by some such missile. This was, I suspect, in 1906, when processions of Conservative supporters had marched through the streets shouting 'All we want is tariff reform!' In this same election, as I later learned, groups of Liberals had linked themselves with chains, proclaiming that they were the victims of 'Chinese slavery', ie the system of indentured Asiatic labour in South Africa which was one of the major issues between the parties. All this aroused my interest to such a degree that, later, having to select a subject for post-graduate study, I chose the 1906 election and the government which was elected then.

Already, in November 1935, I was intensely interested in the political battle and never in any doubt where my loyalties lay. My parents having explained that essentially the Conservatives wanted things to remain as they were while the Labour Party wanted to change them I became passionately pro-Labour and did what I could to help to influence my parents' votes, drawing propagandist cartoons which I left about the house. One, I remember, showed a ship bearing the name *Conservative*, its deck piled high with boxes labelled 'Hunger', 'Unemployment', and 'War' – like the Communist Jubilee banner which had so impressed me – while, by contrast the good ship *Labour*, sailing alongside, bore cargoes of 'Food' 'Work'' and 'Peace'. This was to be the last General Election for ten years and also the last in which my parents voted Conservative.

The reasons why the Conservatives won the 1935 election, in spite of the misery which millions of families like ours had suffered, are complex, but no doubt included fear of a Labour government, the last, which had collapsed in 1931, having proved a failure, and a feeling that, gradually, things were beginning to improve. Thanks ultimately to the rearmament drive, the number of unemployed was beginning to decline and for middle-class people in work life was becoming more comfortable. In Newbury, as elsewhere, a great many new houses, invariably with electricity and often with garages, were going up, though for us the idea of buying one, costing from around £300 for the most modest 'semi' or terraced property to perhaps £1,000 for a large detached 'gentleman's residence', was too fanciful to be contemplated. Car ownership remained so rare that I knew only one car owner, the headmaster of St Nicholas, who ran a small Ford 8, on the market at around £100. The first trip in a car, as distinct from the milkman's van or on a bus, that I remember, was provided by a woman acquaintance of my mother's who one Saturday morning offered to take us all for a trip in the country. I rather spoiled the outing by referring to her tactlessly as our chauffeur, a legacy of my 'Mr Warwick' dialogues with my brother, though his car was a good deal more imposing.

With both my brother and elder sister now working our circumstances were not quite as desperate as they had been, though their joint earnings, under £1 a week, were nothing like enough to support a family of six. I remember an incident which brought home to me how hard-up we were, when, most unusually, a neighbour, aged only 14 or so and reputed to be slow-witted, came to our house for some reason. The visit was unwelcome as far as I was concerned for his job was of the humblest kind, sweeping up horse and cattle dung in the Cattle Market, and he smelt accordingly. Evidently, however, it was not badly paid, for he suddenly pulled a handful of silver from his pocket, spread it on his open palm, and remarked 'I've got lots of money. Would you like some?' My father, of course, declined this generous offer, but, given the chance, I might well have accepted.

I am probably more conscious now than I was at the time of the deprivations poverty inflicted on us. New toys of any kind were a great rarity, but somehow a few had escaped the bailiffs or been given to us by sympathetic friends and those few I played with constantly. Usually, however, there was only one of any species of plaything, like 'the jigsaw', a handsome wooden one which we put together over and over again, and 'the engine' , a green Hornby locomotive, lacking any track, which must have been a present to my brother in more affluent times. Once I spent a happy morning using the projecting key which operated it to pull a toy car up a sloping board by means of a string, the only evidence of any interest in engineering I ever displayed. From my father's disastrous days running his own business there survived a paper punch, which, for some reason, we referred to as Alice, a printing set, once used for making notices for the shop window and, ironically in the circumstances, a series of coloured stick-on labels bearing increasingly pained and threatening messages to slow payers, beginning 'This account is overdue. A settlement would oblige', and ending intimidatingly: 'Legal action will follow in the event of non-payment.'

In earlier, more affluent, days my father had made an elaborate toy theatre and occasionally we assembled this and staged imaginary plays on it, though as the whole process was a slow one and monopolised our only table this had to be fitted in between meals. My father also owned an even more impressive source of entertainment dating from Victorian times, a magic lantern, lit by an oil lamp, no doubt used in earlier days to illustrate missionary lectures and travel talks. The slides he had kept were of little interest apart from the one he always put on at the end, a coloured portrait of Queen Victoria captioned 'God save the Queen', which meant it dated at latest from 1901.

Very rarely indeed did we have spare coppers in our pocket but when we did we always went round Woolworths, a national institution which has hardly received its due attention from historians; no visit to a town in the 1930s was complete without making such a circuit and lack of a 'Woolies' was in 1939 to be a major cause of evacuees drifting back to their homes in the threatened cities. The store conscientiously and ingeniously kept to its slogan of 'Nothing over sixpence' [2.5p] though this was stretched to cover such items as a saw, where one paid separately for the blade and the handle, or spectacles, where the frame and each lens counted as individual items. No such complications were needed for toys and every Woolworth's contained a display of marvellous mechanical devices in brightly coloured tinplate which are now collectors' items. The pride of my own small collection was a steam-roller which, miraculously in my eyes, rolled both backwards and forwards on a single winding, and I can remember seeing the unworldly Father Stenning moved to distinctly unclerical mirth by the sight of a fearsome looking crocodile from the same counter, which opened and snapped its jaws shut while waddling threateningly forward. It was intended for a forthcoming Christmas party at St John's infant school, but I liked to picture this amiable reptile going through its routine on the vicarage carpet.

I was the mildest and least aggressive of children but, perhaps because of the atmosphere at the time, had a passion for military toys; the rearmament drive soon to occupy the country had been anticipated a No 78 Camp Close. I delighted in a toy rifle which had cost the usual sixpence [2.5p] and was supposed to be cocked by 'breaking' it between stock and barrel. This automatic action soon failed, but I found one could still get the spring to work by converting it into a muzzle loader and pushing a poker down inside it. The pathetic cork, tethered by a string, provided as a missile, I soon discarded, substituting a broken propelling pencil, which could land with sufficient force to bring down a pile of bricks. The papers were, from 1935 onwards, filled with photographs showing bomb and shell damage in the Far East and Abyssinia, to which in 1936 Spain was added, and demolition soon attracted me more than construction.

As the likelihood of war against civilians increased, the government announced, in July 1935, the setting up of an Air Raid Precautions Service, usually known as 'The ARP', and I extended my private armoury to keep pace with this development. I bought somewhere a toy bomb into which one inserted a percussion cap so that it went 'bang' on impact, though, disappointingly, not actually exploding, but it would bring down a house of building bricks when these suffered a direct hit. Before launching such raids I gave due warning on a toy siren acquired about the same time. It would emit the oscillating sound already identified as an Air Raid Warning if one blew into it, and I discovered that an inflated balloon would cause it to sound the All Clear for something like the regulation two minutes, long enough to drive everyone in earshot frantic with irritation.

It must have been as a Christmas present that I persuaded my parents to give me, on the argument that it would save money on caps, which at twopence [1p] a box were a serious item in my military budget, a large pistol which fired strips of blank paper, presumably with compressed air. A potato pistol, about which my mother was never enthusiastic since it involved raids on her larder, was a disappointment, failing to make and fire pellets of the raw vegetable – a superior version of the pea-shooters much in vogue at Greyfriars – as the advertisement had promised. I have, however, no complaint about the collection of water pistols which I acquired. A psychiatrist could no doubt offer some simple explanation of why such weapons, along with their big brothers, garden squirts and hosepipes, so attracted me as a small boy, but a sufficient reason is the purely practical one, that the ammunition cost nothing and inflicted no real damage. They certainly gave me and the children I played with, though not, I fear, the rest of the family who were so often our targets, many hours of extremely cheap pleasure. Today's plastic, often misshapen and brightly coloured, water pistols are a sad imitation of those we knew, which, made of black metal, looked real and intimidating, though I cannot recall ever hearing of one being used for criminal purposes, as happens with similar replicas today. I do remember a school story in which a heroic girl saved a collection of sports cups from a burglar by confronting him with just such a weapon. The pride of my collection was a 'repeater' on which, as later with a Sten gun in real life, one could fire a series of individual shots or, in this case by pushing in the plunger at the rear, eject the whole contents in a single splendid burst. At one time, influenced perhaps by the gangster films then so common, I took to carrying a water pistol about the house – 'packing a six-shooter' as the boys' stories would have put it – and even secreted cans of water in cupboards and drawers in case I should ever find myself cut off from a supply of ammunition. These only came to light after one container had rusted, with disastrous results, but my mother was surprisingly indulgent about it. This, after all, was just the sort of prank her hero William Brown got up to and she was probably pleased to find me acting 'like a real boy' at last.

This period, the 1930s, was, of course, the golden age of the 'talkies', as it was of radio. Very typically for a town of its size, Newbury offered a choice of three cinemas. The most ancient, dating from the 1920s, which we knew as 'a flea pit', though this was said more in affection than criticism, was the Carlton, a somewhat gloomy but perfectly comfortable building where the films were, I believe, older and the prices correspondingly lower, than elsewhere. The place where Newburians went for a slightly better evening out was the Regal in Bartholomew Street, opened in 1936, with a programme characteristic of the time: Pathe News, a Donald Duck cartoon and an American gangster film. Grander still was the imposing Forum, built in Park Way behind Northbrook Street and on the edge of Victoria Park, in 1939. It was larger than its rivals, with more than 1,000 seats and, apart from the absence of a cinema organ, almost a luxurious as any of the cinemas recently opened in Reading. Its very first programme featured *Trouble Brewing*, a combination of slapstick comedy with crime typical of the period. In it George Formby pursues a gang of crooks through a brewery, surviving numerous indignities and pausing only to sing comic songs to his own ukulele accompaniment, before, against all the odds winning the girl of his choice.

We did not, I think, yet own a wireless, so I never heard Children's Hour of which so many of my contemporaries have affectionate memories, but one source of pleasure and external stimulus did enter my life each week, purchased by me or, occasionally, I suspect, brought from Herrings as a gift from my sister. This was *The Magnet*, the fascination of which will perhaps be hard to understand by those who know it only through later re-issues or from such travesties as comic-strip cartoons or versions rewritten to make them more 'topical'. Over the 32 years of its existence, from February 1908 to May 1940,[1] this twopence [1p] a week boys' magazine must have enriched the lives and enlarged the vocabulary and knowledge of hundreds of thousands of boys from narrow, impoverished backgrounds like mine and have provided for them, as it did for me, a harmless means of escape into a more enjoyable, interesting and exciting world.

I am infuriated by the ignorant individuals, often pompous elderly schoolmasters and immature journalists, who dismiss *The Magnet* as a 'comic', implying that it consisted of crude drawings telling a story in a single page, with only a few short and often exclamatory words, housed in balloons, for text. *The Magnet* was most emphatically nothing of the kind, but a solid read of perhaps 20,000 words, such as any teacher today would be delighted, if not incredulous, to find his younger pupils enjoying. The characters were admirably drawn, the story ran for anything up to twelve episodes with such ingenious and unobtrusive repetition that each could be enjoyed by itself, and the English drew on an extensive vocabulary and was enlivened with not merely English but Latin quotations and references. I have sometimes counted 20 or more in a single issue and the magazine's critics, who have clearly never actually seen a copy, would, I have no doubt, be hard put to it to identify the source of many of them. From where, I have often wanted to ask them, was one of the author's favourite references, to 'a Peri at the gate of Eden' taken and who was the sister Anne to whom some Remove boy looking out to see if anyone was coming was so often compared?*

It was thanks to Charles Hamilton, who under his pen name of Frank Richards wrote almost every *Magnet* single-handed, that I was first introduced to many now familiar quotations, from Shakespeare, Milton, the Bible, and many less obvious sources, thanks to him, not to my school, that I learned, and can still remember, the opening words of *The Aeneid* and many another Latin or English tag. I was delighted many years later to be able to pay tribute to this extraordinary publication and its creator in a BBC radio programme, to make a pilgrimage to the house where he had lived and written his classic stories, and to interview both the housekeeper who had cared for him and the niece who remembered him, with great affection, and had inherited his copyrights.[2]

The Magnet was by far my greatest source of pleasure between the ages of about eight and ten and helped to give me a passion for reading which has never left me. Apart from the occasional articles on football I relished every word of it, carefully rationing the amount I read to prolong my enjoyment. After it became available, each Friday evening, I would allow myself then, and on Saturday, only to read the central section, *The Greyfriars Herald,* a double page spread nominally from the school magazine, the supplementary story,

---

* The answers, for which I am indebted to the *Oxford Dictionary of Quotations*, are respectively Thomas Moore (1779-1852) and Charles Perrault (1628-1703), the original of the latter being in French.

when there was one, and the advertisements which offered items of supposed interest to schoolboys such as remedies for blushing, and a variety of practical jokes, 'black face soap', metal inkblots and stink bombs. Once I wrote off for the latter, the money coming from an unexpected present, but they were out of stock and I was sent itching powder instead, which I never dared to use. The main story in the magazine I saved up for Sunday morning, when I read it through while lying in bed, the best moment of the week.

I can date precisely the moment when I became a *Magnet* addict, for many of the series have been reprinted and a formidable array of reference books covers the magazine's history. I came in in the middle of what *Magnet* enthusiasts will readily identify as the Smedley series, about a temporary master at Greyfriars who was leading a double life as a burglar and I can still recall a dramatic scene in which the villain, fearing exposure, brings down a bludgeon upon the boy he believes is about to unmask him, so that 'it would have cracked his skull like an eggshell', or some similar turn of phrase. He is, of course, thwarted – only in one very early *Magnet*, long before my time, did anyone actually die – and captured, for our hero is on watch and has left a bolster in bed to deceive the intruder. (Later, seeing this actually tried in a school dormitory, I am bound to say I found the substitute pillow unconvincing, but by that time I was becoming disillusioned with *The Magnet* for other reasons.) This must therefore have been around early June 1934, when I was aged eight-and-a-half. Frank Richards is literally on record as saying – in the BBC Sound Archive excerpt used in my programme – that he did his best work in the 1930s and though I did not particularly care for *The Worst Master in the School,* largely because it involved crime rather than purely school adventures, it was followed by what is generally considered to be the finest series he ever wrote, *The Popper's Island Rebellion,* which began on 16 June 1934 with a story of which the mere title is vintage Richards, hinting at the delights ahead, *The Bunking of Billy Bunter.* The central theme was the Remove's mass walk-out from Greyfriars to set up camp for the summer term on an island in the River Sark to prevent Billy Bunter being unjustly expelled. Although once again a sub-plot, which was to be used in innumerable stories, about an escaping bank robber, intruded, the series had all the ingredients which the author handled best, being school-based, centred on Billy Bunter and set largely in the open air. I should certainly have hated to have been in the Remove at Greyfriars, where, as a non-games-playing 'swot', I would have had a thin time, and living rough on a Kentish island would have been even worse, but any good story demands a suspension of disbelief and supplies a means of escape from reality and this *The Magnet* provided in abundance.

The Magnet was said to make its chief appeal to errand boys and office boys, then two large categories of employment for school leavers, but my own experience suggests that its attraction spread across all classes, except, significantly perhaps, the one from which most of its characters were drawn. I probably came to it younger, and left it younger, than most readers, but I have nothing but agreeable memories of the hundred of so *Magnets* I read over the two years when it was the centrepiece of every weekend. The rich cast of characters Frank Richards created became almost as familiar to me as members of my own family and I can still admire his skill in devising appropriate names for his characters, to which, as he told an interviewer, he attached great importance. They still seem to me incomparably superior, in *suggesting* a character rather than crudely defining it, to Sheridan's malicious Sir Benjamin Backbite or Trollope's imaginary solicitors Bideawhile and Slow. How infinitely subtler are names like Bob Cherry, for the most extrovert member of the Famous Five who dominated the Remove, Horace Coker, for their traditional butt, the good-natured but bone-headed, fifth-former, and Paul Pontifex Prout, for his overweight, pompous form-master? The characters display, too, a depth which is probably unique in children's fiction. Coker, despite his 'short way with fags' and general stupidity, is bold as a lion and at the same time devoted to his indulgent Aunt Judy. The chief friend and lieutenant of Harry Wharton, another admirably apt name, Frank Nugent, is charming and loyal but with a fatal streak of weakness. As for the immortal Billy Bunter, whose name has now passed into the language as a synonym for a fat person, even George Orwell,[3] who in 1940 published a now legendary and highly critical article on *Boys Weeklies* acknowledged that 'Bunter...is a real creation' and commended 'the subtlety of characterisation' of the stories in general. He also complained of the predictability of some of the supporting characters – 'Wun Lung, the Chinese boy...is the nineteenth century pantomime Chinaman...portrayed with a pigtail...Fisher T. Fish is the old-style stage Yankee', but here, I fear, this Old Etonian writing for the highbrow literary magazine *Horizon*, missed the point. What particularly delighted readers like me was the comforting way in which Frank Richards fulfilled one's expectations. The Christmas series, 1935, the last Christmas I was able really to enjoy *The Magnet*, set in a snowbound mansion in Cornwall, was all that anyone could ask, with huge log fires, tables groaning with food and a ghost. The ghost, was, of course, a disguised human, up to no good; Frank Richards, unlike many more famous authors, never cheated by introducing the supernatural and, most obligingly, the ghost did not appear on Christmas Day itself, to spoil the festivities. As 1936 began, *Harry Wharton and Co in Brazil* was delighting *Magnet* readers with a burst of sunshine and providing all that ten year olds like me expected from South America, namely a revolution and dangerous reptiles. (Billy Bunter, I recall, came upon one unfortunate native tied up by villains and left to be eaten by alligators, but, overcoming his terror at the nearness of these fearsome reptiles, cut the captive free with his pocket knife; he was, after all, a public school man, if hardly in the traditional mould.) That summer international events intruded into the peaceful world of rural Kent with the arrival of 'Muscolini's Circus', Italy at that time, rather than

Germany, being our likeliest enemy. Before long *The Signor's Secret* is revealed; the circus proprietor is duly unmasked as a spy.

When I returned to *The Magnet* as an adult I found the old magic had gone. I was instead conscious of how little my own school had been like Greyfriars and now found repellent the aspects of its fictional life I had taken for granted, like the snobbish assumption that domestic servants were humorous individuals who dropped their 'h's, and that the poor were undeserving and probably dishonest. (As I wrote in my radio script, if the Famous Five encountered a tramp they were more likely to throw him into the nearest ditch than give him half-a-crown [12.5p].) Above all, I disliked the incessant violence, from bumpings and punchings to the constant resort of Mr Quelch, the Remove's form-master – 'a beast but a just beast' – to the cane. Corporal punishment was indeed common, particularly at boarding schools, for many years after the period in which *The Magnet* stories were set, but even for its time the beatings were overdone. Once, I can recall, in a story published in 1933 which I have only recently read, Bunter is given 'six' three times in a day, so that his skin can have had no chance to heal between thrashings, an episode which crosses the line into the realms of unreality and sadism. In this, as in other areas, as George Orwell points out, Frank Richards took the easy, repetitive, way out, and I felt even as a boy, as I have already mentioned, that the stories would have been even better without the gunmen and safe-breakers to whom the ordinary rules clearly did not apply. This strange obsession with crime – much less justified in the 1930s than today – is, however, typical of its era and almost all the Will Hay films, immensely popular at that time, revolved round some such situation as a gang trying to steal the crown jewels or blow up parliament.

All criticism aside, the weekly *Magnet* was the great delight of my childhood and occasionally there was the added joy of a 'fourpenny', a complete, almost book-length, story in a smaller, paperback format. Twice I wrote letters to *The Magnet* and was deeply impressed to receive back beautifully typed and courteous replies by return of post, answering in detail all the points I had made. I still have both letters. One politely explained why Bunter did not, as I had suggested, use his powers as a ventriloquist to extract himself from difficult situations – he was, I was told, simply too stupid to think of it. My second suggestion, conscious as I was of how thoroughly we were drilled in getting words right at a school far less grand than Greyfriars, was that Bunter's misspellings were overdone. The answer was flattering. Many readers, it was pointed out, were less accomplished at English than my letters showed me to be and enjoyed such mistakes.

It is a gift of *Magnets* which stands out in my mind as the finest personal present of my childhood. My mother returned from one of her rare visits to relatives with every spare inch of her suitcase crammed with old copies of *The Magnet*, and *The Gem*, the to my mind much inferior magazine written by Frank Richards under another pen-name, Martin Clifford, about a different school, St Jim's. How my mother managed to stagger home with this heavy burden I remain uncertain, but she clearly felt well rewarded by the delight with which I fell upon this unexpected bounty. Some of the series were incomplete but they introduced me to a whole range of new stories including such classics as *The Downfall of Harry Wharton*, published in 1932, just before I had discovered the magazine.

Although she never quite developed my devotion to them, my daughter, a generation later, for a brief period read the Greyfriars stories with pleasure, and I found a quiz involving such questions as 'Who occupied Study Number One in the Remove passage?' and 'At what station would you change to travel to Friardale?' an ideal occupation for long car journeys. (The answers, as every true *Magnet*-ite will know, are, of course, Harry Wharton with Frank Nugent, and Courtfield Junction.[4]) I constantly found in the army and later that a reference to Greyfriars established a bond of common interest and, while writing the BBC programme mentioned earlier, was delighted to be the guest speaker, entrusted with proposing the toast to the immortal memory of Frank Richards, at the annual lunch of the society devoted to boys' paper enthusiasts.

---

[1] *The Magnet Companion* p.77
[2] *Good Old Greyfriars*. See list of scripts.
[3] Orwell, Vol I pp.505-15
[4] Butcher p.46 and endpaper map

11

PANTOMIME

Newbury's Marvellous Pantomime

Headline in Newbury Weekly News, *2 January 1936*

The Christmas holidays of 1935 were the most enjoyable and memorable of my childhood. They saw the start of what was to become a local institution with which we were to be deeply involved, the annual Newbury pantomime. The inspirer, author, producer, director and star of the pantomime was a prominent local character, France Belk - emphatically *not* Frances, as she always insisted. The owner of a dancing academy near the station, close to the site of the town's first cinema, France Belk was to have as large an influence in enlivening the leisure activities of Newbury as the cinema pioneer James Tufnail. In January 1936 she was a youthful 38, of vast vitality and remarkably varied talents, who, in a different environment, would surely have become a nationally known figure. There was nothing in her background or parentage to explain her success. Her father had been an engineer at Newbury Gas Works, while her husband, the amiable Jack, came from a family of Sheffield motor manufacturers and earned his living as a salesman of car accessories. He was by no means a mere appendage to his wife, but, most unusually for the time, he was always ready to take second place to her and it was through the France Belk Academy of Dancing, his wife's creation and her exclusive province, that the family name became known. Just as anyone wanting to learn shorthand and typing went to Mrs Spackman so anyone eager to dance went to France Belk - I never, I think, heard her referred to as 'Mrs Belk', again exceptional in the 1930s - whether as a shy five-year-old acquiring rudimentary movement skills, a tap-dancing puppy-fat-laden schoolgirl, or clumsy adolescent trying to master the then indispensable intricacies of ballroom dancing. No doubt the 'panto' was initially conceived as a showcase and advertisement for the school of dancing, but it soon became much more, *the* annual event of the year, the climax of the months of activity which preceded it and the great talking point for those that followed.

There was always something flamboyant and larger than life about France Belk and I always found her intriguing, especially after, as a child, I heard whispers about some great scandal in the family's recent past that had attracted national attention. This, I soon learned, involved not France herself but her daughter Lorna and another legendary Newbury woman, Esther Luker, headmistress of what she liked to call Newbury Girls' school, though officially it was still the County Girls' School and in the town was always known simply as the High School.[1] Miss Luker and France Belk were in attitudes and personality poles apart. France Belk demonstrated that a woman could make a success of her own business and master-mind a large scale theatrical project but she was always a man's woman, not above getting her own way with the aid of feminine wiles, fluttering eye-lashes and an occasional display of petulance. Esther Luker, by contrast, was a somewhat grim figure, not noted for her sense of humour, dedicated to the cause of advancing the claims of her sex to equality without much regard for the male establishment. Along with her forward-looking belief in the feminist cause went a stern conviction that women should demonstrate their moral superiority by behaving with a more than male propriety, with 'her girls' setting the whole town a suitable example. The result of the collision of the easy-going Belks with the rigidly correct High School headmistress was the great Newbury scandal, of which what follows is likely to become the definitive account, since the sole press report is tantalisingly vague. All the participants are now dead and would, I am sure, have been delighted for the truth to be told at last.

France Belk had herself attended the High School and entered her daughter, Lorna, for it at the age of five. A lively-minded child, Lorna had by the age of nine conceived the idea of compiling a school magazine but when, with another girl a year older, she put the idea to Miss Luker it was turned down, a not unreasonable decision in view of their age and inexperience. The two girls thereupon produced what would now be called an underground newspaper, of which the principal, if not the sole, item - no copy seems to have survived - consisted of a cartoon featuring Miss Luker in a distinctly indelicate pose. Her reaction when this fell into her hands was predictable, and is described in the then famous campaigning weekly *John Bull*, which took up the case, no doubt making matters worse; at that time to involve the press in such a dispute seemed unforgivable. (The *Newbury Weekly News*, for whom this could have been a big story, seems tactfully to have ignored the whole affair, in the best local newspaper tradition.) *John Bull* had no such inhibitions, automatically siding with the embryo journalist of the High School:

The crude products of their childish hands were found by their headmistress…and drastic action followed. The older girl was forthwith expelled. The other child [ie Lorna] was submitted to a cruelly intensive course of punishment for over a fortnight. Instead of being permitted to assemble for prayers, she had to remain in a small cloakroom every morning to await a call to the classroom. After each lesson she had again to return to the cloakroom, was given lines to write and forbidden to participate in recreation or games.

By the standards of the time Miss Luker had acted humanely, being prepared to take Lorna back into the High School fold in return for an apology. It was apparently Jack Belk, usually overshadowed by his wife but on this occasion taking a firm stance of his own, who forbad his daughter to admit her guilt and when he approached the governors of the High School to intervene and overrule Miss Luker they, not surprisingly, refused to do so. *John Bull*, equally unsurprisingly, seized the opportunity to denounce this apparently old-fashioned, heartless and intransigent headmistress in terms which kept on the right side of the laws of defamation but certainly implied she was ill qualified to be in charge of a girls' school. Its issue of 16 April 1932 devoted nearly a full page to *The Girls who were EXPELLED*, accompanied by a drawing of an innocent-looking child in a ballet skirt and such promising sub-headings as 'Mental Torture' and 'Secret Meeting'. Lorna's whole life, it was suggested had been blighted by her harsh treatment:

> She became obsessed with the idea that she had committed some unforgivable sin. Her sleep at night was broken by restless spells of mental torment and she even thought that the minister at church on Sundays directed his sermons especially at her...Ten minutes talk from one who understood and sympathised with the problems of childhood...and varying phases of mental and physical growth would have made all the difference...These two children are deprived of a secondary school education unless their parents can arrange to send them to Reading, some twenty miles distant...Newbury County Girls' School is supported by the public funds...The Department of Education can do no less than grant a full and public enquiry into this case without delay.[2]

Governments in 1932 were less easily moved by press criticism than they are today. The plea was ignored. Miss Luker stayed, Lorna Belk went and only now, I believe, has what she actually did been put on record. According to her own account, relayed by her mother to my parents, she had been shown a drawing of Miss Luker naked and had then drawn a bath round it, adding the caption - surprisingly witty for a nine-year-old - 'Filthy Luker'. Miss Luker retired only two years later, in 1934, though she was to survive until 1969 and reach the remarkable age of 97.[3] Today her name lives on to identify the buildings which once formed the High School and are now part of the comprehensive which has engulfed both High School and Grammar School.

Her memory was still fresh in the High School in 1936, the year my twin sister joined it to have, happily, a less tumultuous school career than Lorna Belk's. This was the year of *Cinderella*, a triumph for Lorna's mother, which marked undoubtedly a victory for this jolly, stage-struck extrovert over the ultra-respectable elderly ex-headmistress. The pantomime was by any test a remarkable achievement, easily surpassing, both in size of cast and overall quality, the professionally produced pantomimes I have seen since as an adult. All the traditional elements of the genre were there, romance, music, knockabout comedy, transformation scenes, sentimental solos, audience participation and, above all, every type of dancing, from ballet to tap, cunningly blended to enable every member of the Dancing Academy not merely to take part but to appear to advantage. At ten I was overwhelmed by *Cinderella,* my first experience of a live stage performance, and as I grew older, and began to enjoy watching the chorus for something more than their colourful costumes - always a great feature of France Belk productions - and rhythmic precision, I realised that my first reaction had been well founded. The *Newbury Weekly News* headlined its review, on 2 January 1936, 'Newbury's Marvellous Pantomime' and urged its readers: 'Don't start to scoff because this is a home-made pantomime. Go and see it. You will come away marvelling as I did.'

The writer went on to pay a well-deserved tribute to the person responsible, recognising that this was a landmark in the town's theatrical life:

> The whole idea originated in the fertile brain of one little woman...She wrote the book, she arranged the dances; she trained the principals, the chorus and the troupes of dancers; she designed the dresses and the costumes...she rehearsed the players, the singers, the comedians and in fact the whole company until they were dead tired; she made them into one homogeneous ensemble and created the brilliant stage pictures with which the show abounds. France Belk has a genius for inventiveness, organisation and execution. She has a wonderful flair for colour schemes. In fact in many ways she had the audacity and cleverness of a Cochran. [*]

Reading this report I can still, after 60 years, see again some of the scenes that captivated me then. I remember the 'huntsmen...wearing scarlet brassieres, black trunks and smart white tricorne hats', who also caught the reviewer's eye, 'Baron de Numskull', whose name seemed to me the last word in wit, 'made up to look like a well-known baronet', no doubt that great patron of amateur theatricals and our family's loyal friend, Sir 'Freddie' Carden, 'the bailiffs...reduced to their nightshirts', who 'make their exit as a sheik on a camel' and not least the devastatingly pretty and accomplished girl who played the title role and was to remain the star of subsequent pantomimes for as long as I remained able to attend them. Like every child on his first such visit I was puzzled that the principal boy, Prince Charming, was visibly a woman, France

---

[*] CB (later Sir Charles) Cochran was the outstanding producer of West End musicals and other spectaculars of the time.

Belk herself. She was even then perhaps a little old for the part, but it was universally recognised as her due and, as the *Newbury Weekly News* reviewer put it, 'She can always be relied on to fit in anywhere.' In later years it was at first the schoolboy humour which attracted me: the outsize drawing-pin on a chair in a schoolroom scene, and the little local jokes: 'Where is France?' 'In the dressing-room changing for the next scene.' After another year or two what delighted me was the chorus of teenagers about my own age, dressed in short skirts, while they sang one of the hits of those years; *Ten Pretty Girls*. But that first year I was simply captivated by the general atmosphere of light, colour and spectacle. Seeing *Cinderella* was the most exciting experience of my life so far and I was impressed to see my father's name in the programme as 'Property Master', which in fact under-stated his role, for France's husband, officially WR Belk, was listed as 'Stage Manager', a polite fiction, dropped in later years. Thereafter my father received what was in every sense his proper credit.

Peggy and I were admitted to the dress rehearsal and both enjoyed it so much we pleaded to be allowed to attend another performance, but by then news of the sensational show to be seen at the Corn Exchange had spread for miles around and there was not a seat to be had. As a consolation prize we were taken to see our first-ever film, *Alice in Wonderland*. This must have been the 1933 version which *Halliwell's Film Guide* (tenth edition) describes as an 'intriguing but disappointing version of the nonsense classic, keeping to the Tenniel drawings by dressing an all-star cast in masks, thereby rendering them ineffective.' I now think even this critical assessment was over-generous. I enjoyed the novel experience of sitting in a cinema after being shown to our seats by a torch-bearing usherette, but I thought the film, which was, of course, in black and white, utterly nonsensical. I was not entertained but merely bewildered and irritated by the sight of grotesquely dressed actors pretending to be animals when they clearly weren't; the glorious, dazzlingly colourful and lively performance, involving real human beings, on offer at the Corn Exchange seemed to me far more convincing and indeed more realistic than the drab, monochrome fairy story. I reacted to *Alice in Wonderland* as a year or two earlier I had responded to *The Little One's Budget* with the feeling that I was being talked down to in a positively insulting manner, and, though, as I shall describe, I later came to appreciate films more, the cinema never did hold for me the fascination it seems to have exerted on so many of my contemporaries. This first essay in movie-going also implanted in me a distaste for Lewis Carroll's classic that has never left me; clever it may be, quotable some lines in it certainly are, but amusing, so far as I am concerned, it is not. I have ever since, as mentioned earlier, detested fantasy of all kinds, finding in the real world cause for interest and excitement enough. That in 1997 CR Tolkien's *The Lord of the Rings*, about a mythical world of strange non-human beings, should have been acclaimed as the outstanding book of the century fills me with incredulity and dismay.

To return to the Newbury pantomime, important though it was to me it was even more valuable to my father. France Belk may, I suspect, have been one of those who helped us when our fortunes were at rock bottom and my father's annual involvement with the pantomime did much to help restore his self-respect. For a few weeks each year he again had a useful occupation, with his hobby, that of amateur stage-manager, becoming almost a second profession. From the early planning meetings, through the visits to select scenery from the firm of Capes of Chiswick, which now became a name almost as familiar to me as Kodak, through the stressful dress rehearsal and the, by comparison, almost routine performances that followed, to the predictable triumph of the last night, he became a changed man. For this period, which covered the Christmas holiday, he was once again playing a recognised part in Newbury affairs and respected by all around him. He was even able during the week of the actual run to enjoy an occasional meal out and an even rarer drink, in which, as I grew older, I sometimes joined him.

In between pantomimes - and France continued to produce some form of annual entertainment for 26 years[4] - she remained a loyal friend, sometimes arranging, at times when he might not otherwise have had a coin in his pocket, for him to man the box office at other productions and thereby earn a pound or two. Although by no means reluctant to disagree with her on technical matters, so that I became used quite early in life to hearing talk of 'tabs' and 'flats', 'practical doors' and 'backcloths', my father clearly admired France Belk. My mother welcomed their friendship. She was convinced, she told me once, that there was nothing remotely improper in the relationship, and I am sure she was right. I never saw France, for all her theatrical exuberance, as much as kiss 'Longy', as she called him, but, as my mother so sensibly recognised, 'going to see France' provided my father with a harmless, indeed beneficial, opportunity to forget his basically depressing situation. I never in fact knew my father to as much as look at another woman and I was astonished, and faintly shocked, when I was in my early twenties, to hear him comment on a girl friend of mine: 'Her legs are her best feature.' Like most children, I had never really thought of my parents as sharing the same desires as the rest of us.

The pantomime, from 1936 an annual event, was to become the high spot of my year, the bright interlude between Christmas and the inevitable return to the grey misery of boarding school which I shall describe later. It was not long before I was able to have the chance to help behind the scenes and I spent many happy hours in the Studio, as her home, with large room below and living quarters above, was known, often with Newbury friends playing some part in the production. I can recall helping to paint 'props', like cardboard boxes which had to be transformed into chests containing pirates' treasure, while in the middle of the floor some small children were being rehearsed in one of those affecting scenes that invariably brought 'Ooohs' and 'Aaahs' from the audience, and in another corner their mothers busily stitched away at their costumes as rosebuds or butterflies. France herself was undoubtedly present, as she always was, and I can remember discovering for the first time the existence of copyright as she wrote for permission to use some commercially published song, and of the survival of the censor, as she dashed off a cheque to the Lord Chamberlain's office for the fee payable for his reading and approval of the script. For many years afterwards nothing could be performed on any stage without his permission but I do not think he ever raised any objection to any of our innocent jokes and dance routines.

My most responsible post, still a humble one, was that of 'brace boy', helping to move the 'flats' which formed the scenery and to screw into the floor the fittings which held up the struts supporting them. I always had a secret fear that one might fall down and wreak havoc on the actors below but it never did, though I must have left my mark on the boards of the wings of the Corn Exchange and often wondered why some less destructive method had not been devised. Much later in life, as I have mentioned elsewhere, I became, briefly, theatre critic for a national tabloid newspaper, but I did not enjoy the experience and have never come remotely within reach of being stage-struck. Ever since that first, magical sight of *Cinderella* it has been the amateur, and more recently the professional fringe, theatre, which has attracted and interested me.

Newbury was not in the 1930s a very exciting town. Little was made of its interesting past, even less of its actual and potential attractions and, as has been made clear from my family's experiences, most of what was done for its less fortunate citizens was due to private kindness rather than public enterprise. The pantomime, the product of one woman's imagination and drive, became, however, so much a part of the town's life as to become almost an official institution, and I have of it nothing but happy memories. It provided a glamorous oasis in our basically drab lives, even more valuable after the outbreak of war in 1939, and for me it had a special significance in causing me for the first time to become aware of the attraction of the opposite sex. I still cherish the programme for the 1943 production of *Dick Whittington* endorsed by one particularly pretty girl, 'With love from Rosamund'. She had, I believe, enchanted me, a susceptible 17 year old, while dressed as a snowball in one of France Belk's great set piece ballets, 'The Frozen Lake'.

This great Newbury character did not live as long as her old adversary Miss Luker. She died in 1976, aged a mere 79, but a Belk Society, of survivors of the pantomime, a steadily declining number, still meets regularly. I was delighted to be invited to be present, on 12 April 1995, at the scene of her greatest triumphs, the Corn Exchange, at a ceremony to honour her memory.[5] The building, both back stage and front of the house, had been so improved that I could barely recognise the wings where I had so often stood as a shy schoolboy, gazing enraptured at the chorus, or the once shabby dressing-rooms, through the doors of which, if one was lucky, even larger expanses of female flesh might occasionally, if illicitly, be glimpsed. It was a pleasure to see again, though now conventionally clad and in middle or even old age, several of the performers who had delighted me then, including the still attractive Rosamund, now happily married. The mayor was far too young to remember the pantomime himself but unveiled a plaque to its founder, which described her as 'a remarkable woman', a tribute I heartily endorse.

---

[1] Garlick p.133
[2] John Bull p.19
[3] Garlick p.133
[4] *Newbury Weekly News* 20 Apr 1995
[5] *Newbury Weekly News* 20 Apr 1995

12

VERY FOND OF BOOKS

Norman told me that he is very fond of books.

Report in the Reading Evening Gazette, *10 June 1936*

King George V died on the evening of Monday 20 January 1936. 'The glorious reign' had brought for us, just as the dissenting banner at his Silver Jubilee had proclaimed, nothing but 'unemployment, hunger and war'. We could not even afford a wireless, so did not hear the famous bulletin declaring that 'The king's life is moving peacefully to its close' which was just the type of elegant phrase that appealed to my mother and, after reading it in the newspaper, she often quoted it to me later. (It represented in fact a monumental piece of Establishment hypocrisy; the king, we now know, was being helped on his way by his doctor to ensure the news of his death made the last edition of the *Times.*) I have no recollection of hearing of the king's death but the clearest memories of his funeral, for the pupils of St Nicholas, with those of other Newbury schools, were assembled in the Corn Exchange that morning, Wednesday 28 January, to hear the service being broadcast from Westminster Abbey. We had to sit on the floor, which was hard, and the proceedings seemed to go on for ever, without even our usual mid-morning milk. I remember some children, thoroughly bored, passing the time playing noughts and crosses, combining irreverence and lese-majesty. Dimly I wondered, already a firm Labour supporter, what the dead king had ever done for me, though everyone then had great hopes of the incoming monarch, Edward VIII, ill-founded as they were soon to prove.

We had in any case no time to spare for anything except the rapidly approaching 'scholarship', now a mere two months away. As the great day drew nearer the tempo of preparation speeded up under our admirable form-mistress Miss Fanny House, a dedicated and talented teacher, formerly Head of the separate girls' junior school. I still wince at the elementary misspellings one now sees every day in public notices and advertisements, as well as in books and newspapers, and am appalled at the readiness of young assistants in shops to resort to a calculator for even the simplest transaction. An inability to spell or to do elementary arithmetic would, we were assured and certainly believed, condemn us to a life of second-rate employment and inferior social status.

Every day began with two tests, one of twenty mental arithmetic problems, the other of twenty words to be spelt correctly. More than a couple of mistakes brought down dire warnings and patient repetition of the proper answers. Mr Pyke himself took an increasing number of our lessons, some of them directed to examination technique, and I attribute to his excellent coaching the fact that throughout my life I have remained a good examinee. Berkshire, he reminded us, was proud of its history, and we should seize any opportunity to write about it.* It was now that I first learned of the White Horse cut in the Downs above Uffington, of the prehistoric group of stones not far from it, known as Wayland Smith's Cave, and, in the same richly historic landscape, of the Blowing Stone, used to call out the local fighting men or, more mundanely, to summon home their cattle. I was later to be grateful for this solid grounding in Anglo-Saxon history, and, in teaching us about King Alfred's campaigns against the Danes, Mr Pyke's teaching made me burn with patriotic pride and awakened in me a sense of the romance and interest of our nation's past.

We were also well drilled in geography and I recall with what joy I first used the newly-learned word 'confluence' three times in one 'composition', earning a mild reproof about overdoing a good thing. I received a similar warning following my excessive use of the image of a glass of beer, with which I rewarded an imaginary character as he made what must have been an increasingly uncertain progress through the Berkshire countryside. 'Too many glasses of beer,' was Mr Pyke's pertinent comment, an observation which I have repeated in different circumstances since. Our headmaster cautioned sagely against choosing subjects which looked easy but were full of pitfalls. Give a miss, he advised, to questions like 'What would you do if suddenly given five shillings [25p] to spend as you like?' If you disposed of it all at once, he pointed out, you would be left with a very short answer, while doling it out in tiny amounts would be tedious and repetitive. It was sensible, common-sense teaching like this which helped to explain why year after year St Nicholas, drawing on by no means the most prosperous or intellectually promising area of Berkshire, made such a respectable showing in the Special Place exam.

Mr Pyke, like many outstanding schoolmasters, had his blind spots and eccentricities, notably a tendency to confide in his pupils information better kept to himself. He informed us, for example, that he had received 'less than a ten shilling [50p] note in change' from £100, after his late wife had received treatment, unhappily unsuccessful, in a local nursing home, Ingleside, in St John's Road. Indiscreet in my turn, though with more excuse, I reported this to

---

* No one foresaw, of course, that on 1 April 1998, like other historic counties before it, it would, for no good reason, be summarily abolished, though Newbury gained in status as a result.

my mother, who, as I have mentioned, sometimes worked there, and she, with a rare loss of tact, mentioned the incident to the home's owners, who were, understandably, annoyed at the size of their bill being disclosed. I also felt then, as I do now, that Mr Pyke behaved somewhat oddly in interrogating one small boy who asked to leave the room during the first lesson of the day what he had had for breakfast. The child's reply, 'Cheese, sir', astonished me – Whoever had heard of anyone eating cheese at breakfast? – but satisfied our headmaster. 'Ah yes,' he said knowingly, 'it must have been the cheese that did it' and the applicant was duly 'excused'. On another occasion he behaved, I felt, both insensitively and unjustly, when he offered a reward of half-a-crown [12.5p] to the first child to answer a question correctly. Amid the forest of eagerly waving hands, not least mine, he selected that of the one unquestionably middle-class child among us, an immaculately dressed little girl called Sybil, who had, of all of us, the least need of such almost undreamed of riches. I was less shocked at the time than I am now by Mr Pyke's publicly proclaimed outrage when some St Nicholas children were caught playing 'doctors and nurses' in a local park. The subject was so taboo that I never discovered precisely what they had done but believe it was merely a case of routine, indeed healthy, sexual curiosity, on the lines of 'You show me yours and I'll show you mine.' Mr Pyke behaved, however, as though the City Park had witnessed orgies rivalling those of ancient Rome. He put in hand a massive enquiry in which all the children in the same age group were closely interrogated, though I answered tactfully, and truthfully, that I had heard about the incident but did not know who was involved or what they had done. Mr Pyke accepted this – as I shall mention again later I was, throughout my schooldays and indeed later, invariably assumed to be far too backward sexually to know what my contemporaries were up to – but did succeed, without my help, in identifying the boy he considered the ringleader. This harmless nine year old was first reduced to tears by a public denunciation worthy of the Inquisition then warned that he had blighted his whole future. 'I will do all I can,' thundered this stern moralist, 'to ensure that this boy does not get a scholarship.' We almost shed tears ourselves at this terrifying threat, the equivalent in our society of a capital sentence, and, even more absurdly, Mr Pyke linked this essentially trivial misdemeanour to a sensational murder case then filling the newspapers, which he would have done better to encourage us to ignore, though it enables me to date the incident precisely, as occurring in the summer of 1935.[*] The Rattenbury Stonor case remains a *cause célèbre* and indeed years later inspired a play of that name by

---

[*] George Stonor, an uneducated 18-year-old handyman, murdered his employer, a 68-year-old retired architect, having fallen in love with his employer's wife, Alma Rattenbury, who encouraged his feelings for her. He was sentenced to death, but later reprieved; she committed suicide. The guilty couple were felt to have breached the rigid social barriers of the time as well as those of sexual propriety.

Terence Rattigan, but it still seems to me an odd choice as the text for an address to a school assembly of seven to ten-year-olds. Mr Pyke, however, assured his juvenile audience that ending up on trial for murder was the all too likely fate of children who played 'doctors and nurses'. This prediction has happily proved false so far as his pupils were concerned and even the boy he had denounced has, so far as I know, lived a happy and blameless life ever since.

Although our sights were set on the Grammar School and High School, Mr Pyke's greatest love was for his old boarding school, Christ's Hospital, and one of his innovations at St Nicholas derived, I imagine, from his years there, the introduction of a 'house' system.[1] Lacking a supply of famous old boys and girls, our houses were named after four rectors of St Nicholas church, including the current one, Canon Wilfred Cooper. Sadly, I cannot now recall what house I belonged to and if house rivalry was encouraged it made little impact on me.

Second only to his affection for Christ's Hospital was Mr Pyke's devotion to his former training college at Reading. Of its academic merits he said nothing, though it had clearly not done too badly by him, but he liked to recall the initiation ceremony at Reading, which could almost have been borrowed from Greyfriars. This began with the new arrivals being roused from bed in the middle of the night only to find their slippers filled with jam, the start of a series of ritual humiliations which ended with immersion in a cold bath. This was the first information I ever received about student life and for a time it dampened any enthusiasm I might have felt for higher education.

His acknowledged oddities and self-indulgence apart, and teaching has always seemed to me such a demanding job that these can readily be forgiven, Mr Pyke was a highly effective headmaster. The atmosphere of the school encouraged hard work and orderly behaviour, but was certainly happy, and I cannot recall any bullying or stealing in all my time there. Nor indeed can I remember any punishments and if beating was ever inflicted I was certainly unaware of it.

Our form, 4A, was in any case far too busy that year to have time to get into trouble. Our form-mistress, Miss House, was as good a teacher as Mr Pyke and a better balanced individual. She would tackle head on any mildly embarrassing subjects which arose in a lesson and her attitude was, I now appreciate, thoroughly sensible. Once there was some sniggering when the adjective 'bloody' came up in class, but Miss House instantly pointed out that this was a perfectly acceptable word in its proper context and not when used – this was her precise phrase – 'as a swear'. She was equally forthright when a mention of a 'closet' produced a similar reaction among her pupils. It could, she observed, merely mean 'cupboard' and even if it did mean WC what on earth was so comic about such a useful object? I remember an enlightening moral discussion which she introduced after a reference in a book we were reading to a servant being instructed to say her employer was not at home, even when she was. Was the maid guilty of lying and, if so, should she refuse to do so? I was interested to learn the answer, being unhappy about the Camp Close practice I have described earlier of deceiving unwelcome callers like the rent collector. Miss House, I believe – and who could have said otherwise when jobs were so precious? – ruled that the maid had to do what she was told. Not telling the truth was indeed wrong but here it was the employer who was morally at fault.

Learning by discovery, now fashionable, was not much encouraged at St Nicholas, where there was really no time to spare to find out for ourselves what our teachers could impart so much more memorably and efficiently. I do, however, recall the class being challenged to find out what word described someone who could write with either hand. As so often, it was the Longmate twins who found the answer, 'ambidextrous', though this information came, I think, not from my mother but from that fount of knowledge – this was often a job for those who had come down in the world – the insurance man.

We were never allowed to forget that St Nicholas was a church school. Every day began with a short act of worship, introduced by a firm order from Mr Pyke 'Close your eyes!', and including a suitable hymn of the 'All things bright and beautiful' variety. After notices had been given out the whole school dispersed to its classrooms to the music of the school piano. Parents could, if they wished, keep their children away from this, the first event of the day, and scripture lessons, for the same reason, followed immediately afterwards. I cannot recall any of my schoolmates who took advantage of this concession, keen dissenters, like my great friend Keith's parents, preferring to send their children to a non-church school.

Because of our school's Church of England status Canon Cooper, a gentle, kindly, man was often in the classroom to ensure that the teaching given was doctrinally sound though I viewed him with suspicion, aware that the true faith was dispensed nowhere except at St John's. Several times a year, as on Ascension Day, the whole school attended a service at the so-called 'parish' church. Accustomed as I was to the ritualistic splendours presided over by Father Stenning this always seemed very tame to me, but the rector did his best to suit his style to his audience. I can still remember seeing him display in the pulpit a large letter 'I', on a totally blank background, to illustrate how a good Christian child should appear to an observer, and a second 'I' almost invisible amid the surrounding blots, the consequence of sin, its nature unspecified.

School outings of the kind now taken for granted were unknown. Only once, apart from the visits to church, were we taken outside the grounds, to visit the Newbury Museum. Like most others at the time – here is one area of life which has dramatically improved since my childhood – the collection consisted of a sad jumble of subjects and periods, amateurishly arranged and presented, with nothing to excite the imagination or create any feel for the past. Stuffed birds, fossils, flint arrowheads, fragments of pottery, all were flung down side by side as if designed to confuse as well as bore the visitor. I recall only one object of interest to us, a first world war grenade, sitting incongruously amid the birds' eggs and the prehistoric bones. A few years later even this had gone, required for sterner service in training the Home Guard, and, I believe, has never been returned. If this was the past, I remember feeling as I wandered from one dull and muddled showcase to the next, it had little to offer me; books about former times were interesting, these objects merely boring. I still believe that one authentic and properly dated document is worth whole galleries full of uncertainly identified objects, often used as the basis for a pyramid of dubious theories. Certainly neither natural history nor archaeology has been among my subsequent interests.

March 1936 was an important month for Europe. On the morning of Saturday the 7th German troops marched into the Rhineland, in open defiance of the Treaty of Versailles, throwing down a challenge to Great Britain and France which was not taken up. This was, we now know, the moment when the drift to war might have been halted, for Hitler's own generals questioned the wisdom of this open act of aggression and the advancing troops, had any resistance been offered, were under orders to withdraw. In fact retreat, under the pretext of conciliation and appeasement – though why the Germans were to be appeased for having started the first world war and then been indignant at having lost it I never understood – were the order of the day, as of all those which followed. I cannot remember the subject ever being discussed either at home, where, as I have said, we had no love for the Germans, or at school, where we were more interested in the war in Abyssinia. The process which was to place us all in mortal danger and to force all my male contemporaries into uniform was now well under way. At ten years old, however, even a politically aware child like myself could be forgiven for not realising the full significance of what was happening and we had in any case far more urgent preoccupations. The great event for which we had so long prepared, the scholarship exam, was now only two weeks away.

Whenever I smell ammonia now I remember the night before the exam for my mother was determined that Peggy and I should go into the room where our future was to be decided clean and tidy, and our worn clothes were carefully mended, then lovingly pressed and sponged with ammonia. The faintest trace of that pungent smell brings back to me that crowded little room and my mother's determination to give us the best chance she could. Years later, when I recalled the incident to her, she remarked: 'I knew you might be the poorest children there but I didn't mean you to look like it.' The selection process itself occupied two days and there was a two hour gap between the morning and afternoon sessions each day. We were told not to go home, my mother perhaps fearing the journey might tire us, but ate our lunch which, a great treat, included a bar of chocolate each, in Victoria Park.

I still have the General Paper which we took between 2.10 and 3.40 pm on Saturday 21 March 1936 and since it is so typical of the time and so well illustrates the standard then expected of a ten year old I give it in full:

1. If you want to cross a road, how would you try to escape being run over?
2. Name some places of great historical interest in Berkshire and write a few lines about any *two* of them. Why is Berkshire known as the Royal County? Explain the terms 'Accession' and 'Coronation'.
3. Where are the following places and what are the chief industries connected with each? Newcastle, Sheffield, Grimsby, Belfast, Burton-on-Trent, Southampton.
4. Write very briefly what you know of any three of the following:
    (a) Doomsday (*sic*) Book.
    (b) Magna Charta (*sic*).
    (c) Cardinal Wolsey.
    (d) The Pilgrim Fathers.
    (e) Robert Clive.
    (f) William Wilberforce.
    (g) Earl Haig.
5. Answer any three of the following questions as briefly as you can:
    (a) What alteration is made to clocks at the end of 'Summer Time'?
    (b) Why are trees on high ground in England often found leaning towards the North-East?
    (c) Is it healthier to live in the country than in the town? Give your reasons.
    (d) What are the Cardinal Points? How would you find them on (i) a sunny day, (ii) a starry night.
6. Name some of the chief wild flowers of early spring.
    How does Nature arrange for the distribution of the seeds of the Thistle, Blackberry, Sycamore?
    Explain the terms (a) Arable Land, (b) Pasture Land, (c) Down Land.
7. For what do you think the reign of King George V will be chiefly remembered?

Apart from the natural history question, on which I cannot recall we had received any coaching, none of Mr Pyke's pupils can have found this paper very intimidating and I positively enjoyed the English paper, which required the candidate to make up a story involving a car. Now those hours composing our private soap opera and my brother's years of service at Martin and Chillingworth's garage came into their own. I had no difficulty in producing a suitably dramatic tale which involved a Ford V8, as driven by the fictional Mr

Warwick, the height of motoring sophistication. Thanks to its superb brakes this vehicle, in my composition, narrowly escaped a disastrous accident and all the characters involved lived happily ever after. Elsewhere we were offered a choice of subjects, and, thanks to Mr Pyke, I kept well clear of 'How I would spend five shillings' and settled instead for 'The Happiest Day of My Life', recalling every detail of our brief trip to Bournemouth five years earlier, still the only time in my life that I had seen the sea.

I have always enjoyed written examinations, though usually doing poorly at *vivas* and selection boards, and felt reasonably confident that the exam had gone well, though after it, I believe, we settled down to work almost as hard as if it were still to be faced. I had no inkling, however, of *how* well I had acquitted myself until a few weeks later, on what must have been the afternoon of Tuesday 9 June 1936, I was walking home and had, I remember, just opted to vary my usual route by going up the Old Newtown Road instead of the main road, when I was overtaken by a master on a bicycle, that same Mr Collins who a year or two before had decorated my untidy work with a 'Where there's dirt there's danger' label. (I now remember him for a very different reason. A few years later he was to join the RAF and die as a prisoner of the Japanese.) Mr Collins asked me to return to school and, obedient as always, I did so, not knowing the reason. I have no recollection of the scene that followed, but Mr Pyke was no doubt in high glee, enjoying the proudest moment of his professional career and I am glad in retrospect to think that I had thereby unwittingly repaid the debt to him of which I am now conscious. According to the account which appeared that day in the Reading *Evening Gazette*, it was its reporter who brought him the news that, as its headline put it, 'Newbury Boy heads List.' I appreciate now that the paper, only recently launched, was eager to increase its circulation in Newbury and thus gave unusual prominence to a fairly minor story. But story it undoubtedly was, for never before had someone from relatively rural Newbury beaten the supposedly brighter products of larger and better known places like Reading and Windsor to become 'Top of the County.'

I was, I suppose, pleased to know I had won a scholarship, but the significance of not merely achieving this but bringing glory to the school and town by coming first did not really sink in, indeed it is really only now that I understand the reason for what seemed a great and unmerited fuss. This reaction was, quite wrongly, attributed to modesty, which certainly did me no harm.

My mother was, as it happened, away for the day on her sole holiday of the year, a day trip with the Mothers' Union, and we greeted her off her coach with the news, though I cannot remember her response and was, I suspect, more interested in seeing if she had managed to bring us back a present. Once home, I went out to play as usual on the Green – 'Not showing any side,' muttered approving neighbours, though I was still genuinely unaware that I had done anything out of the ordinary. Realisation began to dawn, however, when I was called back to meet the rector of St Nicholas, who had nobly trundled his old push bike up Newtown Hill to offer me his congratulations. He had no sooner gone than a reporter from the *Evening Gazette* arrived. I still remember his surname, Black, but have no recollection of the subsequent interview, though he described me as 'unexcited', which was certainly true. I had heard so often that it was reaching the Grammar School which mattered that one's place in the list seemed unimportant.

Mr Pyke knew better. I have often wondered if it was at his suggestion that I was given a hero's welcome when I entered the playground next morning and was hoisted on to the shoulders of my classmates to be carried in triumph into the hall. Here I was immediately summoned to the platform at the end and once prayers were over was ordered to stand on the table behind which was Mr Pyke. While I wobbled uncertainly on this unfamiliar perch Mr Pyke eloquently described the glory I had brought to him and to the school. This was, he said, a proud moment in the history of St Nicholas. He went on to heap praise not merely upon me but upon my twin sister, for Peggy had also won a scholarship. We were, he said, a model to all those present, not merely industrious at our school work but helpful at home. Did we not jointly do the washing up each evening before settling to our homework? 'Which of you,' he asked, 'washes and which dries up?' This was not a question I had anticipated but I responded that I preferred the tea towel, which seemed the right answer. As for my future, this could, Mr Pyke assured my schoolmates, only be dazzling. 'This boy,' predicted my headmaster in terms that clearly impressed his audience, 'will one day earn more than I do.'

That evening I found myself, for what was to be the only time in my life, the subject of a newspaper placard. 'We interview boy scholarship leader,' proclaimed the *Evening Gazette* poster outside Herrings the newsagents. (Miss House's prediction that the son of that business, my friendly rival John Herring, would 'make up in arithmetic what Norman Longmate gains in English', had not quite been fulfilled. He had come eleventh in the county, a creditable performance, but overshadowed by mine.) The real triumph, however, was Mr Pyke's. St Nicholas had secured more scholarships, for the second year running, than any other school in Berkshire, including no fewer than six of the top fifty. They included the boy involved in the 'doctors and nurses' incident, whom Mr Pyke had evidently failed to harm as he had threatened. Understandably this was not mentioned in the *Gazette* report where he explained, with admirable brevity, 'the secret of the school's success. "It is simple", he said. "I have some good scholars, willing teachers and excellent parents. Last year we had 95 per cent attendance of the children, which is a great help."'

These observations appeared at the end of Mr Black's account of his interview with me, which was, somewhat embarrassingly headed, 'Newbury's

Brainiest Boy is an EeeGee'; he had been delighted to discover that I was a member of the paper's club for child readers. This cost nothing but brought two benefits, the ability to read the coded message which appeared each week in the children's column and receiving an annual birthday card from our leader, Auntie Baa. Re-reading Mr Black's story almost sixty years later, after having worked as a journalist myself, I give it full marks for accuracy, even though it wrongly implied that Mr Pyke and I were interviewed together and my headmaster, I feel, emerged as a distinctly more interesting figure than I did. The unflattering photograph which decorated the story (not taken by my father) shows a distinctly serious, introverted looking child, an impression borne out by the text:

> Both Norman and his headmaster, Mr GF Pyke, were unaware of the honour brought to the school when I called to congratulate the young scholar...
>
> He was shy and unexcited, but his headmaster hid nothing of his excitement and pleasure.
>
> 'He has brought a great distinction on the school,' he told me, 'and we are proud of him. He is a smart and willing worker, full of concentration and I think and hope he will go a long way...Only recently I told the boys that I wished that one of my pupils would be top boy in Berkshire.'
>
> Norman is ambitious. He told me that not only does he want to go to Christ Hospital *(sic)*, but he is also aiming to get to Oxford University as well.
>
> For one so young he has clear cut ideas as to his future. 'I want to be an accountant,' he said, 'because I like arithmetic. I also like geography and history, too.'
>
> Norman...will be 11 next December. He told me he is very fond of books.

I have no recollection of the official letter notifying my parents that Peggy and I had 'passed the scholarship' reaching our household. It must have come before the detailed results were published, for the copy sent to a schoolmate's parents, signed by the Secretary of the Berkshire Education Committee, is dated 2 June 1936. Since this document was so important to its recipients, it merits quotation in full:

> Dear Sir or Madam,
> I beg to inform you that, on the results of the recent Special Place examination, my Committee have decided to offer your child...a Special Place Scholarship at Newbury Grammar School [or Newbury County Girls School] from the beginning of the Autumn Term, 1936.

> Under the Regulations of the Board of Education, Special Places are defined as places which, in cases of financial need, will carry total or partial exemption from tuition or entrance fees.
>
> If, therefore, you desire to apply for partial or total exemption from tuition fees, the enclosed form should be completed and returned to this office immediately and, in any case, not later than 9th June 1936. My Committee will then notify you whether your child will be accepted as a special place holder without payment of tuition fees, or, alternately *(sic)*, what fees will be charged if you accept the Special Place offered.
>
> Parents accepting Special Places for their children will be required to sign a form of undertaking (1) to adhere to the rules of the school, (2) to pay such fees as may be required, (3) that it is their intention to keep their children at a secondary school up to the age of sixteen, and (4) to give a full term's notice of intended withdrawal.

Apart from its interest as an example of the bureaucratic prose of the period – and for parents who had not been to a grammar school themselves, no doubt the vast majority, it must have been heavy going – this letter reveals much about the social as well as the educational conditions of the time. The requirement to keep their child at school for two years after he or she reached school-leaving ie earning, age must have deterred some parents, especially since the cost of uniforms, books and other essential extras had to be added and it was not at all uncommon for a scholarship to be turned down. At this time four out of five places at the grammar school and High School were fee-paying and though the cost was modest – £7 a term or £18 a year – this would certainly have been enough to shut Peggy and myself out of secondary education for good.

Two days after the first *Evening Gazette* report the *Newbury Weekly News* carried the story, duly recording my success, but there was no interview and no photograph and little was made of the fact that this was a 'first' for the town.[2] The paper, I now suspect, was reluctant to follow where its upstart rival in Reading had led. (It was indeed to see it out. The *Evening Gazette* has long since vanished; the *Newbury Weekly News* has celebrated its centenary and is still going strong.)

Others in Newbury seemed more impressed that a Newburian had come first among, I think, seven hundred or more candidates, and I still have a letter, dated 15 June 1936, written on behalf of the managers of St Nicholas:

> I have been asked to tell you how pleased they were to hear of your outstanding success...They wish me to convey to you their heartiest congratulations upon your achievement in obtaining first place in the whole county and hope you will be very happy in your new school.

What in fact was my new school to be? I was duly interviewed by the headmaster of the Grammar School, T Rutherford Harley, a pleasant man, and I was impressed by the ivy clad red brick walls of the main building, reminiscent of the quadrangle at Greyfriars as depicted in *The Magnet*. Seven years later, in a retrospective essay about my childhood, a valuable aide-memoire which I shall quote again, I recorded that 'I spoke rather nervously to the headmaster and, after being questioned by another master, as I came out into the space in front of the school I realised the indefinable difference in atmosphere between the secondary and the elementary school.' What prompted this reflection I am uncertain, but Mr Harley was reported to have said afterwards, 'Of course, he'll never come here,' and so indeed it proved.

---

[1] Newton p.14
[2] *Evening Gazette* 10 Jun 36, *Newbury Weekly News* 11 Jun 36

13

TO MAINTAIN AND TO CLOTHE

To admit, maintain, educate, clothe etc…so many boys and girls…as the rents and profits shall be sufficient to maintain.

Bequest of John and Frances West, 18 November 1720

It was undoubtedly due to Mr Pyke that I did not attend St Bartholomew's Grammar School, to give it its correct title, but went instead to his other old school, Christ's Hospital, which was held out to us as an educational Jerusalem, the nearest to academic heaven to which any child could aspire. Years later I was surprised to find a memorial plaque erected to him in the entrance to the school chapel. The explanation lay, I discovered, in a legacy of which this had been a condition. 'George Frederick Pyke (Middleton A 1901-1908)', as the tablet described him, without any other inscription, having founded the Newbury Old Blues Association in 1928 and subsequently seen its ranks swollen by his former pupils, had been loyal to his old school to the last.[1]

His devotion only reflected in an extreme form a view widely held in the town. The corporation was intensely proud of the Christ's Hospital connection. Occasionally members of the Education Committee would pay the school a visit and, as I was to experience, seek out 'their' boys, though, if what happened to me was typical, they never took the slightest interest in one after one had left, whatever one's academic achievements. On Christmas morning, in a provincial parallel to the imposing St Matthew's Day parade through the City of London, Housey boys, in uniform, were expected to join in the mayor's procession from the Municipal Buildings to the parish church, and afterwards were entertained by him in the Major's Parlour and presented with a new shilling, the same largesse as the Lord Mayor distributed at the Mansion House. Everyone in the town had at least heard of Christ's Hospital, so one was spared the embarrassing misunderstandings, which I shall mention later, that the ambiguous name and anachronistic uniform sometimes caused elsewhere.

Curiously, however, reflecting the school's own practice at that time, nothing was done to engage our interest in earlier Newbury Old Blues, whom I concluded must have made little mark. At least one in fact had been a man of solid achievement, John Septimus Rose, at the school from 1807-1813 and subsequently Surveyor-General of Western Australia, a noted explorer who had mapped much previously unknown territory and laid out the city of Perth and other towns.[2] He was never held out to us as an example; simply to get a place at the school was sufficient glory in itself.

Christ's Hospital in 1936 consisted of two quite separate schools, administered through a common governing body. The main school, for about 830 boys aged from nine to 19, occupied a large rural site near Horsham in Sussex, while the girls' school, with some 250 pupils, was on an enclosed campus in the centre of the small, rather Newbury-like town of Hertford. The Newbury connection was not explained to us at the time, but had been established by John West, who was not, as I for long supposed, an Old Blue or even a Newbury man. Born in Twickenham on the western outskirts of London, in 1641, he was, around the age of 17, apprenticed for eight years to a member of the Clothworkers' Company, emerging from his articles in March 1656, two weeks after getting married in the City church of St Gregory by St Paul's.[3]

John West's bride was Frances Mickell, widow of a scrivener, a form of lawyer cum merchant banker, who had died during the Great Plague in September 1665. She had been born Frances Seakes (or Sakes) around 1643, and (though some uncertainty remains) was probably the grand-daughter of one mayor of Newbury, Gabriel Cox, and the niece of another, his son Gabriel Cox the younger, who occupied the position four times between 1643 and 1667, and faced all the complications of the Civil War and the Restoration. Frances Mickell, nee Seakes, had, it turned out, made a wise choice of second husband. John West established a highly successful business in providing capital for new ventures and rose rapidly through the Clothworkers' Company until, in 1707, he was elected its master, a post held earlier by Samuel Pepys. Pepys was himself a governor of Christ's Hospital, taking an active part in managing its affairs, and John West also became a governor, in 1681. He was apparently close to Pepys for he was one of the witnesses to Pepys' will.

John West died childless in 1723; his widow survived him by only a year. They had already agreed the terms of a bequest to Christ's Hospital to come into effect on their death and on 18 February 1724 the Council of Almoners formally accepted the legacy:

> We find that the said John West and his wife by indentures…for the 18th and 19th days of November 1720 did convey…certain houses and ground and the…rents in St Anne's Westminster and also in and near London annually to £241.8s 0d [£241.40] to the use of the said governors of Christ's Hospital for ever, to admit, maintain, educate, clothe etc in the said Hospital so many boys and girls (three fourths always to be boys) as the rents and profits shall be sufficient to maintain.[4]

The terms of 'West Gifts' as they were known, were to have important consequences for Christ's Hospital, for the donors had specifically, and unusually, referred to girls as well as boys and Frances West had indeed arranged a totally separate scholarship to the school specifically for a girl from the City of London. Much later, as I shall describe, these conditions were to prevent Christ's Hospital becoming an all-boys' school and thus not merely to strike a blow for women's education but to leave open the possibility of its ultimately becoming co-educational.

Whether they had particularly longed for a daughter is unknown, but clearly their lack of a family pressed heavily on the Wests for they specified that anyone who could claim descent from them should be given precedence in the allocation of Christ's Hospital places and also left pensions for life to any descendants in need who could establish a valid connection with them. These, too, Christ's Hospital came to administer.

It was not until 1728 that the first children were admitted under the scheme and thereafter the overall numbers varied according to the funds available. From the first, however, following the Wests' own wishes, more children were accepted from Newbury and Reading than from Twickenham. The reason for these proportions remains a mystery for Twickenham was John West's native town and though his wife had Newbury connections why he favoured Reading is also unknown. We often speculated on the subject and one romantic story, which apparently originated in a Reading newspaper, pictured the young cloth-worker as a latter-day Dick Whittington, making his way on foot from Newbury to London with a bundle on his shoulder, being treated with kindness at Reading en route and being entertained rather less generously at Twickenham. The more cynical suggested that he had halted often on the way and had decided the public houses at Reading and Twickenham were the best.

From the first the vacancies were eagerly sought after and for many years election to fill them meant what it said. In 1880, for example, the competing parents published addresses soliciting support in the *Newbury Weekly News* and the bells of St Nicholas tolled throughout the poll to remind eligible burgesses of the need to vote.[5] The winner, among five candidates, received 288 votes, the runner-up 178, which indicates a high degree of public interest. This system of open selection ended in 1912, when the number of Newburians at the school reached a peak of 42. In that year the scheme was revised, the maximum number of places was fixed at 24 each for Newbury and Reading, with 12 for Twickenham, and the selection began to be made by written, competitive examination and interview, though with 'kin' still given preference. I could make no such claim, but have often wondered how I would have fared had the result still depended on a poll. No doubt everyone who knew my mother would have voted for me, but perhaps my father's business failure, though it had left me just the type of child West Gifts were designed to help, would have been held against his son.

The mystique with which Mr Pyke had surrounded Christ's Hospital and its high reputation in Newbury help to explain why neither my parents nor I questioned his decision that I should accept a place at Christ's Hospital, though I was, I now realise and I feel they should have realised then, temperamentally unsuited for boarding school and especially for such a traditional and old-fashioned establishment as this one. But, according to the essay about my childhood which I have already mentioned, I narrowly escaped another year of misery, for it seems I passed the written examination in 1935, when I was nine, only to be turned down at the subsequent interview. I have no recollection of this but can date my second attempt precisely for in the interview which Mr Pyke gave to the *Evening Gazette* on 9 June[*] he stated: 'Today he sat for his oral examination for entry into Christ's Hospital, Horsham, and he should get through.' This indeed I can well remember, though, curiously, it is not associated in my mind with the 'top of the county' news which reached me that same afternoon. The examination itself took place in the imposing surroundings of the Municipal Buildings and seems to have combined written tests with a selection interview. I recall being required to draw a map of India and was, I later learned, the only candidate to include Ceylon. This prompted a question as to its principal export, which I answered correctly, ie tea, and I was then asked about the Middle East and, after referring to its output of oil, was asked how this was extracted. I artlessly replied, 'You just drill a hole in the ground and it squirts out,' which caused some friendly laughter. The really important question, I now realise, was 'How do you feel about going away to boarding school?' which I answered in textbook fashion, declaring my eagerness to receive the best possible education so I would get on in the world.

It was no surprise to me when Mr Pyke's prediction was fulfilled and, with offers from both the grammar school and Christ's Hospital safely secured, I was able to settle down to enjoy my final weeks at St Nicholas. Spoiling my hitherto impeccable attendance record, I was for a short period absent through illness, for reasons to be described in a moment, but when I returned I was still shrouded in glory. I recall Mr Pyke touring the classrooms to read out a congratulatory letter I had received from the school governors and to display the five pound note, the first, as he rightly said, most of us would ever have seen, raised to buy me a present. At the time I valued more, however, a totally unexpected letter from our old benefactor 'Uncle John' Stoodley, offering congratulations to Peggy and myself and enclosing two ten shilling [50p] notes, 'one for each twin'. Here was wealth beyond even the dreams of the Special Place examiners, with their meagre and imaginary five shillings [25p] to spend, as much as my brother then earned in a week. I still look back with gratitude on this extraordinary act of generosity, which ranks with the arrival of the Rotary

---

[*] It was datelined 'Wednesday' and appeared on that day, 10 June, but my clear recollection is that the reporter interviewed both Mr Pyke and me the previous evening. Newspapers, as I learned later, often like to give stories a false appearance of immediacy.

food hamper as an outstanding moment of my childhood, and admire my parents' refusal, hard up as they were, to accept even a penny of our money.

My success brought another gratifying result of which I only learned much later. A few months earlier I had gone into a boys' outfitters in Bartholomew Street with my mother, carrying *The Magnet* which I had just bought at Tufnail's next door. The shopkeeper rudely remarked – I was, after all, a customer – 'Reading rubbish like that will do you no good!' – a thoroughly stupid and ignorant observation; in fact, as I have shown, I owed much to *The Magnet*. I resented the insult, as much on my mother's account as my own, and was delighted to learn that she had later returned to the shop and remarked to this insolent tradesman 'It doesn't seem to have done him much harm, does it?'

That spring I had been too preoccupied with my own affairs to pay much attention to what was happening elsewhere but at the end of May, while still waiting for the scholarship results, I was caught up, like the rest of the nation, in the patriotic upsurge of excitement which greeted the maiden voyage of the *Queen Mary* from Southampton to New York. Somewhat similar acclaim had surrounded the ship's launching on Clydebank, back in November 1934, which seemed to mark the nation's faith in the future and even, perhaps, the end of the depression. By 1936 the great 80,000 ton liner was venerated almost as much as the royal personage after whom she was named and when she set out to gain the Blue Riband for the fastest ever Atlantic crossing public interest was intense. There were daily reports of her progress until the triumphant moment, on 1 June, when she finally docked in New York, the coveted honour duly achieved and Britain's place as top dog in the maritime, if not indeed the whole, world, duly re-asserted. These stirring events had their echo in the classroom of 4A at St Nicholas, when the wireless and gramophone company HMV invited schools to enter a competition to write an advertising slogan linking their products with this already famous ship. While most of the class came up with such predictable and uninspired entries as 'Both British and Best' Peggy and I returned to school armed with far more imaginative suggestions, thanks to the co-operation of my brother. This time, I think, we, or rather he, might have won for both his proposals seemed just what was wanted: 'One rules ocean waves, the other sound waves', and 'HMV makes the records; the *Queen Mary* breaks them.' Tragically, for the first and only time I can remember, the school let us down. Miss House forgot, or could not be bothered, to return the entry forms and I can still remember my sense of outrage, followed, when I told her of this betrayal, by Peggy's tears, as our form mistress tore up our lovingly lettered slogans and threw the pieces into the wastepaper basket.

Another, similar, competition which also belongs to my last year at St Nicholas was set by Cadburys, the chocolate manufacturers. A prize was offered for the best essay from each school and I won that given to St Nicholas with a cunning reworking of the material they had sent us, ending with a sycophantic tribute. 'Surely we should be grateful to Cadbury's,' I wrote, 'for our bedtime cup of cocoa?' Cadburys agreed and I received what I now think was rather a meagre reward, a box containing one example of each of their bars then on the market. These were my first literary earnings since the penny I had been given two years earlier and I enjoyed them more than any since. I had planned to pass off the bars I liked least, of plain chocolate, to my sister but Peggy's tearful response soon put paid to this notion and, on parental insistence, though I got the lion's share, the fruits of my labour were shared out among the whole family.

I have little recollection of international affairs at this time and no inkling that the promising career Mr Pyke had predicted for me was likely to be interrupted by my having, like my father, to turn soldier to resist the Germans. The signs were, however, clear to see for those not blinded by self-deception and illusion, from which my parents were always free. They never showed any faith in the Germans having reformed, a view I inherited and hold to this day. As the *Evening Gazette* made clear they were not alone in showing much more perspicacity than the politicians and – even worse – the pacifists of the time. That same issue which had recorded the scholarship result had carried alongside them a very different story headlined 'Peace Resolution Storm'. One member of the Bradfield Rural District Council, it was recorded, had asked his colleagues on the council to endorse a resolution sent from the mayor of Nelson in Lancashire calling upon 'the peoples of all countries...to urge their governments to abandon the competition in armaments, and seek the solution of all international disputes by peaceful means'. This was three years after Hitler had come to power and withdrawn from both the last Disarmament Conference and the League of Nations, and a year after Italy had invaded Abyssinia, so it is pleasing to record that, unlike the credulous Lancashire pacifists, the villagers of Bradfield were not deceived. 'Is Nelson in England or is it somewhere in New Zealand?' enquired the vice-chairman, and 'a suggestion "to put it in the wastepaper basket"' was greeted with 'cries of "Hear, Hear"'. The ludicrous letter was duly 'allowed to lie on the table', ie ignored.

I had hardly learned of my acceptance by Christ's Hospital when a sheaf of instructions and lists of requirements appeared from my new school, including the demand that I be vaccinated. This practice was already going out of fashion, though no doubt it had made sense when the school was housed on a cramped site in the insanitary City of London instead of amid the healthy open fields of Sussex. The results were to leave me with a degree of sympathy for the anti-vaccination campaigners who had made such a nuisance of themselves when vaccination first came into vogue. Far from being the 'mere scratch' the doctor concerned promised my inoculation 'took' with such spectacular effect that I fell quite seriously ill and still bear a large scar on my arm to mark the site. Since, later, in the army I had a wide range of inoculations without ill effect I am inclined to feel the doctor concerned was somewhat inexpert, though he was unapologetic when I was taken back to him. My violent reaction, he declared, vindicated the school's policy, for it showed that had I caught smallpox I would have died. It may be that the work and tension of the preceding few weeks had now caught up with me; such at least was my mother's explanation. Whatever the reason I was clearly exhausted and ordered to take things easy for several weeks, remaining at home to read, lie down after midday dinner and, just as in the advertisements about 'night starvation' take Horlicks every night. I was allowed back to school only for a morning to be photographed with the other scholarship winners and the resulting photograph, somewhat ravaged by time, still survives.[*] There I stand in the centre, looking wan and small, especially beside my rival, the already somewhat plump and puffy John Herring.

This was a busy, as well as financially difficult, time for my parents with both their youngest children having to be simultaneously kitted out for their new schools. Peggy's needs were less extensive than mine but she still needed a High School uniform. Somehow, perhaps with the school's help, since it often had to cope with scholarship girls though never before, I think, from Camp Close, she learned of a family with a daughter at the High School who had outgrown her blouse and gym slip, and these were duly altered to fit my twin sister. Other items were, I believe, found, or paid for, by those loyal friends, the Stoodleys. That still left her first term's books to pay for but happily the school had well established arrangements for these to be bought secondhand.

My requirements were altogether greater, and, looking back, it amuses me to reflect how precisely my experiences paralleled those of the thousands of upper class children who were at this time similarly preparing to leave home for prep or public school. It is strange to think how No 78 Camp Close was now caught up in the same activity as many a stately home, though there cannot have been many boys about to go away to school who, like me, went shopping for the items on the list of essentials not merely with their mother but with a councillor – perhaps the chairman – from the local education committee.

The process, despite the large number of items, from a dozen handkerchiefs to, I think, football boots and stockings and a sunhat, did not take long, for the councillor simply led us from his office across the road to the cheapest outfitters in the town, Beynons in the Market Place, of which now only the upper frontage still remains. Once, I have learned since, it had supplied the inmates of Newbury workhouse, including the children, with their clothing.[6] Nothing, that I can recall, was tried on, our escort merely reading out the list of required items to the salesman and, when any choice existed, automatically ordering the cheapest. My mother, no doubt relieved not to be paying the bill, did not demur but it soon emerged that there were a whole host of items which we would have to find ourselves. One, costing I believe, all of 3s 6d [17.5p], was a box of Cash's name tapes, which involved visiting the grandest of

---

[*] See illustrations.

Newbury shops, Camp Hopson. My mother bought the smallest possible number you could order, 36, then found she was short of the minimum needed to mark all my new clothes and I can remember seeing her unpick the extra tape on the side of the box to give her one more, and replacing it with plain white tape with my name in marking ink. I was embarrassed by that unofficial tape, but in the event the box was deposited with the matron and went unremarked. I was less fortunate with my toothpaste. My mother cleverly found in Woolworths one brand, Skuses, cheaper than the rest, costing a mere 3d [1.5p], half the price of the traditional Colgate's or Maclean's. This deviation from the norm was to be duly noted and cruelly commented on by some of my schoolmates.

Other requirements proved harder to fulfil. No shop in Newbury stocked the 'Revised Version' of the Bible on which the school insisted, and this had to be specially ordered. A prayer book was easier to obtain and Father Stenning generously offered to pay for both. As for a trunk, my father managed to discovered an unwanted one among his old acquaintance. It was, I imagine, brought home by hand and repaired, my name being neatly painted upon it – the sort of job at which my father excelled. Storing the trunk in our cramped little house must have presented a greater problem and I cannot recall how it was solved, but 'getting Jim ready for school' seemed to dominate our lives that summer.

I have two final memories of St Nicholas. The school sports day was made the occasion for Mr Pyke's regular review of the previous three terms and a report duly appeared in the *Evening Gazette* for Thursday 30 July 1936, headlined 'Newbury School's Fine Record'.

Canon Cooper, Rector of Newbury, presented the prizes at St Nicholas Junior School, Newbury, yesterday afternoon...

Among its pupils is Norman Longmate, the boy who was at the head in the county scholarships this year.

As many as 78 scholars had a perfect attendance record for the year...

Mr GF Pyke...said they had had a very successful year. Their all-the-year attendance was 95 per cent, which was remarkable. Three years ago the school obtained 11 county scholarships, but this year they had gained 22.

On behalf of the teachers and managers Canon Cooper presented a wristwatch to Norman Longmate...Every boy and girl who received a scholarship was rewarded with a present from the teachers and managers.

I do not remember this occasion, but I have a clear memory of my last meeting with Mr Pyke as one of his pupils. I called at his study to withdraw the money I had deposited in the school savings bank. After three years it now amounted to 2s 9d [13.5p]. I believe he showed me then the comment he had just written on my final school report, scrawled in red pencil far beyond the space allowed for it. 'Never forget in your prayers,' it ended, 'your loved ones at home,' an exhortation reminiscent of Tom Brown's father preparing his son for life at Rugby. Unlike Mr Brown, Mr Pyke failed to warn me that I might 'see a great many cruel blackguard things done and hear a great deal of foul bad talk',[7] timely though such a warning might have been. I was none the less impressed by his solemnity and equipped, as it seemed, both financially and spiritually, for the future, left St Nicholas in high spirits.

To this experience there was a sequel. The wristwatch proved an excellent one. It was to stand me in good stead in many examinations over the years and – as the *Newbury Weekly News* reported – was used to time my speech when, many years later, I successfully sought nomination as prospective Labour candidate for the town. Although I soon gave up the candidature I still have the watch. Less enduring has proved the honours board in the hall on which it was the custom at St Nicholas to enter the names of each year's scholarship winners, my name being added in 1936 in red, instead of the customary black. St Nicholas school still exists, though in other premises, and the hall still stands, but the honours board, alas, has gone. Its existence apparently affronted a later, more egalitarian age. When I tried to obtain a photograph of it I was told that it had been torn down and, when last seen, was being used to patch a hole in the floor of the bicycle shed.

---

[1] Dec 1994 p.223
[2] Apr 1966 pp.176-7
[3] *The Charities of John and Frances West*, Typescript, CH, 15 August 1991
[4] Christ's Hospital archives. Report to Council of Almoners
[5] Garlick pp.115-6
[6] Garlick p.106
[7] *Tom Brown's Schooldays* Chap IV

PART II

A REMARKABLE SCHOOL

A Short History of Christ's Hospital 1552-1936

Consideration seems to be justly due to the past history of so remarkable a school...Christ's Hospital is a thing without parallel in the country.

Report of the *Schools Inquiry Commission, 1867-8*

14

LODGING AND LEARNING

They devysed...an hospitall for them where they should have meate drincke and cloths, lodging and learning.

Account by the Treasurer's secretary of the founding of Christ's Hospital in 1552

The school which, thanks to the benevolence of John and Frances West and the enthusiasm of George Frederick Pyke I was now to attend, was overwhelmingly the product of its past. This already stretched back nearly four centuries. Christ's Hospital owed its existence to a sermon preached before the boy-king Edward VI, then aged 14 and a half, by Bishop Nicholas Ridley late in February 1552. The bishop, later to be martyred by Edward's half-sister Mary, drew the king's attention to the plight of the numerous homeless poor, especially children, on the streets of London, whose numbers had visibly increased since Edward's father, Henry VIII, had abolished the monasteries which provided them with relief. As a result, a committee of prominent citizens was set up under the Lord Mayor of London to raise funds for a new foundation to cope with the problem, as the secretary to its first treasurer later described:

> They devysed to take out of the streets all the fatherless children and other poore men's children that were not able to kepe them and to bringe them to the late dissolved house of the Greie ffryers wch they devysed to be an hospitall for them where they should have meate drincke and cloths, lodging and learning and officers to attende uppon them.[1]

'Hospital' meant merely a place of shelter and funds were rapidly raised from the members of the original committee, by sermons preached throughout the City and by a general appeal, which included collecting boxes in both churches and taverns. The initial appeal was so successful that Christ's Hospital, as it was named, was able to open its doors on Wednesday 23 November 1552 to its first 380 children.[*] More than a quarter were babes in arms and many it was said, were 'taken from the dunghill', ie were abandoned infants or children

---

[*] *Christ's Hospital Book* p.7. *Christ's Hospital. A Short History* p.3 says 260.

living rough in the streets. By Easter Day, 2 April 1553, those old enough were already in the 'blewe coats' which were to become their trademark, then the normal wear of Tudor schoolboys.

Christ's Hospital formally came into existence on Monday 26 June 1553[*] when Edward VI is said to have signed the charter formally incorporating it, though the authoritative *Victoria County History* for Sussex, supported by an Old Blue medical historian, suggests that in fact, thanks to the syphilis inherited from his father, his fingers were 'so painful and ulcerated that he could not hold a pen'.[2] Other iconoclasts accuse protestant historians of giving Edward the credit really due to his Roman Catholic successor.[3] The accepted, official story, however, recognises Edward VI as responsible and his birthday, 23 October (12 October old style), is celebrated by Christ's Hospital as Founder's Day.

At first a school and a shelter for homeless children may have existed on the same site, and confusion as to the true nature of Christ's Hospital has persisted. 'That's the school for paupers, you know!' a contemporary of mine recalls hearing one woman say to another as he passed them in a London street, which, though once true, was so no longer. Some of those rescued were far from grateful and would 'steale oute and falle to their old occupacon', ie begging, only to be forcibly brought back and 'sharply punyshed'. From the beginning it was laid down that all the boys should be taught to read, write and prepare accounts and that 'such of the children as be...very apte to learning, should be reserved and kept in the grammar school in hope of preferment to the university'.[4] The very first Christ's Hospital exhibitioner, ie scholar, reached Oxford in 1566 and went on to become a clergyman; already the school was providing a unique route upward for a few – a very few – of those it accepted. An early benefactor, Lady (or Dame) Mary Ramsey, whose husband was Lord Mayor in 1577-8 and also President of Christ's Hospital, described it in her will as 'a free Writing Schoole for poor men's children'.[5] This included girls, indeed an unsubstantiated tradition asserts that the very first child admitted was female. They occupied, however, a subordinate position for it was laid down that, in addition to being taught to read and write, they were to be 'instructed in all such works as become their sex and may fit them for good wives', which meant doing the sewing and mending for the whole establishment.[6] From the beginning the bare minimum was spent on domestic help and both boys and girls were expected to undertake most of the chores themselves, a policy which was to continue.

Christ's Hospital was also unique in other ways. Its location in the very heart of London and the presence in the streets of the Bluecoat Boys, as they

---

[*] Christ's Hospital Book p.3. Chapman p.280 says 10 June, a discrepancy not explained by the change in the calendar in 1752, when 3 September was followed by 14 September and eleven days were 'lost'.

were immediately known, made it a popular charity, regarded by Londoners with particular affection and a few of its pupils also rapidly became successful and famous. The City was the most obvious source of advancement, but a few Old Blues[*] achieved distinction in the professions, such as William Camden, who in 1586 published his pioneering historical work, *Britannia*, in Latin, and in 1593 became headmaster of Westminster. Camden's father was an artist, proof enough that already one did not have to be destitute to gain admission and almost from the beginning a small element of middle-class children seems to have been accepted. It was probably from these that the very small group who went on to enter the universities and the professions was drawn. The introduction of the Elizabethan Poor Law in 1601 also had a marked effect on the school's intake for it placed responsibility for supporting destitute children, like other categories in need, upon individual parishes.[*] Henceforward the school ceased to admit babes in arms and took in most of its pupils from around the age of seven upwards, mainly from ordinary, but low income families, the test from the beginning, though not always rigorously applied, being that the parents, or the guardians of an unfortunate orphan, needed assistance to educate their child. The foundation still supported, however, a number of deserving adults, like 'Blind Alice' and her guide, John, described as 'this innocent idiot'.[7] In 1609 a play based on the pair, a familiar sight in the City streets, was produced under the title *John in the Hospitall* and John's appearance on stage, in school uniform and beard, brought the house down.[8]

Why the original uniform was retained after it had become an anachronism has never been explained, but in the beginning there were obvious practical reasons, notably its publicity value and the assistance it gave in identifying runaways. More important still, it marked out the wearer as the recipient of charity, like the red flannel jackets, tall hats or other outmoded garments which were until recently compulsory for the occupants of many almshouses. In 1638 a yellow lining, of the same bright shade as the stockings, was added to the Bluecoat 'to avoid vermin', which were supposed to breed in 'white cottens'[9], and, although hardly for this reason, this school did indeed survive the Great Plague of 1665 with a mere 32 deaths. In the Great Fire, in 1666, however, the managing committee's minute book recorded, 'this Hospital of Christ's was almost consumed...excepting the four cloisters...and about three wards' and although no-one was killed 200 children had temporarily to be moved elsewhere.[10]

Among the buildings badly damaged was the Great Hall and its restoration was paid for by the first Old Blue Lord Mayor of London, Sir John Frederick, previously MP for the City of London, and, an almost greater honour, President of Christ's Hospital for 22 years. A successful merchant, Frederick's career,

---

[*] See *The Workhouse* p.15 on the origins and effects of the famous '43rd Elizabeth' which established the Poor Law.

from Bluecoat Boy to Lord Mayor, had a Dick Whittington quality about it and he was the first of five Old Blues who became sufficiently rich and respected to achieve this high office.*

It was not till almost 1700 that rebuilding on the old Greyfriars site was complete. The finest of the new buildings was the Writing School, designed by Nicholas Hawksmoor, but Sir Christopher Wren served as a consultant to the whole project and was made a governor in recognition of his help.

Although, strictly speaking, only children in obvious need qualified to enter Christ's Hospital, the governors were already concerned that too many from the lowest stratum of society were being admitted. From 1676 entry was restricted to 'children of Freemen of this City'[11], which implied a stable rather than impoverished home, for to be a freeman was essential to making one's way in the world, whether as a skilled craftsman or as a merchant. He (or more rarely she) was required to have completed a seven year apprenticeship and thereby qualified to practise a trade or open a shop in the City. Freedom also carried with it other privileges, including the right to vote, to avoid impressment in the Navy, and even the chance of becoming Lord Mayor.

In August 1673 the school had become doubly 'royal' with the granting by Charles II of a charter to the new Royal Mathematical School established within Christ's Hospital to train boys as naval and merchant navy officers. The real driving force was Samuel Pepys, a constant friend and ultimately a vice-president of Christ's Hospital, and the immediate result was to encourage the teaching of mathematics, essential to navigation, and instruction in drawing and painting, another useful accomplishment for a sailor in a pre-photographic age. (The custom of an annual visit to court by RMS boys to show off their recent work was kept up until late in Queen Victoria's reign.)[12]

Perhaps on the analogy of a black cat or a soot-stained sweep a Bluecoat was regarded as a symbol of good luck and from 1694 to 1826 boys from the Royal Mathematical School were used to draw the tickets in the public lottery.[13] A surviving illustration shows one with his left arm tucked into his girdle out of harm's way and an attempt to persuade one boy to secrete a ticket in the sleeve of his coat was said to have been unsuccessful.

Inside Christ's Hospital the 40 'mathemats' or 'King's boys' had a fearsome reputation for terrorising their schoolmasters, and they in turn went in dread of their Master, William Wales, a Fellow of the Royal Society who had made his name as an astronomer and explorer while sailing with Captain James Cook. Wales was of a type all too common at Christ's Hospital, a talented and

---

* The others were elected in 1840, 1904, 1905 and 1997. The last-named, Richard Nichols, at CH shortly after my time, had, in the best Housey tradition, been sent to the school by a livery company, the Salters, after his father, its Clerk, had died. After leaving he became a successful solicitor and Master of the Salters' Company. (*Housey* Spring 1998 pp.1-3)

respected teacher with a pronounced strain of brutality towards his pupils. 'All his systems', Charles Lamb recorded in his classic *Recollections of Christ's Hospital,* published in 1835, 'were adapted to fit them for the rough element which they were destined to encounter. Frequent and severe punishments were expected to be borne with more than Spartan fortitude...No occasion of laying on the lash was ever let slip.'[14]*

Wales was credited with having saved the school from being sacked when, in June 1780, at the height of the anti-Catholic Gordon Riots, he persuaded the prisoners whom the mob had released from Newgate Jail that Christ's Hospital was not, as they had supposed from the boys' uniform, a Papist seminary, a misconception which, as I shall describe later, has persisted to our own day.

In 1818 the King's Boys ceased to be a separate entity and were dispersed throughout the school and by the time I entered it, more than a century later, the Royal Mathematical School was wholly integrated, though boys who had entered the school by this route, often the sons of naval officers, still had a distinctive badge on one shoulder of their uniform.[15] I knew only one boy entitled to wear it. Thanks to his pronounced stammer, he was known – I have altered his real name – as 'C-C-Corcoran'. I often reflected what a hard time he would have had trying to give orders in a flat calm, let alone a howling gale.

During the second half of the eighteenth century two major changes occurred in the composition of the school. In 1761 the 200 youngest boys, aged from seven to ten, were moved to Ware and then to Hertford, to which in 1784 all the girls from London were also sent. The Hertford premises were rebuilt and extended between 1795 and 1798, but as a later Headmistress recorded, 'the girls were entirely segregated from the boys behind a high wooden fence and only saw them on Sundays in church'.[16]

At Newgate Street, which some boys entered direct though others arrived via Hertford, the half century which began around 1780 was later regarded as the Golden Age of Christ's Hospital and those who attended it in that period as the Golden Generation[17]. Charles Lamb and Samuel Taylor Coleridge both entered the school in 1782, James Leigh Hunt in 1792 and one of the most famous of nineteenth century journalists, Thomas Barnes, who edited *The Times* from 1817 to 1841, and established its reputation as 'The Thunderer', in 1796.[18] The school also produced in this period what a later Old Blue author, Edmund Blunden, described as 'a wonderful number of lesser writers',[19] literature and journalism being professions in which private means and influential connections were not required to succeed. It turned out, by contrast, few eminent statesmen and lawyers, but a considerable number of successful businessmen, clerics and

---

* Lamb, most confusingly, wrote several accounts of his schooldays, in one of which, indefensibly in my view, he falsely claims to be someone else, critically reviewing one of his own previous articles. The bibliography of the *Christ's Hospital Book* (pp.376 and 387) leaves the reason for this troublesome literary lie unexplained.

schoolmasters as well as university professors, some of whom became heads of colleges. A characteristic of Old Blue writers, as I have mentioned earlier, is an obsession with their schooldays. Lamb, Coleridge and Leigh Hunt all wrote about them at length and Thomas Barnes was for ever dealing with Christ's Hospital issues in the columns of *The Times*. There was already a large literature about the school, including an early school novel, *The Fortunate Bluecoat Boy*, set in the 1720s, published around 1789. It tells the story of a handsome senior who catches the eye of a rich widow. She duly marries him and 'translates him into the life of a gentleman', the aim of every true thinking CH boy but not a career option recommended in my day.[20]

Thanks to Lamb and the rest, life at Christ's Hospital at this time is extremely well documented. It is clear that a minority acquired an excellent education but that an extraordinary degree of violence on the part of the masters was tolerated, noteworthy even for the time. This is explained to some degree, though not justified, by the school having in its earliest days taken in so many 'unhappy children...' in Daniel Defoe's phrase, coined in 1722, 'bred up for the gallows', where indeed some of their parents had perished.[21] Lamb, Coleridge and Hunt are all agreed on the almost insane behaviour of the famous James Boyer, a clergyman, like so many flogging-prone schoolmasters, and an Old Blue, who as Upper Master in the Grammar School, in effect Headmaster, became a school legend. Coleridge admitted later to still suffering nightmares as a result of his treatment.[22] Leigh Hunt had one of his teeth knocked out by Boyer 'in a fit of impatience at my stammering' and observed that the master would regularly 'beat about the head and ears' a 'sickly-looking, melancholy boy' who later died insane.[23] All three pay tribute to Boyer's qualities as a teacher of the classics, but his habit of shouting 'Od's my life, Sirrah, I have a great mind to whip you!' at any unfortunate who caught his eye can hardly have created a relaxed atmosphere, nor the appearances of Mrs Boyer in the classroom, urging her husband on with cries of 'Flog them soundly, I beg!'[24] Leigh Hunt compared James Boyer to one of the 'tyrannical schoolmasters...described...by my friend Charles Dickens'[25] and I have often wondered if he was not the model for Wackford Squeers in *Nicholas Nickleby*, published in 1838-9. The comparison with Dotheboys Hall was often made by Old Blues of later generations, including mine, as I shall describe later, while the epigram composed by Coleridge on Boyer's death was still being quoted, perhaps nostalgically, by at least one master in my day. I give Leigh Hunt's version: 'It was lucky that the cherubs who took him to heaven were nothing but faces and wings, or he would infallibly have flogged them by the way.'[26]

To Christ's Hospital at this period, and for long afterwards, the answer to every problem of childhood or adolescence, including religious doubt, was violence. Coleridge's father was a clergyman, a category always given preferential treatment though outside the normal income limits, but his son decided that, having lost his faith, he would prefer to apprentice himself to a shoemaker. He enterprisingly ran away to offer his services to one in the City, but his intended employer promptly brought him back to Boyer, who immediately knocked the future poet down, then flogged him for professing himself 'an infidel'. Coleridge had in fact got off lightly, as Charles Lamb discovered. On *his* first day at Christ's Hospital, aged seven, he was shown 'a boy in fetters...I was told he had *run away*'.[27] Lamb was next taken to see 'the dungeons...little, square, Bedlam cells where a boy could just lie at his length upon straw and a blanket'. Here, he learned, anyone who had made a second attempt was imprisoned in solitary confinement and near or total darkness, seeing no one except the porter who brought him bread and water and the beadle who took him out twice a week to be flogged. Any boy who made a third attempt was allowed to leave but paid a heavy price for his escape. He was ceremonially stripped of his uniform, dressed in 'uncouth' jacket and cap resembling those of a lamplighter, a foretaste of the type of occupation he could now expect, and taken round the hall by the beadle 'clad in his state robe' who flogged the victim in front of each group of his schoolmates in a 'long and stately' fashion. Once, Lamb recalled, the beadle had to be fortified with brandy after 'turning rather pale', presumably ordered by the two governors who were required to be present 'not to mitigate...but to enforce the uttermost stripe'.[28] The offender was finally, and formally, thrust out of the gates and 'made over...to his friends if he had any...or to his parish officer'. Lamb witnessed, and was disgusted by, the whole horrible ritual, which reveals something of the unique character of Christ's Hospital. To have secured a place there was to be privileged and to reject what Lamb himself described as 'Christ's Hospital's bounty' was to display an almost criminal ingratitude which, in view of the school's name and origins, verged on blasphemy.[29]

So effective had the school been in publicising the belief that anyone admitted to it belonged to a fortunate elite that people outside, though generous to Bluecoat Boys encountered in the street, tended to treat those who ran away rather as if they had escaped from its close neighbour, Newgate Street prison, though it was a good deal easier to conceal a prison outfit than the distinctive Tudor uniform. This presented an almost insuperable problem, as I was later to discover for myself, for would-be runaways, but five who escaped in a group in the 1860s ingeniously overcame it, and, a contemporary recorded, 'cut off the skirts of their coats and...made them into trouser legs', thereby also obscuring the giveaway yellow stockings. 'By this means [they] eluded pursuit' but 'were...eventually compelled to take to some trees by an old gentleman who stood underneath with a loaded gun, while he sent for the police...This crew were all birched in Hall.'[30] By Christ's Hospital standards they had been treated mercifully, for to mutilate the sacred uniform was almost as unthinkable an offence as to run away.

The belief that one's obligation to Christ's Hospital overrode all lesser loyalties was well established by the end of the eighteenth century, as Coleridge has recorded:

> 'Boy!', I remember Boyer saying to me once when I was crying the first day of my return after the holidays, 'Boy! The school is your father! Boy! The school is your mother! Boy! The school is your brother! Boy! The school is your sister! The school is your first-cousin, and your second-cousin, and all the rest of your relations!'[31]

The Christ's Hospital family was expected to endure a remarkable degree of discomfort, even compared to other schools. Attitudes which had perhaps been appropriate in the earliest days, when unwashed, ragged urchins were being brought in off the streets – and often trying to escape back to them – survived, like the uniform, long after the conditions which had justified them had disappeared. The adjective mostly commonly used to describe life at Christ's Hospital has always been 'spartan', whether applied to living conditions or the general treatment of the pupils. The former could perhaps be justified on the grounds that money donated by charitably minded people ought only to be spent on bare essentials, but for the latter there was less excuse. Coleridge calls the discipline 'ultra-Spartan' and is equally scathing about the food. 'Except on Wednesdays I never had a bellyful,' he wrote to a friend.[32] A hundred and sixty years later this was still, as I shall mention, the one day when we had a reasonable meal. (Coleridge left before, around 1800, potatoes, so important to us, were added to the diet by, as it happens, a doctor who had previously practised at Newbury.)[33]

The accommodation also remained primitive, another enduring tradition, initially established at a time when Christ's Hospital was more orphanage than school and those rescued from destitution were grateful, or at least expected to be grateful, for any shelter at all.

When public criticism developed, however, it concerned not the way in which Bluecoat boys were treated, but how they were recruited. Although some came via charities like West Gifts, the main entry route was 'presentation' by an individual or institution who had acquired the right by a recent, or more probably, past, donation. Christ's Hospital was by now a prized part of the London landscape and enough of its former pupils, though mainly drawn from poor families, had made their name in the world to establish its reputation as a nursery of talent. A small middle-class element, notably the sons of London freemen, usually people of some standing, and the clergy, had long been admitted but in 1811 a particularly blatant abuse occurred when the son of a rich London physician who could not possibly require financial assistance in educating his family was found a place. A number of citizens submitted a petition to the Lord Chancellor, the Visitor of Christ's Hospital, urging him to intervene and bring back the school to its original purpose, that of providing shelter and free instruction 'to the children of poor and needy beggars'.[34]

Coleridge, a son of the rectory who clearly did not relish being bracketed with such company, replied with a powerful article in the *Courier*, a newspaper of some importance; its proprietor also owned the *Morning Post*.[35] He readily admitted that 'The admission of Dr Warren's son...was against the true principles of the foundation', but went on to set out the school's purpose in terms far removed from those of its founders:

> We venture to assert that such an education...if actually confined to the lowest and most necessitous classes, would be a curse to the country and not a blessing. For its constant effect would be to call off hundreds yearly from the plough and the dray, to life them up into a class which is already overstocked, and where, in nineteen cases out of twenty, they would be worse than useless...
>
> Hence, the governor is equally mistaken in his sense of duty who presents a child from the lowest class of society, as he who presents the child of a man of fortune or flourishing merchant.[36]

Coleridge's contention was that the school's distinctive role was to cater for those who fell between the two extremes:

> The true and specific purpose of Christ's Hospital is...to preserve in the same rank of life in which they were born, the children of reputable persons of the middle class who, either by the death or overwhelming calamities of their parents, must otherwise have sunk down to a state, which to *them* would be penury and heart-breaking...To preserve and not to disturb or destroy, the gradation of Society; to catch the falling, not to lift up the standing from their natural and native rank.[37]

Coleridge's school contemporary, Charles Lamb, writing two years later in the *Gentleman's Magazine*, took a similar line, arguing that 'A sprinkling of the sons of respectable parents' – Lamb's own father had been a lawyer's clerk – 'has an admirable tendency to liberalise the whole mass.' He even defended the uniform as 'a badge of dependence' guaranteed to keep out the rich. 'While the coarse blue coat and yellow hose shall continue to be the costume of the school...the sons of the aristocracy...will not often be obtruded upon this seminary.'[38] The Tudor costume, as a sign of charity, could, in other words, be relied upon to exclude the rich and well-born.

That the reputation of the school as a singularly harsh and even brutal place might discourage parents never seems to have been considered, although references to it recur throughout its history. 'I always thought the boys in the

Bluecoat school were treated with great severity,' observes the son in an imaginary dialogue with his father in *Recollections of a Bluecoat Boy*, published in 1829 by the Rev. William Scargill, a Unitarian minister, who had been at Newgate Street around 1800, the golden age of the floggers, but the fictional father will have none of it. 'They were never more severely treated than the boys of any other public school and...at present, I understand, that corporeal punishment is almost discontinued', a monstrous untruth.[39]

Whatever those actually attending it thought, Christ's Hospital undoubtedly enjoyed in the early nineteenth century both a high public profile and a favourable public image. It was fortunate not merely in its conspicuous central location but in the fact that so many Old Blues had become successful journalists, forever ready to sing their old school's praises. Thus Coleridge in the 1813 article quoted earlier argued that Housey boys were deservedly popular in the capital:

> The tradesmen and householders of London look with an eye of peculiar affection on the Bluecoat Boy, as he passes along the streets on one of his leave days;...the boys seem to meet with friends and relations everywhere, and are...distinguished by their civility, good manners, and modest pride at equi-distance from the rudeness and insolence of the great public schools and the abject manners of common charity children.[40]

Although, as will emerge again later, there was an exceptionally wide gulf between the most successful Old Blues and the rest, who often severed all connection with it once they had left, among a proportion of its ex-pupils the school attracted a remarkable degree of loyalty. As early as 1629 a group of Old Blues had 'dyned together...in the greate hall' and there was a distinctly modern ring about the Building Fund, opened in 1803.[41] In 1828 the Benevolent Society of Blues was founded, devoted to helping the less successful, and indeed still exists. Already the paradox was apparent that those Old Blues who had done best were now too well off to send their children there, but they could, and did, sing the school's praises and bequeath it money in their wills.

A classic example was Thomas Middleton, who, having entered the school, around 1779, from a suitably humble background had left as a grecian in 1788 after being taught by the fearsome James Boyer.[42] Having followed the traditional upward path for the classical scholar via Cambridge, where the school supported him with a £60 a year exhibition, into the ranks of the clergy he had been appointed first-ever Bishop of Calcutta, a vast pioneering diocese covering all the territories of the East India Company,[43] and in 1821 he repaid his debt to the school with a handsome gift of £400, 'My donation', the Bishop wrote, 'to the noblest institution in the world and my imperfect acknowledgement of what I owe to it.'

12: My Mother with my brother and elder sister, c. 1921

13: With my best-ever birthday present, aged around seven

14: My childhood home, No.78 Camp Close

15: Showing a rare interest in games, during school holidays, c. 1937

16: The family blackberrying. This photograph won my father a prize in a newspaper competition

17: With my sister, date unknown but probably c.1941

18: The former St Nicholas school, Newbury, photographed in 2000

19: St Nicholas scholarship winners, 1936. My rival, John Herring is on the right in the back row, my sister is on the left of the front row and I am third from the left in the second row

20: At the Tower of London. September 1936, on my way to be admitted to Christ's Hospital

21: Outside the Manual School at Horsham, a few weeks later

22: Happy Berkshire Boy, 1936

23: Unhappy Bluecoat Boy, 1937, but my bands are now fastened correctly

The governors were always as ready to spend money on imposing public buildings as they were loathe to disgorge it to make the children's lives more comfortable. In 1795 a 30 year rebuilding programme had begun which was to include a new Grammar School and Mathematical School, the most imposing of the new buildings being the Dining Hall, of which the foundation stone was not laid until 1825. Its roof was the second largest in the country unsupported by pillars, surpassed only by Westminster Hall[44], and Thomas Barnes in *The Times* greeted the occasion with an adulatory leading article describing his old school as 'that ancient and magnificent establishment...that noble institution'.[45] To those attending it the benefits were less apparent. The building programme had included new living quarters, or Wards, large dormitories with a few tables and benches at the end, but, as the school's future historian who arrived at Newgate Street 70 years later, in 1893, discovered, 'they were places from which we were sternly banished all day long, although we had no dayrooms, studies or any other place to spend our time...During the longer periods of leisure we played "Housey rugger"', described later, '...or "spadged"', ie walked aimlessly about.[46]

After the completion of the new buildings little changed at Christ's Hospital for the rest of the century. A Commission of Enquiry, investigating major charities, studied the school in 1837, but its 300-page report made no significant recommendations. The governors, especially the inner ring of Committee Governors, presided over by the Treasurer, who himself resided on the site, continued to manage the school, with the Headmaster enjoying little authority outside the classroom, and the ordinary masters, who left for home each afternoon, none at all. The grecians, originally so called because they learned Greek as well as Latin, remained a small elite destined for Oxford or Cambridge, when they finally left at the age of 19.[47] They lived in small separate rooms, had a 'swab', or fag, to look after them, and enjoyed numerous privileges, from upholstered seats in Christ Church, Newgate Street, which served as the school chapel, to a regular allowance to buy items for their private teas. This last, known as 'Q Shot', which I shall mention again later, survived into my time, though there is still some uncertainty about the correct name. The purpose, however, was clear. A letter dated 1805 refers to grecians having to 'buy themselves...tea, sugar, knives and forks, vegetables', the cost being met by a once-a-term payment.[48] The grecians were almost unbelievably grand, living a life remote from the rest of the school and in no sense prefects, like those introduced by other schools, following Dr Thomas Arnold's reforms while headmaster of Rugby, from 1828-41. Christ's Hospital was run by the monitors, burly and often brutal 15 year olds, waiting to leave for jobs in the City or elsewhere, by the beadles, ex-policemen who watched the boys but did not organise their activities, and by the Dames, uneducated women in charge of their domestic arrangements in the Wards.[49]

In spite of its situation in the heart of London, Christ's Hospital remained behind its encircling wall and prison-like gates a closed and self-sufficient community. For a time it even had its own currency, valid only at the school shop. Boys with homes in London were often given leave to visit their parents for the afternoon but those living elsewhere might see their families only two or three times in all the six or seven years of their schooldays.[50] Holidays, including Christmas, were merely periods without lessons spent at school, since the governors considered that having once accepted a child 'on the foundation' they had accepted full responsibility for feeding, clothing and housing him, or, more rarely her, until he or she left.[51] As late as 1830 'at least' one hundred were on the '"friendless list"...without parents or friends', never receiving a parcel or a visit, for whom the school was their sole home.[52] But even for those with families, it became, far more than a normal boarding school, the centre and ruler of their lives, with even the majority, who did have parents, being treated as if they *were* orphans. Sir John Millais' painting *The Bluecoat Boy's Mother*, exhibited at the Royal Academy in 1867, admirably conveys this situation.[53] It shows a woman gazing as sadly through the Newgate Street railings at her newly admitted, Bluecoat clothed, son as if he had just been carried off to prison.

There was an occasional whole day's leave for everyone, a custom continued, though reduced to once a year, into my time. By then the school no longer attended, as it had formerly, the Royal Exchange on Easter Monday or Tuesday, as some distant benefactor had laid down,[54] bearing a badge reading 'He is risen', which the less pious amended to 'He is a rifleman'. The other big event of the year was St Matthew's Day, 21 September, when the whole school marched from Newgate Street to the Mansion House to receive from the Lord Mayor a shilling, a piece of cake and a glass of wine. The date was 'time-worn' even by CH standards; St Matthew's Day had been the occasion when new governors were appointed since 1577.[55]

The Bluecoat boys, as they were universally known, remained, as in Charles Lamb's time, popular figures in the streets of London. To compensate for the street urchins who shouted 'Mustard pots!' at the sight of their yellow stockings there were tips from good natured citizens who regarded them as public pets, especially the famous 'Bob Gent' who would press a shilling into their hands with the explanation, 'In memory of Charles Lamb'.[56]

The occupants of Newgate Street were certainly in need of all the kindness from strangers they could get for throughout the nineteenth century, and especially until its last quarter, the regime was unrelentingly harsh. From 1819 onwards the old, shared, beds, were gradually replaced by single ones, still in use until the 1980s[57], but the washing facilities until the very end remained, in the view of one user who arrived in 1898, 'primitive and...too closely connected with shoe-cleaning'[58] and the lavatories were always inadequate. Food was poor and insufficient, even by ordinary boarding school standards, indeed the Dining Hall with its meagre fare, on which all witnesses agree, eaten in imposing surroundings, beneath a magnificent roof and vast wall painting, of which I shall say more later, epitomised the contradictory nature of Christ's Hospital, at once so splendid and so mean. The custom of 'trades' whereby the work of serving meals was done by the boys themselves, sounded reasonable enough, though undertaken to save money, but meant that – as I later confirmed for myself – that one might well go hungry. 'When I was "jack boy",' recalled one who entered the school in 1859, 'I hardly had time to take a mouthful of dinner', a 'jack' being the large leather jug used first for beer, then water, and constantly in demand.[59]

Dining Hall was also the scene of another characteristic Christ's Hospital custom, the Public Supper, originally intended to enable the ordinary Londoner to see how his donations were being spent and, incidentally, perhaps, to engender a proper feeling of gratitude among their recipients. By around 1860 the occasions had been restricted to four Thursdays in Lent and were closely regulated but 'going to see the lions fed' remained a popular outing for the visitors, who lined the walls and wandered round the tables as the boys ate their bread and butter and drank their milk, no extra food being provided though the tables were decorated with flowers. Finally the boys marched out in files, led by the 'trades' boys bearing baskets containing any uneaten bread, and the Dames.[60] On the way they bowed, or in the women's case curtsied, to the distinguished visitors. This was defensible when, as sometimes happened, a member of the royal family was present, but the whole procedure became increasingly resented, especially by the Dames, who found it humiliating, and in 1876 they formally asked to be excused from taking part. The governors turned down their request 'in view of the antiquity of the custom', at Christ's Hospital an unanswerable argument.[61] The Public Suppers survived until 28 March 1901, after which, somewhat hypocritically in view of their unpopularity, a black-bordered 'obituary' appeared in *The Blue*, with a melancholy, if prophetic, footnote: 'The old order changeth, yielding place to [the] new.'[62]

One aspect of school life at this time, and earlier, was universally criticised by those forced to endure it, though it could be explained, if hardly justified, by Christ's Hospital's claim to be a religious, as well as an ancient and royal, foundation – a description which still continues as the traditional 'Housey toast'. Even those destined for Holy Orders themselves felt the resulting Sabbatarianism was overdone. 'I had as much religious education squandered on myself,' recalled one schoolmaster, 'as...would have turned a whole regiment of dragoons into missionaries.' Twenty years after he had left, in 1848, remembering 'the gloom and dreariness of our Sundays...I shudder at the recollection of them,' he wrote. Much of the day was spent in Christ Church, seated 'on narrow planks with no back' or kneeling 'on hard boards', but there were also sermons, Bible reading and prayers in the Hall and the Wards, until the day 'appropriately closed...with a singing of the burial anthem'.[63] The boys' only recreation, in their brief period of leisure, was to stand inside the gate and speculate, or bet on, the likely destination of the next bus to appear.[64]

During the second half of the nineteenth century minor changes occurred in many aspects of school life. In 1853 the new steel pens were introduced in place of the old quills and around the same time, although breakfast still consisted merely of 'a crug of bread with dripping', china plates and bowls replaced the traditional wooden platters.[65] In 1859 although Sunday otherwise continued in all its grim rigour, the singing of the Burial Anthem at bedtime ceased. There were even some modifications to that most sacrosanct of institutions, the uniform. One boy who arrived in 1864 found the former separate, lawyer or clergyman style, bands had now been replaced by a new type 'fastened to our shirt collar by means of a pin' and required to 'lie evenly one over the other', the form they were to retain until 1970. This period saw two other, by Christ's Hospital standards, major changes. In 1865 the bright yellow female-style petticoat worn by the boys beneath the Bluecoat and supposed, as mentioned earlier, to discourage vermin, was discarded, but custom was preserved, and unwanted intruders discouraged, by providing a lining of similar colour for the coat itself.[66] Another, even more visible, alteration, had been introduced a little earlier, in 1857, when 'the little black worsted cap, usually carried in the hand' was scrapped, though in use since the very beginning. The reasons were purely practical. The cap had been notoriously liable to fall off and had more often been used as a face flannel than to cover the head. Henceforward, although hats were then almost universally worn, Christ's Hospital boys went bareheaded. It was claimed that, in consequence, they never went bald in later life, an agreeable legend, seriously examined by the *Strand Magazine*, but in fact untrue.[67]

The Bluecoat itself, however, remained unchanged even though every new out of school activity made its impracticality more apparent. An example was military-style drill, which had become popular in workhouse schools as a supposed means of generating smartness and self-respect. When writing *The Workhouse* I learned how, in the 1850s and 1860s, a great enthusiasm for military drill, though as a form of exercise rather than to facilitate movement, swept the local authority Guardians responsible for workhouse schools. Near miraculous results were claimed from adding a drill sergeant to the list of workhouse functionaries. 'Their whole nature seemed changed,' claimed one school superintendent of the boys in his charge, their 'dull, listless, unintelligent air' being replaced by 'a quick, sharp eye and ear, a smartness and pride in [their] personal appearance...Their marching in their weekly walks was the pride and talk of the town.'[68] Some workhouses even adopted a new uniform to show their inmates' new skill off to full advantage. Christ's Hospital's outfit was distinctive enough already, but drill did provide yet another means of reminding the boys of their subservient status, and of rendering the school's processions through the streets even more impressive. Not for the last time the demands of the uniform conflicted with those of innovation. An illustration dating from 1858 shows a long line of boys parading in 'Hospital dress' with their gowns, absurdly and impractically, rolled up on their girdles behind them.[69] Nor was the change popular. Drill was, not long afterwards, the Headmaster reported, 'discontinued...on some supposed ground of distaste for it on the part of the boys', and as an interference with their play-hours', but this, of course, cut no ice with the governors and in 1870 it was reintroduced and a full-time drill Sergeant was added to the staff.[70] Drill henceforward became an inescapable and distinctive feature of Christ's Hospital life, yet another means of setting the Bluecoat School apart from the public schools it was in other respects increasingly attempting to emulate.

---

[1] *CH Book* p.6
[2] Dec 1986 p.260
[3] Dec 1983 p.51
[4] *CH Book* pp.8-11
[5] *CH Book* p.13
[6] *CH Short History* p.10
[7] *CH Book* p.12
[8] Picture in *CH Book* p.27
[9] Morpurgo p.35
[10] *CH Short History* p.4
[11] *The Fortunate Bluecoat Boy* p.vii
[12] *CH Book* xxxi & illus.p.248, Morpurgo p.47
[13] Apr 1962 pp.120-3
[14] *CH Book* p.66
[15] *CH Book* p.37
[16] *CH Book* pp.340-2
[17] *CH Short History* pp.8-9 & *CH Book* p.99
[18] Hunt, *Essays* p.xi. *CH Book* p.145
[19] *CH Book* p.xxxii
[20] *The Fortunate Bluecoat Boy* pp.vii-vii
[21] In *Colonel Jack* – See *The Fortunate Bluecoat Boy* p.vii
[22] *CH Book* p.127
[23] *CH Book* p.77
[24] *CH Book* p.113
[25] *CH Book* p.129

[26] *CH Book* p.124
[27] *CH Book* p.114
[28] *CH Book* pp.115-6
[29] *CH Book* p.179
[30] *CH Book* p.218
[31] *CH Book* p.113
[32] *CH Book* p.113, p.71
[33] *CH Book* p.32
[34] *CH Book* p.175
[35] *Oxford Dictionary of English Literature* pp.120 & 533
[36] *CH Book* pp.175-6
[37] *CH Book* pp.175-6
[38] *CH Book* pp.178-9
[39] *CH Book* p.116
[40] *CH Book* pp.176-7
[41] *CH Book* p.181
[42] *CH Book* p.183 & pp.41-2
[43] *Dictionary of the Christian Church* pp.899 & 1097
[44] Morpurgo p.34
[45] *CH Book* p.174
[46] Allan pp.29-30
[47] Sep 1854 p.192
[48] May 1954 p.113 & Apr 1951 p.118
[49] *CH Book* p.215
[50] Morpurgo p.30
[51] Jan 1968 p.55 & Dec 1982 p.54
[52] Jan 1968 pp.55-6
[53] Reproduced in *CH Book*, facing p.239
[54] *CH Book* p.160
[55] Morpurgo p.37
[56] Morpurgo p.77
[57] Dec 1982 p.54
[58] Sep 1954 p.192
[59] *CH Book* pp.201 & 207-8, *A Book of Housey Slang* p.13
[60] *CH Book* pp.209-12
[61] Seaman p.142
[62] Jul 1951 p.191
[63] *CH Book* pp.230-1
[64] Apr 1950 p.125
[65] Sep 1970 p.293, Sep 1969 p.288, Sep 1969 p.298
[66] *CH Book* p.202 & Summer 1995 p.250
[67] Mar 1972 p.264 & *Strand Magazine* Vol. XXXIV, Dec 1907
[68] *The Workhouse* p.188
[69] *CH Book* facing p.238
[70] Seaman p.80

15

A THOROUGH REFORM

For a thorough reform in the management and discipline of the school, we think that the removal from London is indispensable.

Report *of the Christ's Hospital Inquiry Commission 1877*

Outside the walls of Newgate Street Victorian England was by the 1860s witness to vast changes, in social attitudes as well as technology, and in 1858 the government had launched the first of a whole series of investigations into the national provision for education at every level, from 'cheap elementary instruction' to the great public schools.[1] In December 1864 the Schools Inquiry Commission under a former Liberal minister, the future Lord Taunton, was set up to examine the state of secondary education, then provided by 798 'endowed grammar schools',[2] giving special attention to eight major institutions, Christ's Hospital, to which most time was devoted, being bracketed with Dulwich College, Manchester Grammar School and King Edward VI's School, Birmingham. As the largest, wealthiest and among the most ancient of the group it received special attention, and the nine Commissioners who visited Newgate Street, were enormously impressed, if not overawed, by its mere age and scale, as their vast *Report*, published in 1868, made clear:

> Some consideration seems to be justly due to the past history of so remarkable a school...Christ's Hospital is a thing without parallel in the country.[3]

The specialist, salaried Assistant Commissioner assigned to study the school in detail was less impressed. Daniel Robert Fearon has otherwise no significant place in educational history. He did not appear in the national *Who's Who* when it was launched later in the century and failed to earn a posthumous entry in the *Dictionary of National Biography*. His only book, *School Inspection*, is long forgotten. But DR Fearon, aged 30 during the three months he spent investigating Christ's Hospital early in 1866, remains the one individual to see the dismal reality of deprivation and wasted opportunities that lay behind the venerated facade of Newgate Street. The son of a Suffolk vicar, Fearon was himself the product of one of the crop of new public schools set up in spacious rural sites for upper-middle-class children in the mid-Victorian period; he had in fact been at Marlborough, founded in 1843.[4] He had followed the classic route into the public service, taking a 'first' in Greats at Balliol and, after briefly reading for the Bar, becoming an Inspector of Schools, from which he was seconded to act as Assistant Commissioner to the Schools' Inquiry Commission. (He was to end his career a Charity Commissioner and member of the Athenaeum.)

Fearon, though acknowledging the school's high reputation, nevertheless conscientiously scrutinised in detail the way Christ's Hospital was managed, its academic performance and the boys' life outside the classroom. His findings on all these subjects were scathing, a rare breath of reality in a stagnant atmosphere of complacency and self-congratulation. He was critical of the dominance of the past. 'The school, like a great machine, works on mechanically as it has been set agoing...It has no principle of vitality within itself.' He was critical of the Headmaster's subservience to the Treasurer and Council of Almoners; 'The influence of the Upper Grammar Master [ie Headmaster]...is at Christ's Hospital no greater than that of a junior assistant master in any other school...This is a very bad state of things'.[5] He was critical of the school's much-vaunted scholastic achievements, pointing out that it sent only five boys a year to university, financed by its own exhibitions, but their needs distorted the whole curriculum, so the vast majority of boys, destined to leave at 15, were receiving an education not 'consistent with commonsense and modern enlightenment'.[6] Out of school, matters were even worse. There were no dayrooms or similar amenities and no proper playground, so that 'the Bluecoat boys do not know how to play', while on Sunday, with no opportunity for country walks, 'The boys have nothing to do but lounge about the cloisters.[7] A fives court would help,' he suggested, but to provide proper space for cricket and football, 'a fine piece of grass' was needed and 'nothing but removal into the country would give them this'. Once that occurred the argument for 'some peculiar style of dress...easily recognised' in the streets of London supposed to afford 'much protection to the boys when out on leave in the town' would vanish.[8]

But Fearon's proposed reforms went much further. The boys' preparatory school at Hertford would remain but the Newgate Street site would be sold and the school's endowments be used instead to finance 'a great system of middle-class education for the Home Counties'. It made no sense to have a large boarding school in the City of London when so many of the population now lived outside it. Instead, five new schools, each containing 300 boarders and 300 day-boys should be set up in five rapidly-growing towns such as Chelmsford, Guildford, Maidenhead, St Albans and Sevenoaks, 25 to 30 miles [40 to 48km] from the capital, funded by existing grammar school foundations in the area and by Christ's Hospital, the governors of which would retain the right to nominate, and maintain, half the boarders. By this bold stroke, claimed Fearon, 'All the present evils of the London situation would be avoided. The physical education of the boys would no longer be neglected; contact with the day schools and increased competition for scholarships would greatly develop their intelligence.' Only such a drastic plan could ensure that 'the future of this splendid foundation shall be truly worthy of its great and glorious past.'[9]

Fearon's proposals, despite these fine words, really amounted to abolishing Christ's Hospital and were not accepted by the Commissioners, whose Report, when it appeared in 1868, produced little change. Its chief value lies in the 'Domesday Book' survey it provides of Christ's Hospital at this time. The Commissioners established that Christ's Hospital was vast, with 445 boys (and 18 girls) at Hertford and another 775 at Newgate Street, a total roll of 1238, that it was rich, with an annual income far larger than that of the other schools investigated with it, but that much of this came from Donation Governors, who earned the right to present two children and to join the governing body in return for a once-for-all gift of £500.[10] They were expected, however, only to nominate children in need of assistance, and it was established that in the three years from 1862 to 1864 200 entrants had come from families with an income below £100 a year, another 200 from those earning £100 to £200 and only 16 from parents earning more than £400. Some 300 children were from white collar backgrounds, notably 'tradesmen and deceased merchants'. 84 were the sons of clergy, always a favoured category, 79 the children of other 'professional men' and 39 had military or naval officers as fathers. The tendency, complained of in the past, for children to be drawn from higher up the social scale than the founder had intended, was still evident. 'I should say that now there are many more children from the professions...than formerly,' admitted the Treasurer.[11]

Overall around 230 places were filled by West Gifts, Royal Mathematical School scholarships for the sons of naval officers, and other, sometimes local, charities restricted to particular categories or locations. The remaining 1000 were occupied by children 'presented' by City Aldermen, who could have five or six children each at the school at any time, corporate bodies like the livery companies, and – the largest single category – those nominated by Donation Governors. Here was one curious, distinctive feature of Christ's Hospital, which was to continue into the next century. Its other unique characteristic, of which the general public was far more aware, was the Tudor uniform which, the Commissioners made clear, was not a minor peripheral matter but was closely linked to the whole nature of Christ's Hospital. One eminent witness, the Rev Dr Haig Brown, Old Blue, governor, and Headmaster of Charterhouse, Christ's Hospital's nearest neighbour, described it as 'a positive nuisance...The only thing I was thoroughly glad of at leaving was that I got rid of the dress, so that I could walk along the streets...without being stared at.'[12] The school's President, the Duke of Cambridge, not surprisingly, took a different view. He robustly defended the traditional Bluecoat on the grounds of 'old established habit', the protection it gave the wearer 'from many temptations and many inconveniences...in a large town', which were not defined, and, most important of all, that it discouraged 'lads of a higher class...entering Christ's Hospital. In fact, it keeps it a charitable institution instead of its being an ordinary public school.'[13] This was the same argument, as mentioned earlier, as had been advanced by Charles Lamb 50 years earlier. Daniel Fearon, however, rejected it. Boys entered Christ's Hospital, he contended, 'too young to...feel much of the stigma...of a charity dress' while parents prepared to exploit the system were 'not likely to be affected by their children's annoyance' if they did dislike it.[14]

The School Inquiry Commissioners' Report, when finally published in March 1868, recommended sweeping changes in the way Christ's Hospital was supervised and run, including a drastic reduction in the size and powers of the governing body.[15] In 1865 there were no fewer than 477 governors, including Queen Victoria who had, contrary to the rules, presented a boy, presumably not a member of her own family, who still, at the age of seven, 'did not know his letters.'[16] This total should be sharply reduced to 21, with the Donation Governors being phased out. No recommendation was made about a move to the country and the sensitive question of the uniform was left to be decided by the new Board of Governors.

The Commission, reporting in 1867, acknowledged that Christ's Hospital was unique. Clearly it was not a 'public school', in the conventional, fee-paying sense, for those from well off families were excluded. It was not a local day grammar school, for it offered boarding education from which only a very few would go to universities or enter a profession. But it provided much more than the ordinary elementary school, financed by a parish or local charity. It possessed indeed some of the characteristics of them all and the commissioners decided this situation should continue but that its sights should be set higher than at present. While it might continue to serve as a 'third grade' school, for boys destined to leave at 14 upwards, and a 'second grade', one for those leaving at 16 to enter commerce or a profession, its main role henceforward should be, in the words of a later historian, to provide 'a ladder up which many of the ablest boys of the lower-middle-class would ascend to the Universities'.[17] To achieve this transformation entrants should be recruited by competitive examination at 13 from schools all over the country. Meanwhile the overall numbers should be reduced, Hertford should be sold off and the handful of girls should be transferred to day schools in London.

None of this happened. The principal result of the 1868 *Report* was instead a major expansion and improvement in Christ's Hospital Girls' School, to be described later. But, following the Taunton Commission, Parliament passed the Endowed Schools Act, which became law in August 1869, and created a new body, the Endowed Schools Commissioners, who had powers to persuade, or, in the last resort, compel schools with private endowments to accept changes the Commissioners considered desirable. Christ's Hospital sent a deputation to the ministers responsible, who included the greatest educational reformer of the century, WE Forster, to plead for Christ's Hospital to be excluded, but it failed. The government's only concession was to agree to allow affected schools to prepare their own Draft Schemes for reform for the Commissioners' approval.

During the next decade, while new subjects were introduced, along with, for the first time, external examinations, various minor improvements were made in the school's recreational facilities. In 1868 a school band was founded, in response to a request from the boys, the first instruments and the bandmaster's salary being paid for privately by the Treasurer;[18] members of the governing body, though reluctant to spend the foundation's funds on amenities for the children in their care were prepared to be generous with their own money. Drill, abolished as unpopular, was soon afterwards, as mentioned earlier, brought back. The combination of marching, uniform and band produced just that type of disciplined, army-style display in which the governors delighted and in July 1871 the Council of Almoners formally adjourned 'to witness the parade of the boys to music in the Hall Playground and their march (as recently introduced) into the Great Hall to dinner'.[19] This was the origin of the ritual of Dinner Parade which still in my time dominated the Housey day.

The chief beneficiary of the 1868 *Report* was, ironically, since the Commissioners had wished to uproot it, Christ's Hospital Girls' School. To the governors this had long been regarded as a source of embarrassment rather than pride and it had only escaped being closed down altogether because the Wests had specified that at least 18 of the places financed by their bequest must be filled by females.[20] The unique, saving virtue of Christ's Hospital Boys' School, the opportunity it gave them to rise above their origins, was wholly lacking at Hertford. 'The subjects of instruction as at present used,' the then Headmistress of the Girls' School had told the Commission of Enquiry, in 1866, 'have been found suitable to the class from which the girls have generally come.'[21] 'The standard in 1870 was that of an old-fashioned charity school,' wrote a later Headmistress.[22] Most girls left at 15 and any who remained till 16 and showed academic promise were sent to finish their education elsewhere.

The school had, however, happily copied the worst aspects of Christ's Hospital, London. 'Punishments were relatively as severe as in the Boys' School....' admitted the Headmistress just quoted, 'even for such trivial offences as gossiping.'[23] The uniform, too, though different from that of the boys, had barely changed since the seventeenth century, but while the Bluecoat was widely respected, at least in the streets of London, the girls equally anachronistic outfit, consisting of 'a green or brown skirt, a blue woollen bodice and green apron...white cap and collar' merely, the same authority considered, made them 'conspicuous' and objects of ridicule.[24]

Significantly, it was discarding the antiquated uniform which unlocked the floodgates of reform. In March 1875 the governing body, reluctantly forced to admit that the girls' school was 'no credit to the Hospital in its present...condition' agreed that the traditional outfit should be scrapped in favour of 'a neat, useful dress...more assimilated than at present to that worn by other young people', a visible sign of the transformation that now began. Numbers were raised, initially to 50 – they ultimately reached around 280 – and a new 'Principal Mistress, able to undertake general English education, French, Drawing' was appointed, along with other qualified staff, the curriculum later being widened to include science.[25] A whole series of improvements in living conditions was introduced, so that before long the girls, with a dayroom for use out of school hours, and playing fields nearby – cricket was introduced in 1878 – were in the provision for out-of-school activities better served than the boys.[26]

Christ's Hospital, London, meanwhile, was slow to cater adequately for sport, for reasons rooted in the school's nature as well as its cramped site. As a later Headmaster wrote, 'the idea that it was justifiable to expend charitable funds upon games was slow to take root at Christ's Hospital', and even the Duke of Cambridge admitted there was no room for a cricket pitch on the cramped 5 acre [2 ha] site, of which half was occupied by buildings.[27] There was also, and always, that perpetual obstacle to progress, the uniform. 'Football matches were played before breakfast,' recorded one Old Blue, at Newgate Street from 1869-75, because 'the wearing of jerseys instead of the cumbrous long blue coats was then alone permitted'.[28] The oldest boys did not take part because 'the grecians...were not allowed to endanger their precious limbs upon the asphalt'.[29] On the rare occasions when the school played an outside team it was almost invariably beaten.

Within the walls of Newgate Street a distinctive form of football played with a spherical ball but involving hands as well as feet, and known as 'Housey rugger' evolved,[30] with the gymnasium door and an archway serving as goals, though as the game was played on an asphalt space between the buildings 'concussions and broken limbs were not unknown'. To reduce the risk of injury the practice of 'tackling high' rather than low was encouraged, to the astonishment of opponents who later faced Old Blue teams.

Situated close to the Thames, Christ's Hospital could well have developed a rowing tradition, but a Boat Club, established in 1861, was nearly stifled by the Council of Almoners, who were horrified at the suggestion that its members should wear 'Boating Flannels' on their way to and from the river and only reluctantly accepted that rowing in Tudor dress would be impractical if not dangerous.[31*] Only after a fierce argument with the Headmaster was it reluctantly agreed that the grecians could wear 'private' clothes, on such outings and on certain other occasions, as when attending university interviews.

---

[*] This was clearly true. At one time an annual swimming race was held between boys in school uniform, but it was abandoned for good after one competitor, thanks to his clothing, nearly drowned, a martyr to tradition.

At other times, even during the holidays, for a non-grecian to be caught out of uniform was grounds for instant expulsion. Behind this draconian policy lay the belief, to which the President of Christ's Hospital, the intensely conservative Duke of Cambridge, was committed, that it was above all the uniform which gave Christ's Hospital its distinctive identity and kept it true to its founder's purpose. It was little wonder that, as the non-Old Blue historian GC Coulton observed, 'A passion for conspicuous dress, in reaction from the monotonous Bluecoat uniform' was 'a marked characteristic' among Old Blue undergraduates at Cambridge in the 1870s.[32]

Perhaps because it raised no problems about dress the best provision for games at Newgate Street was for swimming. Until 1869 the boys took the long walk to the open-air Peerless Pool at Islington, a distinct misnomer since it was notoriously cold and covered 'with green slime and smuts'. Then a bath was built at Newgate Street, though it was too small for races, for which Lambeth Baths had to be used.[33] Two enduring traditions had by now been established. The boys bathed in the nude, as was, of course, common among Victorian males, and a stern attitude was adopted towards non-swimmers, who were encouraged to learn by venturing out of their depth with a porter on duty 'to rescue the distressed by extending a long wooden pole.'[34]

When athletics began to come into fashion the main events were at first 'Climbing the Ropes' and 'Stone Gathering', but from 1876 the annual Sports took place on a rented field at Herne Hill. The only sport for which there *was* room was Fives, two courts being constructed in 1871 as a direct result of the suggestion of that great but unacknowledged benefactor of Christ's Hospital, Daniel Fearon.[35]

In 1868, a few weeks after the *Report* of the Taunton Commission had appeared, a new Headmaster, the Rev GL (George) Bell, was appointed, an Old Blue classicist and mathematician who went on to become headmaster of Marlborough.[36] In the intervening eight years he introduced a number of innovations, from physics and German to a reduction in the number of services on Sunday and a bread and cheese snack at bedtime. In 1869 he was invited to join the newly founded Headmasters' Conference and over the next few years Christ's Hospital acquired other marks of the public school: a debating society, an old boys' association, the CH Club, an annual Speech Day and Concert, a school song, the *Votum* (Vow) and, of enormous value to me in writing this book, a school magazine *The Blue*, first published in 1870.[37] To another institution established a little later, I feel less gratitude, the Christ's Hospital Fire Brigade, founded with the help of the famous head of the London Fire Brigade, later Sir Eyre Massey Shaw, immortalised as 'Captain Shaw' in *Iolanthe*.[*] I shall describe later how I became familiar with the school's ancient

---

[*] See *Iolanthe,* Act II. Shaw was present at its opening night, 25 November 1882.

buckets and hand pumps, the very ones, I suspect, bought at Shaw's suggestion.[38]

Although now required to remain into the evening to supervise prep the staff still played no part in the general life of the school[39]. On his final Speech Day in 1876 George Bell expressed the hope that his successor 'might see the day when Blues should worship in their own chapel, when their Masters should live among them and...when the boys should find their playgrounds close to their doors,' a modest enough blueprint for the future but one which clearly involved leaving Newgate Street.[40]

This issue had dominated all others for years. A vote by the Council of Almoners in December 1869, directly after the Inquiry Commission's *Report*, in favour of a move, had rapidly been reversed. In 1872 the doubters had been won over by an offer for the site of £600,000, double their own estimate of its value, from the Mid-London Railway, but this had fallen through. It made little sense to make overdue improvements to buildings likely soon to be abandoned and what was called the Christ's Hospital Controversy – Should the school leave its ancient home for the suburbs or countryside? – was soon a matter of public debate.

The only significant change in the last quarter of the nineteenth century was the introduction, around 1878, of normal holidays spent at home.[41] Life in term time for the 775 boys aged ten to 19 crowded into Newgate Street remained exceedingly tough despite the improvements introduced by George Bell. How tough was now to be tragically and publicly demonstrated. On the morning of Wednesday 4 July 1877* a twelve-year-old boy called William Gibbs was found hanging from a ventilator cord in the school Infirmary. An outcry in the press and questions in the House of Commons followed and the Home Secretary set up a high-powered Commission of Inquiry, under Spencer Walpole MP, which included WE Forster MP and John Walter MP, former editor of *The Times*. Its terms of reference included investigating 'the discipline and management' of the school as well as the suicide itself, and it undertook its task with speed and thoroughness, seeing 63 witnesses and meeting nine times in a fortnight, so that its Report was ready by 10 August.[42]

William Gibbs, it soon emerged, had been a troublesome boy who would today have been accurately, if euphemistically, described as possessing special needs. His own parents – his father was a glass painter in Hoxton – had at various times 'chained him to the fire place and fed him upon bread and water' and carried him to a previous school 'trussed and tied'. Every school he had attended, including Christ's Hospital, Hertford, had been glad to see the back of him. Yet William was the sort of boy who might have been expected to enjoy the rough and tumble of boarding school life. He was a good swimmer and athlete, had joined the school band and showed some promise, though clearly not a future grecian, in arithmetic and geography.[43] He was, however, a liar, a thief and a disruptive influence – one 'crime' for which he was caned on the hand was mockingly repeating the drill-sergeant's words of command – and he proved too much even for the traditional Christ's Hospital methods of taming a rebel. In the last few days before his death he had been repeatedly caned by masters, struck on the face by a monitor, punched until his nose bled by another boy, and, after running home to Hoxton on 23 June, been formally birched, 'receiving eight strokes on the bare bottom'. Faced with a further summons to the Headmaster, and no doubt a further flogging, William had run away again, warning his father he would hang himself if sent back to Christ's Hospital. When he was nevertheless returned and locked up to await a further birching – the Treasurer decided to be 'merciful' and substitute this for expulsion – he duly carried out his threat.[44]

The inquest verdict was 'suicide while of unsound mind'; the school had, on the face of it, got off lightly. But poor William's death was to bring about what decades of criticism and debate had failed to achieve, for the Commission of Inquiry highlighted again all the faults that the Taunton Commission had identified ten years before and that the school authorities, which meant the Treasurer and Almoners for the Headmaster still had no real power, had in the meantime done nothing to remedy. No fewer than three Old Blue headmasters of other public schools gave evidence. George Bell, now at Marlborough, declared his 'feeling...that the satisfactory solution of the problem is to remove the school out of London. I felt it so when I first came', to Newgate Street, 'and every year that I stopped deepened my impression.'[45] The Headmaster of Charterhouse, having presided over its move to Godalming from Clerkenwell in 1872, said that in 1866 he had believed Christ's Hospital should stay where it was but now had changed his mind. The Headmaster of Blundells, appointed to the post at the remarkably young age of 26, considered 'that the absence of resident assistant masters is a very bad thing indeed' producing 'a most lamentable backwardness in the whole tone of the lower school'[46], but in London, the Commission heard, it was 'impossible' to accommodate such staff on site. The Commission made detailed enquiries into the nature and number of the floggings administered in recent years and solemnly inspected the birch used, but, somewhat feebly, were 'not prepared to advise the absolute discontinuance of corporal punishment at Christ's Hospital'.[47] They expressed the hope, destined to be disappointed, that 'such punishments should be diminished as far as possible, so as to lead and persuade the boys by kind treatment rather than compel them by the rude methods so much in favour in former times'.[48] They wanted to see the authority of the 15-year-old monitors limited – William Gibbs had given his fear of them as a reason for running away – with the grecians supervising younger boys' activities instead of holding aloof from them. The Headmaster should, as elsewhere, be able to appoint the teaching staff – the Treasurer had argued that 'Those who pay their salaries ought to have the selection and the dismissal of them' – and he, not the Warden, usually a retired officer, and the Beadles, should be responsible for discipline.

With the staff no longer non-resident a new relationship should develop between them and the boys:[49]

> The younger masters at least might join in the games, and thus a sympathy and confidence might grow up, which really has been found to exist in other schools, but which can hardly be expected in a school where the intercourse of masters and boys is systematically confined to hearing lessons and inflicting punishment.[50]

None of these desirable changes, however, could be achieved without another, far more fundamental, the uprooting of Christ's Hospital from its historic home. About this proposal the five members of the Committee were positively apologetic:

> We should not enter on this subject were it not that...such removal bears strongly upon the matters into which we are directed to enquire. It has been pressed upon us by eminent authorities...that this removal is absolutely necessary in order to enable the Headmaster, with his staff of assistant masters, to exercise control over the boys, which is so advantageously exercised in all other large schools...We feel a great unwillingness to aid in destroying the ancient traditions and venerable memories of the place. But these associations may be too dearly purchased, and for a thorough reform in the management and discipline of the school, we think that the removal from London is indispensable...Probably all the defects in management and discipline which are complained of at Christ's Hospital, and which cannot be effectually cured while it remains in its present cramped situation, would disappear under the government of an able and judicious Headmaster, if once the school were removed to a spacious site in the country.[51]

Christ's Hospital was always newsworthy and the Report attracted widespread attention. The *Annual Register* neatly summed up the Committee's conclusions as publicised in the press:

> They find many serious causes of complaint in the general management of the school but these, they say, are...faults inherent in the system. They recommend the removal of the school.[52]

Henceforward those struggling to prevent the Bluecoat Boys leaving Newgate Street were fighting a losing battle, especially after, in 1881, the Charity Commissioners had produced what became known as the 'first scheme' for the foundation's reorganisation. A bitter and protracted battle followed as the governors disputed the Commissioners' right to dictate to them on the grounds that 'Christ's Hospital was much more than an educational institution' and in particular defended the traditional right of the Donation Governors to select their own nominees to attend it.[53] An amended 'second scheme' duly came into operation on 1 January 1891. This required the Council of Almoners to provide 'buildings suitable, in the case of the Boys' School for 700 boarders, in the case of the Girls' School for 350 boarders, in the case of the Preparatory School for 120 boarders...within a convenient distance from the City of London'. Although the Council of Almoners and Treasurer still retained the final authority the Headmaster was now given power to decide on 'the method of teaching...and generally the whole internal organisation, management and discipline'[54] of the school and there was a major change in the admission arrangements, with 179 places allocated to children from London elementary schools, the selection process being conducted by the London County Council[55] through the type of 'Special Place' examination I have already described in the case of Berkshire. These 'LCC scholarships' soon became the traditional source of the brightest children and the major source of future grecians.

The standard was certainly high. The future journalist John Middleton Murry, one of 30 candidates from London Board, ie elementary, schools, competing for only six scholarships in 1900, found himself asked to identify a passage from *Tristram Shandy* and to name some of Tobias Smollett's novels. He did both successfully but still only came second in the final list.[*]

Meanwhile life at Newgate Street continued unchanged. One annual ritual, much enjoyed but revealing the violence that lurked below the surface was the celebration of Bonfire Night. 'For days before 5th November,' one Old Blue of the 1887 to 1892 generation has recorded, 'we were busy making truncheons out of brown paper wrapped round a ruler to form a tube. The cylinders were filled with paper balls and tamped down hard.' On the great day 'the air was full of flying truncheons...with hundreds of boys wrestling, pushing and fighting, either to protect their own or destroy another Ward's Guy.'[56] Later various Wards in turn became 'Guardians of the Guy', being deemed to have won the resulting battle if the effigy emerged intact from three full circuits of the playground. Sometimes a currently unpopular individual was substituted for Guy Fawkes. 'One such figure chosen by us,' recalled a boy who left in 1899, 'was the editor of a leading London daily paper...Strapped to a chair mounted on two bed-poles and wearing his silk top hat and frock coat, he was trotted round the big playground before breakfast six times,' as the prelude to a 'terrific battle' later in the day, which left 'plenty of minor casualties on both sides'.[57] It was no doubt the latter which caused, around 1900, the suppression of the whole tradition.[58]

---

[*] Murry vindicated his selection, duly winning an Oxford scholarship in classics and becoming a major figure in London literary society. He later married the writer Katherine Mansfield.

A more enduring custom which still flourished in my time involved violence on a lesser but more personal scale, the Bonfast. This had become established when the school only enjoyed one real holiday at home each year, the mid-August vacation, the approach of which led to almost unendurable excitement. In addition to the calendars, crossed off each day, common at boarding schools, Christ's Hospital had a well observed tradition to mark the shortening gap to the end of term as one Old Blue explained to the readers of the *Illustrated London News* in 1857. When the end of term was only 50 days off, he explained, all his Ward mates would 'turnover', ie beat, 'the boy whose bed was marked with the number of the days that August was distant…and so each boy was served (and not unwillingly) till August was only three days off and then turning over was indiscriminate.' At least one master, not ready to let such a chance slip, joined in caning the unfortunate Bonfast Boy for no other reason than his school number.

The deficiencies of Christ's Hospital, London – its inadequate facilities and tradition of violence – as well as its private language, were neatly illustrated by one revealing anecdote recounted by Middleton Murry, one of the very last to arrive there in January 1901. While queuing up for the lavatories he confessed incomprehension when asked by an older boy 'Have you got any bodge?' 'There was a moment's dead silence, while he stared at me dumbfounded. Then he slapped my face, well and truly. "That's a fotch," he said…'And bodge is paper. Have you got any?"'[59]

The last decade of the nineteenth century was dominated by the search for a new site, while the die-hards struggled to prevent the move going ahead. The most determined opponent was the school's own President, who at a public meeting at the Mansion House predicted 'absolute ruin' if the boys ceased to be 'seen by this great community of London'.[60] Other objections voiced in the press were that poor parents would no longer be able to visit their children, that employers would be unable to drop into Newgate Street whenever they had a vacancy to fill, or governors wander in from their offices to keep an eye on 'their' school, and, somewhat curiously, that the school would no longer 'be within easy reach of Her Majesty and the Princesses'.[61] There was general agreement that the Tudor uniform would not survive in the country – indeed, suggested one Old Blue, a future bishop, despairingly, 'it might be better to introduce at once a more appropriate costume'.[62] By June 1892, after considering more than a hundred different properties, the Council had decided, both bravely and far-sightedly, to purchase a 1200 acre [486 ha] site two miles [3.2km] south of Horsham in Sussex, from the Aylesbury Dairy Company for £47,500.[63] The critics were outraged. The site was too big, too far from London and potentially unhealthy. 'If the Aylesbury Dairy Company could not farm their cows, at a profit,' it was asked, 'could it be a good site for boys?'[64] A timely outbreak of scarlet fever, which caused the school to be closed for nine months from October 1893, made Newgate Street seem less appealing and an offer by the London, Brighton and South Coast Railway to build a special station for the school, with a cheap day return from London costing half-a-crown [2s 6d, 12.5p] answered the 'remoteness' argument[65]. A determined campaign by a governor in favour of a 15 acre [6 ha] plot at Wimbledon, which he just happened to own, finally failed.[66] From six competitors, the future Sir Aston Webb, later president of the Royal Institute of British Architects, was chosen to design the new school, along with a less well-known figure, Ingress Bell.

The foundation stone was duly laid, with elaborate Masonic ceremonies, by the Prince of Wales, the future Edward VII, on Founder's Day, 23 October 1897,* in 'bitterly cold and bleak' conditions which showed the Sussex countryside at its very worst.[67] Before leaving London the school was treated to a valedictory sermon from the Archbishop of Canterbury in St Pauls. 'He...told us,' one of those present recalled, 'that there were certain bad customs among us which he begged us not to transplant into the country. What these bad customs were, other than owling** and fotching, we were at a loss to know.'[68]

On the last day of the Lent Term, 18 April 1902, the boys said farewell to the school's ancient home in a most untypical orgy of sentiment, formally shaking hands with the Headmaster, who was retiring, before the grecians, each holding a lighted candle, 'beat the bounds' by kicking the walls at various well-known spots, and 'having solemnly extinguished their candles...marched up and down three times, singing lustily *Auld Lang Syne*'.[69]

During the extended Easter holidays which followed, one boy returned for a nostalgic look at the now empty premises. Already four hundred years of history were being obliterated and amid the 'piles of planks and scaffold-poles' stood a poignant notice:

GOOD, OLD
BRICKS
FOR SALE[70]

---

* Not 1896 as stated by Morpurgo p.75.
** The *Dictionary of Housey Slang* defines an 'owl' as 'A hit on the head with a closed fist'. A 'fotch' is described earlier in this chapter and will be mentioned again later.

[1] Woodward p.461
[2] Morpurgo p.69
[3] *CH Book* p.339
[4] H. Cox, *Who's Who In Kent Surrey and Sussex,* 1911
[5] Seaman p.53
[6] Seaman p.56
[7] Seaman p.57
[8] Seaman pp.57, 59
[9] Seaman pp.60-1
[10] Seaman pp.50, 46
[11] Seaman pp.47-8
[12] Seaman p.60
[13] Seaman p.59
[14] Seaman p.60
[15] Seaman p.69
[16] Seaman p.48
[17] Seaman p.62
[18] Jun 1998 p.105
[19] Seaman pp.82-3
[20] Morpurgo p.25
[21] Seaman p.51
[22] *CH Book* p.342
[23] *CH Book* op.cit
[24] *CH Book* p.343
[25] Seaman pp.97-8
[26] *CH Book* p.344
[27] Seaman pp.119, 58
[28] *CH Book* p.224
[29] *CH Book* p.222
[30] *CH Book* pp.225-6
[31] Seaman pp.92-4
[32] *CH Book* p.261
[33] Seaman pp.120-1
[34] *CH Book* p.228
[35] Seaman pp.120-3
[36] Seaman p.71
[37] Seaman p.82
[38] Seaman p.95
[39] Seaman p.92
[40] Seaman p.112
[41] Morpurgo p.30
[42] Seaman p.20
[43] Seaman pp.22-4
[44] Seaman p.25
[45] Seaman p.38
[46] Seaman p.35

[47] Seaman p.40
[48] Seaman p.40
[49] Seaman p.31
[50] Seaman p.40
[51] Morpurgo p.70 & Seaman p.41
[52] *Annual Register*, 1877 p.81
[53] Allan pp.7-8
[54] *CH Book* p.247
[55] Morpurgo p.125
[56] Jan 1970 p.72
[57] Jan 1960 p.57
[58] Apr 1960 p.109
[59] *CH Book* p.265
[60] Morpurgo p.74
[61] *CH Book* p.250
[62] *CH Book* p.204
[63] Allan p.80 & *Short History* p.11
[64] Allan pp.80-1
[65] Allan pp.80-1
[66] Allan pp.82-3
[67] *CH Book* p.252
[68] *CH Book* p.257
[69] *CH Book* p.254
[70] *CH Book* pp.257-8

16

TRANSPLANTED

It was he who mastered the herculean job of transplanting Christ's Hospital from its almost parochial city background to the green acres of Sussex.

Philip Youngman Carter, at Christ's Hospital 1916-21, on the Rev Dr Upcott, Headmaster 1902-19

On Thursday 29 May 1902 Christ's Hospital Boys School assembled, re-united, in its new home near Horsham. The girls had been left behind at Hertford, but the 120 smaller boys, aged eight to ten, were now accommodated in the Preparatory block at the western end of the Avenue, where they lived a separate life from the main school, 700 strong, aged from ten to 19, though few boys stayed on after 15.

The boys had been met on arrival at the brand new and imposing six platform station by the impressive figure of their new Headmaster and led up past the former cowsheds, now forming the gym and swimming baths, across the seemingly endless but as yet unmarked out playing fields to the Avenue and their new homes in the boarding Houses.

This populist gesture was untypical. So too was one which followed soon afterwards, for by a happy chance the school had hardly arrived in its new home when, on 31 May, the South African War officially ended, an event celebrated by what was to become a tradition on great national occasions, a bonfire on Sharpenhurst Hill which overlooked the new school. The Headmaster presided and led the singing of *Rule Britannia*, in striking contrast to his customary aloofness.

The Rev Dr AW Upcott was a curious choice as first Headmaster for the newly re-formed school. Most unusually, he was not an Old Blue and he was far from being the open-minded and progressive innovator the situation demanded. Upcott was, though Queen Victoria had just died, a Victorian figure, the last, as it turned out, of the school's clerical headmasters, with the then customary doctorate of divinity and classics degree, though the Christ's Hospital grecians in their arrogant way dismissed him as a poor scholar and considered his teaching 'an insult'.[1]

But Upcott's other defects were not yet apparent. Instead, what everyone was immediately conscious of was the unaccustomed sense of space and a feeling of liberation. 'To me the new school seemed like heaven by comparison with...London and Hertford', testifies one boy, aged 13 at the time of 'the Great Trek', with an 'almost miraculous improvement in the whole atmosphere'.[2] On all sides everyone sensed a new beginning. The Royal Mathematical School, for so long virtually a separate establishment, was now integrated into the main foundation, its members identified merely by a distinctive shoulder plate, and the grecians lost much of the almost lordly status they had formerly enjoyed. They were indeed worse off, losing their separate common room and independent way of life and becoming in effect the senior monitors in each House.

The architects had ingeniously incorporated some features – statues, a wall, part of a cloister – brought from London in the new buildings, and much of the equipment also came from Newgate Street, including the Dining Hall tables, the unyielding wooden-slatted beds and the clumsy metal settles. Numerous traditions had also survived the move, including 'trades' and punishment drill, though the old disciplinary machine of Warden and Beadles was now replaced by that of resident masters and school sergeants. Marching, with greater distances to cover, featured far more prominently in daily life than before and the uniform, despite the forebodings of the traditionalists, had not been left behind in London.

The surroundings, however, were totally different. To the sharp eye of the travel writer EV Lucas the new buildings resembled 'an arrogant brick town'[3] and the only one which, much later, pleased the great architectural authority Sir Nikolaus Pevsner was the station which he considered 'actually a better building than the Hospital itself'.[4] When, in the 1940s, I wrote as an exercise, an essay on the architecture of Christ's Hospital, what struck me then, as it does even more strongly now, was the contrast between the generous provision made for 'learning', in the shape of classrooms and laboratories, and the meagre penny-pinching policy adopted towards 'lodging'. The Charity Commissioners had indeed struck out some of the softening ornaments and architectural flourishes proposed by Webb and Bell,[5] but they could hardly be blamed for the living conditions which, even when they were brand new, a party of visiting architects described as 'spartan', that word so often used of both Newgate Street and Horsham. The design of the Houses had clearly been influenced by the 1877 Commission of Enquiry which had proposed that 'for the sake of economy...the present system of placing boys in large wards', though with more space between the beds, should continue. (The Commissioners were also responsible for suggesting that 'the masters' house might be built with doors opening into every ward', though, as I make plain later, in my house at least this proved ineffective.) A dayroom was at last provided, but only one for all 50 boys in a House, and the washing facilities, changing rooms and the rest reflected the Victorian age, now past, rather than the new century.

The physical separation of the houses, their independence jealously guarded by their new housemasters, removed one benefit of the companionable squalor of Newgate Street, the ability to make friends throughout the school. Now began the ludicrous practice of restricting one's choice of friends to the few people of the same seniority in the same house. 'For one in Peele to make a friend in Maine [at the far end of the Avenue] was not only frustrated by distance but incurred the risk of suspicion of moral turpitude,' recalled one Edwardian Old Blue.[6]

An equal parochialism extended to the school itself. The school was a major employer in the area but kept itself aloof from other contact with the locals who were often, as I discovered 30 years later, ignorant of the most elementary details about it. Similarly, membership of any outside organisation was discouraged. The Old Blue just quoted remembers when Dr Upcott, addressing the assembled school in the Dining Hall, 'called down the wrath to come and fire from heaven on some unnamed boy who had dared to write to the Horsham scoutmaster to ask him to form a troop at CH'.[7]

The uniform, despite the gloomy predictions of *The Times* and other opponents of the move, survived unaltered, but one colourful opportunity for individual expression rapidly disappeared. For swimming in public, recalls the same observer, 'we wore Edwardian varied costumes of our own choice', but those were now replaced by 'standardised bathing triangles',[8] though presumably, only, as in my day, when visitors were present.

In many respects the move seemed to have achieved all that the reformers who had campaigned for it had hoped. Frustrated games players welcomed the almost unlimited space available for cricket and later football and there was so much land available that the first pitches were said to have been allocated on the basis of the first house-captain to arrive in a desirable area staking his claim, as in a goldfield. The masters, just as planned, were soon involved not merely in sport but other out of school activities and a spirit of forward-looking expectation prevailed in the newly built Masters Common Room; in Newgate Street, with its daily exodus at 4.15 pm one had hardly been needed. Half of the 40 staff were also new, and mainly young, with no temptation to look back nostalgically to Newgate Street and free as yet of the traditional schoolmaster's cynicism. One master who arrived in 1904 and was to spend his whole career there, like several others, recalled this period 50 years later as 'a sort of renaissance, a veritable springtime of energy and hope'. Some of his colleagues 'seemed to my young eyes,' he recalled, 'to burn with loyalty to the school' and 'made a complete surrender of their own interests in the service of the boys...Few of them found time or inclination to marry. Marriage was a betrayal and children a reprehensible distraction' – though, as he acknowledged, 'it was by no means easy for a young master to marry' on a modest salary of £150 a year.*

When not under the eye of their housemasters the boys had frequent contact with the new matrons, who had replaced the somewhat Dickensian figures of the Ward Dames. Their duties were now domestic and medical, not disciplinary or pastoral, but they were no doubt even more underpaid than the masters. They feature little in the recollections of Old Blues though one at least, a few years later, showed how times had changed. She actually gave a house-captain she considered impertinent a slap on the cheek so that 'Small boys...whispered as she swept past, "She fotched a grecian!"'[9] Not all the grecians, however, meekly accepted their newly reduced status. Another, reproved by his housemaster for entering the house by the central door, a privilege reserved for the staff, is said to have 'replied haughtily: 'But I saw Mr Smith passing that way and he is a mere usher.'[10] **

To one six year old, visiting an older brother in the Prep in 1905, the school seemed 'a desert of ugly brick with tiny new trees struggling to grow along the Avenue', but the reaction of those who remembered Newgate Street was different. One who had spent five uncomfortable years in London felt that at Horsham by contrast, 'Everything was spiffing!! The Science School! The Showers!'[11] This first euphoria cooled a little as the new arrivals realised that they were now cut off from their parents and friends. An afternoon out in Horsham once a term was a poor substitute for the old system of passes for Wednesday and Saturday afternoons which had enabled boys who lived in London to go home and everyone, if they could find a relative or friend to sponsor them, to visit such places as Madame Tussauds and Kew Gardens. Horsham was a pleasant enough town but offered no comparable attractions and its citizens received the newcomers with polite indifference rather than enthusiasm. I never heard of anyone meeting a 'Bob Gent' on its streets, or any similar benefactor, like the kindly individuals who, on spotting a hungry looking Bluecoat boy in the City, would take him to the nearest pastry cooks to stuff himself with whatever took his fancy. These unavoidable disadvantages apart, not everyone preferred their new home. One who had made the move after two terms at Newgate Street confessed to looking back with regret to the rough and tumble of before breakfast rugger played on the asphalt. Now the day started

---

* Of the three masters who joined the school at this time and who later taught me one (ACW Edwards, quoted above) was excellent, one (C Blamire Brown) totally incompetent, one (E Hyde), was by then, during the second world war, adequate but uninspired. About a fourth (HA Rigby) I remain undecided. I shall say more of all four later.

** The grecian involved is said to have been the subsequently famous educational psychologist, Cyril Burt. The rule still existed in my day, though manifestly absurd, since the door gave on to the Grecians' Path which 'button grecians' could use. A photograph in the illustrations shows me in front of the forbidden door.

much less enjoyably with a 'half-hour [of] study followed by half an hour in Chapel.'[12]

By the time Christ's Hospital left Newgate Street the regime of almost continuous Sunday services described earlier had become somewhat less demanding but at Horsham, having now, at last, its own chapel the school made full use of it. The young John Middleton Murry, totally lacking, as he later acknowledged, in 'religious susceptibility' found that in place of the single Sunday morning service at Christ Church, Newgate Street, 'when,' he recalled, 'my own main office was...tickling the feet of a bigger boy during the sermon...there was morning chapel every day and an evening chapel for the saints' days. This was one of the innovations which we felt it our duty to resent.'[13]

One sermon at this time became legendary. The preacher was a science master WR Kelsey, 'a wizened creature with an Edwardian black beard, who carried his head perpetually on one side' and whose 'genteel accent...made him a mimic's joy', his favourite exclamation being mocked as 'Oew!' 'Late in life he took Holy Orders...which automatically put him on rota to preach in chapel':

> This duty he performed once only, for in pulpit he was seized with a divine frenzy which proved a wild verbose tap in which the washer refused to function.
>
> After an hour – it was a Sunday evening and we were hungrily awaiting tea – he came to the likely words, 'And noew...' – we rose to our feet as a body – 'I come to my seventeenth point'. We re-seated ourselves with a sigh...
>
> When he reached his twenty-fifth point the Headmaster, whom we had all been watching with one eye, passed a note to the school Beadle, a colossus called Lovegrove, who moved majestically out of chapel and rang a bell in the quadrangle without cessation until a messenger recalled him. Kelsey, thus reduced to ignominy and ultimate silence, became wildly popular. Hitherto he had been a figure of fun cultivated only by the *cognoscenti*, but now he swept to fame and affection as the school's personal comedian.[14]

Such diversions were all too rare, so that even those who were not natural agnostics were often left feeling 'that the time that they had spent upon their knees at school was sufficient to last them through life', for the new Head was determined 'to beg or bully his charges into communion with their Maker' and 'to build a great school after the Rugby pattern'.[15] To one of his charges, at Horsham from 1907-17, the Head seemed 'a reincarnation of Dr Arnold', a comparison not intended as a compliment. 'On Sunday he preached "Suffer little children to come unto Me", but on Monday it was "Come unto me little children and suffer".'[16] Another Old Blue, proposing the health of the school of a Founder's Day dinner 60 years later, compared his old headmaster to the fictional Dr Grimston in RH Anstey's famous school novel *Vice Versa*, first published in 1882.[17] 'It was Grimston's boast,' recalled this distinguished Old Blue, 'that "I will instil a spirit of cheerfulness into this school even if I have to flog every boy for as long as I can stand over him".'[*]

Upcott's nickname, 'The Butch', short for 'butcher', speaks for itself.[18] Oddly, early in his time as Headmaster he had produced 'an almost miraculous improvement in the whole atmosphere of the school', believed one of those present, by assembling it in the Dining Hall to hear what became known as 'Upcott's Edict'. This called for a major reduction in corporal punishment of all kinds, especially the unofficial violence practised by the monitors, and a threat to beat bullies personally. This had a profound effect for 'his burly frame made the prospect of being caned especially unpleasant.'[19] In due course, this observer recalls, one victim 'was required to display himself in the dorm' of Thornton A, 'and we viewed with awe and wonder the multi-coloured weals and appraised the accuracy of their application'. In fact Upcott had by his, and the school's standards, been merciful. The beaten boy had committed an offence, unspecified but not hard to identify, for which his partner had been expelled.

Here is another example of the school's reluctance to get rid of offenders whom elsewhere would almost certainly have been sent packing, since, as mentioned earlier, it was recognised that to strike someone 'off the foundation' and transfer back to his parents the whole cost of maintaining, as well as educating him – girls rarely seem to have merited expulsion – was primarily to punish them; it also involved a most unwelcome acknowledgement that a school which had been taming troublesome children from rough backgrounds for several centuries had failed. This policy had its compensations for the Headmaster for Dr Upcott showed absolutely no reluctance to do his duty, as he saw it, of not sparing the rod. He so often and so vigorously resorted to the cane that the school historian Professor Morpurgo, refers, in an apt phrase, to Upcott's 'pious sadism'.[20] Several, though by no means all, of the staff followed their Head's lead. Corporal punishment, it soon became apparent, was one Christ's Hospital tradition at least that had successfully been transplanted into new surroundings as the master, quoted earlier, who arrived full of hope – and high ideals in 1904 discovered. 'When I entered my first study', he later recalled, 'I found in it three pieces of a furniture, a desk, a chair and…in a corner, a perfectly new cane.'[21]

The disposition towards violence of all kinds was reflected in the numerous words relating to it in the Christ's Hospital vocabulary. One term which, significantly, survived the move was 'titch'.[22] In London any master with a

---

[*] *Vice Versa* was made into an excellent film, released in 1947. James Robertson Justice, who played Dr Grimston, bears a notable resemblance to photographs of Dr Upcott.

more than average penchant for beating boys was known as 'Titchy', as in 'Titchy Smith', probably derived from the term 'tight breeching' for being beaten, used at Hertford.

A correlation between Holy Orders and a predisposition to flagellation has often been remarked on. One of Upcott's pupils, quoted earlier, thought him typical in this respect of 'parson headmasters'[23], while the most notoriously cane addicted Head of the century, Geoffrey Fisher of Repton, actually became Archbishop of Canterbury. The removal of the Preparatory School to Horsham meant that the smallest boys, aged eight, now entered via Prep A or Prep B. Those assigned to the latter soon realised they had been lucky. The housemaster of Prep A, a clergyman, readily resorted to the cane, while his colleague in Prep B, not in holy orders, was of a kindlier disposition. At the far end of the Avenue, in my future House, Peele A, the housemaster's clerical collar rightly gave warning of a belief in corporal punishment and the monitors, themselves allowed to beat boys, could refer offenders to him when they felt their own arms inadequate to do justice to the scale of the offence.

A rare exception to the clerical enthusiasm for the cane was the Rev. Kelsey, mentioned earlier for his interrupted sermon, who had assumed the cloth only late in life. So noteworthy was his restraint that when he left it was publicly acknowledged, as the future artist Youngman Carter has described:

> I spent a happy week illuminating an address which one of the grecians...had decided to present to him. It was gilded and decorated with more twirls than a five-pound note.
>
> 'An humble address,' it ran, 'thanking the said WR Kelsey, deacon in Holy Orders, in that he has never at any time used bodily or corporal violence upon the person of his pupils...'
>
> At the presentation (which was performed with strict formality) the little man remained magnificently unmoved. 'Oew, thanks,' he said and stuffed my master work into his pocket, unread. [24]

Specialising in the classics, as I observed and shall describe later, also seemed to encourage a tendency towards violence. One member of Peele B from 1909 to 1917 described six decades later, when he had risen to the very top of his profession, as an engineer, and achieved a knighthood, how he suffered 'a year of acute misery under "Plum" Moore in LE [Little Erasmus] B...While he terrorised us with threats, blows and detention or even worse, we could hear our next destination in succeeding years in the sound of Leonard Dale shouting his head off next door. Why was Latin the only subject that could only be taught by terrorism?'[25]

Upcott's denunciation, in the speech already mentioned, of monitors who kept order by force had little effect, as one boy who arrived 14 years later, in 1916, discovered:

Caught by the monitor during prep on my third evening whispering to my neighbour at the juniors' table, I was sent for and stood trembling before his august table.

'Will you have a fotch or a couple of owls?' he inquired dispassionately...In my ignorance I opted for 'owls', which turned out to be two blows on the top of the head delivered with a toffee hammer. The traditional punishment was generally administered with the knuckles, but this particular bully had been given authority 'to pull the house together'.[26]

As for that other Housey institution the 'fotch', if handed out skilfully it was, this new boy discovered, 'very painful and on occasion in my time, perforated a boy's eardrum. It was a forbidden practice, but of ancient lineage' — sufficient justification at Christ's Hospital for any kind of excess.

The ultra-modern kitchens at Horsham were proudly displayed to visitors with impressive statistics about the volume of provisions they handled, but the move had brought little improvement in the daily diet. Breakfast one day a week still consisted of bread and dripping, the ultimate in 'charity' foods, while, with the abolition of the late night snack of bread and cheese the day ended even more hungrily than before. The main meal still hardly justified the pompous formality of Dinner Parade which preceded it. 'One thing in my time,' an eminent Old Blue knight, at Horsham from 1906 to 1914, told a Founder's Day audience, 'was almost unrelievedly bad...the food. At the advanced age of 54 I still sometimes wake in the night screaming under the incubus of a nightmare,' that of being offered 'a plateful of baked minced beef and ham....Whatever else it was, it was neither beef nor ham.[27] Another witness from an overlapping period, 1906-17, has described shuddering at the memory of 'fish and slosh', boiled fish followed by tapioca, served regularly as the main meal one day a week.[28] The only decent dinner he could recall was provided by pea soup and duff ie suet pudding, served each Friday. (By my time, 20 years after he had left, it appeared each Wednesday. Who could justly accuse the school of never making changes?)

What was achieved at Horsham in those first years of the century was, despite the continuing dominance of the classics, a significant widening of the curriculum. The Science School, occupying one side of the quadrangle, offered, when it first opened, the finest school laboratories in the country, under an outstanding Head Science Master, Charles E Browne, affectionately known as 'Uncle Chas'. In contrast to the beating and bellowing of the classics masters, Browne and his colleagues adopted the newly fashionable 'heuristic method', of encouraging boys to learn by personal experiment. The same principle led to an even bolder innovation, the opening in 1908 of a novelty then unique in public schools, the Manual School. This was 'originally designed,' as one of its early beneficiaries has recorded, in the belief 'that the theoretical aspects of science are more easily grasped when accompanied by practical experience' and that 'if he is to devise and carry out his own experiments every boy must have some manual skill'.[29]

The opening of the Manual School was followed by an even more far reaching innovation, the creation, announced by Dr Upcott in person, of 'a Technical side'. Among those who responded was a future President of the Institution of Civil Engineers, whose unhappy experiences while learning Latin have been quoted earlier. He felt immediately at home with, and respected, the first Head of Engineering. 'Usherwood,' he recalled 60 years later, 'became my saint.'[30]

TS (Tom) Usherwood, a London University engineering graduate, was clearly one of those outstanding teachers whose influence is not merely life-enhancing but life-changing. The Old Guard despised him and his pupils, as the same witness recalls. 'When the Technical Side was started a classical master called us hewers of wood and drawers of water...The BAs on the staff rather despised the BScs, but these...were really better educated...Usherwood...knew more about art, literature, music, ballet and drama than any of the Arts degree masters from older universities. Most of his boys obtained scholarships, which in those days were few and far between.'[31]

The Manual School, a school historian admitted in 1937, 'in its early days was referred to by the old-fashioned die-hard as a place for occupying boys who can use their hands but not their brains'.[32] This was certainly how it was regarded in my day by a Headmaster even less sympathetic to its aims than Upcott.[33] The latter deserves all the more credit therefore for tolerating, if he did not truly encourage, these new specialisms, for they went against the whole ethos of his great hero, Dr Arnold. Like other Victorian public school headmasters, Arnold had regarded science as 'the enemy at the gates' liable to undermine religious belief and thus frustrate their great aim of producing 'Christian gentlemen'.[34]

The most famous engineer produced by Christ's Hospital during Upcott's regime left before the Engineering School had been founded. BN (Barnes), later Sir Barnes, Wallis was part of the 'crossover' generation who had been at Newgate Street and his school career reveals a great deal about the nature of Christ's Hospital in his years there, from 1900 to 1904. He ought, like many others who were to achieve eminence, never to have been admitted, for his father, though disabled, practised as a doctor and employed his own maid and nanny. Nevertheless his son was awarded a presentation, though, because of his poor Latin, placed in a lower form than his general ability merited, causing his father to protest to the Headmaster, an act comparable, observes Wallis's Old Blue biographer to 'disagreement with God'.[35]

Wallis had an early experience of the school's medical care, after being sick in Dining Hall one dinner-time. 'He was,' his biographer records, 'taken across to the Infirmary and allowed to lie down. As for sympathy there was none.

"You know what's the matter with you,'" he was told, "'You've eaten too much cake.'" In fact, as Wallis well knew, 'it was not gluttony that had caused his pain', but migraine, an inherited condition from which he was to suffer all his life.[36]

Wallis, one of the first occupants of my own House, Peele A, was left in no doubt about the underlying philosophy of Christ's Hospital when he was prepared by his housemaster, a notorious beater as mentioned earlier, for confirmation:

> [The Rev DF] Heywood had added his own question to the Catechism:
> 'What, boy, is your principal ambition?'
> With his eyes firmly upon the housemaster's clerical collar Wallis had given the answer that in the circumstances he thought was expected from him:
> 'To get to heaven, sir!'
> Heywood had rounded upon him in fury.
> 'No, no, no, boy!' To get on, to get on!'[37]

In spite of these disconcerting experiences Wallis 'soon came to participate, with pleasure and ease...in all that Christ's Hospital had to offer', and even became a monitor, almost his last act being to send a boy to his housemaster to be beaten. But ultimately the school failed him. He had come top, or almost top, of his class in a whole range of subjects, including English, History and German, but it was in Science that he was outstanding and the Head of Science proposed that he should 'stay on to become the school's first-ever Science Grecian', destined, however, for the University of London rather than Oxford or Cambridge. Barnes Wallis's father, too, though an Oxford graduate – a further indication he really had no right to be sending his sons to Christ's Hospital – wanted Barnes to go on to a modern university but his wishes were also disregarded.

The incident is significant. Accustomed as it was to dealing with working-class parents who were humbly grateful to the school and meekly accepted whatever it decided, the governors and successive Headmasters had never taken kindly to articulate members of the middle class who dared to criticise anything it provided. 'Most parents were overawed...perhaps only professional parents had the temerity to beard the Governing Body,' one historian of Christ's Hospital has written, instancing a clergyman who in 1868 was brave enough to protest against the poor quality of the food and an army captain who, even more surprisingly, objected both to the inadequate diet and compulsory drill before breakfast which, he alleged, had reduced his son to 'a bag of bones'.[38] Dr Wallis's concern for his son was regarded as equally irrelevant. The promising 16-year-old Wallis was 'shuffled out of Christ's Hospital' to become a four-shillings [20p] a-week apprentice in a shipbuilding works.[39]

Not surprisingly, for nearly 20 years he had no further contact with his old school. Then, demonstrating once again the power of long dormant loyalties, he revisited it and became the passionately dedicated of Old Blues. 'It's the most wonderful school in the world,' he wrote to his future wife in 1923, 'I love it and so does everyone who went there,' a manifest untruth.[40] Wallis ultimately reached the highest post in the governing hierarchy, that of Treasurer, and become involved not merely in raising finance for the school but in personally designing the improvements to the buildings he had known as a schoolboy. When, as instructed by his housemaster, he had duly 'got on' and become a household name following his invention of the 'bouncing bomb' used against the Ruhr dams in 1943 and the success of the film *The Dam Busters*, released in 1954, the school made the most of its connection with him.[*] Later in life, by now a Fellow of the Royal Society, like so many Old Blue scientists, and a knight, he attended the Beating of the Retreat, a newly created tradition, on the last Sunday evening of the Summer term. As the now elderly figure appeared the band broke into *The Dam Busters' March* and, one parent who was present assured me, there was not a dry eye in the Quad.

Although Christ's Hospital had, as described earlier, possessed a Drawing School since early in its history this was, in the early years at Horsham, regarded with almost as much suspicion as the Science and Manual Schools, and until 1910 the scene inside the building was much as it had been at Newgate Street. The pupils, recalled one who joined the school in 1906, 'sat on long benches at long high desks…facing an enormous blackboard, never used but to publish the name of some recent criminal…In front of this, clamped to a vertical rod, was a skeleton cube of which you had to make a freehand drawing…any attempt [at] "measuring", earning a fotch or an owl, or, if repeated, detention.' It was therefore 'a shock' to enter the same room after the arrival of a new Drawing Master (later Head of Art) to find the former 'gloomy darkness' replaced by 'unaccustomed daylight' and, in the place of the former uninspired tyrant, to be 'greeted pleasantly by one HA Rigby'.[41]

Harold Rigby – he never seems to have attracted a nickname – rapidly achieved what another witness, at CH from 1907-1917, remembers as a 'transformation…We found separate tables, with sheets of paper and paints' while the new master rapidly consigned to a bonfire the previous exercises, 'by accident' destroying 'one of the hated pots' previously set as subjects for those who had progressed from drawing cubes. '"Oh dear, I have dropped it!" he commented when 'it fell to the floor below, littered with earthenware'.[42]

Dr Upcott's successor as Headmaster later explained that one of the reasons he had applied for the post was the existence of the Manual School and Art School, 'then unique' among public schools. He was impressed by his Art

---

[*] On the significance of the much publicised attack on the dams see Chapter 18 of my book *The Bombers*.

Master, whom, on his tours of the school after his appointment, 'I usually found...painting delightful pictures in one corner, apparently as oblivious of the boys as they were of him. An HMI [His Majesty's Inspector] who spent a morning in the Art School came in to lunch full of enthusiasm. I asked him what Rigby *did*. "Well," he said, "he only spoke to two boys all the time. They asked him where something was and he said he didn't know."'[43]

Rigby's 'hands-off' approach, of neglecting boys who showed no aptitude for his subject, deeply impressed the future illustrator and book-jacket designer, Phillip Youngman Carter, at CH from 1916-21. He refers in his autobiography to 'that beloved school' and describes Rigby as 'the vital figure' in his school life, who 'offered to any boy a true approach to taste and appreciation of beauty, but...on the take-it-or-leave-it principle.'[44] It was Rigby's own boast 'that he never taught any boy anything' but tried to create an atmosphere in which boys were inspired 'to walk in their own way'.[45]

For those devoid of artistic talent this approach failed. Nor was anything done to promote Art Appreciation as a subject in itself. With the staff, however, it was different. One young master, attracted to Christ's Hospital by the reputation of the Art School, recalls how Rigby persuaded his colleagues in the Common Room 'to spend their profit on the sale of drinks...on original water colours by living artists', which he himself chose, the start of what is now a valuable collection.

Outside Christ's Hospital the world in these Edwardian years was changing dramatically. 'In 1909,' recalls the eminent engineer cited earlier, 'no master and certainly no parent could afford a car, although Monsieur Bué [the senior French master]* had a motor cycle...A motor cycle in the Avenue was a matter for excitement.'[46] Even greater changes were on the way. 'In 1911 the first London to Brighton Air Race flew over us during cricket, guided [by] and barely missing the Water Tower...We ran along under the planes as they ploughed very slowly at their best speed a few hundred feet above us.'

Christ's Hospital's private language had largely survived the move. 'Kiff', still used for 'tea' in my day, had as recently as around 1890 also been used for cocoa and coffee, allegedly being derived from the Greek *kuphos*, meaning 'a drink of uncertain extraction.'[47] Another usage, however, understandably, dropped out of use at this time, 'phrart' for 'potato', its last recorded use being at a Founder's Day dinner in 1901.[48] In London the grecians alone had used the nickname 'Housie' for the school itself, but after arrival at Horsham the need developed for a rallying cry to be used to encourage the Christ's Hospital team from the touchline.[49] 'Blues' proved short lived, being heard, or deliberately rendered, as 'Booze', and soon even the humblest new boy was using the new name 'Housie!' For a time, when used as an adjective, as in 'Housey flab', ie

---

* Henri Bué was famous in his day for a classic translation of Lewis Carroll, *Alice au Pays des Merveilles*.

butter, it had a somewhat derogatory ring, but the word achieved official status after being used by the then Headmaster at a Founder's Day dinner after the first world war and was soon appearing in school notices and documents.*

No words were more part of the CH tradition than 'fotch' and 'owl', both of which have already been defined. The former was said to have originated with a Scottish beadle at Newgate Street who would cry 'Gie ye a fetch'" as he administered summary justice to boys arriving back late from half day leave.[50] The origin of 'owl' is unknown. As already mentioned, though 'Upcott's Edict' had supposedly banned monitors from using both, offenders were often, as in an example given earlier, offered a choice between them. When this happened to Barnes Wallis, his biographer has recorded, he 'chose always to be owled for he knew his skull to be thick', and likely to leave his assailant 'nursing bruised knuckles'.[51] Even when the monitors complied with the new rules the long established tradition, one boy, 13 at the time of the move, has described, was kept alive by 'unofficial bullies' who would 'order the luckless small fry to stand at attention, to be bowled over by a swinging "fotch" or have his skull nearly cracked by hard, descending knuckles in…an "owl"'. Another boy, in Thornton A from 1908-12, remembers one 'senior who carried in his pocket a brass locker knob…and for occasional amusement would crack' his favoured victim, 'on the head with this implement'.[52] (The offender, to universal rejoicing, was ultimately expelled, though for other misdemeanours.)

Within a few years the humane atmosphere which had followed the Great Trek from London had begun to fade, but around 1912, following the arrival of a new Medical Officer, Dr GE Friend, of whom I shall say much more later, a second, if minor, wave of improvements began. The most obvious, and appreciated, changes, were in the food, as one observer, previously quoted, in Peele B from 1909-17, has recorded. Now for 'breakfast, butter with every meal and with porridge on the previous meatless days. Sausage, ham and fish as before, but rather more. Tea: Butter with every meal with jam or paste, home-made, on different days. This really did cheer things up…We still saved up…to buy a pot of blackberry and apple jam at the Shop for four-pence-halfpenny [2p] to reinforce the spoonful of jam dispensed by monitors. (Four at 1d, [0.5p], with another to pay a halfpenny [0.25p] for "scrapes".'

A major step away for the old 'workhouse' tradition of Newgate Street was the provision for the first time of proper footwear. 'When our clogs needed soleing,' the same Old Blue has described, 'we had to walk to the Shoe Shop, a squalid corner of the Gym building. Confronted by a heap of other people's buckled shoes, already mended, we had to scrabble among ourselves…until we

---

* I have followed the convention throughout this book of using 'Housie' for the noun and 'Housey' for the adjective, which was the practice in my day, but the latter is now often used for both, as in the current *Housey!* newsletter.

could find someone else's cast-offs which were not too painful to wear...[Now] we were each given a permanent number to mark all our things. We were issued with a new pair of clogs each term...When these were mended we got our own back!'

Almost as astonishing, since the new playing fields had made almost incessant games-playing not merely possible but obligatory, 'just before the [first world] war we were allowed on Monday two hours for voluntary work in the Manual School, instead of compulsory rugger...Our housemaster said, sadly, that we ought really to be punting a pill about in such unusual freedom', and by my time the concession had vanished.[53]

The first world war had hardly begun when, on 6 August 1914, the whole school was requisitioned by the army to house German prisoners, though they soon turned out to be mainly 'meek and mild waiters and barbers...rounded up as they tried to make their way back to the Fatherland' rather than the ruthless uniformed Huns of popular legend. Eventually 630 arrived but, as the school's historian recorded, 'the Vice-Chairman of the Council was not going to have a little thing like a war interfering with the liberties of CH,' an attitude which, as I shall describe, was to be repeated in the second world war. By the end of the month, pressure in Whitehall had led to the unwelcome arrivals being transferred to 'a barbed-wire compound on Sharpenhurst', and an assurance 'that the last thing the government desired was that Christ's Hospital should be interfered with or occupied'.[54] The school duly blacked out its windows against Zeppelin raids, though no bombs fell nearby, cultivated allotments, produced aircraft parts in the Manual School, and accepted an influx of elderly and short-sighted temporary masters often incapable of maintaining discipline. Its main contribution to the war effort, however, was in releasing younger teaching and estate staff, and older boys, to serve in the Forces, which until 1916 consisted solely of volunteers. All too often, sometimes within weeks, the same names were heard again in Chapel, as one Old Blue, at CH from 1916 to 1921, has described:

> Dr Upcott's beard became a snowy fleece of the softest silk, setting off the scarlet robes of a Doctor of Divinity with medieval richness. In all the world there was no more dignified nor tragic figure than that of the Headmaster reading from the high altar the roll of the dead at the conclusion of evensong, whilst the bugles in the wintry quad beyond sounded the Last Post.[55]

For Upcott's hearers it was 'the prospect of a jamless tea with execrable margarine' to follow which dominated their thoughts, for to provide inadequate food was now patriotic and in this respect at least Housie was not found lacking. 'One cubic inch [110gms] of margarine, four ounces [55gms] of bread and two ounces [220gms] cake, or if we had no cake, eight ounces of bread and one spoonful of plum and apple jam but no margarine – this was typical of our evening meal', recalls one former inmate of Coleridge B.[56] For one Barnes B boy, at school from 1915, the ultimate in unpleasant gastronomic experiences was 'torpedoed whale' an unidentifiable fish 'in a vicious (sic) pink sauce'.[57] Another Old Blue, who arrived in 1916, could 'vividly remember...experiments with grass' in his 'acute hunger. They provided,' he discovered, 'very little sustenance; moorhens' eggs, parboiled by keeping the single hot tap in the changing-room running over a tin mug full of them, were a better bet.'[58] On grave occasions in the Dining Hall more daring spirits were publicly beaten for stealing turnips from neighbouring farmers.' The girls at Hertford were no better off, 'with at least two meatless and fishless days a week...no tea, no eggs' and, much unappreciated, 'vermicelli, known as the "Diet of Worms"'.[59*]

Games at Horsham continued until the school was beaten on the playing field by an unprecedented margin by the supposedly inferior Merchant Taylors, day boys who mainly ate at home.[60] 'Our own bones became so thin,' recalls one sufferer, who had joined Barnes B in 1915, '[with] 13 of the first XV and half the second XV in the Sicker with broken bones, that Dr Friend had all rugger cancelled.'[61]

The increased incidence of fractures among schoolboys due to nutritional deficiencies was just the type of subject to appeal to the new doctor. As he himself pointed out, the school community provided a large scale laboratory for his studies, equipped with 800 unwitting guinea-pigs:

> In a school run on the lines of Christ's Hospital it is possible to trace the contacts in most epidemics until the third or fourth batch of cases...as one can find the whereabouts of any boy for any hour of the day. My experience is that dormitory and dayroom are more probable areas of infection than classrooms, with the exception of the art and manual schools, but that the tuckshop is a congregational danger-spot that unfortunately defies too often the efforts of the epidemiological detective.

The world-wide epidemic of influenza at the end of the first world war provided Dr Friend with an ideal opportunity to put his theories to the test. Trips into Horsham were banned and it was only against the doctor's wishes that visits from parents continued, but Dr Friend's chief weapon was the still novel one of wholesale inoculation. In the best school tradition this was compulsory, though parents could object and for this and other reasons only 77% of the 819 boys – 633 – were ultimately given injections. The academic staff and estate workers were given a choice and only 13% – 34 – agreed to receive the vaccine, but

---

* The Diet of Worms was the occasion in 1521 at which Martin Luther formally defended his doctrines in front of the Emperor Charles V, declaring 'I can do no other'.

these totals proved sufficient to keep the disease beyond the ring fence. 'During the term', ie from September to December 1918, 'there was less illness recorded at the school,' an Old Blue doctor has observed, 'than at any time since 1898.'

This success, revealed in the *Lancet* in 1919, made Dr Friend's name and had lasting consequences. He became a firm believer in the value of nasal douching and of compulsory nose-blowing. This latter became a distinctive Housey institution, of which I shall say more later.[62]

The Armistice in November 1918 was celebrated in the already traditional way though, symbolically in view of the short-lived peace which was to follow, 'the victory beacon on Sharpenhurst faded in a torrent of rain'.[63] The school, like the country, was in a sad, depressed state. Christ's Hospital had been stripped of its ablest masters and senior boys, and the cost of defeating the Germans had been heavy. 17.8% of the 2105 Old Blues known to have served in the Forces had been killed, ie 375, and another 238 were wounded, some of them several times, the overwhelming majority of casualties being in the infantry. The records indicated once again how many boys lost all contact with Christ's Hospital on leaving. The true number who had joined up was probably 'at least 3,000'.[64] In 1919 Upcott left, worn out after 17 years as Headmaster and broken by the loss of so many of his former pupils. He became Archdeacon of Hastings, but like several later Headmasters, did not long survive leaving Horsham. He died in 1922, little lamented, at least by Old Blues, who remembered his defects rather than his achievements. Among those who later decided they had been unjust to Upcott was Philip Youngman Carter, who in his autobiography, published in 1982, 61 years after he had left Christ's Hospital – an even longer interval than in my case – attempted a balanced judgement of the man who had, as he still recalled, 'punished me...mercilessly...for an offence of which I was completely innocent'.

> It is only now that I see the austere old mandarin with his silky white beard in a perspective which is sufficiently removed. It was he who mastered the herculean job of transplanting Christ's Hospital from its almost parochial city background to the green acres of Sussex and establishing it as one of the great public schools. There must have been mountains of prejudice against any break in custom...What the school needed...was precisely what it got, a strong-minded, forward-thinking diplomat clothed in all the outer trappings of traditionalism.[65]

[1] *CH Book* p.270
[2] Jan 1963 p.39
[3] *Short History* p.13
[4] Jul 1986 p.196
[5] *CH Book* p.251
[6] Feb 1972 p.76
[7] Feb 1972 p.75
[8] Mar 1983 p.111
[9] Jul 1983 p.179
[10] Morpurgo p.79
[11] 1997 Founder's Day Programme p.10
[12] Ibid
[13] *CH Book* p.273
[14] Carter p.20
[15] Morpurgo *Wallis* p.50
[16] Mar 1983 p.111
[17] Feb 1972 p.74
[18] Jul 1984 p.184
[19] Jan 1963 pp.38-9
[20] Morpurgo *Wallis* p.50
[21] Jan 1956 p.43
[22] Nov-Dec 1947 p.57
[23] Mar 1983 p.111
[24] Carter p.20
[25] Mar 1983 p.111
[26] Carter p.14
[27] Dec 1949 p.36
[28] Jul 1984 p.182
[29] ie Barnes Wallis *CH Book* p.319
[30] Mar 1983 p.111
[31] Feb 1972 p.76
[32] Allan p.100
[33] Feb 1972 p.76
[34] Morpurgo *Wallis* p.36
[35] Op.cit. p.27
[36] Op.cit. p.47
[37] Op.cit. p.54
[38] Seaman p.137
[39] Morpurgo *Wallis* p.57
[40] Op.cit. p.147
[41] May 1971 pp.149-150
[42] Ibid
[43] *CH Book* p.356
[44] Carter pp.12, 17
[45] Jan 1968 p.6
[46] Mar 1983 p.111

[47] Dec 1992 p.216; *Housey Slang* p.13
[48] Dec 1951 p.52
[49] Autumn 1968 p.272
[50] Nov-Dec 1947 p.57
[51] Morpurgo *Wallis* p.46
[52] Jul 1984 p.184
[53] Mar 1983 p.111
[54] Allan pp.108-12
[55] *CH Book* p.285
[56] Jan 1970 p.86
[57] Dec 1987 p.187
[58] Carter p.15
[59] Dec 1986 p.259
[60] Dec 1987 p.187
[61] Dec 1987 p.187
[62] Hull pp.67-74
[63] *CH Book* p.287
[64] Mar 1992 pp.67 & 77
[65] Carter p.16

17

DOWNS AND WOODLANDS FAIR

Praise Him for our spacious dwelling,
Ringed with downs and woodlands fair…

School hymn, Praise the Lord for our Foundation, *1933*

In September 1919 the man generally considered to have been the best Headmaster of Christ's Hospital, at least until very recent times, took over at Horsham, WH (later Sir William Hamilton) Fyfe. A classicist, though not a clergyman, Hamilton Fyfe had a conventional background, having attended Fettes and taught at Radley before becoming an Oxford don, but proved himself miraculously free of preconceptions. The new Head and his school soon proved remarkably at one. 'I had been…continuously happy' he later wrote of the eleven years that followed[1] and, astonishingly, since so many boys of every generation have disliked their time at Christ's Hospital, I have found no critics of Hamilton Fyfe. With the 'Old Guard' masters he was less successful. '"Common Room" at first looked loftily askance at these unorthodox methods,' he wrote of the innovators he admired, 'but in time the infection…spread to other masters, who began to abandon the belief that text-books and their own voices were the only legitimate instruments of education.'[2] Fyfe rejoiced in the classlessness of Christ's Hospital, though pointing out that 'Housey (*sic*) is not completely democratic because the sons of rich parents are excluded'.

The artistic minded Philip Youngman Carter, whose mixed, but essentially hostile, feelings about Dr Upcott have been quoted earlier, had no such doubts about Upcott's successor. He considered Fyfe 'One of the great men of this age…The prototype of all that is good in modern education…This clearly was a new era and a new inspiration…We who were of his time pride ourselves on having known the vintage years.'[3]

Carter himself was one of the first beneficiaries of the new regime. While Upcott had jibbed at making Barnes Wallis a science grecian, Fyfe, far more bravely, made Youngman Carter a deputy grecian in Art, jocularly 'knighting' him 'with a roll of cardboard…"Arise, Sir Dep., the first of your species in the history of the school."'[4] A new department was set up entitled '"The Arts and Crafts"…to provide the out-of-the run specialist with a working education while giving him long periods to devote to a chosen subject. Unfortunately this attracted such a collection of oddities, misfits and perceptive idlers that it became suspect from the moment of birth and immediately produced its own ignominious stigma'.[5] Here was another case of history repeating itself. A form of boys who did not fit comfortably into any existing academic category, known as 'the Middlers', had existed in London until the name was dropped as derogatory, while non-specialists who lingered on beyond School Certificate in my day were known by an even more offensive nickname, 'the General Dregs', officially the General Deps. Fyfe was more successful with other non-traditional subjects. 'A wave of culture swept over us, largely instigated by a new English master, RC Woodthorpe,' observed Youngman Carter. Woodthorpe later became famous in Christ's Hospital's annals as the author of the crime novel *The Public School Murder*, published in 1932, which Carter, a dedicated Old Blue, considered provided 'an intelligible if jaundiced picture of the school in that epoch'.[6] Although some features of Christ's Hospital, such as the chapel and the Doctor's Lake (renamed) are clearly based on CH the plan of the fictional Polchester suggests it was an amalgam of various places,[7] though one character at least, the uninspiringly named 'Mr Smith' was undoubtedly drawn from life, for the author confessed as much to the original, mentioned already, 'Teddy' Edwards.

The CH connection proved much more valuable to Woodthorpe than it did to me when, many years later, I set my own *A Head for Death* in a thinly disguised Christ's Hospital. He was taken up by Youngman Carter's far more famous crime-writer wife, Margery Allingham, to whom he dedicated a subsequent detective story, *Death in a Small Town,* which was clearly Horsham.[8] The author then moved on to become literary and arts editor of the Labour *Daily Herald*, edited by the Headmaster's brother Henry. William Hamilton Fyfe made no secret of his own Socialism, remarkable in a public school headmaster of the period.

A test for many local authority schools was the existence of the Corps, which, in the prevailing climate of revulsion against all things military, some decided to ban. Fyfe's attitude was ambivalent. He 'let it be known,' recalls one observer, 'that if any boy did not want to join the OTC he would be exempted if he could make out a good case', but only one 'very bright grecian' is known to have succeeded.

Religious doubts were treated with unprecedented tolerance. 'After Confirmation...with some trepidation I went to his study and told him that I could not grasp the concept of the Holy Trinity,' remembers another of Fyfe's pupils. 'Rather to my surprise he replied, "And nor can I."' Fyfe was even tolerant on the subject of sex. When one 17 year old's admiring note to Fyfe's daughter was intercepted her father good-naturedly asked the writer to a meal to get to know her better. 'I consider myself very fortunate in having had WH

Fyfe as my Headmaster,' one Old Blue quoted earlier has observed. 'He was benign, humorous, approachable and highly intelligent.'

Most revolutionary of all was Fyfe's defiance of the most notorious of school traditions. 'In Newgate Street and at Horsham well into this century,' its own historian has written, 'CH was infamous even among generally brutal public schools for the severity of its discipline'.[9] Under the new regime beating was, regrettably, not banned altogether, but, wrote Fyfe in the retrospective survey quoted earlier, 'I never aspired to corporal correction.'[10] It was indeed 'correction' which he sought, not pretexts for inflicting pain. One house-captain, sent to the Head after missing Chapel, an offence his housemaster felt too serious to deal with, bravely confessed he had simply overslept, and was told: 'So did I my boy; come and have dinner with me this evening.'[11]

Fyfe's enlightened approach proved far more effective than Upcott's perpetual flogging, as Youngman Carter saw for himself:

> Punishment was no longer a matter of a five-barred gate of red weals on the buttocks, to be exhibited secretly before an avid and often fee-paying audience. A rap from Fyfe was more likely to be in the form of some memorable saying: 'My dear fellow, how very silly of you to get caught. A beating would not suit your dignity or mine. If you happen to be an ass, please try to conceal the fact from us all'. He had very few second offenders to deal with.[12]

About the diet and accommodation Fyfe could do little, since these were the concern of the governors. Much was hoped of the appointment of the first Lady Superintendent in 1922, supposed to bring a feminine touch to the catering, but neither she nor her successors achieved much, to judge by conditions when I arrived in 1936. Fyfe also evidently failed to stop the excessive emphasis on house loyalty which, as a matter of discipline, *was* within his control, but he did try to widen the intellectual horizons of what had become an inward-looking, as well as physically isolated, community. A Modern Literature Society was founded, visited by famous actors and playwrights, and, in 1920, a literary magazine, *The Outlook*, into which, from 1924, the poems and essays which had sat somewhat uneasily alongside the official news in *The Blue* were 'siphoned off'.[13] The first, duplicated, issue, contained a poem by Edmund Blunden and 'a Sitwellian offering' by Constance Lambert,[14] but curiously for a school with so strong a literary tradition *The Outlook* was to have a chequered history, for long periods failing to appear.[15] It still retains a special place in my affections for reasons which I mention later. Under Fyfe music also flourished, with Constance Lambert, later well known as a composer, conducting the school orchestra 'with verve and...brilliance.' He had refused the Head of Art's suggestion to concentrate instead on becoming an artist. His father, he pointed out, was a Royal Academician, his brother intended to be a sculptor, and 'Two in the family is enough.'[16]

That Christ's Hospital under Fyfe was not quite the idyllic place such accounts suggest is made plain by the experiences of (John) Keith Vaughan, who entered Prep A in October 1921 – he was a month late because Dr Friend had, characteristically, insisted he must first have his tonsils removed – just after Youngman Carter had left the senior school. Hamilton Fyfe wished, he later wrote, to weed out before admission boys who, though clever, 'were altogether unsuited...for the life of a boarding school'.[17] In the case of Keith Vaughan, the most successful artist Christ's Hospital has so far produced, he failed miserably. Intellectually this sensitive nine year old clearly merited a place and he also qualified financially, for his father, a civil engineer, had walked out on the family, leaving his wife to bring up two small sons – both went to CH – on £60 a year alimony and her income from 'doing fine sewing for Hampstead ladies'.

The future painter arrived full of apprehension for, his biographer records, 'he was still wetting his bed and must have dreaded the prospect of sleeping in a dormitory'. The reality proved far worse, however, than his forebodings and he never forgave his mother for failing to respond to his 'daily letters...begging her to rescue him or he would die.' Her sole intervention probably made matters worse. When Mrs Vaughan wrote 'to the school to protest against Keith being bullied, the culprit, a boy of nine, was given twenty or thirty vicious strokes with a cane "from the knees to the shoulder" by the housemaster, who lost his temper because the boy dared to struggle'.

Keith Vaughan's experiences will have an all too familiar ring to many generations of Old Blues. From his time in the Prep he remembered 'compulsory games, bullying, flogging, ragging and coarse sexual jokes...Rugby in particular gave him nightmares'.

> Nearly fifty years later, when drunk, he recalled the brief respites offered by prayer and prep and 'the smell of the long deal benches in Prep A against which I pressed my forehead in agony and longing for oblivion'. Night-time, when the others in the long dormitory were asleep, became the magic time when he was free to be himself and so he became a lifelong insomniac.

Promotion to Peele A, a traditionally tough house, brought no improvement and the arrival of adolescence added to his problems. 'Very handsome in a slightly feminine way' Vaughan was seduced at the age of 13 by an older schoolmate whom his mother had naively asked to explain the facts of life to him and who 'set him off on a lifetime of masturbation', an offence allegedly meriting expulsion. Vaughan's reaction to the discovery of sex went far beyond that of a normal schoolboy and continued into adult life. At the age of 47 he recorded in his *Journal* that he had already written '40 typed pages...on the purpose, pleasure and techniques of masturbation.' Significantly he justified this by a reference to the Marquis de Sade. Vaughan had discovered at school the pleasures of masochism after the helpful friend already mentioned had obligingly caned him 'for allegedly neglecting his studies'.

This was one need Christ's Hospital was well equipped to satisfy. 'The whole school, according to Vaughan,' his biographer records, 'seems to have throbbed with homo-erotic tensions which periodically erupted in ritualistic beatings. Several of the masters were also pederasts...He [Vaughan] concludes: "They were about as degenerate and perverted a group of men . . . as were ever likely to be in charge of the education of boys."'[18]

Here is a very different view of the 'golden age' of the Fyfe headmastership quoted earlier and Vaughan himself summed up the effect of 'eight years of concrete misery' as 'a lasting fear of hostility in others, a mistrust of strangers and a maddening desire at all costs to ingratiate myself and earn the goodwill of everyone.' Yet the very brutality of his environment encouraged his creative development. 'Music and art', comments his biographer, 'were pursued', according to Vaughan, 'not just because of his aptitude for them but because they too were solitary consolations.'

The above writer, who had not been there, is notably more sympathetic to Christ's Hospital than his subject had been. 'The school's academic curriculum,' he observes, 'seems to have equipped him rather well for life, in spite of his reluctance to acknowledge it...The music teachers were excellent...A lifelong interest in books...also began during those years.' Vaughan sang in the choir, learned the piano, played the part of a fairy in *Iolanthe* and of a 'dizzy flapper' in Galsworthy's *Loyalties*. Above all, the school recognised and fostered his artistic talent. If not, as his biographer asserts, 'the first sixth-former to specialize in art whom the school had ever had' – Youngman Carter, just ahead of him, makes the same claim, as quoted earlier – Vaughan certainly received every encouragement. A small exhibition was staged 'of his drawings of cliffs and rocks' and *The Outlook* carried some of his woodcuts and linocuts and, in 1924, used one of 'boats against clouds' on its cover, his first published work. Vaughan himself later identified in some of his adult paintings the features derived from influences received at school, including the urging of the Head of Art, HA Rigby, to 'put more in'. More important, however, were the Brangwyn paintings, described elsewhere, which were still being finished at the time Vaughan arrived. He was particularly struck by those showing that ultimate in masochistic expression, the martyrdom of St Stephen and St Alban, although, according to his biographer, 'his experiences at this Protestant school seem to have expunged any Christian beliefs he might have had when he arrived'.[19]

'Vaughan's schooldays made a lasting impression on his personality', his biographer believes, and Vaughan's own *Journals* confirm. He left, in 1929, at the age of 17, under the inflexible rule which ejected those not destined for university at this age, and worked for a time for a London advertising agency, before becoming a part-time tutor at a College of Art and ultimately a full-time painter. He was soon associating with the leading artists of the day and rapidly established himself as a member of the Neo-Romantic movement, which applied modern techniques to traditional subjects. Vaughan ultimately acquired an international reputation and in 1965 was awarded the CBE; his works still command substantial prices. He remained, however, one Old Blue of whom it was difficult for the school to boast. A pacifist during the war, he was throughout his life a self-obsessed, sex-obsessed and promiscuous homosexual, given to what he called 'lust-sleuthing', ie picking up complete strangers in public places. Thirty years after leaving he did re-visit Christ's Hospital and in 1975 even offered to return there to lecture on art but by now, his biographer recounts, 'was too ill to make the journey which might have completed his reconciliation with the establishment that had made him miserable for so long'. Two years later, aged 65, impotent, lacking further ambition as a painter, and with terminal cancer, he took his own life, having earlier written his own, sad, epitaph, 'The well is dry.'[20]

I admired Keith Vaughan's work – the naked males, of which he was so fond as a subject, apart – long before I knew of his connection with Christ's Hospital or learned that there had been talk of his, and my, old house commissioning four of his paintings, though this came to nothing.[21] I must now, however, return to the history of Christ's Hospital after he had left it.

Sadly, for both himself and the school, in 1930, Fyfe moved on to become Vice-Chancellor of a Canadian university, a frustrating experience which his wife described as 'like cutting cheese with a razor'. He was succeeded as Headmaster by the 34-year-old HLO (Henry Lael Oswald) Flecker, whose 25 year reign covered the whole of my own time at Christ's Hospital. Only much later did I learn his background. A clergyman's son, he had been educated at Dean Close School, Cheltenham, had been a classical scholar at Oxford, and an assistant master and housemaster at Marlborough, where he had come close to stifling the career of a future Poet Laureate. 'He read out my verses to the set of boys,' wrote a former pupil, by then Sir John Betjeman, 'making fun of each line as he went along,' an action which left its victim with a 'morbid fear' of critics,[22] and perhaps contributed to Betjeman's well publicised loathing for his old school. Three years as Headmaster of Berkhamsted followed (equally loathed, incidentally, by its most famous old boy Graham Greene) before HLO Flecker's move to Horsham.[23] This was to prove one of the longest headmasterships in the school's history, but even his first nine years, before the war gave an excuse for inactivity, were not a time of innovation. An obituary tribute in *The Blue* claimed HLOF – I still cannot think of him simply as 'Flecker' – had encouraged the teaching of biology, geography and mathematics, and aimed, in his own words, to provide 'A first-rate education for boys less well-endowed with purely intellectual qualities'.[24] This is the very reverse of the opinion formed by some of his staff, which I shall quote later, nor did I see any sign that he was, as his obituarist claimed, 'a ready recipient of new ideas'.[25]

The new Headmaster was fortunate in that he had hardly taken over when, in October 1930, the New Science School was opened, a brand new block housing biology laboratories and geography classrooms, planned before his arrival. The ceremony was performed by the school's President, the future Edward VIII, who arrived by air, the very model of a modern Prince of Wales,[26] though the three-sided quadrangle thus formed was given a backward-looking name, the Garden, after one of the asphalt playgrounds at Newgate Street; in practice we always called it the New Quad. In 1932 another new building was added in the same area, the Dominions Library, which revealed that Christ's Hospital still had the capacity to attract sudden and large donations, for it resulted from a visiting Australian asking what he could do to assist the school. On 'being told that one need was for a "Colonial Library"' for the benefit of 'boys intending to emigrate', he instantly wrote out a cheque for the £5,000 required.[27] Apart from its intended purpose it also provided a useful venue for small meetings, like those of the school debating society, and the 1930 Society, formed as a Sunday afternoon discussion group by Hamilton Fyfe, but under his successor becoming more ambitious in its aims. I shall mention both organisations again later.

The extent to which HLOF failed to keep up the momentum of the movement begun by Hamilton Fyfe to make Housie a more civilised place will be evident from the detailed account of my own experiences which follows. But even in his first years as Head he did little to achieve reform, or even to recognise that it was needed. Of more living space and privacy, which were admittedly not his to provide but for which he could have privately campaigned, of a more relaxed regime with less ferocious discipline, which were within his area of authority, there were no signs. 'Flecker was a good administrator' was the opinion most commonly expressed of him. An admiring former Senior Grecian, later a public school headmaster himself, observed that the Head 'even rested with intensity' and that 'his unsparing efforts made him intolerant on occasions.'[28] The truth is that we were all, boys and masters alike, in awe, if not actually scared, of him.

HLO Flecker was undoubtedly, as I shall describe, a man of deep religious, and specifically Anglican, conviction: I always expected him to become a bishop on his retirement. He was, as I make clear later, very different from the 'sanctimonious sadist', as Youngman Carter described him, who had preceded him.[29] While Dr Upcott had wanted to make Christ's Hospital more like Rugby, HLO Flecker's model was more probably Marlborough. There had traditionally been close connections between the two. It was an old Marlburian who became Flecker's closest subordinate at Horsham, and no fewer than three Senior Grecians went on to teach at Marlborough, while he readily recruited Old

Marlburians to the staff.[30] Undoubtedly his main interest, like that of most of his predecessors, lay in the classical grecians. He was civil to those achieving scholarships in other subjects; in boys of lesser attainments he had no interest. In a long retrospective essay, *Fifty Years at Horsham*, in that Bible of Old Blues, *The Christ's Hospital Book*, in 1953, my old Head acknowledged that 'of our five "streams" the lowest two are...what modern educational jargon describes as "Modern School" rather than "Grammar School" boys...and have to undergo no more than a simple test in the "three Rs" and a medical inspection'.[31] This was the situation that had existed ever since the end, around 1600, of the earliest, 'orphanage' phase in the school's history, but it was clearly not one he cared for.

HLOF claimed that 'though migration has made Christ's Hospital more like other public schools, it has retained a great measure of distinctiveness'. He instanced 'its traditional dress', where 'the only change made since London days is in the pattern of the shoes', the requirement on boys to undertake domestic duties, like bed-making and waiting at meals, and marching.[32] These, as will emerge later, were all features of my schooldays of which I was highly critical and that HLOF should have defended them is proof enough that he was no great, or indeed minor, innovator.

This was the man, who had then been Head for six years, and this the school, 384 years old, which I was now, in September 1936, to enter as a timorous ten year old. Three years before my arrival the school's private hymn book had been published, containing the school hymn, *Praise the Lord for our Foundation*, written many years earlier by Dr Upcott to a tune composed by the Director of Music. Far more than the older school song, *The Votum*, written in London, this expressed the essence of Christ's Hospital:

> Praise the Lord for our foundation
> Praise Him for our holy name...

acknowledged the then still recent move:

> Praise Him for our spacious dwelling,
> Ringed with downs and woodlands fair...

and boasted of the school's long history:

> Praise Him for the unbroken story
> Linking present with the past.

These references, and the general emphasis on looking back were significant. In its general spirit and ethos, in what might today be called its 'culture', Christ's Hospital in the 1930s still bore many resemblances to the institution into which those first orphans and street urchins had been removed, often unwillingly, back in the 1550s and to which generations of London schoolboys had returned with sinking hearts over the intervening 350 years. Along with Christ's Hospital's many virtues, to which in later chapters I shall try to do justice, it suffered from one overwhelming disability; it was to an extraordinary degree, not merely the product but the slave of its past.

---

[1] *CH Book* p.355
[2] Ibid p.356
[3] Carter p.22
[4] Carter p.26
[5] Carter p.25
[6] Carter p.26
[7] Dec 1997 p.255
[8] Mar 1998 p.75
[9] Morpurgo p.91
[10] *CH Book* p.355
[11] Mar 1998 p.80
[12] Carter pp.23-4
[13] Dec 1992 p.236
[14] *CH Book* p.288
[15] Jul 1980 p.149
[16] Carter p.22
[17] *CH Book* p.359
[18] Yorke pp.28-9
[19] Yorke p.31
[20] Yorke p.267
[21] Yorke p.32
[22] Dec 1989 p.194
[23] *Daily Telegraph* 'Peterborough' column 20 Aug 1998
[24] Jan 1959 p.5
[25] Ibid
[26] Allan p.98
[27] Dec 1994 p.223
[28] Jan 1959 p.8
[29] Carter p.15
[30] Mar 1983 p.210, Jun 1957 p.139
[31] *CH Book* p.337
[32] *CH Book* pp.337-8[32] *CH Book* p.355
[32] Ibid p.356

PART III

BLUECOAT BOY

*Dressed for the first time in this treasured
uniform the boy is truly a Blue, a Housey boy,
a member of a world-wide and age-old community.*

JE Morpurgo, Christ's Hospital, *1984*

CHRIST'S HOSPITAL

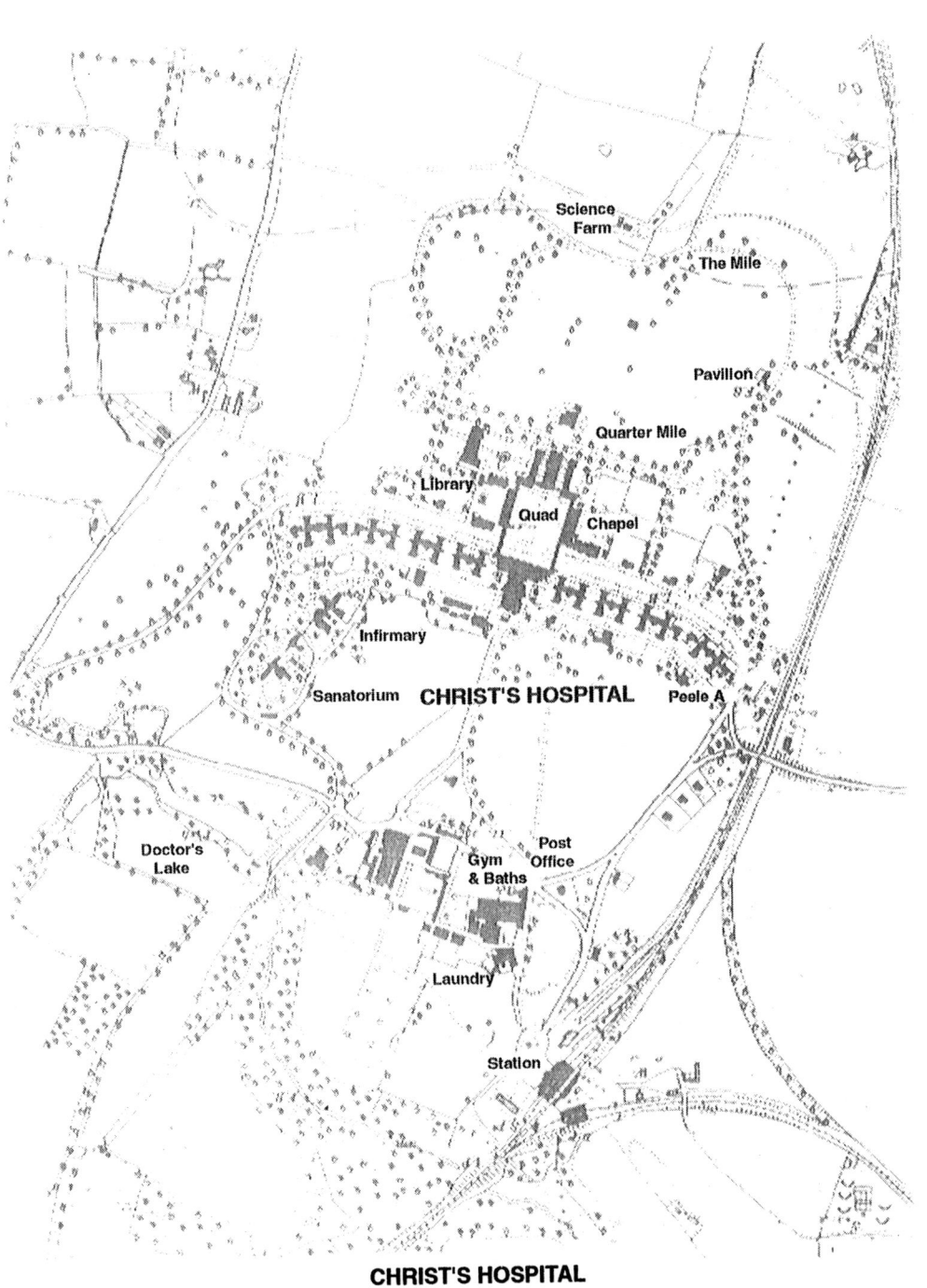

This plan shows the lay-out of the school as it appears to a visitor approaching from the station.
The map is therefore shown pointing approximately south, not north.

18

OLD WORLD HABIT

Old world habit, civic glory,
Time-worn customs, newly cast.

Praise the Lord for our Foundation, No 79 in Supplementary Hymns *for use in Christ's Hospital Chapel*, 1933

The transition from my old life to my new one began with a treat. I was required to attend with my father at the school offices in Great Tower Street in the City for the formal admission ceremony, and somehow he had saved enough to give me a day out first. This was my first visit to the capital and I was fascinated by everything we saw and especially by the two places we toured at my request, the Tower of London and Madame Tussauds. I can still remember my first, indeed only, sight of the Crown Jewels and of being allowed – an indication of the momentousness of the day – to visit the Chamber of Horrors. A photograph taken at the Tower that morning, Friday 18 September 1936, shows a cheerful, bright-faced little boy, very different from the miserable-looking creature I had become a few weeks later.[*] The climax of my day in London was to be led into the imposing Courtroom in Great Tower Street, where all the boys, each with his father behind him, were lined up to face a row of elderly adults seated behind a long table. In the middle was a shrivelled figure who seemed to me so ancient that I wondered if he would live long enough to complete the entry formalities and he was silent so long that I felt uncertain as to whether he were alive at all. Finally he roused himself with what seemed a massive effort to deliver in a weak but wholly audible voice the vital formula: 'Your sons are all admitted free of charge.'[**] At that moment, I went, like many thousands of poor boys before me, 'on the foundation', becoming a beneficiary of the piety of Edward VI and the benevolence of John and Frances West.

From Newgate Street we must have gone to Victoria and thence by train to Christ's Hospital station, built specially for the school's use, but I have no recollection of the journey, being still overawed by the impressive ceremony in

---

[*] See illustrations.
[**] For an account of the similar experience of the future artist Phillip Youngman Carter twenty years earlier see Carter p.11.

which I had just taken part. This was, I realise in retrospect, almost the last time I was to feel proud and happy at being a Housey boy. I made no record at the time, but four years later, aged 14, described what followed in an essay: 'A New Experience':

> I stepped onto the platform from the train which had brought us down from London and, together with a large number of other new boys and their parents, passed out of the station. In front of me the winding road seemed to stretch out like the new school unfolding before me. A stream of people were plodding up that incline which leads up from the station, not going too fast, as though they were dubious of their reception, and yet not dawdling, for fear of being left behind. Everyone was looking about them, noting with interest the building marked Laundry and the neighbouring Gymnasium and Swimming Baths…Then we pass through a white gate and are inside the grounds of our home for the next few months. On either side of the path are the playing fields with boys playing on them and other boys watching, while here and there are groups walking about, glancing at the cavalcade winding its way towards the Dining Hall. Walking towards the Dining Hall we notice the buildings all around and the task of learning one's way about among them seems hopeless. But the Dining Hall makes the greatest impression. At first it seems immense with an enormous picture seeming to cover most of one wall. Before we can fully take in all its features someone calls out our name and we temporarily part from our respective parents. Two or three of us bound for the same house are observed by some boys who seem to be awaiting us. They lead us to what we are told is the Wardrobe and are here given the strange uniform we have thought so much about, and led back to our house…We are shown the dormitory, introduced to the matron, who gives us each a number and then dressed in those same strange looking clothes which give the school its name. How heavy the coat feels and how strange it all seems! Then our 'nursemaids' show us the house, tell us various people's names, (What a hopeless task learning all their names seems), we meet our housemaster, are allotted a locker, helped to unpack and then march up to tea. None of us eat much, for we are all too interested in taking in everything we have learnt. Then after tea the hardest part arrives as we say goodbye to our parents and are left in this strange place, which we hope we shall like. The evening wears away in the dayroom and then we climb the stairs to bed and our first day at Christ's Hospital is over.

Spelling mistakes apart, I have reproduced this exactly as I wrote it, as I have all later contemporary documents I quote elsewhere, and it still seems to me a fair account, but my English master, often generous in his praise, was not impressed. 'Rather dull,' was his verdict. 'I should have thought it affected you more than this.' He was right. Perhaps already I was suffering from reluctance to acknowledge my true feelings about the school and certainly I can now recapture more vividly than I did then my impressions of that September afternoon.

I was struck first by the sense of space. The playing fields on either side of us as we plodded up from the station seemed vast. The Dining Hall appeared enormous and I was deeply impressed, as most visitors are on seeing it for the first time, by the huge painting which covers almost the whole of one wall. This did not, as I supposed at my first, awed glance, depict the foundation of Christ's Hospital by Edward VI but commemorated the foundation of the Royal Mathematical School by Charles II, a century later. I did not know then that it incorporated a visual untruth, since it showed Charles's brother, James II, who had succeeded him, and indeed lost the throne, by the time Antonio Verrio had finished it, in 1690, after six years' work and much nagging by the governors. This huge canvas, brought, though I did not know this, from London, seemed to confirm that all I had heard about the grandeur of Christ's Hospital was true and that I was indeed privileged to be about to exchange my mundane shorts and shirt for the historic uniform shown in the picture. [1]

This reaction even survived my next experience, actually putting on my Housey clothes. The Wardrobe adjoined the Dining Hall, and resembled an army quartermasters' stores, then still unfamiliar to me. I was bewildered by the rack upon rack of dark blue coats surrounding me as I tried several on, and remember the uneasy, stiff, feeling as, afterwards, I walked clumsily and self-consciously back to my house, Peele A, the most distant one as it turned out, before emerging from it to say goodbye to my father in the privacy of the space behind it. He did not linger over the parting and later praised me for having shed no tears as several other new boys were all too audibly doing. 'You were, ' he told me later, 'a real brick.' Future separations were to be very different, but on that first occasion I was borne up by the prospect of the glories supposedly awaiting me, the splendours I had already witnessed, and by sheer curiosity.

On one subject this had already been satisfied, not very reassuringly: what the Christ's Hospital boy wore in addition to his famous blue coat. My underclothes still consisted of ordinary pants and vest, bought, as I have described, at Beynons, but there all resemblance to normal twentieth century garb ended. The white shirt I had acquired from the school was large and shapeless, with wide open sleeves, not tapering to the cuff, and lacking all buttons both there and at the front, which was a mere slit. At the neck, even more strangely, one wore bands, twin starched rectangular objects that had to be perfectly aligned with each other; for them to be askew so one could see both was a sure sign of a new boy. These I had already learned, though hardly taken in, would only achieve the required degree of precision if the ends were held in the mouth while one thrust a long safety pin through the collar round one's neck, and the top of one's shapeless shirt. To wear 'fudge bands', pinned perfectly together before one put them on and then simply tucked in, was, I was warned, a serious offence, and easily detected by simply pulling at the offending object, which came away in the hand instead of half throttling the unfortunate wearer. Below the waist one wore thick knickerbocker style breeches with buttons at the knee, bearing a portrait of Edward VI. Below these went the heavy yellow stockings which were also as famous as the blue coat itself, in thick wool, folded over at the knee. Only the shoes, solid black walking wear, with leather soles, were normal, and these I discovered were a fairly recent innovation, replacing the original, more elegant buckled type. Another reassuringly normal garment was the black woollen slipover provided for winter wear, the only concession made to climatic changes. Over the whole outfit we wore what was officially the 'gown', though always known to us as a 'Housey coat', and round the waist one's 'girdle', a narrow leather strap with metal buckles.

Progress up the school brought minor changes, rarely obvious to outsiders. On entering the Upper Fourth, at around 14 or so, and thereby becoming a member of the Upper School, entitled, for example, to use the school library, you acquired your 'broadie', a wider girdle held in place by a silver buckle. One had to pay for this oneself and it cost a sizeable sum, 3s 6d [17.5p][2], but the whole girdle then remained your property.[*]

To become a grecian, which elsewhere would have meant entering the sixth form but at Christ's Hospital implied you were in the select stream expected to go on to university, meant no external change in your preliminary years as a probationary deputy grecian or deputy grecian. Real glory followed, however, on becoming a full 'Button Grecian', which meant you had secured your university scholarship and justified the school's faith in you. The ordinary 'Housey coat' was now exchanged for a far more impressive one, with turned-back velvet cuffs, a cutaway collar to show off one's bands and large buttons all down the front.[3] Once, grecians had also worn more expensive, softer breeches, but by my day they were the same as everyone else's. For all boys, whatever their age or rank, no hat was provided. Far worse, however, was the fact that no form of raincoat or overcoat was supplied, the 'Housey coat' being regarded as a dual, indeed quadruple, purpose garment, to be worn indoors or out, in heatwave or snow, so that, the slipover already mentioned apart, we were dressed exactly the same whether the temperature was in the eighties Fahrenheit (the thirties Centigrade), or below zero, and whether soaked with sweat in swelteringly hot classroom or shivering with cold on some rainswept touchline. In the past Housey clothes had also been worn for games, as I have mentioned, but even in the 1930s only games clothes or, on 'Corps' days, of which I shall say more later, out-of-date Army uniform, brought any escape from this ridiculously impractical outfit.

Curiously, just as the school was intensely proud of its history but never taught us about it, so no explanation was ever offered as to why we were still dressed like Tudor schoolboys. Nor was anything said of the various minor

---

[*] I have promised mine to the Christ's Hospital collection of the Newbury and District Museum. A museum seems to me the proper place for the whole antiquated outfit.

changes made over the years which showed that the uniform was not wholly sacrosanct.* I still do not know why and when the lighter blue shown in old paintings was replaced by the near black of the twentieth century uniform, nor the originally loose fitting bands, fluttering separately like a clergyman's or lawyer's, gave way to a pair sitting tidily on top of each other. Nor am I clear when normal shoes replaced the buckled footwear earlier generations had sported. But with these trivial exceptions our outfit had not really changed since 1552 and I remember hearing, with inward amusement, the tribute paid to the Lady Superintendent, responsible for the domestic side of our lives, on her retirement. She would, claimed the speaker, be remembered for making a major improvement in Housey uniform, the provision of a pocket in the lining of the coat to accommodate a fountain pen. It seemed to me a somewhat insubstantial achievement for so many years of supposedly outstanding service.

I have given much space to the uniform because it must balk high in the recollection of anyone who has worn it and because it is regarded as of vast significance, not merely by the school's critics but by its keenest admirers. Thus the school hymn, which I have quoted earlier, mentioned the 'old world habit' – bored boys sometimes added an 's' at the end, giving the phrase a totally different meaning – as something for which the Almighty was to be thanked:

> Praise him for th' unbroken story,
> Linking present with the past,
> Old world habit, civic glory,
> Time worn customs newly cast.

Putting on the blue coat had always had a symbolic significance. It was only when a boy was, in the traditional term, 'clothed', that he 'went on the foundation' and became an object of its care.[4] The uniform had often, mistakenly in my view, been considered essential to the school's survival. Thus the school's latest historian, Professor Morpurgo, in his 1984 edition of the standard, 1937, history, *Christ's Hospital*, gives, with all the authority of a Donation Governor and almoner, the classic, traditional view:

> Dressed for the first time in this treasured uniform the boy is truly a Blue, a Housey boy, a member of a world-wide and age-old community, possessor of a promissory note on a rich future and heir to four centuries of tradition,[5]...Tudor bluecoat and yellow stockings are precious to the Boys' School, and to all who have ever worn them of much more significance than aliens will believe possible...They are (and it cannot be said too often) the prime symbols of continuity, the most immediate evidence to the equality of all Blues, and among the most compelling influences which assure every boy

---

* See Chapter 14.

in the school that equality is beyond challenge, that, from wheresoever he comes, however deprived his background, however disadvantaged his family or miserable his home circumstances, he is settled with all his contemporaries and with all their predecessors in the aristocracy of Christ's Hospital.[6]

My introduction to 'the aristocracy of Christ's Hospital' came via a boy from a background similar to my own; his father, I learned much later, worked for a wholesale confectioner in Twickenham and he had reached Christ's Hospital, like myself, via the West Gifts route. Pitman, as I knew him, was my 'nursemaid', it being the sensible custom to appoint a second-year boy to assist each new boy to settle in. The relationship officially ended after a fortnight, during which the nursemaid was liable to be blamed for any of his charge's shortcomings and misdemeanours, but in our case was the start of a life-long friendship, indeed the relationship was to be almost duplicated when, eleven years later, I arrived as a freshman at the same college as my old nursemaid had entered the year before. Here indeed is one respect in which my experience has followed that of Charles Lamb. 'The Christ's Hospital boy's friends,' he wrote around 1820, 'are commonly his intimates through life.'[7] Apart from my former nursemaid, sadly long dead, my closest life-long friend has been someone who was a contemporary in my house and another close and lasting friend came from its immediate neighbour; getting to know boys further afield was not encouraged. While revising the present book I was contacted by a Peele A friend whom I had barely seen since schooldays. He suggested 'a walk such as we used to have', and I duly found that, after half a century apart, the old intimacy was immediately restored. Other Old Blues have had similar experiences. Christ's Hospital, I believe, affects its pupils even more deeply than other boarding schools both because of its unique character and because they have not previously been 'inoculated' to living away from home by attending a prep school first.

The first of the 'friends for life' who was to impress his personality upon me was my nursemaid, Robert Percival Pitman, as he proudly signed himself in my autograph book. Bob, as I knew him after leaving school, and I, hit it off from the first, though he was in disposition very different from me, casual, untidy and ill-organised to an extent that often infuriated me and which sometimes alienated even the most tolerant masters. He took very seriously his duties as my guardian and mentor and my introduction to this new world would have been far more unpleasant without his help. At the end of term I described to my father how helpful Pitman had been to me and he bought me a penknife to give him, which so delighted its recipient that his widow still recalls his talking of it.

Pitman's first task was to see that I was properly turned out and did not disgrace him by displaying separately fluttering bands or an over-loose girdle. We spent a lot of our lives dressing and undressing and great importance was attached to putting on or taking off one's clothes in the prescribed fashion. After removing breeches and underpants, pyjama trousers or games shorts had to be pulled on *before* removing shirt and vest, and on dressing a similar routine had to be followed in reverse. Another requirement was to wear one's pullover over the braces, never below them, although the latter procedure saved much time and trouble. Shoe laces, it was laid down, must be inserted at right angles to the row of holes, not herring-bone style. Failure to obey such rules was a punishable offence, often involving yet more changing of clothes, and so deeply were these rules and rituals imposed upon us that I still feel uneasy if I do not keep them. They had, I imagine, originated in the distant past when many boys entered the school never having worn normal clothes.

The same strict regulations governed the procedure for keeping us clean, no doubt for similar reasons, and even in the 1930s there must have been many other boys who came, like me, from homes without a proper bathroom or hot water supply. Thus when I had my first bath at school Pitman was on hand to teach me the accepted drill, beginning, I think, at the neck, which had to be well scrubbed before one moved on to the ears and face itself, and followed by the armpits before the chest and arms. It was quite an elaborate routine, designed to ensure that no area was omitted. One was, however, given a choice of day for one's weekly bath and I opted for Friday on the grounds that this was the first treat of the coming weekend. Here, too, for many years after leaving school I felt compelled, whatever other baths I had had, to continue the practice every Friday night.

Having confirmed that I was suitably clean and properly dressed Pitman's next duty was to introduce me to the lay-out of the house. My first impression of space rapidly disappeared and I realised it was a confusingly crowded and noisy place, but what struck me even more was the overwhelming odour of carbolic soap, the result of pre-term scrubbing by the domestic staff.

The lay-out of the house block was, I now discovered, not difficult to master. Each block formed an 'E' with the centre stroke missing, the 'A' house being to one's left as you faced it from the Avenue, the 'B' house to the right. In the middle were the matron's room, adjoining a large walk-in wardrobe where we kept our best coats, taken out only for Sunday and occasions like Speech Day, a sewing room occupied by the maids, and bedrooms for all the staff of the house, including the junior housemaster, whose study was on the ground floor. Attached to the block on either side was the senior housemaster's house, assuming he was married, for some houses, lacking such accommodation, had bachelor housemasters, with a mere study and bedroom to themselves.

In Peele A the senior housemaster's house was separated from the boys' area by a door of traditional green baize and there was also a door linking the senior dormitory, on the first floor, to the housemaster's bedroom floor, but, for some reason, it was never used. Our housemaster was, as I shall describe, prone to pay sudden visits to the dormitories but we usually had some warning of his approach. Had he chosen to make use of this private corridor more than one career might have been cut short, but the architect's foresight in providing it remained unjustified.

At the front of the House, occupying most of the front of the 'E' I have described, was the dayroom, where most of our lives outside the classroom were spent. Here we sat silent for prep and nightly prayers, played board games, read, practised what hobbies there was room for, chatted, fought and, when old enough, made use of the half-size billiard table situated at one end, an oddly luxurious item in this highly functional environment. Round the walls were small lockers, assigned according to one's house number, the sole concession to privacy and individuality the school afforded, since it accommodated all one's possessions except 'tuck'. When I arrived this was kept in one's overnight case in a boxroom, a useful overflow repository for other possessions, but, on hygienic grounds, the boxroom became used for other purposes and a special tuck cupboard was provided in the corridor outside the day room. When food began to disappear from this, which was made up of small individual cubby-holes, suspicion hung heavy over several unpopular boys, notably one notorious as the house thief, and our housemaster set in hand the type of massive investigation to which he was prone though, as usual, it achieved nothing. A more acute boy remarked, however, on the curious circumstance that it was only the spaces nearest the ground which had been raided and the true culprit, the housemaster's small dog, by now swollen on a diet of illicit cake and biscuits, was unmasked.

Above the lockers were the rows of battered books which made up the house library, the sole source of recreational reading for all boys in forms below the Upper Fourth, ie in their first two or three years. Most of the dayroom was taken up with five or six long and solid wooden tables, surrounded by upright wooden benches. In the dayroom as elsewhere seniority was all. One started off with a seat at the table near the door, then gradually progressed up the dayroom until if one survived long enough one reached the top table and acquired the valuable right to sit on the ledge behind it with one's back to the window, the only place in the building where one could read with a reasonable degree of comfort and undisturbed.

To concentrate on anything, even playing a game, in the body of the dayroom was almost impossible since it was simply too small for the number of occupants. At most times it contained various groups of boys shouting, fighting, trying to make models or to practise some quiet pursuit like stamp collecting; some were even working, despite all the difficulties. A particular hazard was presented by boys stretched on the floor with a rifle, aiming at a target held up some distance away, for reasons I explain later. Such exercises took up a great deal of floor space and inevitably the recumbent boy might get trodden on, or someone might come between him and his target, with noisy, if not more violent, consequences.

Beyond the dayroom lay the senior and junior changing rooms, separated by a washroom with washbasins and a communal trough in which the more exhibitionist older boys, to my great alarm as a new boy, liked to stretch out and romp naked. It must have been here that I first discovered the meaning of puberty, and I can remember that to me the tall, hairy 16 and 17 year olds who disported themselves there seemed enormous and hardly members of the same species as me, let alone the same House. Behind the changing rooms was the bootroom, a grim and dingy area where there was a locker for each boy's shoes and facilities for shoe cleaning. Opposite this was a small junkroom, the true purpose of which I never found out, but items left there tended to be regarded as communal property, unlike the undoubtedly personal contents of one's dayroom or tuck cupboard locker.

Behind the House, separated from it by the sort of ventilation space to be found in out-of-date hospitals and apartment blocks, were the lavatories, consisting of a row of urinals and four small WCs, one in each corner, shielded by a small door, with a gap below and above. This area was always known as 'the bogs' and, especially since our lives operated to such a tight schedule and the school facilities were even worse, the provision was obviously inadequate for 50 boys. At the end of my first year the 'new bogs' were added in a block tacked on to the existing one, offering a further row of WCs, and providing a little more privacy since they opened on to a passage. This, and the addition of the tuck cupboard, already mentioned, were the only improvement in the fabric and amenities of the house that took place in the seven years that I was there.

For the school as a whole there was, however, a major addition in 1937, in the shape of new buildings for the Preparatory School. The Prep had always been a place apart, with a recognition that the eight to ten year olds who occupied it required closer supervision and a slightly milder regime than the inmates of the other houses, though, 'because of the tininess of the inhabitants', a school historian explained, 122 boys were crammed into its single block in place of the 102 fitted, not very comfortably, into the rest.[8] Now, as *The Blue* for March 1937 reported, 'magnificent new buildings' were added, not indeed to improve the living quarters, but to provide the sort of recreational facilities that we so notably lacked: 'Manual Rooms in which the boys can do fretwork, painting and cardboard cutting, a Nature Room where caterpillars, fish and insects can live and be studied, a Hobbies room where stamps can be catalogued and Meccano models built' and of value to the whole school since it came to be used as a theatre, a 'Hall...where on wet afternoons games of all descriptions can be played.' There were also new classrooms of notable 'lightness and cheerfulness'.[9] I shall mention the Prep block again and it clearly demonstrated what vast strides school design had made in the 39 years since the main building programme at Horsham had begun.

To return to Peele A, which was identical with what were then known as the senior, ie non-Prep houses, the first and second floors were taken up by the senior and junior dormitories respectively, each containing about 25 beds, with one small cubicle in each for the house-captain and his deputy, the second monitor. At either end of both dormitories were the 'lav ends' containing communal washing facilities, consisting of a flat trough housing removable metal wash basins, with a bath at one end, open to view, urinals, also public, and a single WC, partly shielded by a screen at the side but open at the front. Privacy, the curious undressing routine apart, was clearly not something on which my new school set much store.

To return to my first evening, at 8 o'clock, though I cannot remember it, I must have attended my first 'duty', the simple evening prayers with a Bible reading and grace, which rounded off the day. This was the time for the housemaster to make any announcements, or to single out individual boys for praise or censure, but I cannot remember any on that occasion and immediately afterwards the juniors went to bed, leaving the seniors to settle down to another hour of prep. With the attentive Pitman no doubt leading the way I must have gone upstairs, changed, somewhat apprehensively, into my pyjamas in what seemed the vast dormitory, and then have been instructed to wash in the prescribed fashion. I was then pushed into position in the line stretching down the middle of the dormitory of boys awaiting matron's inspection. We were required to strip off our pyjama jackets and bend down to submit our necks and ears to her gaze, then hold out each wrist in turn, turn it over, and then lift up first our left foot and then our right for her approval. Sometimes a boy must, I suppose, have been sent back to wash some inadequately scrubbed limb again but I cannot remember this ever happening and I certainly passed muster that first evening.

Finally, still excited rather than apprehensive, I must have climbed into bed, before the cry of 'Lights out!' at 8.30, when the dormitory was plunged into darkness apart from the lamp over the monitor's table.

Looking back, I can recall only one uneasy moment that first evening, strange though everything seemed. This had occurred when Pitman, anxious to be friendly, had asked me what football team I supported. I had even then no interest whatever in sport and replied with the only name I could think of, 'Arsenal', which seemed to satisfy him. I spent the rest of the term fearful he or some other boy might ask a question about 'my' team which would reveal my ignorance.

I do not recall feeling homesick that first evening. What I had found most upsetting was the noise in Dining Hall and indeed the whole experience of communal eating, as well as the public undressing and half-naked line-up in front of matron at bedtime. I had, however, sufficient sense to anticipate that I would get used to both, as Pitman, so far my only real contact with my schoolmates, clearly had done, and he seemed a nice enough and normal boy. Above all, I can appreciate now, I was still sustained by the novelty of my situation and the feeling that I was privileged to have come to Christ's Hospital and that if I disliked anything about it this must be my fault and not the school's. No doubt some furtive tears were shed that night in the junior dormitory of Peele A, perhaps by a returning second-year who knew what to expect, but my eyes remained dry and, in spite of the unaccustomedly hard bed, I rapidly fell asleep.

[1] Allan pp.65-67
[2] Morpurgo p.35
[3] Morpurgo p.79
[4] June 1973 p.158
[5] Morpurgo p.127
[6] Morpugo p.140
[7] *Christ's Hospital Book* p.65
[8] Morpurgo p.90
[9] Mar 1937 p.151

19

FORM TWO DEEP !

Order given to marching boys before entering Dining Hall, 1936

At 7 am on the morning of my first full day at boarding school I was roused by the distant pealing of the school bell, followed by loud cries of 'Get up!', the second word being drawn out over several seconds and delivered at full pitch so that it penetrated the deepest slumbers. No one that I can recall ever defied this summons and in any case the next half hour was so packed with activity that a rapid response was essential. Nose-blowing on command followed, when we stood at the end of our beds and, three times in succession, raised our handkerchiefs to our noses and on hearing the order, 'Blow!' did our best to dislodge any accumulated contents. I shall say more about this curious custom later.

Following nose-blowing I followed Pitman into the lav end for the morning wash which began our day, but, except for new boys like myself, kept under scrutiny by their nursemaids, it was a hurried affair, with boys jostling each other for use of the inadequate number of large metal basins, or to find a space to spit in the communal trough after cleaning their teeth. After washing, one's bed had to be stripped and the bedding arranged in a prescribed pattern, rather as on inspection days in an army barrack room, but at Christ's Hospital every day was an inspection day and the somewhat unyielding mattress had to be folded over in the specified arch-like fashion, with 'bolio' beneath it and blankets, neatly folded, again according to a traditional pattern, at one end of the now exposed wooden frame. By 7.25 this ritual had to be completed and, washed and tidy, one had to be outside on the pavement of the Avenue. Then, to shouts of 'On parade!' we shuffled into the road and formed up facing the house in two rows, with the tallest boys on the right and left and the smallest in the middle. The monitor in charge then ordered 'Number!', whereupon the first boy on the right of the line shouted 'One!', his neighbour 'Two!' and so on until the tiniest ten year old on the far left piped up with a squeaky 'Twenty-four!' or some such figure. We were next instructed to 'Form fours!', whereupon the even numbers moved a pace back and another to the right, the resulting four lines being then told to 'Right turn!' If the manoeuvre was not performed with sufficient alacrity and smartness we might be forced to repeat it before being commanded to 'Quick march!' A similar scene was repeated in front of every other house until 16 squads were converging on the Dining Hall, being duly ordered 'Left wheel!' as they approached the doors and then 'Form two deep!' a repetition in reverse of forming fours, to create a file narrow enough to go through the entrance. Thence we were actually allowed to make our own way to the house's allotted table. At that time each was large enough to seat the whole house and ran across the room at right angles to the side walls. We sat on backless benches, strictly by seniority, with the most junior boys at the centre, so that throughout one's school career one found oneself seated with the same people as one progressed steadily towards the ends. At the midday meal the chair at the end was occupied by a housemaster, but at other meals by the house-captain or senior monitor.

On that first morning I was too bewildered by the whole procedure and the accompanying noise to have much understanding of what was going on, so I was taken unawares by the blow from a gavel from the supervising master to command silence and the further two blows which signalled the grecian standing in the pulpit at the centre of one side to begin reading grace. There was a similar procedure at the end so that, quite apart from the daily service in chapel and 'duty' in the evening, we thanked God, or more immediately, those 'founders and benefactors' of whom we were so often reminded, a total of six times a day for being fortunate enough to be where we were. At breakfast that first Saturday I felt hopelessly at sea, but the ever present, ever helpful Pitman pushed me into the proper, humble place in the middle of the seated boys and prompted me as to what was happening. No doubt he also explained the mysteries of 'trades' and the 'kiff-bowl' of which I shall say more later, but nothing he said can have diminished my realisation that, if this first meal was typical, I faced a hungry future.

After breakfast on that first day we almost ran back to the house; Peele A being the furthest away we always had to hurry. Here we had to make our beds, another new experience for me, though Pitman instructed me so efficiently that I can still turn a neat 'hospital corner'. An extremely high standard was insisted on, at least as demanding as anything I subsequently encountered in the army, and there was one refinement not required in the barrack room, 'poling' our 'bolios', or stiff bolsters which took the place of pillows, with the long wooden rod kept at the end of each dormitory, two beds having their bolsters pressed into place simultaneously. The beds were then inspected, and the blankets torn off any considered unsatisfactory, with their owners forced to make them again.

The brief interval after bed-making was the classic time to visit the lavatory. The *Health Rules* displayed in the lav ends of each dormitory, which we were required to learn by heart, attached great importance to this event. 'A daily bowel movement is essential to health,' I can still recite, 'though', it was acknowledged, with an unaccustomed concession to personal freedom, 'the actual time of day you go to the lavatory does not matter.' My housemaster, a Frenchman, a race notorious for their abdominal obsession, was much concerned that the boys in his charge should do their duty in this respect. He would periodically deliver a homily to the house on the subject, and, using a curious idiom which invariably produced suppressed giggles, would occasionally ask some boy whom he suspected of defecatory slackness; 'Have you had your rear in today?' [*]

There was, I soon discovered, a strong incentive to use the house facilities at the intended time because most masters were very reluctant to let boys 'be excused' during a lesson and, if permission was granted, one had to use 'the school bogs', a block of solid, cheerless, brick toilets set in the centre of the car park. The comparatively civilised lavatories in the classroom blocks were reserved for masters' use. Those for our use had no doors, merely a short stretch of wall on either side with a large central opening, leaving the user on public view. This prospect appalled me and, as I know that others reacted in the same way, must have undone much of the *Health Rules*' exhortations to regularity, especially at that time when each house offered only four WCs for the use of fifty boys. Later I understood the reasons for the doorless lavatories, and for the barely shielded one adjoining each dormitory and the inadequate doors, over which the tallest boys could certainly see, in the main house toilets, but this was little consolation and for me, as for so many Old Blues, the inadequate provision for this basic need remains one of my abiding memories, as it had done for those who faced the even more defective facilities of Newgate Street.

'There were never enough loos,' confirms a contemporary who left in 1942. 'It was not uncommon to miss out on the opportunity to meet one's needs and go through the morning in discomfort because of the pressures of the timetable.' When you did find one vacant privacy was still lacking for 'The doors had no locks and it was common for juniors to sharpen the ends of their girdle so that it would fit in the latch and prevent it being opened. We used to put our coats over the doors to indicate occupancy but it was very common for passing boys to flick the coat over the door. The occupant then jumped up under rather inconvenient circumstances to prevent his coat from falling on to the usually wet floor.'

A Peele A contemporary was even more deeply affected. He told me many years later with what satisfaction he had threatened, as a factory inspector, to prosecute firms who provided for their employees the same doorless facilities as

---

[*] I have learned since the housemaster of Maine A used a variant of this expression, asking his boys 'Have you been to the rear today?'

Christ's Hospital. In industry they were illegal and he regretted being unable to return to his old school and take it also to court.

To return to my first day, after bed-making and the more or less statutory visit to the lavatory we were marched to Chapel, about which I shall say more later. I was surprised at having, for the second time in less than two hours, to parade outside the house and march down the Avenue. On this aspect of school life I shall also comment again later.

After Chapel on that first day we again hastened back to our houses to collect books for morning school. I imagine I ran with the rest, though I had as yet none to fetch, and Pitman must then have escorted me to the classroom where the examination was held to settle in what form I would start my Housey career. I shall recount the results in due course. At the time I enjoyed sitting at a desk again and being confronted with a question paper, a familiar situation in an otherwise unfamiliar world.

By now I was beginning to gain some appreciation of the lay-out of my new home, though much of it still remained to be explored. Its backbone was the Avenue, about three quarters of a mile [1.2km] long, of which about a third curved away towards the entrance lodge – an impressive building surmounted by the school crest – at its eastern extremity, where it joined the Worthing Road. Along the main half mile were arranged the boys' houses, with four blocks located on the Avenue on either side of the central area formed by the Quadrangle. At the opposite end of the Avenue from my house was the preparatory school, or 'Prep', whose members shared the Dining Hall with us but otherwise lived a largely separate life. Between the Prep and the Quad lay Maine, Barnes and Lamb blocks, then, beyond the Quad, in that order, Coleridge, Middleton, Thornton and Peele. Each block was sub-divided into an 'A' and 'B' wing, with in the central area the matron's room and assistant housemasters' studies and bedrooms. The two wings contained the boarding accommodation, with in each a dayroom. Behind this were the changing rooms and lavatories, with the two dormitories, for the senior and junior boys respectively, above.

The boys' houses, on the northern side of the Avenue, faced the houses of the married masters on the far side, of which by far the grandest was the Headmaster's house, which adjoined the Chapel and the Quadrangle. This was the main, and most striking, feature of the whole design and the claim made in a recent booklet about the school that it 'contained monumental buildings of architectural distinction – Chapel, Dining Hall, Big School – which have stood the test of time and remain an inspiration to those who use them today' is not exaggerated. Unlike so many large institutions, Christ's Hospital, Horsham, had not grown piecemeal over the years but had been laid out on a systematic plan in a single style, consistent and coherent, if undistinguished.

The heart of the school was formed by the Quadrangle, with, in the centre, a statue of Edward VI, brought from London. Around him stood smaller statues of those now legendary Old Blues Coleridge, Lamb, Middleton and Maine. The northern side of the Quadrangle was occupied by the Dining Hall, with lesser buildings to either side containing the Masters' Common Room and the Court Room, used on occasions like Speech Day, with behind it the Kitchens and Wardrobe, and towering above them all, the Water Tower, visible for miles over the surrounding countryside. On the far side of the Quad was the main school assembly building, Big School, surmounted by the school clock and linked by bridges at first-floor level to a classroom block on either side. The two other sides of the Quad contained the Cloisters, with, behind them on one side the Old Science School, smelling permanently of chemicals, and on the other, the west side, the Chapel, with beyond it the Headmaster's house. Behind Big School was the Music School, its purpose easily identifiable long before one reached it, from the sometimes anguished sounds produced by inexpert hands on piano or violin. For such tuition there was a charge, the only school activity which was not entirely free, but the musically minded could also develop their skill in the Band Room, where instruments, and instruction, cost nothing. It had, I later learned, though the information was never of any value to me, a secondary importance in that it was one of the few places where one regularly met boys from other houses.

Gradually after those first few frenzied days I mastered the remainder of the school's geography. Adjoining the main Quad. to the east was the car park, already mentioned, with the Art School to one side and the Library to the other, and beyond the Library the 'New Quad' or 'Garden', already mentioned, but this name was never used. On its left, ie eastern side, was the modern New Science School, dedicated to biology laboratories, which with their ever present aura of preserving fluid smelt no better than those in the Old Science School, and to the geography department. This faced the back of another classroom block. The far side was open, giving a view of the Quarter Mile, a straight road running parallel to the Avenue, and of Big Side beyond, with at one extremity the so-called Science Farm, though I suspect this was always a misnomer, and to the far right the school Cricket Pavilion which, except as a Home Guard, I never entered in all my years at the school.

Almost every building on the whole vast estate had, I now realise, something to reveal about the distinctive character of Christ's Hospital. I only discovered some time after my arrival, for example, that the small church-hall-like building behind Lamb was the Scout hut. No Peele A boy ever entered it because our housemaster objected to the Scouts on the grounds that, as a school-wide organisation, they would weaken house spirit.[*] I was soon, however, to get to know the inside of the Manual School, in the same area, where what would now be called craft subjects were taught, and beyond the Manual School, what we

---

[*] Here he was following in an earlier tradition. See Chapter 16 on Dr Upcott's attitude to the Scout movement.

called 'the sicker', officially the Infirmary, an ugly, somewhat shapeless three storey building of vaguely sinister appearance and large enough to meet the medical needs of a small town. Just like a town, Housie had, too, I learned, its isolation hospital, detached from the Infirmary, known as 'the san' or sanatorium. This lavish provision, far more than other schools found necessary, was, I now realise, probably a survival of the days when epidemics could spread like wildfire through the all too aptly named wards in Newgate Street, and reflected, too, the tradition that the school's care for its pupils should be all-embracing with free medical and, if necessary, in-patient, treatment for everyone 'on the foundation'.

The governors may also have been influenced by the grim predictions made at the time of the move that the Sussex clay on which the school was built made it unsuitable for its purpose –'gravel soil' was a notable selling point of fee-paying prep schools – but their pessimism happily proved unjustified.[1] The Almoners had, however, undoubtedly listened to the critics who had proclaimed the need to provide space for physical recreation. Behind each house lay 'the asphalt', where we engaged in ten brisk minutes of PT, or physical training, every morning and were encouraged to play at other times, the favoured activities being roller-skating, which I never mastered, and, on Saturday evenings in the summer, asphalt cricket.

The great glory of the new Housie, however, was the lavish space available for organised games. Each house had its own rugger and cricket pitches, either in the area between the back of the house and the Post Office, or on the far side of the Avenue, adjoining or beyond Big Side, where the pitches used by school teams like the 'Housey First' and 'Housey Second' were located, though I never played on either. Here, too, in the Lent Term, the long jump and other facilities needed for athletic events were laid out.

Sport was to be at the root of many of my most painful recollections of Housie, as it is with so many of my contemporaries, but my first acquaintance with it seemed reassuring. On the afternoon of that first Saturday of term, 19 September 1936, I was still sustained by a sense of novelty as (with Pitman on hand to see that I followed the proper order in discarding my Housey clothes and pulling on my brand new games outfit) I dressed, for the first time in my life, in football shorts and boots. I also put on the plain red jersey which identified Peele A, somewhat resenting the fact that we did not, for a reason I never discovered, have a colourful pattern of stripes like every other house, but, instead resembled Garibaldi's famous 'Red Shirts' who set out in 1860 to liberate Sicily. I must have made an unimpressive figure as, highly self-conscious and slightly shivering, though it was a sunny afternoon, I falteringly made my way to the house pitch. Here I made for the first time close acquaintance with my housemaster, to whom I devote a separate chapter later. He had, I have learned since, been an outstanding rugger player as a young man, and it cannot have taken him long to realise that I was unlikely to bring his house much distinction on the games field, but he conscientiously drilled us in such hitherto arcane procedures as passing the oddly shaped ball while running down the field – it had, he stressed, to be passed backwards, not forwards, which seemed to me strange if one wanted to reach the opposing team's 'try line' as rapidly as possible. I quite enjoyed the novelty of this, and it was already a relief not to be wearing the bulky and burdensome uniform which, even in September, was uncomfortably hot.

Hitherto my only experience of any form of sport, apart from a few races once a year on St Nicholas Sports Day, had been helping to kick a soccer ball about in the playground wearing ordinary school clothes and shoes. To play a game with an odd shaped ball and to be required to deliberately fall on it while it was being 'dribbled', a word new to me, by another player, or to hurl oneself upon a boy who was carrying it, known as 'tackling', was more interesting than frightening. I have often felt since that I might even have enjoyed rugger, or at least have disliked it less, if games had been more imaginatively organised so that those with a marked lack of aptitude for them could have been assigned to separate teams, drawn from the whole school. This, however, would have meant bringing boys from separate houses together, thus violating a basic Housey principle – though, curiously enough, outstanding, and even promising, players, did join all-school teams.

As for soccer, I doubt if I would have enjoyed it much more than rugger, and I soon realised, despite my nursemaid's question about my favourite team, that interest in this supposedly working-class sport was not encouraged, belonging, as it did, to the world from which we had emerged, rather than the one to which we now aspired. A soccer enthusiast in another house, however, arriving in 1945, resented the same attitude and, a natural rebel, later challenged it. 'I used to organise pick-up games on Sunday afternoons,' he has recalled. 'These were soon banned on the grounds that we were wearing out the rugby pitches. When we moved to play on waste patches, this too was forbidden. Kicking a round ball was akin to joining a trade union. Just not done.'

---

[1] Allan p.85

20

STRAIGHT AND SQUARE

Plane one edge straight and square and then complete the face mark.

Carpentry instructor at Christ's Hospital, 1936

My life now rapidly fell into a closely regulated pattern, covering three areas: the house, the sports field, and the classroom. It was in this last, as the most familiar, where from the first I felt most at home and, one or two fearsome or incompetent masters apart, it remained for me throughout my schooldays a welcome refuge from what rapidly became the horror and discomfort of the other two. On my first morning, as already mentioned, I had sat the internal examination which assigned new boys to the appropriate class, an even more important decision at Christ's Hospital than elsewhere, since it largely settled whether we would ultimately join the small elite known as grecians, destined for Oxford and Cambridge, or remain with the solid majority who would leave school at 15 or 16. The Housey system did not, as I was to witness, rule out the possibility of a later move upwards or, though I cannot recall such a case, downwards and at the time I had no idea of its significance. As it was I found myself assigned to the top entrance level for boys of my age who had not yet learned any Latin or French, 3A. (If there were first or second forms they must have been confined to the Prep.) Had I already started on a foreign language I might have gone straight into the Lower Fourth, or LF, and skipped a year.

The term 'grecian', as already mentioned, originally identified boys who learned Greek as well as Latin. These two ancient languages were still at the heart of the Housey curriculum and proficiency in them was regarded as the real yardstick of intellectual ability and – more important – as by far the likeliest means of gaining university entrance, which meant winning a scholarship in a highly competitive examination. Mere places did not in our day, for boys of our background, exist. By the 1930s the ability to produce, and cap, classical tags was no longer the hallmark of the educated man, but, perhaps longer than most, Christ's Hospital tended to have classicists as its headmasters and to value Latin and Greek above all other subjects. Like so much else, this belief went back, at least in part, to the school's golden age. The reason, asserted Charles Lamb, that 'the Christ's Hospital boy feels that he is no charity-boy' lay 'in that measure of classical attainments which every individual at that school...has it in his power to procure.' [1] By my day no one except classics specialists learned Greek though it was, for a time, after I had left, taught instead of Latin.

The reason, sensible enough, was that it was by then so rarely offered that the pass mark was encouragingly low, and a similarly practical argument, that it was supposedly easier, explained the school's practice of teaching German as the normal foreign language rather than French. Useful though my schoolboy German has proved since, I found great difficulty later on in trying to master French from scratch and have never acquired the faintest facility in speaking it. As it was, I enjoyed my first encounter with a foreign language, due to a master regarded with affection then, and since, as a 'character', Arthur Rider, who would enliven lessons by hurling chalk at inattentive pupils, and greet mistakes with shouts of 'Tripehound!', a rough anglicisation of the German 'Schweinhund!' which wartime films were soon to make familiar. I shall say more of him later.

It was the sensible practice at Housie to assign boys to 'sets' according to their proficiency in a particular subject, so that, at least after that first, largely diagnostic, year, one was working with those of similar ability. What impressed me most in that first term was the smallness of the classes, invariably under 20, so that it was impossible to coast along in amiable idleness. The basic subjects held no terror for me and I enjoyed Latin and German for their novelty, though well aware within a few weeks that I would never make a linguist. I also, with less regret, realised that 'manual' – what would now be called 'craft' – subjects were not for me, and Mrs Curwood's despair at my ineptitude in her raffia lessons was soon being echoed by that of the good natured middle-aged man who now tried to teach me the basic elements of carpentry.

I have explained earlier how, in 1908, Christ's Hospital, ahead of its time, opened a Manual School, built on the same lavish lines as the Infirmary. In the upper reaches, which we juniors never penetrated, there was a Drawing Office, where mechanical drawing, whatever that was, was said to be taught, but the few engineering grecians and 'deps' seemed doubly remote to us, from their subject as well as their rank. I was surprised to be having such lessons at all and concluded, unjustly I now know, that the school hoped to equip us as carpenters or plumbers if even the City refused to accept us. Manual rapidly proved one of the many subjects at which I was no good, so that, far from acquiring an understanding of the unique satisfaction that using one's hands can give, it left me with a fresh feeling of failure.

Apart from one or two senior masters, like the Head of Engineering, CWS Averill, BSc, (known from his slightly grizzled appearance as 'Bonzo') and his immediate subordinate, the staff of the Manual School held a somewhat uneasy place in the Housey social structure, ranking roughly with the head groundsman, the school drill sergeants and the bandmaster. This last achieved fame later in my time at Housie by having an affair with the wife of a particularly unpopular master. The shock could hardly have been greater if the chaplain (an eminently respectable man) had run off with a kitchen maid. The general reaction, however, was that this public humiliation served the cuckolded husband right.

Most of the Manual School staff could have given lessons to many of the 'real' masters in conscientiousness, ability to communicate and sheer kindness. I still remember with affection the woodwork specialist, TS Leaney – known as 'Leaney senior' since his son was also employed there – and I am still grateful to him for having drilled into me the functions of various tools and the names of different types of joint, knowledge that has enabled me to understand the conversation of do-it-yourself enthusiasts today, if not to share their interest.

I must, I now realise, have been a sad disappointment to this amiable and patient individual, of whose appearance and teaching technique one of my contemporaries has left a vivid account:

> Short in stature, well past his first youth, a pink hairless, head attached to his trunk without apparent benefit of neck...he looked like a slightly sinister Humpty Dumpty...When he advanced on you, crooning quietly to himself, the sunlight gleaming on his spectacles and a razor-sharp chisel curving curlicues in the air before him, it was difficult not to dive for cover under the bench. [2]

This boy clearly got further through the syllabus than I ever managed:

> We were taken step by step through the course – first the forthright mortice and tenon, then the cunning dovetail, the four-holer egg stand on its cruciform base, then the heavy teak penholder, soapy with polish.
>
> Finally came the stool, which incorporated all we had learnt so far, with the added embellishment of a veneered pattern of our own choice and several coats of sticky varnish...It was too small to be sat on...and had no other discernible purpose. It was not so much a stool as an ikon. [3]

In that first term one began by making a wooden box, with a sliding lid, to familiarise one with the use of the basic tools. Shaping the sides was the very first task and I can still hear in my mind TS Leaney's ritual chant; 'Plane one edge straight and square and then complete the face-mark', this being the pencil scrawl that identified the surface to go outside. He was moved to despair rather than anger – I never saw any boy struck or even threatened in the Manual School – when one planed off too much wood or sawed a piece so badly it had to be shortened in a second attempt. He did once say that if I wasted any more wood I would have to pay for the replacement, a terrifying prospect, but one that never materialised. After the box came more ambitious exercises, notably making a wooden doorplate, something not much in evidence in our council house. This involved using a chisel to secure a neat curve at the ends and, I believe, an electric drill, something then not to be seen outside a factory or workshop, to pierce holes at the corners. A friend recalls how his first attempt to obtain an adequately level edge on a five inch [12.7cm] plank ended up with him surrounded by wood shavings and a small sliver of the original in the vice. 'My child,' lamented Leaney senior as though recording some unthinkable crime, 'you've planed the wood away.'

Basic woodwork supposedly mastered, though I am sure my mortice and tenon joints must have had some surreptitious help from Mr Leaney to hold together, one moved on to metal work, the first object to be made, designed to accustom the pupil to the use of files and metal punches, being a keyhole plate. I was no better at this than at making a shoe box, though as it took more work to ruin the materials the results were less disastrously inadequate, but learned one useful lesson, to treat power tools with respect. When the time came to drill holes in the somewhat curiously shaped keyhole plate I tried to hold the edge in my bare hand, instead of the proper heavy pliers, and gave it a bad gash, my first and last industrial injury.

In the summer term, by unhappy chance, we were in the forge, a popular location in the colder months since one was surrounded by furnaces and it was the one place in the school one could be certain of being warm. The experience demonstrated the grotesque impracticality of our uniform and I doubt if even a Tudor blacksmith ever looked as unsuitably dressed as we did, sweating in our heavy knee-breeches, thick winter-weight shirts, yellow stockings and constricting white bands as we heated up metal rods with a bellows and hammered them into shape on an anvil. Our Housey coats we were allowed to discard, to protect them rather than us, but it was wretchedly uncomfortable none the less. I proved no more successful in the forge than in the carpentry and metal workshops and once melted away the whole of the raw metal we were supposed to work into shape, but emerged at the end of term with the fruits of the simplest exercise, a poker. Others completed far more complex tasks, like shaping two separate metal bars and then fastening them together to form a pair of tongs. The forge was an even more dangerous place than the metal workshop. The friend whose lack of planing prowess has already been mentioned incautiously gripped a poker, as instructed by Leaney junior, to take it out of a vice only to find it was red hot, a fact concealed by the sun shining on it. He immediately plunged his smouldering hand in cold water to be reproved a second time, being told: 'Worst thing you could possibly do,' the current doctrine being to keep burns away from water.

Some boys did soldering and pewter work, but I have no recollection of either nor, to my great regret, did I spend any time in the Print Shop, which I should have enjoyed. One contemporary who did experienced 'great fun setting up the type.' He can date the period precisely as early June 1940 because the class was instructed to write a poem about current events and then produce a printed copy. His began, he recalls,

'In Norway now, the British have drawn back.'

In charge of printing was the deputy head of the Manual School Major WD Harrup, whose chief role in the life of Christ's Hospital was as Commanding Officer of its OTC detachment. His service during the first world war on the Western Front had left him with a legacy of shell shock. Major Harrup was considered 'genial', a term of high praise, and his pupils, who never included me, soon came to ignore his habit of walking up and down behind them while they were at work muttering to himself 'Come on now boys, over the top!' interspersed with the warning: 'They're shelling again!'

The Art School was as much a novelty to me as the Manual School but, surprisingly, proved even more disappointing. This was due entirely to the Head of Art, HA Rigby, of whose impact on the school on his first arrival 25 years earlier, I have written earlier. By now his distinctive method of teaching had become accepted and meant that new boys like me lacking any talent for drawing were given the minimum of attention. It was claimed in Rigby's obituary in *The Blue* that he believed every boy possessed 'a spark of creativity and saw it as his sacred duty to fan that spark into flame', but nearer the truth was the experience of a contemporary, who, on seeking guidance from the Art Master, was told brusquely, 'Go away, boy. Leave me alone!'

GAT Allan claimed in his book about the school written at this time that the Art School was 'where our budding RAs enjoy the atmosphere of real Art – Morris tapestry, period furniture, the best of pictures',[4] but if any of these existed they were never pointed out to us and Art periods were a time of amiable idleness. Though not unwelcome at the time I now feel that here was an opportunity lost. One does not have to be an artist to appreciate art and here the school did nothing to encourage us. Outside the Chapel, and the huge Verrio in the Dining Hall, there were no paintings to awaken interest in the subject and no formal lessons in art history or appreciation. This I have since greatly regretted, as attending exhibitions and buying such modest pictures as I could afford has been a continuing pleasure of my life.

The Art School staff, like, to a lesser extent, those who taught English, were expected to provide a dissenting, even slightly anarchic, element in our over-regulated, rigidly conformist lives. I saw no signs of eccentricity outside the classroom on Rigby's part, but they were evident in abundance in his assistant and successor, Adrian Kent, who arrived in 1939.[5] Although he had been at Rugby, Kent (I cannot recall any nickname) had soon shed its inhibiting influence at the Slade School of Art and as a teacher at Dartington Hall, a pioneering establishment I mention elsewhere. He had hardly arrived when he was questioned by the police, who had been warned that a German spy was allegedly measuring the ground around Sharpenhurst, presumably for an airborne landing. Kent had in fact been pacing about 'with long strides round a field trying to warm himself up' between sessions spent at his easel, but, when asked to confirm his identity by naming the German master, found the name had slipped his mind. It was said in an obituary tribute to him, on his death in 1977, that he tried to identify each boy's needs. 'Art is different and Adrian Kent got this over to us.'

Kent himself was also very different from the usual Housey schoolmaster. He did not fit in well into our rigidly timetabled society and could be seen frenziedly cycling down the Avenue to his first class with pyjama legs still visible beneath his trousers and hastily applied cycle clips. But it was in the classroom that this revolutionary influence was most felt. If Rigby had rescued the Art School from long outmoded teaching methods, his successor carried the process a stage further, encouraging boys to venture outside the classroom and introducing them to the joys of the *avant-garde* in art. One unappreciative pupil who arrived in 1941 joined a small contingent who on the pretext of 'sketching nature' would make during Art classes for 'the nearest tube entrance' and occupy an area used as 'a smoking rendezvous', returning confident of not being detected since 'the Art Master...smoked like a chimney himself and thus the smell of our tobacco reeking breath meant nothing to him'.[6] The same group were equally unappreciative of their teacher's attempt to widen their artistic horizons. 'One had of course to remember to scribble some asinine drawing on the sketch pad...the more idiotic the better, as Mr Kent would rhapsodize over anything which he regarded as abstract. Providing one showed enthusiasm he was patent and gentle with even the most obvious...duffer.'

It was perhaps this individual who gave the only encouragement I ever received in the Art School after I had devoted most of one term to painting an orator on a soapbox addressing a mob in a park. The master was kind enough to praise my unusual choice of subject and the vigour of my execution, but he must have known, as well as I did, that it was a crude daub, useful only in confirming my total lack of artistic talent. It does not surprise me that the school has produced so few artists. The whole atmosphere was inimical to the production of art and the lack of privacy provided almost insuperable practical difficulties. (My housemaster, asked to allow a boy to leave the grounds to sketch or paint, would certainly have forbidden any such activity as potentially immoral, or involving contact with someone not in Peele A.)

Music was a totally different matter. The explanation, as so often, lay in the past, as Edmund Blunden made clear in his *Introduction* to the *Christ's Hospital Book*:

Music itself...was a subject of instruction at Christ's Hospital in early days largely because it was a means of getting on in the world. The musician as a professional had good hopes of employment in Elizabethan England and later. Even the general education in singing was maintained – so it seems – on the principle that such music helped to attract the person of rank and fashion into the roll of admirers and benefactors. [7]

The band, as I have mentioned earlier, dated back only to 1868, when it had been founded more as an aid to discipline than to encourage musical appreciation. By the time I reached Christ's Hospital it was probably the best of any school in the country, with unfortunate results, for this encouraged the perpetual parading and marching which other schools found unnecessary. Boys who actually belonged to the band, however, regarded it differently. Repeatedly, contemporaries have mentioned to me their mastery of an instrument, and membership of the band, as the most enjoyable element of life at Christ's Hospital. Nowhere was this enthusiasm greater than in Peele A, for band practice was one inter-house activity in which even Noel Sergent could not prevent his boys from participating.

Although musical appreciation was not taught, active participation, by singing in the choir or playing an instrument, particularly in the band, was positively encouraged, and the opportunities to do so, and to hear first-class performances, were probably better than at most other public schools. The school had had some exceptional Directors of Music, including the one who was in charge in my time, Dr CS ('Beaky') Lang, whom I spoke to only once during my whole time at school, in the first week, when I was, like all new boys, tested for the Chapel choir. He heard me sing, winced, and politely dismissed me.

My generation and those immediately preceding or following it, were, however, to produce a number of outstanding musicians. I well remember Ivor Keys, said to be one of the youngest, if not *the* youngest ever, Fellows of the Royal College of Organists. 'Famous musicians listened spellbound,' ran one newspaper report of a visit by outsiders to hear this prodigy. Others to achieve distinction were the composer Constance Lambert, Sidney Carter, who wrote, or adapted, the now incessantly performed, and in my view over-rated, *Lord of the Dance*, the conductor Colin Davis, the BBC Controller of Music, the late William Glock, both later knighted, and a fellow Newburian and West Gifts' scholar, Brian Trowell, who became Professor of Music at Oxford. The Housie of my time also produced two authoritative writers on music, the former MP Bryan Magee and *The Times* columnist Bernard Levin, while my house produced a future professional singer, much disapproved of by my housemaster for his pacifist opinions, Wilfrid Brown.

Here was one area at which Housie excelled which left me entirely unaffected. My admired ex-nursemaid, Bob Pitman, made periodic attempts to open my ears to what I was missing, but, so far as I was concerned, being asked to name my favourite composer was as embarrassing as having to acknowledge support for a particular football team. I now feel grateful that I discovered early in life that music gave me no enjoyment and have reflected on the many hours I have saved through not having devoted any of my time to attending concerts and listening to broadcast music, or more precisely, pretending to listen: I have noticed how often in the houses of professed music lovers the radio is blaring away in the distance while my hosts are in another part of the house.

A consequence of the antipathy, not so much to music as to music-lovers, which I discovered at school, has been the satisfaction of discovering characters in fiction, or prominent individuals in real life, who openly admit indifference, or actual hostility, to concerts and the like. My pleasure in CS Forester's Hornblower books was immensely enhanced on reading that his hero found having to sit through a musical recital more trying than any battle. I much admired the provost of my Oxford college, Sir John Masterman, and liked him even better on reading in his autobiography that he had always found music pointless. Later I worked closely with the BBC's best Director-General of recent years, Sir Hugh Greene, without discovering that he detested music to such an extent that he had to be coaxed into putting in an annual duty appearance at the BBC's Promenade Concerts and then, being tone deaf, nudged to make him rise when the national anthem was played. [8]

Useless as I was at games, indifferent to music, at the bottom of the class in manual subjects, not much above it in German or Latin, I had made a by no means distinguished start at what I had expected to be a paradise. What saved me then, as later, was being able, even as a ten year old, to retreat into the world of books and to restore my academic self-respect by being recognised from the first as having some aptitude for the 'soft' but by no means despised subjects, English and History. Although little was done to make us aware of it at the time, the school had a strong literary tradition, rooted indeed in its even stronger classical bias, as I have described earlier. Christ's Hospital had produced no major novelists but several Old Blues, most recently Edmund Blunden, at Horsham from 1909 to 1915, had achieved eminence as poets, and many more as journalists, since this was a profession where one could make a start and a name, however humble one's background. I shall say more of Old Blue journalists of my generation later. [9]

It would not be surprising if those of a literary disposition were even less happy at Housie than the usual schoolboy, though even here there are 'pro's as well as 'anti's. Edmund Blunden rose to become senior grecian, ie head boy, before leaving school to fight on the Western Front, and was ever afterwards a passionate advocate for it, testifying in his *Introduction* to the *Christ's Hospital Book* to 'the feelings of gratitude, of admiration and of delight' which its compilation had given him.

Blunden survived the first world war. The best known Old Blue poet of the second was less fortunate. Keith Douglas's time at school overlapped with mine, though I was several years his junior and in a different house, so never knew him. He was notoriously 'difficult' at school and, another contemporary told me, detested the place; by a nice irony, he ended up with a keen Old Blue, Edmund Blunden, as his tutor at Oxford, before being killed in Normandy in 1944.

While I was growing up in Camp Close another future author, destined to be far more successful, Richard Adams, famous for the classic *Watership Down* and other bestsellers, was, as mentioned earlier, enjoying what he describes as an 'upper-middle-class' upbringing – his father was a successful GP – barely a mile away, in the prosperous Newbury suburb of Wash Common. After attending the kindergarten at the High School, as a fee-paying infant, Richard Adams moved on to Horris Hill, a local prep school with a national reputation. His autobiography, which encouraged me to press on with the present book, vividly recreates its atmosphere. 'We were,' he writes of his schoolmates, 'disgustingly snobbish little boys...The Horris Hill word for anyone not considered a gentleman was a "rustic". This automatically included all workmen, shopmen, servants and so on.' Even Adams himself was suspect for his 'father was the school doctor – a sort of servant' and he heard other boys sniggering when he artlessly admitted that his mother prepared the family meals; this was, of course, a job for 'cook'.[10]

Horris Hill was not unique in its snobbishness. I can remember the secretary of one Christ's Hospital sports club recounting the response he had received after writing to another public school to propose a fixture. 'We've played Cranleigh and St John's, Leatherhead,' his correspondent wrote, 'but we've never even heard of Christ's Hospital.'

Its classlessness has always been one of Christ's Hospital's most endearing, and enduring, qualities. It was this that attracted some of the best members of staff to it, and its most outstanding headmaster, Hamilton Fyfe, as he described it in a broadcast in 1950:

> Alone among the schools which we insist on calling public because they are private, it admits only boys whose parents are unable to pay the fees normally charged elsewhere. Poverty cuts diagonally across the classes. So a parent of a boy at Christ's Hospital might be a burglar, or a bishop's widow.[*] When the new boys assembled, they were like a lot of little sheep and little goats, a living exhibit of class distinction. When they left school you couldn't tell t'other from which.[11]

---

[*] Fyfe was fond of this phrase, which he used again in *The Christ's Hospital Book* in 1953. He claimed there (p.358) to have admitted 'the son of an unemployed burglar...compulsorily unemployed'. He also accepted a candidate who, when asked why he wanted to go to Christ's Hospital, replied 'Better 'eadmorster, Sir.' (p.359)

English society between the wars was permeated with snobbery and even at Christ's Hospital some housemasters, including my own, were said to have a soft spot for a mother who was evidently 'a lady' and for a boy from a social background a cut above the rest of us. Overall, however, the school was a remarkably classless place and I cannot remember anyone, boy or master, ever referring to a boy's home background. Until my last few terms I had no idea of the occupation of the parents of even my closest friends. A common factor, I then discovered, was what would now be called having a single parent. Of my own year and the one immediately following it in Peele A, the only contemporaries with whom I was supposed to associate, three had widowed mothers, one of whom supported herself as a district nurse, and one came from a broken home, with a mother who ran a succession of small businesses, such as a pets' beauty parlour. The father of another friend was a small builder and the Peele B boy I got to know best came from a council estate in Dagenham, where his father was a school caretaker.

If any of the parents of the boys I knew were making a contribution to their fees this was never mentioned and, with the single exception mentioned below, all conformed to the long-established requirement of the governing body 'that no child will be admitted whose parents or next friends are not, in the opinion of the Council of Almoners, in need of assistance towards his education and maintenance'.[12]

The parents highest up the social ladder tended to be clergy, and one son of the vicarage who entered Peele A with me duly took Holy Orders himself on leaving school. In my house at least only two boys appeared to come from a background that should have disqualified them, for they had been to a fee-paying prep school and one had even been abroad, something unheard of among ordinary families at that time. He would sometimes remark 'I've been there!' when an exotic location like Madeira was mentioned, until this became a much mocked catchphrase. We talked little about our families, but my impression, confirmed in a few cases by later visiting the homes of school friends, was that, with a very few exceptions in both directions, the boys entering Housie in the 1930s were from the lower-middle class, typically the sons of small tradesmen living in modest, probably three-bedroom, semi-detached houses, the social stratum to which my family had belonged before my father's business failure had caused us to plunge down the social ladder. Boys who came visibly, or, more commonly, audibly, from the working class were few, though I knew of one West Gifts' entrant from Newbury whose father was a corporation dustman, and the mother of a Peele B boy revealed herself to be a costermonger when she turned up wearing the Wellington boots which were the badge of her trade. (I have often wondered what the reaction would have been at Eton or Horris Hill.) Occasionally a group of boys would publicly interrogate another about the precise size of the front garden at his home – mine was, I fear, by far the smallest anyone owned up to – or the cost of his last Christmas present. I shall describe in a later chapter one malicious incident inspired by someone who had discovered that my parents were exceptionally badly off, but this was more bullying than a display of class consciousness. I can recall only one other occasion when a reference to parents caused embarrassment. One friend, still shocked by the experience, described to me how he had entered a room at home to find his father dead of a heart attack. This made a deep impression on me, too, for I had hitherto hardly realised that parents might actually die.

---

[1] *CH Book* p.58
[2] Jul 1987 p.122
[3] Jul 1987 p.122
[4] Allan p.100
[5] July 1977 p.111
[6] Mar 1986 p.127
[7] *CH Book* p.xxxi
[8] Frank Gillard in 'Radio Lives', BBC Radio 4, June 1993
[9] Nov 1980 p.230
[10] Adams p.129 & p.153
[11] Apr 1951 p.145
[12] Morpurgo p.10

21

LOCK UP 4.30

Regular notice on winter Saturdays, Christ's Hospital, c. 1936

My dominant impression of that first term is that we always seemed to be hurrying somewhere. A contemporary's chief recollection, by contrast, is that we were for ever carrying something, but often the two were combined, as we dashed from house to classroom laden with books, scurried to or from the house pitches carrying sports gear, or marched into tea laden with jars of jam or other delicacies, sometimes clutching one in each hand to our Housey coated chests as we 'doubled' along the Avenue to the Dining Hall. My housemaster would no doubt have been horrified to learn that I constantly regretted that I had not been allocated to Coleridge or Lamb, situated on either side of the Quad, who had the same time as us to travel a far shorter distance. When in my second year Peele A carried off an unprecedented number of cups, including not merely the various running trophies but almost every other award, it did not surprise me, though my house master attributed our success not to the imperatives of geography but to his constant obsession, 'house spirit'.

 The daily timetable seemed, indeed I suspect was, constructed to leave us as little time as possible to ourselves, the assumption being that boys with even a few minutes to spare invariably got into mischief. The school's rules reflected an intensely held conviction that if a boy from one house met a member of another they must both be up to no good. Looking back this is, I think, one of the absurdities which I find hardest to forgive. There were, I have discovered since, many like-minded boys in other houses with whom I might have developed life-long friendships, or whose acquaintance would at least have helped to make our unhappy lives more tolerable but, as it was, even getting to know one's exact contemporaries was made as difficult as possible. It is this experience, of encouraging petty parochial loyalty at the expense of a wider view, that has made me throughout life more interested in the larger unit than the smaller. I never displayed at university that college loyalty to which so many attached importance; local government, whether as a functionary or a councillor, has never attracted me, local history, though necessary enough, seems to me important primarily as contributing to the national picture. Finally, to anticipate a later period of my life, local radio still seems to me a time-wasting, money-wasting aberration actually harmful to the real, nationwide BBC.

At the age of ten I did not, of course, engage in such philosophic reflections but I already found irksome the emphasis on the house at the expense of the school in which my housemaster indulged to a degree which now seems paranoiac. Happily what happened in the classroom was outside his control and, as he taught French, it was to be many years before I met him in that context, but much of the day was inevitably centred on the house. I have already described the early part of our routine, which left us around 9 am attending our first lesson, or 'period', followed by a second, with, as usual, barely time to get from one room to another. At 10.30 am we had ten minutes to get back to our houses – a comfortable amount for occupants of Coleridge or even Middleton, a rush for Thornton and a frantic dash for Peele A – and to change into games clothes and muster behind the house for a further ten minutes, hardly more demanding, of vigorous PT, or physical training. PT was cancelled when it rained and I can still recall how joyfully I would hear the three chimes of the school bell which signalled this relief, and meant instead the comparative luxury of another ten minutes of lessons and a comfortable amble back to the house. Usually, however, there was no escape and after PT a scramble back into our clothes followed, hastiest of all for members of the Junior School, aged up to about 13, since they had to find time to call into Dining Hall for milk and biscuits. Two further lesson periods followed and, at 12.15, we were, in theory, free till lunchtime.

'Twelve-fifteen' was a sacred part of the day, a 40 minute interlude in our rigidly structured schedule, a time for meeting masters to hand in work, for school society meetings, for band practice, for working off punishments, as described later, and even, occasionally, for leisure. This peaceful time ended all too soon with some boys mustering in Dining Hall for 'trades', also to be explained later, and, for the rest, the big event of the school day, Dinner Parade, when each house paraded in the Avenue and then marched in columns of four into the Quad while the band played some suitably military tune. I can still hardly hear *Blaze Away, Colonel Bogey* or most evocative of all, *Sussex by the Sea,* without involuntarily lifting one arm and stretching out a leg to forestall some shouted criticism from one of the monitors marching beside us. Particular importance was attached to 'dressing', ie keeping in line with the three boys in one's own rank, and other common causes of complaint were not lifting one's arms high enough, not stamping one's feet loudly enough, or 'forming two deep' in a ragged fashion when the four ranks were reduced to two as we approached the Dining Hall doors. If the house was considered to have become slack in such matters extra parades were ordered but in my experience – and I spent nearly four years in the army immediately after leaving school – the standard of drill insisted on surpassed that of any military regiment, indeed Housie retained the complications of four ranks long after the services had, sensibly, opted for the simpler and more flexible three.

This incessant marching about was, like the uniform, such a distinctive feature of Christ's Hospital that it merits special examination. HLO Flecker, writing in 1952, declared that 'The midday Dinner Parade is a grand sight, as the boys converge on the Dining Hall from the Eastern and Western Avenues, played in by their remarkably good band.'[1] This may have been true, and the sight of their son marching immaculately alongside his schoolmates may have caused the parental heart to swell with pride, but my old headmaster's claim that 'The school marches to Chapel and to meals, because that is the quickest and most orderly way to get 834 boys to the right place at the right time' requires further scrutiny.

At the time I accepted this tradition as just another strange feature of the wholly new world I had now entered, but having discovered in the army how much less often we were marched about than at school, and how other even larger schools managed without such military style manoeuvres, now believe the practice grew up for quite different reasons, as I have explained earlier. We still, in 1936, had to parade four times a day, with even more marching for additional functions or as a punishment. Basically, I suspect, the reasoning was the same as in the 1850s when military style drill had first been introduced. Lining us up, shouting orders at us and marching us about was part of that incessant regimentation, from rising bell to lights out, in which the school delighted, a sign of that *recta disciplina*, ie proper discipline, commended in the *Votum*. I have described earlier how it had come to be adopted and, like the uniform, for which there had in the early days been far more justification, marching had survived to be an anachronism. At the time, so conscious were we of our good fortune in being at Christ's Hospital at all, that neither were resented but both, I now believe, were by the 1930s unnecessary, encouraging that backward-looking narrowmindedess which was the school's worst feature.

After dinner we walked, instead of marching, back to our houses, but were soon being dragooned again into something I dreaded far more than marching, games. Compulsory sport was universal at that time in public schools but Housie, as always, had to outdo the rest and I know of no other where every weekday afternoon was occupied by games or some equally unavoidable activity. Shortly after dinner a notice would be posted in the house setting out the afternoon's programme. Usually, in the Winter Term, it was rugger practice or a rugger match; three house Fifteens, with the odd boy away in the 'sicker', training with a school team or acting as referee or linesman, comfortably took care of all fifty boys. Sometimes the whole house, or part of it, was assigned to gym, which I detested even more. Only the preliminary walk or run across the playing fields to the group of buildings beyond the school Post Office was enjoyable. Once there we were subjected to a variety of what I came to regard as tortures. Worst of all was 'the horse', which involved an individual performance in front of the whole group, beginning with relatively simple vaulting but rapidly becoming more complex until one was being required to stand on one's head on top of this insubstantial padded object, a procedure which seemed to me then, and seems to me still, to be thoroughly dangerous. 'The rope', which involved climbing up it hand over hand, was not too bad, since one could go at one's own pace and, once at the top, simply came down again, but 'the beam', which meant creeping like a tightrope walker, arms outstretched for balance, along a narrow plank suspended at varying distances from the floor, was distinctly frightening and I have often wondered if the severe phobia about heights and climbing ladders which I suffered later in life had its origins in these hazardous sessions. Some boys undoubtedly enjoyed gym and performed the sort of dazzling displays now familiar in coverage of the Olympic Games on television, but it was, happily for me, the custom to grumble about it, and, as in the whole sports programme, too little allowance was made for our differing ages and capacities. It now seems strange to me that the streaming so successfully practised in the classroom was not extended to other areas of school life.

Half the time at the gym was devoted to PT, which was not too bad since the movements were mainly familiar from our morning sessions, and, though occasionally masters took such classes, our sessions were mainly directed by two ex-servicemen known as 'the sergeants', who wore a quasi-military uniform and affected the speech and demeanour of old-fashioned NCOs dealing with exceptionally stupid and idle recruits. They were also employed to take messages round the school and visited each classroom every morning to summon boys to see the headmaster, a very rare event causing intense speculation as to the cause, or, much more common, to collect the names of those due for punishment. The sergeants occupied the same dubious middle ground in the school hierarchy as the bandmaster and Manual School instructors and were, I believe, so far as the nature of their duties allowed, kindly men. The senior and more vociferous, Sergeant Usher, briefly known as 'The Crusher', though this never really caught on, liked to assign nicknames of his own to any boy who caught his eye. He would address me as 'Longboat', which I welcomed as giving me some form of personal identity and being prompted by goodwill. I realise now that coping with a non-athletic boy like myself must have been a real trial for him and in the autobiographical novel I wrote immediately on leaving school, *First Bloom,* the portrait I gave of his dual role in the life of the school was not unkind:

To a class during a tedious period his loud 'Any absentees, sir?' was frequently a welcome interruption. A new and nervous master might ask hesitatingly if he might have a little stationery, [delivering such orders was another of the sergeants' duties] and when the form started eagerly to suggest 'Three packets of pencils, sir, Mr Brooker always used to supply us with them!' or 'Don't forget the small notebooks, sir!' 'The Crusher' would quell them with a glance and enquire cheerfully if there were any for punishment drill. If the form were a hardened one, a shocked murmur of protest would be heard to circulate at the mere thought.

Once in the gym Sergeant Usher was no longer the servant but the master:

The period always began with running round the gym and 'Lup Ri, Lup Ri!' he would cry, varying it sometimes with 'Drip drop, drip drop', pausing perhaps to deliver some witticism and an injunction to 'Come and see me on Friday!', the weekly punishment parade being held after school on that day.[*]

Rugger and gym were the staples of our games afternoons but occasionally an activity was substituted which I could actually enjoy, although it was much disliked by the keen games players. This was the house run, a thoroughly sensible form of exercise which enabled everyone to go at his own speed and, an enormous advantage, took us beyond the ring fence out into the unspoiled Sussex countryside. Most runs from Peele A began and ended beside the large hill overlooking the school from the far side of the railway which formed the western boundary of the grounds, Sharpenhurst, which in First Bloom I renamed Brackenhurst. Sharpenhurst, with Shelley Wood below it, always represented for me 'the downs and woodlands fair' described in the school hymn and it must feature in the recollection of many Old Blues. It was from here that the crossover or 'Great Trek' generation, who had previously known Newgate Street, first looked down, as one of them has described, on their new home, 'a discord of natural green and...the arresting brilliant red of new bricks',[2] and it was on its summit that a giant bonfire was lit to celebrate great national occasions. The hill dominated the view from our end of the Avenue and always seemed to me to symbolise the wider world which lay so near to us and yet so far away. I felt to this gently curved stretch of Sussex countryside a loyalty the school itself never commanded, as the description I wrote of it in *First Bloom* confirms, though it describes the landscape on a summer day, not in autumn as I first saw it:

---

[*] In fact, as I mention later, there were two, but the school in *First Bloom* was, in theory, fictional.

The green turf-covered slopes of Brackenhurst Hill slumbered under the afternoon sun....Middlestone [ie Housie] was as if it had been swallowed up in the raw clay that its arrival had disturbed. There was not in the distance any sound of boys playing at the nets, of the shouts of others watching the railway line, or setting off on their Sunday rambles over the full-breasted curve of Brackenhurst – a hill, and yet more than a hill, a friendly door through which to pass to the country beyond, a heaven-made slope for long toboggan runs when the roofs of Middlestone, now red in the distance, were bowed beneath the snow of Winter. Brackenhurst held its own secrets. Every fold in its surface seemed to be as a wrinkle in the facet of a ripely genial old man, content with the wisdom of his years, but sympathetic and kindly towards the follies of youth. On moonlit nights, when one looked from the high windows of Blake's [ie Peele A's] upper dormitories, Brackenhurst seemed to have a message, the eternal message of the unchanging permanence of the earth: I was here before men heard of Middlestone, I shall be here when they have forgotten her.

Edmund Blunden, in a poetic foreword to a booklet by one of our geography masters, *The Country Round Christ's Hospital*, published in 1934, shortly before I arrived there, wrote of 'the kindness that rules this countryside' and contrasted the rural setting the school now enjoyed to the city streets through which the boys had once had to escape before they could enjoy the same delights, and to which, inevitably they had to come back:

> But all too soon the Wen again receives
> The captives, and the dreary gate clangs to.[3]

'So what's changed?' I would have asked had I known these lines then, for returning back inside the ring fence caused just that sensation of despair that the poet had evoked. Perversely perhaps, it was that ghastly sense of confinement – open prison it might be but it was prison still – within the school that first made me conscious of the countryside. At home in Newbury I had taken for granted the presence of footpaths and commons almost on our doorstep. Now that our life was so regulated that every minute spent outside the school, on a walk or a house run, was precious, simply to be in open fields away from Housie was a pleasure, the start of a lifelong hobby of walking for enjoyment, the source of many friendships. Natural history and the minutiae of the habits of birds, animals and plants, never attracted me. It was the landscape itself I loved and love still and to turn from a sweeping view to study a single bird or flower seemed a kind of profanation, a substitution of the minor and trivial for the vast and impressive.

Leaving the grounds had the paradoxical result of making me appreciate the school more. I am almost embarrassed to read now my account of this reaction at the age of 18 for it could have been written by the most besotted of Old Blues:

> There were many afternoons when the Downs were hidden behind a curtain of mist, and the wind hurled its burden of rain viciously into the face of any who dared venture out, that the House, or a part of it, with Conway near the rear, buttoned up its jerseys, and ran over the lime-bearing fields, along dreary country roads, through winter woods already lit with the prospect of Spring, and so through ditch and hedge back to the long iron fence which bordered the school. It was at the moment when one emerged from a wood or turned a bend in the road, to find in the distance the orderly symmetry of Middlestone, with its tower reared against the sky in the centre of the pattern, that it seemed not unlike a home.

Housie it is clear was already taking an insidious hold upon my emotions despite the increasing unhappiness I felt at being there. Here lay the roots of that mixture of feelings which I have already mentioned and shall refer to again. For the moment, of course, I had no such insight and simply registered each new experience, usually disagreeable, as it occurred. Some games afternoons I positively enjoyed. These were those devoted to a game which features in Victorian and Edwardian school stories under such names as 'French and English' or 'Prisoners' Base', since it involved two teams which each attempted to capture the members of the other, or to release captives held in the opposing camp. If played in the grounds this provided an opportunity to use the copses which were normally out of bounds, and no doubt our housemaster would have forbidden access to them even for this purpose had he been aware of it, but, as I was already learning, there was a tacit agreement between all age groups to keep him in the dark about what we did.

Even heavy rain did not prevent games. On these occasions the heavy tables in the dayroom were pushed to one side to make room for yet another hour of PT including such hallowed favourites as 'Flip flop', 'Running on the spot' and – slightly daring this, though it merely involved bending forward and swinging both hands together to left or right –'Dung shovelling'.

No one admitted to liking PT, though I vastly preferred it to rugger or gym, but what really provoked a universal profession of disgust was an announcement that the day's activity was 'Farm'. The school possessed in fact two farms, one on the Horsham side of the site near the Post Office, which actually, I believe, produced milk and perhaps meat for our consumption[4] but with which we had nothing to do, the sole reminder of the Dairy Company which had once occupied the whole area, and the other, then known as the

Science Farm, set up on Big Side when we arrived. The laudable intention had been to enable boys used to city life to learn some understanding of agriculture by the 'heuristic' method, mentioned earlier, ie encouraging the pupil to find things out for himself.

The same high intentions no doubt explained the presence on the Farm of a small weather recording station, but in my time no attempt was ever made to capture our interest in this and on a visit after I had left I found that both the glass globe, designed to measure the hours of sunshine, and the metal rain gauge, lay in ruins.

Even by 1936 the Science Farm itself had already deteriorated into a few dismal patches of cabbages and root vegetables, mainly onions and potatoes. These seemed to require constant digging, planting and weeding but I cannot recall that we ever actually harvested anything and there were, in my recollection, no cereal crops and certainly no animals, except perhaps some chicken. In theory it was possible for an intending farmer to specialise in the subject but, as the school's historian Professor Morpurgo has written, 'an agricultural grecian would have been an inconceivable contradiction in terms'[5] and though, we did, I believe, have one or two 'farm deps', or 'ag deps' ie deputy grecians or lower sixth formers, they commanded no respect. However it had started out, the Science Farm by the 1930s was a place where each house in turn laboured like a chain-gang clad in games clothes and, I seem to remember, rugger boots, since we had no wellingtons, doing little except dig for purposes never very clear, in the solid and unyielding Sussex clay. In my first term I was, humiliatingly, considered – indeed was – too small to handle a spade and, like a village child in an earlier age, found myself spending hours picking up stones. 'Farm' was in my opinion better than games but boring and I was not bold enough to enliven it by throwing potatoes at other boys or half audibly mimicking the instructions given us by the Farm's presiding custodian, the aptly named R. Seed.[*] 'Gaff' Seed – short for 'Gaffer' – as we referred to him, was an amiable, gnarled man who looked, dressed and sounded like a stage farm labourer. In *First Bloom* I rechristened him Clay:

> Mr Clay...was one of Middlestone's most interesting characters. He was an old man, whose life had been given to farming, and he now spent the winter of his days in labouring and directing the labour of others on the School Farm. He was invariably clad in a torn shirt, and trousers which were stuffed below the knees into an aged pair of gum-boots, and sometimes wore on the back of his head the battered relic of a sun hat. His witticisms were

---

[*] We delighted in the appropriate names of several school employees. The Estate Agent was Mr FG Partridge and the Chief Engineer, responsible for the electric wiring, Mr WT Strand. Mr Partridge was succeeded, less appropriately, by Mr JF Codd.

enthusiastically applauded and eagerly passed on. When there were prayers in chapel for 'those who serve this school on the estate' a picture always sprang into James's [ie my hero James Conway's] mind of Gaff Clay, stumping along the paths of the Farm with an uprooted carrot in his hand and an outraged expression on his face. The school regarded him with affectionate amusement. He...seemed to have been planted in the Sussex clay and to have grown through the years of Middlestone's residence there to his present condition. It was as impossible to imagine the Farm without Gaff, as it was to imagine the school without the Quad. On this occasion [ie the scene in the novel I was describing], however, he passed by with no more than a cautionary 'Mind those onions now!' and advanced on a small boy in the distance who, blissfully unaware of approaching authority, was throwing stones idly towards his companion in the next row.

Two or three times a term the school First Fifteen played at home against another school and we were required to turn out and cheer it on with shouts of 'Housie!' Later, since they meant ordinary house activities were cancelled, I came to welcome such occasions but my memory of the first such match I witnessed still stands out in my memory, sixty years later, as one of the unhappiest afternoons of my life. Because our uniform was so clearly impractical for standing about for long periods in wet weather if it was raining on a 'Housie First' afternoon we wore games clothes, ie shorts and a thin jersey with plimsolls on our bare feet. That particular afternoon the rain streamed down unceasingly and along with the other spectators I was soon soaked through and shivering, barely able to make out our side's mud-stained and sodden jerseys from their opponents' and certainly unable to raise even the most muted cry of encouragement. I thought as I shook with cold and felt the rain beating relentlessly on my face and body how, but for being privileged to secure a place at Christ's Hospital, I might have been at home, sitting by the fire looking forward to reading *The Magnet*. Now the best I could hope for, and I longed for it ardently, was to go down with some disease like pneumonia and be removed to the 'sicker'. I have never been so wet and miserable in my life, though I was to take part in several winter exercises in the army and to go on many all-day walks later in life in which the rain was equally unrelenting. Eventually another new boy and myself found an open sided hut a little way back from the touchline and here we sheltered, technically at least still watching the game, until help arrived unexpectedly, in the shape of a kindly-faced plumpish woman I vaguely recognised. She ordered us both to go back to the house and get dry and, when we hesitated, reassured us: 'If anyone asks why you are there, say that Mrs Sergent sent you!' This was the first encounter I remember with my housemaster's wife and I found later that my first impression of a thoroughly sensible, good-natured woman, was not mistaken.

There was, I learned that afternoon, an alternative in such situations to standing in games clothes in the pouring rain for an hour and a half, or wearing – though we were not given the option – our heavy daily uniform, which would soon be soaked through and leave one in damp clothes for the rest of the day. It was, though no one had told us before our arrival, permitted to own a raincoat and wear it over one's games clothes on such occasions, though not, I think, over one's Housey clothes, with or without the ankle-length coat. One's head, of course, continued to get wet, the cap once worn with the blue gown having been scrapped, as mentioned earlier, seventy years earlier and never replaced.

Adjustment to the uniform features large in my memories of that first year. I remember on wet days using the 'tube' to walk in the dry to and from school only to have to dash through the rain the last few yards to one's classroom, unless it could be reached via the Cloisters, and then sitting about in one's rain-sodden uniform, though, if it were really soaked, we might by a considerate master be allowed to take our Housey coat off and leave it draped over a desk. Similarly, on a very hot day, when it was impossible to concentrate because of the oppressive discomfort of our winter-weight garments, we might take our coats off and sit around in our exceptionally-wide, workman-style braces. This had been considered distinctly vulgar on my council estate, perhaps implying one could not afford a belt or a second, lighter, jacket or shirt, and, though the practice is now, alas, widely tolerated, even in public places, I still find it highly offensive.

My initial reaction to rugger, that it would not be too bad, was soon revised. I found the daily practices on muddy pitches, often in a freezing downpour, no fun at all and when, after a few weeks, teams were picked from boys within the house for an impromptu game I was invariably one of the last to be chosen. I also came to realise that the game was positively dangerous. Being trampled on in the scrum, or hurled to the ground by a determined tackle, rarely happened to me, since I usually managed to keep out of the way of the ball, but later in my schooldays I witnessed two incidents that thoroughly alarmed me. In one an older boy – happily he was one I detested for his bullying – was struck in the testicles by a rugger ball in full flight and doubled up in agony on the ground. Far worse was the fate of another boy in our neighbour, Peele B, of whom I shall say more later. He was no more a games-lover than I was but proved less adroit at keeping out of trouble and I can still recall the sickening sound of hearing his leg being broken as another boy fell on him during a loose scrum. The stretcher on wheels kept in the foyer of Big School for just such emergencies was duly sent for and I can remember seeing my friend Ivan, white-faced and in pain, being loaded on to it and wheeled off, like a Victorian Saturday night drunk.

Games played a large part in the life of all boarding schools at that time, though Housie, as I have already suggested, was probably more sport-obsessed than most, but where I think it can most justly be criticised is in the poor provision made for those like myself who might have made a reasonable showing if given the chance of playing non-team games against other boys of comparable ability. Tennis would have been the obvious solution with the additional advantage of equipping us socially for the outside world in which the tennis clubs and, higher up the ladder, the tennis party were important institutions. Later in life, though with no eye for ball games, I enjoyed an occasional game with a fellow 'rabbit' but I had no such opportunity at Housie and left not even knowing the rules. The only individual game which we had a chance to play was fives, usually once every two or three weeks, when the house was simply placed out of bounds for the afternoon and we were required to choose some suitable physical activity; mere walking, alas, would not be considered adequate. The house, however, while crammed with far more expensive cricket equipment could provide only a couple of pairs of fives gloves and usually playing involved the painful use of a shabby right hand glove with a large hole in the palm just where one struck the ball. Much later, in the army, I discovered I was a first class shot with a rifle, and in my final year or so at school this might have provided an acceptable choice of sport but again no such opportunity was provided. Those who were no good at rugger or cricket were assumed to be useless in other areas, too. As a result I left school hating all sport and have regarded it with contempt ever since. I certainly owe it to Housie that I can follow what is happening in a rugger or cricket match – but equally that I have absolutely no desire to do so.

The best times of our week were on Saturday after games and Sunday afternoon. On Saturday, between games and tea, there was 'lock-up', which arrived progressively earlier as the days grew shorter. 'Lock-up' demonstrated the Christ's Hospital system at its most restrictive, for during it we were forbidden not merely to leave the house but the dayroom; even to go out to the lavatories required permission from a monitor and would be refused if any other boy was already there. The dayroom, with fifty boys aged from ten to nineteen crowded into it, was cramped and noisy but at least we were left to ourselves, a rare event at Housie, to read, play board games, or indulge in any hobby not ruled out by lack of storage space. Some boys achieved miracles in finding odd corners for their possessions; one brought back a train set for a term, though there was no real room to lay out the track, some managed to accommodate butterfly nets and collecting jars, stamp albums were common and one boy even, miraculously, built a radio. There was also a period of leisure after tea, but this tended to be filled with 'scavenging', the collecting up by hand of all the litter scattered about the house, the rota of scavengers being directed by that overworked maid of all work, the trades monitor.

Another regular occupation at this time, often on Saturdays, was one of the numerous inspections to which we were constantly subjected. Every night there was the nightly ritual of shoe-cleaning and I duly learned from Pitman the correct, or at least the school, way to clean our black shoes, which was not as easy as it sounded since no aprons were available and one could easily soil one's coat or our voluminous, buttonless shirt sleeves if one removed it. Blacking – to refer to 'polish' was the mark of a new boy and invited derision – had to be extracted from the large tins kept in the boot-room (there was, I remembered, one at Greyfriars but there the house page boy did the actual work) and applied in a strictly established procedure. It had, I recall, to be rubbed in very thoroughly then polished with the same brush – this, I was informed, was absolutely essential – until it began to reveal a shine, when the polishing brush came into its own. The laces, if not correctly tied, ie straight across, had then to be made ready and we lined up in a queue in front of the particular monitor whose task this was, to display our shoes and turn them over, in accordance with a strictly prescribed mantra of 'Round! Up!' and, if all were well, 'Right!' Prep followed, then it was time for 'duty' and bed, with a last few precious minutes to read before lights out at 8.30, after the second line-up of the evening, already described, when we presented our neck, hands and feet, this time bare, for approval by matron.

Since our uniform was worn both indoors and out for all purposes except games, including the nightly 'scavenging', it was more often dirty than not. This provided the school with another opportunity to use it as a means of filling up our time and imposing additional discipline. Our long blue coats might have been designed to attract dirt, but the school had apparently never heard of dry cleaning, which was what they required. So several times a term, in the precious interval between games and tea on Saturday afternoon, we were required to hunt down and scrub with hot water and Housey soap every intrusive stain. Then, surrounded by the aura and odour of cleanliness, one had to present oneself to a monitor for approval. So rigid was the separation between houses that I did not realise others were undergoing the same ordeal even more frequently until I read an account by a Barnes B contemporary:

> The hated coat inspection took place each Wednesday. When coats were new, the cloth had sufficient nap to make it slightly easier to remove grease-marks. On the well-worn fabric of older coats the grease would stick like glue. Scrubbing it with a brush merely buffed it to a high polish. The monitor in charge of inspection would lose his patience and eventually his temper, causing many a surreptitious tear to be shed.[6]

Although the major repairs, like mending tears and darning socks, were undertaken by the house maids, we were required to sew on our own buttons and here, too, the traditional blue gown being loaded with them, provided a regular source of occupation and potential punishment. Sewing was not at this time a skill required of any male and here CH, albeit for the wrong reasons, was ahead of its time. Pitman patiently taught me how to thread a needle and sew on a button, but no thimble was supplied and my recollection is that one had to push the needle through with a Housey button.

Apart, of course, from economising on domestic staff, which, during the war became patriotic as well as economical, requiring us to do for ourselves what boys at other boarding schools had done for them – or was not found necessary at all – had its origins in the past. Coat-cleaning, nose-blowing, shoe-inspection, scavenging and the rest all had no doubt begun at a time when the school took in boys from the streets who needed to be taught habits of personal cleanliness and tidiness. Apart from coat-cleaning, which took up so much of one's leisure and has left me with a life-long distaste for our ridiculous uniform, I did not, being a naturally tidy person, find these restrictions particularly oppressive; only later did I realise that other, more rationally dressed, schools managed without them and that for all my contemporaries in day schools and normal boarding schools Saturday afternoon was a time for enjoyment rather than an ordeal of frenzied scrubbing.

On Sunday afternoons, between dinner and letter-writing at 4.30, 'hanging about the house', compulsory at most times, was forbidden and one was expected to go for a walk. On this one occasion in the week permission to leave the grounds, usually so hard to obtain, was readily given, though even then some places remained Out of Bounds, for reasons not always clear. Why, we wondered, were we not allowed to enter the attractive coppice known as Shelley's Wood, though the poet's connection with the area was tenuous, just across the railway line from Peele A? The reason why the deep, secluded gully near the doctor's house, beyond the ring fence in the Horsham direction, known as the Lag, was forbidden to us was easier to explain. It was, I learned later, the traditional spot for illicit smoking and, as a highly law-abiding boy, I never set foot in it until learning to fire a Sten Gun there, as I shall describe in due course.

Letter-writing, between the Sunday afternoon walk and tea, was to me a wholly welcome interlude of silence, for once one's letter was completed it was permissible to read a book. Some boys made heavy weather of this weekly chore, but I was happy to keep in touch with my parents and my letter arrived as regular as clockwork every Monday morning, just as theirs to me turned up on a Saturday, usually with a parcel of what Mr Quelch of Greyfriars called 'comestibles'.

Happily our letters home were not censored and though none of mine – in contrast to Robin Hull's[7] – have survived I suspect that at the beginning they concentrated on the novelty of my experiences and registered more surprise than dismay. I can remember only one phrase from my first letter home and it must, I believe, have delighted my mother, with her conventional view, which I so often failed to fulfil, of how a schoolboy ought to behave. 'It's a good job,' I recall writing, 'that I brought your jam and cake with me, for the grub's awful!'

---

[1] *CH Book* p.338
[2] Allan p.86
[3] *CH Book* p.300
[4] Allan p.102
[5] Morpurgo p.78
[6] Dec 1988 p.195
[7] See *A Schoolboy's War* for numerous examples.

22

BREAD AT THE SHOP

They're serving bread at the shop!

Christ's Hospital street cry, c. 1936

In 1936 I was exceptionally small for my age and had an appetite to match, but one of my sharpest recollections none the less is of always feeling underfed. Boarding school food in this period has often been castigated by those who endured it, but just as Christ's Hospital had, for reasons I have already discussed, adopted the compulsory games and ferocious discipline of 'real' public schools even more enthusiastically than their originators, so, too, it was happy to outdo them in the meagreness of its diet. At the time we blamed the Lady Superintendent in charge of the school's domestic affairs, but I now believe that we were unfair. It was the governors who dictated how much, or little, money should be spent on food, as on such essentials as beds and dayroom benches, and they were still steeped in the 'charity' tradition to which I have already referred. None, indeed, was more zealously maintained. Hardly an Old Blue until the last few decades has written of his schooldays – even when in other respects he enjoyed them – without denouncing the inadequacy of the meals. The testimony on this subject is both unanimous and overwhelming. 'The food, by tradition, was execrable,' one of my contemporaries has written, 'and wartime shortages made it worse.'[1]

I have already described how, while carrying out research for *The Workhouse*, I instantly felt on familiar territory: the conspicuous uniform, the hard beds in large dormitories, the cheerless dayrooms, the unrelenting schedule and lack of privacy, all were reminiscent of the workhouse system of 1834. Most of all what links the two institutions together is the smell, the all-pervading antiseptic aura so well known to workhouse inmates, which greeted us at the start of each term. The memory of it causes my heart to sink still, creating in me, as in the newly arrived pauper, a sensation of overwhelming dismay at the months of misery which lay ahead.

I found echoes of school too when working on my book *The Waterdrinkers*, published in 1968. Beer had been throughout the nineteenth century a recognised part of the diet at public schools but in the 1890s a campaign was launched against it by the temperance movement, which recruited the school physician of Rugby to denounce it. 'Supper with beer...,' he told a conference in 1891, 'starts a vice which is as infectious as measles.'[2] Housie, never inclined to half measures or reluctant to save money, soon afterwards abolished not merely evening beer but supper as well.

When I arrived at Horsham the last meal of the day was at 6 pm on a weekday, 5.30 pm on a Sunday, with not so much as a biscuit or cup of cocoa thereafter, so that by bedtime, far from thinking about 'vice' – though that managed a showing, too, as will be described – we were obsessed by a more basic appetite. The school physician, Dr GE Friend, of whom I shall say more later, is on record as asserting 'A hungry boy is a healthy boy', and had this been true, Housie in the 1930s would have been a model of good health.[3]

An article in *The Blue* long after I had left, acknowledged, a little unnecessarily, that 'by reason of its origin as a charity school and ever present need to husband its resources, Christ's Hospital has always believed in plain and even hard living.'[4] In my time this doctrine still prevailed. We often debated what dish was the worst provided and here we were again following in a long tradition. One Old Blue, though he had left in 1932, admitted in 1989 to 'dislike which has lasted half a century' for a master who had forced 'an unfortunate victim to eat up his serving' of Apple Charlotte, an 'unpalatable mish-mash of whole apples, tough skins, cores and sometimes stalks'. His own worst memory was of another of the school's many 'culinary horrors. Did any minced beef ever have such a proportion of tooth-bouncing gristle?'[5]

Not to eat up what was offered was clearly an offence and though monitors, as fellow sufferers, turned a blind eye, not all masters were as tolerant. The Thornton A Old Blue just quoted remembers one who 'if he thought too much had been left on the plates at any meal' would 'stop the issue of pocket money and bar access to the luggage room in which tuck had to be kept'.[6] My own housemaster, being in charge of Dining Hall, was uniquely well placed to keep an eye on us, but largely, as I shall describe, contented himself with admonition, perhaps more aware, as a Frenchman fond of his food, of the shortcomings of the Housey cuisine.

Nowhere was the gulf between the governors' perception of what they were providing and that of the boys in their care more evident than in the case of our diet. According to the Clerk, GAT Allan, writing in 1937, the school was well fed, with no less than 7s [35p] a week being spent per head.[7] Where the money went I cannot imagine. My mother, as I have described, had managed to feed us on considerably less than that and I now looked back to the years at home as a time of comparative plenty. At Christ's Hospital at this time the food was not merely often poor in quality and inadequate in amount, but – a defect which could easily have been overcome – totally predictable. Sunday breakfast apart we knew precisely what we would get for every meal of the term and anticipated many of them with as much foreboding as appetite.

Breakfast consisted of either porridge or a meat dish, never of both. On Tuesday, a high spot, there was bread and marmalade with the porridge, on Thursday it was accompanied by bread and dripping, a true charity dish, not served even in the workhouse, where the diet was in many respects superior to ours. On another morning there were kippers, or rather a single, small, evil smelling object at which even the hungriest rebelled, fish, presumably cheaper than meat, being a common feature on our menus. Dinner, at 1 pm, consisted of two courses. By far the best day of the week was Wednesday, with a thick pea soup for the main course, with no meat or vegetables. It was followed by the best pudding of the week, either suet roll, which we called 'currant duff', with custard, or 'chocolate duff', a chocolate pudding with chocolate sauce. Dinner on other days involved a repellent looking Housey stew, fish pie, which was tolerable, or haddock, which was so unpleasant in appearance, shrivelled and yellow, with such a repellent smell, that I never touched it and indeed could not bring myself to eat this fish until I reached retirement age. Unpopular, but regular, puddings included prunes, a fruit I have only now begun to enjoy, rice pudding, of glutinous texture and made with far too little sugar and milk, a repellent yellowish grey in colour, and, nastiest of all, semolina, which I have never eaten, then or since. Hungry as we were, few boys ever touched their portion and I remember one upturning his plate and passing it along the table to demonstrate that the semolina was solid enough to stick to it. Unfortunately it fell off on to some unfortunate's lap, occasioning a more than usually frenzied bout of coat-cleaning.

Tea in those days meant bread and jam, the latter a low-grade mixture that even looked unappealing and contained so little fruit that we speculated about its identity. It was closest to plum and when I learned of the notorious 'plum and apple' served to the troops in the trenches in the first world war I decided that the school had acquired cheaply the stocks left over at the armistice. Unlike other meals, however, it was possible to improve tea by bringing in private supplies. Jam, Marmite, chocolate spread, sardines, baked beans, all had their supporters and it was even possible to have a boiled egg, though this meant a troublesome trip to the kitchen. I recall one boy creating a dish of his own, inviting all those around to contribute an ingredient to two universal mixtures, one sweet and one savoury. He claimed the results were delicious but the experiment was not repeated.

The two items of which we were not kept short were tea and bread, the former being the sole drink on offer at both breakfast time and at tea itself; coffee, other than 'Camp', which we very occasionally had at home, I never tasted until after leaving school. Housie had always had a large private vocabulary; far bigger than that of other schools, and much of this concerned food, reflecting the extent to which this subject must have dominated the thoughts of successive generations of Blues. Significantly, now that the pupils are no longer permanently hungry, this ancient language has died out, but of the two hundred entries in *A Book of Housey Slang*, published in 1994, many relating to food were still in everyday use in my time. Butter in the 1930s and 1940s was always 'flab', and a slice of bread 'a crug', a term sometimes used in Victorian times as an alternative to Old Blue. The 'crug-boy' who sliced the bread and distributed it from a basket carried on the shoulder had been a centrepiece of the old public suppers, but this term had disappeared with them.

'Kiff' for tea, however, was still in constant use, though the liquid itself was not highly regarded. 'Kiff', one of my contemporaries later wrote in *The Blue*, 'looked like brown paint and came in a variety of flavours. At its best it was an addictive thirst-quencher on a hot summer afternoon. At its worst, it was sour and pungent, as if it had been infused from old dishcloths. In one thing it was consistent only – it never tasted like tea.'[8]

Nor did the receptacle in which it was served remotely resemble a tea cup. For some reason, never explained, what masqueraded as tea at Housie was served in a 'kiff bowl', a large shallow basin, measuring five and a half inches [14.6cm], by two and a quarter inches [5.7cm], marked by a blue ring around the rim and the school crest, though these disappeared during the war, when decorating china was forbidden.[9] When tea first came into general use it seems likely that the school opted for these bowls as being cheaper and longer lasting than normal cups and saucers, while reminding us of the 'charitable benevolence' which prevented us going thirsty. Here again I have found my knowledge of workhouse history helpful. Its female inmates were notorious when they went into domestic service for smashing the china they handled, being accustomed only to metal plates and mugs.

Christ's Hospital had, in 1843, abandoned its wooden platters and leather drinking 'jacks' in place of china, which was perhaps considered more than enough change to be going on with,[10] but why the clumsy kiff-bowls were introduced instead of seizing the opportunity to adopt a standard mug I never discovered. Since that time the design had remained unchanged. Coming as I did from a poor home with the minimum of crockery, none of it matching, I found nothing unusual in the general simplicity of the domestic equipment, but the bowls – they were what dogs drank out of, not schoolboys – did come as a shock and I still regard them as symbolic of Christ's Hospital's determination not to move with the times. Inevitably the contents of the bowl rapidly became cold, while to drink from it involved holding the side between right thumb and forefinger, almost inevitably immersing the former, with results I shall mention later.

At home, however close we were to hunger during the week my mother had always contrived to make Sunday dinner something of an occasion, but at Housie there was no longer this weekly treat to which to look forward. Sunday breakfast, though inadequate, was at least varied, sometimes consisting of a single slice of German sausage but occasionally, eagerly looked forward to, a real fried sausage, plus bread and 'flab', with no jam or marmalade. Dinner on Sunday was appalling, the main dish being a slice of tough and often fat cold beef, plus repellent-looking reconstituted or reheated mashed potatoes. I came across many references to dehydrated potato when writing my account of everyday life during the war, *How We Lived Then*, but I have often wondered whether, as I suspected with the jam, the school had discovered some private source of supply, perhaps from first world war army stocks, so that we experienced this long before it came into general use. The Ministry of Food version, however, was far superior to that served to us. 'Cold gag' had an even longer pedigree, being singled out for critical mention in Charles Lamb's classic *Recollections* of the 1780s. Here he described how 'the fat of certain boiled meats' was considered so disgusting in his day that 'a boy would have blushed, as at the exposure of some heinous immorality to have been detected eating...his allowance of animal food, the whole of which...was little more than sufficient to allay his hunger'.[11]

I have sometimes speculated that the meat served to, and spurned by, us was the very same Lamb's generation had rejected, miraculously preserved and re-offered to each new generation of Housey boys. Certainly it almost rates a history of its own, for it features in a curious and, in my view, unsuccessful, book, published in 1987, which attempts to link the fictional Greyfriars with the real Christ's Hospital. In Daniel Green's novel, *Bunter by Appointment*, one of Billy Bunter's ancestors founds the family fortune in a highly appropriate manner by collecting unwanted fat from his schoolmates' plates in Newgate Street and selling it to City pie-makers. The story seems unlikely. The Bunters were notorious snobs and if the family had ever been poor enough to have a child at Christ's Hospital, London, would surely have kept quiet about it.

Lamb's contemporary Coleridge, an even more passionately 'pro' Old Blue, also complained years later about the food. 'Our diet was very scanty...,' he wrote to a friend. 'Our food was portioned; and, except on Wednesdays I never had a bellyfull. Our appetites were damped, never satisfied.'[12] That Wednesday should, 150 years later, still be the culinary highlight of the week, says much of the tyranny of tradition at the school, like the survival of both the name and dismal reality of 'cold gag'. Our food remained, too, 'strictly portioned' and for a house to run out of any item was considered a great disgrace to the monitor doing the serving, and much resented by neighbouring houses, which were expected to go short to make up the deficiency.

Sunday ended hungrily with, as I have mentioned, our last food at 5.30, and has left me with a loathing for cold beef and indeed for cold meat generally. How, I have often mused, can anyone bear to serve, say, pork cold, when it is so delicious hot?* Apart from such prejudices nurtured in the Dining Hall – and watery, mushy cabbage and hard, under-cooked carrots must be added to the list already given – I did acquire a useful skill on which friends and dinner companions have often remarked, the ability to eat very rapidly. Like another giveaway sign that I shall mention in a moment, the ability to empty a plate in record, even impolite, time is common to many Old Blues. Robin Hull has acknowledged how 'fifty years later, he is still the first person to finish a meal', thanks to a skill originally acquired on the 'few occasions when second helpings were available and one needed a clean plate to get them.'[13] This was essential if one was to fit in one's 'trade', which I shall describe later, while not missing out on the possibility of 'seconds', of which, such detested items as haddock apart, there was never enough. What helped us to survive was that, just as with wartime rations, there was invariably someone who did not like a particular dish or ingredient. There was eager competition for the skin of the sausage which one boy invariably discarded, while another who disliked pea soup enjoyed a rare popularity every Wednesday. It was, however, regarded as an offence by our housemaster not to eat everything on offer so the soup-hater had to smear his plate with a tiny amount, hungrily watched by the rest of us, in case it was later inspected.

One ingredient that was never denied us was salt and this was much in demand for masking the taste of much that was served to us. My closest Old Blue friend is also a salt addict and when we see anyone helping himself to more than the usual amount we invariably speculate as to whether he might have attended our own old school.

What I missed most, apart from the bedtime drink which had been an important occasion in my family, was eggs, although they had only been an occasional treat at home. Housie, however, did not serve a single egg in any form from the first day of term until the very last, when a hard-boiled egg graced our breakfast as a going-home treat. As I have mentioned, a boy recently taken out by his parents might occasionally get an egg cooked for him at teatime, but for most of us the ration remained at three a year, all served on the very days on which we did not require cheering up.

The adjective constantly used to describe the school of my time is 'spartan', defined by the dictionary as 'rigorous, frugal, militaristic'[14] and these were certainly all too apt. The contemporary already quoted, who arrived at Horsham in 1941, later decided that the description he then read 'of the Siberian gulag was just like Christ's Hospital. He was cold, he was always hungry and frequently frightened.'[15] As a preparation for life in the services the Housey regime was probably unsurpassed. 'My nearly nine years of Housey

---

* Perhaps Charles Lamb had the same thought. See his *Dissertation on Roast Pig* in *The Essays of Elia*.

routine fitted me well for three campaigns in Burma', testified one Old Blue, who left as war broke out in 1939, and later joined the commandos.[16] Another survivor of the same era recalls the diet as 'POW camp-like'. Coming from a fatherless home 'sans pension or social security, we did not truly starve,' he observed. 'That only happened at CH.'

My junior school headmaster, Mr Pyke, had often described to me his favourite delicacies while at Housie, namely a mixture of cocoa and sugar, a substitute for chocolate, and condensed milk, eaten straight from the tin. I duly tried these, but with no particular pleasure. We all ate all the sweets we could, less from self-indulgence than sheer hunger. Getting served in the shop for someone like myself who could barely reach the bottom of the wire mesh protecting the counter was difficult but the kindly woman who ran it kept an eye out for smaller boys, wedged at the front and feebly waving their coin-clutching hands above their heads, and I can still remember my regular order: 'Two' [ie two pennyworth] 'of chocolate chewing nuts and a Wonder Bar', also, I believe, costing twopence [1p]. Both items have now, I believe, vanished from the shelves, but we were the first generation to enjoy two enduring inventions of the 1930s, the Milky Way costing 1d [0.5p], and the Mars Bar, priced at 2d [1p]. I still feel a debt to the Mars Company and a contemporary who later became a consultant to the firm told me of his delight at finding on the boardroom table bowls of Mars Bars instead of the then still common cigarettes.

By far the most popular line the tuckshop ever stocked, however, consisted of inch-thick [2.5cm] hunks of bread, generously smeared with butter. So hungry were we that when the word spread down the Avenue 'They're serving bread at the shop!', which happened at most about once a term, eager hordes would pour out from the back of each house and converge on the shop doorway, through which another crowd of boys, each holding his treasure – we were strictly rationed to one slice per customer – would also be streaming. Some would already be taking hearty bites, too hungry to wait till they got back to their house.

Presumably on grounds of potential infection, trying to supplement our inadequate diet from outside sources was discouraged. We were, I recall, forbidden to buy from any 'itinerant vendor', the continuance, I imagine, of a similar rule designed to prevent Housey boys from Newgate Street patronising the hot-chestnut-sellers and muffin-men then common in the City streets. The only such salesman we were likely to encounter was an ice cream man, though I cannot recall ever seeing one in our rural location – and, why, I now wonder, should we not have bought from him had one appeared? I used sometimes to fantasise about the confrontation which would have ensued had a 'Stop Me and Buy One' merchant on his tricycle bravely pedalled down the Avenue and halted to ring his bell invitingly outside the Headmaster's house.

A distinctive feature of Housie at that time, and one already well established before the school left London, was 'Trades', the system whereby all the domestic work of the Dining Hall, except actually cooking and washing up, was done by the boys themselves. Its great virtue was clearly a massive saving on domestic staff, its worst feature that those carrying out trades, unlike servants, were given no extra time to eat, which was, after all, what meals were for. At Newgate Street the most detested job had been that of 'jack-boy', who 'had to run up and down the long refectory tables, filling up the "piggins", ie mugs for his Ward-mates, to the detriment of his own dinner.'[17] His nearest equivalent at Horsham was the 'kiff server'. 'Owing to the weight and heat of the bowls and the absence of handles,' believes the critic of Housey tea quoted earlier, 'serving kiff was the most unpleasant and unpopular of Dining Hall trades'. Since, as mentioned earlier, a full bowl, much less two, would not be carried without immersing part of one's hand, 'kiff-servers could always be recognised by their clean, pink thumbs.'[18]

Everybody in the house after his first term who was neither a monitor nor a 'swab', ie a monitor's fag, had a 'trade' assigned to him. They varied widely in popularity and were allocated according to a traditional system which gave the easiest jobs to the smallest boys and those which involved speed and agility to the largest. Table-laying was a popular trade, since this excused one from marching in to the meal concerned though it was a recognised part of the table-layer's responsibility to clean still soiled knives and to polish spoons and forks on the edge of the tablecloth. Other boys cut 'crugs' or distributed the large flat plates of jam or small portions of 'flab' along the table. After the meal began and the large containers of food were brought in boys with the appropriate trades lined up to collect the food from the monitor serving it. Later, which made this definitely a job for the best or most ruthless runners, they had to jump from their seats on the cry of 'Seconds out!', seize the nearest two extended plates and dash down to the serving table to fetch any food left over before the supply ran out; a boy hoping for a 'second' who failed to get one was all too likely to blame the plate carrier. There were also some disagreeable features of the system which could make meal times a dreaded ordeal. Trying to carry two laden plates at speed was an acquired skill – even in the busiest restaurants the waiters are not actually required to run – and often when crockery arrive from the kitchen it was scaldingly hot. I can recall seeing boys attempting to carry a plate in each hand while using the skirts of their Housey coat as a form of oven cloth. It was an unsightly spectacle, often ending in disaster – whereupon a cry of 'Housey crockery!' would go up from everyone in earshot of the resulting crash – but showed that our bizarre uniform did have some advantages after all. Preparing the list of trades, so that each boy had one suitable for both his seniority and his ability, was an enormously intricate task and the job of trades monitor, who had none of the privileges of a real monitor but far more responsibility, exposing him to almost inevitable unpopularity, was universally acknowledged to be the worst in the house.

Hungry though we invariably were much of the food served was so inedible that large amounts were left over and 'skiffage', collecting up these rejected fragments, was, like kiff-serving, much disliked, for reasons the same Old Blue makes plain:

> Skiffage was carried out by a team of three, one collecting up dirty plates, one bearing a long spoon and an aluminium tray into which he scraped the left-overs, and one carrying the plates in a stack, under which he tottered like a mobile Leaning Tower of Pisa. This job demanded strength and dexterity, but being unpopular was always performed by small juniors, who distributed about them a miasma of greasy particles which later proved almost impossible to clean off Housey coats.[19]

Every Old Blue of this era has his own memory of his least favourite dish. Robin Hull has particularly painful recollections of so-called 'skiffage pie', supposedly made from the rejected scrapings of the plates from earlier meals, but even this, though 'extremely unpopular' was not uniquely unpleasant:

> Housey stew consisted of tough gristle floating in a sea of fat, fish came stewed unappetisingly in a thin milky fluid and then there were the horrors of macaroni cheese…whose memory after fifty years still makes Robin shudder…and 'worms in carbolic' as the boys called the spaghetti they were offered. Years later Robin had nightmares about tearful sessions when he was forced to consume these awful dishes.[20]

Any opportunity for a meal away from Dining Hall was eagerly seized. I can still remember a 'gut', defined by the *Book of Housey Slang* as 'A feed provided by an Old Blue for the members of his house,' though this particular one was financed by a junior housemaster to mark his marriage. Here was a feast of all the delicacies we so rarely saw, including unlimited ham and cheese, cakes and sweet biscuits, washed down by orange squash. The glories of a Thornton A 'gut' were recalled in 1989 by someone who had left in 1932: 'A large tin of salmon between four, a tin of pineapple chunks between two, numerous pots of jam, extra butter.' Surely few gifts can ever have been more appreciated.[21]

There were also two occasions during one's first term when something better was substituted for tea in hall, though one of these presumably only occurred when a housemaster was married. In Peele A, soon after being rescued by Mrs Sergent, as I have described, from being a sad and soaked spectator at a 'Housey First' match, I found myself invited to tea in her house along with other new boys. Rumour had it that this was a kind of social assessment to see how one handled an ordinary tea cup and saucer, or if one ate with one's mouth open. I suspect, however, the real motive was to help us feel at home, though if so it failed. I can remember only a feeling of awkwardness which left us tongue-tied and unable to do justice to the food, served by a maid – sufficient in itself to leave us ill at ease. I have clearer memories of tea that term at the Headmaster's house, where Mrs Flecker entertained simultaneously new boys from several houses. Here, too, we were admitted by a maid in cap and apron and the occasion that followed was difficult, if not grisly, enlivened only by the discovery, reported to us by the first guest to visit it, that the lavatory was of a low-flush kind, operated by a handle at the side. This was the first time any of us had encountered such a novelty and it provided proof, we agreed, of the Head's position in the world. Boy after boy now begged to be excused, until our hostess must have feared we were suffering from some mass digestive disturbance.

We would have been even more nervous had we known that our hostess kept a 'guest book' in which she recorded her impressions of the boys she had entertained. 'I was,' she told *The Blue* in her nineties, 'grateful to any who would talk and not just eat', but excessive conversation earned the comment 'too chatty'. She recalled, too, that it was the basic, filling food that made most appeal: 'Those plates of bread and butter which you all liked to devour!', an observation which speaks for itself.[22]

The great event of the term for all of us was to be taken out by our parents. There was, I think, no actual ban on this happening more than once, but most families could in any case only afford one visit. It was, I think, my father who took me out that first term – my parents never, I think, came together – and I remember that, as most boys did, I opted for lunch at Wakefields Cafe in the centre of Horsham, an excellent establishment which has now disappeared. For my main course I asked for scrambled eggs on toast, which became a termly tradition, thanks, of course, to the absence of eggs from our regular menus. I have retained a passion for them ever since and when, late in life, forced after a heart operation to adopt a low cholesterol diet, found that limiting my consumption of them to two or three a week was by far the worst sacrifice required of me.

That first outing remains in my mind for another reason, for my father took me to the cinema, a splendidly imposing Odeon with, I still recall, a curious white stone tower outside it. On boasting of the visit afterwards I was advised by other boys to keep quiet about it, since we were, they believed, not supposed to enter such centres of potential contagion, physical or moral, in term time. Terrified of having my parents' visits banned, on subsequent days out we merely walked in the park or went on bus trips.

With the approach of the fifth of November I eagerly waited to see fireworks appear at the shop, for Bonfire Night was still a major occasion in the world outside and was always a jolly event at Greyfriars, invariably meriting a special issue of *The Magnet*. I looked hopefully for logs to be piled up on Big Side for the expected bonfire and at first supposed Pitman must be joking when he assured me that, so far as Housie was concerned, 'gunpowder, treason and plot' had indeed been forgotten. I had, as mentioned earlier, much enjoyed the occasion at Camp Close and still feel cheated of the Bonfire Nights I would have enjoyed at home. My sense of deprivation would have been even greater had I known then, as I do now, how important an event this annual celebration had been in the Newgate Street year.*

Apart from being taken out, the chief, indeed almost the only, pleasure in our lives was 'Films'. Every two or three weeks, we were marched into Big School on a Saturday night to the tune of a lively record which I have never heard since but even now echoes in my head. The cinema represented, of course, the great means of escape for the whole population during that bleak decade, the 1930s, but to none of its audiences can it have been more important than to the eight hundred boys incarcerated within the ring fence at Horsham. When I first attended a films evening, in September 1936, there was only one projector, so that several times during a performance the lights would go up while the reels were changed, but I welcomed this as prolonging the experience and postponing the evil moment of return to the real world. I cannot remember any talking, much less bullying, during films; it was a time of blessed escape and security, like chapel without the prayers, and it does not surprise me that for so many of my generation dedication to the cinema has become almost a religion of its own.

The standard of comfort was much below that of even the ancient Carlton at home, with all but a few seats at the back on the same level, but, to the school's credit, the films, one of the few activities for which we had to pay, since the cost was deducted from our pocket money, were admirably chosen to appeal to their audience. Although many of the productions of that pre-war black and white era now seem absurdly stiff and dated this was a golden age in the British cinema and most of the films we saw were British. The censor's certificate which ushered in our hour or so of escapist bliss was a guarantee of a performance free of crudity, bad language and violence, all of which featured all too greatly in our daily lives, and I would have liked to prolong the opening credits to make the evening last longer. Showing them at the end, when we were about to be re-immersed in the real world, was nothing like as enjoyable. I supposed at the time that I was almost alone in regarding Films as an oasis in a hostile desert, and it was not until long after I had left school that a Peele B friend, by then a television producer – his devotion to the moving image had proved life-long – confessed to me that it was only those Saturday evenings which, in his early years at Housie, had kept him sane.

---

* See Chapter 15.

After the exciting moment when the lights had been switched off the evening began with a 'short', often a cartoon or a *March of Time* documentary, a style of visual journalism which is still acclaimed. There was never, as in the ordinary cinema, a 'B' feature, nor a newsreel and, of course, no trailers for the next programme, but the 'full supporting programme' we did enjoy was perfectly suited to our taste. I can recall only one such item which bored us, a 40 minute travelogue, though it seemed much longer at the time, made by the Ceylon Tea Board, *Song of Ceylon*, and released in 1934. This wound its weary way through one tedious section after another until *Part Four: The Buddha* appeared on the screen, greeted by a spontaneous sigh of boredom from the whole audience.

With the start of the main film a stir of anticipation ran through the expectant ranks of schoolboys and reading in *The Blue* the titles of the films we were shown in that first year I am carried back to my hard bench in Big School, its discomfort unnoticed, and the smell and feel of the packed ranks of boys all around me. That first term my few moments of escape from a life I already detested came while watching *The Lives of a Bengal Lancer* (released the previous year), *The Scarlet Pimpernel* (1934), *The House of Rothschild* (also 1934) and the movie which *The Blue*, in a retrospective review, described as 'the most universally enjoyable film...*The Ghost Goes West*' (released 1936).[23] The title which made the deepest impression on me, however, perhaps because it showed a world which made ours seem almost civilised, was *Sanders of the River*, produced in 1935 and admirably reflecting the attitudes of the time. It is now criticised for its patronising view of the African race but we were unaware of this and I remember it as a gripping story about a District Officer efficiently ruling his area, which breaks into rebellion when the false rumour spreads, by tribal drums, that 'Sandy is dead'. Everything about this film, from its presentation of the selfless, and no doubt public-school-educated, District Officer, played by Leslie Banks, to the singing of the noble black man, Paul Robeson, and the final climax in which the rebels are quelled by the last minute arrival of a river boat crammed with riflemen, delighted us. It did not surprise me when the house captain of Peele A in my first year, JCD Lawrance, whom I much admired, later joined the Colonial Service and I pictured him in just such a situation. (Lawrance, incidentally, proved the very model of an Old Blue, going up to Oxford, marrying the daughter of a housemaster, serving with distinction in the war and finally retiring to live near the school. He recalled me, when I met him one Old Blues Day, as an exceptionally small and apprehensive new boy, useless at games, but believed to be bright, an accurate enough portrait.)

Films were to remain an enduring delight through my schooldays. My second term was not quite so rich as my first, although the films chosen included one acknowledged classic, *A Night at the Opera* (1935). I have never, however, cared for the Marx brothers or the type of comedy they represented and preferred *David Copperfield*, released in the same year. In the following year, as *The Blue* for December 1938 records, we saw a number of popular films released during 1937, including *The Prisoner of Zenda, One Hundred Men and a Girl, Captains Courageous*, and, my introduction to Will Hay and his regular supporting actors, Moore Marriott and Graham Moffat, as respectively a querulous old man and extremely fat young one, *Oh Mr Porter*. I think we enjoyed even more, however, the films in which Will Hay presided incompetently over a totally anarchic school, so different from our own, like *Boys will be Boys* (1935), *Good Morning Boys* (1937) and *The Ghost of St Michael's* (1941). We were a model audience. Dramatic moments were greeted in rapt silence and I can remember no interjections of the kind that sometimes enlivened Saturday morning matinees in the world outside. The only untoward response I witnessed was a scene which showed Will Hay being passed over the heads of his pupils while hands groped in his trouser pockets. Their owners were in search, as was made clear, of his keys and money but the incident was received with knowing and anything but innocent laughter.

I can recall only one really bad choice, *Green Pastures*, an attempt, daring in its day, 1936, to present heaven and God through the eyes of a simple-minded negro. Its showing represented, I suspect, a triumph for the evangelising Christians on the staff, one of whom introduced it and urged us to treat it with respect, but we considered it a waste of a precious film evening and the production left me with a distaste for Biblical films I have never lost.

Although we all tried to catch up on the latest releases in the holidays, we inevitably missed out on many subsequently famous titles and I have been grateful to television for, late in life, enabling me to fill these gaps. But it was the occasion, not the film, which was important to us and I can still feel the excitement that swept through Big School as the film company's trademark flickered on to the screen: the Big Ben of London Films, the female portrait with the elaborate hat seemingly about to fall off of the Gainsborough company, and – more rarely – the angry lions of MGM or the sweeping searchlights of Twentieth Century Fox, all marked the gateway to an hour and a half of enchantment. 'What a wonderful escape from the realities around us,' remembers another Old Blue of my generation, who can still remember the sense of anti-climax as 'the lights went up in Big School and we were rushed back to the house'.

The school did little to encourage us to take an interest in the world around us. At some time later in my schooldays freak conditions created a unique appearance to the trees and flowers, with every leaf or blade loaded with a separate covering of ice. The girls at my sisters' school were urged by the mistresses to go and study this once-in-a-lifetime phenomenon. The reaction at Housie was very different. I recall, with other boys, innocently peering at the unexpected spectacle presented by the bushes in the copse beside the house when our housemaster leaned out of this window to shout at us to move on. To him, boys lingering near a shrubbery could mean only one thing. I feel indignant still that because of his refusal to allow a wireless in the house I was deprived of the experience of hearing the many historic broadcasts made during my schooldays, an important part of our heritage. Happily the newspapers provided a means of discovering what was happening beyond the ring fence. The choice of papers, subject to the housemaster's veto, was left to a consensus of house opinion, which had at that time settled on two now defunct titles, the *Daily Sketch*, for light relief, and the *News Chronicle*, for more serious coverage. They lay about the dayroom, often divided up into four page sections, and reading them became another valued means of escaping from my environment.

Experienced masters spoke of what they labelled the 'sticky' period of the term, with the excitement of the beginning merely a memory and its end still a distant dream, but, almost incredibly, the latter did at last begin to approach. The games fanatics and the bullies were as eager to go home as the still bewildered new boys, now out of their nursemaid-sheltered period but still readily identifiable by their ill-pinned bands and general air of bewilderment. As the days were crossed off one by one on our homemade calendars excitement steadily mounted, aided by a succession of traditional rituals. In 1936, however, they were somewhat overshadowed by the sudden eruption early in December of the Abdication crisis. Curiously, I now feel, our housemaster did not seize the opportunity to deliver to the house one of the homilies in which he delighted, though 'duty' would have been an obvious theme. Perhaps as a Frenchman he felt that marrying a divorcee was a minor affair, or regarded what the king of England did as none of his business. I still find it hard to forgive him for not giving us the chance to listen to the former king's famous broadcast, but that day, Friday 11 December 1936, is fixed in my mind because of an English lesson that afternoon. I recall putting up my hand to ask my form-master as he entered the classroom, 'Is he going, sir?' and, though Roy Macklin was probably the least royalist-minded member of the staff, the solemn, almost funereal tones of his reply: 'Yes, I'm afraid so'.

For us, however, the event which, wrongly as we now know, cast the country into gloom, was soon overtaken in our minds by 'Swizzling Sunday', a custom said to have been brought from London. (Oddly, it does not appear in *A Book of Housey Slang*, but was certainly observed until well into the 1940s in my house.) On that day, the last Sunday but one of term, the dayroom was converted into a giant mart with boys trading their unwanted possessions for cash, or bartering them for some item of similar value. I can recall no particular bargains, but knives, string, books, and, for those lucky enough to possess them, such cherished items as fountain pens, electric torches and butterfly nets, changed hands; food, too valuable to be disposed of, was, I seem to recall, tacitly excluded. As in a Victorian street, there were also boys prepared to undertake unpleasant commissions for cash. One I remember offered to drink Housie ink on payment of a penny from each observer of the spectacle, a transaction which cost him nothing except discomfort, and I can still remember the sight of his blackened teeth contrasting oddly with his white bands.

Before 'Swizzling Sunday' I had discovered the Bonfast, mentioned earlier, and wrongly stated by *A Book of Housey Slang* to be 'confined to the Prep' and to date only from around 1910. As in London, the approach of the holidays was marked by inflicting the same number of blows as remained till the last day of term on the boy who held that particular house number. I can recall much discussion as to whether it was better to have a very high number like 49, which merited only very light blows and might with luck go unnoticed altogether, or a very low one, where only four or five blows could be inflicted, but these inevitably severe. If the occasion was noticed in time, bumps might be substituted for the traditional pummelling on the back or, in the Prep, a knee in the bottom. My own number, 26, was considered ideal, since it merited neither a very large number of blows nor exceptionally heavy ones. This basically harmless custom could easily be abused. A Barnes B boy, who left in the same year I did, has recalled how 'one very nasty lad', with a number in the forties, 'landed up in the sicker'.[24]

The first official sign of approaching liberation was 'luggage in advance', a phrase which for years after I had left school could still arouse in me a keen sense of anticipation. One evening during prep a monitor took the names of boys in alphabetical order to prepare the list submitted to the Southern Railway. That first term I was too shy to call out my name in front of the whole house at the proper moment, thereby earning a chorus of jeers, but happily this was soon forgotten in the general euphoria which the approaching end of term induced.

Soon afterwards there was packing, with our trunks being carried up by willing pairs of boys from the Tube where they were stored. No one seemed, however, to have realised that empty trunks weighed less than full ones and, when packing was complete, our eagerly labelled trunks lay stranded in the upper, junior dormitory, until we managed to manhandle them to the fire escape at one end, normally out of bounds, and propel them, toboggan-like, down the stone steps to the ground floor. I was conscious, as my battered second-hand trunk collided with each corner, how ill my parents could afford to provide a new one, and I now feel aggrieved that, in its eagerness to economise on domestic staff, no arrangements were made to assist even tiny ten year olds like me with our luggage. I suspect that the back pain from which I have periodically suffered for much of my life had its origins in this and similar occasions at school – I shall mention another a little later – when we were expected to carry weights well beyond our physical capacity. At the time struggling with one's trunk, knowing one would in a few days be following it home, made the discomfort worthwhile.

A consequence of going to boarding school was that I was always away from home on my birthday, which fell on 15 December. Housie, typically, made no concession of any kind to such occasions, even for small boys newly away from home, but my parents nobly did their best to ensure that I did not feel forgotten. I received a shower of birthday cards from Newbury acquaintance, no doubt prompted by my parents. My mother tactfully intercepted one from 'Auntie Baa' of the *Evening Gazette* Children's Club, but sent me a particularly handsome parcel of food. I recall giving away a reasonable proportion of it, then taking most of the rest up to afternoon school with me to eat at tea time, using an upturned atlas as a tray. This caught the attention of one of the house bullies who denounced me to a sycophantic crowd for my alleged greed; even the recent beneficiaries of my bounty failed to stand up for me and the incident cast something of a cloud over my eleventh birthday, but nothing could blunt anyone's awareness that the end of term was now less than a week away.

And so, an almost unacceptably glorious fact, the round of last lessons began. Even the sternest masters devised some form of recreation, reading poetry we had selected, singing German songs or recounting stories of their own school or undergraduate days. On the last Saturday afternoon of term our very last activity consisted of a house run over Sharpenhurst, accompanied – a favourite device of Lawrance's – with episodes of PT and, finally a game of 'Follow my leader'. Various people led this in turn and when we stopped in the middle of a small wood Lawrance, in response to the general spirit of Saturnalia or to try and build up my self-confidence, instructed me to move to the front and take charge. I have a vivid recollection of the horror I felt and how desperately I led the 50 boys behind me through thickets, up steep banks, and across water-filled ditches, finally, in desperation, halting to perform a 'flip flop' exercise, of which I thought Lawrance would approve. Happily he did so and the general opinion seemed to be that I had acquitted myself better than anyone had expected although, until I became a monitor and had to do so regularly, I was not asked to lead a run again.

And so, at last, the final afternoon of term arrived There was a distribution of journey money, when almost any amount could be asked for. This was an especially unusual experience for me since the official at Newbury responsible for seeing I was credited with the proper amount – 15s [75p], the minimum being 10s [50p] – always failed to do so. Week after week I saw a circle drawn around the amounts against my name in the housemaster's ledger, meaning that I was in deficit. Once or twice I was actually refused any cash, though I would not have been overdrawn had Newbury Council been more efficient. Our tickets home were also paid for by the council, the money, for some mysterious reason, being disbursed by the Estate Office, located between the Post Office and the railway station. This walk, from the house to Mr Partridge's office to collect the precise amount needed for my fare, then on to the station to buy the ticket, which I was to repeat another 20 times after this first experience, was to become for me the highlight of every term, along with the return walk with the ticket safely in my pocket. Then we all had an extra bath and changed into our best uniform, marching to Big School for the prize-giving for the boys who were leaving that term. This was followed by the last tea of term – no better, alas, than any other – and the Leaving Service, of which I shall say more later, and the day traditionally ended with games of 'Murder' in a darkened house. Hardly had the lights been switched off that the screams of the victim would rend the blackness, the lights would go up and the boys nominated as detectives would carry out an inquisition in the dayroom, until the culprit was identified and denounced. Lawrance, from the same motives as had led to my being appointed leader on the run the previous Saturday, named me as a detective in our game and I found myself almost paralysed with embarrassment at having to point the finger of suspicion at boys vastly senior to me, but in the unique atmosphere of the last night of term this was taken in good part. For once goodwill and real 'house spirit' prevailed and I seem to remember that refreshments were provided, in the form of lemonade and biscuits, before we went to bed.

Next morning we were up very early, for the bulk of the school caught the 'Housey Special' to London, but the 24 strong Newbury party left on a later train for Guildford, where we changed trains, and thence to Reading, to change again, from the alien Southern Railway to the reassuring embrace of the Great Western. It must have been around midday on Monday 21 December 1936 that our slow, local train entered Newbury station and, with unspoken but mutual relief, we ceased to be a group of Housey boys and became again individuals with homes of our own. By tacit agreement we saw as little as possible of each other during the holiday; school and home we already recognised as different worlds, best kept apart.

---

[1] Hull p.43
[2] *The Waterdrinkers* p.132
[3] Jul 1996 p.159
[4] Jan 1957 p.33
[5] Mar 1989 p.61
[6] Mar 1989 p.61
[7] Allan p.97
[8] Dec 1988 p.195
[9] Nov 1973 p.260
[10] Jan 1957 pp.35-8
[11] *CH Book* p.60
[12] *CH Book* p.71
[13] Hull pp.128-9
[14] *Chambers Dictionary* 1993

[15] Hull p.37
[16] Dec 1989 p.196
[17] Jan 1957 p.33
[18] Dec 1988 p.195
[19] Dec 1988 p.195
[20] Hull p.44
[21] Mar 1989 p.65
[22] Mar 1998 p.82
[23] Mar 1937 p.152
[24] Dec 1986 p.264

23

HOLIDAYS NOW ENDING

I certify that my son has not been exposed to any infectious disease in the holidays now ending.

Health certificate signed by parent or guardian, c. 1937

My mother had somehow contrived to provide a memorable meal for my first dinner at home and this became a tradition. It was always the same, roast beef as on a normal Sunday and Snow Pudding, a jam based dish with a white topping for which I have failed to find a recipe since. I hope this feast may have helped to reconcile my brother and sisters to my reappearance, which, since the house was small and funds still desperately limited, must have had unwelcome repercussions for them, though they never gave any hint of this.

Some Old Blues have admitted to comparing their necessarily modest homes unfavourably with the impressive buildings and spacious surroundings of Christ's Hospital and, more fundamentally, contrasted their own restricted backgrounds with the centuries old traditions of their new school. The classic statement of this attitude, often quoted since, was made by the literary critic J Middleton Murry, friend of DH Lawrence and husband of Katherine Mansfield, who was at Housie from 1901-1909 and therefore experienced both Newgate Street and Horsham. His autobiography, published in 1935, reveals that he became a passionately 'pro' Old Blue, the Charles Lamb of his generation. Like Lamb, and so many of us, he came from a lower-middle class background, which he described as 'black-coated proletarian'; his father was a clerk at Somerset House. Middleton Murry had a low opinion of his home and elementary school:

> We lived in a jealous and sterile seclusion. From this I had emerged in virtue of a board-school education as sterile as the life from which it rescued me...At no point had it touched my dormant imagination...With my entry into Christ's Hospital all this was subtly changed. From disinherited, I became an inheritor. I was received into a tradition and knew the meaning of solidarity: suddenly, I, the spiritual waif of modern industrial society, was endowed with ancestors – and noble ones, named and nameless. When I

stared at the simple tablet in the cloister: 'Here lyes a Benefactor: let no one move Hys Bones', there was an inarticulate upheaval in my soul. [1]

I had no such revelation. Only while writing the present book and learning something of the history of Christ's Hospital have I begun, feebly and dimly, to understand Middleton Murry's experience. Certainly I did, during that first holiday, realise afresh how cramped my home was and, at the purely superficial, physical level, make unflattering comparisons with my recent surroundings. I missed the constant hot water and the proper baths available at school, and even having my own bed. Here I shared the double bed in my parents' room with my father, while my mother slept, uncomfortably, as it was too short for its occupant to stretch out, downstairs on the battered old sofa which had survived our earlier misfortunes; evidently the bailiffs had not thought it worth taking. I suspect that for blankets my mother used our thin and ragged overcoats, though, I am now ashamed to say, I never troubled at the time to find out or reflected how this nightly separation must have affected my father. (On the other hand, I now reflect, my absence for nine months each year meant that such inconveniences were only temporary. Our house, designed to sleep five, could never adequately accommodate six.) One 'luxury', however, taken for granted at school, my mother had, as she proudly told me, been able to provide. We had a toilet roll in the lavatory, a sign on our estate of relative affluence, since most people relied on torn up newspaper.

My overwhelming reaction that Christmas of 1936 was that, for all its deficiencies, I had been happier at home than I was at school, and far happier at St Nicholas; at Horsham I was both wretched and despised and lived a far more restricted life than the fortunate boys who had failed to get a West Gifts' scholarship. As it was, far from drawing unflattering comparisons between home and school, I tried as far as possible to forget the latter, and remember that first Christmas holiday as a happy time, marred only by a reminder of the school's close connection with Newbury. We were expected, if not actually required, to join in the mayor's formal procession to church and to return afterwards to receive a ceremonial chocolate and a brand new shilling [5p] from His Worship's hands in the mayor's parlour in the Municipal Buildings. That first Christmas I was not inclined to demur. A year or two later, when the prospect of an extra shilling was perhaps less tempting and my fear of meeting anyone who had known me at school was more intense, I only attended after some argument with my parents, who never understood how much putting on the school uniform cast a blight over an otherwise festive day. One year I delayed so long that we had to hurry to arrive for the procession and I was sick during the service and had to walk out. I never went again. No overt retribution followed but not long afterwards my father was buttonholed by a councillor to be told I was not 'fitting in' at Housie, and thereby, it was implied, bringing discredit on my native borough. Clearly the council felt they were not getting value for the money spent on my handkerchiefs and underpants.

That Christmas brought, I believe, a 'real' Christmas dinner, of a chicken, a turkey being still far beyond our means, and an evening of family games, like *I Spy, Mrs Brown's Cat* and *Family Coach*. One is supposed now to look back on such occasions with nostalgia, but, as mentioned earlier, I have never cared for 'pencil and paper' games and think that making one's own entertainment is overrated. How fortunate, by comparison, are modern families who can watch television together and then discuss the programmes.

Early in January 1937 the second Newbury pantomime, *Dick Whittington*, was staged, but for me it lacked the magic of the first and my enjoyment was overshadowed by the approaching end of the holidays. Already a gulf was opening up between me and my former friends, no doubt an inevitable consequence of going to boarding school. I can remember my mother, thoughtful as ever, asking two or three boys from the Grammar School with whom I had been playing not to discuss some event, perhaps going to a film, scheduled to take place after I had gone back to school and, whenever I compared my lot to theirs, I concluded I had had much the worst of the deal. Other boys I knew at school were even less fortunate and found themselves virtually friendless in the holidays.

I recall having the same thought, of the vast superiority of day school to boarding school, on the journey home for another holiday, when a group of girls en route to a local grammar school, probably in Guildford, got into our compartment. They were cheerfully talking about what they would do at the end of the day and not at all apprehensive about the lessons immediately ahead; that any child could be happy at school seemed to me, after my recent experiences, incredible. I remember a similar thought when, a term or two later, I met my sister one day from the High School. No one seemed to be scurrying away to escape bullying, no one was being marched about or loudly criticised, and a friendly relationship seemed to exist between girls of different ages and between all ages and the staff. Day school, I became convinced, was an infinitely more civilised place than boarding school, and though the former may have deteriorated since selection ceased, and the latter have been forced to become more humane, I hold this conviction still.

In contrast with school where I had made no close friends, my choice, as already explained, being in practice restricted to the five other boys, two from outside and three from the 'Prep' who had entered Peele A with me, I had several friends at home. Small though the house was, and extremely poor as we were, my mother made every visitor welcome and it so happened that the three boys of whom I saw most were all only children and eager for company. With my twin sister, Peggy, we formed a group who were often together, for not merely were our holidays much longer than those of the children who had gone on at ten to the council school, but attendance at the Grammar School and High

School set us apart from all the others around us. One of the three, Gerald, lived on the estate and was little better off than us. A second, Harold, was the son of the owner of the local shop and thereby cut off from the children of its customers, who were also largely its creditors. The third, still a close friend, was Keith, socially a cut above the residents of Camp Close for his father taught at the council school and lived in his own detached house a few minutes walk away in Monks Lane.

With this small but unchanging group I walked every holiday on Greenham Common or ventured a little further afield, to Donnington Castle, learned to ride a bicycle and, as we grew up visited the cinema, helped with the preparation for the pantomime and even, though such events were rare, once or twice, in late adolescence, attended parties and discovered the opposite sex. For the other boys, the presence of my twin sister was, I now realise, especially as we all grew older, an added attraction, though she was rarely responsive, but perhaps her very coolness increased her appeal. How different my life might have been, I have sometimes thought, had one of my three Newbury friends had a sister. As it was the female sex was to remain a mystery to me for many more years.

I remained on very good terms, however, with both my sisters, especially the elder, and with my brother. During my first term at school a notable change had taken place in my brother's life, hoisting him out of his manual job, as a petrol pump attendant, into the ranks of white collar workers, as a clerk. I can recall my father proudly recounting how he had spoken to Gordon's employer at the garage about the proposed move. When the latter had offered another half-crown [12.5p] a week to retain my brother, my father had replied: 'It's not that. He needs a real job, which he hasn't got here!' This was true enough, but was all too typical of my father's clumsy approach, alienating people who merely wished to be helpful. My brother's new employer was very much a part of Newbury history: 'Plenty and Son Ltd, Engineers, Manufacturers of Marine Engines, Contractors to War Department, etc.'. Founded in 1790 it was probably the oldest established company in the town, at first making ploughs, then lifeboats, then marine engines, its reputation being consolidated by the first world war.

Gordon kept the letter recording this major change in his life, which occurred around his twentieth birthday. The text admirably reflects the working practices of the time:

With reference to your application of today for post of Junior Clerk, if you care to come to us for a month on trial, we shall be glad to offer you the post at a salary of 15/. per week to commence, and shall be glad if you will make a start with us on Monday 2nd November. The hours are from 8 a.m. until 5.30 p.m.

Fifteen shillings [75p] a week was hardly a fortune but for Gordon this move was a triumph. At the garage, lacking all mechanical aptitude, he had been a fish out of water with no prospect of advancement. Office life suited him far better and, he was always respected and well liked by his colleagues, though not naturally gregarious, while his curious dietary habits made it hard for him to meet potential friends over meals. In the 1930s, however, this was less of a barrier than it would be today, for few people had money to spare for entertaining and even to offer a visitor a cup of tea was a generous act, which might involve the host later going short.

The classic route out of manual work, or of advancement if one already had a white-collar job, was to acquire what are now called 'office skills', which we knew as 'shorthand and typing'. These were not taught at grammar schools or, more surprisingly, in council schools, but Newbury was fortunate in possessing a dedicated and accomplished teacher of 'commercial subjects', Mrs Spackman, whose classrooms overlooking the Market Place were as essential a part of the town's life as the France Belk Academy of Dancing. Mrs Spackman's charges for evening classes must have been modest, for both my sisters and Gordon attended them, and I still have the certificate awarded to him, on 16 May 1938, for passing the shorthand test for fifty words a minute. I do not think he ever had the chance to make use of this knowledge but it was the first and indeed only formal qualification he ever received.

After the disillusionment and unhappiness of my first term no holiday could ever seem as precious as that of Christmas 1936, but over it hung the shadow of my impending return. I can still remember every stage of that miserable process, which was to be repeated another twenty times over the next few years. First came my mother's careful inspection and repair of the clothes I was taking back to school, then the packing of my trunk and its collection by the GWR van. How dismal those letters LIA, for Luggage in Advance, which had so delighted me a mere four weeks before, now seemed. However much I tried to slow down the passage of time the last full day of my holidays seemed to arrive with extraordinary speed and there came that horrible moment on the last afternoon when my parents signed the Health Certificate to confirm that I had not been in contact with any infectious disease 'during the holidays now ending', a dismal phrase sufficient by itself to reduce me to tears. I could rarely enjoy whatever small treat was arranged for my last evening. Then next morning the hours ticked remorselessly on until the moment when I had to dress in my hated uniform and set out with whichever parent was escorting me to walk to the station. Once I was in such a distressed state that my father hurried out to 'The Rook' which we never patronised, to return with a single glass of port in a bottle. I duly drank this and, thus fortified with alcohol, like a first world war soldier going over the top, was at last persuaded to make the journey down the hill to the station.

Often we took the path that ran through the fields, away from the road, because I was in no state, tear-stained and perhaps still sobbing, to be seen by passers-by. Once, when my father was working again, my mother had the job of getting me on to the train. Much more intelligent and sensitive than my father, she realised, I think, that it was more than the normal dislike of the beginning of term – I had, after all, positively enjoyed day school – which rendered me so desperate. I tried, unsuccessfully, to make her understand how totally intolerable life at Christ's Hospital was and how utterly unlike the idealised picture she clearly still had of it. Knowing how much she would sympathise with my dislike of the frequent swearing I told her of this and of how my refusal to join in, which was true enough, was one reason for my being persecuted. I also tried to describe the bullying behaviour from which I suffered, but it was, I now realise, for someone so innately good and so lacking in experience of evil, almost impossible to understand. She tried to cheer me up by assuring me that when I was grown up the very boys I most detested might come to me in search of work, a prediction regrettably not fulfilled. She was, I now realise, handicapped by her assumption that this was how all children returning to boarding school behaved and indeed told me once of reading the memoirs of some famous individual who had confessed to shedding a furtive tear long into his teens before returning to public school. My misery on this occasion must, however, have made some lasting impact for, just after the start of that term, I received a letter from my father recounting how he had got home on the day term began to find my mother in tears and sternly denouncing me for my 'lack of grit'. I can now sympathise a little more with my parents' failure to respond to what some parents would have recognised was not mere end-of-the-holidays gloom but a real cry for help. Appallingly hard up as they were, indoctrinated as they had been with the belief that a Housey education was a passport to security and riches, conscious of the enormous sacrifices that they and, inevitably, my brother and sisters also, had made to give me my chance, I still feel that they should have recognised that my distress and despair were more than mere home-sickness, especially when my unhappiness increased, instead of diminishing, with every term. It would have been embarrassing, if not unprecedented, to abandon a West Gifts' place once gained. The scholarship I had won at the Grammar School had no doubt now gone to someone else. Nevertheless the rules could and, I believe, would have been stretched to accommodate 'Berkshire's brainiest boy' a term, or even several terms, late. More serious would have been the effect on the family budget. At Housie even my books and uniform and pocket money were provided. Apart from the weekly food parcel I cost my parents nothing. At home, I would have been yet another mouth to feed while only two of the four of us were earning and neither my father nor my mother had any regular work. Yet had my mother realised how overwhelmingly wretched I was she would, I believe, have managed somehow to rescue me. As it was I had, tearful and apprehensive, to return term after term to a place I hated.

What would undoubtedly have consoled me, had we ever talked of such matters, would have been to learn that other new boys had reacted just as I did. Only much later did I discover that more than one had told his parents he did not wish to return and one boy in my house was so persuasive that he was taken away after his first term. At the end of my first or second year I was taken by my mother to meet a boy about to go to Housie to tell him what to expect. With the two mothers sitting beside us over tea I did not dare to tell him the truth and to refuse at all costs to take up his place, although, as the idolised only child of a widowed mother, he might well have got his way. As it was, he went to Housie, hated it – 'I'm not going back there!', he told her, bluntly at the end of his first term, but was forced to do so – and left at the earliest opportunity. I lost touch with him but, years later, his mother confided in mine how deeply hurt she had been that he had got married without telling her, or inviting her to the wedding. This, I have always suspected, was his belated revenge for his mother's failure to respond to his distress as an unwilling Housey boy.

Years later when writing about the history of medicine I came upon a description of a patient awaiting an operation before the days of anaesthetics. It ran something like: 'He counted the days to his ordeal, listened fearfully for the surgeon's knock upon the door, counted his steps upon the stair and to the bedside.' This echoes my feelings as the end of the holidays approached and I feel sorry now for my unfortunate brother and sisters who must have dreaded the gloom that descended on our house three times a year. My wretchedness at the start of my second term was still a novelty, to them as to me, but proved entirely justified. In *First Bloom* my hero's overwhelming thought as he arrived, in the dark – somehow this made it worse – of a January evening was 'It has begun again'. So indeed it had and the period which followed, from January to March 1937, still stands out, sixty years later, as the worst of my life.

My feelings have been well captured by an Old Blue of a generation only just before mine, Sydney Carter, who was at Housie from 1926 to 1933. Clearly, like me, he had been brought up on the myth of Greyfriars and had found Christ's Hospital a disappointment:

> The bell is calling and the London train
> Is fading homeward. I am left alone,
> My bands are crooked, and a coward wind
> Is wailing through my bone.
>
> The bullies in The Magnet and The Gem
> Were all substantial but I face a lout
> Without a body; being homesick is

> A thing Bob Cherry never knew about.
>
> Oh, haloed heroes of the world of school
> Tom Brown, Tom Merry, intercede for me!
> Make me glad that I'm a Bluecoat Boy,
> And dull this ache I feel for Battersea.[2]

The impact of these magazines on my generation is also revealed by the reaction of a contemporary at Horsham from 1941-48:

> Frank Richard's tales of Greyfriars...created for me, and no doubt for many other avid readers of *The Magnet*, the image of public school life we brought to CH. In the event the school proved to be a strange hybrid. Aston's Webb's masterpiece gave nothing away to the mythical Greyfriars or the real-life public schools in its outward aspect but lost out badly on domestic detail...Nowhere to be found at CH were those spacious studies in which the Famous Five toasted crumpets and chastised Bunter...The dormitories were spacious and airy...but the stoutest Greyfriars heart would have quailed at those beds, which I always suspected were picked up as a job lot at the Dotheboys Hall liquidation sale....Most of the masters were vintage Greyfriars and there was little difficulty in placing our Quelches and Prouts. However we found that the Housey boys were less like the characters in *The Magnet*, than those in plebeian publications like *Hotspur*. Of Lord Mauleverers there was none.[3]

Homesickness provided a convenient explanation for the unhappiness from which so many boys visibly suffered but was not the real cause. It was not so much that I wanted to be back in Newbury but that I desperately needed to be somewhere else than Housie, which, during my second term, I realised I detested, not because it was a boarding school but because it was a thoroughly unpleasant place. As the comparative immunity from punishment and persecution – the dominant elements in our daily life – I had enjoyed as a new boy disappeared, I was now exposed to the full rigour of Housey life, and hated it. What depressed me most was not that life seemed unendurable but that no reason seemed to exist why it should ever get better and had I known I was destined to stay in the house for another seven years and become indeed its longest serving member, though without the respect and position such seniority should have brought, I might have been even more strongly tempted to end my existence then and there. I did not, of course, know the sad story of James Gibbs who had been only a year older than I now was when he had preferred suicide to life at Newgate Street, but I do recall dark stories of a more recent death, when one master was said to have given up his house after one of his charges had killed himself rather than face further bullying. The tale I heard was that the victim had cut his wrists in bed and been discovered lifeless in his bloodstained sheets next morning. Robin Hull heard of a similar case, when 'as a sanctuary from bulllying...a young boy stabbed himself with a penknife...The episode occurred in another House almost as remote as a foreign country and...was hushed up.'[4] At least one suicide occurred after I had left, though the newspaper reports left the reason unclear and it is only fair to observe that such tragedies also occur among day school pupils and even at universities. Nevertheless this was the only occasion in my life when I have ever seriously entertained such an idea and that I could have done so at the age of eleven speaks for itself. I found that I instantly identified with the hero of *George Brown's Schooldays*, by Bruce Marshall, published in 1946, which describes life in a school not at all unlike Housie around 1914. Although the author, who had been at Glenalmond before the first world war, stated that 'I understand that the abuses so common thirty years ago no longer exist'[5] the portrait he painted was still entirely recognisable, indeed is by far the best account of boarding school life I have ever read. In his novel George Brown has actually hoisted himself up on to a window sill and is preparing to jump to his death when he is discovered by a sympathetic master who persuades him to think again. In my case I got no further than eyeing the Southern Railway line that ran close to the house and listening attentively to boys who claimed that a Housey button left on it could readily be flattened and converted into a sixpence by a train, though it would bear the wrong monarch's head and would not, I suspect, have passed the most cursory inspection.

I am not sure now how serious my thoughts of suicide were, but my unhappiness was sufficient to drive me to a crime almost as heinous in the Housey calendar, to run away – the indirect cause, as I now know, of James Gibbs's death, though, happily, I did not then know how savagely it had been punished. What finally persuaded me to this desperate step – at Greyfriars boys ever only ran away to save the family from ruin or to attend a sick parent – was what seems in retrospect a comparatively trivial matter, my introduction to 'trades'. My particular duty was, if my memory is accurate, to lay out the 'kiff bowls' or plates and collect them up again just before the meal finished. Frequently there were not quite enough to go round and, after first obtaining permission from the Dining Hall Warden to leave my own table, I then had to go on a tour of other houses to find any with a surplus. This meant obtaining permission from the monitor presiding over that table, although at eleven I barely dared to approach my own house-captain let alone any other, and finally take back the missing crockery or cutlery and distribute it to those impatiently waiting for it – impatiently because any delay would jeopardise their chance of 'seconds'. By the time I had sat down in my place it was almost always time to leap up again for the second part of my 'trade', to collect up the used items, so that at meal after meal I had only a few mouthfuls of food and sometimes none at all. If the boys around me were aware of the position they probably regarded it as a joke which improved with repetition and I was far too shy too approach the trades-monitor and alert him to my dilemma.

I can remember precisely the moment when having endured Christ's Hospital for one whole term and two weeks of a second, I decided I could stand no more. I had written to my father setting out my difficulties and on a Saturday morning I received his answer, which was essentially 'Grin and bear it'. He said reasonably enough that for me to be given preferential treatment in regard to 'trades' would make matters worse and drew a comparison with guard duty in the army in the first world war, which he had hated but had to put up with. By the last lesson of the morning, biology, my despair had given way to unstoppable tears and the master, a kindly man, sent me back to my house to calm down. Here was my opportunity, for there was still a half hour or so before school ended and before I could possibly be missed. I realised that in Housey clothes I should rapidly be spotted – it was, I have always believed, to prevent boys running away that the uniform had been retained – so I made myself as inconspicuous as I could. I exchanged my yellow uniform stockings for the dark blue ones worn for football, the only time in my life I have willingly put on an item of games clothing, and replaced my Housy coat with a dark raincoat. By happy chance, which seemed at the moment almost divine intervention, I had brought one back that term as an 'extra' to wear on occasions like the wet games watching afternoon I have described earlier. My parents could not have afforded the 15s [75p] it cost, but Father Stenning, still, I think, seeing me as a potential recruit to his profession, had generously paid for it, as for my prayer book and Bible the previous term.

Thus in dark socks and raincoat, buttoned up at the top to conceal my bands, I walked undetected to the station and boarded a train for Guildford, unnoticed by anyone. I did not buy a ticket for fear of later enquiries at the booking office, and doubt if in any case I had cash sufficient for the fare, but I had some vague thought that if I got far enough I was more likely to be sent on to Newbury than brought back. My plan was, however, frustrated by the good nature of two railway workers who, checking the doors before departure, noticed me alone in a compartment and asked if I was on the right train. They had perhaps seen boys in my situation before, for they then asked if I was running away, which I readily confirmed. 'Was I a fag?' was the next question; perhaps they had read *The Magnet*, too. I decided that to explain the whole 'trades' system and my reasons for rejecting the school would be too complicated and replied that I was. 'I've always thought it was hard on the younger boys,' one then remarked to the other, and their sympathy and kindness, in contrast to the indifference and active hostility which seemed to have surrounded me since the beginning of term, had their effect. They would, I think, have turned a blind eye if I had asked, perhaps even paid my fare. As it was, remembering my father's letters, I realised that if I did get home I might be sent back again and, reluctantly acknowledging that the system had won, made my way back to Peele A.

The house was empty as it was by now the dinner hour, so I rang the bell of the housemaster's house and when the maid asked: 'Do you want to see Mr Sergent?' I answered in words his wife still remembered many years later, 'No, but I think he'll want to see me.' For some reason my housemaster was not at his usual post of duty in the Dining Hall but at home enjoying a family lunch, which I was invited to join. He had, I later learned, been told by the master concerned of my sad collapse in biology class and had gone round the house shouting for me to show myself, doubtless concluding I was hiding somewhere. To my surprise I was not punished or even reduced to fresh tears by a sharp telling-off. I have realised since that Noel Sergent was probably relieved to see me back safe and well, since for a boy to run away or come to worse harm must be a black mark against his housemaster. Noel behaved in fact very decently; his neighbour in Peele B, I have no doubt, would not have let pass the chance of inflicting a sadistic thrashing. As it was no one else ever learned what had happened, except Lawrance, who genially asked me when we were briefly alone, 'How far did you get?' I believe that if the truth *had* leaked out my stock would actually have risen, since most of my contemporaries were, I suspect, longing to do the same. Perhaps Lawrance had a word with the trades-monitor about my duties, or it may have been that I had become more adroit at them. At all events I did at subsequent meals at least manage to get something to eat, and, much though I longed to, I never summoned up the courage to attempt to run away again.

Only on reading *A Schoolboy's War*, mentioned earlier, have I realised that other boys reached a similar degree of desperation. One 'tiny, scholarly child', ie a small boy like me, 'ran away regularly three times a week in his first term in Middleton A'[6] but this obvious cry for help – a phrase not yet in common use – went unanswered and perhaps in the end he decided, like me, that it was easier to endure school life than escape from it.

The rest of my second term was only wretched to what I now recognise as an average degree of misery and I never sank back into that trough of total desolation I had plumbed in January. A slight easing in the burden of games helped, for though both rugger and gym continued the emphasis was on athletics and running. Here, relay races apart, one could go at one's own speed in heats with boys little better than oneself, but my house, as I have mentioned, excelled in such activities and there were plenty of boys for the various house teams.

One event that term even made me feel that at least this particular activity might be quite pleasurable. This was the inter-house steeplechase, run over a gruelling course of several miles through the surrounding countryside. It was well organised, with a board set up outside the Music School where the course began and finished, on which cardboard cut-outs in jerseys showing the various house colours were moved according to the reports sent in by observers and relayed by signal detachments of the Officers Training Corps, for whom this provided annually their finest hour. There was mounting excitement as the painted figures were moved along the board until the first bedraggled and panting contestants stumbled almost exhausted into sight and across the finishing line. I never ran well enough to be part of the Peele A team, my only sporting regret, but I remember the Steeplechase as one school tradition I thoroughly enjoyed and – a bonus not contemplated by its founders – doubly welcome because on that afternoon we were excused all ordinary games.

---

[1] *CH Book* p.280-1
[2] *CH Book* p.290
[3] Jul 1987 p.123
[4] Hull p.100
[5] *George Brown's Schooldays* facing p.1
[6] Hull p.101

24

A DRAMATIC DIVERSION

Another excellent House Concert. Thank you, Peele A.

Review in The Blue, *June 1938*

The Lent Term was not all work and athletics. Each house, or occasionally a whole block, staged a senior and junior play and rehearsals took up much of the second part of the term, reaching their climax with the assembly of the stage, from the dayroom tables pushed together. Curtains were somehow mounted above them and exits behind the stage were provided on either side via the tiny studies for the house-captain and his deputy which occupied the far corners of the dayroom. To reach the windows a series of steps was constructed from the Grecians' Path outside, the only time ordinary mortals could use it, by removing numerous settles from the dormitories and piling them up on top of each other. This readiness to press whatever was available into service for a different purpose reminded me later of the conditions in Nelson's navy, when the midshipmen's trunks were lashed together to form an operating table for the surgeon. At the time I was only conscious of how heavy the metal settles with their thick wooden lids were, and I have wondered since if moving them from the dormitories down to the Avenue outside and then hoisting them into position to form a pile higher than the smallest boys may not have completed the undoing of my back which heaving our trunks around had begun. When the settles were finally disposed of many years later with the introduction of proper wardrobes I bought one as a souvenir, and found it was still far too heavy for me to lift unaided into a car boot.

Carrying the settles downstairs and subsequently returning them to their proper place in the junior dormitory was such an ordeal that I still wince at the memory of it, and how we kept our clothes together during their absence, since they were our only bedroom furniture, I cannot now recall; presumably, as would have happened in the workhouse, they were simply laid on the floor. A minor inconvenience was the lack of tables for several days, which made doing prep almost impossible. The more considerate masters set learning by heart exercises. The rest expected us somehow to show up properly written work from benches and window-sills.

But house plays brought into our lives an interest, excitement and break in routine which justified almost any other deprivation, as the hero, Conway, of my novel *First Bloom* described:

> Each house strove hard to outdo its neighbours in the quality of its acting and, if possible, in the lavishness of its settings. Work was impossible, for all the dayroom tables were commandeered for the stage, and at frequent intervals the juniors were herded outside so that the seniors might rehearse their thriller with all the secrecy that tradition demanded. And at last, the burly youths who had been despised hitherto for spending time in trivial work in the Carpenter's Shop [ie the Manual School], came into their own and made the lives of all intolerable with their demands for screwdriver or string. The house scenery, rescued from the honourable if dusty retirement in which it spent the rest of the year, took up its annually insecure stand upon the stage and, after much cursing and universal loss of temper, the dayroom would be filled with visitors, old boys, and a selection of bored but faithful masters...
>
> No one ever paid any attention to the junior play...for the real business of the evening was the senior play. Usually it was a thriller, though occasional bold producers sometimes presented Shakespeare or pantomime, and invariably at some time or another someone forgot his lines. Just who this should be, and at precisely what moment the hazardous trip across the open country of improvisation should commence, were questions which interested the experienced members of the audience far more than the detection and dénouement of the criminal in the play. But Conway realised little of this and he was deeply impressed when the house captain appeared, as he usually did, as the hero, and when monitors, doing their best to look at ease, appeared on stage in borrowed evening dress. Masters who had been cajoled into lending furniture or properties for the play would sit wondering when the first wine glass would fall, or who should be the actor to demolish their best table lamp with a dramatic gesture. Not least of the transformation House Concerts effected was in what was to Conway the astonishing change of sex which could turn the House treble into a demure bride, or a girlish-looking senior into a blushing heroine. With the somewhat reluctant fall of the final curtain, and the hearty and tuneless rendering of the National Anthem, the illusion was shattered. Actors who had a little while ago seemed like adults now shook off their years with their costumes and expressed their relief that 'the bloody business' was finished, or their regret that it had not been an even greater success. Only the 'women', drinking their lemonade with the garments that testified to their sex still upon them, seemed to have

remained in the stage world, while a few and no longer innocent seniors eyed them as if hungry for even this substitute femininity, as indeed they were.

The junior play in 1937, if *First Bloom* is to be trusted, was written by our junior housemaster, CJW Parkin, a convenient arrangement which ensured that parts were provided for all who needed them. This now forgotten work, *A Musical Extravaganza*, revolved round a series of characters bearing the names of musical terms. My ex-nursemaid Pitman played the leading role of Crochet, while another plum part, Sonata, went to a good looking new boy with a fine voice. The remaining new boys, including myself, were Gossipers and, according to *First Bloom*, I contributed only two remarks to the evening's entertainment, the first being that certain ladies under discussion had 'eyebrows black as ravens' and the second that the villains had been 'seen in the Market Square'. I do not seem to have made much impression for in the following year, in *Have You Anything to Declare?*, set in a customs house, I had no lines at all, playing the role of a silent, henpecked husband burdened with his wife's suitcases, which he dropped one by one as she upbraided him. I must have done this adequately for I earned a gratifying round of applause, and by 1939 I had a real part, as the Hon. Guy Sydney in *Something to Talk About* by Eden Phillpotts, one of the least talented dramatists of the twentieth century. This performance was notable for being disastrously under-rehearsed and remained in my mind as the worst performance by amateurs I had ever seen until I attended one many years later of another Eden Phillpotts' play, *Yellow Sands*, by a West Country company, who were far worse than us; a singer had to be taken through his song line by line by the prompter and a 'cottage' was only prevented from falling down by an actor leaning against it. Our offering was, however, bad enough. I recall that at one point a boy had to bring in a golf bag, which he duly did on cue, but unfortunately a minute or two later the actor who had received it delivered the same line again. The audience waited expectantly to see what would happen and this time, in a notable piece of mime, the 'butler' again came on and solemnly, having no golf bag to deliver, presented a non-existent one. To their great credit, the audience did not laugh, the tradition being that the juniors were treated with indulgence, but I recall wondering if we would be stuck in a kind of time warp with the same scene being enacted again and again until someone took pity on us and rang down the curtain. Happily the third time round the offending actor managed to get his lines right and the play staggered to its end, while the incident clearly did the 'butler' no harm, for he ended his Housey career as senior grecian, ie head boy.

I must, as on the sports field, have lingered on in the junior league long after I ought to have joined the senior play, for I can recall having a minor part in *Smithers G has a Dream*, a topical work by our housemaster, Noel Sergent, staged in the Lent Term of 1941, the blackest period of the war. This was based on the imaginary adventures in Nazi Germany of a Housey boy who had fallen asleep until roused by the customary morning summons of 'Get up!', a single line which the boy assigned it played for all he was worth, like an Islamic imam summoning the faithful to prayer. This was, I think, the only occasion on which house plays were influenced by the world around us. 'Throughout,' wrote the Peele B reviewer in *The Blue* that June, 'we were brought face to face with Nazi tyranny and Boche cruelty.' This verdict must have delighted the play's author, who seized every opportunity to denounce the hated Germans, then in occupation of his native land, but I believe that, basically a kindly and conscientious man, he also used his position as producer to drag into the limelight normally obscure and despised members of his house. I was therefore given the leading role of Dr Goebbels, only to be displaced after a few rehearsals by a boy at least as unpopular as me and, I must admit, a far better actor. The following year I was compensated by being given the principal part in a play about an unsuccessful modern artist, Mr Slightly Green. I enjoyed playing it, though I can only remember a single line, where the painter complained: 'It was a real one-man show. I was the one man.' The Peele B reviewer merely observed that 'At Peele A's concert we saw Fame affecting the artist', omitting my name, a slight that still rankles for this was the last time I ever trod the boards at school or elsewhere. My experience had been sufficient to show me that, unlike several of my contemporaries, I had absolutely no aptitude in that direction – though I cannot recall suffering from stage fright and thoroughly enjoyed the applause at the end. I certainly did not foresee that I would later, although briefly and not by choice, become theatre critic of a national newspaper.

A sure indication that I lacked the true thespian's outlook was that I always preferred watching other people perform to acting myself and I did not feel slighted at never being offered a part in the senior play, rehearsing for which tended to dominate – after due obeisance had been paid to the great god sport – the second half of the Lent Term. Tradition required that its title should be kept secret, not merely from other houses but from all those not actually in the cast, including most particularly our own housemaster. I can recall Noel's eye being caught, as well it might be, by the crudely lettered title on the brown paper cover which concealed one play text, *Noises in the Dark* by More Farts, but, surprisingly, he let it pass. Usually he had no cause for anxiety. In 1937 the choice fell on *Someone at the Door*, a regular stand-by for amateur companies which was to be performed again before I left. In 1938 we put on another conventional three-act thriller, *The Amazing Dr Clitterhouse*. ('A keen and clever cast, led by the amazing Mr Hatten.' ie our house-captain, wrote *The Blue*'s reviewer that June. 'Another excellent House Concert. Thank you, Peele A.') In 1939, the year of the imaginary golf-bag in the junior play, the seniors opted for another regular choice, *The Ghost Train*, admirably suited to a schoolboy cast and audience. Pitman, oddly, since there was never anything feminine about him, appeared as a woman, while another female part was played, more predictably, by a dark, strikingly good looking boy who, as I shall mention later, was subsequently to be involved in a major scandal and narrowly escaped being expelled. 1940 saw Peele A performing *The Dentist's Chair,* of which I remember nothing, but it was the Lent Term of 1941 which provided a classic victory over Noel and one which must have blunted much of his pleasure at the success of *Smithers G has a Dream,* performed earlier the same evening.

Turkey Time had survived the Lord Chamberlain's scrutiny when first produced in 1931 and would today hardly merit being banished to 'adult' viewing time on television, but it 1941 it appeared the height of salaciousness. It was, except as another weapon in the undeclared war that was permanently in progress against our housemaster, a poor choice of play for most of it must have been above the heads of the bulk of the audience. This counted for little, however, against the fact that Noel was successfully deceived as to its nature until the moment the curtain rose. The name of Ben Travers, already famous among British theatre goers for his saucy farces, meant nothing to him and the title probably suggested an innocent comedy set in a country house at Christmas. *Turkey Time* is in fact typical of its day, essentially innocent but laden with innuendo. Its climax, if I remember correctly, was the scene in which one character, probably an elderly spinster aunt, picked up a pair of discarded panties – shed in some complicated twist in the plot for some wholly respectable reason – and held them aloft with the horrified exclamation: 'Knicks!' This line reduced the audience to hysterics, and Noel, who had been watching from the centre of the audience, at first with incredulity as the nature of the play dawned on him, then with a face of thunder was, according to those around him, hard put to it not to leap to his feet and declare the entertainment over. The cast, anticipating some fearful retribution, must have begun to wonder if the whole elaborate joke had been worthwhile, but the situation was saved by the Headmaster, who normally visited each house play in turn for a few minutes. He turned up at the interval for *Turkey Time,* laughing loudly at every dubious line, and staying to the end, when he vigorously applauded. Noel, torn between pride in his house's success and embarrassment at its cause, finally calmed down. Once the Head had left he professed himself 'disgusted' and 'ashamed that my house could put on such a performance' but that proved the end of the matter – or almost so. The following term the wound was reopened, perhaps by collusion with the culprits, by the reviewer from our neighbouring house, who began, 'Well, perhaps we ought first to pay a tribute to the broadmindedness of their censor, and to maintain that Peele B chose Ben Travers first anyway, so there!'

This was true enough, as I shall describe in a moment. So far as Peele A was concerned, in 1942, with Noel no doubt demanding to see the text of the proposed production before approving the senior dormitory's choice, respectability was restored with a repeat of the comedy thriller *Someone at the*

Door, which built up to a most satisfactory, and wholly sexless, climax. When the slow-spoken, somewhat stolid boy (later a clergyman) playing the part of the village policeman opened the door on to a stage littered with murdered bodies to ask in yokel-like tones 'Is there anything wrong here, soor?' he brought the house down. I often wondered if he ever had a similar triumph with a sermon.* The Peele B reviewer, writing in *The Blue* for June-July 1942, considered the evening 'a great success, mainly due to Pitman', who played the leading role and I remember how the final lines of the play involved his telephoning the *Daily Express* with news of the sensational crimes which had just occurred. To the unseen speaker at the other end he replied 'Sub-editor? Sub-editor, hell! Get me Lord Beaverbrook!' There was an odd foreshadowing of his later career for my friend was later to become a well known name on that very newspaper and (not usually to his satisfaction) to be frequently telephoned by Lord Beaverbrook himself. Bob Pitman gained an equal success in the following year, this time as the sinister villain in *Love from a Stranger*, and I often reflected, if he had followed his first inclinations and gone to the Bar his histrionic talents would have been put to greater use than in Fleet Street. I can recall him staging a mock trial in a changing room where one boy was charged with borrowing another's football jersey and hugely enjoying himself as prosecuting counsel.

Thanks to the rigid segregation of the various houses the only other house concerts we saw were those staged by Peele B, but, for unexplained reasons, it possessed at this time a reservoir of acting and production talent. Two close future friends of mine, a future Peele B house-captain, Peter Scroggs, who, after Cambridge, managed the Arts Theatre in that city and then became a television producer, and Ivan Yates, who finally became a journalist, were both constantly commended. As early as June 1940 they were being singled out for mention in *The Blue*. 'The hiccups were so realistic that Peele B's house funds must be sadly depleted', wrote the reviewer of the former's performance in *The King can do no Wrong*, and of the latter in *The Distant Drum*: 'Yates acted a difficult part well.' I remember this latter play for providing me with the first authentic shiver down the spine I received from any theatrical performance. The story revolved round a family who regularly heard a ghostly drum playing before any sudden death, and a boy with a drum was posted a very long way away on the playing fields and then steadily tramped towards the house until eventually the noise from just outside the dayroom was deafening. As it stopped, the central character on stage, involved in some family scandal, shot himself. The build up of tension was superbly handled, so that, as the gun was fired in the sudden silence one almost expected the suicide to be real, and I often used this incident as a yardstick by which to measure comparable *coups de theatre* when professionally reviewing plays later in my life.

---

* For the Rev. Roger Whitehead's obituary see *The Blue*, Dec 1999, p.248.

In 1941, as mentioned earlier, Peele B produced, as a rival to *Turkey Time*, a somewhat milder Ben Travers farce, *Rookery Nook,* a great hit when first put on in the West End in 1926 and since revived. I can remember another future friend, destined to become senior grecian, colonial police officer and finally publisher – sadly, he turned down the chance to join MI6 – who as a boy enjoyed dark and girlish good looks, giving a dazzling performance as the flighty young woman, Poppy Dickie, round whom the plot revolved. The moment when, supposing the man entertaining her to be alone, she burst in dressed in her underclothes, carrying a charity collection tray, with a cry of 'Flags for the lifeboat!', to confront some staid visitors, or perhaps the vicar, was a triumph comparable only to the 'Knicks!' moment in *Turkey Time*. But it was not all double entendres. Peele B gave such an impressive production of that great, and somewhat tedious, stand-by of amateur companies, *George and Margaret* in 1942 that it was, most unusually, repeated for the benefit of the whole school during the summer term. 'Yates…,' conceded the reviewer somewhat grudgingly in the June *Blue*, 'seems to have the makings of a good amateur actor…Irving [Richard Irving, another future house-captain and post-school acquaintance, now dead] and Scroggs were just themselves – what better entertainment could we wish?'[1] The outstanding house play of my time at Housie was undoubtedly Peele B's production of *The Importance of Being Earnest*, with Ivan Yates as Lady Bracknell and his delivery of the classic line 'A handbag?' is still talked about by those who witnessed it. Years later the cast, by then middle-aged, held a reunion, attending a professional production of the same play at Guildford. They compared notes on their careers, agreeing, one of those present reported to me, that, even if not happy at Housie, it had not done too badly by them, since all had made a reasonable mark in the world. The same was undoubtedly true of another acclaimed Peele B actor of my time, Bernard Levin, who was to achieve fame in quite another sphere, as a journalist.

The life of a professional actor was not one the school encouraged boys to contemplate. One future headmaster, Michael Marland, who arrived at Housie the year after I left, has recorded the headmaster's unsympathetic response to his declaration that he wished to go on the stage. 'You don't act well enough,' he was told, 'to convince us that you are working.'[2] When Marland wished to use the school's name in the troupe of boys he formed to tour church halls performing Shakespeare he was forbidden to do so and they became instead 'The Elizabethan Players'.

The theatrical profession being, like journalism, one in which talent is more important than riches, might have been expected to attract Old Blues but perhaps the regime I have described stifled such impulses. At all events the school has produced only one actor this century who has become a household name, the film star Michael Wilding, though several others of my generation or one shortly after it reached the West End and can still occasionally be seen when the films in which they appeared are repeated on television. Among them is Robert Crewdson, (CH 1936-44), who played a German in *The Guns of Navarone*, the Rev. W Tenniel Evans, (1937-44), who, most unusually, combined a career on the boards with being in Holy Orders, Roger Allam (1964-70) and Jason Flemyng (1978-83). The best known of Old Blue scriptwriters is probably the television dramatist Clive Exton (1940-45).[3]

In my time drama was not regarded as a serious subject in its own right, or even as an additional educational resource, but merely as a means of diversion. Comedy or strong and simple stories were what we craved. More intellectually demanding productions were few. Barnes A in the Lent Term of 1941 put on *The Ascent of F6* by WH Auden, but this was a rare exception; more typical was Thornton A's *Strife*, by John Galsworthy. Elsewhere along The Avenue, however, routine fare by Edgar Wallace and another crime play, *Mr Pym Passes By*, remained the rule. By my last Lent Term, 1943, the mixture remained much as before, with yet more Ben Travers, in the shape of *Thark*, another stock thriller, *I Killed the Count*, and, a brave but probably over ambitious choice, Bernard Shaw's *The Doctor's Dilemma*.

The school possessed at that time no custom built theatre though the Prep contained a small stage. Only Big School, however, could accommodate us all and it was here the masters or grecians commonly put on a play at the end of the summer term. The former were the more enjoyable if only for the pleasure of identifying normally fearsome members of the staff in spite of their costumes and make-up. I recall DM Macnutt, a master of whom I shall say much more later, in a minor play by Shaw, *Passion, Poison and Petrifaction*, sounding as cold and pompous as he did in everyday life, and a hardly more impressive production of *Androcles and the Lion*. (By contrast, an 'entertainment' put on by the masters consisting of music hall style acts, in one of which one was supposed to be fired from a cannon, was a great success. A little Shaw, I concluded – and was to confirm later as a West End critic – goes a long way.) In July 1940, despite the distractions of the threatened invasion and the claims on their time of the newly formed Home Guard, the grecians staged *Lady Precious Stream*, providing, according to the review in *The Blue*,[4] which appeared in November 'one of the most delightful evenings we have experienced since the beginning of the war'. From this judgement I must dissent. Described by its own author as 'a very ordinary play written solely for the commercial theatre in China'[5] it left me with a prejudice against all things Asiatic. In my opinion later experience has amply justified this. I have never visited the Far East, nor had any great desire to do so, and have a horror of Chinese food, Indian music and everything Japanese. The roots of this hostility lay in *Lady Precious Stream* for it provided my first experience of the conventions of Chinese drama, in which horsemen were represented by characters lifting their feet like horses' hooves and scenery was dispensed with altogether. I still view such productions, like those without proper costumes, with deep suspicion. What has one paid one's money for if not to be transported into a different world? I was, I recall, bored by the tedious artificiality of the play but remember it for one reason only, a scene in which, after two characters had agreed to marry, a placard was carried on to the stage reading 'Nine months later'. I am sure its significance was lost on the smaller boys – indeed I am not sure that, at 13, I appreciated it myself. The meaning was not however lost on the Headmaster. While a few older boys glanced apprehensively towards him to see how he would respond the urbanely sophisticated HLO Flecker, so much more broadminded than many of his staff, threw back his head and roared with laughter.

The grecians' choice in July 1943 was far more to my taste, *The School for Scandal,* still my favourite play of its period, and my two future Peele B friends were both involved and on form. 'Scroggs,' wrote *The Blue* in its delayed review in November, 'was engaging as Charles in his acting and singing', while 'Yates is to be congratulated upon a vivacious and intelligent rendering of Lady Teazle.'

Poor Ivan! He found Housie as unsympathetic an environment as I did and got on even worse with his housemaster, Macnutt. Later he achieved some success as an actor at Oxford and became President of the Union and a prominent member of the Labour Club, before making his name as a political correspondent. He had, quite early in life, become Assistant Editor of the *Observer* when killed, tragically and pointlessly, while crossing the road. The last service I could perform for him – we had become close friends by then and, as best man at my wedding, he made a typically accomplished speech – was to write his obituary in the magazine of the school he had detested.[*]

Acting gave boys with no natural aptitude for games a chance to make their mark and enjoy the sweet music of applause and, bearing in mind that in the 1930s and 1940s drama was not considered a serious academic subject but rather a distraction from real education, Housie did not do too bad a job. The standard of our amateur productions, especially those for the whole school – another argument against the petty parochialism I have criticised elsewhere – was high and by the time one left one was likely to have discovered if one had any latent talent for acting and to be familiar with at least the more popular plays of the time as well as a few classics. I still feel grateful to Housie, though this would have happened equally at Newbury Grammar School which had an outstanding reputation in this area, for introducing me to one source of lifelong pleasure, the Savoy Operas. It was Pitman who opened my eyes to their delights and, most appropriately, the first I enjoyed, *Trial by Jury,* was the earliest to achieve success, at the Royalty Theatre, London, on 25 March 1875,[6] though I first saw it in the Prep Hall, Christ's Hospital, on 5 June 1942. *The Blue* observed that 'It was like the good old times to hear Gilbert and

---

[*] Jun 1975 pp.163-4. See also *The Times*, 14 Feb 1975.

Sullivan at Housie again. All concerned are to be congratulated on this very sporting and successful attempt to dissipate the War Feeling.' My former nursemaid, by now a close friend – we were aged 17 and 16 respectively – was singled out for commendation:

> The Usher RP Pitman, duly saturnine and severe – a good actor this – sang his Bias song with humour and expression and got the audience and Jury well and truly into the Proper Frame of Mind. He was always in the picture.[7]

I was even more taken with *HMS Pinafore*, in February 1943, a colourful interlude in the bleak winter of my last year. Again *The Blue* was enthusiastic about my friend: 'RP Pitman as Sir Joseph Porter made a great hit,' recorded the next edition that March. *Patience*, with the aesthete triumphing over the obviously games-playing Dragoons, delighted me, and I also remember a series of extracts from various operas, including the song from *Princess Ida*, in which one character, Arac, discards his heavy and elaborate armour piece by piece. In the Housey version Home Guard uniform was substituted, with steel helmet doing duty for the original ornamental version, battledress blouse for red tunic, and so on. By then, as I shall describe, I was in the Home Guard myself and this performance stands out in my mind as the only occasion when modern dress has added to a play's effectiveness.

Gilbert and Sullivan proved something of a bond with my father who, though as unmusical as myself, had stage-managed all the well known Savoy operas for the Newbury Operatic Society and many other operettas as well, like *Miss Hook of Holland* and *Merrie England,* all of which I accordingly got to know and enjoy. But, as for many essentially non-musical people, Gilbert and Sullivan remained my real love and I have found his contemporary references have often given added interest to my reading since. It needed little perception to identify Oscar Wilde, whose work, as I shall mention, I got to know later in my school career, with Bunthorne in *Patience*, but I was delighted years later, while writing about the second world war, to realise that the fire boat Massey Shaw was named after the Chief of the London Fire Brigade mentioned in *Iolanthe*, to whom I have referred earlier.[8]

When I remarked to my history master that I had been much taken by the inscription on Gilbert's monument on the Victoria Embankment, 'His foe was folly and his weapon wit', he, very properly, urged me to identify the source. And so I did, though with disappointing results. The author was Anthony Hope who had died, largely unremembered, in 1933.

We were never taken to see professional productions outside the school and lacked the opportunities which day boys, at least in London and the major cities, enjoyed to attend them on their own, but occasional entertainments were provided in Big School by visiting performers. The most notable was the annual visit, which ended with the war, of the London Symphony Orchestra, the smaller boys being taken to hear its final rehearsal, but this did nothing for me. I much more enjoyed an evening filled by the Stock Exchange Glee Club, or some such society, which included some lively 'rounds' and comic songs, presented by a genial raconteur who told a succession of excellent and wholly respectable funny stories. We were, of course, unlikely to provide a critical audience and I can remember only one entertainment that dismally failed, a marionette show. Puppets of all kinds have always seemed to me a pointless form of entertainment, only surpassed in tedium by that most contemptible type of performance, mime. I had never enjoyed Punch and Judy shows and only duty, later in life, caused me to watch the famous television series *Bill and Ben, The Flowerpot Men*, while on the one occasion I was sent to see a West End puppet show, as a drama critic, I failed to file a review. My mentor Pitman shared my views and I can recall how we were both overcome with laughter at hearing that a college contemporary had gone on to produce puppets, though only, as it turned out, before graduating to grand opera. I recall Bob's effective mimicry of our acquaintance trying to coax more emotion out of one of his cast: 'Oh come, darling, you're still giving a rather wooden performance!'

---

[1] Jun 1942 p.76
[2] Jul 1996 p.168
[3] Board in CH Museum
[4] Nov 1940 pp.3-5
[5] Ibid p.3
[6] *Gilbert and Sullivan Complete Plays* p.42
[7] Jun-Jul 1942 p.75
[8] *Gilbert and Sullivan Dictionary* p.32 and *Complete Plays* p.236

25

NOT OUT

In this first summer term, Conway was told repeatedly...that cricket was the most important thing...in the world of school.

Extract from First Bloom – *relating to 1937*

No subsequent term ever exposed me to the same near suicidal bottomless despair I had experienced between January and March 1937. The summer term that year contained an unforeseen bonus that almost turned me into a royalist, the Coronation, on Wednesday 12 May 1937. By some sad oversight the school had no official part to play in this historic ritual, but instead we were sent home for a couple of nights. This was like an end of term in miniature and I remember it all vividly, from being released from school five minutes early to catch the Guildford train to walking into Newbury that evening, with a strong sense of playing truant, in search of that Saturday's edition of *The Magnet*. This was, however, the last time I bought the magazine. I had by no means grown out of it, but Greyfriars, having proved so different from Housie, had lost its earlier appeal.

That first year was exceptional. Of our three terms it was the summer which I came to detest most, thanks solely to its dominant activity, cricket. I had managed to stay reasonably out of sight during rugger practices and had, as already described, almost enjoyed the running which took up much of the Lent Term, but cricket was an individual sport where one's shortcomings could not be hidden. In *First Bloom* I described how the game came to take over our lives on those long, often sunlit and, I came to feel, endless days:

In this first Summer term, Conway was told repeatedly, and by sheer weight of repetition came almost to believe...that cricket was the most important thing, if not in the whole world, at least in the world of school. In every house in Middlestone, and in almost every house in every school, there were those who, like Conway, found that the universal cricket mania made their lives a misery. In the two previous terms, games on a half-holiday had always finished by four o'clock, leaving two hours of freedom before tea. In the summer, even if the feeble junior game had dragged to its weary conclusion, it was almost a duty to watch the senior match. When some distinguished personage visited the school and obtained for it an extra half-holiday, it meant for Conway only an extra hour- and-a-half's drudgery on the cricket field, instead of a comparatively peaceful time in the classroom. It was not that he liked work but that he hated cricket. The love of sport prevailing at Middlestone affected his development no less than that of those new boys who seemed to have been born to take a bat in their hands. But instead of teaching him to love cricket it inculcated into him a dislike of the game and all it stood for.

When we were not actually playing cricket we were preparing to play it, watching others play it, or ministering in some way to the perpetual demands of the pitch on which it was played, and above all the sacred 'square' between the two wickets. Of all these activities infinitely the worst was fielding practice, as my hero discovered:

To him it seemed a waste of a fine afternoon, when the sun made the metal of the rails beyond the pitch sparkle, to be out on this space, listening to a lecture from one of the monitors. His thoughts wandered while the voice continued to enlarge on the importance of Conway learning to play cricket, but when it ceased, he came back to earth with a start. He found a ball was being flung at him, for him to catch, once, twice, on and on, time after time, and as soon as he returned it, his instructor hurled it back harder. He missed it once and it blacked his eye, while the relentless monitor continued to point out how utterly Conway deserved this.

My memory of that first term – under this stern regime my ability to catch a ball did dramatically improve, as I recall my father remarking in the following holidays when we were throwing a tennis ball back and forth – is of constantly bruised fingers and of frequent minor damage to my face and other parts of my body after failing to intercept this dangerous missile. (It is gratifying to see, on television today, professional cricketers cravenly cowering behind solid helmets and vizors like medieval knights. If they are, very sensibly in my view, frightened of the ball why go on to the pitch at all?)

Other aspects of the game also made little appeal to me, as my alter-ego James Conway, describes:

There was not only the horror of fielding, but the equal horror of being put up, as it seemed, as a target for someone at the other wicket who was resolved on his destruction. 'Even people who are poor players', Conway said three years later, when he had secured emancipation from the chains of the cricket field, 'seem to enjoy batting. The only pleasure I ever found in it was lying in the grass before I went in and after I came out, and the closer together these two occurrences were, the greater my satisfaction.'

This was not, I fear, what our housemaster considered 'having a good spirit in house games' and I came to dread our daily musterings on the house pitch:

> Sometimes the new boys were drilled in the Nets, sometimes they were able to spend a restful afternoon watching a house game, sometimes there was the glorious freedom of 'rolling' when after twenty minutes of lazy locomotion up and down the pitch beside the rollers the afternoon was free. These periods were times of contentment, for if the senior in charge was easy-going, conversation and chocolate helped the time to pass pleasantly. Up and down, up and down, from one white crease to another and back again, with the drowsy June sun making the green of the grass stand our more vividly and the windows of the trains sparkle as they flashed by on their way to the coast.

I looked forward to 'rolling' afternoons, which came round only every ten days or so, though this activity, as I shall describe later, was also used as a punishment. Not officially punitive but far more demanding than some disciplinary penalties was another regular activity, 'watering the pitch', for the wicket on the house playing field was like a sacred god that needed constant sacrifices. To provide this particular oblation we were required to raid the dormitory for the large, metal basins we used for washing, fill them to the brim and stagger out to the pitch with them, in a seemingly endless stream. The load was both awkward and heavy and can have done no good to the backs of small boys too small to bear it, as I certainly was for my first year or two. Once, I remember, the monitor in charge ordered us to go into Peele B to get additional basins, so he could speed up the rate of water delivery, and we were intercepted by matron. This was undoubtedly an offence, since the permission of both housemasters and perhaps of matron herself should have been sought first, but we were far too junior to question our orders, and matron's response seems to me excessive. I can still see her, positively trembling with rage at the supposed outrage we had committed, her voice shaking with emotion as – I recall the words verbatim – she cried incredulously: 'How dare you come into Peele B house?'

It seemed impossible to get away from cricket. Unlike rugger or athletics it had no finite length and it needed only one or two good or keen players in a team to keep it going indefinitely, at least on Saturday when there was no afternoon school. I never decided whether batting or fielding was the worse; with bowling, apart from some compulsory sessions at the nets, I was rarely entrusted. To stand at the crease while another boy hurled a hard ball in your direction seemed bad enough, but, if you got out too rapidly you might be blamed for the team's defeat, and far worse, the game might go into a second innings.

My lack of aptitude for the game rapidly became apparent but Housie was always reluctant to recognise any deficiency in any direction, especially in the sacred area of physical exercise, and week after week, those members of the house third eleven who were clearly destined for better things found their enjoyment of the game spoiled by having to play with myself and other 'rabbits', whose sole desire was to be out as quickly as possible and field in the quietest corner of the ground. The abler performers had their revenge, however, leaving the weaker ones to carry back to the house the pads and bats they simply discarded at the end of the game, and week after week I struggled back across Big Side barely visible beneath a load of stumps, bails and other equipment.

Occasionally in that first term and later I was required to act as scorer, which was at least preferable to playing, though sometimes malicious spectators would try to obscure one's view of the pitch, an example of 'bullying by proxy', for one was liable to be punished for keeping the score inadequately. My real problem on that first occasion, however, was that I did not as yet understand the umpire's signals and, however much I attempted to concentrate, found my attention wandering. It was all so extraordinarily trivial and boring! One was required to keep a record of every ball so that the bowling analysis could be studied later and promising players identified, but I did not realise this till too late and accordingly had to fabricate a whole game, working backwards from the final scores and trying to ensure it tied in with the points at which the various wickets had fallen. Lawrance duly studied this masterly piece of falsification in detail and without identifying it as such, and, if he commented on it to the boys concerned, whom I had credited with byes, maiden overs and even the occasional boundary to which they were not entitled, they accepted his unmerited congratulations in silence. Even more difficult was performing a similar feat for the opposing team, since I had not even known their names. Happily Lawrance failed to discuss this with his opposite number in the house concerned merely remarking to me my efforts had been unnecessary; it was only one's own side for which bowling details were required. For years afterwards I was afraid that someone would stumble on this piece of deception, but happily that term's scorebook was soon filled and remained closed. I suspect it survives still, mute evidence to my undiscovered fraud.

As I had already discovered with rugger and running, the only way in which games could become remotely tolerable was to play them with people of one's own level of ability and happily in time most of the players in the third eleven were promoted to one of the more senior games. I described the results in *First Bloom*:

The House Third Eleven tended to be made up of any incompetents not required for either school matches of the two other Blake [ie Peele A] teams and its captain was usually chosen from the hard stratum of burly youths who, though invaluable to the House in the rugger season, were merely a liability during the summer term. Since it was certainly the highest form of cricket any of these gentlemen was likely to direct they made the most of their opportunities. It was a rule at Middlestone that a match which finished before half-past-four must continue into a second innings. If a match showed signs of coming to a premature end both sides usually displayed feverish activity to prevent the unwelcome decease. An extraordinary amount of time would be put into crossing at the end of each over and small boys sent in last because of their junior status would make frenzied efforts to keep their wicket intact...Most ludicrous of all, however, was the cricket when half-past four struck. Weary youths, anxious that their precious half-holiday should not be entirely stolen from them...would attempt by every stratagem in their power to end the game quickly. They swiped wildly at impossible balls and, if this device failed, would even resort to destroying their own wicket with a particularly vigorous stroke, but such extremes were rare, for a house-captain tended to be harsh about such carelessness and it was expedient to enter this self-inflicted tragedy as 'bowled'.

Ultimately, though far from burly still, I became, through sheer age and seniority, captain of the Peele A Third Eleven, though the nearest I ever came to a 'captain's innings' was a score of five. I never put myself on to bowl, knowing the result was likely to be an embarrassing catalogue of 'Wides' in the score book, and modestly gave myself the least demanding position on the batting orders putting myself in last – in the Third Eleven final wicket stands were unknown. I also assigned myself the easiest fielding position as long-stop behind the wicket-keeper though he all too often missed a ball. The deep field, favoured by some unenthusiastic players, I distrusted. Occasionally some show-off would send a ball towards the boundary, or, far worse, would hit a high catch which I knew with certainty that I would miss. The best position, without question, was to be umpire, a job filled in the junior games by batsmen already out or waiting to go in. Some players took enormous pains over 'taking guard' on first going in, a procedure which always seemed to me thoroughly unsporting, since it was, I felt, part of the game for the player to decide for himself where to put his bat. I happily responded to all such requests, however, which served that important purpose of wasting time, and waved my hand vigorously to one side or the other as a guide to the batsman at the far wicket, though I doubt if this did him much good for I could never remember, and still cannot, which was the 'leg' stump and which the 'off'. Was 'leg' *my* left or the batsman's? Nor did I ever master such arcane terms as 'silly mid-off' and when allocating positions to the fielders would direct them by a lordly wave of the hand until there seemed to be a reasonable spread across the pitch and no one was at 'short slip', which seemed to me dangerous. 'Square leg' I would allocate in a loud, confident manner; I knew where that was all right, thanks to it being also the location of one umpire.

In spite of my strong instinct for self-preservation on the sports field – not cowardice, which implies giving way to fear when there is a real reason not to – it was cricket which inflicted on me the only injury I suffered at school, apart from those incurred during fielding practice, a spectacular black eye. I was with other boys from Peele A supposed to be watching a house match and, becoming bored, sought refuge in the long grass some way from the pitch and settled down to enjoy a book. Meanwhile two boys waiting their turn to bat were whiling away the time by playing 'French cricket', which involved one gently bowling a ball to another who would hit it back in the same way. Unfortunately the boy with the bat suddenly struck the ball hard and, having missed the bowler, it struck me sharply and painfully in the face. Though not quite knocked out I can remember literally 'seeing stars' and I sported a markedly discoloured eye for weeks afterwards, which brought me some undeserved sympathy.

Apart from the whole afternoon being liable to be taken up with cricket I hated Saturdays for another reason. In the long light evenings after tea games of asphalt-cricket were organised on the open spaces behind the house, using a tennis ball, which made them at least safe to play, but by that time I had seen more than enough of the game in any form. It was, however, difficult to avoid getting pressed to play if numbers were short, or being expected to watch. To seek out a corner to read, as I preferred to do – Was not six afternoons a week of cricket enough, for heaven's sake? – was to invite social condemnation if not actual bullying. I soon came to look back longingly to the dark evenings of the winter and the hours of lock-up in the boisterous and noisy dayroom.

As a result of those Summer terms, rather than the compulsory games of the Winter and Lent terms, I have retained a lifelong loathing of all sport and a deep suspicion of anyone who displays anything except the most cursory interest in it. In retirement I have complained bitterly to the BBC of it abandoning to cricket for long and largely unpredictable periods its best wavelength, specifically allocated to it to provide a news and current affairs service to the whole United Kingdom. Who, I asked the offending controller bitterly, can spend all day listening to this series of non-events except overgrown schoolboys who ought to be more usefully occupied? The BBC's fanatical obsession with sport and its readiness to sacrifice its audience to cricket, soccer, rugby, racing, rugby, soccer, swimming, tennis or whatever other trivial, time-wasting activity happens to be in progress in competition with real broadcasting, seems to me a lasting blot on its reputation. Thanks to Housie, I hated all outdoor games throughout my life and shall carry my loathing of them beyond the grave, having left instructions in my will that no part of my estate shall benefit any form of sport in any way – for example by purchasing books on the subject for a library.

To return to Christ's Hospital, I still remember my incredulity at hearing a master ask a class if they had noticed how appropriate that day's prayer in chapel had been since it had referred to 'running the race that is set before us' and this was the first day of relay sports. How, I wondered, could a grown man with a real job possibly concern himself with such unimportant ephemera? This was among the incidents that convinced me that I was unlikely to be happy as a schoolmaster, a career I briefly contemplated when in my teens, and one reason I still feel some admiration for our headmaster was that he showed little interest in such matters. It was, I think, a great reflection on his headmastership that he allowed so much importance to be attached to games, but I cannot recall his ever making much reference to them in public, nor was he, in my recollection, a frequent attender on the touchline during major matches.

Hostile to cricket though I have remained, I am aware how much pleasure it has given to many people, as spectators rather than as players, and at university I was amazed to meet several people including my fiercely non-athletic friend Ivan Yates, whose leg had been broken by rugger, as I described, and whose short sight made him a poor cricketer – who still followed the game. (Ivan indeed, as President of the Union, played in a game of 'Members versus Staff' which I declined to do.) The school cannot entirely have extinguished such impulses in myself for, hard to believe though I now find it, I remember in the summer holidays of 1938, when I was twelve, following with rapt attention the broadcast accounts of Len Hutton's record-breaking Test innings of 364[1] and even bowling at an impromptu wicket set up on the open space enclosed by our council estate. (I used a soft ball, however, and, with no batsman at the other end this was hardly cricket by any test.) Later, in middle age, I even came to enjoy watching village cricket in Hampshire or Dorset, so different in character from the tense primadonna displays I had witnessed at school, since the game was now being played, and watched, from choice, not compulsion. I do, I suppose, feel a certain gratitude to Housie for having at least enabled me to understand most of the rules of the game, though I was, and still am, unsure when a player has been 'stumped', and putting 'leg before wicket' seems to me a sensible tactic, as it did at school. The truth is that it was Housie, with its obsession for them, which turned me from a poor player into a games-hater. It had, I know, the same effect on some of my contemporaries. One once sent me, without comment, an advertisement which showed a group of spectators clearly not watching a cricket match. It was captioned: 'They're not talking about the cricket, but about Burroughs gin.' Years later, when commissioning recruiting advertisements for future electrical engineers, I was delighted with one lay-out proposed by the agency which showed the scorer at a school match ignoring the game and instead drawing in the score book an elaborate electric circuit. That indeed, I felt, was the sort of young man we needed in Electricity Supply.

The Summer term cast a shadow over the rest of the year; I could not enjoy the Spring because the cricket-dominated Summer was bound to follow it. Fifty years on, autumn remains my favourite season, as furthest from the threat of cricket, for sub-consciously I still half expect to be forced out on to the cricket field, for pitch-watering or fielding practice, as soon as the warm weather returns, or dragged from my hiding place to participate in a 'friendly' but enforced game of asphalt-cricket. But, conversely, those three months of misery brought a joy so acute that I have never recaptured it. This was the pleasure I experienced on the last afternoon of the Summer term when the house cricket bats, pampered even when not in use, were carefully anointed with linseed oil and wrapped in newspaper, before being laid in the aptly named 'coffin' in the hall for the next two terms.

My first Summer term also introduced me to another Housey institution 'Baths' and its at first dominant component 'Non-swimmers'. Here, too, I feel a mixture of emotions, gratitude for being compelled to learn to swim being tempered with unhappy memories of the methods used. In *First Bloom* I recalled these lessons sympathetically:

> In the break after morning school, in the time before tea in the afternoon, the Baths seemed to be issuing always their peremptory summons to those unfortunates who could not yet swim. The small juniors, blushing for their nakedness, or, if they had been nourished in the Middlestone Prep-school, seeming to rejoice in it, would be urged from one side of the bath to the other, from one end to the other, aided by the exhortations of an artistically clad Mr Maperton [ie Macklin], or a less artistically clad, but more vociferous, mob of seniors.

My recollection now is that I found such sessions deeply embarrassing, since, in the Victorian tradition of 'all males together' manliness, we were compelled to bathe nude. For shy small boys this was bad enough, but far worse was that the masters instructing us did the same. I found being supported at the chest by an adult of the same sex, with my head only a few inches from his all too conspicuous private parts, including pubic hair, which most of us had never seen before, or even heard of, a paralysingly unpleasant experience, which distracted me from concentrating on mastering the simple breast-stroke required of us. My disgust must have been evident to my instructor for he loudly assured me, and all the other shrinking new boys in earshot, 'There's nothing wrong in being naked,' but I silently disagreed then and disagree still. In a House consisting of shy new boys of ten, through teenage adolescents, to mature young men of nineteen compelling them to swim naked together was in my view likely to distress the innocent, encourage the exhibitionist and give satisfaction, for the wrong reasons, to the corrupt. Nude bathing was a cause, I now know, of embarrassment not merely to me but to many other boys, and I still recall as a thoroughly upsetting spectacle seeing all the boys in a non-swimmers class, including the youngest and smallest, climbing out of the water with rigid erections, thanks to the coldness of the water. I was as yet too innocent to enjoy as one of my contemporaries did the spectacle provided by one young art master 'who used to sit on the edge of the swimming pool in the nude, legs up and crushed down concealing...a shameful erection.'

Far worse was the experience of the eleven-year-old Robin Hull, newly arrived in Middleton A, who 'loved swimming' and readily accepted the offer of the senior housemaster of another House to give him extra tuition. The Baths, as the master had no doubt planned, were deserted and 'There was a great deal of body contact' between pupil and instructor until the former was 'drawn forward' by the visibly excited master in a full-scale assault. The small boy, 'frankly terrified...started to cry...The master abandoned his attempted seduction and then gave Robin sixpence [2.5p] not to tell. The sixpence was rapidly transmuted into two Mars bars and the little boy, munching happily, reflected that after all he had got the best of the bargain.'

If the classics bred sadists the performing arts seem to have produced paedophiles: the offender in this case taught music. He did eventually fail to return after one holiday but must have been given a respectable reference for, his intended victim learned, 'he went on to other schools where years later an Old Blue was horrified to find he was teaching his son the piano.'[2]

Significantly, when the school took part in swimming matches against others even though all the participants and spectators were male, it conformed to the visitors' practice and the Housey team appeared in tiny swimming trunks known as 'bathers'. If ours was the natural and healthy mode why, I wonder still, was no attempt made to proselytise? My dislike at having to expose myself probably contributed to my slowness at learning to swim. This involved two landmarks. Until one could swim two lengths of the larger school bath one remained officially a non-swimmer, not allowed to attend the regular House Baths, which were supposed to be enjoyable. A second test followed, to pass which you had to dive in head first and then swim five lengths. It was not, I think, until my second or even third summer than I achieved this and was no longer compelled to attend classes, though still required to go with the house when there was a compulsory session for all swimmers. Having passed the test I soon afterwards swam 20 lengths, with something of the satisfaction I felt about the same time on learning to ride a bicycle. I could, I think, have become a good, if not enthusiastic, swimmer but for the legacy of distaste for the Baths left by the school's crude teaching methods. What I remember best of the many hours I spent in the cold, murky and heavily chlorinated water of the Baths is of expecting at any minute to drown. For some reason the school despised the rubber ring which most non-swimmers used while mastering the necessary strokes, indeed we were not even allowed to provide our own. Christ's Hospital relied instead, no doubt because this has been the method used in London before the tyre-like device had been invented, on a far more primitive type of support, a canvas belt attached to a pole by a line. The pole was carried by the instructor along the edge of the bath, while the pupil went through the motion of swimming, like a tethered fish. The idea was, I imagine, to give the non-swimmer confidence by taking him out of his depth in safety, but I never felt much faith in the belt round my waist, especially as, to punish some inept stroke or to lend emphasis to what he was saying, the instructor would sometimes lower the pole slightly so that one sank beneath the water, frantically spluttering in terror. I can recall small boys crying out in fear at such treatment and I suspect it may have left some with a permanent fear of the water. This is not something from which I have suffered, but it does seem possible, so strange are the ways of the sub-conscious, that the experience may have emerged, many years later, in the totally different phobia to which I am a victim, fear of heights.

That summer term of 1937 gave me my first experience of a long-established Housey tradition, mentioned by Charles Lamb, the Whole Holiday.[3] For weeks beforehand elaborate plans were made to make the most of this one day in the school year when we were free to leave the school grounds and some boys formed little groups to visit such beauty spots as Leith Hill, but, realising they had no funds to spare for me to have a second day out in a term, I always seized the chance for a full day out with my mother or father, as an alternative to the mere Saturday afternoon on offer in other terms. Where we went I cannot recall for certain, but at various times I visited Brighton, Worthing and the picture-postcard village of Amberley with one of my parents and I have had an affection for all three places since.

Returning to Housie after the Whole Holiday was almost as bad as coming back at the beginning of term and we were all reluctant to let the holiday atmosphere disappear. A House tradition was that the monitor responsible would select some particularly absurd passage from the Bible for Duty that evening, a favourite being one from the Book of Daniel in which the writer described how King Nebuchadnezzar had 'commanded, O peoples, nations and languages, that at what time ye hear the sound of the cornet, flute, harp, sackbut, psaltery, and all kinds of music, ye fall down and worship the golden image that Nebuchadnezzar the king had set up'. This tongue-twisting list of musical instruments was repeated four times in six verses and by its last appearance, even if the reader had managed to keep a straight face, giggles were invariably to be heard among his audience.[4]

One other break in our routine in the Summer Term, Field Day, did not yet involve me and I will mention it later, but from my first summer I was indirectly affected by two other regular events, Old Blues Day and Speech Day. They occurred on successive Saturdays, on both of which we were deprived of the use of the Dining Hall at midday and instead were issued with two 'crugs' and a slice of 'corned gag', ie a single corned beef sandwich, with an orange. Like all our meals at that time this never varied from year to year, but the lack of a hot meal that day was a small price to pay for the absence of games, for both Speech Day and Old Blues Day were 'free days', blissfully clear of any organised activity. Old Blues Day was indeed pure pleasure, for instead of having to turn out for Dinner Parade we watched the Old Blues from every house form fours and all the rest and march into Dining Hall behind the house standard, a ritual which, incredibly, I was to perform in my turn after leaving.

Another attraction of the day was that generous minded Old Blues would sometimes wander round the house seeking out the fortunate boy who had inherited their house number and pressing a tip upon him. This was indeed something of a Housey tradition. I have mentioned earlier the 'Bob Gent' encountered by earlier generations in London[5] and I once met a 'Florin Gent' outside Reading station who gave me this substantial coin with the words: 'I was there myself.' Whether he felt I needed consoling or was displaying loyalty to his old school, I never discovered. On Old Blues Day I was less lucky. I did meet the previous holder of my house number on several occasions, but all he ever gave me was a visiting card setting out his qualifications as a financial adviser and suggesting I might make use of his services. I have, I fear, never done so.

That first Old Blues Day, in 1937, I knew, of course, none of the recent leavers who returned, but from my second year was able to identify formerly familiar faces. Occasionally, too, old members of the house returned at other times. I can remember listening to my former house captain, Lawrance, describing his life as an undergraduate at Oxford to a fascinated group, who were delighted by his tales of proctors and 'bulldogs', but to me it sounded altogether too much like life at Housie to be attractive. I remember with more pleasure seeing two boys who had left the year beforehand, whom I had detested, being told off by our housemaster for smoking in the dayroom and how they complied as promptly and obediently with his order to put out their cigarettes as if they half expected to be ordered to bend over for 'six of the best'.

Speech Day was much less enjoyable than Old Blues Day for we were required to take part in a military style march past, for which we rehearsed for weeks beforehand. Apparently for the Lord Mayor and his fellow dignitaries even our usual highly drilled and disciplined parade was not sufficiently imposing and we had instead to lay on a march past more elaborate than anything I subsequently experienced in the army, even for a royal visit. The process began with a special 'sizing parade' when the whole house was lined up in height order before being mustered into the usual fours, to ensure that we made the most striking impression possible on the day. We were duly paraded, with each boy's place now specially allocated, on Speech Day and, having formed fours as usual, were marched through the Cloisters arch into the

Quadrangle, to the accompaniment of suitably martial music from the specially augmented band. This was the climax of the year for the bandmaster and drum-major, who hurled his mace high in the air as he strode ahead of the band, supposedly delighting the Lord Mayor's party lined up on the saluting base on the grass. As each house in turn entered the quad, it was given the command 'Eyes right!' just as on any military parade and the standard of drill was indeed impressive, not surprisingly in view of the ferocious punishment awaiting anyone who let not merely the house but the school down.

I thought the whole ritual impressive in my first year, when I was terrified of not keeping my dressing or getting out of step, or even wandering off to the right while we were looking in that direction, but now find it somewhat repellent. None of the City dignitaries and governors who attended seem ever to have thought to enquire after our welfare or even to make the customary request of distinguished visitors for an extra half holiday, though I recall glimpsing in a transformed Dining Hall some of the delicacies laid out for them, a striking contrast to our crude and scanty rations. (Just so, I have thought since, did workhouse children eye enviously the superior food enjoyed by the Master and Guardians.)

By chance *Radio Times* carried shortly afterwards, on 9 July 1937, as part of a regular series entitled *Samuel Pepys, Listener,* a description of this, my first Speech Day, on 12 June, in the style of the famous diarist. The result is a fair depiction of how this occasion must have seemed to one of the favoured visitors and, incidentally, refers to several subjects I have already mentioned such as the Brangwyn pictures in chapel and the school's commitment to music:

> Come to school, here first of all to service in chapel – a noble chapel and well proportioned, with frescoed pictures out of the Bible round the walls. Picture opposite me was Paul and others staggering ashore at Melita from their shipwreck. And one of the men's faces (but whether Paul's or noe I cannot say) was exactly such a face as the artist might have studied from the life on Folkestone pier emerging from the Channell boat after a choppy crossing. Musick good, singing likewise….Soe to lunch in the great hall – a good lunch with good table company and all merrie…Presently, after seeing the boys march past my Lord Mayour, we all into the great school-room where we were very well entertained with musick, singing and play acting. Herein one notable thing was Dr Vaughan Williams his being present in the audience unknown to most of us (and heard some of his own musick done). But the conducteur spyed him out and had him on to platform to make his bow, amid the generall acclamacioun. And another notable thing was one of the boy musiciens, Keys by name (But Lord how apposite!) his being already an FRCO; since he was 14, I was told. Alsoe we had a very good bright speech from Lawrance the chief Grecian, befittingly and most welcomely seasoned with Attick Salt.

'Attick salt' is defined as 'wit of a dry, delicate and refined quality' and the senior grecian's oration, required by tradition to be delivered after learning by heart, without notes, was an annual ordeal. This was indeed Lawrance's year. At the end of term he played the lead, successfully it need hardly be said, in the Leaving Grecians' play, *Youth at the Helm,* while that other current Housey hero, Ivor Keys, 'enlivened the intervals with pianistic frivolity'. As a New Boy, aged eleven, I no doubt attended the latter event, but played no part in Speech Day, and two other distinctive features of the summer term I remember with positive distaste. On very hot days it was the fashion to proclaim an enthusiasm for cold baths, compulsory at some public schools throughout the year. Peele A had happily not adopted this unpleasant practice, as some other houses had done, but it was hard to refuse to take part in the supposedly voluntary dip on summer evenings, though I now suspect that, as so often, a few extroverts bullied the rest of us into doing something we secretly detested. Thus, with other shivering eleven and twelve year olds I lined up naked and shivering to plunge in turn into the chilly water only slightly warmed by those ahead of me in the queue. Cold baths were supposedly effective at damping down pubescent emotions but I doubt if they succeeded; on the contrary these lines of naked boys, eyeing each other's physical development, were an ideal forcing ground for our still quiescent sexuality.

Cold baths were one of the many unpleasant features of the Summer Term and the long light evenings also encouraged another amusement which singularly failed to divert me or, I suspect, most of the others who felt obliged to participate in it. This I now realise also contained a powerful, if covert, sexual element, and made ingenious use of our bed numbers, as I described in *First Bloom,* giving the monitor a fictitious name:

> Sometimes in the long summer evenings Brown held a semi-sadistic lottery in the junior dormitory, when all the bed numbers were gathered in a hat and drawn out in pairs, the owner of the first card being permitted, indeed directed, to beat with a slipper the owner of the second. On those delightful nights when sleep seemed as reluctant to come as the day to die, small boys writhed in ecstasies of anticipation while waiting for the numbers to be drawn. Since public opinion would have condemned any attempt to use the luck of the ballot as an aid to paying of old scores, the actual chastisement of the unfortunate boy was never brutal, and the possibility of 'old Jack', [ie Noel Sergent] entering the dormitory while it was proceeding added a conspiratorial relish to the whole affair.

The long evenings also made it possible to read in bed before settling down to sleep, which has remained a continuing pleasure, and Sunday, when the cry 'Get up!' was not heard until 7.55 am, provided a further opportunity to read in peace. *The Magnet* had left me for the moment disillusioned with school stories and my favourite author at this time was Percy F Westerman. The remoteness from my experience of his naval and military adventure stories appealed to me, and I was perfectly prepared to be heroic by proxy if not in real life. Occasionally Noel Sergent or the junior dormitory monitor would read to us as a Sunday evening treat. Noel read admirably, as he did most things he attempted except, for reasons I still do not quite understand, being a housemaster, and I can still hear his splendid rendering of *Moonfleet* by J Meade Faulkner, an excellent choice. One sunny Saturday evening of that first summer term I remember the two most senior boys in the house, admirable products both of the Housey system, Lawrance and Hatten, walking up and down the dormitory exchanging humorous reminiscences of, I think, OTC camp. These seemed to me the height of wit and I became more in awe of these almost god-like creatures than ever.

The summer term demonstrated once again the impracticality of our uniform. In winter we had been inadequately protected out of doors and had to sit in soaked outer garments inside. Now we sweated miserably in our heavy woollen outfits, sometimes presenting an unsightly spectacle of coats draped over the backs of our chairs, while we suffered miserably from our winter weight vests, shirts, stockings and knee breeches, held up by the wide and coarse working men's braces I have already described. The evenings brought, however, some relief for it was now permitted to wear 'flannels', ie shorts or long grey trousers with a sports shirt and blazer, instead of Housey clothes, while – a recognition that our out of date attire was a positive handicap to learning – these were also allowed for boys taking examinations.

My memory of that first Summer term is that the sun always seemed to be shining, much to my despair, for rain alone could liberate us from morning PT, and, far worse, long afternoons of cricket. I also recall, however, some admirable lessons in English, which I had the good fortune to be taught by WR (Roy) Macklin, one of the three outstanding masters from whose instruction I was to benefit at Christ's Hospital and to whom I still feel a debt of gratitude.

Roy Macklin, who did not, I think, have a nickname, represented for us the ultimate in what would now be called 'trendiness', a rare distinction in ultra-conformist Christ's Hospital. He wore, like a stage artist – my 'Mr Slightly Green' was modelled on him – a sombrero and brightly coloured jackets and, far worse, permitted his wife to go about in trousers, the first woman, I believe, to do so at Housie. More important, he was an inspired teacher, although he occupied a frustrating position, for no one was allowed to specialise in English after School Certificate, so, unlike his colleagues, he lacked the satisfaction of seeing his pupils gain Oxford or Cambridge scholarships.

Every first class teacher, I now realise, needed the qualities WRM displayed, a proper regard for accuracy in the treatment of his subject, along with a personal enthusiasm for it fierce enough to inspire others. He was as stern about misspellings and sloppy grammar as the admirable Miss House had been at my junior school, but delighted in English literature and especially poetry, reading verse, particularly Shakespeare, aloud, with a passion to which even the dullest could barely fail to respond. He lent me that term my first 'grown-up' book, *The Collected Short Stories of Sherlock Holmes*, and though I am no longer a particular enthusiast for Sir Arthur Conan Doyle's famous creation, this was only the first of a series of introductions to names unfamiliar to me. From that very first year he encouraged me to believe that I had some natural talent for writing, all the more welcome because the general consensus among both masters and boys seemed to be that I was hopeless at everything, but invariably mingled his praise with shrewd, and sometimes fierce, reproof, as I shall illustrate later.

None of my exercise books for this period survive, but I do recall being instructed to write a poem on the hot weather that term, and a few lines stick in my mind because of the reference to the iced orange soft drink – 1d [0.5p] a small glass, 2d [1.5p] a large one – which was then our great consolation:

> To the tuckshop there will be a rush:
> We all would like a Khula Krush.
> Though we take off our coats in third period,
> If we are not careful our heads will nod.

Our heads did indeed nod – I can recall falling asleep in more than one lesson thanks to our heavy clothing and the rest of these verses must, I think, have had more merit. At all events they were warmly praised, without for once any accompanying criticism. 'You'll be Poet Laureate one day, Longmate,' Roy Macklin told me, another of the flattering predictions of my boyhood which has remained unfulfilled.

The summer term ended with Prize-giving on the last afternoon, sufficient by itself to make it a popular and eagerly anticipated occasion. The title was in fact something of a misnomer for the main distribution of prizes took place in the winter and the only recipients in the summer were boys leaving that term. The tradition was for the presentation to be made by a distinguished Old Blue, and preferably one recently in the news. One year, I remember, the famous guest failed to appear and the headmaster thereupon invited a junior master, who happened to be an Old Blue, to deputise for him. (The missing man, a wing commander who had, I think, at some time won the world air speed record, duly turned up another year, but we had, I believe, enjoyed more the performance of his suddenly elevated substitute.)

Prize-giving was also the occasion for awarding the various house cups, though the Head never gave any sign of attaching much importance to these. He always, however, thoroughly enjoyed presenting the special trophy assigned to the house supposed during the preceding year to have distinguished itself most, not merely in games but in work and general conduct. The results were read out in reverse order, providing a public rebuff for those named first, though it was the housemasters who tended to show more embarrassment than their boys. I cannot recall that Peele A ever came bottom but had it done so the house would have rejoiced, unreasonably, at Noel Sergent's humiliation, indeed for a house to score exceptionally low marks was regarded as a distinction of its own, by its members.

The term ended with the Leaving Service in chapel, always, as I shall describe, a moving ceremony, but especially so in the Summer when 70 or 80 boys might make the journey in chapel to collect their Bible and hear the headmaster's solemn charge. Along with relief that some of the older boys who had made my life unhappy were leaving was mingled a sense of awe in my mind, for my hero, Lawrance, was among those going, and other school figures far too eminent for me ever to have spoken to them. I cannot believe that, clad in my best clean-smelling Housie clothes, my ticket home in my pocket and the prospect of using it next morning, my own eyes were damp, but I was certainly aware that having completed a year at Housie was a landmark in my life and one never to be forgotten.

---

[1] *Chronicle* p.500
[2] Hull p.122
[3] *CH Book* p.300
[4] Daniel 3 v 5-10
[5] Morpurgo p.77

26

A DOSE OF BLACK DRAUGHT

Soft, spongy gums mean ill health sooner or later.

Extract from Health Rules *displayed in dormitories at Christ's Hospital, c. 1937*

I have a clear recollection of the first morning of the summer holiday of 1937. It was bright sunshine and I was walking with my twin sister and Newbury friends along the then peaceful road towards Newtown and the Swan Inn, barely daring to contemplate the wonderful fact that I did not have to return to school for a full seven weeks. At that time, like other independent and grammar schools, Christ's Hospital had no half-term breaks but two substantial, four week, vacations at Christmas and Easter and a full seven weeks from the end of July until mid-September.

In retrospect the weather that summer seems always to have been fine and we spent many days walking in the country, which at that time came almost to our estate, and especially on the as yet unspoiled Greenham Common, a mere mile away down a quiet lane. When I was indoors I read, mainly books borrowed from the public library or the 'B', threepence [1.5p] a week, shelves of the local Boots. The range of books for boys of eleven was limited, but, though now weaned from *The Magnet*, I read many hard-cover school stories. I can remember only one, however, that seemed to echo my situation, in which one boy, unpopular for his ineptitude at games, demonstrated what a total rotter he was by stealing a plough and digging deep furrows across the First Eleven pitch the day before a major match. He was, of course, severely punished, but he privately became my hero. I also borrowed my sisters' books, especially the Chalet School series by Eleanor Brent Dyer, not because I had the faintest desire to be a girl, but because they were set abroad, comfortably remote from Sussex, and were also pervaded by a generally humane atmosphere. For similar reasons I derived enormous pleasure then and for the rest of my childhood from the stories of Arthur Ransome. Few boys can have been less inclined to go camping on the Cumbrian fells or sailing a small boat on Lake Windermere, but I could immerse myself within seconds in the solid, comfortable, middle-class world occupied by John, Nancy and the rest and could readily identify with the slightly eccentric Dick, not much good at tying knots, but useful when more intellectual skills were required and known to the others as 'The Professor'. These were very much books of the period, the classic which gave its name to the whole genre, *Swallows and Amazons*, being published in 1930, and *Winter Holiday*, the first I discovered, in 1933. A new Arthur Ransome – the last, *Great Northern?*, was not published until the year I became an undergraduate, 1947 – remained a major event for me. Over the years no other author has, I think, given me as much pleasure and I was delighted in my sixties to go on a holiday entitled *Swallows and Amazons Forever* devoted to visiting the sites which inspired him and, incidentally, to win a prize for my detailed knowledge of the books. Other children's books made little appeal to me. I detested *The Jungle Books*, as I have all such anthropomorphic works ever since, and, though his poetry has given me much pleasure, acquired a lifelong distaste for Kipling's prose. At school I can remember Pitman trying to arouse my enthusiasm for an illustrated edition of *Alice in Wonderland*, but though I dutifully laughed at each grotesque picture, I found the book tedious, just as I had disliked the film, and it merely confirmed my aversion, already mentioned, to fantasy of all kinds.

None of us, I think, had a holiday away from home that year, but I was wholly content not to be at school and all too soon the dreaded day of return to Housie arrived. It was, unusually, a Saturday and extremely hot, both of which seemed to make the already disastrous occasion worse, and putting on our heavy uniform added to my discomfort. When we changed trains at Reading I decided I simply could not face another term and wandered away from the other Newbury boys, indeed we were already tending to resume our school *personae* and separate. I found a quiet spot by the river, not without difficulty, as one well-meaning passer-by came up to ask me if I felt all right, as I lay down in the shelter of a bush by the Thames and tried to doze off, only emerging when I felt confident the last train to Guildford which could connect with the final service to Christ's Hospital had gone. As so often, Housey uniform made it impossible to remain unnoticed and two helpful men from Newbury, recognising mine as I hung about the station trying to pluck up courage to go home, took charge of me and insisted on buying me a pork pie, for which I fear I had little appetite. I cannot say my parents received me with enthusiasm. My father was, I remember, more concerned to let the school know that I was all right than about my reasons for, in effect, running away. I was allowed to stay for the weekend but on Monday morning firmly despatched back to Horsham.

Once again Noel proved surprisingly understanding, though I now feel that he might justly have concluded from this second attempt to escape that the school would be better off without me. He confined himself to writing in my end of term report: 'I hope that there will be no fuss at the start of next term.' This I was by no means prepared to promise, but for the moment I was spared the full rigours of Housey life as within an hour of my return I vomited spectacularly in hall, more from emotion than in response to the particularly repellent rice pudding served to us. My performance aroused admiration among the boys around me; often we had asserted that this dish made us feel sick, now I had suited the action to the words.

This was the first of two brief spells I was to spend in 'the sicker' as an in-patient and it brought me my first contact with a man destined to become a school legend. Whether Dr GE (Gerald) Friend was a good doctor I am hardly qualified to judge, though his successor is said not to have had a high opinion of his predecessor's medical ability. It was certainly a demanding job, for the school doctor was required to display simultaneously the skills of a Medical Officer of Health in charge of a community of more than a thousand bodies, a paediatrician, a general practitioner, and a hospital superintendent where he was both physician and, for minor conditions, surgeon. It is fair to observe that throughout his long period of office, from 1913 to 1946, the school remained relatively healthy and suffered very few deaths, while he seems to be remembered with universal affection.[1] This was certainly not due to any un-Housey like softness. Dr Friend's approach to every problem, whether a broken limb or constipated bowels, was robust and it was perhaps this no-nonsense attitude which had impressed the governors who had appointed him, as well as his institutional background. He liked to say he had been 'born in prison': his father had been padre at Reading jail. Having taken his first degree at Oxford Dr Friend had acquired an MRCS and LRCP in London and worked at the Victoria Hospital for Children before becoming Medical Superintendent of the famous St George's Hospital in Knightsbridge. He was then offered a post as pathologist by the later legendary (Sir) Bernard Spilsbury, but, wishing to bring up his children in the country, opted instead to devote himself to the living schoolboy.[2] He was to spend his whole subsequent career as Medical Officer of Christ's Hospital, a post which clearly suited him and brought with it the finest house on the estate, Stammerham, overlooking the Doctor's Lake, the waters of which were said to have been used in iron-smelting in the days when this was an important Sussex industry.*

The new doctor rapidly made his mark on many areas of daily life. It was thanks to him, though 'thanks' was the very last emotion I felt when experiencing the results twenty years later, that, around 1917, daily Physical Training was introduced to supplement team games, PT being designed to exercise the whole body and to ensure that every boy was constantly involved, with no idling at the back of the scrum or in the Deep Field. He was also said to have been responsible for improving the quality of the food, though not alas, its

---

- For an informed account of Dr Friend's work see Hull Chapter 4. He sums up: 'Looking back, medicine at Housie was somewhat reminiscent of Dotheboy's Hall. Bowel function was everything. . . "Sicker" had a bleak air, redolent of phenol.'

quantity; after a horrified look at the boys' teeth, he insisted on a change to wholemeal flour for both bread and biscuits. We were still grumbling about the results in my time, the products of the favoured local supplier, Prewett's, being both greyer and more solid than those we enjoyed at home, but the second world war was, as I mention later, to endorse his judgement.[3]

Although I only learned this many years later Dr Friend rapidly established himself as the leading authority on the relationship between diet and growth in adolescent and preadolescent boys. The collection of statistics about the physical development of every boy in the school had begun as long ago as 1874 and become a regular ritual accepted, according to the historian of that period, 'with perplexed humour. "The whole school are being individually weighed and measured"', it was recorded '"The breadth across the chest is taken with some other details. Opinion is vexed as to the objects of this novel enquiry...Some say that each is to be fed according to his size."'[4]

The practice continued after the move to Horsham, though the second Headmaster there, in office from 1919 to 1930, was not impressed. All the Medical Officer's lovingly constructed curves seemed to demonstrate, he commented, was 'that a boy's weight increases as he gets heavier'. Dr Friend's reputation was confirmed by the publication in 1935 of his classic work, *The Schoolboy...His Nutrition, Physical Development and Health,* but he ultimately became sceptical about the value of his own research. When asked what it had taught him he told a future Clerk, GAT Allan, 'I learned that boys grow, some faster than others.' Allan's testimony, however, is distinctly flawed, for though an Old Blue himself, he had the effrontery in his *History* of the school two years later to claim that 'All the food is of the best quality', which must rank as one of the great untruths of the century. Among my contemporaries, at school when this statement was published, criticism of our diet is universal. 'Not enough food and we were always cold' was the brisk summing-up of one of them, now himself a headmaster, whom I asked on Founder's Day 1997 for his dominant memory of our schooldays.

Some realisation of our attitude must, I think, have reached the school authorities but they had a persuasive answer in the figures resulting from 'Weighing and Measuring', which demonstrated that, however ill-fed we were, we all grew remorselessly taller and heavier. It was our cynical contention that the whole process was designed to satisfy outsiders, against all the evidence, that the school was not stunting our growth by starving us. It has since been stated by one Old Blue that Dr Friend had 'inadvertently omitted a nought from the number of calories he calculated were necessary to keep a boy fit and well' and that the error went unnoticed till the second world war. Then the food did, as I have mentioned elsewhere, improve enormously, and it has been claimed since that Dr Friend was 'responsible for CH getting a small additional ration in lieu of potential restaurant meals not taken'.*

Perhaps the best tribute was that of 'Gaffer' Seed of the Farm who remarked to one grumbler: 'I see you arrive here as weedy little boys and you leave as fine strapping lads.' I am not sure I could have justly been described as a 'fine strapping lad' when I left, but I was certainly wretchedly undersized though perfectly healthy, when I arrived at Horsham. I have a distinct recollection that when I first climbed on to the Infirmary scales at the start of my first term I weighed a mere 52 lbs [23.6*kg*] which seems extraordinarily small, but may be correct for my party piece as a new boy was to double myself up inside a dormitory settle and close the lid.** I have one now in my hall as a reminder of less happy times and have noted the dimensions, 2 ft 1 in [63.5cm], by 1 ft 5 in [43cm] high by 11½ in [29.2cm] wide, so I must indeed have been an exceptionally small ten year old. By the time I left I had reached normal height, around 5 ft 7 in [1.7m], close to medium height for a grown man and enough to make stupid plays on my surname inappropriate. (Jokes about names, so popular with some journalists, have always seemed to me particularly puerile, though common in that puerile society, school. Who chooses his name? And who, given the choice, would opt for the undistinguished near anonymity of Smith or Jones?)

I came to detest the whole Weighing and Measuring procedure, which added an extra discomfort to the already miserable start of each term and cast a shadow over the joyous week when it ended. On each occasion we were marched to the Infirmary and required to strip to the waist, providing an absurd sight as we lined up in our knee breeches, held up by one hand, to have our weight and height recorded by the versatile and ubiquitous Sergeant Usher. It was not merely natural modesty which made the experience so distasteful to me, but my meagre dimensions. Even when I stretched to my full height this seemed miserably little, while my weight was, at least in my first year, well below that of any other boys in the house.

What was far worse than the routine twice termly weighing and measuring, however, was the requirement added at the end of the summer term – yet another reason for detesting it – to record one's chest expansion. I have wretched memories of hearing Sergeant Usher announce my miserable chest size, invariably below that of my contemporaries, and on one never to be forgotten occasion after I had taken a deep breath it was said to be less than

---

* I have not investigated this point but it was government policy to assume that family rations would be supplemented by meals out in restaurants or works canteens, for which no coupons were required. See *How We Lived Then* p.151.

** This was not such an exceptional feat as it sounds. A future Headmaster, JT (John) Hansford, in Coleridge B from 1931-40, was photographed doing the same at the age of nine and, on his retirement in 1986 was presented with a settle with a suitable inscription. I had to buy mine, uninscribed.

before, a result received by the expectant audience with understandable but humiliating laughter.

Shortly after Dr Friend's arrival a printed card headed *Rules for Health* appeared in every dormitory and it was still much in evidence throughout my schooldays. Having to learn the Rules by heart was common punishment and in one house, a little before my time, a dormitory prank, the placing of holly leaves in the house-captain's bed, led to the whole dormitory being ordered to produce a fair copy of the *Health Rules*, versions being submitted in a variety of forms and languages, including copperplate and Gothic script, German and Welsh. Attention thus focused on them, 'It was realised the *Health Rules* could be set to music...and chanted to the impressive dirge of the *Nunc Dimittis*'. With the pointing of the Psalter as a guide boys could thereafter be heard singing:

> Nature helps to induce sleep by a general slowing of the circulation.
> To get warm in Winter, Do not pile on extra covering
> But lie upon the right side with the legs fully extended,
> Bending the knees impedes the circulation
> And thus makes the feet feel cold. [5]

Such exhortation, of course, came cheaper than providing more comfortable beds or an adequate number of blankets, and a similar attitude was evident in relation to another of Dr Friend's recommendations, the necessity of regularity in bodily functions. Here, however, one may detect a recognition of the reality, for the number of lavatories was, as I have mentioned, absurdly inadequate for everyone to use them at the obvious time, after breakfast and before Chapel. Here, however, the *Health Rules* were reassuring:

> The exact time of day you go to the lavatory does not matter, but some boys need two bowel actions a day to keep them in health.

One practice introduced by Dr Friend was to survive long after his death and was, so far as I know, unique to Christ's Hospital. I have mentioned earlier the part it played in the influenza epidemic of 1918, though Dr Friend's own account was somewhat different. 'I had,' he wrote in *The Schoolboy,* 'found from direct observation that the condition of noses and throats of a considerable proportion especially among the younger boys was decidedly unsatisfactory.' Accordingly 'nasal drill was introduced'. Like so much that Dr Friend did the daily practice of compulsory nose-blowing was entirely in tune with the whole ethos of the school, indeed there might have been sound reasons for it back in the sixteenth century when most of the boys admitted would never have seen a handkerchief. By the 1930s it served a different purpose, enabling the school to begin the day with a disciplined routine which would continue unrelenting until the final cry of 'Lights out!' 13-and-a-half hours later.

Significantly, since it confirms how rigidly we were kept apart from our contemporaries in other houses, many boys were, as indeed I was, unaware that the practice was universal throughout the school. One exact contemporary of mine confessed in *The Blue* in 1996 that he had assumed 'this custom was the special invention of Peele B', while we were blowing away equally vigorously in Peele A, a mere corridor length away.

In fact in every house the day began in the same way, with shivering boys standing by their beds, right arm extended by the side, clutching a handkerchief, which was then, with military precision, raised to one's nose and equally smartly lowered. (I cannot recall any left-handers, but suspect such an aberration would not have been permitted.) The precise procedure – Who should say the houses lacked independence? – varied. In Peele A we were, I seem to remember, given a degree of independence, being simply ordered 'Blow!' and then left to do so until told to stop, with, of course, punishment for an inadequate response. In Barnes A the process began with the imposing order 'Nose-blowing commence!', and continued until the command 'Cease nose-blowing!' [6] In the Prep the procedure was formalised, like some army drill, into a series of movements, following the sequence of orders:

Handkerchiefs out!
Blowing by numbers. By numbers, One!
By numbers, Two!

and so on until the final

By numbers, Six!
Handkerchiefs away!

Dr Friend recorded a drop of 30% in the incidence of common colds following the introduction of his nasal drill, though I can testify that they still remained frequent.[7] Nose-blowing has for many Old Blues come to symbolise the over-disciplined Christ's Hospital of their time, though the practice lingered on, at least in the Prep, until the 1960s.[8] The Peele B survivor quoted earlier described how he was still able at dinner parties 'to amuse those sitting next to' him 'with stories of the rigorous discipline at CH in the 1930s. The *piece de resistance* is always "nose-blowing by numbers"...The trouble is no one believes my story, not even my grandchildren.'[9]

Like many Old Blues I have, despite his eccentricities, retained a great affection for Dr Friend and it must be said that, to his credit, he was always ready to try out new or unfashionable remedies. He had no time for patent medicines of any kind but one boy who arrived in Middleton A in 1923, has recalled with incredulity being prescribed Burgundy in the infirmary, at a time when most of us had never seen, much less tasted, a glass of wine.[10] Another boy found himself in the 1920s one of a number of 'guinea pigs' during a whooping cough epidemic, set to record the number of 'whoops' emitted by the group each day as the doctor tried out some new form of treatment, and to plot the resulting information on a graph.[11] But in divine assistance, in spite of the school's religious tradition, Dr Friend had little faith. He was famous for his reply, when the chaplain, 'worried about a seriously ill boy due for surgery, asked… whether we might say prayers for him in Chapel… "Well, I shouldn't think it will do any harm"'.[12] The prayers were duly said and the boy recovered.

With so much time spent on the rugger field fractures were all too common and here, too, our doctor favoured a firm approach. A whole ward, as in a full size hospital, was set aside for surgical cases in the Infirmary and one Old Blue remembers what happened to a boy in a neighbouring bed with a broken elbow during the doctor's regular round. 'He was saying to the patient "I don't think I like the way this bone has been set", when there was a sharp crack. The patient yelled. The Doc said calmly: "It would have been worse for you if I'd told you I was going to break it again".' [13]

Cold sores, a common affliction at under-heated Housie, were dealt with by equally forthright methods. The doctor, remembers a contemporary in another house, Coleridge A, would 'lever up one corner with tweezers and then deftly…rip off the whole sore, followed by an application of gentian violet to the bleeding hole.' [14] A similar technique was used to combat other complaints. 'Friend dealt with both my boils,' another Old Blue recalls, 'by winkling them out with a scalpel, in the way that one digs our "eyes" when peeling a potato.'[15] One eleven year old who developed a witlow on the top of his left thumb during his first term was horrified to hear the doctor's decision: '"Sister, we'll cut the top of the thumb off. You'd better hold his hand in case it hurts, clean it up and it should be okay." Funnily enough,' recalls the patient 'it didn't hurt,' but he had learned his lesson. 'In no circumstances, I resolved, was I going to go back for more treatment by Dr Friend.' [16]

This resolution proved impossible to carry out, and, after a fall at gym which had left him with a suspected fracture of the arm, he was sent to the Infirmary. 'Dr Friend grasped my wrist with one hand,' he remembers, '[the] elbow with the other hand and waggled the arm about listening intently. Comment: "Can't hear any grating, so it can't be broken. Probably a bad sprain…You can have a sling if you like. Don't fight anyone and it should be all right in a couple of days."'

Excessive stoicism in the face of such tough treatment was ill-advised. *The Blue* recorded on Dr Friend's departure, shortly before Miss Flack's – the end of an era for the 'sicker' – how one small boy, given a fierce prod, and asked, 'Does that hurt?' bravely gritted his teeth and replied 'No, doctor'. The doctor's response was unappreciative: 'Well, it ought to.'

24: 'The Garden' at Newgate Street

25: Newgate Street entrance, with top-hatted beadles. The statue of Edward VI is now at Horsham

26: Dinner Parade at Newgate Street

27: A 'Ward' at Newgate Street, combining sleeping quarters and living area. The dormitories at Horsham were equally bleak, but there was now a separate dayroom

28: 'Hall Play' at Newgate Street, the main recreational area

29: Transplanted. Big School and classroom blocks at Horsham

30: The Quadrangle at Horsham showing the Dining Hall and, on the left, the Chapel

31: Interior of the Chapel, showing Brangwyn paintings.
Normally masters occupied the back row of the pews

32: Dining Hall interior, 1935. The Verrio painting is on the left, the pulpit on the right. The boys standing up are doing 'trades'

A boy suffering from styes, which had to be lanced nearly every week for a year, was alarmed to be told by Dr Friend of a new treatment recommended in the *Lancet* which involved plucking the patient's eyelashes to cause the stye to break. 'After pulling out five of my lashes the doctor gave a squeal of delight. "It does work!" he exclaimed.' The longer term remedy he suggested was to 'stop using the school swimming baths. "That water's no good for anyone."' This boy, exceptionally, managed to follow this advice but even Dr Friend was unable to achieve a general ban on 'House baths' and 'non-swimmers'.

The Friend treatment for persistent colds which blocked up the nose was simple, and successful.. 'Stuff a tube up one nostril,' he advised, 'pour saline solution into it...and let it run down the other nostril.' [17] The future Professor Hull has described 'having', in the 1940s, 'to undergo this horrible regime':

> A large Winchester [bottle] was stored on a high shelf from which a fine rubber tube conveyed the douche solution into the patient's nostril. Boys were obliged to run this fluid with much choking, spluttering and eye-watering into each nostril in turn while trying not to inhale and drown. The experience, performed in public view in the treatment room, was almost as humiliating and generally horrible as gym.[18]

Like many people who had been innovators when young, Dr Friend was by this time addicted to medicines, like the notorious Black Draught, which were going out of use elsewhere. The same witness describes as 'lethal stuff' the solution of carbolic in glycerine, a 'foul tasting medication that made him gag', with which his throat was once painted. (Later, when himself a school medical officer, the victim used a milder substitute.)[19] Dr Friend's preference was always for the heroic remedy, favoured chemicals used in douching being the strong smelling eucalyptus and the purple coloured Potassium Permanganate, a favourite of mine in my brief period of interest in chemistry because of its striking colour. Dr Friend did not despise such traditional aids to diagnosis as requiring one to 'Say ninety-nine!' but at Housie this served a secondary purpose. When a boy uttered these words as the doctor listened to his chest it was said that he would detect the tell-tale signs of illicit smoking.[20] The remedy in such cases was likely to be of a kind not available to the medical profession outside, a private report to the patient's housemaster, but for other complaints treatment might instantly follow diagnosis. One boy waiting in the usual queue in the surgery witnessed what happened when 'the boy in front complained of a bad pain in the stomach. Like a flash Dr Friend punched him in the stomach, the boy broke wind... and went away cured.'[21]

To gain admission to the Infirmary, whether as out-patient or in-patient, one had to visit the matron's office, the first line of defence against malingerers. The matron in my time bore the Dickensian name, although I learned her Christian name only much later, of Adeline Flack, which suited her admirably.

When, the victim of ill-health herself, she finally retired, in 1946, the tribute in *The Blue* was even further from the truth than most such eulogies.* 'Miss Flack,' claimed the author of this ill-deserved valediction, 'interpreted her duties with breadth of mind, teaching courtesy and unselfishness and loyalty and all the graces... "No boy," wrote one housemaster of long experience, "ever came back from a stay at the Infirmary without being a better member of his house and of his school."' [22] My own impression was that, like a number of the masters, she simply did not like boys, or indeed the male sex, though a friend's mother, visiting him as a patient, found herself given a welcome that was not merely warm but embarrassingly affectionate. I felt on the few occasions I met her that she regarded herself as part of the school's disciplinary system and management – the Infirmary certainly ran like clockwork – rather than as the provider of care and comfort to small boys. If, as I suspect, she regarded it as her duty to make the Infirmary as unwelcoming as possible it was one she performed effectively.

Miss Flack was disliked by her staff as well as her patients, as a former Hertford girl who worked in the Infirmary at Horsham as a nurse from 1941-2 has confirmed. 'Miss Flack rude at dinner,' she noted in her diary. 'Row brewing, most unhappy.' Her subordinates, it was observed later, 'took turns to be out of matron's favour' and it was perhaps fortunate for them they could not suffer her favourite punishment, the order, '"No jam for tea!" as she caught some unfortunate misbehaving in his ward'.[23]

Once past the matron's office one joined a long queue in the surgery, with no nonsense about a private consultation. The examination by the doctor, and often the resulting treatment, took place in earshot and full view of those still awaiting attention, as part of the overall process of discouraging unnecessary resort to the Infirmary. Once I was kept waiting so long I was overcome by the ether hanging in the air and began to collapse, until the boy behind me – I can still remember these precise words – caught the attending nurse's ear with the striking announcement: 'This person seems about to faint.'

The school was, understandably in view of the harshness of our daily lives, concerned that no one should get a 'pass' excusing him from games, or, even worse, gain admission to the far softer life of an inmate of the Infirmary, without being truly ill. Those who had hoped, back in 1913, that the new Medical Officer might be easy to deceive were soon disappointed. He noticed, his son remembers, how 'soon after his arrival...there appeared to be an outbreak of German Measles in one of the houses. The odd thing was that the rash disappeared overnight.' He soon diagnosed the cause, 'beating the chest with a hairbrush', and prescribed the cure. 'A dose of castor oil and an immediate return to school with a note to the housemaster.' [24]

---

* She in fact survived till 1977 and the age of 81.

This was a foretaste of the policy the new doctor was to follow throughout his long career at the school and purgatives of all kinds, the harsher the better, played a large part in our lives. The clue to good health, in the school's view, was clearly not a good diet or rational clothes, but the regular functioning of the bowels. Each week on Sunday evening we were required to swallow under matron's supervision a large spoonful of what was officially labelled 'Sulphur and Treacle' though we knew it as 'Brimstone and Treacle', and very unpleasant it was. The scene as boys lined up awaiting their turn to have a large spoonful of this viscous dark brown mixture thrust into their mouths by a stern-faced matron, clutching under her arm a large earthenware jar, was irresistibly reminiscent of an illustration from *Oliver Twist* or *Nicholas Nickleby*, while it would have required an illustrator of the genius of his Phiz (HK Browne) to have done justice to the variety of grotesque facial expressions displayed by the pyjama-clad victims as they swallowed this obnoxious medicine. One Old Blue remembers how 'the sulphur used to settle as a congealed mass at the bottom of the large stoneware containers. By the time the juniors were served all the treacle had disappeared and heaped dessert spoons of almost neat sulphur were forced down the throats of the victims.'

Sulphur and Treacle remained, another of Dr Friend's sons has acknowledged, 'one of his pet forms of treatment' and, with it going out of fashion elsewhere, he was anxious to secure his source of supply. This he managed to do, applying to the famous pharmaceutical firm of Maclean to ask if they would make it for him. 'This we did,' his son, then a manager at Macleans, recalls, supplying '2 cwt [102kg] at a time, packed in 7 lb [3.2kg] stone jars, which Goodall [presumably an Estate employee] used to trundle to the houses in his handcart.' [25]

Obtaining adequate quantities of another medicine, with similar properties, presented fewer problems since, as one Old Blue discovered in 1995, amazingly it is still in modern dictionaries, but not on sale in Boots. This was Gregory or more correctly, Gregory's Powder, named, the same victim of it, at school from 1927 to 1936, discovered, after Dr James Gregory its inventor, who 'became Professor of Medicine at Edinburgh in 1776 and eventually the top medical authority in Scotland'. The whole experience clearly left its mark upon this unappreciative patient:

> If a boy was off colour matron would mix a pinkish powder with water and say: 'There you are. Drink that down!' It was the most unpalatable medicine imaginable and could only be likened to brick-dust and water. [26]

About this being the nastiest medicine known this informant was, however, wrong, for the school had two other weapons left in its armoury in the perpetual battle against malingering, and one at least surely deserved the 'most unpalatable' accolade. The milder of the two by a long way was a medicine still familiar, at least by name, today, castor-oil.[27] This remained Dr Friend's medicine of first choice for almost every ailment and it was a heavy blow for him when, late in the war, it began, like everything else, to become scarce. One boy who remarked to the doctor during a private conversation while helping with 'weighing and measuring', that he seemed to prescribe this less than formerly was told the reason, 'Trouble is,' explained Dr Friend, 'that when they made the film *In Which We Serve*', released in 1942, 'they used castor oil mixed with soot in all those scenes where the men were in the water after being sunk. Must have wasted enough castor oil to have lasted me for years.' *

What, however stands out in the memory of all Old Blues of my generation and seems to me to detract for ever from the doctor's reputation for humanity and enlightenment, was his use, on in-patients only, of a mixture which I thought then, as I do still sixty years later, to be uniquely horrible, justifiable only in *extremis*, with death the likely alternative. I can well recall seeing tough rugger players in their late teens cringing away from the nurse holding out the glass containing the hated medicine or even bursting into unmanly tears. That I did neither, but accepted my first dose of the remedy as the price of staying in the Infirmary, makes me realise even now how much I must have detested the daily life of the house from which I had briefly escaped.

One of my contemporaries, at CH from 1935 to 1940, has equally vivid recollections of a similar ordeal:

[I remember] the practice of dosing every boy on admission to the Infirmary irrespective of his ailment, with some filthy dark liquid known universally as 'Black Draught'. Thereafter the same medicine was administered on every third day throughout the patient's stay…Everyone in my day accepted that its purpose was to discourage malingerers…You knew if you were ill enough to get to bed in the sicker you would get Black Draught…I once dragged myself to the Infirmary with all the symptoms of some gastric infection. Within an hour of getting into bed, pulse and temperature taken, nurse appeared with the usual remedy. I swallowed it, but my churning stomach simply couldn't cope and ten minutes later rejected the lot.

Feeling rather pleased at the apparent escape from the dreadful effects the stuff used to have on the system, I was horrified to be presented with a similar quantity of castor-oil.

The second exception [to the Black Draught every three days rule] was a boy I came across who was a semi-permanent resident of the sicker…His arm was always in a sling and he had some infection of the bone necessitating surgery. In view of his special circumstances, he told me, he had to take Black Draught only once a week. [28]

---

* As another of Dr Friend's sons, Philip, a well-known actor, had been in the film the explanation is almost certainly correct.

What was Black Draught? I still remember an intensely bitter, thick, dark brown, somewhat oily liquid, closely resembling in appearance the motions it was designed to promote, and, like the reluctant imbiber of Gregory Powder, was sufficiently impressed by it to make further enquiries later. The name I had supposed to be a nickname, but learned from the helpful Royal Pharmaceutical Society that it was in fact 'an officially recognised synonym for *mistura sennae composita'*, of which the largest ingredient was an 'Infusion of senna', to which were added 'liquid extract of liquorice', 'aromatic spirit of ammonia', magnesium sulphate and cardamom. This fearsome concoction made its first appearance in the *British Pharmacopoeia* in 1867 'and so,' in the words of the Society's curator, 'is very likely to have been in the repertoire of Army doctors in the Crimea a few years before'.[29] By the second edition of the *Pharmacopoeia*, in 1885, the use of Black Draught had been endorsed by the General Council of Medical Education and it had, it seems likely, become part of the Medical Officer's stores at Newgate Street, though it is possible that Dr Friend, with his passion for laxatives, revived its use.

Little pretence was made that this horrible medicine was required on purely medical grounds. 'When lead swingers appeared at the Infirmary on end-of-term examination day,' remembers one Old Blue who left in 1944, 'he would give them a choice; a dose of the dreaded "Black Draught" and a day in the sicker or milk and biscuits and back to face the music.'[30]

In spite of Dr Friend's remedies, life in the Infirmary was infinitely pleasanter than that outside, thanks largely to the nurses, who were the very reverse of the matron who supervised them. Nursing has traditionally attracted the prettiest and most sweet-natured young women and though those in the CH Infirmary were no doubt cautioned by Miss Flack against being over indulgent their natural feminine kindness would constantly break through. I well remember the kindly efforts of two nurses to persuade me, an unhappy eleven year old, soon after I had entered the Infirmary and was allowed to eat again, to tuck into a plate of roast lamb and roast potatoes, the sort of delicacies we never saw in the Dining Hall. Unfortunately both had been soaked in mint sauce and, like the rest of my family, I had always hated vinegar. Overwhelmed by this unaccustomed kindness, I was too embarrassed to explain the reason for my reluctance to eat, and insisted, what was manifestly untrue, that I was not hungry. A most frustrating battle between patient but determined nurses and tearful schoolboy followed, which left them convinced that I was trying to starve myself to death. This was untrue, though I might have done so had I thought of it. As it was, Dr Friend, after accurately diagnosing my no doubt common complaint, that I hated Housie, sent me back to Peele A. He spoke to me in such a sympathetic way that I dissolved in tears, whereupon, a kindly man, he promised to tell my housemaster that I seemed to be more than normally unhappy – though this can hardly have been news to Noel.

All that happened was that I was invited to tea by matron one Sunday. She was, I am sure, well meaning, but less motherly, though much older, than the Infirmary nurses and I found it impossible to explain to her the real depth of my misery. Unhappily, too, she served fish paste sandwiches, as unwelcome to me as vinegar, so I left no happier than I had arrived.

Disappointingly, my time in the Infirmary did not include a sighting of the spectre said to haunt it. 'On every Thursday evening,' wrote a later visitor in a profile of the institution in *The Blue*, 'the tormented ghost of Lamb wanders pitifully through the drab and eerie corridors...wailing heart rending cries of anguish.' [31] Charles Lamb did indeed suffer a painful accident at Newgate Street requiring his removal to the sick room but it was not fatal and how he had managed to move to Horsham, and why he restricted his appearances to Thursday, were not explained. However the author of the report just quoted testified that 'there are often very odd noises in the Infirmary's corridors at night time. Often a footstep noise sounds outside the duty room, making the nurses' hair stand on end.'

We also visited the Infirmary to see the school dentist, occasions I almost enjoyed since they meant an afternoon away from games, They were, however, all too rare since the school considered that dental care was something parents ought to pay for, and the school dentist was expected merely to conduct regular inspections of our teeth; the school, here ahead of its time, had been providing these since 1880.[32] He also dealt with emergencies but most of his work consisted of reminding us of the need to care for our teeth, underlining the exhortation in Dr Friend's *Health Rules*. 'Softy spongy gums,' we were warned, 'mean ill-health sooner or later'. Regular sessions with a toothbrush, night and morning, were, we were told, essential, and to omit to brush your teeth was, in the junior dormitory at least, a beatable offence. To these common sense instructions the school dentist added his own catchphrase, in the best Housey tradition: 'Brush your gums until they bleed.'

Only long after I had left did I discover the dentist's name, TC (Tom) Stretton, and that he was of some standing in his profession, being an instructor at the Royal Dental Hospital.[33] His particular specialism was extractions, so that he must have found his school visits rather frustrating for when needed these must mostly have been done in the holidays.

He must also, I now realise, have found conditions at CH very different from those he was used to in his academic work and private practice for the room allocated to him – it hardly merited the name of surgery – was poorly equipped, even by the standards of the time. I well remember the inadequate lighting and the already out-of-date drill which roughly resembled the upright portion of a spinning wheel, and was operated, like a sewing machine, by a treadle. This the dentist pressed with one foot to provide motive power for the drill, balancing on the other foot as he struggled, painfully slowly, to excavate a sufficient hole for an emergency filling. I sometimes wondered if I could have imagined the existence of this old-fashioned appliance but have seen one since in a junk shop window. It had, I imagine, been brought from London and dated back to the days before electricity. Tom Stretton was described in his obituary as 'a kind-hearted dentist', who 'in his quaint way...bullied the boy who neglected his teeth'.[34] I would endorse this tribute, for I had a good deal to do with him, though I received most of my treatment in Newbury.

Compared to Housie, visiting the dentist at home was almost a luxury, and I was sent to a practice with a modern surgery, overlooking, as it happened, the pleasantest part of Newbury, the Water Bridge. A session involving more than a single filling took in those days what seemed hours and anaesthetics, usually by slow-acting injection, were only provided for extractions. (Happily I never needed one at school.) I doubt if anyone who did not live through that era of what now seems prehistoric dentistry can imagine the foreboding, pain and subsequent discomfort which every visit to the dentist then involved, or the extraordinary sense of relief one felt on reaching the end of a course of treatment. Once a series of appointments which had stretched right through my four weeks of holidays finally ended along with them, and I recall feeling cheated that I could not for once gloat over the fact that I need not come to the dentist again.

Part of the treatment I required involved the fitting of a dental plate with a wire hook to frustrate the efforts of one wayward tooth to grow at the wrong angle. In the rough and tumble of Housey life, or as a result of deliberate bullying, my plate was often damaged and, when repaired, I had to go to the school dentist to have it refitted. He would greet me as 'the champion plate-breaker', a kindly remark which I welcomed. I have often thought since that dentists have not been given by society the status they deserve, having found them, with rare exceptions like one long vanished Newbury practice nicknamed 'the butchers', to be kindly, dedicated and innovative professionals, genuinely concerned for their patients.

[1] Nov/Dec 1946 p.2
[2] Dec 1987 p.187
[3] Dec 1992 p.224 but says Friend arrived in 1912
[4] Seaman p.136
[5] Mar 1987 p.49
[6] Dec 1987 p.187, Jul 1987 p.121, Cartoon May 1970 p.115
[7] Dec 1986 p.259
[8] Jul 1987 p.121
[9] Lent Term 1996 p.163
[10] Dec 1986 p.259
[11] Jul 1986 p.196
[12] Jun 1992 p.143
[13] Jul 1987 p.126
[14] Dec 1987 p.188
[15] Jul 1987 p.126
[16] Jul 1987 p.126
[17] Jul 1987 p.126
[18] Hull p.74
[19] Hull p.74
[20] Dec 1987 p.188
[21] Jul 1987 p.126
[22] Mar/Apr 1947 p.59
[23] Dec 1997 p.255
[24] Dec 1987 p.187
[25] Dec 1987 p.187
[26] Dec 1995 p.228
[27] Jul 1987 p.126
[28] Dec 1987 pp.187-8
[29] Letter from the Curator to the author
[30] Dec 1987 p.188
[31] Jan 1969 p.60
[32] Jan 1969 p.66
[33] Sep 1966 p.203
[34] Sep 1966 p.203

27

NOT READY FOR WAR

We were not ready for war and Czechoslovakia was not worth a European catastrophe.

Speaker at Christ's Hospital Debating Society reported in The Blue, *November 1938*

My second year at school from September 1937 to July 1938 was for me basically uneventful. For the nation it was very different. The first school debate that term, which I was too junior to attend, was on the motion that 'Britain's rearmament was justified.' Perhaps reflecting opinion in the country, the result was a tie, until, 'the president gave his casting vote against'.[1] Others showed more prescience. That November saw a visit from 'Mr BN Wallis (Peele A, 1900-04)', who 'lectured to the 1930 Society,' ie all the more senior boys in the school, 'on the subject of flight', making special reference to 'his first two aeroplanes the Wellesley and the Wellington,' which, he claimed, uninhibited by false modesty, were 'far above all others, not only in the matter of beauty but also of performance'. The following June, *The Blue* for July 1938 recorded, 'some of the senior engineering boys from CH were privileged to view the works of Messrs. Vickers (Aviation) at Weybridge, and see these aeroplanes being made'. No doubt later some members of Wallis's former audience were destined to fly, and perhaps die, in them, for the deteriorating situation in Europe was becoming impossible to ignore. In March 1938 Austria had been forcibly incorporated in the Reich. The following month Housie took its own steps towards rearmament: the Officers Training Corps acquired its first wireless sets. For those of us who did not yet belong to the Corps another item of news was of more interest: that the railway line from Horsham to Portsmouth was being electrified.

Life in Peele A changed little that year. Lawrance, house-captain in my first year, was succeeded by a boy of similar temperament, who, most exceptionally, was also senior grecian. In its *Cricket Notes* for November 1938 *The Blue* wrote of the now departed Hatten: 'Sheer pluck made him a most useful batsman in a crisis and a brave fielder in the suicide position.' Surely no Housey boy could have asked for a finer testimonial.

My first surviving school exercise book dates from January 1938 and confirms that this was for me a distinctly inglorious time. 'Very careless indeed' is the comment against the earliest history essay I have kept, on 'Norman architecture' and my last that term, on 'Peter the Hermit', which ended robustly 'so the cross triumphed in the end', was deflatingly endorsed: 'I don't think so'. My work thereafter seems to have gone from bad to worse, with a piece on the history of Scotland marked with the grim word 'Detention', which meant I had to join other boys guilty of poor work in a special class one afternoon. I cannot pretend this distressed me too much, since it meant leaving games early, as did a 'Bring Up', when a whole form was similarly treated, though the master also suffered since he had to supervise it.

Both were harsher punishments for boys who enjoyed games, as one Coleridge A contemporary described:

> Those unending hours of one's precious free time on a sunny Saturday afternoon, the silence unbroken save perhaps by the buzzing of an insect, were made even more interminable if the master awarding the detention had set no work to be done. The invigilating master's reaction...varied; some would set a piece of work – to write an essay on 'A day in the Holidays' was quite common – but others would instruct the unfortunate to spend the time pondering on his misdeeds.[2]

That I should have merited such punishment in what was, along with English, supposed to be my best subject is not, I think, a proof of idleness, though the history of Scotland was not a topic of much interest to me then or later, but an indication of how miserable I must have been. Part of my unhappiness was due to the one totally incompetent teacher I encountered at Housie, C Blamire Brown. 'Blam' as he was universally known, had arrived in 1912, a young man with curling brown hair, lean athletic build and quick movement but by the time I knew him, perhaps soured by ill health, he had changed dramatically. *The Blue* admitted in its obituary that he had 'aged early, and 'was not at his best perhaps in class,' a damning verdict on any schoolmaster.[3] As an older boy I found him civil, if uninspiring, but for younger pupils he was disastrous, displaying no aptitude whatever for his chosen profession except the ability to keep a class totally silent in terror of him. The hours I spent under his tuition, as an eleven and twelve year old, and again at 14 to 15, were the only ones of my school career to be totally wasted and, worse, gave me and other boys a dislike of Latin which, properly taught, could be an enjoyable subject. There must be many Old Blues who feel, as I do, a reminiscent shudder at the memory of the hours wasted in that stuffy little classroom in the corner of the classics block, while that plump, ponderous, unsmiling figure squatted on his rostrum, scowling at us.

Blam's customary practice was to pretend to take offence at some elementary mistake early on in a lesson and then to sit in sulky silence glowering at the class, which was too terrified to move until the end of lesson bell released it. Occasionally he would rouse himself to make some such remark as 'What you small boys require is a good beating!' after which he would relapse into his usual near comatose state. This was, however, to be preferred to the rare occasions when some faint realisation of why he was supposed to be there would trouble his conscience. I can recall a painful dialogue between himself and a boy who made a mistake in converting a Latin preposition into an adverb:

'How would you blunt a knife?'
'Leave it out in the rain, sir.'
'How would you blunt a chisel?'
'Do the same, sir'.
'How would you convert *post* into an adverb?'
'Add *ea* to it, sir.'
'Then how would you convert *ante* into an adverb?'

I am not, in retrospect, impressed by this example of Blam's teaching technique, if only because there are so many exceptions to every rule in Latin. Later in my school career, having been drilled in grammar by another fearsome, but this time competent, teacher, Macnutt, I began positively to enjoy the language under a real enthusiast for it, AH Buck, and I still feel great satisfaction in puzzling out a Latin inscription or footnote. So much Housie has achieved, but no thanks to C Blamire-Brown.

This, my second year, marked my academic low point at Housie, reflecting both my unhappiness and the lack among my masters that year of anyone who inspired, or even appeared to like, me. My father, meeting my housemaster at mid-term, was told that I was not exerting myself in class, and that term my report was endorsed by Noel Sergent: 'Disappointing. He has not yet learned to work as he should.' It was true, but no one thought to ask the reason.

When, thanks partly to better masters and the recognition on my part that I never was going to escape from Housie, my work began to improve, a new and recurrent source of criticism was my handwriting. 'Longmate,' I remember one master telling the class as an example of what they should avoid, 'writes a bad, small hand.' I have in fact seen many worse since, above all that of my fellow Old Blue Ian Trethowan, whose amendments to the drafts I submitted to him when he was Director-General of the BBC I found totally illegible.

How Trethowan was allowed to leave school writing so badly I have never understood. Housie had traditionally regarded good handwriting as important. Already by the eighteenth century, in addition to the Grammar School, which concentrated on the classics, and the Royal Mathematical School, it possessed a

Writing School, devoted to calligraphy as well as elementary arithmetic and book-keeping. As the *Christ's Hospital Book* explains, the brightest boys were from the first marked out for 'the college fellowship, the country parsonage, the schoolmaster's desk', but these were the exceptions:

> Many other children to whom Christ's Hospital extended her bounty were bred for the commercial world, in which often only a few minutes' walk from the cloisters – they duly obtained employment as clerks…These scholars understood by 'writing' not so much prose and verse as calligraphy to catch the eye, and fill the ledgers, of wealthy merchants.[4]

Although the typewriter had by my time long since transformed City offices, the traditional emphasis on good handwriting remained. One term several masters complained about mine, to such effect that the Education Committee of Newbury Council, to whom my report was initially sent, added a formal note when forwarding it to my parents: 'Your attention is drawn to the references to bad handwriting in the attached report.' What, I have often wondered since, was my father supposed to do in response? Beat me? Arrange private tuition? I now understand better what prompted these small town councillors, the Newbury equivalent of City aldermen, to complain as they did. Poor handwriting was something these shopkeepers and minor business men could understand; the literary talent with which I was also credited by the school was beyond their experience and, if noted at all, probably considered positively undesirable. True to form, when I did later achieve some academic success the Newbury councillors ignored it.

So close was the connection between Newbury and Christ's Hospital that I found myself in the following term required to do private handwriting exercises and to submit them to my junior housemaster, a pleasant young man who was as embarrassed by the whole procedure as I was. He nonetheless conscientiously examined my weekly offering of down-strokes and pot-hooks, copied from a writing primer that was issued to me. The requirement ceased after a single term and, having learned to type at the age of 18 I have never since written by hand a line that I might type – indeed to do so seems to me a form of discourtesy to the reader.

Regrettably I never learned if the Newbury councillors were aware of another school policy, the deliberate attempt to rid boys from the town, and indeed from elsewhere, of their distinctive accents. The school's aim was for us all to speak the then universally accepted 'BBC English' using an 'Oxford Accent'. Here I believe Christ's Hospital was entirely right, for no one could have foreseen a time when a positive premium would be put on speaking badly, or expensively educated people from cultured backgrounds would deliberately affect a proletarian type of speech.

Much of the improvement in our accents came from our being immersed in a linguistic melting pot in which, as in everything else, most people rapidly came to conform to the norm. In my house at least failure to do so was not resented. One boy with a Cockney accent, though he came in fact from Edgware, was cheerfully greeted with cries of 'wotcher!', a word supposedly often on his lips, but he took it in good part.

Thanks to my mother we all spoke in an acceptable accent, but my native town had left its mark upon me and other Newbury boys in the shape of what one master described as 'that horrible Berkshire "o"' and this the school made stern efforts to eradicate, attempting to convert our elongated 'ooh' or 'ewe' vowel sounds into a sharper, full-rounded 'oh'. I can recall sitting with other boys and chanting the sentence 'Thousands and thousands of lousy brown cows, browsing about on the South Downs.' If 'thousands' emerged as 'thewsands' this would be cruelly mimicked by the presiding master and he must have had some success with me for I have an embarrassing recollection of a neighbour remarking to my mother one holiday, 'Ooh, I love to 'ear 'im talk'.

This year, my second at the school, was destined to remain the most miserable I experienced and the end of the summer term, in July 1938, was particularly welcome. I can recall sitting alone (as I usually was) on the grass of Little Side, looking towards the Infirmary on the last Sunday afternoon and writing home: 'I feel like singing gaily.' It was in fact, not only the prospect of impending release that had raised my spirits but the promise for the first, indeed only, time in my childhood, of a seaside holiday. I remember in the last maths lesson of term our master HWC Armistead, an excellent if demanding teacher, asking each boy in turn where he would be going. I was not obliged to join the doleful but truthful minority who confessed they would be staying at home but was able, to answer proudly, 'Ventnor'. It was true, though I did not explain the circumstances. My father, finding no work in Newbury, had taken a job for the summer with a photographer on the Isle of Wight, developing and printing the holiday snapshots brought in by customers or by the firm's own photographer who roamed the beaches and promenade. I was, I knew, to join my father in his boarding house for a whole week.

This, I now realise, though I was to share his room and indeed his bed, must have put some strain on the family finances, for my father was able to send home from his earnings 25s [£1.25] a week, a modest enough sum but, with Freda's and Gordon's contributions from their even more modest wages, sufficient to enable us to keep financially afloat. My twin sister, perhaps with some help from the Girl Guides, which she had recently joined, and a gift of pocket money, something we never normally enjoyed, from my brother, was sent off to Guide camp, while I was despatched to Ventnor, via the ferry across the Solent. It was an extremely hot day and, for some reason, presumably because my father wanted to show me off, I wore Housey clothes, which I discarded as soon as I arrived and only put on again to go home. My father had a room in a typical boarding house where salad featured prominently on the menu, and I disappointed the landlady, who kept referring to healthy schoolboy appetites, by showing no enthusiasm for it; it still seems to me hardly to merit the description of food at all. I remember a wet Sunday evening in the lounge, a fit setting for a Terence Rattigan play, when I delighted my father and the other residents by asking loudly: 'Dad, what time do the pubs shut?' I spent a somewhat lonely week, since my father was at work all day, but on the Saturday we travelled home together, as the season was coming to an end and my father was, I think, weary of being away from home. I can today well understand the mixed welcome my mother gave him, delighted to see him but painfully aware that she was now once again deprived of any regular income.

In fact he did soon afterwards get a new job; the worst of the recession was at last ending. This new employer was a small photographer in Didcot, which meant a long journey each day, and my father's real skill with the camera was not required as he worked solely in the darkroom on routine developing and printing, as at Ventnor. It must also have been galling for him to have to work for someone who occupied just the position, of self-employed small businessman, he had filled himself only a few years before. But at least he was once again contributing to the family budget, and things were less desperate than they had been, for my brother's income had also increased. He had, as I have mentioned earlier, shown a real aptitude for office life and the typed letter offering him a better paid appointment with Edmundson's Electricity Corporation, dated 28 May 1938, still survives:

> With reference to our interview yesterday, we confirm your appointment as Clerk in our General Office at a commencing weekly wage of 35/- [£1.75] and shall be glad if you will commence your new duties on Wednesday week, June 8th. The appointment is subject to the Company's standard conditions of employment, and is determinable by either party giving to the other one week's notice.

The move, respected though Plentys was, represented a real step up in the world. Edmundson's, a major electricity wholesalers and the Wessex Electricity Company, responsible for distribution in the Newbury area, were often bracketed together and jointly formed one of the best employers in the town, traditionally offering job security, the outstanding benefit one looked for in the 1930s, a recognised career structure and such uncommon amenities as a pension scheme and a sports club. My brother, though never naturally sociable, settled in rapidly and happily in his new post, and was to remain in it, despite various changes, for the rest of his life, interrupted only by six years following the same occupation, pay clerk, in the RAF.

I always felt that fate had dealt him a very poor hand but I cannot remember his ever complaining about this or indeed the more minor inconveniences of life.

He would stay silent even when he might reasonably have solicited sympathy, as when suffering from toothache. It was presumably his deep religious faith which made him ready to accept what seemed to me his basically unenviable lot and the more I look back on his life the more I respect him. He was careful with money, as anyone brought up in our circumstances and suffering from my father's mismanagement of his affairs, was likely to be, but he was the major earner in our family and our lives would have been a good deal less agreeable had he been less ready to spend for the family benefit cash he might have saved for a rainy day, of which we had known so many.

It must have been around this time that we acquired our first wireless set. My brother's first attempt to buy one ended in embarrassment, for only a day or two after he had signed the hire purchase contract it was cancelled. The reason, he had to explain, was 'because of dad', for, being under the age of 21, my brother had had to give my father's name as guarantor and this the lending company had refused to accept in view of his dismal financial record. A little later, however, my brother was able to obtain a set, and he also, I believe, met the regular expenses it involved – not merely the 'never-never' payments, but the licence, costing the substantial lump sum of 10s [50p] a year, and the costly batteries needed to obtain a signal. The 'HT', for High Tension, battery was a solid, slab-like object bigger than most present day radios, and cost 17s 6d [87.5p], a major expense as it needed to be replaced about every three months. The low tension 'accumulator' required charging every week, at 4d [2p] a time. I remember on many occasions accompanying my brother on this regular mission, one of us gingerly carrying the fragile, rectangular glass container filled with sulphuric acid, to a neighbour's garden shed, crammed with batteries being recharged. It was an early lesson in the importance of being 'on the mains' and a reminder of the short sightedness of the Newbury Corporation in forcing its tenants to use gas, for Camp Close had been built at the very middle of the period, between 1920 and 1938, during which the number of electricity consumers multiplied twelve fold. [5]

Apart from the expense of using a battery-operated wireless, we would have been much better off had electricity been laid on, for my brother, as an employee of the industry, would, I believe, have qualified for a substantially reduced tariff. It was, I suspect, the inconvenience of having constantly to have the wireless batteries recharged or replaced, along with that of the troublesome ritual of lighting the gas or, outside our living-room, using candles, which first aroused my interest in the whole subject of electricity supply, on which I was later to write a number of books. Electricity was in the inter-war years, I came to realise, a test case of one's political stance, and a symbol of what I increasingly felt to be a contest between the modernisers in society and the traditionalists. I did not, of course, then know that national control of the whole system had been proposed at the end of the first world war, nor that the lines of transmission towers being erected at this time to bring the benefits of electric power to every corner of the countryside were the work of a single national authority, the Central Electricity Board, set up in 1927.[6] I was however, vaguely aware, thanks to my brother's employment, of the silent revolution that was in progress and at this time to have a house with sufficient rooms and electricity was the utmost height of my ambition.

Later both my elder sister and I were, like my brother, though in different capacities, to join the electricity supply industry and by my teens I had no doubt that the need for the country to enjoy a single, unified electricity system, nationally, not locally, controlled, was a powerful argument for state socialism. A year or two later I discovered the 'pylon school' of poets, consisting of WH Auden, Cecil Day Lewis, Louis MacNeice and Stephen Spender, then a group of young left-wingers rejecting traditional poetic imagery in favour of the praise of roads and power stations. I warmed to Spender's *The Pylons*,

> 'those pillars
> Bare like nude, giant girls that have no secret',

published in 1933.

But, even if we lacked electricity, we now had the wireless and it vastly enriched our lives. My brother had retained his interest in the medium since his childhood 'Radio Circle' days and he was an enthusiast for the popular 1930s' occupation of 'twiddling the knob' in search of the exotic foreign stations listed on the waveband selector. Why anyone should want to listen to Hilversum, much less Belgrade, I never understood but we certainly tuned in on occasion to the BBC's only real competitors, Radio Luxembourg and Radio Normandie.[7] I can also recall listening to English language broadcasts from Moscow, which seemed positively daring if not actually subversive.

None of this made much appeal to my mother. She enjoyed comedy programmes and Outside Broadcasts of national occasions, but what really delighted her was when things went wrong, the BBC then being regarded as the epitome of correctness in behaviour as well as speech. I do not think we had our set in time for the classic 'Fleet's lit up' broadcast made by a drunken commentator in May 1937, and still being talked of in the 1960s when I joined the BBC myself, having moved on from electricity to broadcasting, but we enjoyed our share of 'technical hitches', as any unscheduled incident tended to be described. When a presenter, by a slip of the tongue, referred to Victor Silvester's Bathroom Orchestra, instead of 'Ballroom', no listener can have laughed more heartily than my mother. She also happily related to me hearing another famous BBC faux pas when a delay in presenting a George Formby programme with the signature tune 'When I'm cleaning windows' was tactlessly explained by the remark, 'I'm afraid the windows in question are not yet quite clean enough for the BBC', an admirable but libellous ad lib for which the BBC had to apologise.

My mother was not hard to amuse. 'He's shot him!' she would comment cheerfully when some sudden bang intruded into a silent interval between programmes, and she loved the simple good humour of Arthur Askey. 'Arthur!' she would comment warningly, as if he could hear her, when he seemed likely to overstep the limits of propriety, as in his regular comment at the end of his famous Bee Song, 'It's a silly b. song, isn't it?' The word for which 'b' stood, though often heard on our estate, and regarded as the ultimate in obscenity, was never broadcast or, of course, uttered in our household. I can, however, remember my mother recounting with shocked pleasure how she had heard a librarian at Boots Library reproving a more junior one who had helped her to choose a title on the 'B' shelves – an 'A' subscription was beyond her means: 'B customers must choose their own b. books!'

Making ends meet must have involved my mother in a constant struggle, but she never uttered a word of complaint. 'Life is good!' she would sometimes declare, when it seemed anything but. Somehow she managed to ensure that I received a parcel each Saturday during term, visible proof that I was not forgotten at home, and my twin sister went off each morning to Newbury High School looking not too different from the other girls, though she was the only pupil from Camp Close. The High School contained, like the Grammar School, a fair leavening of scholarship pupils and the authorities were as helpful as they could be in passing on secondhand books and items of uniform but inevitably there were other extras to be paid for and keeping Peggy at the High School must have involved a constant struggle.

It was probably during the summer holiday of 1938, though it may have been a year or two later, that an incident occurred which brought home to me how hard up we were. My Uncle Tom, my mother's brother, of whom she had always been fond, and his son and daughter, came up from their small Somerset farm to visit us. This was a rare day out for them as for us, and only after we had all got on the bus to take us up the hill did I learn, from a whispered conversation between my parents, that they did not have a single coin between them. It seemed we would have to ask our guests to find not merely their fares but ours as well, but happily I had saved a large sum, 1s 6d [7½p] from my school pocket money. Deeply embarrassed, I passed this privately to my father and it was just sufficient, with adult fares costing 2d [1p] and children's 1d [½p], to pay all our fares.

The sacrifice, if realised, was not reciprocated. The visitors brought, I believe, some fruit and vegetables from the farm, which had cost them nothing, but though we took them on a tour of the town before they left, this time going down the hill on foot, and entertained them to both dinner and tea at home, my uncle gave none of us a tip, though we gallantly and untruthfully assured each other that we had not really expected one. Nor, to the best of my knowledge, did he do anything to help his sister financially. Humble though our house was, I suppose it may have seemed superior to the oil-lit farm with its outdoor privy from which the visitors came, and farmers are, I have realised since, notoriously more ready to accept money than to part with it.

My third year at Housie began in September 1938, when I entered the 'B' stream of the five which made up what the school in its quaint, perverse way called the Little Erasmus. The name was, typically, not explained to us and I later assumed it to be a tribute to the Dutch scholar who died in 1536, but it fact, Housie-like, the explanation was more parochial. Erasmus Smith was a seventeenth century merchant whose benefactions largely financed the rebuilding of the Newgate Street school a century later.[8]

The LE, made up of 13 and 14 year olds – like my former heroes, the Remove at Greyfriars – was traditionally one of the most troublesome classes in the school. I can remember a masters' entertainment in which a senior master, dressed in Housey clothes, sang a song recording the misdeeds of one imaginary member which began:

> 'I'm one of the boys of the LEA,
> I'm a bit of a lad in my own little way…'

and went on to record a series of failures -'I've been a non-swimmer for nearly three years' – and misdeeds. I certainly qualified under the failures count, but, my attempt to run away not being generally known, was regarded as tediously law-abiding. I can, however, remember a sense of real intellectual excitement that year thanks to the LEA having one of the pleasantest, ablest and most stimulating members of the staff as its form master, qualities which at the time I barely appreciated.

Looking back sixty years later it is, I think, possible to make a fair judgement of the staff of Christ's Hospital in my years there, from 1936 to 1943. There were perhaps three or four outstanding teachers of a calibre I might not have encountered in the state system. There was also at least one, the contemptible Blam, and perhaps one or two others, who would not have survived a term in a less indulgent environment. In between were a mass of solidly competent masters, conventional in their methods, successful in drilling into ordinary boys the essentials of their subjects, and in enabling them to face the universal test of School Certificate, and, in the case of future grecians, the more demanding Higher Certificate, followed by the real goal to which our efforts were directed, an open scholarship at Oxford or Cambridge. The younger staff, if fairly free with the cane in the manner of most public school teachers of the time, were usually pleasant, amiable individuals, happy to move on after a year or two, often to more senior posts in day schools. The older masters tended to be duller, often resigned to rising no further in their profession, and ready to accept the school as it was, with no desire for innovation or reform.

The LEB's form master defied this classification, in being both long serving and enlightened. Most unusually, he did not have a degree, but taught several subjects in a sound, straightforward fashion, combining solid instruction in essentials with imaginative exercises in a way which marked out the born teacher. I owe 'Fred' Haslehust a lasting debt for without the remedial operation he now undertook I might well have failed School Certificate in Latin, then essential to qualify for university entrance, and thus fallen at the first of the obstacles between us and Oxford.

I can still remember Fred's incredulity as he discovered that in the previous three terms under Blam we had covered none of the prescribed syllabus and that he therefore had to begin by making good the damage inflicted on us by his idle and inept colleague. He set to manfully, so that we mastered two years' work in one, and also, as I shall describe in a moment, taught admirably what I considered my subjects, English and History. Fred also served as a supernumerary assistant housemaster to Peele A and we occasionally saw his two increasingly attractive daughters, soon known to the whole school as 'the Haslehust twins'. They must have carried off many schoolboy hearts and eventually, most appropriately, one married the excellent house-captain of my first year, JCD Lawrance.

Fred Haslehust was a kind man and I remember my first encounter with him on the sports field when I was serving as linesman at a house rugger match. I was far too shy to thrust myself in front of the spectators, all senior to me, but Fred dragged me forward and gave me a brief pep talk to the effect that it was more important that I should see what was happening than anyone else. Thereafter I welcomed this somewhat despised assignment, which enabled one to be honourably occupied without actually having to venture on to the pitch.

Later I also came to appreciate Fred's quiet cynicism. He was the first, though not the last, master I heard remark that the real purpose of a public school education was to make a boy so inured to injustice that he would be well prepared for the world outside. I also recall his ill-concealed religious scepticism. Once, when the chaplain had delivered a favourite prayer about loving God more dearly and knowing him more nearly, Fred added an audible but far from pious 'Yours sincerely' which both shocked and delighted us.

But it was as my form master that Fred had his greatest influence on me. Although I normally excelled at English he discouraged any tendency towards swollen headedness. 'I don't doubt you know what it means,' he told me dryly when I had written an excessively long sentence to explain the meaning of 'precocious', 'but writing too much is as bad as not writing enough.' He constantly preached that one should tackle difficulties even at the risk of getting the answer wrong. I was told off for leaving a blank when *sangfroid* came up during dictation, but commended for attempting to spell *insouciant* even though I did so incorrectly. He was, very rightly, a stickler for accuracy and, for the first time since junior school, I found myself having to write out lists of words I had spelt wrongly, among. them 'deign', 'prodigious' and 'manoeuvre', which, embarrassingly for a military historian, still sometimes defeats me.

In late September 1938 I was still immersed in beginning of term gloom when we were caught up in the Munich crisis. My clearest recollection is of the trial black-out which, with its own generators, Housie was able to carry out independently. One evening during prep the lights gradually began to go dim and one boy was instructed to stand on a table to see if he could read by the now barely visible light bulb. He could not. It was obvious that if we were to continue to work the windows would have to be covered.

This experiment, and the issue of gas masks, imposed by the government, were the only visible concessions Housie made to what was happening, and even the most senior boys, likely to be called up if the worst happened, were given no opportunity to hear the broadcast news bulletins and other important announcements. Happily, individual masters were less oblivious to the needs of the time. Fred Haslehust made no secret of his view that we were in our present danger because of the ludicrous leniency we had shown to Germany following the first world war, an opinion I wholly shared, as I do still.

My already intense interest in politics was merely heightened by the Munich crisis. I find that on 26 September 1938 I wrote in an exercise book, in answer to some unspecified questions, the names of Neville Chamberlain, Lord Halifax, Duff Cooper and Hore Belisha, two arch appeasers, one realistic patriot and the then Secretary of State for War. The following day we were set an essay entitled 'Herr Hitler' – evidently Housie, like the BBC and *The Times* felt he merited the courtesy of a title – and I still feel that, at the age of twelve and a half, I showed a far truer grasp of the situation than the 67-year-old prime minister and his advisers:

> The most obvious fact about Herr Hitler is his greed. Offered by the Anglo-French plan was the part of Czechoslovakia with a large majority of Germans. Even the Czechs were prepared to give this. But, rejecting this peaceful offer, he asked for more. He would ruin Czechoslovakia by taking a great portion of the country…Czechoslovakia would no longer be a nation; with mineral wealth taken and used by Germany against the rest of civilisation. He started his expanding campaign by marching into first Rhineland and then Austria while French soldiers in the Maginot Line watched and ARP became more extensive in Britain. Jealous of our Empire, he is expanding that of Germany at the expense of small states, and when these are conquered he will aim at larger countries.

Showing considerably more prescience than the then ambassador in Berlin and most of the House of Commons, I spelt out the consequences of surrender in terms Winston Churchill, who was to denounce the Munich settlement as 'a total and unmitigated defeat...a defeat without a war', would surely have approved:

> In Czechoslovakia are the colossal Skoda munition works. If he is given all he wants no steel mines will be available to Czechoslovakia to supply the factory. When he need go but a few further miles to reach them and Prague will he stop?...Unless war comes now it will be but a few years before it commences and then his army will be stronger than now...He should have been stopped when he built more guns than the allowed number by the Treaty of Versailles, but people said 'Let Germany live' and this is the result...so it looks as if a 2nd war will come and August 4th 1914 will change to October 1st 1938.

In this final prediction alone I was wrong. Instead, on the day when I had thought the war would start, the newspapers carried news of Chamberlain's capitulation to Hitler the previous day, but the jubilation shown in Downing Street on the evening of Friday 30 September, and subsequently in the House of Commons, found no echo in the Little Erasmus classroom at Christ's Hospital. By the time I got my essay back the crisis was over. Fred Haslehust, always anxious to discourage conceit, marked it 'Not bad', but privately told me that it was the best of the class and that he shared my sentiments. But even with a war likely to break out soon he kept his eye on essentials, correcting my spelling of 'militarism' and reproving me for not writing out 'second' in full.

Three weeks later we were set another controversial topic for an essay, 'The Causes of the Great War'. This prompted from me another, equally justified, denunciation of Germany, in which I listed all her crimes since 1914, not forgetting the violation of that 'gallant little country' Belgium, the shelling of the English coast that December, and the ignoble scuttling of the German fleet after its surrender. The 'barbaric culture' of our former enemy was, I concluded, unchanged:

> Germany under Hitler again prepares to make a second try at European power. By a mere display of armed force Britain has been terrified. Peace is bought, but at what a price. Britain's honour is sold by Chamberlain to Germany. He is acclaimed as the peacemaker but he is really leading us into a snare. Suffering under a delousion *(sic)* that Germany wants peace and not Europe he pins our hope on a worthless scrap of paper. Only one way can peace be brought to troubled Europe. That is by Germany being completely squashed and disarmed.

It was not, however, enough for Fred to have one's heart in the right place. This time he took me to task for not having properly planned my essay in advance and he was even more severe on 'Germany and the Jews', written on 15

November 1938 which ended by urging the government to prepare for war. When I wrote of Germany 'pulling the tail of the British lion' he admonished me 'Don't write journalese' – not the last time I was be told this at school; later, working in Fleet Street, I was to be urged to cultivate a 'racier' style, ie to use more journalese rather than less. 'Don't rant,' he counselled me. 'I asked for an essay, not a violent piece of propaganda. But at least you try.'

I was still too junior to attend the School Debating Society when, a month after Munich, it debated the motion that 'This present government ought to be replaced'. Amazingly, the appeasers won, defeating the motion by 42 votes to 29. 'We were not yet ready for war,' asserted one speaker – hardly a reason for supporting the government which, had left us unprepared it seemed to me – 'and Czechoslovakia was not worth a European catastrophe.' But there were, even at Housie, some dissenting voices. The master who occupied the chair, the Hon. DS Roberts, of whom I shall say much more later, vacated it 'to show', in the words of *The Blue*, 'that Mr Chamberlain had been a great man for 24 hours only'.

It was, I think, that Christmas, 1938, that Aunt Maud came to stay. Normally we saw her only in the summer. I date it because I know that I was supposed to be past the age of tears but nevertheless burst into loud sobs on overhearing her suggest to my father, after I had gone to bed, that he could save a whole £1 three times a year by leaving me unvisited. I now realise these days out, his only holidays, were probably as welcome to him as to me, but in any case the prospect of being deprived of my solitary interlude of happiness in the otherwise unadulterated misery of my three months' exile left me so distressed that my mother hurried upstairs to find out the cause. My parents were, I now realise, in a difficult position for Aunt Maud may have helped us out with small gifts and somehow the incident was smoothed over. It confirmed her, I suspect, in her dislike of me and certainly seemed to justify my detestation of her. 'Old maid' she may have been but she could nevertheless, I believe, have shown more understanding of my situation and more sensitivity and generosity in dealing with my parents. How very differently would my mother have behaved had her situation and that of her sister-in-law been reversed.

By mid-January 1939, after the blessed interlude of the pantomime, I was back at school and again fascinated by international affairs. These were forcing their way even into such subjects as grammar and I find that a sentence set for us to parse, ie analyse into its component parts, that year ran as follows:

> Though (conjunction), we are agreed that the attitude of Germany towards the Jews (adverbial clause) is indefensible, it is difficult on the spur of the moment (prepositional clause) to suggest a remedy.

More directly to the point was an essay on 'Dictators', set that month, which was assessed as 'Not bad in places'. Routine compositions made, however, little appeal to me, and I performed poorly on the subjects of 'The Wind', 'Breakfast', 'Cutlery' and 'Cats'. Fred commented unkindly on the last-named: 'You drivel on without much design or purpose', a cruel verdict I have sometimes quoted to myself since when cutting some prolix first draft.

On 14 March 1939 Hitler occupied the rest of Czechoslovakia, thereby proving the critics of the Munich Agreement to have been right, and two weeks later, on 31 March, Neville Chamberlain gave the pledge to protect Poland which seemed likely to make war inevitable. For me the closing part of the term was dominated by a private triumph, for I entered, and won, a competition mounted by the *Daily Sketch* to write an appreciation of a children's book, restricted, I believe, to readers under the age of 14. I cannot now remember my subject, but it was probably *Tom Brown's Schooldays,* which, with its mixture of sport, bullying and piety, appealed to me as depicting a world not unlike that I knew at Housie. My house-captain, a civilised individual, AH Davies, thought the event worth recording in the house's entry in the March 1939 issue of *The Blue*, the only time my name appeared in it until the term I left:

> We must extend our congratulations to Longmate on his sudden, unsuspected and magnificently rewarded advance into the world of letters; and to the *Daily Sketch* for realising his undoubted literary talent.

The 'magnificent reward' consisted of a set of six well-bound children's classics, of which I remember *Black Beauty, Grimms' Fairy Tales* and *Gulliver's Travels,* for none of which I much cared. However, it was pleasant to be noticed for once as good at something and I remember my housemaster taking me aside to urge me to read more classics, such as Dickens, advice which may help to explain why I have felt a lifelong distaste for this in my view overrated author.

For Noel this was a year of triumph, with the 'house spirit' he so longed to develop at last in evidence. Peele A in 1938-9 housed in its dayroom no fewer than six cups covering every major sporting activity: football, cricket, relay sports, individual sports, PT and Gym, and shooting. I had contributed nothing to any of these, to the vexation of my old nursemaid, who in the same House Notes that recorded my journalistic success had been commended for his performance in that term's Steeplechase, 'Pitman especially doing good work'. Bob, as I now think of him, still regarded me as his protégé and had not abandoned his hopes of turning me into a proper games-playing, music-loving all-rounder of the type Housie hoped to produce, though he was to be disappointed. I continued to be anything but the carefree, insouciant – I knew the meaning of the word now – risk-taking teenager he hoped to turn me into.

One's LE year had a special importance in that during it every boy had to decide in what subjects he would begin to specialise in the following year. This was also when the school finally decided whether one was grecian material, ie of university calibre, or destined to leave after School Certificate. The moment of choice was a solemn occasion, for the headmaster toured the classes in the relevant year and called us up one by one to ask, 'What do you want to be when you leave?' Expecting a realistic answer from 13 year olds was asking a great deal, and since this was the first time most of us had, in three years or more, spoken to the Head it was a terrifying experience. There was often with HLO Flecker a sense of suppressed anger only just kept in check and I remember one boy who tried to evade committing himself was firmly put in his place and compelled to reply.

The truth so far as I was concerned was that I really did not know. I no longer wished to be an accountant; the two subjects I liked, English and History, which would have been appropriate to my second choice of career, journalism, were not available as options; and I was a poor performer in those that were: classics, foreign languages and mathematics. This left only science, and teaching being the one profession I had encountered I said I would like to be a science master. The Head expressed surprise, but raised no objection.

My housemaster's reaction was different. He reminded me that I had always done best in Arts subjects and suggested that since my Latin was poor I should opt for modern languages. I did not dare point out that my German was little better than my Latin and that there was an overwhelming argument against starting French, that it would mean being taught by him. So I stuck to my guns and was duly assigned, come September, to the Science School.

The pressure on any boy who showed any aptitude for the classics to concentrate on them was intense. One Old Blue, who later acquired a doctorate in psychology and had wanted to specialise in science, found himself, against his wishes, 'put down for classics' because, having learned it previously, he had been top of his class in his first year. 'Flecker never allowed me to change subjects' he recalled in 1994, 'and in the end I did not make it in Latin and Greek.' He left before becoming a grecian, despite the efforts of Blamire-Brown, whom he 'hated', to teach him Greek and 'Macnutt, who tried to improve my performance with a stick'.[9]

There is much evidence that the 'options' procedure was unsatisfactory. My poor performance at Latin saved me from being forced, unlike many of my contemporaries, into specialising in it, but I had, as I was to demonstrate, no real aptitude for science yet was not discouraged from pursuing it – indeed, as I have pointed out, the only subjects for which I had shown any aptitude were not available. The truth is that the classical tradition hung so heavy over the school that anyone unable to follow it was regarded by the headmaster as inferior. One boy, shortly after my time, was told 'Don't be ridiculous', when he confessed his ambition to become 'a research chemist', and was told 'I'll put down pharmacist', though in fact, he later reported in *The Blue* 'I...have indeed spent most of my working life in research laboratories.'[10] The Headmaster even had a low opinion of the medical profession. 'Flecker...seemed to think boys who opted to do medicine were second class,' complained one doctor in *The Blue* in 1991, for whom the 'injustice...at being', with other science grecians, 'denied our "Buttons"', the outward sign that one had been accepted by a university, still rankled 44 years later.[11] It was essentially the same complaint as that made in Edwardian times, that no subjects counted except Latin and Greek and no universities except Oxford and Cambridge.

To be both a late developer and to wish to join the medical profession aroused the school's scepticism. 'I have never been so certain of anything in my life as I am when I say young Hull will never, never, become a doctor,' his form-master, GM Malins, whom I mention critically elsewhere, told Robin Hull's brother. After taking the examination a term late to improve his chance 'of passing one of two of the seven subjects' 'young Hull' confounded everyone with a 'seeming miracle', a School Certificate that included seven credits and a distinction, thus easily achieving 'Matric exemption', the importance of which I explain elsewhere. The school, having shown one of its worst characteristics, a readiness prematurely to write off potentially talented boys, now displayed one of its best. 'Suddenly,' Robin Hull has recorded, 'I found myself getting attention from some of the most able teachers', and, promoted to Deputy Grecian he was set firmly on the path which was to lead to a scholarship to St Mary's Hospital, London and a university chair in General Practice.[12]

Journalism, which so many Old Blues had practised successfully, was not highly regarded. 'But my boy, journalists aren't gentlemen!' one master told WL (later Sir Linton) Andrews, a future editor of the *Yorkshire Post* and Press Council chairman, when he taught himself shorthand at school.[13] In fact my generation was to prove exceptionally rich in producing recruits to what was not yet known as the media. My nursemaid, Bob Pitman, after briefly contemplating the law as a career and a short period as a schoolmaster, found his true vocation as a book critic and columnist in Fleet Street. So, too, did my Peele B contemporary, Bernard Levin. Overlapping with me at Housie, though I did not know him, was Ian Trethowan, the first Old Blue to become Director-General of the BBC. He only just qualified for admission, in 1933, for his father's income, of 'a little over £400 a year', was close to the acceptable limit, and he was, he later learned, 'accepted on the basis of an unusually good English paper'. Having 'only just scraped enough School Certificate passes' it was decided, however, that he was not Oxford or Cambridge material. His main interest lay in cricket and rugger, but having, at 15, 'uttered a well-known four-letter word' after tripping on the field, he was sent off and 'told afterwards that,' as Trethowan recounts, 'I would never play for the school again'.* Apart

---

* Trethowan himself remarks in his autobiography how he would later 'spend a fair amount of time at the top of the BBC trying to keep that same four-letter word off television and radio'. The letters of apology or explanation when he failed were often, incidentally, drafted or approved by me as a member of the BBC Secretariat.

from his enthusiasm for games which proved, for once, of practical use, for he spent some time as a sports correspondent, the future journalist gained, like so many products of Christ's Hospital, a lifelong interest in music, but in his central ambition the school gave him no support. During the holidays, in his last year at school, he was already selling items to the 'London letter for a provincial evening newspaper', edited by a family friend who was also an Old Blue, George Christ (pronounced to rhyme with 'grist'). *But the headmaster was not impressed. 'He had,' Trethowan discovered, 'no sympathy with my particular aspirations...During what proved to be my last term he told me there was a job on offer with a whisky firm and he strongly advised me to take it...I declined and...his parting words were: "You're making a big mistake. You'll never make a journalist."' Trethowan left soon afterwards and found his own first job, as a 'tape-boy', distributing ticker tape through the newsroom, at the far from prestigious and now defunct *Daily Sketch*. His career began in earnest soon afterwards on the *Yorkshire Post*, edited, as mentioned earlier, by another Old Blue. Trethowan believed half a century later that Christ's Hospital's chief legacy to him was 'an insatiable relish for history' thanks to a master I have already mentioned, ACW Edwards.[14] It is hardly surprising that the then Director-General showed no great affection for his old school when in November 1980 I helped to organise a dinner of BBC Old Blues to celebrate his recent knighthood. Most of the seven who attended were also unenthusiastic about their schooldays and three others declined the invitation altogether.

Although the tough regime over which he presided might have seemed to provide an admirable training for life in the services, HLOF had no enthusiasm for such a career. 'I agree to your wish to go for a soldier,' he told one Peele B boy who left in 1937, 'but I think you will never achieve what I achieved, which was Lieutenant-Colonel at the age of twenty-one"!** Flecker had served with the Gloucestershire Regiment in the first world war. 'Actually I did,' remembers the officer concerned, who survived the disastrous retreat from Burma in 1942, when 'others had just faded away.' They had not, he observed, had the advantage of learning to go hungry or 'had the fringe benefit of being in Prep B and Peele B, with the maximum distance to walk/march several times a day to and from chapel, classroom and Dining Hall.'[15]

A recurring complaint among Old Blues of my generation is of the premature and rigid separation of boys into potential grecians and the rest. This began, one of my contemporaries believes, even before the crucial 'Options'

---

* I owe my own debt to George Christ, who wrote an extremely favourable review of my *How We Lived Then* for *The Blue*, although indignant at its critical references to Christ's Hospital. He paid me a generous, if back-handed, compliment: 'Housie . . . must have given Longmate a tolerable education to have enabled him to produce such a well written and worthwhile book.' (May 1971, p.163)

** This was presumably the result of exceptionally heavy casualties.

began, one of my contemporaries believes, even before the crucial 'Options' interview at the age of 13 and 14, thanks to the tendency to regard boys who entered via the Prep, with its high proportion of 'presented' boys, as intellectually inferior to those who had gone straight into the main school, often by competitive exam. The curious 'presentation' system had other consequences. This boy, though doing well, found himself forced to leave before his seventeenth birthday because his governor wanted his place for another protégé, though he reached university eventually and remains 'grateful to Housie for the education received'. The school suffered, he believed, from the 'charity school ethos of get-on-or-get-out', but a reunion of boys from his house provided ample evidence of the unreliability of the initial 'sheep and goats' divide. Among the 'failures' whom the school had required to leave prematurely he identified a doctor, several engineers with degrees, a lawyer 'involved in property development' who 'clearly could have bought up all the rest of us' and the deputy headmaster of a well-known public school, who had managed to enter Oxford long after leaving school. 'Had you suggested to Oily,' he commented, 'that John and the others...would have taken an MA at Oily's alma mater he would have thought you utterly mad.'[16]

---

[1] Nov 1937 p.10
[2] Mar 1988 p.69
[3] Jan 1962 p.7
[4] *CH Bk* p.xxx-xxxi
[5] Taylor p.343
[6] Mowat pp.29-30
[7] Briggs II p.350 et seq
[8] Morpurgo p.19, Allan p.14
[9] Dec 1994 p.230
[10] Dec 1994 p.231
[11] Dec 1991 p.203
[12] Hull pp.202 & 213-4
[13] Mar/Apr 1945 pp.67-8
[14] Trethowan pp.6-8
[15] Jul 1996 p.159
[16] For the origin of this nickname see Mar 1994 p.72

28

CALL THE ROLL, SERGEANT-MAJOR!

Order given at the start of every OTC parade.

Christ's Hospital, Summer Term, 1939

It was, I believe, during the Easter holiday of 1939 that I wrote my first, and almost my only, play. This contained only one act and was inspired by the growing threat from Germany. The dramatic climax consisted of a young German boy, who had seen the candle he had lit in front of a religious statue – my brother's influence was surely evident here – being blown out by an atheistic Nazi, uttering aloud a prayer: 'Oh Lord, bring down fire from heaven, as you did before.' My twin sister and our regular friends obligingly took part in this pious, propagandist work, which I directed, and we performed it in front of our indulgent parents. Everything that summer seems, at least in retrospect, to have been overshadowed by the visibly approaching war, and the government's announcement, made on 26 April 1939, of its decision to introduce conscription, initially in the form of six months' compulsory military training for 20 year olds, provided a suitably bleak accompaniment to the start of a new summer term. [1]

I was not alone in being outraged at what now seems to have been a long overdue change of policy; like many others at that time, I saw no inconsistency in castigating the Chamberlain government for not resisting Hitler only to abuse it when it at last showed signs of doing so. The Labour Party's official explanation later was that it had no confidence in the government's ability to use the extra forces it was raising. It was certainly true that Neville Chamberlain had gone back on his word, having repeatedly promised never to impose compulsory service in peacetime and for my father, hitherto a loyal Conservative, this proved the breaking point. He vowed never to vote Conservative again, and never did.

Back at school conscription provided an obvious choice of essay topic for the current-affairs-minded Fred Haslehust and I find that on 16 May 1939 I wrote for him a fiercely anti-Chamberlain diatribe, recounting the prime minister's pledges not to introduce it, the last as recently as 25 March, and denouncing him for 'deliberately telling the country untruths'. I dismissed the prime minister's claim that two pending by-elections would prove that the country was behind him by pointing out that both were being held in safe Conservative seats. The real test, I argued, would come in North Southwark, with its much smaller majority.

I was right about North Southwark, where a Liberal-National, ie Conservative, majority of 79 became a Labour one of 3,270, but about conscription, I was, I now believe, wrong. What embarrasses me still is not this misjudgement but the almost hysterically anti-Conservative tone of my essay, which earned from my form master the handsome mark of 24 out of 30. This was, I now think, undeserved as this extract suggests:

> As Mr Atlee *(sic)* so concisely puts it, there is to be conscription of men, but no conscription of wealth. The nation not only loses its freedom...but is not even consulted as to whether it wants conscription or not. The people affected by the decision have not even got the vote. Young men from universities who should be learning to govern and become good citizens are to be forced to learn to kill each other. They are to be taken from the universities and paid for learning the art of murder, the sum of one shilling per day. Chamberlain had once more betrayed the nation's trust in him. If at the next election the Socialists win the Conservative party will have him to thank, who destroyed the freedom of the British nation.

What strikes me now is how passionately interested in politics I had become. When we set each other current affairs quizzes in the classroom, Fred would caution me not to ask too many questions on the identity of ministers, for I could reel off the names of the parliamentary secretaries of even the most obscure departments. I was by no means alone in this. Pitman matched me in my knowledge and so did Ivan Yates, both future journalists and Labour parliamentary candidates, but the latter being all of 30 yards [27m] away along the corridor linking Peele A to Peele B, we had no opportunity to exchange opinions. Both of us, I realised, when we at last got to know each other, found in our fierce party loyalty the sort of satisfaction our schoolmates derived from supporting 'their' football team, and in being concerned with politics, and on the Left, we were also rebelling against the whole Housey ethos, of beating and compulsory games, poor food and petty rules, Macnutt and Blam.

Oddly enough I cannot remember having contemplated becoming a politician myself, though I was often accused of 'being a red', and a few months after this I wrote a long essay on the political situation that I had some vague idea of getting published as a pamphlet. It went over much the same ground as my essays in class, denouncing the Munich Agreement and criticising the government for not making more effort to secure Russia as an ally against Hitler. This work, which, ashamed of its crude partisanship, I later destroyed, somehow got to the attention of our junior housemaster who publicly, and courteously, debated these subjects with me in the dayroom as the rest of the house gathered round to listen. This proved a popular occasion for, engrossed in argument, the time passed unnoticed and the house went to bed long after the normal hour.

Housie was now, like the rest of the country, gearing itself up for war. This was an interesting time to be a schoolboy and nowhere more so than in Peele A at Christ's Hospital with its fiercely anti-German housemaster. Noel Sergent, for all that we mocked him, had been proved right about 'The Boche', and having fought against him in the first world war was eager to prepare his house to do its duty in the second. Here for once, though we privately, and most unjustly, questioned his military credentials, Noel and his house were at one. He fully shared the official anxiety about the use of poison gas and I can remember a most welcome interruption to prep one evening when, after his usual preliminary cough, he delivered a lecture on the principal varieties we were likely to encounter.

The gas masks distributed at the start of the school year, during the Munich crisis, were now reissued and we were instructed in how to put them on and remove them. I was an apt pupil and still wince when I see someone in a film pull the mask *upwards* off the face by the rubber facepiece instead of *downwards* by the straps. I happily practised preventing the mica eyeshield clouding over by thinly spreading soap over the inside and must have bored my family in the subsequent holiday by lecturing them on anti-gas precautions whenever I got the opportunity.

A curiously unrealistic set of notes was circulated on how to behave during an air raid. If caught out of doors, I remember, we were supposed to hide under, or even climb, a tree, though I thought even then the likelihood of a German airman singling out an individual Housey boy for attack was remote. Noel, going further than the official guidance, warned us that we must steel ourselves when war came for some gruesome experiences. 'I, who have seen many such horrible sights...,' I remember his beginning one such homily, in his slightly too correct English.

Some things, of course, were too important to be disturbed by a mere war. Cricket continued unrelentingly and I remember one match which could have come straight out of *The Magnet*. Our house-captain, AH Davies, having 'carried his bat' through a whole series of stands with weaker partners, finally found himself with the weakest of all, and set himself out to monopolise the batting, skillfully hitting a single at the end of every over so that he continued to face the bowling, until, to well merited applause, he scored the winning hit.

The summer of 1939 saw my last Whole Holiday and it was my mother who took me out; my father's employer having refused my father the day off, then professed surprise when he turned up for work. We went, I remember, to Brighton, visited the aquarium and put pennies in the slot machines in the amusement arcade. These have all long since been supplanted by more sophisticated devices but seemed at the time amazingly inventive and daring. I recall the crane which hovered tantalisingly over some costly looking piece of jewellery but invariably in the end scooped up only a few tasteless but brightly coloured sweets. My mother sportingly, if disapprovingly, allowed me to invest a coin in a peepshow entitled 'The Last Drop', in which one saw the door of the condemned cell jerkily opened, the executioner and chaplain shuffle into view, and the prisoner pushed on to the trapdoor, only for the scene to go dark as it opened. My mother's attention must have been diverted when I also tried out the 'What the Butler Saw' machine. On this one turned a handle to produce the impression of a film, showing the antics of a maid, though they seemed distinctly tame even to an inexperienced adolescent like me. Much better value was a machine where, for the usual penny, one could 'drive' a car by means of a steering wheel connected to a pen travelling along a diagram of a busy street. This was ejected at the end and I found that I had ploughed my way through several other vehicles and even the odd brick wall or two, my first intimation that I was not a natural driver.

In June 1939 I reached the age of 13 and a half and thereby qualified for admission to the Christ's Hospital company of the Officers Training Corps. According to the school's Clerk and historian this was a 'a flourishing contingent, purely voluntary, though most boys who are physically fit join it.'[2] Enrolment was in fact automatic and compulsory and, one Quaker apart, I never knew of anyone excused membership. This was hardly to be expected. Every public school had its OTC, though some local authorities refused to have a unit in their grammar schools, on the grounds that this would encourage militarism. They were, I believe, mistaken, for reasons I set out in *First Bloom*, written while I was experiencing 'the real thing' in the army:

> The OTC was compulsory at Middlestone and, as cynical intellectuals observed, this was as well, as it helped to inculcate into the sensitive a contempt for all things military and, in the less sensitive, an attitude of amusement. At its head was a self-righteous and sternly important major, whose school position was a mere sinecure, for he was perpetually in uniform. He had a deep voice, which contrasted well for entertainment purposes with the higher pitched, but equally unintelligible, tones of the permanent regimental-sergeant-major attached to the school OTC. The latter...was of exceptionally slender build and his legs were remarkably thin, so that in puttees, which he always affected, they looked ridiculous.
>
> The start of a parade at which he was presiding was an occasion not to be missed. Strutting self-importantly along the parade ground he was wont to halt with a tremendous stamp and announce: 'Ite Arkers!' [ie 'Right Markers!']. A few flustered youths detached themselves from the throng at this summons, and stumbled out in response to the command. Usually they

contrived to sort themselves out incorrectly and titters could be heard among their waiting comrades, while the 'sagger-magger', as he was always described, in the manner of an obsolete Oxford slang, glared balefully towards them and was blasphemously silent. 'Un ADE!' [ie 'On parade!'] he thundered at last and the Middlestone contingent of the OTC tramped on to its markers and, after much shuffling and military formalities Major Jennings appeared. A voice which might more justly have come from the depths of an episcopal chest, a portly self-satisfied voice as of a bishop pleased with his sermon and his dinner, gave its orders, and the business of the afternoon commenced and continued till about quarter to four, when little groups of temporary soldiers began to drift across the playing fields to their houses, discussing in lurid language but bored tones the various humorous incidents the afternoon had produced.

In spite of the opportunities for entertainment it provided, the Officers Training Corps, later renamed, more democratically, the Junior Training Corps and later still demoted to becoming the Combined Cadet Force, was never popular. Part of the reason lay in the out-of-date uniform, which made us look, as well as feel, as if we were about to set out for Flanders or had strayed from the cast of *Journey's End*, RC Sheriff's famous anti-war play of 1929. Corps achieved indeed the extraordinary feat of making Housey clothes seem relatively sensible and the outfit in which we were required to deck ourselves out once a week had already been abandoned by the army in favour of the more practical battle-dress, just as it had scrapped the ancient four-rank drill formation which Housie retained.

Our OTC uniform consisted of knee breeches not unlike those we wore all the rest of the week but in a thinner, khaki coloured fabric, a usually ill-fitting jacket with brass buttons down the front, a flat, peaked cap, heavy boots and puttees, long strips of cloth about two inches [5cm] wide which had to be wound very carefully in overlapping folds up one's leg from just above the boot to just below the lower hem of the trousers. If one's puttees were not fastened properly they would unravel and trail behind one or trip the wearer up. A very high standard of smartness was demanded and metal cap badge and tunic buttons had to be highly polished with a brightness that would surely have attracted the attention of enemy snipers, if not artillery, from miles around. On inspection days boys would often carry a button stick – a 'U' shaped metal strip with a slot in the centre – on parade, along with twists of the invaluable polish-impregnated wadding called Duraglit, the sight and smell of which still reminds me of those military afternoons. It was then possible furtively to buff up your buttons at the last minute, just before the inspection began.

The best features of our equipment were the small arms, also dating from the first world war, consisting of the excellent Lee-Enfield rifle, still virtually unchanged when I joined the army in 1944, and the long 'carving knife' bayonet, also used in both wars and only replaced by the 'meat-skewer' type late in the second. More exotic weapons which might have captured our interest, like Bren and other machine guns and grenades, were never, understandably, put at our disposal, and I can only remember seeing drawings of revolvers and pistols. We spent in any case more time on drill, in which, thanks to our daily parading, we reached a higher standard than in weapon training but there was a good deal of instruction in elementary tactics, delivered by masters and NCOs with the aid of booklets bearing titles like *The Platoon in Attack*.

The Commanding Officer of the Corps, whom in *First Bloom* I called Jennings, was Major WD Harrup, whose contribution to the work of the Manual School I have already described. Somehow he had persuaded himself that his troops were not conscripts, for one Old Blue has recalled hearing him say to 'the visiting brass-hat...during a Corps inspection..."Oh yes, all completely voluntary," his first revelation that 'adult incorruptibility' was a myth.[3] I saw nothing of him except on Corps afternoons but he was an effective instructor. His fruity voice lent itself to mimicry and I can still hear one boy repeating Major Harrup's most recent fragment of military wisdom: 'The difference between a reconnaissance patrol by day and a reconnaissance patrol by night is that one is carried out by day and the other by night.' I recall being exhorted to remember – and I felt no inclination to disagree – that one must *not* on a reconnaissance patrol get drawn into fighting. He also stressed that the 'getaway man' was not at the rear of the patrol but next to last and that it was his duty to run away if trouble were encountered, a role for which I felt an instinctive sympathy.

The 'sagger-magger' in *First Bloom* was also taken from life and was so completely identified with his full-time job that we barely knew his name. His hour of glory came, as indicated in the quotation earlier, each Corps afternoon and he was credited with a legendary, though perhaps apocryphal, joke. It was related that once when the Corps contingent was on its way to camp the private supply of toilet paper he had prudently added to the laden trek cart had fallen off and the sagger-magger had thereupon clicked his heels together as at the start of every parade and in his usual stentorian tones had issued the order: 'Call the roll!' In contrast to the traditional personality associated with his rank he was, I think, a kindly man, indeed it was later my experience in the army that warrant officers, having reached the top of their particular tree, were not nearly as fearsome as their reputation or as the ranks immediately below them.

Perversely, instead of finding a bond with my housemates in despising Corps, I actually enjoyed it. Sitting in a classroom being lectured on elementary tactics, or practising them in the surrounding countryside was, after all, better than games. The local farmers were less enthusiastic about this latter activity and I can recall one being distinctly unimpressed for the explanation I gave for having forced my way through his hedge and trespassing on his field that I had been ordered to do both by my platoon commander. I never made much of a showing at drill but the more academic side of military training, like memorising the names of geographical features, or learning by heart a few essential military rules and commands, held no terrors for me. I can still distinguish a valley from a re-entrant and both from a saddle, and recite such useful rules for judging distances – though I would not now swear to their accuracy – as 'At one hundred yards the outline of the body begins to taper, at two hundred yards the shape of the face is blurred.' I could still, if required, though the occasion seems unlikely to arise, give the correct sequence of commands to an infantry section required to lay down fire, immortalised in the mnemonic DRINK. This stood for Designation ('Number One Section'), Range ('200 yards'), Indication ('Five-o'clock from that bushy-topped tree'), Number ('five rounds') and Kind ('Rapid', perhaps omitted), followed by 'Fire!' The essence of giving effective commands, we were taught, was to keep them as short as possible, or, as Major Harrup put it – this was before the days of political correctness – 'Imagine you're a Jew sending a telegram!'

The account of the OTC which I gave in *First Bloom*, as seen through the eyes of my hero James Conway, was notably more sympathetic than that of most other Housie institutions:

> There were times when there was a lecture in a classroom and a friendly NCO, who might but for military necessity now be drowsing over a novel in the comfort of his study, helped the time to pass pleasantly enough, and out of doors on a rather misty afternoon in November there was a good deal of amusement to be found in walking about on Big Side estimating distances, for usually the fool of the squad disappeared into the fog and, on being retrieved by a harassed instructor, who saw his squad dissolving before his eyes, would remark innocently: 'I thought it was fifty yards you said!' Grahame [my hero's closest friend] was in the same squad as James, and on sunny afternoons in the summer term...they sat together at the back of a squad at an open-air lecture, and speculated on the possibility of ever having to put the knowledge they were presumed to be acquiring to practical use...But all too often a whisper of 'Jennings is coming!' galvanised the instructor into a frenzy of questions and the audience at whom they were hurled were startled into an alertness which made whispering impossible.

There were two big events in the Corps year. I have only vague memories of the first, the Annual Inspection, conducted by some visiting general who was charged with the twin duties of assessing our military competence (usually passable) and inspiring us with fighting spirit (usually nil). The portrait of such an occasion in *George Brown's Schooldays* rings entirely true. If no-one actually quoted *If* to us they might as well have done so. I have, however, the clearest recollections of the second major military event each summer, Field

Day, which also features large in many public school novels, indeed one actually has this, so typical of the institution, as its title.

It is my first Field Day which I remember best. We were issued with haversack rations, consisting mainly of the unspeakable 'cold gag' normally confined to Sundays, and transported to a neighbouring estate, Denne Park, which still bears the same name. Here, after much deployment of patrols and outposts, designed to catch the umpire's eye while escaping that of the 'enemy', we charged forward and climbed a fence, during which we would undoubtedly have been massacred by any enfilading machine-gun, and then hurled ourselves flat before our final assault. This was less for tactical reasons than to give us an opportunity to fire off our remaining blank cartridges before the exercise ended. We were strictly warned against discharging them too close to the target for fear of inflicting real injury – 'Twenty yards, the length of a cricket pitch, is the safety limit', we were told – and in later years were issued with fire crackers instead, a poor substitute.

Another Field Day stands out in my mind as the most exhausting single day of my whole school career. Rain not being anticipated we had left our greatcoats behind and we were not issued with army style groundsheets which would for once have been useful. (In the army these did duty for raincoats and very unpleasant they were. Whenever old film is shown of the British Expeditionary Force marching up to the front in 1939 thus inadequately protected against the pouring rain my heart goes out to the soldiers concerned.) That morning we were soaked in an unforeseen storm, then issued with our heavy greatcoats just as the sun emerged at the start of a scorchingly hot afternoon. By the time Field Day ended we were soaked to the skin for a second time with sweat, but back at Peele A we had no time to rest for an extra parade had been called for the whole house to punish it for alleged slackness. So, after an exhausting day, we were marched up and down again, this time in Housey clothes, until those who had taken part in Field Day, by now barely able to stand, were allowed to go. I doubt if any prison in the country, much less any other school, ever imposed such unrelenting exertion upon its inmates; certainly serving in the army during the war I never experienced such a day.

I cannot recall anyone ever pointing out to us that the military knowledge we were supposed to be acquiring might soon be put to use in earnest. Our great target was a far more modest one than leading troops on the battlefield, that of passing Certificate A, the War Office equivalent of School Certificate, which more or less guaranteed a commission in the unlikely event of one wishing to join the army. More immediately, it opened up the prospect of becoming an NCO in the OTC, with corresponding privileges. As well as displaying the sort of topographical and basic tactical knowledge I have described, the candidate was, I believe, required to reach a minimum standard of marksmanship and it was the custom to practise for this with an unloaded rifle aimed at a paper target. I became accustomed to seeing some senior boy stretched on the floor of the dayroom and taking aim while a second gave him directions, rather as if he were a cricketer taking guard. Mostly, however, we did not take Corps very seriously and in Chapel the prayer about 'putting on the whole armour of light' would invariably be audibly rendered by someone as 'putting on the armoury light' and be good for a chuckle.

The summer holidays of 1939 coincided with an intensification of the nation's preparations for war. I was probably the most cheerful member of the family for I had felt Munich to be a disgrace, but my vigorous advocacy of the necessity of fighting was not well received at home. All of the family were as clear as I was that Germany had to be stopped, but my father, who had had to waste years of his life in the army in the first world war, my brother, of an age to be called up almost at once, and my elder sister, who had just got engaged to a young man in the same age group, all hoped, I believe, that somehow war might be avoided. Had I realised that it would drag on long enough to involve me – indeed I was destined to serve far longer than my father had done – I would no doubt have been less enthusiastic.

The international situation apart, this was not a bad time for my family. My father around this time again got a regular job, and one which suited him admirably, managing a photographic business in Northbrook Street, a mere hundred yards or so from his own former shop. According to family tradition the vacancy had occurred because the previous incumbent was an army reservist who had been recalled to the colours, and, as I can now appreciate, for my father to be working in his own profession but in a business owned and ultimately run by someone else, was an ideal arrangement, relieving him of the financial responsibility he was so ill equipped to carry.

Apart from a brief period when my sister's fiancé worked as his assistant, my father ran the business single-handed, so that he had to leave the shop unattended when needed in the studio above, and, for longer periods when filling outside commissions, usually weddings, still the backbone of any small town photographer's trade.

The business was known as Blandford's, after the owner, and adjoined a ladies' hairdresser in the next door shop, which also belonged to her. The two shared premises behind them and here was located the darkroom where my father, back in his natural element, spent much of his time. 'D and P', Developing and Printing the amateur film brought in by customers, was an important source of income. The shop also sold films and cameras and undertook minor repairs. These most commonly involved Box Brownies and the somewhat superior folding Kodaks, of which the front pulled out, bellows-like, before use.

Since the demise of my father's own business no dramatic changes had occurred in the photographic world. Although photographs were sometimes coloured by hand, and there were rumours of colour film, of which the quality was said to be poor, almost all photographs were still in black and white. To achieve a professional result involved using a plate camera, setting it up on a tripod behind which the photographer disappeared, under a black cloth. Focusing was a slow business, but eventually, after the warning 'Stay very still!' or, for children 'Watch the birdie!', the slide covering the plate was pulled out with a jerk, the cap covering the lens was whipped off, not to be replaced for several seconds, or in a suitably dark environment, minutes later.

Even in Newbury, however, new technology was making strides. A few years before, 'flash' photographs had required the use of a flat, open metal tray, loaded with aluminium powder, which was ignited by pulling a trigger to set off a percussion cap. I had always enjoyed seeing this process and admired the dexterity with which my father fired the flash at the same moment as he exposed the plate in the camera. Now he needed a flash-gun, resembling an electric torch held upright, with a reflector behind what looked like an ordinary electric light bulb but, when switched on, gave a momentarily blinding light. As soon as the bulb had been discarded and replaced by a new one the process could be repeated. I had previously only seen such up-to-date equipment in Hollywood films showing American news cameramen and it impressed me deeply.

The business did not provide a car and it was inconceivable that my father should own one, so his cumbersome equipment had to be loaded on to a bicycle, or carried by hand to and from buses and local trains just as when he had owned his own business. Indeed progress had made it even bulkier for at some stage in his years at Blandfords he acquired a set of mains-operated lights with high wattage bulbs, a feebler version of those used on film sets. On many occasions when I was at home I travelled with him to some village hall to perch on a chair holding one of these lights at arm's length as he recorded a silver wedding party or an amateur dramatic production.

I look back on these excursions with pleasure for several reasons. They helped to give me a love of the Berkshire and Hampshire countryside, so much of which, at least close to the town, has now been built over or despoiled. I was impressed by the great respect with which the customers who were having their wedding or family reunion recorded treated my father, who was given the deference due to an acknowledged expert. And, I realise, my father enjoyed our cooperation, for, our joint loathing of the Germans and the Conservatives apart, we had little in common. I suspect that, being increasingly conscious of the poverty to which the failure of his business had reduced us, and resentful of his refusal to recognise how unhappy I was at school, I all too rarely made him aware of the affection I felt for him.

To return to the summer holiday of 1939 I can remember only one incident and this I think may belong to a slightly earlier period. This was an afternoon my friends and I devoted to 'killing Hitler'. Between us we devised every possible means we could think of for executing the *Führer* in effigy, an old wooden doll or discarded puppet doing duty for the arch-enemy. He was, I recall, drowned in a bucket, stoned to death, shot by a popgun loaded with a lethal missile – in fact an old propelling pencil – defenestrated by being dropped from a height, hanged, and finally run down by the toy armoured car which, as I have described, I had acquired several Christmases before and now outgrown.

The events of that August must have left their mark on my imagination and memory for thirty years later I could still remember them in detail and civilian life during the war became the subject on which I was to specialise as a historian. For several months the government had been issuing information leaflets to every household and I became a great enthusiast for doing everything the authorities advised. I much regretted that, being in a 'safe' area, we did not qualify for an Anderson shelter in the garden, nor had we space in our undersized house to construct a refuge room as *The Protection of Your Home against Air Raids* advised, but whatever we could do we did. My elder sister's boyfriend, a tough young man – he was an Assistant Scoutmaster – in his early twenties, dug out a private shelter for us in the allotment facing our house, with Gordon and myself giving inexpert assistance. We duly installed an escape hatch at one end and constructed a roof from an old door covered with earth, though, lacking lateral support to hold up the bare walls, this would, I suspect, have proved a death trap had a bomb landed anywhere near to it. Inside we installed a home-made bench, and I confess to looking forward to the time when we might occupy this in earnest.

I must, I think, have made myself a nuisance in the house by trying to find other precautions to take. I cut up strips of paper and pasted them on the windows, supposedly to prevent their shattering dangerously in the event of blast and also amused myself setting up a totally unnecessary internal alarm system, with a bell push by an upstairs window, connected to an electric bell in the living room. (Dick in *Pigeon Post*, published in 1936, had inspired me to get this rusty old appliance to work, just as he had done; it had, I imagine come from my father's now long defunct shop.) My twin sister and three male friends were cajoled into taking part in frequent rehearsals, being required to dive under the table when the bell rang. Understandably, with no bombers yet in sight, they tired of this game more rapidly than I, manning the look-out post in a bedroom, did.

What was happening in the town outside, as war drew remorselessly nearer, was even more exciting. I was much struck by the physical transformation of several buildings, including two immediately adjoining St John's church, which we visited every Sunday, though as the crisis deepened I walked into town every day to keep track of the latest changes. The disused pub on another side of the same corner now came dramatically back into use as an auxiliary fire station, with intriguing looking trailer-pumps, towed behind vans, parked there. On the opposite side of St John's Road a former school, long derelict, became a First Aid and Decontamination Centre. I rejoiced, I fear, in the notices directing casualties to the appropriate entrance, the admission procedure being different for those merely wounded and those contaminated with gas. Everywhere there sprouted walls of sandbags, the great symbol of the time.

But it was gas, so mysterious and so sinister, and on which, since the lecture on it at school, I felt myself an authority, that lent real excitement to all these preparations. I delighted in recalling that (if my memory is still correct) phosgene smelt of musty hay and Lewisite of pear-drops, and in describing the appalling blisters Mustard Gas inflicted on unprotected skin. There can have been no family in the country better drilled than mine in the use, and care, of gas masks.

It was, I think, during this holiday that the Newbury ARP services held a full-scale exercise, which I watched avidly with other more sceptical spectators. A large chalked circle had been drawn in a road close to the canal – it was a quiet area not likely to cause much disruption to the traffic – to represent a crater blocking the road. Oddly, this had apparently been caused by a gas bomb, for the decontamination squad now appeared, encased in waterproof oilskins and heavy-duty, military style, respirators, much superior to the civilian version. I felt full of envy of the last item, little appreciating that, before the war was over, I would, as a soldier, be similarly equipped.

The war apart, this must have been for my mother the happiest time she had known for years. We were still hard-up, but to my father's regular income was now added a larger contribution from my elder sister, who had recently moved from her ill-paid, if agreeable, job in a newsagents to a somewhat better one as assistant in a shoe shop. It must have been around this time that, a proud moment, my mother felt able to tell our long term benefactor, mentioned earlier, that we could now manage without the weekly 5s [25p] that had kept us afloat during the worst years of the depression.

For my father, too, the prospect of war once accepted, this must have been a happier time than for years. He was again doing a job he enjoyed, and supporting his family, while when he got home from work on the sunny summer evenings of that last August of peace he was busy making an elaborate blackout for the living room; the other rooms, unlit or using only a feeble candle, could be adequately obscured with curtains. From somewhere he had found an old screen and this he successfully converted into a series of separate shutters, painting them, as recommended in Public Information Leaflet No 2, with a mixture of size and lamp black. They were held in place by a wire with hooks at either end and he was justly proud that when put in place for the first time, they fitted beautifully. We had the best blacked-out house on the estate and one much envied, to my secret delight, by Aunt Maud when she came to stay.

I was deeply stirred by the posters which, on 31 August, began to appear on walls all over the town, dramatically headed, 'By the King, a Proclamation', calling out those army and navy reservists not already summoned back to their units. Next afternoon, Friday 1 September 1939, the day Hitler invaded Poland, I stood opposite Newbury station watching the pitiful procession of evacuees filing off the trains towards the reception centre in the council school once attended by my elder brother and sister. Our house was far too small to accommodate an evacuee, but that evening we stared awe-struck at the silent wireless after instructions had been broadcast to re-tune it to new wartime frequencies.

Saturday was an anti-climax and our Sunday morning I have already described in the opening chapter of *How We Lived Then*. Testifying to the strangeness of the times, we invited in our radio-less neighbours, there being a tacit understanding on the estate that each family respected the privacy of those around it. Like the rest of the nation we listened to Neville Chamberlain's broadcast in silence and, still quiet and thoughtful, stood up for the national anthem at its end.

I was much impressed when my father received a pass from the new Ministry of Information authorising him to photograph military installations and bomb damage and giving him access to places denied to ordinary civilians. I have regretted ever since that I did not suggest to him he should make use of this to keep a pictorial record of the war as it affected his home town, as similarly placed photographers did in other places. My mother, a natural writer, would have been ideally placed to keep a day to day record of a housewife's war, but these possibilities did not occur to me and were lost.

We ate our Sunday dinner, on 3 September 1939, so far as I was concerned, with undiminished appetite and I can remember remarking at five o'clock in announcer-like tones, 'France is now at war with Germany!' This reminder was not well received by my elder sister or my elder brother, for obvious reasons, nor indeed by my twin sister, privately, she has since acknowledged, fearful of air raids. My parents made no comment on my cheerfulness, grateful perhaps that I was not yet displaying the first signs of end of the holidays gloom. The truth was that, apart from whole-heartedly supporting it, I thought the outbreak of war might lead to my return to school being postponed, but in this I was destined to be disappointed. Others I learned, when term began, as scheduled, in mid-September, had been far more unfortunate, with their holidays actually being cut short, as *The Blue* recorded that November:

> On August 26th, the school was opened for such boys as preferred to leave their homes in dangerous areas. Gradually about 300 came back and great activity by masters and boys saw some 20,000 sandbags filled and used to strengthen the Tube and Office.

---

[1] Taylor pp.444-5
[2] Allan p.103
[3] Mar 1997 p.69

29

STRANGE ALTERATIONS

Some strange alterations to the timetable loom ahead.

The Blue, *November 1939*

The war made little immediate difference to our daily life at school. We were already so regimented that there was little room for further restrictions and later, as will emerge, wartime conditions were to lead to a vast improvement of the Housey regime in many directions. The one major change that I did not appreciate, and was to remain for me the most unpleasant feature of the whole war, was the black-out. I now discovered, like many thousands of other people, that I suffered from 'black-out blindness', ie such poor night vision that I simply could not find my way about after dark. Though Double Summer Time, when it came, greatly minimised the nuisance by prolonging the hours of daylight, there were many weeks in both the Michaelmas and Lent terms when we had to walk up to afternoon school, and march into tea, in total darkness. Marching down the Avenue, unable to see the boys to my left or right, or ahead or behind me, was a nightmare and when, as happened if we were late, we were ordered to 'double', chaos could follow. It was easy to trip over the boy in front and then a dangerous pile-up could develop, especially since we were usually carrying one, or even two, jars of jam clutched to our chest and had no hand free. In some such accidents at shelter entrances in the cities unfortunate victims were stifled to death and I feel now that Housie was lucky to escape any major accident. The obvious remedy, that we should give up marching for the duration, at least after dark, never seems to have been contemplated.

Indoors, the black-out caused less problem, thanks to the efforts of the early returners, as described in the first wartime issue of *The Blue*, that November:

> A combination of beaver-board shutters, brown paper and blinds made the ground-floors of the houses inhabitable after sunset...The chapel, the laboratories and many classrooms will remain unused after sunset and some strange alterations to the timetable loom ahead.[1]

The new shutters, though very efficient at preventing the escape of light, had no means of ventilation and had to be taken down during the evening for a ten minute break to allow the windows to be opened. During this time we sat in total darkness, during which there was much shouting of insults, some surreptitious bullying and, I suspect, though I was still too young to be aware of this at the time, some furtive sex. Upstairs the monitor supervising each dormitory was encased in 'the box' consisting of blankets enclosing his table, the rest of these large rooms being lit by a few dim, heavily obscured bulbs, a meagre level of illumination which made it easy to engage in illicit activities.

Most classrooms were blacked-out, but to take the place of those that were not some late afternoon lessons were held in a dayroom and after a few weeks an ingenious new timetable was introduced to minimise the disruption to any particular subject, the worse sufferers being the science staff. Theory could, of course, be taught in the dayroom, though under difficulties, but practical demonstrations or experiments were impossible. Some unknown benefactor therefore invented the Eight Day Week, which replaced the normal six day school timetable. The first Day 1 was a Monday, and the first Day 2 a Tuesday, but, Sunday being ignored, the next Monday counted as Day 7 and Tuesday as Day 8, with a new week beginning again with Day 1 on Wednesday, Day 4 on Saturday and so on. It worked very well, so long as the boy responsible for changing the sign in the dayroom to remind the house what number day it was remembered to do so. If he failed or got the day wrong, confusion resulted, as a verse in the first wartime issue of the school literary magazine, *The Outlook*, confirmed:

> English and German
> And Science and Greek –
> But heaven knows when
> In the eight-day week.

The underground 'Tube' linking the houses provided a ready-made air raid shelter and it was now divided off by sandbag walls, to prevent a bomb in one section spreading destruction along its whole length. Each block of an 'A' and 'B' house was allocated one section, and though they were supposed to keep separate this did mean that we saw, as yet only during rehearsals, a little more of our contemporaries in our neighbouring house. Some of the small rooms, of mysterious purpose in peacetime, which opened off the Tube, were now converted into latrines – 'the lats.' – by the addition of chemical closets.

The Tube had at one time, it was said, included a spur running to the Infirmary which in 1924 had been bricked off and abandoned after the roof had collapsed, burying a boy, whose ghost was still said to haunt it.[2*] An even more gruesome story had him walled up like a miscreant nun, for some monstrous misdemeanour. Both tales were undoubtedly false, but the blocking off of the main Tube was a nuisance for we now had to run the whole distance from house to classroom or Dining Hall in wet weather and sometimes in the black-out, an experience I dreaded. Often we arrived drenched and had to hang our coats over the back of our desk to dry, which, with the windows sealed off, soon made the atmosphere damp and unpleasant.

In those first months of the 'phoney war' life for many families revolved round their wireless sets for news bulletins were now broadcast from early morning onwards and even at such unfamiliar times as 4 pm. In Peele A we remained reliant on the newspapers but word of major events would spread from more fortunate houses, and it must have been in this way that we learned of the first event that made a real impression on us, the sinking of the aircraft-carrier HMS *Courageous* on 17 September, with the loss of 500 men. 'So this was war!' I remember one classmate commenting dramatically in one of our first English essays that term. On the whole, however, the war affected the content of lessons very little, though I still recall with embarrassment beginning an exercise involving a description of the view from a window with a topical reference to black-out shutters, and, far worse, the would-be humorous piece I wrote, in the laboured style of the *Punch* of the period, entitled *ARP in Our Village*.

If we lacked up-to-date news our housemaster made sure we were not kept short of comment. Throughout the war he tried to keep up our martial spirits with talks in the dayroom, not wholly unwelcome as they were delivered in mid-prep. Noel's analysis of recent events was nothing if not partisan, since it invariably showed his native France in a favourable light, though he took an optimistic view of events generally. In this, of course, he was not alone. Just as in the first world war there were people who predicted that it would end by Christmas and I can recall one master reminding us that some politicians had been publicly hinting, 'It might all be over sooner than you think!'

It was in this same fatuous spirit that the government that winter risked making Russia our enemy as well as Germany, an act of stupendous folly that would surely have led to our destruction.[3] I was as hostile to Russia following her attack on Finland on 30 November, not realising she this act of aggression was designed to protect her flank, as everyone else, but this did not prevent my being subjected to some topical bullying for being allegedly 'pro-Red'. On the whole, however, this was a less miserable term than its predecessors for at least one of the worst bullies in the house had left. He had boasted of being a Fascist

---

* The account in *The Blue*, cited here, is unfortunately written in a facetious style which blends useful fact with obvious fiction. A proper history of this interesting architectural curiosity, now disused, is yet to be written.

and had singled out for persecution smaller boys known to be on the left politically. When I next saw his name it was in the Roll of Service which now began to appear in *The Blue*, for he had become an NCO in the army. Presumably he had changed his opinions but I felt sorry for his men.

Somehow the school had managed to squeeze in the members of the Westminster Choir School, but their arrival made very little impact upon us. They maintained their separate identity for lessons and, I think, games, and though they lived with us, two to a house, and took part in chapel services, their presence brought no change to our way of life. Being already in the country, evacuation had otherwise no effect upon us, though the motion carried by the Debating Society, by 34 to 28, 'That evacuation is a blessing in disguise,' showed that the revelations of scandalous social deprivation it had produced had not left us unmoved. I was now old enough to attend debates but have no recollection of this one and what I remember best of the first wartime term is my new form master, MR, later the Rev. Michael, Warneford-Brown, whom *The Blue*[4] and the school staff list[5] also variously rendered as Brown and Warneford Brown. 'Warny-B', as we nicknamed him, was a young man still in his early twenties who had arrived straight from Oxford and he was one of the masters who had a real influence upon me. He arrived uncontaminated by the usual pedagogic cynicism, bursting with enthusiasm, with long, somewhat uncoordinated limbs, a permanent smile, pink complexion and bright red hair, the subject of many schoolboy jokes. At first we thought him somewhat odd and played him up but he speedily asserted an unobtrusive authority and gained our warm respect. In *First Bloom*, where I prematurely ordained him as the Rev. Templemore, I tried to convey the impression he had made on us:

> The Rev. Templemore was soon a school personality, with his thick, flowing, usually disordered hair, a nose long and crudely designed, and a mouth open in an affable smile at the world's agreeableness. His appearance was sufficient to create a disturbance at any school function, whether it was a concert, a lecture, or one of the rare addresses from the headmaster. When the first shock of surprise had worn off, Middlestone soon began to love its 'Temple' and his sayings were circulated with an enthusiasm out of all proportion to their value. It was reported that he had threatened to report a boy to 'the Usher', and had sat in bemused bewilderment at the howl of laughter which followed.[*] On another occasion his chair suddenly collapsed beneath him, and the class, uncertain whether to laugh or sympathise, was treated to the spectacle of seeing a huge shock of red hair, even more disordered than usual, followed by a great mouth smiling benevolently at a

---

[*] The mistake was understandable but seemed to us irresistibly funny. Usher was, as I have mentioned earlier, the school sergeant's surname.

world which could provide so pleasant a surprise in the dull routine of existence, rising Venus-like from behind the desk.

'Warny-B.' had arrived at Housey brimming with energy and full of teaching ideas already commonplace in other schools but still viewed with suspicion at Christ's Hospital. One of them was that we should try to perform Shakespeare rather than merely read him, and my first experience of this technique impressed me so much that I recorded it in *First Bloom:*

> On one celebrated occasion he set three burly members of the form dancing, book in hand, round the waste-paper basket in the middle of the form-room floor, in an effort to render the first scene of *Macbeth* more vivid. He seemed unaware that the spectacle of three of its members solemnly prancing round an overflowing waste-paper basket chanting in tones which they believed to be demonic 'Fair is foul and foul is fair!' was one likely to affect the sobriety of even the gravest form. But Templemore realised the danger and for a short time was excessively severe with his classes...for the owners of the classrooms beneath complained no less of the noise of hilarity than of the noise of feet and, with the coming of the summer term, the Upper Fourth commenced to study *She Stoops to Conquer.*

This, too, we performed, though on stage in Big School and without an audience, in what was normally free time, but Warneford-Brown's enthusiasm made even the dullest boys – and there were few in this 'A' stream class – eager to participate and he was even more successful in arousing interest in another of his innovations, a form magazine. We spent many periods discussing its contents, with 'Warny-B' tactfully suggesting that boys with no literary aptitude might instead contribute jokes. Some of these were so familiar that we groaned when we heard them. ('An optimist sees a silver lining in a cloud of mustard gas' was one topical but unoriginal suggestion.) I was deputed to write a political article and planned a detailed indictment of the Chamberlain government, but events overtook me. By the time the contents of 'The UF' – ie Upper Fourth – 'Magazine' were complete it was the summer of 1940, the war had started in earnest, and the school office, which was to have provided typing and duplicating facilities, could reasonably plead more urgent commitments. I doubt if the magazine would have seen the light of day in any case, since it was the sort of inter-house activity frowned on by the school 'Old Guard', and another of 'Warny-B's' schemes also came to nothing, the proposal that we should fill in some of the gaps in our knowledge of English literature by being set a holiday task. Although participation in some form of camp was encouraged, and indeed became almost compulsory, Housie had no tradition of setting school work for the holidays, and Noel Sergent professed himself opposed to the idea on principle, apparently regarding it as un-English, or conceivably un-French. At all events the somewhat impertinent entry proposed for the abortive form magazine never saw the light of day: 'There is no truth in the rumour that the U F A (Upper Fourth A) are to do holiday work.'

Newbury, when I returned to it at the end of term, seemed less affected by the war than it had been in September. The fighting had still not started, there had been no air raids and many of the evacuees had gone home. The only rationing so far introduced, of petrol, did not affect us or anyone we knew, and food rationing, though threatened, had not yet begun. Our patriotism remained unwavering but we were beginning to wonder what all the fuss had been about, especially as the most militant action so far undertaken by the government had been to scatter leaflets over Germany. I can recall my mother, the kindliest of persons, expressing regret that we were dropping paper, not bombs. The official line of trying to distinguish between an evil Nazi minority and a basically decent, if easily led, mass of Germans made no appeal to us. My father considered the whole lot unredeemably militaristic, who if they had not chosen Hitler would have found some other bloodthirsty leader, a view I entirely shared, while my mother's attitude was shaped by her concern for her family. She told me later that among the three most painful occasions in her life had been receiving back a parcel of his civilian clothes when my father joined the army in 1916, and again when my brother and I joined up successively in 1940 and 1944. Here we were at last for the first time since my birth reasonably settled at school or in work and in a house, however small, we could afford, and now all this was to be wrecked thanks to the Germans' refusal to live in peace. Quietly, and so far as a decent, church-going Mothers' Union member could, she hated them, as did all of us.

Although my brother's impending call-up somewhat overshadowed it Christmas 1939 was the happiest I could remember. It was, I believe, this year that I received the most handsome present of my whole childhood, a microscope set, which my father was able to order at trade price, and which joined a growing collection of chemical equipment deployed in our bathroom, on the shelves built by my father when he was forced to use it as a darkroom. I now anticipated becoming a scientist, partly because this seemed appropriate to wartime, when we were constantly being told that science held the key to victory, partly because, as I have described, Housie had offered me no real alternative, but also because my closest Newbury friend, Keith, destined to gain a doctorate of science and to become a university professor, influenced me in that direction. Both in appearance and temperament, above all in his practicality, he much more closely resembled Dick of the Arthur Ransome stories than I did. Under Keith's direction, we combed Greenham Common on the look out for brush fires, just like the Swallows in *Pigeon Post*, studied the level of water in the locks of the canal, for which Keith was already an enthusiast, and produced a more scientific version of the game of Pooh Sticks, though I had then never heard the name, not merely floating sticks beneath

Newtown Bridge but trying to measure their speed. We also surveyed imaginary new roads with home-made chain and my sister's Girl Guide compass, as close as we could get to my heroes' exploits in *Secret Water*, published that year.

I had enjoyed my first term as a science specialist, due in part to the excellent teaching; the Science School carried none of the deadbeat 'passengers' found in other departments. More than the actual subject, however, it was the idea of science that appealed to me at this time. Unlike English it sought firm answers and dealt with the real world, with no place for fantasy, which I despised; in contrast to both the classics and modern languages, it functioned by reliable rules, without incessant and frustrating exceptions. I dreamed of making some great discovery that would immortalise me and, incidentally, make those who had given me such a hard time at Housie look thoroughly foolish.

The Lent Term of 1940 stands out in my memory because of the snow. This was one of the most severe winters of the century and it was easy for both sides to forget that they were at war with the mere struggle to keep warm uniting both of the still inactive armies. At Housie, morning after chilly morning, the 'No PT' bell rang out its welcome message over the snow-covered Quadrangle and Avenue and afternoon followed afternoon in which no games could be played on the frozen pitches. We were sent out instead to indulge in quasi-military exercises, good-natured affairs in which boys showed off their knowledge of elementary tactics learned in the OTC and mustered us into sections and patrols to ambush each other with snowballs. Occasionally there was PT in the dayroom in the afternoon, but mostly this was a blissful interlude from rugger, during which, with the opposing armies likewise paralysed by snow, the war seemed suspended. One unpleasant reminder of the summer to come intruded itself, for instead of water-carrying to keep the cricket pitch green we were put to staggering out into a swept portion of the asphalt with the same wash basins full of hot water, which, it was claimed, would freeze more thoroughly than cold, and this was tipped down to form a massive slide. Anyone stepping on to it in the black-out was likely to suffer a nasty surprise, if nothing worse, but I was reconciled to the activity with memories of Greyfriars stories in which Billy Bunter had suffered a similar fate.

The Blue for March 1940 looked back on this, for me, gloriously games-free term from a somewhat different perspective:

> Snow-bound rugger pitches. Pitches thawed and flooded; pitches wind-dried but frozen. Cup-ties postponed and abandoned; seven-a-sides struggling, only to be stifled; the steeplechase...dropped; one fine day of sports training and again the snow; even the fives-courts fickle; PT the exception rather than the rule...Against this frustration optimism is the only defence.

The author of the Peele A House Notes also, for once, had no physical triumphs to record:

> We could describe our activities this term in one word, but we prefer to say that Heaven has hampered our athleticism with snow – and it's still snowing!

But the war was not totally eclipsed by the weather for now the first of a long procession of Old Blues on leave from the forces began to appear in the dayrooms they had so recently left. 'We had a glimpse of brilliant uniform,' noted the Peele A House Notes that term, 'and...a short while ago...we saw Hatten, Lawrance and Foxton all together', names which have already appeared, or will soon appear, in this narrative. Other new items mentioned what was to become a regular feature of almost every issue henceforward, the departure of some young member of staff for the forces, or the return from retirement of some elderly master, like the legendary 'Dido' Hyde who took so poor a view of my handwriting.

The first stirrings of the great movement towards social equality which the war was to produce were evidently being felt even at Housie, that innately conservative society. In February 1940 the Debating Society considered the motion, 'That if we are to build a better England the public and preparatory school systems must go.' This was a theme which was to fascinate me for years and the mover was the Head of History, DS Roberts, whom I have already mentioned for his anti-Munich views. The result, predictably, was a victory for the status quo, but by a surprisingly narrow margin, of 32 votes to 26. *The Blue* considered however that 'the weight of oratory seemed to lie with the proposers, who seemed, after a masterly summing up by Mr Roberts, to have won the day.'

---

[1] Nov 1939 p.2
[2] Apr 1967 p.138
[3] Taylor p.469 footnote
[4] Nov 1940 p.2 & Jun 1941 p.126
[5] CH *Alphabetical List*, 1942

30

MORE BORING THAN GLORIOUS

We were warned that the LDV would be more boring than glorious.

The Blue, *July 1940*

On Tuesday 9 April 1940 the Germans invaded Norway and Denmark. I have no recollection of hearing the news, which may have arrived during the holidays, but, like my schoolmates, and the whole country, expected our army to emerge victorious from this long awaited encounter with the enemy on land. We were at first incredulous, then stunned, as a series of defeats followed, with heavy losses in ships, men, aircraft and, above all, prestige. Disillusionment with the government, which had been consistently wrong about Hitler before the war and had now once again under-estimated him, was bitter and universal. I well recall hearing a former junior housemaster, who had returned to visit us after a brief excursion to Norway, describing in the dayroom the fiasco of the campaign, with guns being landed with the wrong calibre ammunition.

The real start of the war in the west, the German attack on France and the Low Countries, on Friday 10 May 1940, coincided with the climax of the great inquest in Parliament on the government's catastrophic failure. As it happened, my mother was in Downing Street, then open to the public, that day, taken to London as a treat by my brother, before he was called-up. After he had pointed out No 10 to her she was searching in her handbag when she found her wrist gripped by a policeman, who supposed her to be reaching for a missile. That such a respectable middle-aged woman should have been suspected of such an intention bore witness to the tension of the time, and her narrow escape from arrest became a cherished family joke.

There was, however, nothing remotely humorous about the events of the next few weeks. Our housemaster's appearances during prep were no longer received with ill-concealed derision, since, with the only wireless in the building, he had access to the latest news, and I can remember the gravity with which he informed us that the Germans had captured Abbeville, on 20 May. The name meant nothing to us, but he was right to see the event as significant, for it meant the

Germans had reached the coast, at the mouth of the Somme, and that the British army was now encircled, with its back to the sea.

We had, of course, been denied the chance to hear the classic broadcast by Sir Anthony Eden (later Lord Avon), on 14 May, calling into existence the Local Defence Volunteers, who ten weeks later became the Home Guard. The school, however, reacted as it had always done, and was to do throughout the war, ignoring inconvenient niceties about volunteering or legal rights, something that, in the school's opinion, you surrendered when you put on your school uniform. The Housey LDV was no more a truly volunteer organisation than the Corps, though no doubt – as was not the case for the Corps – everyone eligible would readily have come forward of their own free will. In fact all boys aged 17 and upwards were simply enrolled *en masse* in 1940 and anyone who reached that age thereafter was curtly informed he had joined without any nonsense about being invited to do so. The school unit might indeed have been more use than most of those formed at the time, for all the boys concerned had at least had some elementary military training and a uniform, even if it did belong to the first world war. More valuable still, the OTC possessed that most rare and valuable of articles at that dark time, rifles, though it was not long before most of them were removed to arm other LDVs who needed them even more.

The Blue, having given a whole page to a report of a cricket match against St John's Leatherhead, dismissed the preparation for the sterner fixture against the Germans in a few lines:

> Several masters and most of the boys who are of age are engaged in Local Defence work; and thanks to the energy of the OTC officers many masters and neighbouring villagers are brushing up their musketry to deal with possible parachutists.[1]

The account which I gave in *First Bloom* is fuller and more dramatic and reveals that, with the school bell silenced along with others – church bells were now to be used as an invasion warning – the buglers of the band, whose finest hour had hitherto been sounding the Last Post on Armistice Day, now had an even sterner duty:

> One summer evening towards the end of the term James had gone to bed early. A practice of the LDV was being held and, as a bugle was heard in the distance, blown if truth were told a little uncertainly by a member of the school band, the older boys emerged from the beds in which they had been feigning sleep and poured off, clad in hastily snatched garments, towards the OTC armoury. James, looking from the window, reflected that the crowd of men now rushing on foot or bicycle towards the storehouse of the rifles was typical of the spirit that was abroad. Masters, who had believed that their fighting days were long past, boys, young and adventurous but thinking,

perhaps, of forgotten essays and neglected proses, groundsmen and servants of the Estate – all surging in a democratic throng, united in a common purpose, to arms.

For those of us too young for the LDV, life, and even School Certificate and school exams, continued as usual, while the 17 and 18 year olds who formed the Housey company of the new force faced the trials of Higher Certificate and forthcoming Oxford and Cambridge scholarship competitions, as usual. But there were diversions, as *The Blue* recorded in that month of destiny, June 1940:

> Two barriers of various obstacles have been erected, one on the south side of the Mile and one across Big Side, to discourage hostile aircraft from landing.[2]

These pyramids of planks were designed to rip the wing off any enemy glider or troop-carrier, but for the moment did nothing more destructive than stop hard-hit cricket balls in mid-flight, so that a new local rule was introduced counting such a collision as a four-run boundary.

The playing fields themselves were, to my disappointment, considered sacred and with one exception, to be mentioned later, managed to escape the 'Dig for Victory' campaign to which truly patriotic citizens were sacrificing their lawns and flower beds. Housie was, however, always happy to offer its pupils' labour, quite properly, to the war effort and 'Farm' now became a more frequent and respected activity. 'There is...a party of thirty or forty boys digging on the Science Farm...three or four days a week...,' *The Blue* recorded in June. 'We fully expect to have calls made on us for harvesting during the summer holiday.'[3]

Already the war was bringing a whole series of improvements to our lives. A marked enhancement of our diet, as I shall describe later, followed the application to the school of the food rationing scales laid down by the Ministry of Food, and it was now becoming easier to escape outside the ring fence. Parties of boys were sent to help widen the nearest water barrier, the River Arun, part of the overall plan to prevent German tanks roaming at will about the countryside which I have described in my book *Island Fortress*, and it was now that a Peele B friend, and future house-captain, first caught his seniors' eye when he suggested that, if arms were short, they should paint themselves with woad like Ancient Britons and line the water's edge to scare off the enemy. This was indeed, though I could not know it then, to be a fruitful period for me personally for it aroused the interest in contemporary events that many years later was to inspire a number of books including *The Real Dad's Army*, on the Home Guard, and *If Britain Had Fallen*, on the whole summer of 1940.

As I have stressed in my first book about wartime life, *How We Lived Then*, although the war resulted in many deprivations for children it had great compensations, not least that it was an interesting time to be young. At Christ's Hospital, as I have mentioned elsewhere, it in many ways improved our lives, though one loss in the summer of 1940 was the usual Whole Holiday, which shrank, I believe, to a mere half day to be spent within the grounds. It was easier to keep us in, however, than to keep the enemy out and I vividly recall one summer morning, though it may conceivably have been in a later year, when a German bomber suddenly appeared very low over the middle of the Avenue in the post morning school period we called Twelve-fifteen. We eagerly stood and identified it, as, I think, a Junkers 88, before it disappeared as inexplicably as it had arrived. That dinner time a message was passed down from boy to boy 'Don't write home about it!', but I doubt if it was heeded and in any case there was no secret about the Germans making exploratory flights over Sussex. In retrospect I think we were lucky not to have been attacked, for the house blocks and Quadrangle, with boys marching between them, must from the air have resembled a barracks. Marching could have been scrapped as a precaution for the duration but was too well entrenched as a tradition to be abandoned.

My great delight at this time was, like many of my age group, aircraft spotting and my pocket money largely went on the illustrated booklets, costing from 6d [2.5p], which showed the silhouettes of both British and German types currently flying. German aircraft appeared all too rarely for my taste – I saw only another two or three, flying-bombs apart, during the whole war – but a reminder of the nearness of the Continent came during the Dunkirk evacuation when we could clearly hear explosions from the embattled port 90 miles [144km] away, just as people in London occasionally heard the barrage on the Western Front during the first world war.

We were in no danger of forgetting the danger the nation was in. Night after night Noel Sergent appeared, increasingly grim-faced, to report on the deteriorating situation as reported by the BBC. One evening his usual cough ushered in the news that the new French prime minister, Paul Reynaud, had declared that 'only a miracle can save France'. This left us unmoved for, justly or unjustly, we felt that our supposedly invincible ally had let us down and deserved its fate. A little later Noel was back. He did not, he said, want us to go to bed despondent for it now appeared that Reynaud had also said that he believed in miracles.

If so, he was destined to be disappointed and so grim had the news now become that a little later, for the only time in the whole of my seven years at school, a wireless was brought into the dayroom for us to hear it for ourselves. The occasion was the account of the terms imposed upon France by the Germans, so must have been on or around 17 June. Our housemaster had discovered that one boy had, against all the odds, managed to build and store a wireless set of his own, which Noel described as 'the Bailey apparatus', naming its constructor, a future mathematics grecian, and I can well remember how we gathered in the sunlit dayroom round this curious looking collection of valves and wires on a plain wooden base. We were silent as the anouncer's voice recounted the details of our beaten ally's humiliation, and finally summed up: 'They amount, in a word, to the complete capitulation of France.'

It must, I now realise, have been a bitter moment for Noel, hearing in a foreign country of his homeland's total surrender to the hated Boche, but I fear we did not appreciate this at the time. He was the only Frenchman most of us had ever met, he had not impressed us and we were inclined to feel that what had happened to the French army and government proved that we had been right about France all along. The universal reaction was – including, had we known it, that of King George VI, as he confided to his mother on 27 June[4] – that we were better off without allies. Although Churchill himself has since revealed that he considered whether it might not be his duty to make peace with Hitler, such a possibility, I believe, never entered the head of any boy at Housie, or indeed that of any of my fellow citizens. At 14 and a half I could see well enough that we were losing the war but that we might ultimately be beaten seemed inconceivable.

The real world was now breaking in upon the play-acting and make-believe of our military training. By a pleasing irony one of the first victims was the OTC, as the *OTC Notes* in the July 1940 *Blue* sadly recorded:

> The OTC can claim to have helped towards winning the war, as a cancelled camp and General Inspection bear witness to the fact that we have caused the powers that be as little trouble as possible, and released several officers for more important duties. Meanwhile we have tried to carry on our usual work efficiently and keenly.[5]

Claiming to cause little trouble seemed a sad decline from the days of the Corps' greatest glory, but the truth was it had now been upstaged by an upstart new body:

> A more direct contribution to the war-effort has been made through the medium of the LDV, in which we have formed a section, including most of the senior NCOs and cadets together with masters and employees from the Estate, under the command of the Headmaster. On the strength of this we have added an occasional night operation for members of the LDV to our normal OTC training, and have had additional practice in the message sending and weapon training...We were warned that the LDV would be more boring than glorious, but Miss Stevenson's [the Lady Superintendent's] rations mellow the inner man, and in the Classical Grecians' room we sleep and dream of Bacchic orgies.

It was clearly convenient that Major Flecker, as he later became, should be appointed commanding officer of the new unit. He had served on the Western Front in the first world war, and could hardly be expected to take orders from an assistant master. He remained, however, Headmaster of Christ's Hospital first and only second CO of the LDV. The boys in Coleridge, opposite his house, were delighted when one evening he rushed from it 'to give the Canadian officer leading a convoy down the Avenue a most almighty rocket', as one remembers.[6] Sussex might be threatened by invasion but the defending forces were not, it was made very clear to them, to make use for that purpose of the road that ran through Christ's Hospital.

The LDV rapidly became yet another claim on the older boys' time, but the younger ones, like myself, were, I fear less concerned about its self-evident unreadiness to face the German army in the field than the fear that if the invasion started before the end of term the summer holidays might be postponed. We need not have worried. As sunlit week followed sunlit week and the Channel offered a smooth and tranquil surface to the would-be invader, such as earlier generations of enemies had awaited in vain, the Germans still failed to set sail.

I can recall a lively correspondence with my father that summer, for both my parents wrote to me every Friday and I replied each Sunday, a practice continued, so far as my mother was concerned, until her death in 1966. My mother's letters were mainly, but not exclusively, concerned with domestic matters; my father and I tended to discuss current events. That summer we were totally at one in our hatred of the Germans and in our desire to see the new government mobilise the whole nation against them, without allowing the rich and idle to escape their share of the burden. My father had come to despise the party he had so long supported, while I remember expressing the hope that trenches would be dug across the lawns of stately homes, as well as in the public parks, though feeling little confidence that this would happen.

During the summer holidays all the Housey boys in Newbury were approached about forming a work party to fill sandbags at a local school, the *Newbury Weekly News*, whose chief reporter had two sons at Housie, describing those who responded as 'the flower of the nation's youth'. I was, I must confess, not among them. I would have been happy to help but the prospect of being even in the holidays among boys who had known me at school, with all the reminders such a situation would involve, and perhaps even some out of term bullying, was not to be borne. My mother put down my refusal to indolence or lack of patriotism, a heavy burden to bear, but, for all her intelligence, she always failed to understand how deeply unhappy I was at school.

Although there were, I believe, a few warnings that summer, they soon, in Newbury as elsewhere, tended to be ignored. Only on 7 September 1940 did everyone begin to take air raids more seriously with the start of the blitz, which seemed likely to be the prelude to invasion. I was almost prepared to forgive the Germans for threatening to land for around the end of August a letter arrived from school suggesting that parents who lived in districts comfortably removed from the coast, like Berkshire, might prefer for the moment to keep their sons at home. My parents kept this possibility from me until they had decided to agree to it, and the moment when I learned my return to school had been indefinitely postponed was one of the happiest of my life. I recall hearing my father dictating his reply to my elder sister's fiancé, who had brought in his typewriter for the purpose, and in the blissful few weeks that followed this machine became my favourite source of recreation. Plans for me to receive tuition from my friend Keith's father, a schoolmaster, came to nothing and I was able to fill my days listening to the radio and at last following the war in detail, which it had been impossible to do at school.

Much of the news at the time concerned the effects of the German air raids on Britain, which were played down, though at the same time much – too much, we now know – was made of the RAF's destruction of enemy aircraft. Meanwhile the BBC carried constant reports of British raids on Germany, the importance of which was even more greatly exaggerated. For me, however, this was the pleasantest time of the war, indeed of my whole schooldays. Following my brother's departure – he had joined the RAF on 15 May – I had the use of his bicycle and, cycling round the countryside during the long hours of daylight, which later in the war, with permanent Summer Time in force and Double Summer Time added for much of the year, became even longer, I had ample opportunity to observe how a peaceful market town was preparing to become a battlefield. I did not appreciate at the time how Newbury occupied a key strategic position, just as it had in the Civil War three centuries earlier, with the road from Southampton and the coast joining at the Broadway the main east to west route between London and Bristol. The Kennet and Avon Canal, running right through the centre of the town, was, as I now understand, part of the so-called GHQ line behind which the defending commander planned to make his final stand. Crossing the canal was the water bridge, and this, a little later as more artillery became available, was commanded by an anti-tank gun, permanently mounted on a specially built base, erected in the middle of Northbrook Street just outside my father's shop. During air raids the crew would man machine-guns pointed skywards, a most impressive sight. Every bit of the town had its interest to offer, however, and I remember particularly the tree trunk barrier mounted on a metal pivot at one end and on a large wheel at the other, which was installed half way down the hill leading down into the town from our estate. On one side it was overlooked by a firing aperture cut into a garden wall, on the other by a machine-gun position set up behind sandbags in the upper window of a large house to the right of the road. I suspect that at this time the weapons for all these defensive points were still lacking, but there was no lack of preparations to be seen, and at crossroads near many of the villages I visited by bicycle sandbag strong points, often of great complexity, blossomed like those familiar to me from first world war photographs. Though to my disappointment Newbury escaped the ringing of the church bells in the false invasion alarm of 7 September – an occasion on which I drew in several subsequent books and which formed the subject of my first radio programme about the war – one of our neighbours was called out and I became more zealous than ever in my reconnaissances, assessing fields of fire and dead ground around the local pillboxes with all the confidence of a year's experience in the OTC.

It must have been early in October that the school decided that invasion was unlikely and, having suggested to parents that they should keep their sons at home, now, in its arbitrary way, wrote a peremptory letter announcing that any who were not promptly sent back would be deemed to have left. Nothing would have pleased me more; apart from my general dislike of my school I had realised that summer that it was only at home that I could follow, even in a way, enjoy the war. However the threat was enough for my father and so four weeks or so late, I was taken back to school, for perhaps suspecting that if left to myself I might, as on a previous occasion, never get there, my father insisted on delivering me in person.

I well remember my sense of dismay as I entered the house and heard someone call out in tones of total contempt: 'The weed's back!' This was my welcome as in October 1940, now approaching my fifteenth birthday, I began my fifth year at the boarding school I hated.

---

[1] Jun 1940 p.133
[2] Jun 1940 p.134
[3] Jun 1940 p.134
[4] Wheeler-Bennett p.460
[5] Jul 1940 p.172
[6] Mar 1991 p.54

31

CARRYING ON

Air raids have naturally influenced our life this term…We are doing our best…to carry on the usual activities of the School.

The Blue, *November 1940*

The school to which I returned, belatedly and unwillingly, in October 1940, was in many respects different from the one I had left in July. The war had taken its toll of some traditional holiday activities. 'OTC camp was, of course, impossible,' lamented the first edition of *The Blue* that Michaelmas Term. 'The Scouts Camp had to be reluctantly abandoned.' Meanwhile what would now be called 'community service' had begun. 'Mr Warneford-Brown took a few helpers to a medical mission to the Kentish hop-fields.' To look forward a little, this excellent master, whose qualities I have already described, was to suffer a permanent injury thanks to the war, being shot in the arm by an over-zealous sentry while serving as a naval chaplain.

This was the legendary winter of the blitz, which had begun on 7 September and was to continue until the following May. Night after night the German bombers droned overhead on their way to and from the capital. Happily only a couple of small bombs were dropped on the school grounds and these in a distant corner, close to the bird sanctuary, doing no damage. Housie was later to suffer from a flying-bomb, as I shall describe, but this was not to occur until after I had left.

That autumn and winter of 1940 the school, if not actually in the front line, was not far away from it and *The Blue* for November struck the authentic 'Britain can take it' note:

> Air raids have naturally influenced our life this term. Suffice it to say, however, that we are doing our best, consistently with a reasonable measure of security, to carry on the usual activities of the school. The timetable suffers wonderful changes; films have to be seen by boys in small batches in the Science Lecture Theatre; football games are subject to other whistles than the referees'; chapel and meals are sometimes brought to an untimely end; but the school goes on. [1]

At first the whole school had slept underground, in the tube, which, like its London namesake, now really came into its own. By the time I got back the windows of the lower, normally the senior, dormitory, had been protected and the whole house slept there, in cramped but reasonable comfort, unless the Home Guard watcher posted on the chapel tower sounded the 'Imminent Danger' alarm and everyone was roused to file sleepily downstairs to the tube. In fact most nights we remained undisturbed, planes clearly making for London being ignored, and the Peele A *House Notes* in the December *Blue* took a philosophic view. 'Now that we are encaged in wire netting,' observed the writer, 'We are allowed the doubtful privilege of sleeping 43 to a bedroom, but at least we have real beds.'

For boys with homes in London it must have been, as I hardly appreciated then, a worrying time and *The Blue* carried that November its first 'Bomb story', typical of the period:

> TR Cloke, Maine B 1926-32, has had the misfortune to have his house totally destroyed by a bomb, and ten days later his father's house, to which he and his wife moved, was also damaged...He is now waiting to be called up for training as an RAF pilot and doubtless hopes to return good measure for the loss he has sustained.

The obituary section the following month carried its first report of a civilian Old Blue, 'killed by enemy action at Deptford Central Library while engaged on work connected with public assistance', a worthy but not obviously heroic end. More in the Housey tradition was the death of a former member of my house who, having shot down five enemy aircraft in 21 sorties 'during the Dunkirk operations' as air-gunner in a Defiant, an astonishing feat considering the inadequacy of this two-seater fighter which was later withdrawn, had gone on to give his life at the height of the Battle of Britain:

> His untimely end came during a battle with a large force of Messerschmitts over Kent towards the end of August, in the course of which two of the enemy met their doom at his hands before his own machine was hit and crashed. Worthily indeed did he display the traditions and spirit of Housie to the end. [2]

That month *The Blue* carried for the first time a new, but henceforward regular, item, *News from the Forces* and obituaries of Old Blues killed in action or on active service, ie of accidents or disease while in uniform, took up an increasing amount of space. Sadly, from the beginning of 1942 *The Blue* was published only once a term instead of twice, and each issue was also reduced in size, thanks to paper rationing, so that little space was left to describe the impact of the war on the school's daily routine.

Every few weeks the headmaster would mount the pulpit during evensong to read out the latest additions to the Roll of Honour, a custom begun during the first world war.[*] HLO Flecker, standing in the pulpit in his black gown and red hood, made a striking figure, and the ceremony was particularly moving during the winter, when, despite Double Summer Time and the re-scheduling of services, it seemed always to be dark, or getting dark, as he rose to his feet and intoned solemnly the introductory text: 'Greater love hath no man than this that a man lay down his life for his friends.' Here was an archetypal Housey text, combining the Christian, and public school, theme of sacrifice with our private requirement to 'Love the brotherhood'. At these words we got to our feet, while the Head read out a list of those recently killed, with, just as at the Leaving Service, Christian name as well as surname, but now with rank and service added. The most typical of these descriptions were 'Flying Officer', or sometimes, 'Pilot Officer', 'Royal Air Force Volunteer Reserve' and I was struck by how few by comparison, just as in the lists in *The Blue*, were the casualties from the Army and Navy, indeed in the list published in November 1940 no recent naval deaths were recorded, while the only soldier mentioned had become a prisoner of war. By contrast five Old Blue airmen had recently lost their lives. These proportions were to change somewhat with the launching of new campaigns on land, but, equally, the expansion of the bombing offensive was to result in more RAF deaths and it was clearly this service which suffered first and most.

Occasionally a civilian was mentioned, like one who, while waiting to enter theological college, had volunteered to escort children being evacuated to Canada on the ill-fated *City of Benares*, which was torpedoed around 10 pm on 17 September 1940, with the loss of 73 children and many adults, a tragedy which effectively ended such transatlantic voyages. *The Blue* that November told the story of Michael Rennie, who had left Thornton A the term before I entered Housie, recounting how he 'dived in again and again' to rescue drowning children. When rescue finally came in sight nearly 24 hours later he 'collapsed and fell...dead into the water which filled the water-logged lifeboat. His last words were; "Hurrah! Here comes the destroyer. Thank God."' [3] I remember being deeply moved by this story and have heard other Old Blues describe reacting similarly to the heroism of another Old Blue, a doctor on a destroyer sunk while escorting a convoy to Russia in February 1944, though this occurred after I had left. *The Blue*, much later, told the story of this latter day Captain Oates:

---

[*] See Chapter 16.

Having managed to climb onto one of the few Carley floats to have come through the sinking, he set about hauling others aboard. The float soon became overcrowded. Remarking almost casually: 'There's not enough room for us all,' the doctor slipped over the side into the sea and was never seen again. [4]

The Christmas holidays of 1940 arrived while the war was at its bleakest and the blitz at its height. I can remember standing outside our house in Newbury one night – it must have been Sunday 29 December 1940 – and seeing the red glow in the distance where the City of London had been set ablaze, all of 60 miles [96 km] away. I did not then know that the whole area where Christ's Hospital, Newgate Street, had stood for so many centuries was at the heart of the blaze and that, if it had not moved 38 years before, it would now have become mere rubble and ashes.

I was now just 15, as patriotic as the next boy, if not rather more so since I devoted to following the war the energy some others dissipated on sport. During the summer it had been Dunkirk which had thrilled us and inspired me to write a poem of which I can now remember only one line, commended by 'Warny-B':

'Working in a tumult of devastating sound'.

By the time we got back to school it had been the turn of Fighter Command and I again recall a single line, this time with embarrassment, of the verses I wrote in praise of its pilots:

'winging their way to victory up the sky'.

Now, in that dismal winter of 1940 to 1941, only Bomber Command seemed to be hitting back at Germany, although we now know the effect of its raids was vastly exaggerated. At the time, however, the impression given by the headlines was that the enemy was being so heavily pounded he must soon surrender and the names of the regular targets became as familiar to me and my Newbury friends as those of local villages. 'The marshalling yards at Hamm,' we would joke, as we crossed the railway bridge beside the modest sidings of Newbury station. What I remember best, however, about that Christmas was the latest France Belk pantomime mounted at the Corn Exchange, in defiance of the black-out and the risk, if not of bombs, at least of air raid warnings. The chorus contained many girls of my own age and if not yet positively disturbed by their proximity to me in the wings as they waited to go on, I was certainly aware of it.

Back at school, our nights were still being governed by the *Luftwaffe* as the February edition of *The Blue* confirmed:

The senior dormitories have been protected by wire netting and nearly all the boys of each house sleep there. The alarm system has varied slightly, but at present the 'Jim Crow' on duty in the chapel turret gives the alarm to the school office, which warns the school by a bell rung in the dormitory of each house and in each section of the tube. [5]

The novelty of such nocturnal disturbances had long worn off as it now seemed unlikely that Housie itself would be bombed and the first sleepy progress from the dormitory tended rapidly to become more noisy and boisterous. Our broken nights brought another change in our routine, a regular rest period after lunch. This was highly welcome to me as it reduced the length of time available for games, but very few boys seemed to take advantage of the chance to enter the normally out-of-bounds dormitory. The two or three who did often had it to themselves to read or otherwise amuse themselves, a blissful interlude of peace.

We had the black-out to thank for another major improvement, as the same issue of *The Blue* recorded:

Owing to the more stringent black-out enforced this winter, tea in Dining Hall had to be put as early as 4.30 during the darkest weeks. A supper, consisting usually of soup and bread, was served in house dayrooms at 7.30 and met with general satisfaction. [6]

The soup – I cannot recall ever seeing any alternative – was collected from the kitchens in large cauldrons, each carried by a pair of boys, a welcome opportunity to get out of the house. Our housemaster, I am sure, disapproved, especially where two boys about whom he had 'a theory' were assigned to the duty together. Except on really dark nights, when I could not see where I was going, or in bad weather when, once again, we missed the tube, I enjoyed soup fetching and found even boys who normally went with the crowd congenial company on such occasions. Precisely what soup we would get on a particular night added a new subject for speculation to our restricted lives. Celery was not appreciated, the start of a lifelong dislike as far as I was concerned, but 'thick juice', officially oxtail, was acceptable, and even our great gastronomic treat, pea soup, may, I think, have appeared occasionally.

This highly welcome, and long overdue, extra meal was merely one sign of the significant improvement in our diet caused by the war. In 1938 a new Lady Superintendent, already mentioned, Miss JB Stevenson, had been appointed but her arrival brought at first no change in the tediously predictable menus and their absurdly restricted range. If she did desire to feed us better her attempts were frustrated by lack of funds or the conservatism of the governors. The Ministry of Food had more success. Food rationing, imaginatively planned and efficiently administered, was one of the great benefits of the war, leaving the vast majority of people infinitely better fed than they had been before, and even

Housie, hitherto at the very bottom of the culinary heap, gained enormously from it. Increasingly, after the start of food rationing, at first affecting only a few items, in January 1940, it must have become obvious to the authorities that we were receiving far less than the ration of many essentials and as controls grew more severe the quality and variety of our diet steadily increased. Even 'cold gag', that horrible Housey tribute to the sanctity of Sunday, an apparently immovable tradition since the time of Charles Lamb, was replaced by minced beef, which, in inadequate amounts but at least edibly now began to appear in Dining Hall under the grandiose name of Scotch Collops. Meat being rationed by price, not weight, and mince presumably being cheaper than even the toughest joints, the school may thereby have saved money. We also benefitted from 'points' rationing for tinned and packaged food, 'points' being available to be spent on a range of items, from highly-pointed canned meat to low-pointed macaroni and baked beans. If we saw corned beef before the war it was as a single tough and all too thin slice, one per boy, as a Sunday morning breakfast treat or as our 'packed lunch' on occasions like Speech Day or Field Day. Now a delicious new dish of corned beef cooked with onions, the latter presumably from the school farm, replaced pea soup as our favourite main course, one I have tried to recreate many times since. Baked beans and macaroni cheese were sometimes served instead of jam at tea time, converting this into a reasonable meal and, most fortunately, fish became scarcer than before the war so the uneatable cod and noxious smelling haddock which had so nauseated us now largely became a memory. Kippers and herrings, though the allowance remained strictly one per boy, we did still see, though less frequently, but there was another, sensational, change, the addition to our diet of eggs. Before the war, as mentioned earlier, we had been allowed one a *term*. Now, even when the egg ration was at its lowest, everyone in the country was entitled to at least two a month, supplemented by a generous allowance of dried eggs, and the school found itself forced to make regular use of what had hitherto been regarded as a luxury. I well remember the first occasion when scrambled eggs were served at breakfast. Noel Sergent, as Hall Warden, recognised this was a historic occasion and made a speech to urge that this unprecedented gastronomic bounty should be fairly distributed. 'Today you have buttered eggs,' he began, instantly, in his infallible way, alienating his audience. What on earth, we wondered, was wrong with the honourable old English name of Scrambled Eggs?

Around this time we enjoyed an even more sensational dinner: cold chicken. This was never repeated and, though no explanation was offered – as always the school failed to make us see our own experience in a wider context – it was no doubt that the school's stock of chickens had just been slaughtered for lack of feeding stuffs. What, I have wondered since, had become of all the eggs they must have laid over the years, when our total consumption was three a year per head?

Fats rationing made no difference to us, since the weekly amount of butter or margarine now allowed was more than adequate to supply the miserable little pats of 'flab' served out at breakfast and tea. The sugar ration was, similarly, no hardship, while as for bacon and ham, we had never seen the former and the latter only in the form of an occasional small slice at Sunday morning breakfast. Bread and potatoes, regarded by the Minister of Food[*] as his staple 'fillers' for the nation, had always fulfilled that role in our lives and the tea ration was more than adequate to continue the watery brew slopped out into our 'kiff' bowls at breakfast and tea; 'kiff' and 'crugs', ie slices of bread, had always been the only items of which the supply was unlimited. Now we learned that the grey bread we had eaten in Hall was wholemeal and healthy and soon, in the shape of the 'National Loaf' all our fellow citizens were obliged to eat it too.

Before the war we had occasionally, I think, been given an apple in place of jam at tea but I cannot recall that other fresh fruit, the traditional sign of a well-balanced diet, but expensive, had ever featured on the menu. Here too, the enlightened policies of Lord Woolton, the nation's first and best Minister of Food, left their mark upon our tables. When, late in the war, oranges were briefly available on the basis of one or two for each child's ration book, Housie could hardly refuse its share, although I have no personal recollection of seeing any before I left.

The war, and especially rationing, based on the manifestly fair principle of basic shares for all, with extra for people with special needs, is usually credited with creating a new readiness among all sections to demand their rights in exchange for the sacrifices they were making, and to this great sea change in opinion even Christ's Hospital was not immune. It was in the Dining Hall that I witnessed the only occasions of rebellion against authority during all my years at school. The target on both occasions was 'The Hag', as we unkindly labelled the Lady Superintendent – though some houses favoured an even more offensive term, 'The Bitch', also applied to an unpopular matron[7] – and she was, I suspect, unjustly blamed for the shortcomings of others. One morning, no doubt due to some accident in the kitchen, the porridge tasted so strongly of soap as to be uneatable, even by hungry schoolboys. 'The Hag' was sent for and, as she entered the Dining Hall, a rare event, she was loudly hissed, each table taking up the protest as she passed until the whole Dining Hall was in uproar and she turned and retreated to the kitchens. Had Noel Sergent ordered the school to leave, or threatened punishment, he would, I think, have been defied. A hungry boy, as Dr Friend might have remarked, is a determined boy. At all events, Noel sensibly announced that a mistake had been made, the

---

[*] For a fuller account of the strategy and details of wartime food rationing see *How we Lived Then*, Chapter 13. On CH's adoption of wholemeal flour see Chapter 26 of the present book.

rejected porridge was collected up, and some form of replacement substituted. A day or two later there was another protest, when we came into tea to find dishes of dripping on the table in place of the customary 'flab'. Dripping had replaced butter or margarine at breakfast on one morning a week as long as anyone could remember, but to have it appearing at tea as well was too much. A spontaneous but school-wide boycott of it followed. That day we had raw bread and tea for our meal, and the repellent whitish-grey slabs of dripping in their cheap tin dishes were sent back untouched apart from the words 'No thanks' carved on them. The sacrifice proved effective. Dripping never appeared at tea again, and talk of an 'Anti-Hag League' to carry on a continuing campaign for better food came to nothing.

Air raids had given us more liberty, in the shape of access to the dormitories and more contact with other houses; food rationing had vastly improved our diet; now, by a splendid irony, the war weakened the power of that hitherto unchallengeable institution, the OTC. *The Blue* for February 1941 lamented the recent changes in terms reminiscent of those regular soldiers who longed for the fighting to stop so that they could get back to 'real soldiering'.

> The Corps is feeling sad. It is no longer an Officers' Training Corps, but plain Training Corps, Junior division. It is menaced by the rival growth of the ATC [Air Training Corps], which has hardly yet been born, and of the Home Guard, which is at last showing signs of life. It has suffered irreparable loss of officers...Our shooting has suffered owing to wartime conditions...We shall soon have forgotten the existence of a shooting VIII, the possibilities of a Field Day, and the realities of a Camp, while memories of General Inspections...hover in the remote past. However, we can always content ourselves with the confidence that while Housie continues to feed the ranks and staffs of our forces throughout the Empire, Britain cannot go down. [8]

The OTC's change of name followed the launching by the government of two rival organisations, the JTC, or Junior Training Corps, which was not confined to the grammar and public schools but designed for recruits to all ranks, and the Air Training Corps, offering boys aged 15 and upwards a similar preparation for service in the RAF. I shall say more about the ATC later.[*]

The Lent Term of 1941, a pivotal period for the school in the way it was affected by the war, witnessed another development, recorded in the same *Blue*:

> A strip of land of some five acres to the east of the Post Office path is being ploughed for national requirements. Lamb A are thus dispossessed for the

---

[*] See Chapter 40.

time being of their cricket and football pitches and Middleton B of their football pitch.[9]

Five acres [2 ha] was a meagre contribution from a campus covering 1200 [486 ha] but it was a start and I watched with delight, and recorded in a snapshot, a horse-drawn plough turning over the soil to put it, at last, to a more useful purpose than games. On one of the affected pitches, behind the tuckshop, I had often, on House Out of Bounds afternoons, filled in the weary hours with ineffectually practising place-kicks, the only part of the game one could indulge in alone, well knowing that I would never be required to do so in a real match.

The war was also leaving its mark in other, less traumatic, ways than the sacrifice of playing fields. *The Blue* for February 1941 recorded the addition to our lives of 'First Aid Classes and more and more fire-fighting practices, with Mr Strand's agility on the fire escape as one of the highlights.'[10] Three motor-cycles were now to be seen about the grounds, their first appearance, I believe, the staff's response to petrol rationing. But the main influence of the war followed the insatiable demands of the services for more men, as masters disappeared in mid-term, while the space devoted in *The Blue* to news of Old Blues who had already joined up grew ever longer, as did the CH Roll of Service, recording the names of the most recent recruits.

Although it was often said that this was the civilians' war, the truth was that, as always, it was primarily and above all that of the fighting men. It was those who joined the Services who made by far the greatest sacrifice of their normal lives and ran by far the greatest risk of being killed.[*] The demands of the Forces seemed insatiable and were visible at Housie in the frequency with which the younger masters disappeared, often in mid-term, and the new faces to be seen in the Common room and classrooms, often belonging to former schoolmasters who had thought their teaching days were long over, but occasionally to men past call-up age, or medically unfit, who had never faced a class before but now heroically filled the gaps from a sense of duty. Some of the 'dug-outs' as the Forces described elderly officers recalled to duty from retirement, already knew their way about the school, like the much-loved maths teacher, 'Dido' Hyde, who had taught at CH in the first world war, but the newcomer I saw most of, after his arrival in the Lent Term of 1941, was A Featherstonehaugh, whose name provided us with a perpetual source of amusement. (Later I used it, for similar purposes, in a detective story.[**]) When, in the army, I came across someone else with this name, I found, as we had really known all along, that it was pronounced as written. My form, Great Erasmus A, preferred, however, to believe that our new German master should

---

[*] See *How We Lived Then* p. 84 for the statistics which make this clear.
[**] *Strip Death Naked* (Cassell, 1959) pp.4-5 which features Sir Geoffrey Featherstonehaugh, a Whitehall Permanent Secretary threatened with blackmail.

be known as 'Feeston Ho' or 'Ho' for short, though another school of thought insisted that Featherstonehaugh should correctly be rendered 'Fanshaw'. Whether the name's owner knew of this speculation I never learned but he was an amiable, long-suffering person, of whom I shall say more later.

A sterner reminder of the war than the arrival of elderly masters was the premature departure of senior boys for the forces, from which they would often return, if commissioned, to show off their new uniforms; Other Ranks were less frequent visitors. I remember one visit from a former house captain of Peele B, who came back to his old house in all the glory of a Commando officer's uniform and proceeded to demonstrate one of his newly acquired skills by organising a boxing match, the only occasion I witnessed such a contest at Housie. Unfortunately, at least one of the contestants singularly failed to display the Commando spirit when thrust into the ring, formed at one end of the dormitory by piling up mattresses. Weary of being battered he simply climbed over them and, quite literally, ran away through the door, clearly determined to fight no more. What happened to him I never discovered but the fights which did take place, and one which I later saw in the army, forced upon almost equally reluctant combatants, one of whom fouled his shorts when struck, left me with a profound distaste for what still seems to me a disgusting activity and I am grateful that Housie never added it to our existing sports.

Meanwhile, the space devoted in *The Blue* to the CH Roll of Service, listing the latest recruits to the Forces, and to news of those already in uniform, grew steadily longer. So, sadly, did the Roll of Honour. That February saw, most unusually, an obituary of an 'Old Bluess', as we called those who attended our sister school at Hertford, a woman 'killed instantaneously' by a bomb while she was helping East Enders in a Mission House in Wapping. More typical, however, were the deaths of a sergeant-pilot, lost in action in a Hurricane 'keeping guard over a convoy', one of six heroic pilots who tackled eighty enemy aircraft – 'as help arrived from the mainland, the Huns broke and made for home' – and of a squadron leader 'killed in action on HMS *Illustrious*'. The other four recent military deaths were also all of airmen. Flying, it was clear, was by far the most dangerous of wartime occupations.

It must have been around the end of the Lent Term that an event occurred which made a deep impression upon me and made me realise for the first time that I might actually be killed myself. One evening Noel Sergent entered the dayroom during prep to summon to his study a boy in, I think, his second or third year in the house, the younger brother of a boy whom I had known, and liked, in my first year, which was his last. This twelve year old had often talked of his brother, now in the RAF, and now returned in tears, to pack up his books and go to bed. Noel then came back and, for once enjoying our full attention, explained that he had just had to break to him the news of his brother's death. He paid the dead boy a brief tribute and ended: 'I want you to comfort Leslie Foxton in his sorrow and to remember Terry Foxton as someone who died fighting not merely for his country but for civilization as well.' There were no derisive murmurs after Noel had gone; for once housemaster and house were at one.

Nine months later *The Blue* carried the full story of the death of this former member of Peele A and it left me much moved. I quote it almost in full because it so admirably catches the spirit of the time and so well illustrates the kind of influence to which impressionable boys were subjected in 1941:

> Just after tea on March 22nd we [ie an RAF base in Malta] were raided by a large formation of Ju [ie Junkers] 88s, and Terry took the flight up to have a crack at them. After they had chased the bombers some way out to sea they were themselves attacked by about twice their number of ME [Messerschmitt] 109s and the usual dog fight followed. Terry went straight for the tail of the nearest Hun and had just set it on fire when he was himself attacked by two more, one of which must have got him, for he dived straight into the sea. We think he must have been killed outright by a cannon shell...The Jerry that got Terry was immediately attacked and crashed in flames.
>
> He was a great loss to the Squadron.[*]

---

[1] Nov 1940 p.2
[2] Nov 1940 p.25
[3] Nov 1940 pp.23-24
[4] Mar 1996 p.67
[5] Feb 1941 p.62
[6] Feb 1941 p.62
[7] Hull p.66
[8] Feb 1941 p.68
[9] Feb 1941 p.63
[10] Feb 1941 p.63

---

[*] The death of Flying-Officer JHT Foxton is recorded in *The Blue*, June 1941, p.149. For the full account, from which the above quotations are taken, see the Nov-Dec 1941 issue, p.27.

32

INSPIRING SUNDAYS

'A particularly inspiring Sunday is always liable to be followed by a particularly depressing Monday.'

Headmaster of Christ's Hospital addressing confirmation candidates,
March 1941

Chapel had been a constant part of my life at Housie since the very first morning. A short service was held every weekday and every evening there was 'Duty' in one's house, before the juniors went to bed and the seniors settled down to another hour of prep. On Sunday there was a service morning and evening, each lasting about an hour and, of course, compulsory, with, for those who had been confirmed, a voluntary early morning communion at 8 am. All this was in line with the intentions of our founders, and featured first in the traditional 'Housey toast' said on formal occasions:

The religious, royal and ancient foundation of Christ's Hospital. May those prosper who love it and may God increase their number.

I never resented Chapel being compulsory. On the contrary, like many other boys, I welcomed our frequent attendance there as a time of refuge, free from bullying or harassment. As a High Anglican I regretted the design, of pews facing inward to a central aisle, instead of towards the altar, but this arrangement had a practical advantage. Each house occupied the same block of seats at every service, with members of the staff occupying the rear row. Our own housemaster, his junior, and sometimes his wife and family, sat on the far side of Chapel, facing us, so that he could keep a vigilant eye on the conduct of his house. I welcomed this supervision, and once, after I had choked with ill suppressed coughs throughout one evensong, Noel Sergent, most unexpectedly, excused me from games for the next few days.

The form of worship was middle-of-the-road Anglican, with a tendency towards the High rather than the Low. The surpliced choristers and servers with whom I was familiar at home were unknown, but the liturgy was based on the Book of Common Prayer, adopted in 1662 when Housie was already more than a century old. This superb compilation, with its stately and near-poetic English fitly enshrining the marvellous doctrinal compromise achieved by Cranmer, has always seemed to me an argument for the superiority of the Church of England, if not indeed for the existence of God, and I feel grateful that my schooldays were enriched by the glories of the Prayer Book before the act of National Apostasy [*] which rejected it.

The teaching of what was then called 'divinity', now 'Religious Knowledge', was often indifferent and sometimes, as I shall describe, positively bad. In chapel, however, the services, apart from the over emphasis on music at the expense of worship, could not be faulted. The *English Hymnal*, the preferred choice of High Anglicans, was our main source of hymns, and, to cater for our particular needs, *Supplementary Hymns*, known to us as 'The Supplement', adopted as recently as 1933. This introduced me to a number of worthwhile poets, such as Robert Bridges and Henry Vaughan, and it was from the list of acknowledgments that I first discovered the existence of copyright. I still delight in the elegantly phrased disclaimer in the *Preface*:

> We have spared no pains in endeavouring to discover the owners of Copyright. If, in spite of this, we have innocently infringed such right, we can only crave indulgence.

I was even more taken with the *Preface* to the *Christ's Hospital Psalter*, a selection of versicles and psalms, with accompanying music, made especially for our use:

> The pointing used in this Psalter is an attempt to effect a compromise between the accepted rhythmical form of the Anglican chant and the natural flow and elasticity of the English language...With full knowledge that the compromise here effected will seem cowardly to the radical and an outrage to the conservative, we yet believe that it will appeal at once to many and in time to all.

Chapel provided other opportunities for 'education by stealth'. I can recall how affronted the headmaster was when the school sang during one Saturday morning practice

> Now thank we all our God,
> With hearts and hands and voices.

---

[*] A sermon by the Rev. John Keble at the University Church, Oxford, on 14 July 1833, under this title, in which he denounced the proposed suppression of ten Irish bishoprics, is generally regarded as launching the Oxford Movement to restore the traditional practices and beliefs of the Church of England.

'No, no!' cried HLO Flecker from his stall, 'Catherine Winkworth was one of the greatest hymn translators of the nineteenth century. She would never have written that vulgar "s" after "heart".' Apart from those who, like me, found in the language used in chapel a real source of inspiration, many others must have responded to the musical tradition which inspired and sustained it. The Director of Music, Dr CS Lang, tended, like many musicians, to regard services as primarily an occasion for musical display. Worship came a bad second if not regarded as an intrusion. Dr Lang's hour of glory came at the end of chapel every Saturday morning when the whole school practised the works to be sung on the following day and, in the Christmas term, the carols and *Messiah* to be performed at its end. I found his loud instructions, directed solely to the musical aspects of a hymn, wholly unsuitable in this consecrated place. I can remember the whole school stumbling into an embarrassed silence, mingled with titters, when he tried to persuade us to sing of that 'happy land…where troubles never cease' instead of 'never come'.

The explanation of Dr Lang's nickname, 'Beaky' was self evident. 'His most notable feature', one of my contemporaries has recorded, 'was his nose, a world-class contender in the heavyweight division', made more conspicuous by the 'pair of horn-rimmed spectacles mounted on its crest'. The impression the Head of Music made was underlined by 'his voice, perpetually hoarse from shouting at choir and orchestra and croaking snatches of the work in hand to illustrate the way he wanted it performed.' [1]

His own contributions to our musical repertoire were modest, though they included, the same observer remembers, 'a spirited arrangement of *Joshua won the Battle of Jericho*' and 'a setting of some verses by GK Chesterton…the last line of each, declaimed with great passion, being "I don't care where the water goes if it doesn't get into the wine",' though, as this observer remarked, 'few of us could have recognised a glass of wine if it had been put in front of us.' I was impressed by the realisation that several of the settings we used of the *Te Deum*, the *Venite* and the *Nunc Dimittis* had come from his pen, though we more commonly sang 'rival' versions by outsiders, such as *'Stanford in B flat'* and *'Walmisley in D minor'*.

A leading part in the musical life of the school, and, after his ordination in 1941, its religious life was played by the Rev WCM Cochrane, whose nickname 'Corky' or 'Corks' was prompted by more than a liking for alliteration. I hardly knew him, but he had a reputation as a kindly housemaster, known to take boys out for meals or even, in deep secrecy, for a drink at one of our two local pubs, the *Bax Castle*. (The other, the *Fox and Hounds*, has now, for no good reason, become the *Boar's Head*.) 'Corks' was credited in *The Blue* after his death with having inspired many boys with his own deep love of music and after Dr Lang's departure in 1945, though I had left myself by that time, Cochrane succeeded him. Battle was soon joined between him and the Headmaster, who would complain about 'too much music going on'. To this his

Director of Music would reply with thunderous blasts, with the heaviest stops pulled out, on the chapel organ, loud enough 'to rattle the panelling on the back of the Head's stall'. Cochrane was, none the less, one of a number of staff who left after the arrival of a new headmaster, and he became parish priest in an Essex village. An Old Blue who visited it after 'Corks's' death heard from 'the ladies doing the flowers' in his former church a somewhat backhanded tribute: 'A lovely man – but the pub was close by.'[2]

Although I found elaborate settings, particularly descants, and anthems, an actual barrier to worship, I enjoyed the rousing hymn tunes which the musical staff failed to tamper with and I often furtively studied the words of hymns during sermons. I also benefitted from reading the details of their origins. What, I wondered, was the 'Foundling Hospital Coll. (1796)' from which *Praise the Lord! Ye heavens, adore him* had apparently been taken? And was the S Johnson who wrote *City of God*, still my favourite hymn, the famous Dr Samuel Johnson who compiled the first English dictionary? (It was, however, years before I learned the answers. The Foundling Hospital, an even poorer man's Christ's Hospital, had been established by the philanthropist Thomas Coram in 1745, but has long since been closed, while the hymn-writing Johnson's dates, 1822-1882, assigned him to the century after the great lexicographer.)[3]

Apart from the Leaving Service, a distressing occasion for those directly involved, the one chapel occasion which everyone enjoyed was the Carol Service on the last Sunday afternoon of the Christmas term. It was well planned and admirably staged; such big set pieces Housie, with its centuries of tradition, always got right. From a surviving leaflet I can reconstruct the first wartime Carol Service, on 17 December 1939, held in mid-afternoon because of the black-out. Rousing, traditional hymns, like *In the Bleak Mid-winter* and *Ding Dong! Merrily on High*, which even the least musical could enjoy, were interspersed with less familiar works like *King Jesus hath a Garden* and *Love came down at Christmas*, which gave the choir, and especially the trebles, a chance to excel. This was emphatically Dr Lang's occasion and in 1939 he had personally written two of the hymn tunes as well as master-minding the whole performance. An attempt was also made to further our musical education, with a violin recital and organ voluntaries from Bach at the beginning and end of the service, while I also discovered for the first time some of the poets whose work had been drawn on for the hymns, including George Withers (1588-1667), Christina Rossetti (1830-1894) and the Victorian giant, Alfred Lord Tennyson (1809-1892).

To be enjoyed to the full the Carol Service needed to be celebrated in seasonable weather and this must have happened at least once during my schooldays for the description I wrote for *First Bloom*, nominally set in 1942, seems to have been founded on actual observation:

This year even the weather seemed to lend a special charm to the music which usually emerged from the Chapel windows to wage a gusty battle with the December gale blowing outside. Snow was falling all the morning and when in the afternoon the bell[*] summoned the school to its devotions, it still drifted down, not too consciously, not too swiftly, but settling with determination, hushing the tread of the houses as they filed into the building.

James felt strangely at peace, as he sat waiting for the service to begin. It was only three o'clock on a winter's afternoon, but already it was growing dark. The lights of the traditional Christmas trees placed on either side of the altar shone out brightly against the black oblongs of the windows above. The lights in the chapel caught the panelling and appeared to give age to it. The deep glow of the electric lights sought and found an answering glow in the black folds of the masters' gowns, in the red hoods [of an Oxford MA] that most of them wore above. It drew a special sheen of glory from the purple gown [signifying a Doctor of Music] of the Music Master, who stood waiting, baton twirling impatiently in his fingers, for the choir to arrive.

They came at last. Their footsteps as they marched along outside the chapel were quieter than usual, for the snow which had blown off the surface of the quadrangle on to the cloisters through which they were moving, muffled the sound of nearly a hundred pairs of feet, tramping towards the West Door. They filed in. The cold outside had given an added glow to the cheeks of the young trebles, who came first, and boys of eleven, twelve or thirteen who for the past term had seemed ugly in their appearance and stupid in their behaviour, now took on an aspect almost cherubic. The fair hair of the young boys, their fresh glowing cheeks and bright eyes, whose reverent look could not altogether conceal a lurking joy at the nearness of the return home, seemed a fitting complement to their startlingly white surplices and warm red cassocks...

The choir took their places. The deep voice of the headmaster began to recall the familiar story: 'Let us go, even unto Bethlehem!' The beauty of the words was soon swallowed up in the beauty of the music. *The Messiah* had, as usual, been extensively drawn upon:

There were shepherds, abiding in the fields,

Keeping watch over their flocks, by night...

The voices seemed to breathe simplicity and innocence...Handel was forgotten for a moment...The trebles, who seemed to James's emotional mind as if at any moment they might themselves take wings, rise up on the strength of their melodious voices, and be gone, sang

Angels from the realms of glory

Wing your flight o'er all the earth....

---

[*] This confirms the date as being probably 1942. The ban on church bells had been lifted that November to enable the victory at El Alamein to be celebrated.

Choruses from *The Messiah* followed, and the trebles'
   Unto us a child is born, unto us a son is given
Was followed by the deeper wave of the tenors and basses'
   And the government shall be upon his shoulder.
The school sang one of the jolly boisterous carols in which generations of worshippers have relieved their spirits after a year's confinement of them, and sat down to recover their breath for the final triumphant *O come, all ye faithful!*

Our religious education outside chapel was a great deal less satisfactory. My first divinity teacher was a clergyman known as 'wet smack' because of the mild-mannered way in which he reproved his classes and he was notorious for asking anyone who sought 'to be excused' 'Do you merely wish to make water?', a phrase we found irresistibly funny. Another, far more admirable, cleric was universally known as 'Boggy' from his initials, 'WC', to distinguish him from another master of the same name, Johns. He confessed to me once, when I was much older, that he would have preferred a far 'Higher' form of service, which aroused my sympathy, but he was not well equipped to deal with the natural curiosity of adolescent boys. Once, when a mention of circumcision came up in class he aroused our hopes by beginning 'To be perfectly frank...' and then went on to be anything but frank, describing it as 'a cut on the private parts'. This left us more bewildered than ever. Despite the close proximity in which we lived none of us (except presumably the few Jewish boys) had any understanding of the term and it was not until years later that I found out what it meant.[*]

It was assumed that on reaching the age of about 14 a boy would wish to be confirmed, though, if my memory is correct, it was deferred in my case until I was 15, no doubt on the assumption that anyone not in a house first or second team was not yet qualified to join the Anglican First Eleven. I cannot recall, as a friend claims to have done, hearing someone being asked 'Do you want to be confirmed? If not, why not?' but the intention to become a confirmation candidate certainly had to be announced publicly, with a monitor calling out the names of those considered eligible in alphabetical order, as if preparing the Luggage in Advance list at the end of term.

Being confirmed, if not actually compulsory was expected, like joining the OTC. For me the decision posed no problem, but it was very different for my old nursemaid, who, from his earlier piety, had now swung round to professing himself an atheist. He had, I discovered, never been baptised, which at that time seemed like professing oneself illegitimate. In resisting pressure to conform to

---

[*] Robin Hull, though younger than me, was better informed. In the Prep the subject was clearly of compelling interest, boys so marked being known as 'Roundheads' to distinguish them from the un-circumcised 'Cavaliers'. (Hull p.42).

the majority's behaviour he was carrying on a family tradition. His father, he revealed to me – a brave confession in the middle of the war – had been sent to prison for refusing to serve in the army in the first world war, his objection – too subtle a concept for the tribunal to grasp – not being on religious grounds but on a simple refusal to take human life. Bob was no pacifist, but so proud of his father's courage that he had kept, and indeed showed to me, the charge sheet recording his indictment for refusing to put on his army uniform. Oddly enough, later in life, when my faith was beginning to wane, Bob's re-emerged and he was baptised in hospital just before he died of leukemia, at the age of 44. Had he survived a few hours longer he would also have been confirmed, a whole thirty years after all the rest of his Housey generation.

In Barnes Wallis's day, Peele A boys had been prepared for confirmation by their housemaster, a cleric, but happily Noel was not so qualified for had he been his house would probably all have professed unbelief en masse just to affront him.[*] As it was we were sent to the chaplain, the Rev WC Johns, the final polish being provided by a talk the day before the service from the Headmaster, our first meeting with him since our 'Options' interview. I was impressed by 'Oily' then, as on every other occasion when I had dealings with him, and can still remember what he said. Feelings of religious exultation were, he warned us, to be distrusted, as a particularly inspiring Sunday was liable to be followed by an exceptionally dismal Monday. He cautioned us, too, against people who boasted of their faith, telling the story of a woman who had prayed passionately for a hill obscuring her view to be removed and, when she found it still there, declared in disgust: 'I knew all the time You wouldn't do it!' This talk remains in my mind for another reason, as the first occasion I heard the word 'paradox', which the headmaster then defined. At last, I felt, we were being treated as grown-ups, in contrast to the approach of most of the clergy on the staff.

I was deeply moved by my confirmation, and by the bishop who confirmed us, Dr George Bell of Chichester, an enlightened and respected cleric. (The cynical Mr Haslehust described him dismissively as 'our local priest' but for once 'Fred's' humour failed to amuse me.) Dr Bell had an exceptionally high-pitched voice, and according to Robin Hull, 'to bell' became school slang for speaking in this way. I still remember, as he does, a soon legendary sermon on a text drawn from Ezekiel Chapter 37 on the Valley of Dry Bones, for the preacher 'kept repeating "Bones, dry bones, nothing but dry bones" in his falsetto voice. For years afterwards, everyone squeaked "Dry bones" whenever the bishop's name was heard.' It is generally accepted that Dr Bell would have become Archbishop of Canterbury in 1944 but for his opposition to the strategy

---

[*] On Wallis's confirmation interview see Chapter 16.

of indiscriminate bombing begun in 1942, on which he was, on both military and moral grounds, entirely right.*

The fact that I was, by pure chance, the first boy to have the bishop's hands laid upon him seemed to make the event even more special and in *First Bloom*, three years later, I tried to recapture the sensations of Saturday 8 March 1941:

> The service, like most services at Middlestone, was short, dignified and at times beautiful, and as, very conscious of his extremely clean body and Sunday clothing, he rose from his knees before the bishop to return to his place, he felt an uprush of exultation pass through him. Everything else seemed as clean as his own carefully scrubbed hands...as the following figures, now kneeling so innocently before the white robed ecclesiastic as though they had put their sins behind them. He heard that voice, infinitely tender, commending his soul to God: 'Defend, O Lord, this Thy child with Thy heavenly grace, that he may continue...' He knelt down and found himself praying fervently...
>
> He rose from his knees a moment later. The chapel seemed flooded with sunlight, as the beams of the midday sun played on the white marble of the altar, on the white robes of the bishop who was seated before it. The warmth of noon seemed to permeate the building, in through the stained glass of the east window, as the clear voices of the trebles, whose features now shone with a light that was almost angelic, began the hymn 'O holy spirit, lord of love.' James felt for the first time...a great spiritual peace.

No doubt part of the impact that confirmation made upon me was due to the service being followed by my being taken out by my father, who was staying at a house occupied by an estate worker, one of a group known unimaginatively as the Works Cottages. This was almost as primitive as our house at home, and as it was wartime my father had brought his food with him. The eggs and sausages, no doubt from the famous Newbury firm of Griffin, we enjoyed at breakfast after my first communion remain one of the most memorable meals of my life.

I felt closer to my father that weekend than I had ever done, or was to feel again, and I regret that I did not seize the opportunity to discuss his own faith with him. Thanks to the war, which in 1941 seemed likely to last for ever, there was clearly little point in talking about my future. I realise now how much my mother would have liked to have seen me confirmed but they could not both have afforded the trip. Her devotion to the High Church wing of the Church of England remained unwavering to her death, though she drew the line at my brother's more extreme practices. I suspect she never said a 'Hail Mary' in her

---

* See *The Bombers* pp.374-7. The title of the relevant chapter, *Worse than a Crime?*, sums up my own attitude.

life, while she was far too kind-hearted to join the Easter prayers at St John's, recited by Gordon and the other servers with relish, which asserted that all who did not accept the Catholic faith – or in our case the Anglican version of it – would 'perish everlastingly'.

One consequence of my confirmation was that I severed my links with the school Christian Union, a small group of boys – no masters were ever present – who met once a week in a borrowed classroom to pray together and to listen to an outside speaker of evangelical opinions. Oddly enough I had been introduced to it by Bob Pitman who had regarded his duties as nursemaid as including responsibility for my spiritual development. The Christian Union was, by Housey standards, a very recent innovation, dating only from 1927, when two boys had approached the then headmaster for permission to set it up. [4] After Pitman had dropped out, my closest friend in Peele A became an enthusiastic member, and ultimately head, of the CH Christian Union, later following its founder into the East African mission field. I attended regularly for several years, partly out of loyalty to him, partly for much the same reason that I enjoyed going to chapel, that the meetings provided a peaceful interlude in our stressful everyday lives. Robin Hull bears out my conclusion. 'There was,' he observed, 'much piety among the boys' partly perhaps because attending such voluntary activities as early morning communion and the meetings of the Christian Union 'left less time for unpleasant things to happen'.[5]

In *First Bloom*, where I called my friend Graham, I traced this purely negative part of my spiritual development through the eyes of my *alter ego*, Conway:

> Right up to the time of his confirmation, there were few meetings which he did not attend. He watched the arrival of the weekly speaker with his vigorous greetings to the senior members, he heard his talk which, whatever his subject, usually ended with the text 'Behold I stand at the door and knock' and a trumpeted 'Let us pray', delivered as though the speaker desired to include in his exhortation any who had not yet seen the light and might be spending Sunday in the farthest corner of the playing fields.
>
> Another favourite text with speakers was that which referred to 'the salt of the earth'. Even in his first term Conway heard more than once that he and the others who attended regularly were 'The salt of school life'. Glancing round him, it seemed that they were an uninspiring collection of people for so great a distinction. Was their language or behaviour so different from that of anyone else?

As I grew older, this disillusionment deepened and, as confirmation classes clashed with Christian Union meetings, the latter inevitably took second place, as 'Conway' recorded:

Its speakers seemed to him, with a mind now broadening, and with his naturally critical outlook strengthened by the more orthodox addresses of the priest now preparing him to be confirmed, to be merely wordy rather than helpful, and now that its numbers had dropped to a mere dozen, mostly rather bewildered juniors who had a feeling that attendance was in some vague way helpful to their school career, there was not even the comfort of being in a nondescript crowd. Added to this was his irritation at speakers who conducted their talks by means of questions.* He never forgot one speaker who pointed at an embarrassed small boy and demanded: 'Who do you say can save us?' The poor boy thus addressed murmured, not without some triumph at giving an answer which he knew to be right...'The Lord Jesus Christ!'...The speaker inserted his thumbs in the armholes of the waistcoat of his dark blue Sunday suit, and repeated with gusto, as if smacking his lips at the memory of some particularly savoury morsel he had eaten for lunch: 'The Lord Jesus Christ!' He went on to relate how, at 8.30 am on Thursday the 16th of March 1933 he had seen the light. James decided that he was finished with CU and not even Graham's continued attendance could change his resolution.

Today I suspect that part of my distaste for the Christian Union was based, though I hardly realised this at the time, on a suspicion that some of the speakers found close physical contact with young boys more attractive than rescuing their souls. Robin Hull observed that 'at least one master used his outward religious fervour as a cloak for homosexuality' and knew of a boy who 'dramatically forsook the Christian Union after attempted seduction by this master'.[6]

Looking back I wince at the memory of some of the tracts I read during my encounter with the evangelicals. One, I remember, urged the reader to submit his prayers to 'the heavenly GPO, the Great Prayer Opportunity'. I still recall the mnemonics recommended to us to ensure that our prayers were properly structured, namely PATH for 'Praise, Ask, Thank, Hear' and ACTS, 'Adoration, Confession, Thanksgiving, Supplication', this latter, politely putting one's requests last, seeming the more courteous. At 14 I did for a time conscientiously pray to be converted, as other members of the Christian Union, including my friend 'Graham', claimed to have been, and, when I chided him with the fact that no such change occurred, he replied that this must be because I lacked the necessary faith, a circular argument impossible to answer. The truth was that I now found my spiritual needs adequately met by chapel, to such an extent that I was reproved by my priest at home for no longer regularly

---

* I still consider this a most objectionable practice. I can now barely enjoy the books of a famous writer who interspersed a lecture with semi-rhetorical questions to the audience such as 'Don't you think so?'

attending church in the holidays. I still occasionally exchanged letters with him and, to our mutual embarrassment, my parents encouraged me to visit him in the holidays. He later complained to them, via my brother, that I seemed to have little to say on these occasions, but eventually accepted that I had no intention of entering the priesthood and these meetings ceased.

I was late coming to adolescence and for me, as for so many, it brought not only physical and emotional imperatives but spiritual problems. Here I was, I have learned since, following in the footsteps of Coleridge who, when he confessed his doubts to the Rev James Boyer was, as I have described earlier, soundly thrashed.[*] I got off more lightly when I fell into dispute with my spiritual mentor, the Rev EK Quick, who taught divinity and who had succeeded the more enlightened WC Johns as chaplain.[7] Quick, unlike some of his other predecessors, was addicted neither to the cane nor the bottle, but was a singularly stupid and small-minded individual, one of the least qualified holders of his important post. One of his pupils who later took Holy Orders himself has commented that while Quick was chaplain the chapel's churchmanship was 'so middle of the road as to be practically invisible', and that he 'even spoke out of the side of his mouth as if passing on some secret message'.[8] A naturally pious child, well drilled in the faith, I found him profoundly unimpressive, and in matters of Christian apologetics he was emphatically no Aquinas. When, in a genuine spirit of enquiry, I fell into dispute with him in the classroom about the doctrine of original sin, which has troubled many believers, he accused me of being an agnostic and added a novel theological argument, that if I did not immediately accept the disputed doctrine he would report me to my housemaster. Noel, I knew, would dislike any suggestion that one of his boys held subversive views, so I instantly recanted.

Quick, a silly, small-minded, man had his revenge for my supposed impertinence on the last afternoon of term. As mentioned elsewhere, the school required us to salute any master we encountered outside the ring fence, and Quick, having encountered me at the railway station while I was buying my ticket, hurried back to complain to Noel that I had not saluted him, which clearly ranked in his eyes with questioning the existence of God.

Noel, though jealous of his house's reputation, was always ready to stand up for his boys if unjustly accused. He readily accepted my explanation that since the station was not out of bounds I had not felt a salute was required but I was none the less sent off to apologise to him for my inadvertent offence, while the last night of term was enlivened by an after Duty homily to the house on the importance of displaying good manners in public. I enjoyed a brief popularity as a law-breaker, too late in the term, alas, to benefit me much. As for Quick, he survived into his nineties and managed to annoy me posthumously by being considered worthy of an obituary in the *Daily Telegraph*.

---

[*] See Chapter 14.

Although Christ's Hospital was a specifically Anglican foundation it managed to accommodate a few boys of other denominations and even of different faiths. Most Jews readily conformed to both attendance at Chapel and our diet though one, a Thornton B Old Blue recalls, was 'allowed to remain looking straight ahead when everyone else turned towards the altar to recite the creed'. The small Roman Catholic contingent in the same house was positively welcomed by the other boys for they were 'permitted to attend their own church in Horsham', and brought back the *News of the World* and similar titles, which, in addition to their notoriously explicit news stories, 'contained proper football coverage, as well as instalments from steamy novels', a perfect combination for adolescent boys.

Actual unbelief was treated less tolerantly than mere dissent. The informant just quoted, found himself, at the age of 14, permitted to decline confirmation on the grounds that he 'felt unworthy' but he remained 'intensely interested' in religious questions and secured 'the top marks in the school for Religious Knowledge' in School Certificate. Afterwards, as a history grecian, he found himself, as I did, 'fascinated by the role of religious bodies, theological disputes and church/State relations', but, unlike me, lost his faith. 'When I asserted my atheism,' he recalls, 'I was told bluntly by the Headmaster that I could either attend chapel or leave school. This was, after all, *Christ's* Hospital. So I contented myself with arguing with the chaplain in divinity lessons.' Even this modest rebellion created problems. While the chaplain 'seemed grateful for the discourse...one boy complained to his housemaster...I was disconcerting him by sometimes winning the argument.'

The war brought changes to our chapel-going as to other areas of our lives. It was announced that, as a great concession, attending morning chapel on Sunday for the over seventeens would become optional, though this was less liberal than it sounded; the school having enrolled everyone of this age in the Home Guard, they were in any case on parade on Sunday morning. In many respects, however, the school's religious life under Flecker was enlightened. Sermons, like collections, took place only three or four times a term, so each was an event, and the speakers were usually as admirably chosen as the films we saw on Saturdays, and suited their material excellently to a congregation aged from ten to eighteen. I can still remember one large black man, notable for this alone when white faces were universal, who had the whole school enthralled with his account of a visit to a chocolate factory and the aptitude tests to which would-be employees were submitted, though, sadly, I cannot recall the point he was making.

Masters often gave addresses at special services for the younger boys, but I can only remember one delivering a sermon to the whole school, my much admired English master Michael Warneford-Brown, by now in Orders, who denounced the pre-war destruction of food to keep up the price. Oddly enough the commodity most often mentioned was coffee, allegedly used to feed railway engines in Brazil, though it must have been a most inefficient fuel and was remote from our experience; most of us did not see a single cup, either at school or at home, from one year's end to the next.

The high quality of the preachers did not guarantee a reverent attitude in their listeners. Perhaps borrowing the idea from PG Wodehouse's *The Great Sermon Handicap*, a group of boys in Peele A decided to hold a sweepstake on all the term's sermons, each contributing sixpence [2.5p], an average week's pocket money, the winner to be the boy whose 'horse' went on longest. I agreed to be treasurer, but the gamble led to acrimony, for one boy, realising that in another minute or two another boy's preacher would have spoken longer than his own, took off his shoes and dropped them on the floor to put the speaker off his stride. How the affair ended I cannot be certain, but I think all the stakes may have been returned.

I can recall no bullying and very little misbehaviour in chapel, if only because of the housemaster opposite keeping a stern eye on his house's behaviour but double meanings in hymns were eagerly seized upon. The phrase 'the matron and the maid', a reminder of our domestic arrangements, often provoked a few sniggers, while a friend could never sing the question in *The Son of God goes forth to War* – 'Who follows in the train?' – without having to stifle a laugh. Even here, however, we were following a Housey tradition. In Dr Upcott's time 'the Beadle who sat in the pew under the headmaster's',[9] an official who had vanished by the 1930s, had regularly been embarrassed by the whole school singing with exaggerated emphasis, while looking towards him,

> By many a deed of shame
> We learn that Lovegrove's cold

instead of the correct 'Love grows cold.'[*] Similar treatment was meted out, at least by his own house, to any boy who happened in my time to have this not uncommon name. On the whole, however, in contrast to the ludicrous over emphasis on worship at Newgate Street, which I have described elsewhere, the chapel services seem to me to have been well planned, and it must have been a singularly insensitive boy who was not to some extent moved by them.

At that time, however, I was less aware of their good qualities and by the age of 17 the piety I had felt at my confirmation two years before had begun to be replaced by scepticism, as is evident from the essay, 'What have twelve years of education done for me?', which I wrote at this time. I had only recently abandoned the idea of science as a career, but as a history specialist, had in the past term become increasingly aware of the significance of faith in Middle Ages:

---

[*] See Chapter 16 for an occasion when this official was employed to help silence an over loquacious preacher.

I am still, despite constant exhortations from psalm, prayer, hymn and sermon to 'hold fast to the faith' very hazy as to what constitutes the faith, and I still have doubts as to whether this omniscient, omnipresent and omnipotent being whom we call God, whom the cynics might described as a cross between an ultra-benevolent Father Christmas and a more than usually villainous pantomime demon-king, does indeed exist. It is education which has made me question a belief which, until quite recently, with the credulous 'mother's knee' type of simplicity, I accepted without thought. All that is hard and questioning and scientific in me rebels at the idea of a being who created all the laws of science and is yet outside them, who formed impartially in his image, Judas Iscariot and Saint Paul, Galileo and Mussolini, who loved all mankind and watched millions of innocent men, their wives and their children, killed senselessly, uselessly and seemingly inevitably. Yet the poet in me never fails to be thrilled by the Communion service, or by the sight of the simple altar of a village church. I waver between atheism and Anglo-Catholicism and it is education that has done this for me, twelve years of teaching that have made me critical of things I once accepted implicitly.

Beside giving me a love of the Anglican liturgy I owed chapel at Housie another debt. The school then did virtually nothing to encourage appreciation of the visual arts, the privileged History Grecians apart, and the walls were bleaker than in many a seminary, which at least offered uplifting images of the Holy Family and of saints suffering martyrdom. There were, of course, the paintings in the Dining Hall, impressive by their mere scale, and, more disturbingly, an odd picture in the library entrance of a naked boy being pursued by a shark while rescuers in a boat try to haul him aboard. A colourful story lay behind this striking scene. Its subject, Brook Watson, was not, as we supposed, an Old Blue. Orphaned at the age of six, he was only fourteen when, serving at sea around 1749, he lost his leg while bathing, but survived, to become, in the classic tradition, a successful merchant, a baronet and Lord Mayor of London.[10] The artist himself, John Singleton Copley, bequeathed it to 'the Royal Hospitall of Christ', but the school sold it, in 1963, after my time, to an American gallery, the artist having been American. I can still recall my astonishment upon coming upon it unexpectedly during a visit to Washington; even on the far side of the Atlantic, I felt, the school was still able to catch up with me.*

---

* A reproduction of *Watson and the Shark* appears facing p.280 of the *Christ's Hospital Book* and on Morpurgo p.63. The sale, for £35,000, plus the provision of a replica which the school retained, was not disclosed at the time and caused much offence to Old Blues when news of it leaked out. (Jan 1970 pp.88-9, & Dec 1991 p.200.)

Chapel, however, was a splendid exception to the general lack of pictures. By an imaginative act of patronage the future Sir Frank Brangwyn [1867-1956] was invited, at the suggestion of the architect, Aston Webb, to fill the large vacant spaces on the walls. Brangwyn's theme was 'the mission and expansion of Christianity...leading to the conversion of our own islands' [11] and he was himself unenthusiastic about the subjects he was required to depict, considering them dull.[12] Dr Upcott, however, approved of the first eight pictures, commissioned in 1913, and the order was raised to twelve and then to sixteen. The final painting was not finished until 1923 and the whole series, the artist confided to a friend, 'nearly did for me', leaving him both exhausted and badly underpaid. For the whole 1680 square feet [156 sq.m] of paintings 8 feet [2.4m] high, with a total length of 210 feet [64m], he ultimately received only £500, so that he was, he complained, actually out of pocket, and he had difficulty in collecting this. The finished work was clearly disliked by many people and here the school authorities were not alone. A series of similar, even larger, panels he painted for the House of Lords a few years later were rejected by the peers on a free vote, and they were bought instead for the Guildhall at Swansea, where, stumbling upon them many years later, I had the same sense of *deja vu* as when confronted by Copley's *Shark* in Washington.[13] Later I had a further surprise encounter with his work when visiting Bruges, which had been Brangwyn's native city and now housed the Brangwyn Museum.

That normally slavish admirer of everything to do with Christ's Hospital, its faithful son, Clerk and historian GAT Allan, made an exception of the Brangwyns, though he added, with truth as well as humility, 'Unskilled as I am in the niceties of...modern "art", any opinion of mine is worthless.' His reason was more practical than aesthetic: 'I think it is a pity to provide boys with grotesque pictures, to be studied during divine service, amongst which may be found apparent caricatures of masters and others waiting to be "spotted".'[14] I can recall no such discoveries though it was the one which faced me every school day for seven years that was most criticised, the final painting, *Let All the People Praise Thee*, featuring a scene in the East End of London, containing 'a hunchback and a cripple drawn from life'. Only occasionally, when seated elsewhere, did I get a chance to study the other subjects but I came to know the various inscriptions by heart and, in 1993, seeing the pillar near M'Dina commemorating the apostle's shipwreck on what is now St Paul's Island off the coast of Malta, instantly recalled Brangwyn's rendering of the scene and the text he provided as caption: *And so they all came safe to land!*

[1] Mar 1989 p.50
[2] Dec 1993 p.222
[3] B Williams p.133
[4] December 1996 p.253
[5] Hull p.110
[6] Hull pp.110-11
[7] Jul 1982 p.185
[8] Mar 1991 p.57
[9] Jul 1983 p.183
[10] Morpurgo p.62
[11] Mar 1994 p.75
[12] Ibid
[13] Jan 1970 pp.88-9 & Dec 1991 p.200
[14] Allan p.94

33

A JOLLY GOOD WHACKING

'Anyone who doesn't do as I say is asking for a jolly good whacking.'

Christ's Hospital housemaster, c.1941

Soon after his arrival the new boy was issued with a slim, blue covered booklet entitled *School Rules*. Older boys often amused themselves in idle moments by going through this, ticking those they had broken, but on first reading it tended to be taken seriously and especially those two catch-all warnings: 'Ignorance of these rules is no excuse' and 'A breach of commonsense is a breach of *School Rules*'. In fact the vast majority of offences one was likely to commit were in the house. The close-packed timetable to which we were subjected, the incessant demands for an unnatural tidiness even in the small areas – such as lockers and beds – we could call our own, above all our absurd uniform, which it was almost impossible to keep perfectly clean, all provided frequent opportunities for inflicting punishment.

Significantly, it was the famous Bluecoat and the equally outmoded shirt, bands and socks which went with it, that featured in most of the penalties inflicted. In Peele A, situated at one end of the Avenue, the standard punishment for minor offences was one or more 'Triangles'. A 'Triangle' involved reporting to a monitor in Housey clothes, rushing into the changing room to change into games clothes, running round the small triangular coppice just outside the nearby gates, changing back into Housey clothes, and then reporting to the watch-in-hand monitor. Four minutes was, I think, allowed for this performance, which was just about adequate if you were an old hand, but desperately difficult for a new boy liable to stick his safety pin into his throat when re-fastening his bands. One way to save time was to use 'fudge-bands', pre-pinned together and not fastened to one's shirt, as described earlier, but an alert monitor was likely to jerk these out, resulting in a doubled penalty.

For slightly more serious offences the standard punishment was 'the Post Office', which required one to run across the playing fields to the distant Post Office. For this, I believe, eight minutes was allowed, again just adequate if one was a speedy runner and an accomplished dresser.

Only while writing the present book did I discover that Post Offices were also awarded in other houses. One Coleridge A contemporary, his house being closer to the Post Office than Peele A, has described how he evaded the full rigour of the routine. 'I soon realised,' he confided to *The Blue* in the 1980s, 'that perspective was lost when the runner was more than halfway down the Post Office path and from that point you could just run on the spot.'[1]

Some houses inflicted 'QCs' or 'Quick Changes' on offenders, which meant reporting in uniform, games clothes and again in uniform, but without the running element in between. The reverse of this, not practised in Peele A, was to omit the changing but to require a boy to run round the track encircling Big Side known as the Mile. Here too, inadequate performance resulted in the original sentence being increased. One housemaster 'taking a constitutional on Big Side' found himself overtaken by a member of his house, running in games clothes. 'What are you doing?' he asked, to be told, 'Twenty-seven miles, sir!'[2]

In Peele A, and perhaps in other houses, the house-captain would periodically decide that the house had become slack and proclaim a *Straf*, significantly, a German term for a sudden and vicious bombardment. I recall this being painted in such frightening terms in my first year that some of the new boys were close to tears of apprehension, and Lawrance, a decent individual, felt compelled to say it wouldn't be quite as appalling as it sounded.

If anything it was worse. For several days, until the monitors got as tired of this trivial tyranny as we did, normal life was suspended and a kind of martial law prevailed during which every rule was enforced with rigid minuteness, whether it was producing perfectly squared 'hospital corners' to one's bed, having one's shoe-laces fastened in the correct fashion, or being lined up outside the house before the normal shout of 'On parade!' Our uniform, as always, provided a rich source of potential faults and woe betide the boy during a *Straf* whose bands were not perfectly aligned or whose coat cuffs revealed a spot after scavenging.

Another frequent feature of such occasions was the locker raid, though locker inspections, to see that the contents, which included our private possessions as well as school text and exercise-books, were tidily arranged, also occurred, usually after prior warning, at other times. During a *Straf*, the door would be opened in the owner's absence and the contents of any locker found to be insufficiently neat would be flung on to the floor, to form a heap with the contents of other lockers, from the solid block, four or five rows high, which occupied one corner of the dayroom. This intimidating chaos would confront the unfortunate owners when they returned, to try to extract their possessions from the jumbled up mess on the dayroom floor, a sight which left me with some understanding of what the owners of bombed-out houses must have felt on returning to their damaged homes. Understandable though the desire to encourage tidiness was, I still feel the locker raids were wrong. This was the one tiny fragment of privacy left to us and if a boy chose to keep it in confusion that was his choice, from which only he suffered.

Similar descents to the locker raids were made occasionally on the settles in the dormitory, supposed to be used only for clothes. One monitor would stand sentry at the dormitory door to prevent anyone entering while the rest worked their way from bed to bed, pulling out the contents of each settle and commenting loudly on any illicit articles – a book, or, far worse, an item of food – they found inside and throwing them on the floor. Once, I remember, during the war, the searchers struck gold, in the shape of a collection of used cartridge cases, retained after a Field Day or perhaps picked up in the street and they could hardly have been more jubilant had they discovered a cache of real, live ammunition.

Sometimes, when the person responsible for some misdemeanour could not be detected, the whole house was punished. An extra parade would be ordered, like that I have already described as following one Field Day, in which numbering, dressing and keeping in step were enforced with particular severity. A brisk pace was kept up the whole time and periodically the order would be given 'Breaking into double time, Double march!', which meant that we had to run, still in our clumsy four rank formation and with the skirts of our coats flapping round our knees – a far tougher requirement than any I ever encountered in the army.

The elaborate structure of rule enforcement which governed our lives was completed by school punishments. The great stand-by of masters for non-academic offences was the 'drill', usually single, but ordering two was not unknown. It was much favoured by my housemaster for misdeeds in the Dining Hall, though the offenders rarely served their sentence, for the unfortunate member of my house who acted as secretary to the Hall Warden was regularly forced to rub out the names of any from Peele A. He faced violence from the boys on the drill list if their names were not erased and reprisals from Noel, and the loss of his office, if he was detected. Happily he never was.

I can recall a typical occasion when I was sentenced to a drill, unjustly as I still think. Pitman had asked me to deliver for him an overdue essay to the house of a master directly opposite Peele A, though it was after lock-up, and I did so quite openly, being intercepted on my return by Noel. He refused to accept my explanation, which he could easily have verified, and accused me of sneaking off to visit a boy in another house, a subject on which, as I have mentioned, he was almost paranoid.

Drill also made use of our impractical uniform, rendering a punishment just about bearable in games clothes into an exhausting ordeal. I am still amazed that no one ever actually collapsed as we doubled round the asphalt by the Manual School in our cumbrous, sweat-soaked outfits. That this never happened must be attributed to the good sense and kindly nature of the ubiquitous Sergeant Usher, who presided over Drill, as well as serving as a classroom messenger, gym instructor, sergeant-major on Dinner Parade and, during the war, NCO in the Home Guard. I cannot recall his ever having a day off. He was far better suited to *his* post than several of the masters were to theirs, and was one of those dedicated, long-serving employees who gave the school its character and a greater loyalty than it merited. Even when he retired, Sergeant Usher's first name was not disclosed. He had joined CH eleven years before me, in 1925, on leaving the Royal York and Lancaster Regiment and the Army School of Physical Training. When finally pensioned off, he could still, it was claimed, 'leap and somersault in the gymnasium with the lissomness of a man forty years his junior'. If some of his much quoted witticisms were the common currency of ex-NCOs, such as 'Keep your eyes up! I picked up the cigarette ends long ago,' he added others of his own coining. 'He was going along with his eyes wide shut' and, to those misbehaving while swimming: 'Next time you come to House Baths, don't come!'[3]

Punishment Drill, to give it its official title, had, like so much else at Christ's Hospital, echoes of the army, but more of the 'glasshouse', ie military prison, than of the normal defaulters' parade. One frequent attender at it, at school from 1939-44, left a vivid account of his experiences in *The Blue*:

> The Drill took place in that blessed interval between the end of morning school at 12.15 and lunch at 1.00 pm. The miscreants would report in full uniform to the asphalt square between Lamb A and the Manual School. After forming us into a squad, reading the roll and, on reaching my name, commenting that I was 'one of his favourite sportsmen', Sergeant Usher would direct us round and round the square at the double. Although of stentorian voice he was getting on in years and preferred to remain in one spot as we doubled round. Sometimes the more enterprising would leave the squad at the furthest point from where he stood and would hide round the corner of the Manual School until the squad came round again, but occasionally the sergeant...would halt the squad and call the roll again and absentees would emerge ignominiously from the bushes, to be awarded yet another drill. At five minutes to one, perspiring freely, the squad was dismissed and offenders...had to run back to their houses to be in time for lunch parade.[4]

Occasionally a boy took the risk of not turning up, but this was hazardous, since Sergeant Usher applied a 'doubling up' principle; one missed drill became two, two became four and so on. One of the school's historians has described how his first drill grew into eight, 'So I learned very early that at Christ's Hospital this discipline business was taken seriously,' a conclusion no Old Blue would dispute.[5]

In spite of his disciplinary duties, the sergeant was regarded with universal affection. When, ten years after I had left, he retired, his final Drill was made the occasion of a ceremonial send-off and sixty volunteers joined the listed culprits to perform a kind of lap of honour 'with more than double that number of spectators fringing the asphalt'.[6]

Sometimes it was decided that the whole school needed punishment, as when some notices had been defaced on the boards in the cloisters and the culprits had failed to come forward. On this afternoon we marched by houses round the Mile, periodically as on a regular drill, breaking into double time. The offenders remained undetected and the whole exercise was futile, illustrating the limitations of the public school code of honour which supposedly prompts a culprit to own up to save the innocent from punishment. My verdict is borne out by that of an Old Blue who experienced a similar occasion in the late 1940s. 'I don't think I ever discovered what the original wrongdoing was,' he admits. Robin Hull was among the sufferers when the boy responsible for flicking a pat of 'flab', ie margarine or butter, at the Verrio picture on the wall of Dining Hall where it remained 'all too visible', failed to own up. 'Oily Flecker was incensed and...the whole school was sentenced to a punishment drill.'[7]

To save trouble, or when other punishments had not been completed, there was always beating. In addition to the masters, all monitors, of whom each house contained six or seven, were allowed to beat boys in their own house – though they had no disciplinary powers outside it, except to report the offender – using any instrument they favoured. For summary justice, such as being late for games, a gym shoe, often the victim's own, was favoured, but for more formal, pre-arranged, punishment a cricket stump, a swagger-stick, borrowed from the Corps, or, in Peele A, the handle of a golf-club, never employed for its proper purpose, might be used. Beating was often defended on the grounds that it 'wiped the slate clean' but I was always revolted by it and when, much later could, as a monitor, have beaten boys myself tried to find some more creative alternative. Once, I recall, I set one much punished and, I now realise, maladjusted, small boy to learn a poem after he had left earlier punishments undone, but he proved as hopeless at this as at everything else.

To many masters my hesitation to adopt the obvious solution would have seemed unintelligible. Christ's Hospital had always had a reputation for vigorous corporal punishment, as numerous chroniclers, approving as well as hostile, have testified, and this was a tradition which was conscientiously maintained in my day. When, long after leaving school, I read of a workhouse school in Hackney where a government inspector reported in 1894, after a major scandal, 'From the time the boys get up in the morning until they go to bed at night they are never out of sight of a cane'[8] I thought at once of my old school. The cane, it is true, was rarely visible but the threat of a beating never lay far away and in the 1930s still seemed almost as much a part of a master's routine equipment as his gown.

My first realisation of this came in my first term and astonished me for the master concerned, who taught Latin, was normally amiable and smiling. Suddenly, however, he produced a metal ruler and fiercely caned on the open hand a normally well-behaved boy guilty of some trivial misdemeanour. The culprit burst into loud sobs and was ordered from the room for disturbing the class, leaving us all feeling uneasy and, in my case, ashamed. I have since discovered that this master, LW (Lionel) Tidmarsh, was as addicted to his ruler as some of his colleagues to their canes. One of his frequent victims, with what has proved to be a life-long inability to learn poetry by heart, recalls how 'my regular punishment in almost every English lesson was to have my flat palm beaten several times with a steel ruler...I vowed that if I ever met Mr Tidmarsh after school I would beat him up.' In his house, Middleton A, wrote a boy who was a member of it from 1934 to 1941, to *The Blue* in protest at the usual adulatory tributes on his old housemaster's death, 'Tidmarsh ruled and taught by intimidation'.[9] Clearly, however, this did him no harm professionally. Like so many CH masters he went on to become a headmaster, first of Lady Manners School, Bakewell, then of Aylesbury Grammar School.

The commonest methods of meting out summary justice in class involved cuffing the culprit's head ('fotching' in Housey parlance), ear-boxing and chalk-throwing. At least one master would hurl a bunch of keys at a boy not paying attention, a potentially dangerous missile. Actual beating, as distinct from casual caning on the hand, was rare. I witnessed only one such incident, the offender being aged about 15, the master who punished him being a decent man and the crime a serious one: the boy concerned had substituted sulphuric acid for water in a beaker, knowing that when water is poured into the acid it spurts up explosively. Another Old Blue of my generation, the *Times* columnist Bernard Levin, described to his readers how another boy had applied a heated test tube to his neck, causing him to yelp aloud, 'six of the best' thereupon being delivered on the spot to the boy responsible.[10]

The worst violence I ever suffered in class was a painful punch in the chest from JEM Massen, head of German, for some poorly completed corrections to an exercise and the unexpected blow having failed to improve my mastery of the language he ordered me to take the offending exercise book to my housemaster, presumably for further punishment, in the favoured Housey tradition. Noel, happily, had no liking for anything German and was almost cordial at my having maltreated the language and fallen out with his somewhat Germanic colleague, brushing the matter aside.

Noel himself, of whom I say more later, belonged to the mainstream of public school masters in regard to beating, as indeed to most other things. A solid, powerful figure, when he set himself out to hurt he certainly did so, but I do not believe that, unlike several colleagues, he derived any pleasure from this. He tended to regard the cane as the last resort rather than the first and his routine beatings, as distinct from those for serious offences, tended to be dismissed lightly by their recipients. No doubt one reason why his threats were rarely taken seriously were that they were couched in the outmoded jargon he believed to be idiomatic. 'Anyone who doesn't do as I say, is asking for a jolly good whacking,' he would tell the house and somehow this phrase, like 'six of the best', diminished the solemnity of the warning.

The school in my day had a staff of around fifty,* of whom about half used the cane occasionally and five or six beat constantly at every opportunity, real or imaginary. None of the ablest teachers, with perhaps one exception, ever resorted to such violence, but managed to maintain perfectly good discipline and achieve respectable academic results without it. The keen caners were sometimes competent, but seldom outstanding, teachers, understandably if I am right in believing that it was the infliction of pain rather than the communication of knowledge that they found the most rewarding feature of their profession. 'Some masters,' confirms Robin Hull, 'had the most ferocious reputations. One liked to bend his victim over under the door handle. Invariably, the gluteal [ie buttock and hip] pain made the boy forget the risk to his head which, after being hit on the doorknob as he straightened up was as painful as his bottom.' The same observer makes the point, a very fair one, that 'the days when a boy was not beaten go unremembered' and that 'there were quite a lot of them', but the readiness with which the cane was used still seems to me inexcusable.[11]

In London, as described earlier, boys had sometimes been publicly thrashed in front of the whole school. This practice had died out by my time and I cannot recall any public flogging, though boys were sometimes beaten in front of their classmates. Repellent though this was, with the beater eager to show off his prowess and perhaps deriving some pleasure from the enforced voyeurs observing it, it had exercised some restraining influence. The worst excesses of all occurred in private and were often surrounded by some personal ritual devised by the master concerned to maximise his personal pleasure.

One factor common to what can now be identified as the serious sadists on the staff was that nothing but the bare flesh would suffice to satisfy them. In Victorian magazines any reference to disciplining maid-servants was likely to attract a number of contributions insisting that it was the employer's duty to force the offending girl to remove her drawers and perhaps her petticoat before she was spanked; any intervening layers of cloth would, it was argued, prevent the blows inflicted having their intended disciplinary effect. Our thick blue coats, heavy breeches and coarse shirts and underpants would indeed have provided a measure of protection, but the true flagellants on the staff had devised a regular procedure to ensure that this did not happen. While normal masters would order a boy to change into his flimsy games shorts before

---

* The School List for 1942 includes 45 male assistant masters and 5 female. The latter never, so far as I know, used the cane.

attending for a beating, the real enthusiasts required him to turn up in school uniform, and then to remove his coat, lower his breeches and underpants and bend forward, usually over a chair, with shirt tail flung up over his back, leaving his bare bottom exposed.

All these preliminaries had the effect of prolonging the master's anticipatory pleasure, but thereafter the technique varied. It was the practice of one master to circle round his victim at this point, cane in hand, until, unnerved by the scrutiny of his exposed genitals, the boy began to become physically aroused. The beater would thereupon, with evident pleasure, begin the prescribed punishment. It was often monstrously severe. 'Any master who inflicted this sort of injury to a boy would be in severe trouble these days,' observes one informant who 'never received "six of the best"' himself, 'but saw the results on those who did....The stripes were of a terrible hue and were on the point of bleeding,' a point in fact often surpassed.

Another enthusiast for corporal punishment was the mathematics master LT Waddams, who went on to a headship elsewhere. One of those who suffered at his hands can still picture his 'cold, cruel eyes' below 'spare pale ginger eyebrows...staring at you just before beating'. Waddams had evolved a ritual of his own for spinning out the whole process, for he would order a boy to go back to his, Waddams's house, in mid-class, to await his arrival. He would then follow him back and, the beating duly inflicted, would order the chastened boy to return to the form room 'at the double', a painful process when newly inflicted wounds were chafed by heavy undergarments. The master himself, invigorated by the experience, would be back at his desk before the boy arrived. 'He must,' recalls one sufferer, 'have sprinted across the grass', a short-cut denied, except on penalty of another beating, to the boys.

One close friend, a consistently well-behaved boy, never in trouble, also remembers the sole occasion he was beaten at school, unjustly as he still believes. He had been released from a game at the last possible minute to attend a 'bring up' and, having had to return to our distant house to change, was, quite unavoidably, a minute late. For Waddams this was enough. The unfortunate Peele A boy found himself ordered into the empty classroom next door and was conscious of the obvious enjoyment Waddams derived from what followed, *his* characteristic when administering pain being not visible pleasure but cold disdain.

Beatings inflicted for poor school work or alleged misconduct in the classroom tended to be of a milder character than those delivered inside the houses. There seems to have been an unspoken convention that the fiercest thrashings should be delivered by those supposedly *in loco parentis* to 50 boys, as a junior or senior housemaster. On the latter in particular there was no restriction and a master who interpreted the pastoral care he owed to his boys as involving frequent and savage beating was free to indulge his proclivity unchecked. (Of the fourteen senior housemasters, excluding the Prep, in the

School List for 1942, five readily resorted to corporal punishment, while a smaller group were, to put it euphemistically, inclined to be over affectionate.)

Actual sadists apart, to most masters occasional beating seemed as natural a part of everyday public school life as compulsory games. The archetypal example in my time was LM (Lionel) Carey, of whom I shall say more in a later chapter. He was not, I think, a sadist in the true sense, rather a conventional individual who was not the man to shirk his duty even, or perhaps especially, when it involved inflicting pain. Carey, too, went on to a headship, of a middle-ranking independent school.[12] Within a year or two, so it was reported to us, many of the staff had resigned, refusing to turn back the clock to the old-fashioned, games-obsessed, cane-centred regime imported from Christ's Hospital.

Thanks to our greater knowledge today and numerous prosecutions the tendency of paedophiles to get together to share their experiences is now well known. I have often wondered whether the little group of sadists in the Masters Common Room ever met to discuss their shared interest, forming, to quote the title of a notorious pornographic novel, *The Whipping Club*. If such a caners' circle did exist its head must unquestionably have been the housemaster of the house adjoining mine, Peele B, DS (Derrick) Macnutt.

Macnutt – his 'official' school nickname, 'Boom' was rarely used – was by far the most famous master of my time at Christ's Hospital, thanks to his second profession, that of compiler of crosswords for a national Sunday newspaper, the *Observer*. Within Christ's Hospital he became renowned for different reasons. More space has been devoted to him in *The Blue* than to any other master of my generation and any reference to him prompts a flood of letters, by no means all laudatory. Macnutt's career began conventionally at a boys' prep school, of which one of his own Peele B boys was later to become headmaster, continued conventionally, at public school and university, and attained a solid plateau of orthodoxy at Christ's Hospital, where he was an assistant master from 1928 to 1963, for much of this time editing the school magazine, running the school athletics, appearing in school plays, apparently a model public school master. Macnutt was in fact the James Boyer of his day,[*] a notable teacher of the classics, respected, even liked, by his older pupils, dreaded by the younger boys, a bully and a brute.

Macnutt had known the Headmaster when the latter was an assistant master at Marlborough, with which Christ's Hospital had close links; Old Blues often did their teaching practice, or started their pedagogic careers at Marlborough, though we were not considered grand enough to play it at games. The two largely shared the teaching of the *crème de la crème* of our society, the classical grecians, and had collaborated in by far the best Latin course of the time, which I describe elsewhere. Along with his abilities as a teacher, however,

---

[*] See Chapter 14 above and numerous references in the *Christ's Hospital Book*.

went a fatal flaw, which today would debar him from the profession if not land him in prison.

I have often wondered whether it was the opportunity to beat boys, rather than any real sense of vocation, which attracted him and some like-minded masters into teaching and specifically to Christ's Hospital. Here was a unique opportunity to teach bright boys in what was essentially a charitable institution, where parents would tolerate whatever happened to them with unprotesting acceptance. The possibility seems far-fetched, but in recent years numerous scandals and court cases have revealed how often children's homes and orphanages, especially those with a strong religious tradition, have attracted perverts to their staff.

Macnutt's position as a senior master, teaching a subject which even clever boys often found difficult but in which some proficiency, for reasons I explain later, was essential, gave him ample opportunity to indulge his proclivity, a method favoured since Shakespeare's day. 'If you do not know your *qui's*, your *quae's* and your *quod's*,' declaims the clerical schoolmaster in *The Merry Wives of Windsor*, first performed around 1600, 'you must be preches,' ie beaten.

Some connection appears to exist between the classics and corporal punishment, for those specialising in other Arts subjects like English and history beat far less, if at all. Certainly, Latin, a difficult subject, which, in its lower reaches, requires precise 'right' and 'wrong' answers, and a vast amount of learning by heart, was ideally suited to providing allegedly idle victims for the type of master who liked to teach by terror and punish with pain.

Like other sadists on the staff Macnutt had devised his own rituals to enhance his anticipatory pleasure. One former pupil has described in *The Blue* how he was required to re-learn the previous night's prep after failing to achieve the required mark of nine out of ten. When he presented himself at Macnutt's study for this second test he found that the required minimum had now gone up to ten out of ten, an almost impossible figure, and, failing to reach it, he duly, he recalls, 'received a beating'.[13] Another victim has similar memories of being 'set a short-answer test in form...miraculously I had all the answers right. Not in the least impressed, Macnutt bade me to his study...explained his doubts as to the honesty of my expertise and ordered me to write the answers again. Was he disappointed that I got them right?'[14]

A 'bring-up', where a whole class was brought back for an extra lesson during a games afternoon, provided a golden opportunity for the beating fraternity, and like his fellow flagellant Waddams, already mentioned, Macnutt did not let such a chance slip. He amused himself by devising a form of lottery in which the reward, if he won, as he usually did, was immediate. 'He would,' remembers one sufferer, 'put a cross against a wrong sentence. You sweated to find the error, but if you failed he would send the offender into the next room to beat him.'

Any reference to Macnutt still brings letters flowing in to *The Blue*. 'There must be many for whom this brings back sharp memories,' the Old Blue editor commented on one such contribution as late as 1993,[15] and in the previous year a poem entitled *The Beating* was submitted to a national poetry competition where the subject set was 'Terror'. It was much later withdrawn, but finally appeared in *The Blue* in 1997, after the author's death, 49 years after he had left Christ's Hospital:

> Behold the fearsome Ximenes!
> With eyes that would a furnace freeze.
> And booming voice and angry frown,
> He seeks me out and glowers down...
>
> My heart beats fast, my mouth is dry,
> For retribution cometh nigh.
> "You've done your work disgracefully.
> Come to my study after tea!"
>
> Before the oaken door I wait,
> My guts in delisquescent state,
> Awash with sweat my brow and palms,
> A tremor running down my arms.
>
> He bids me enter with a roar,
> Then rump in air and head to floor,
> Humiliated, wild with pain,
> I bear the venom of his cane.
>
> I shuffle back towards the house,
> Where friends await, solicitous....
>
> 'Let's see the stripes!' I raise my shirt
> 'Good grief, I bet that must have hurt!'
> 'Oh no!' I nonchalantly drawl,
> 'It really hardly hurt at all.'[16]

Like his fellow flagellants, Macnutt had devised his own technique for making sure his victim suffered the maximum pain. By 1993 *The Blue* was enlightened enough to report on the now dead master's 'habit of beating downwards, so that there was no scope for "swaying" with the wind', ie moving slightly to evade the full force of the next blow.[17] A second account, four years later, accompanying the poem just quoted, similarly described how, after the customary stripping from the waist down, Macnutt 'placed the miscreant kneeling in the seat of an elderly armchair, ankles over one arm, midriff over the other, so that there was no way of "riding" the blows'. Here, one must hope, is the last contribution Christ's Hospital will add to the many it has made in the past to the literature of flagellation.[18]

The editorial comment on the first of the accounts quoted above, 'Rumour has it that he was worse before he married',[19] speaks for itself, as does another aspect of the beating ritual. Having ensured that his victim could not move and his naked bottom presented a clear target, Macnutt would open the interconnecting door into another room and retreat to its far corner. He would then, cane in hand, literally run across the intervening space, shouting, 'I am coming!', which we innocently assumed to be a warning to his victim. The blow which followed was savage, with a brief interval while Macnutt withdrew to his launching point, then the procedure would be repeated another three or five or even eleven, times – beatings seem invariably to have been in multiples of two – until, exhausted, he ordered the bruised and perhaps weeping child to leave.

The convention that the most serious, formal beatings tended to be inflicted by one's own housemaster made no appeal to Macnutt, except in so far as it gave him *carte blanche* to maltreat the unfortunate inmates of his house. These included several who later became friends, among them Ivan Yates, an Assistant Editor of the same newspaper that had made Macnutt's name. Later in life he was still obsessed by memories of his housemaster. 'Did you know this terrible man, Macduff, whom Ivan was always talking about?' an *Observer* journalist asked me after his death. It gave me pleasure to hear the tyrant's name rendered wrongly and it reminded me, too, of an occasion when he had to endure a supposed insult in silence. Ivan had innocently remarked to his housemaster that the Debating Society was having great difficulty in finding a speaker but, having scraped the barrel, had finally, he understood, come up with someone. Macnutt, Ivan told me gleefully, had gone purple with rage. 'I suppose you think that is very funny, Yates?' he had replied, revealing he was himself the last-minute choice.

Another member of Macnutt's house has two memories of his housemaster's obsession with violence. Once, early in his school career, this boy had the misfortune to collect four detentions for poor work in a single term, sufficient reason in Macnutt's eyes for him to be beaten by himself. Deciding that only being sent to 'the sicker' could save him from Macnutt's ferocity the small boy began to bang his head against the wall of the cloisters, only to be stopped by Roy Macklin, one of the kindliest of masters, and asked the reason. The boy concerned broke down in tears and, how he never discovered, his rescuer intervened so that the threatened beating never took place.

A few years later there was to be no such reprieve, when, now aged around 16, the same boy, seeking a quiet place to work, climbed out through the attic above the senior dormitory on to the flat space above the side entrance of the house. This was not against any published rule and the boy concerned was a highly responsible individual, already a grecian and later house-captain. Macnutt, however, inflicted such a savage beating that his victim was left barely able to move. His bottom, he recalls, was scored with deep cuts, with blood flowing down his thighs, and when he was allowed to pull up his underpants again they were soon soaked in blood. This spectacle no doubt afforded Macnutt pleasure but also alarmed him. He had, he confessed, gone too far and offered his victim a bribe to stay away from the school baths where the wounds might be seen by other members of the staff.

Macnutt often reminded me of the self-important Paul Pontifex Prout of the Greyfriars stories, but Prout had a kindly streak and was not remotely vicious, while Macnutt, in my recollection, though also pompous and overweight, was perpetually unsmiling. I can recall him glowering at me after I had put my exercise book on the wrong pile, and, even more vividly, my last encounter with him, in the streets of Horsham. I was then almost eighteen, at the top of the school tree, as a first-parting grecian and, most important of all, on a bicycle, when even the army, for safety reasons, merely demanded that you should sit to attention. This, however, was not enough for Christ's Hospital which had a rule, of which, as I have mentioned, I had already fallen foul, that any boy who met a master outside the school grounds should salute him. Only the most pompous, self-important individuals expected this public tribute in such circumstances, especially from someone so senior as I was, but Macnutt was not to be cheated of his moment of public glory. 'It mightn't be a bad idea if you saluted, Longmate!' he shouted after me down the main street of Horsham. At what other school in the country would an 18-year-old have been subjected to such indignity?

Macnutt's reputation in his distinctly minor art form outlived him. During the 1990s the creator of the fictional Chief Inspector Morse, supposedly a crossword addict, named a character after him, though the imaginary Macnutt, I believe, bore no resemblance to his real-life namesake. Nor did the retirement and obituary tributes to him which appeared in *The Blue* in 1963 and 1971 respectively, though it has made amends since.[20] Macnutt's prowess at composing crosswords has even earned him a place in the *New Dictionary of National Biography*, due to be published around the year 2000. As the author of another entry I was invited to contribute my recollections of Macnutt to the non-Old Blue writing about him. I suggested that the opening sentence of the entry under his name, supposed to summarise its subject's main occupations, should read 'Sadist, schoolmaster and crossword compiler' in that order.

[1] Mar 1988 p.69
[2] Jul 1989 p.136
[3] Jan 1954 pp.5-6
[4] Mar 1988 p.69
[5] Mar 1986 pp.130-1
[6] Jan 1954 p.5
[7] Hull p.47
[8] *The Workhouse* p.180
[9] Mar 1993 p.56 & Dec 1992 p.230
[10] Jul 1993 p.145
[11] Hull p.102
[12] Mar 1953 p.86
[13] Jul 1993 p.141
[14] Dec 1993 p.220
[15] Jul 1993 p.140
[16] Jul 1997 p.174
[17] Jul 1993 p.141
[18] Jul 1997 p.174
[19] Jul 1993 p.141
[20] Sep 1963 p.133 & Sep 1971 p.248

34

FOR NOEL'S IN BED

*'For Noel's in bed
With a cold in his head.'*

Song of Peele A boys during housemaster's illness, c. 1941

Apart from an ability to play games, or the lack of it, nothing made more difference to the happiness of one's life at Christ's Hospital than the house to which one was assigned. A good housemaster could make the grim Housey regime at least a degree more tolerable; a bad, or, more commonly, excessively tough one, could render it almost unbearable. It was perfectly possible, so separate were the various houses, to go through one's whole career without ever speaking to some of the masters, indeed at the end of seven years there were still some of whose names I remained uncertain. But with one's housemaster one was in daily contact, in the formal routine of Duty, in seeking permission to venture outside the ring fence or – a much more serious request, involving questioning about the reasons – to visit another house. Some housemasters left the house, or rather the monitors, to run itself. 'What are the troops doing?' HR ('Troops') Hornsby, of Middleton B, would ask his house-captain, thereby earning himself his nickname. 'In my day we hardly ever saw the housemaster or his deputy,' confirms one boy who arrived there the same day that I entered Peele A. 'Mid B in my time was run by the monitors' – with results I shall describe in a later chapter. The junior housemaster of Middleton B at that time, HD Sills, of whom I shall also say much more in a moment, carried on the non-interventionist tradition when in due time he became senior housemaster of a house of his own, Maine A, at the far end of the Avenue, beyond the Quadrangle, almost as remote as if it had been on another planet. At the other end of the spectrum were the masters who were for ever wandering about their houses, either on the lookout for trouble or, though less likely, because they actually liked boys and considered it their duty. Nearly all masters at some time served as housemasters, the post being welcomed as providing extra income, and sometimes in several different houses, a junior housemaster commonly being moved elsewhere rather than being promoted within the same house. Aptitude for the job, much less matching a master to a particular house, does not seem to have been considered, though whether or not a house had accommodation attached for a family was a decisive factor. Junior housemasters, however, were not invariably resident and I can recall some, already married, with homes elsewhere on the estate, who merely retained a study, as a daytime base, in the house they helped to run. That a man might be competent in the classroom but useless at providing pastoral care outside it was not a factor taken into account. Looking down the list of junior housemasters when I first arrived who went on to become senior housemasters I can identify several with no real interest in caring for boys and at least two with all too much, who should never have been allowed near a dormitory. Here Peele A was lucky. With one exception, mentioned elsewhere, who lasted only a term thanks to his over-affectionate disposition, our junior housemasters were excellent young men – or, in the case of the best of all, women – sensible, forthright, good-natured and as yet untouched by the premature senility and narrow-mindedness which so often affected long serving older masters.

It was, however, the senior housemaster who really set the character of the house and here I now think, though we did not recognise it at the time, Peele A was relatively fortunate. For the whole of my time there we had in charge of us a man who, for all his little oddities – and nowhere could eccentricities flourish more than in a boarding school – was a fundamentally decent person. To realise how lucky we were I have only to recall that at the other end of the short corridor separating us from Peele B was the domain of the appalling Macnutt.

JNB Sergent was himself not lacking in weight and self-conscious dignity and had indeed that innately solid if not pompous air that so often marks out the long-serving schoolmaster. He was, however, as I now appreciate, a fundamentally decent if unimaginative man, with a thoroughly normal and happy family life, to which his surviving daughters testify. He beat occasionally – I have already mentioned his threats to administer 'A jolly good whacking' – but from a sense of duty, not pleasure. Though by no means the greatest influence on my schooldays he was more responsible than any other individual for my daily welfare in the seven years I spent in Peele A and I believe he tried conscientiously to fill the place for all of us of the fathers we had left at home.

I have since discovered that almost everything we believed about him was wrong. We regarded his spelling of his surname as a form of affectation and suspected that some slightly shady reason lay behind his settling in England when he was clearly French, though there could have been no one less Gallic and excitable in his manner. Beside the customary MA, his qualifications listed in the school roll included B-ès-L, which we dismissed contemptuously as 'The French School Cert.', instead of recognising it as the far more demanding baccalaureate. His service in the French army in the first world war, which he sometimes mentioned, we chose to believe had been in some unit well to the rear, like the Pay Corps. In fact he had a distinguished front line record and, though he never revealed this, had won the *Croix de Guerre*. We gave him no credit for his perfect English accent and vocabulary, preferring instead to mock his sometimes excessively formal grammar and use of slightly out-of-date slang. 'Honest Injun?' he would ask, like a character in Kipling's *Stalky and Co* (published in 1899), when questioning some boy's veracity. Once he brought a slice of cake into the dayroom and asked *'Quis?'* – 'Who wants it?' – a routine in which we often engaged to dispose of some unwanted item. Instead of an enthusiastic chorus of *'Ego!'* – 'Me!' – there was an embarrassing silence and the boy who eventually replied, and then carefully scrutinised the gift before eating it, was reproved for discourtesy and ingratitude. This was all too typical of Noel's well-meaning attempts to form a better relationship with his house. There was something so innately stiff about him that, however much he tried to unbend, one felt uneasy in his presence. My father found his occasional meetings with Noel a great trial, with conversation painfully difficult on both sides. His solitary meeting with the Headmaster was, by contrast, a great success, my father pronouncing him 'far easier to get on with'.

Noel Sergent would undoubtedly have been delighted by the description of him in his obituary by a colleague in *The Blue* as 'an English gentleman', though he was passionately proud of being French. He was the youngest child of a French architect-cum-engineer and an English mother and grew up bilingual in the South of France. The family moved to Oxford to assist the sons to enter English public schools, and Noel duly attended the Dragon School and then Repton, going on to graduate at Oxford before returning to the Dragon School as a master and thence moving to Christ's Hospital.

He was, I now appreciate, a man with an extraordinary range of abilities, for none of which we gave him much credit. His facility with our language we took for granted, though, I was told, it was notable enough for him to have been an interpreter at the Versailles peace conference. He was said to have been in the French national high-diving team and to have been of almost equal standard at football, though we rated higher the fact that he was entrusted with training the Colts, an inter-house team of 14 and 15 year olds felt to show promise on the rugger field. He was an accomplished skater, but we attributed, I fear, to his weight rather than his skill the tradition that, as his obituary in *The Blue* recorded, 'on him was the responsibility always of deciding if the ice of the Lake would bear' boys venturing on to it. [1]

Noel Sergent was a competent performer on the clarinet and a more than competent broad-stroke painter, producing the scenery not merely for house plays but for school Gilbert and Sullivan productions, though I doubt if these essentially English works much appealed to him. He wrote, as I have already described, plays for us to act which were admirably suited to both performers and audience, but the jokes, which from any other pen we would have applauded, we affected to despise and would repeat them mockingly to a chorus of groans. He reacted very typically. Instead of ignoring this foolish response he delivered an over-solemn homily to the cast – I can still remember its opening words, 'I say, my men, a word about the jokes...' – to remind us that they would come fresh to those who heard them on the night. We had no suspicion that he was much liked by the women who joined the staff during the war for being far more welcoming to them than most of the masters. Only years later did I learn that he had marked the birthday of one of them, in 1943 or 1944, with an elegant home-made card, which carried an excellent drawing of the chapel and some humorous verses listing various members of the staff:

> Hooray! Hooray!
> So ALL the staff do say!
> Humps and Blam and Poo and Burl:
> Joining fingers skip and twirl,
> Round their birthday girl,
> Hooray! [*][2]

Here was a side of our housemaster, skittish and gallant, we had never discovered, though the house had composed its own verses about him, when he lay ill, and a group of boys wandered from dayroom to changing room singing these distinctly callous lines, to the tune of one of the Brandenburg Concertos:

> Oh let us rejoice and make a great noise,
> For Noel's in bed with a cold in his head
> And he's damn nearly dead.

Why this essentially decent and well meaning schoolmaster should have provoked such constant derision I am still not clear, but another occasion illustrates our attitude all too well. Early in the war the school had, with remarkable open-mindedness, invited a German refugee who had been a spy for his country during the first world war to address us. This man, Captain von Rintelen, had held us spellbound with his account of his experiences, and afterwards a list was circulated inviting anyone who wished to buy his book, *The Dark Invader*, available in a Penguin paperback. Noel was outraged. He urged us not to believe in the speaker's protestations of a change of loyalties, and on no account to enrich him further by buying his book. Without this exhortation few of us, I think, would have done so, for we had no love for the Germans and sixpence [2.5p] was, after all, sixpence, but the opportunity to deliver a public slap in the face to our housemaster was too good to miss, especially as Noel would have the chore of deducting the payment from our pocket money. Every boy in the house, I believe, put his name down and Noel

---

[*] The masters named are CA Humphrey, C Blamire Brown, the Rev H Poole and DH Burleigh.

had to take what consolation he could from the fact that he was proved right; soon afterwards von Rintelen was arrested and interned.

With his intense admiration for the English public school system, it must, I now suspect have been a disappointment for Noel to find himself at Housie, a long way down any recognised 'pecking order'. With its working – and lower-middle – class recruitment area, its barracks-cum-workhouse atmosphere and its bizarre uniform the school was not a promising setting for turning out well-spoken, well-mannered, suitably dressed English gentlemen. Noel, however, did his best. One reason for his hostility to us having contact with boys from other houses was that we should not suffer from the contagion of their bad example; he hoped, on the contrary, that we would visibly surpass the rest of the school in our reputation for courtesy. I remember one post-Duty address in which he proudly informed us that one Peele A boy was renowned throughout the school for his politeness. We stared at each other in bewilderment as to whom this paragon might be. I found myself, somewhat embarrassingly, under suspicion, since I did indeed automatically stand aside to let others pass through a door first, or get a better place on the touch-line, from no higher motive than timidity.

Even more important than letting others go in front of one was treating the opposite sex with respect, a difficult lesson to teach at Christ's Hospital where they were so thin on the ground. As we no longer wore hats even Housie could not require us to raise them, as convention then required, on greeting, leaving or passing a female acquaintance, or even on speaking to a lady out of doors, but it did its best by ordering us to salute, in military style, any master's wife we encountered in the grounds; outside them, as I have described elsewhere, we were required to greet male members of the staff similarly. In my time most masters were still single and we so rarely saw the partners of those who were married that it could be years before you could recognise them with confidence. To be on the safe side we therefore tended to salute any woman in sight, so that matrons, Infirmary nurses and even maids and washers-up from the kitchens, as embarrassed by this gesture as we were, all tended to receive a salute, sometimes altered, when identification seemed doubtful, to a non-committal scratching of the side of the head. When I became old enough to recognise a pregnant woman, which was not something expected of a ten year old in 1936, I invariably saluted her, assuming that no one except a master's wife would have the temerity to reproduce within the ring fence.

So far as our primitive conditions and hurried meals allowed, Noel Sergent was a stickler for good table manners, and here he had a unique opportunity to ensure his house set a good example since, as Hall Warden, he was the only master present at every meal. He often circled his house's table to ensure we were all behaving with proper decorum and eating everything on offer, however repellent. Luckily he was easily deceived by a hastily smeared plate, but I do recall him upbraiding me when I had left some baked beans one teatime; as these are now a favourite of mine, the Housey version must have been singularly inedible. 'Longmate,' he told me, 'you are a little fusspot!', a sentiment that more than one hostess has, more politely, echoed since.

Noel was also concerned that we should all learn to write an acceptable letter of thanks for hospitality, though this was really the responsibility of the English staff. I recall his referring to 'a bread and butter letter', a phrase new to us, which we assumed at first to be a literal translation from the French, and how essential it was to despatch this within a week of being entertained, 'or', as he told us, 'your name will be mud in that house ever afterwards'.

To encourage a proper standard of letter writing he once required everyone in the house, from the most senior to the newest new boys, to write him a letter as if from home, offering a prize for the best. I was much affronted when this coveted shilling [5p] was awarded to a boy younger than me whose letter was full of rambling irrelevances instead of keeping to the prescribed subject, a lost ration book. I had, I discovered, lost marks, in an otherwise perfect letter, for omitting the 'esquire' after Noel's name on the envelope, which he probably interpreted as a deliberate insult, but was due to sheer carelessness. Much later I realised Noel had probably wished, as in the award of parts in his house plays, to encourage a normally despised member of the house, a boy who achieved the remarkable feat of being even more unpopular than I was.

If this was the reason it provides further proof of Noel's conscientiousness and innate good nature, but somehow we never gave him the credit for his good qualities and generation after generation of Peele A boys followed its predecessor's lead in referring to him disparagingly. 'Have you heard Noel's latest?' we would ask each other about some perfectly reasonable remark. One constant campaign which he waged was against bad language, then far less prevalent among either adults or children than it has since become. When I first went to school some masters were almost fanatical in their objection to even the mildest swearwords. I can recall one boy who used the word 'damn' in the hearing of a master during a lesson being held out of doors being ordered to move away from the rest of us, since, he was told, he was not fit to be near decent people, and another referring to '"mad" spelt backwards', rather than use the same word himself. Expressions such as 'Oh God', at least on the lips of a younger boy, invited heavy punishment and I recall a divinity lesson devoted largely to discussing the morality of milder alternatives, the master's ruling being that even 'Crikey!' which was permitted – my usual test – at Greyfriars, was best avoided as having possibly blasphemous origins, though 'Good heavens!' was, I think, allowed. In my last year or so I do recall hearing the now legitimately printed 'f word' occasionally, but a boy who introduced us to the 'c word', still barely acceptable today, was for a time at least shunned as a pariah.

Noel Sergent, never the man to shirk his duty, was keen that his house should set a good example in these matters, as in all else. 'Damn', I recall his telling us in one of his regular evening addresses, was permissible in extreme circumstances, as when one hit one's fingers with a hammer, but 'bloody' was definitely not. At even grosser words he merely hinted. When my friend Bob Pitman became house-captain, in 1942, he was, he told me, given two tasks by his housemaster, of which one was to reduce the amount of bad language heard in the house. Bob himself had never been a great offender in this respect, and even later, in the often foul-mouthed environment of Fleet Street avoided what was so mistakenly called 'colourful' language. He now set out to introduce such novel oaths as 'Great George!', though with no great success.

The other duty laid upon him was to try and create what Noel described as 'a better spirit in house games'. Here, too, he had, I think, little success. Although boys certainly liked to score tries or gain their house colours it was undoubtedly, as seems to me a characteristic of all sportsmen, more a matter of personal glory than of helping one's team. The house often seemed indeed to feel some satisfaction in losing a game on the grounds that it would annoy Noel. His attempts to improve matters merely made them worse. I can recall a typically heavy-handed talk on the theme of house spirit, which contained the words – I have remembered them precisely because few had done less to bring the house athletic glory than me – 'Boys who don't show a proper spirit in house games grow up to be the scum of the earth, conscientious objectors and people like that.' I had known in my first years in the house a boy now serving, as a Quaker, in the Friends Ambulance Unit, who had been excused from joining the Corps. He had been a far more civilised person than many of the games-playing bullies now in uniform and I concluded that Noel had, as usual, got it wrong.

The Blue said in its obituary tribute to him that 'French he sturdily remained, despite his naturalisation...French in his taste in wines; in his exquisite cooking of an omelette'[3], a skill he was once said to have demonstrated to a junior class. His house, alas, failed to recognise his virtues. If we had known, for instance, as I heard years later, that he was, in true Gallic fashion, having an affair with some unidentified lady – whether member of the staff or colleague's wife remains uncertain – we would have respected him more. It was true that under his rule Peele A produced a remarkable number of Senior Grecians, one of whom later testified to his 'fundamental goodness'. This was not an attribute every senior housemaster possessed but, sadly, not one we either recognised or appreciated.

The French master in many schools, including Greyfriars, was a traditional figure of fun, but this was certainly not true of Noel Sergent. 'He would award a punishment drill to anyone not actually sitting down in his class when the bell went,' remembers one former pupil. 'It was not good enough to be entering.' Noel had his own, often mimicked, catchphrase, based on his 'strange rule that all pupils had to have their hands on top of the desk at all times. If any hands strayed below his expression was: "I say, man, hands above board!"' By the time I first entered his classroom myself I was a grecian and too senior for such treatment, but it stemmed, I suppose, from that same obsessive fear of illicit sexual activity that led to his torchlight patrols of the Peele A dormitories.

To the rest of the school the man we knew as Noel was 'Sam' Sergent, a name due solely to an affection for alliteration. Because of his third role, which I shall mention in a moment, he was to be one of the best remembered masters of his generation; although he died in 1954, just before he was due to retire, he was still, along with the unspeakable Macnutt, prompting reminiscences in *The Blue* 30 years later, like this account by someone assigned to his French class following two years under a notoriously poor disciplinarian. It was an experience, he decided, resembling that 'of a German soldier transferred from guard duties in Paris to the Russian front':

> Sam had an overwhelming physical presence. He was very tall, with slightly simian features, massively built yet proportioned like an athlete. A man of few words, and those mostly sarcastic, he towered over us like a francophone King Kong, often literally rendering us speechless with terror. Once or twice a term a wintry smile would flicker across his face, but he betrayed no other evidence of a sense of humour...He set about covering two years' curriculum in one, and being an excellent teacher, as well as a martinet, succeeded. [4]

In the classroom, I must have been as much of a disappointment to him as in the house, for I had no aptitude for languages and found French far more difficult, both to learn and to pronounce, than German. When I encountered him, in my last term, as a first-parting grecian secure of his university place, I recall moving my housemaster to despair. 'I say, old Longmate,' he once addressed me, after my rendering of some straightforward sentence had reduced the other members of the form to near hysterics, 'you may be a fool, but you can't be such a fool as all that.' But the sad truth was that I could.

Yet not all his efforts were in vain. Some of his enthusiasm for French literature and all things French rubbed off on me and I have occasionally struggled since to appreciate them. I remembered his lively rendering of Alphonse Daudets's *Lettres de Mon Moulin* when, late in life, visiting Daudet's native Provence, and Noel's praise of the drink *cassis* caused me to try it 50 years later. One of his favourite themes was the superiority of the French cafe to the average English pub, which he dismissed as 'a horrible place'. We regarded it as a great cheek for a Frenchman to criticise one of our national institutions, but I now think he was probably right. Here was the fundamental reason for the lack of *rapport* between Noel and his house. However perfect his English, however obvious his devotion to English games and customs, he was not, and never could be, wholly one of us.

Noel (or Sam) Sergent's position in charge of the Dining Hall gave him ample opportunity to exercise his authority and for miscreants to try to undermine it. His principal duty was to maintain discipline at meals. Any boy who wished to leave his own table to visit another for any purpose, even to find extra crockery or cutlery or to deliver a message on school business, was required to go first to the Hall Warden's desk for permission. In some houses it was the custom to garble such requests and to boast of having asked, 'May I cut off your head, sir?' instead of 'May I get some more bread, sir?', relying on Noel's alleged deafness to escape detection.[5] In addition to preventing contact between the separate tables, the Warden used his gavel at the beginning and end of every meal, first to call for silence, then to signal the grecian in the pulpit to read grace. Irreverent treatment of these ancient prayers always offended him, and I can recall a typical reprimand delivered to the whole school after one boy had read grace in a grotesque accent, modelled on that of another who was particularly slow spoken and deep voiced. The whole school, given prior warning, responded with a similarly sepulchral 'Amen!', but Noel failed to see the joke. He gave an additional, extra loud, bang with his gavel and delivered a full-scale homily, in over-correct English, of the kind his own house was accustomed to hear after Duty. 'There are those who when they see an ancient oak tree feel compelled to carve their names upon it,' he began – so emphatically that I can recall the precise words, 'Today a similar act of vandalism has been inflicted upon our ancient Housey grace.' We were, I think, suitably chastened, but a generation after mine repeated the offence, for in 1948 the grecian responsible for delivering grace 'mimed the words', while a second grecian 'concealed below the front of the pulpit, spoke them'. The 'great roar of laughter' which greeted this performance left my old housemaster puzzled and he had clearly forgotten the date, April the first. When another master, who was in the secret, enlightened him, Noel 'stormed over to the Office' to complain to the headmaster and the offenders, one of the pair later recalled, were 'sentenced to be deprived of our buttons and the privileges thereto appertaining'. Happily their status was restored before they left. Robin Hull witnessed a similar, more serious incident, which confirms how Dining Hall tended to be the site of any collective gesture of defiance towards authority:

> Once, in protest at some real or imagined injustice, there was an organised laugh. At a prearranged signal, the entire school of 800 boys started to laugh. The laughter quickly got out of control and merged into hysteria, which frightened the staff out of their wits.[6]

Noel also took very seriously his duty to ensure that no food was wasted. One Old Blue has described how, having received a bad hard-boiled egg, and 'desperately hungry' he took it up to the Hall Warden's desk 'to have it changed'. Instead he found himself 'forced to consume' the defective egg, which left him, he found, unable to eat another for many years. [7]

The same boy had, however, a suitably appropriate revenge. Another of the Hall Warden's duties was to condemn cracked crockery taken up to him for inspection, and, to ensure it was not used again, to shatter it with his gavel. The policy 'led inevitably to the occasional' plate or 'kiff' bowl 'having a line pencilled on it', in place of a real crack. 'To the amusement of all those in the know, "Sam" had to hit pretty hard, at least a couple of times, before the…bowl broke in pieces.' [8]

---

[1] Sep 1954 pp.147-9
[2] Lent 1996 p.161
[3] Sep 1954 pp147-9
[4] Dec 1987 p.196
[5] Hull p.45
[6] Hull pp.45-7
[7] Jul 1986 p.195
[8] Jul 1986 p.195

LEARNING PSALMS FOR KAPPA

*You must learn a psalm by Saturday
and say it after tea...*

Song of Maine A boys about their housemaster, c. 1941

So rigid was the separation between houses that we knew little of what went on elsewhere and only now have I realised how comparatively lucky we were in our housemaster. Macnutt's Peele B apart, and the houses ruled at various times by the burnt-out Blamire Brown and the cane-ready Tidmarsh and Waddams, I would, I believe, have had the worst time in Barnes B, presided over with a rod of pliable wood, if not of iron, by the man one of its members recalls as 'the fearsome Lionel Carey'[1].

LM Carey's father had been immortalised in *The Loom of Youth*, that admirably accurate portrait of the public schools of its time, as 'The Bull', a nickname overtly based on his fictional name in the novel, Buller.[2] It was, however, apt for other reasons, as, according to the author of the novel, he 'rushed up and down the field cursing and swearing' and would accuse any team which failed to measure up to his standards of 'shirking'.[3] His son, who had also attended Sherborne and been 'a notable rugby player',[4] followed the parental lead and one Old Blue has described his technique, experienced at the age of 16, as 'coaching by cursing'.[5]

Lionel Carey, with whom, happily, my own contacts were confined to receiving orders from him in the Home Guard, illustrates both the virtues and the defects of the traditional public schoolmaster. He had acquired a degree at Cambridge and was a conscientious teacher, remembered with gratitude by some of his pupils, but his academic interests were limited and his work confined to subjects, or age groups, not considered demanding.[6] He taught a minor subject, geography, and some history, his approach, according to one witness, being 'inclined somewhat to the school of Sellars and Yeatman', authors of *1066 and All That*. 'The British Empire was a Good Thing, and so was the House of Lords,' but the best thing of all was undoubtedly rugger, which his house was expected to play and practise with fanatical devotion:

A new boy entering Barnes B in my day might have been forgiven for thinking he had arrived at an academy dedicated to the study of rugby football, with a little school work thrown in for light relief...Even on Sunday afternoons we were as likely to spend our precious free time booting a ball back and forth as going for a walk or engaging in a hobby.[7]

This boy, a success in Housey terms, came to share his housemaster's enthusiasm, deciding that the game was 'an excellent character-builder, hugely enjoyable to play and watch', and, at worst, all over in 'a brisk eighty minutes', in contrast to cricket which, for all but a few 'prima donnas', was merely 'constructive time-wasting'. It was indeed the character-building which appealed to Carey. He accepted that the members of a rugger team would receive as well as give hard knocks and was scornful of the welcoming claps which traditionally greeted a boy who returned to the field after being hurt. 'It was Carey's dictum', recalls one who imbibed it, 'that "It's his duty to come back if he can breathe."...Many is the visiting player who staggered back on to the pitch, bleeding, shattered but determined, to be met by a stony silence from the massed ranks of CH support.'

Here was a classic example of Christ's Hospital outdoing its rivals in the public school virtues and the same approach permeated the daily life of Bames B. Carey's perpetual enemy was 'spinelessness', for which, in his view, the best remedies were 'fresh air and cold water'.[8] He introduced into his house the custom of a compulsory early morning cold bath, which no other master inflicted on his boys, though, as I have mentioned, his fresh-air obsession was widely shared and would have been defensible, even laudable, if the heating and blankets provided in the dormitories had been more adequate.

Barnes B was not totally without lighter relief. The monitors were, one contributor to *The Blue* has recorded, allowed to keep their gramophone after Carey's arrival, although 'their record collection...for a long time...', those listening upstairs in the senior dormitory soon discovered, 'numbered just two well-worn 78s...Ravel's *Bolero* and *O my beloved Father*, from the opera *Gianni Schicci,* played after the rest of the house had gone to bed:'

As the last palsied echoes of the music died away, a ghostly figure would be discerned proceeding down the dormitory. It was Lionel Carey, wrapped up to the eyebrows against the cold, on Window Patrol. Fresh perhaps from a convivial evening with his crony Fred Haslehust, exuding the faintest aura of Scotch, his gait on the deliberate side of careful, he would ensure that no obstacle was allowed to stand between his charges and the icy currents of character-building air blasting in from the Arctic Circle.[9]

The strict regime in Bames B, one of those who endured it considers, was all the less appreciated in that its neighbour, Bames A, was presided over by 'the kindly old Mr Burleigh':

Our style of break-time PT was frenetic, theirs balletic. For them marching was a means to an end, rather than an end in itself. They did not consider every moment not spent chasing a ball as a moment wasted. They did not subscribe to the barbarous dawn ritual of the Cold Bath. Their monitors had a distinct likeness to normal human beings, unlike rather too many of ours...who tended to resemble demented sergeant majors.[10]

All this dedication failed, however, to earn its just reward; civilised Athens continued to challenge philistine Sparta:

When we were called upon to test ourselves against them on the rugby pitch or cricket field they were as likely to prevail as we were. It was hardly fair or, to quote one of our stuffier house-captains, 'Just not good enough'.

We would have been astonished to discover that the extrovert Carey, never seen without a rugger ball under his arm or a cane, or swagger stick, in his hand, had a totally different image among the children of other masters. One still remembers him as 'Uncle Moke' and recalls with delight the elaborate tales he invented to amuse her sister and herself about the adventures of a Red Indian chief and his squaw, 'Wishee Washee'.* 'Hairy Carey' as we called him – a play on the Japanese phrase hari-kiri then often in the newspapers, as he was not particularly hirsute – was a model of fitness, who looked like a first world war subaltern, but a significant number of his colleagues suffered from some form of disfigurement or disability. Blam had what appeared to be the remains of a bullet hole in one cheek, which we attributed to a German sniper whose aim, regrettably in our view, had been inaccurate; the real cause was less exciting, the removal of a cyst. Fred Haslehust's striking facial scar was, we chose to believe, the result of an encounter with Chinese pirates while serving as a magistrate in the Far East. He had in fact had no such career and acquired this disfigurement in the same disastrous car accident which had prevented him taking his degree. The one time junior housemaster of Peele A, PR Beaven, would intrigue us by removing his glass eye, the result of a laboratory accident as a research student.[11] He had in no way allowed the disability to interfere with his life; he was an excellent shot and highly competent driver. His nickname, I now feel, was somewhat heartless – 'Pop', short for 'Popeye', though on his death the matron of Peele claimed that it was really a tribute to his kindly, paternal manner. It was shortly after my time that a master in another house returned from the war with an artificial leg which he would remove and leave, complete with sock and shoe, outside his cabin while taking boys on a sailing holiday; at school he barely acknowledged its existence, but his nickname was even more tasteless that Beaven's, 'Pegleg'.

The most unkind nickname of my day was reserved for the most visibly disabled member of the staff, who, because of his crippled lower leg walked

---

*This seemed to me so inconceivable that I queried this story with the informant concerned but she assured me that her memory was reliable.

with a curiously jerky gait, which resembled in profile the Greek letter 'K'. 'Kappa' – in fact HD (for Harold, or Harry, Darlington) – Sills seemed odd even in a staffroom containing numerous eccentrics. We speculated about the cause of his deformity, usually attributing it to the currently newsworthy polio, but in fact, I learned later, it was the result of a childhood accident. An Old Blue visitor, invited to visit his home, found a rag still tied to the banisters on the stairs, to mark the spot where, as a one year old, he had fallen headlong to the bottom after a nursemaid had failed to fasten a protective gate.

The young Sills was already a sickly child and, according to family legend, had only survived infancy after the doctor had said in despair, 'Well, give him a little port!' His intended school, Harrow, was ruled out because it contained too many steps and he was sent instead to Uppingham which was enlightened enough to allow him to play golf. He went on to read science at King's College, Cambridge, and thence to teach at Christ's Hospital, a curious choice for someone physically crippled and of solitary temperament. He remained a bachelor throughout his life, returning to the family home near Cambridge during the holidays where he lived until his death with his mother and subsequently with his brother, cared for by a housekeeper in a bitterly cold house.

This cheerless, enclosed and unexciting life, of which I learned only while writing the present book, reflects, and perhaps helps to explain the character of, this essentially sad figure. I cannot recall his ever smiling and he lacked altogether that natural warmth to which boys instinctively responded. Poor Kappa was simply never at ease with either his class or his house and I still cringe at the memory of the final physics lesson of each term when he would try to unbend. While other masters devised appropriate forms of relaxation, like singing German songs, composing historical crosswords, or simply exchanging jokes or anecdotes – good teachers, I had by now realised, were often natural story-tellers – Kappa was reduced to appealing to members of his class to recite a favourite poem. Usually a painful silence followed and, even though we were not working, the end of the lesson was greeted with more than the usual relief.

When I first encountered him Kappa must still have been in his early thirties but he always seemed to belong to the Housey 'old guard', like the prematurely aged Blam, who seemed to have gone into teaching because they disliked boys. A few, by contrast, had evidently chosen it because they liked boys too much, but Kappa appears to me now, as he did then, to have been entirely sexless. Nor, come to that, could I imagine him enjoying a drink. He could clearly play little part in the games which dominated our lives, and obsessed some housemasters, though he gamely took part in what was described as 'basic tennis'. He had, I believe, taken refuge from his infirmity by behaving as though he were already old. 'To me he seemed like Methuselah', comments one of his former house-captains, who found him easier to deal with than more interventionist superiors, since he was only too happy to remain distant from his charges. As another former member of his house, Maine A – next door to that of the perpetually active Lionel Carey, Barnes B – has remarked, it was probably only the shortage of better qualified candidates during the war which had brought him to a position for which he was temperamentally unsuited. Despite his disability, however, he managed to carry out at least one almost indispensable part of a housemaster's duties. He had, it was reported, worked out a means of securing his balance while beating, so that he could swing his cane with the best of them, though not the worst; his house was ruled with strictness but not brutality. We even felt a certain grudging respect for him after he was said to have beaten two senior boys on their very last night at school after they had celebrated their impending liberation with illicit beer, drunk in the traditional resort of law-breakers, the Lag.

Parents found it as difficult as their sons to establish any rapport with Kappa. I remember the mother of a small boy in Maine A confiding in me, in my last term, how much her son disliked his housemaster and how she believed his deformity caused him to resent the normal, healthy boys over whom he ruled. The explanation now seems to me all too credible and explains what vaguely puzzled me then, the feeling that within that cold, unresponsive exterior there was a kinder, more sensitive person trying to get out.

As an alternative to beating Kappa would sentence boys guilty of minor offences to learn a psalm by heart. Just as in Peele A we sang unfeelingly about Noel to the tune of the Brandenburg Concertos, so Maine A resounded to kindlier verses set to a tune from *HMS Pinafore*:

> Never mind the why and wherefore,
> I am Kappa Sills and therefore
> You will learn a psalm by Saturday
> And say it after tea.
> It had better be psalm twenty,
> For I think that will be plenty
> For a little twit like thee.[12]

Just as in the laboratory Kappa was curiously inarticulate when not actually teaching, so his relations with his house represented a triumph of non-communication. One former Maine A boy still remembers how he provided news of a member of the house believed to be dangerously ill in the Infirmary. 'I have to tell you,' he blurted out suddenly after Duty, 'that Byers' – I have altered the name – 'is dead!' No consoling words or memorial tribute followed. The periodic meetings Kappa called of his house monitors soon foundered into uneasy silence, with each side regarding the other with tongue-tied embarrassment. Once, bravely, but disastrously, he tried to instruct some of the adolescents in his charge on the facts of life. Better informed than their bachelor housemaster, they responded with some sophisticated teasing. 'What about VD, sir?' asked one boy with apparent innocence and was told, after a pause: 'Well, I don't really know much about that. But if you ever go to France, make sure you cover the lavatory seat with paper.'

Kappa must have been aware of the nickname so callously given to him. One master who prided himself on his forthrightness would openly greet him by it and one of my informants recalls including it in a list of masters' nicknames which he carelessly left in a physics exercise book. Kappa made no comment except to give him a detention, a favourite punishment of his, since, unlike so many of his colleagues, he beat with reluctance rather than enthusiasm. He must also have overheard the 'Kappa races' which regularly took place between boys in his house. Trying to walk with a halfpenny lodged between the thighs produced a similar gait to that of their housemaster and the competitors, so handicapped, would half run, half walk along the passage connecting the changing rooms, anyone whose coin fell to the ground being disqualified.

In spite of his disability, which ruled out the contribution to our non-academic life the school valued most, on the games pitch, Kappa played a notable part in the out-of-classroom life of the school. As a physics master he was regarded as an authority on all things electrical and I can remember, when the lights failed during a performance of films in the science lecture theatre, his limping off to attend to the defective fuse, to the cheers of the audience, the only time he ever received any such public tribute. He also supervised the emergency telephone network which linked the houses via the Tube. One boy, a jazz enthusiast who had managed to build his own radio, remembers how, when stationed in the drying-room below his house during air raid alarms, he would transmit 'big band music' over the wires to entertain his fellow signallers. The vital connection was provided by the safety pin which we all wore to secure the bands round our neck. 'When Kappa came in sight at any house, the code phrase was "Oranges are in season" and I immediately withdrew the band pin. He found out about this and did not take it any further. The appearance on the network of Harry James and Glenn Miller was attributed to "Band Pin Induction".'

Kappa's real passion was for music, not science or teaching, and it seems sad he could not have made it his profession. 'What he really loved, no doubt a sublimating displacement activity,' remembers one of his house-captains, 'was his piano, which used to crash out on summer nights while his house was abed or working.' One of his then colleagues recalls how, before the war, he and Kappa would escape from Housie to drive up to the West End 'directly after afternoon school', would park 'in Portman Square without the slightest difficulty', listen to Toscanini at the Queen's Hall, later burned down during the blitz, and round off the evening with dinner at the Langham Hotel, also later hit by a bomb though since rebuilt, for a modest 7s 6d [35.5p]. Here is the very essence of a 1930s night out, but that our masters had any lives away from the school never occurred to us.

To everyone's surprise. Harry Sills left Housie in 1947, before retirement age,[13] having become increasingly odd, though the example commonly cited –

that he was seen walking down the Avenue in the rain under an umbrella, a volume of the philosopher Kant open before him – might have added to a more popular master's reputation. He had by now become a vegetarian and apparently found the school, in every sense no place for herbivores, an increasingly unsympathetic environment. He went instead to St Christopher's, Letchworth, a notoriously progressive independent boarding school, which, according to legend, was not merely co-educational but encouraged nude mixed bathing. I doubt if it suited this strange, introverted man any better.

After leaving St Christopher's Kappa qualified as a barrister, but never practised. His closing years were spent on his Cambridgeshire farm with surviving members of his family, enjoying the consolations of music. His departure from Christ's Hospital earned only a brief mention in *The Blue* which referred to 'his shy dislike of the emotional' and 'Spartan hardiness',[14] good public school virtues but not sufficient, alas to make him ever truly accepted by those he taught for 15 years. When he died, in May 1989, he received an even more cursory obituary, which recalled his 'severe physical disability' and 'somewhat withdrawn character'.[15] As will be apparent, however, he features more prominently in my memory, if only for a somewhat negative reason. It was his example which, unreasonably, made me renounce all thought of the career I had earlier contemplated. If this was what being a science master meant, I had decided, I wanted no part of it.

The interesting diversity of characters which a single boarding school staffroom could contain is also illustrated by Harry Sills's predecessor as senior housemaster of Maine A, Arthur Rider, a cheerful extrovert in class, as already described. His nickname, 'Snoopy', reflected another side of his character. 'He used to creep around on rubber soles,' recalls a Maine A contemporary. 'You might be sitting in the changing rooms and feel a clasp round your shoulder, with "And what do you think you're doing?"' This same talent was said to have been recognised by HLO Flecker while head of Berkhamsted, where Rider had been head boy. When offered a senior housemastership at the unprecedentedly early age of 27 Rider replied modestly, 'Aren't I a bit young for it?', to be told brusquely: 'That's for me to decide.' But, according to masters' gossip, there was a price to be paid. The young Rider was believed in the Common Room to be 'Oily's nark', reporting on their private activities and opinions. His house watched with interest the young man 'nipping off pre-war to woo some nurse in the sicker', but the courtship came to nothing, and, after the usual absence during the war, he 'settled into the bachelor schoolmaster ways in due course becoming a Grand Old Man in the Western Avenue'. Simply by surviving, he became even more admired after retirement, until his death in 1997. By then he had achieved the longest continuous period of service on the staff in living memory, amounting to fifty years, and an obituary tribute in *The Blue* described him as 'a very devoted schoolmaster and a very good man.'[16] It omitted, however, one significant detail. Boys who retreated from the demanding daily regime of

Maine A to 'the sicker', until exposed as malingerers by Dr Friend, were said to be suffering from 'Arthuritis'.

Even more long-lived proved another famous Housey character of my time, CF (Cecil) Kirby, an Old Blue from my own tough house, who had returned from university to teach biology and, having finally retired, chose to live near Christ's Hospital, in a house uncompromisingly called 'Kirby's'.[17] He survived into the present millennium, reaching the age of 97. I do not think I ever spoke to him, but can well recall him striding about the school in old clothes and gumboots, or hidden behind a bee-keeper's protective apron and hood, so that at first I supposed him to be one of the farm workers. Kirby's rustic appearance was enhanced by the unprepossessing animals commonly at his heels, proudly described by their owner as 'the worst dogs in Sussex'. Their disposition was as sour as their names were unusual, Chlorine being succeeded by Boodle and Boodle by Lobster. The most notorious of all was Pooch, a true Christ's Hospital pet, which would encourage the Maine B rugger team, one member of it remembers, by snapping at the heels of the rear row of forwards during a scrum.[18]

CF Kirby bore little resemblance to the traditional public school master, at least in externals, and his teaching methods, though I never experienced them, were said to be equally robust and forthright. A picture on the wall of his laboratory depicted a defecating cow, 'captured in the act,' according to *The Blue*, 'of illuminating the eternal verities of the nitrogen cycle,' whereby animals return the nourishment they have taken from the soil. Several of my informants recall how he successfully illustrated the principles of conductivity by ordering his class to join hands and then giving them a mild but simultaneous electric shock. Misbehaviour in the laboratory allegedly attracted summary punishment with a bed-board, another example of how the school economically made a single object serve a dual purpose. 'Known to us all as "Uncle"', another Old Blue of my generation has written, 'he inspired fear, respect and affection, in that order. If you earned a rebuke he had a stinging tongue which was more painful than any beating...You had to respect someone with his polymathic range of knowledge and skills, who could effortlessly recite yards of Virgil and Homer, cultivate a garden, build a wireless set and turn sheep's head stew into a gourmet dish. The affection came later.'

CFK achieved the longevity which silences criticism but not every boy enjoyed his encounters with him, in or out of school. One boy who attended one of the farm camps he organised was horrified, on enquiring where the latrines were, to be handed a spade, and found the whole experience more disagreeable than being at school. Another, however, testifies that 'he ran the camps with clockwork efficiency' and any 'temptation to play the fool' was firmly restrained. 'You could be sure that nothing would ever happen to let down the good name of Christ's Hospital, inside or outside the Ring Fence, when Uncle was in charge.'[19]

Although emphatically not a man to stand any nonsense, CFK had a kindly side. Housie made little provision for enabling younger boys to enjoy the normal recreations of their age group, and one Old Blue remembers with gratitude joining a group of juniors allowed 'to build a big railway layout in his garden.' Others still appreciate his work in running the Signals Section of the Corps, which, in contrast to the rest of it, was actively enjoyed. 'Signalling in the JTC under Uncle's Command,' wrote one admirer, who entered the school in 1941, 'was always as much about initiative and self-reliance as about the techniques of radio and telephonic communication. I learnt more that was useful to me in later life from my membership of the Signals than from any other activity at CH.'[20]

Just as the OTC's uniform, before its transformation into the JTC, had recalled the first world war, so, too, did the Signals' equipment. The telephonic system used to link houses during air raids, already mentioned, made use of the Fullerphone, a robust but outmoded machine which had seen service in the trenches in Flanders.[21] Kirby's signallers must also have been among the last in Europe to use the heliograph, which relied on sunlight striking on mirrors. It had done yeoman service in the Boer War and one Old Blue was gratified to find it still in use in 1940 in the Sudan where, unlike Sussex, there was no shortage of sun.

During the war the real army claimed CFK, but the school was soon providing volunteer guinea-pigs for his military research, as one of my contemporaries, later an engineer, described:

> He...recalls...happy memories of Sunday afternoons in CFK's lab assisting with experiments on model boots of different shapes and sizes, made of wood. The boys measured the force needed to push them into and extract them from wet Sussex clay, plotting the results on countless sheets of graph paper. The final outcome was six pairs of a new type of boot covered in the furry hide of cows' feet because 'Kirby assured us...cows' feet don't get mud on them, it slides off the fur!' A group of older boys from the JTC demonstrated them to a sceptical group from the War Office.[22]

The result, sadly, was disappointing, the idea being turned down, due to a lack of cows, and the inventor's suggestion of substituting plastic for fur, then a novelty, was not pursued. Undeterred, his versatile mind then turned to devising 'a cheap waterproofing system for battledress', probably the origin of the scandalous, and false, rumour that swept the school that 'Major Kirby had, while experimenting in the baths to see how much equipment a soldier could wear and still swim, succeeded in drowning two Canadians.'[23] Even after the dauntless experimenter had returned to his old job at CH, he continued to assist the army, for, at a JTC camp – an occasion at which he was always in his element – 'CFK was asked by the officer in command...to try out a new concentrated field ration on his men...The ration consisted of small biscuits with the flavour and texture of lightly-compressed cement. They were not a success. One of our number, crawling back in agony from the latrine,' reported a fellow guinea-pig in *The Blue*, 'remarked that he now knew what it was like to have a baby.'[24]

If CF Kirby's nickname, 'Uncle', gave little indication of the man, even less apt was that of the geography master, MRD Hallows, most unjustly labelled 'Cissy', a good-natured, mild-mannered, thoroughly decent individual. I remember him with gratitude for his leading walks for the Rambling Section of the Natural History Club, a rare opportunity to escape from the school grounds. He astonished one form, after he had become a member of the pre-war, evangelical Oxford Group, by telling them that he practised resisting temptation by lying naked in bed beside his wife every morning. (Evidently he was not permanently abstinent for he later acquired a daughter.) He went on to become headmaster of the Royal Grammar School, Guildford, an outstanding and ancient establishment then open to everyone of sufficient ability, subsequently, in the name of equality, forced to become independent and fee-paying. When I visited it many years later I found he was still affectionately remembered – something far from true of some ex-Housie headmasters, though a remarkable number did achieve this distinction, no fewer than 23 Old Blue heads being noted in *The Blue* in 1949.[25]

The school, with its extensive vocabulary of slang, was a fertile ground for nicknames. They were rarely flattering. A well-known 'toucher/cuddler', to quote one of my informants, was known as 'Snugs' or 'Hugs' (in fact DH) Burleigh. The master referred to earlier for attempting sodomy in the Baths was aptly nicknamed 'Phallic', his proclivities being well known to us if not to his colleagues, though if any suspected the explanation they chose to turn a blind eye. EG Malins of the Prep was called 'Gad', from his habit of using the ejaculation (much in vogue at Greyfriars) of 'By Gad'. (His children were, wittily but unfairly, described as 'The Gaderene swine'.)

One unexplained nickname was that of FW Wagner, a science master as enthusiastic about cricket as LM Carey was about rugger. One Old Blue contemporary remembers how, while junior housemaster of Coleridge A, he 'spent many hours in the dormitory teaching us to lift the bat up straight and play down the line', efforts which cannot have been much appreciated by those trying to sleep. Wagner was known as 'Og', presumably from the Old Testament character Og the King of Bashan, of whom we sang with relish in chapel, though he 'was an antediluvian' giant while our Og was normally proportioned, if somewhat intimidating in manner.[26]

The nickname 'Jem' for JEM Massen, Head of German, has already been mentioned but he was, more ingeniously, also known as 'The gangster' from the 'very grim figure' he cut in Home Guard uniform, while carrying a Chicago style Tommy Gun,[27] and perhaps something Germanic and intimidating had rubbed off on him from his time at the University of Kiel. (Like so many masters, he was totally different outside the classroom, where I found him kind and considerate.) 'Buggy' for the Rev LH White, founder of the Natural History Society and a keen entomologist, requires no comment. Equally unimaginative was 'Fo-Dry' for the geographer Kenneth Fawdry, and 'One-man' (AL) Creed, for a biology master who invariably pronounced the word as 'wun'. Some names were descriptive, like that of 'Jumper' (JH) Edwards, who introduced modern PT to the school. He was thereby distinguished from the staider 'Teddy' (ACW) Edwards, who taught history and was renowned for his catch-phrase *magna cum pompa*, ie 'with great pomp', though some pedants claimed it was really a veiled reference to the Welsh valley, Cwn Pompa, from which he came. 'Pip' for GW Newberry, who taught history and geography, remains unexplained, while 'Dangle', for another master, who taught mathematics, illustrates the casual cruelty of schoolboys; its owner had a bad stammer as revealed in one much mimicked sentence: 'D-d-d-at angle equals d-d-d-d-at angle!'

Some nicknames were obvious, like 'Bumph' for CA Humphrey, housemaster of Lamb A, 'Shish' for a master with a limp and 'Horse' for one with a supposedly equine profile, but why the elderly 'Dido' Hyde was so called I never discovered – the name belonged to a queen of Carthage who burned herself to death for love, and a less romantic figure it was hard to imagine. He is, however, credited with a typical schoolmaster's pleasantry. When asked by St Peter at the gates of heaven what he had done to merit admission, he would, Dido said, reply, 'I taught the GE 3' – the Great Erasmus Three being a 'maths' set with no aptitude for the subject.[28]

Nicknames given to boys usually reflected their alleged physical characteristics, and were rarely flattering, as in the case of 'Stump', 'Barrel', 'Belly' and 'Girth'. Facial resemblances explained 'Horse', 'Babe', 'Hen' and 'Puss' and hair styles 'Shaggy' and 'Brush'. Our film-going accounted for 'Harpo' and 'Groucho', two boys in my house considered to resemble two of the Marx brothers, in appearance and in style of running respectively. Whether the Coleridge A boy known as 'Lusty' regarded this as a compliment is uncertain, but life must have been a perpetual torment for the boy known as 'Hutch' because he was supposed to smell like the inside of a rabbit's cage, and even crueller was the nickname for a Middleton B boy with a hare lip, 'Hic Ug', the nearest he could get to rendering his own name. Social distinctions rarely inspired nicknames, but an exception was the boy who had acquired his accent in 'the stony ground of Hoxton' and reached Housie via an LCC scholarship. His nickname, 'Blimey' was confounded by his later career as an 'exquisitely articulate academic, politician and broadcaster', though the school would probably have liked it even better had he become a Conservative rather than a Labour MP.

[1] Mar 1991 p.58
[2] Dec 1988 p.213
[3] Waugh, *Loom* p.31
[4] Dec 1988 p.214
[5] Mar 1994 p.74
[6] Dec 1988 p.214
[7] Mar 1991 p.58
[8] Mar 1985 p.93
[9] Jul 1989 p.137
[10] Mar 1991 p.58
[11] Jul 1988 p.138
[12] *HMS Pinafore* Act II Sc I
[13] Mar/Apr 1948 p.65
[14] Mar/Apr 1948 p.65
[15] Dec 1989 p.205
[16] Mar 1998 p.67
[17] Sep 1963 p.132
[18] Sep 1963 p.133 & Sep 1960 p.123
[19] Jun 1991 p.132
[20] Jun 1991 p.132
[21] Dec 1997 p.257
[22] Dec 1993 p.233
[23] Mar 1988 p.50
[24] Jun 1991 p.132
[25] Mar 1949 p.75
[26] Brewer p.910
[27] Sep 1965 p.144 & Mar 1978 p.41
[28] Mar 1974 p.70

36

ARE YOU CALLING ME A LIAR?

Question frequently asked as prelude to bullying,

Christ's Hospital, c. 1941

Conditions at Christ's Hospital, London, might almost have been designed to encourage bullying. The cramped surroundings, the cheerless regime, the school's tradition of harshness, the lack of supervision, all conspired to encourage the more brutal boys to take out their frustrations on those smaller and younger than themselves. With the move to Sussex a happier era seemed to have dawned and, as described earlier, the new headmaster proclaimed a crusade against bullying, backed up by threats of expulsion. Sadly, however, this brave initiative rapidly died, with Dr Upcott himself setting an example of ready resort to the cane. By the 1930s bullying was again rife and, ample though the grounds were, for long periods, as I have described, we were confined to our own house, and often to the dayroom, while our routine was governed by a schedule of petty regulations which made a normally civilised life, founded on self-discipline and the type of public opinion which left the bullies despised rather than respected, impossible.

Bullying no doubt occurred in all schools, especially segregated boarding schools. Like child-abuse, of which it is a variant, with the abusers being near contemporaries instead of adults, it had not then been recognised as a serious problem, but I have no doubt that it was worse at Christ's Hospital than elsewhere for reasons peculiar to the school. Each house contained a wider age range, from ten to nineteen, than the ordinary public school. There were no proper facilities within the house for practising hobbies, reading, or merely 'larking about' with one's contemporaries. Everything possible was done to prevent one forming a friendship with like-minded contemporaries in other houses. And, most important of all, the majority of boys had nothing to look forward to except being forced to leave at 15 or 16. The headmaster, more than one Old Blue and former member of staff have testified, barely bothered to conceal his lack of interest in those who would never join the grecian elite, preferably as classical specialists. With no prospect of exerting authority legitimately, the most vicious among the rejected majority happily dispensed injustice illegally.

There was a clear correlation between lack of school status, which did not necessarily mean, as later careers demonstrate, lack of intelligence or potential, and a readiness to torment others. I cannot recall a single serious bully who went on to become a grecian, though a number did become house monitors and were soon abusing their authority themselves or turning a blind eye to the outrages committed by their old cronies. Throwing one's weight about, unofficially or not, does not seem to have proved very fulfilling. Of the five or six boys who at various times made my life a misery only one has joined the Christ's Hospital Club, and, more understandably, not one, myself apart, of those who suffered at their hands. It has been suggested that bullies and their victims are in some way linked, and it would seem that they certainly share an aversion to the scene of their former conflict and are fearful of again confronting each other, not without reason. My closest, life-long, Old Blue friend, in his seventies, can recall how he was singled out for persecution by an older boy, then much larger than himself. Now, as a burly six footer, he would himself tower over his former tormentor, and has assured me that, should he ever meet and recognise him, would knock him down without hesitation.

Apart from the reasons already put forward, there is another explanation why bullying flourished at Christ's Hospital, that it was tacitly, if not openly, tolerated by a few masters. The more conventional regarded it as part of the toughening up process to which boys lacking the proper public school spirit ought to be subjected; the feebler and more tearful the victim the more he clearly needed encouragement, however cruel or brutal, to 'stand on his own two feet'. Here is further evidence of the distinctive Housey desire, already mentioned, to demonstrate the school's entitlement to a place alongside more famous establishments by copying their worst features.

It is significant that, apart from food, no subject rates a higher place in the special school language than violence, and no words have proved more enduring. The most widely used and best remembered of all Housey slang words in my day was 'fotch', said to derive from a beadle who in London around 1880 had been prone to smack boys' heads with his open hand while crying 'Gie ye a fecht' or 'focht'.[1] Another popular form of attack was to bring the open palm down on another boy's bare back to 'give him a cherry back', and a group of boys might be lined up to see who would yield the most spectacular cherry back when struck. Pinching, kicking, tripping up might all happen at any time of the day, particularly if one had found a quiet spot and was trying to read, but in the changing rooms and dormitories, and those favoured torture chambers, the lav ends, the most popular means of inflicting pain was flicking with the wet end of a towel which, on the bare flesh, could hurt a great deal.

These were the small change of bullying, accepted as a regular part of Housey life, but every house seemed to contain two or three 'professional bullies' who devoted their lives to inflicting pain and are still remembered for it. In my first year the worst offender was a boy of about 16, about to leave, whom I have mentioned earlier. He claimed to be a Fascist and regarded it as his mission to tough up *Untermenschen* like me. I recall him forcing me to stand for much of one Saturday evening during my first summer term on one leg in the senior changing room and, on another – clearly he found the long summer evenings boring – forcing me and another new boy to have a fist fight. I won easily but the victory gave me no pleasure.

After he had left the title of chief bully passed to a boy so sadistic that we discussed, as we very rarely did, his home life. It was said that his father was a clergyman who during the holidays constantly beat his son and that the latter looked forward to returning to school to be violent in his turn. This boy was the Flashman of Peele A and so outrageous were his excesses that, like Flashman, he eventually over-reached himself. One junior had recently acquired a brand new pair of roller skates of which he was extremely proud until the bully removed one of the pair and, by beating it out of shape, made both unusable. The owner was desolate, but powerless, until an older boy, seeing his distress, discovered the cause and, most unexpectedly, confronted the bully. 'They only belonged to ----,' he snarled, whereupon our champion, just as in a school story, punched him in the face. A regular fist fight followed, a hard hitting affair, the only one I ever saw at school, in which both combatants genuinely tried to harm each other. As news of it spread an excited crowd of small boys swarmed into the changing room to watch and, as their enemy was visibly getting the worst of it, began to cheer on their hero and applaud every blow that reached his opponent's face. There was in the air an almost tangible feeling of hatred which was not lost on the boy who had provoked it. Eventually he admitted defeat and withdrew, with battered face and bleeding nose, to try to regain his dignity and, for a time, to behave better.

My house was not exceptional, nor indeed, I suspect, as bad as some. Bullying was in the very air of Christ's Hospital, for a variety of reasons, as suggested earlier. Robin Hull, who entered Middleton A in 1943, at the age of eleven, discovered that 'there was continual harassment of the young by the older boys'. Especially those 'about sixteen...in their last year at school'. He soon learned how effective a whip a 'plaited girdle' made and was savagely thrashed in this way on a walk with two other small boys by one bully, who varied the assault by using 'ash plants cut from the hedgerows'. Two other older boys also witnessed this affair, without intervening, and the victim's injuries were soon common knowledge, thanks to a visit to the Baths, but 'though questions were asked the truth never came out. The code of Christ's Hospital was "No sneaking"', encouraged by 'the risk of...retribution'. Nor were the offenders always school failures. The culprit in the most serious case

Robin Hull heard of, which involved 'holding another boy by the ankles from a third floor dormitory window', was 'everyone's hero', a much respected athlete 'usually quite kind to the small boys'.[2]

As a supposedly clever child, always, until late in my school career, small for my age and hopeless at sport, I was a natural target, and in some form or other I was not to be free of persecution until my final term and even then, too senior, as both a grecian and a monitor, to be physically attacked, my property suffered instead. But I was by no means the most bullied boy in the house. Sometimes the reason why a boy was victimised was obvious. One, I remember, confessed to me he had in his early days at Housie, 'had an accident', ie wet the bed, a mishap that haunted him for years and built up a habit of maltreatment towards him even when its cause was forgotten. A boy in Peele B who suffered from the same misfortune was known ever after as 'Pissy' Patterson – I have altered his surname – a nickname sufficient in itself to earn regular maltreatment. He was already disadvantaged in having as housemaster the insensitive Macnutt who, far from protecting this vulnerable member of his flock, dropped a strong hint to his seniors not to spare him, telling them 'He is just the sort of boy I can't stand.' In Peele A one boy who left early, despite being outstanding in some subjects, also had a rough time, thanks to the misfortune of having evil smelling feet, no doubt made worse by our thick stockings. His mother, he confided in me – the unpopular and the bullied tended to stick together – had suggested he keep his socks permanently damp, but he found this very uncomfortable.

Seldom can there have been an environment less suited to anyone of my temperament than Peele A in 1936. In *First Bloom* I described my first exposure to it, but the description would have been almost equally valid for other houses and for later years:

> Blake was at that time in a bad condition. It had a strong house-captain and strong monitors, but there was a general tradition that the seniors would be left to themselves as much as possible, and that a little maltreatment was good for new boys...During the whole of his first term there can have been scarcely a day when one of those new boys was not at some time in tears, and every moment began to be haunted with the fear that a passing monitor would seize on one of them for a catechism intended to display his wit. The more commonplace forms of persecution...were also practised. Disturbing their rest, tossing them in blankets when the monitor was late in arriving to supervise bed-making in the morning, removing clothing so that they were late for the next function of the day, all these and a hundred forms of petty persecution, each small in itself, but in the mass oppressive, contributed to reduce any sensitive person – and there are few eleven year olds fresh from school who are not thus sensitive – to misery. Conway, observing his companions, noticed that fear of the seniors and the older members of the

junior dormitory soon made them move humbly aside when the worst of their persecutors came near, made them fearful of speaking to anyone above their level, even on official matters. The interference of those above when a new boy was reading, or otherwise occupying himself in his own way, was accepted as so usual that it became regarded as an Act of God.

The father of a friend later told me how one of his first memories of visiting his son was of seeing me in tears. I can well believe it. Although 'buzzing' in public attracted further brutality and mockery there can rarely have been a time when someone was not crying somewhere in the school.

I can remember in my second term feeling total despair that my parents had not responded to my appeal to remove me, even when I had demonstrated my unhappiness by threatening, and indeed trying, to run away. I felt abandoned and alone, not realising Christ's Hospital contained scores of boys who shared my reactions and hated the place to which well-meaning parents had despatched them.

My own first experience of being bullied was of having my bed 'skiffed', which meant the bedclothes being pushed on the floor after I had made it, leaving me barely time to remake it and be on time for chapel parade. As it happened, the attempt to get me into trouble in this way misfired as Lawrance, our house-captain, entered the dormitory just as I was struggling to heave the heavy mattress back into place. He made no comment at the time, but later, after my abortive attempt to run away, he told me this incident had made him realise that I was having a hard time but that to have punished the boys responsible would probably have made it even harder.

Although it has been the custom for every writer describing his schooldays to declare how much matters have changed since he left – and this book is no exception – some of the forms of bullying described in the most famous public school novel, *Tom Brown's Schooldays*, published in 1857, could still be witnessed at Christ's Hospital in the 1930s and 1940s, and even later. I personally witnessed in the junior dormitory of Peele A a worse example of a boy being tossed in a blanket than that described by Thomas Hughes.[*] This took place during the morning bed-making, a period I came to dread, and the unfortunate boy selected for the experience was thrown so high that he was flung right out of the blanket and crashed on the hard wooden floor with a sickening crunch. He was warned of the dire penalties he would suffer if he breathed a word of what had happened and these threats proved effective when,

---

[*] On the 'things have changed' disclaimer see *Tom Brown's Schooldays*, Chapter VIII. On tossing in a blanket see Chapter VI. The custom continued at Christ's Hospital long after I had left and the school seems to have been positively proud of it. The cover photograph of *The Blue* for June 1973 shows a boy being thrown dangerously close to the dormitory ceiling, while p.84 of the June 1975 issue depicts a blanket-tossing out of doors.

a few minutes later, he was violently sick and collapsed in chapel, having to be carried out and removed to the Infirmary. I had always supposed this to be a unique accident but later learned from a Middleton B informant that he had also witnessed occasions 'when the blanket holders did not manage to catch the...boy who landed with a thump on the ground'. I can personally recall seeing a boy forced to sit with his feet in front of him while another hurled a dart on either side of each of them in turn, like a circus knife-thrower. He was, I think, trying to show off his skill rather than generate fear but eventually his aim wavered and the metal point of the dart plunged through his target's yellow stocking into his foot. It was pulled out and, bleeding profusely, the victim was sent off to matron with some cover story which she tamely accepted. The dart-thrower had, I now suspect, some need to assert himself for he liked to persuade smaller boys to demonstrate their faith in him by falling backwards to the floor to be caught half-way in his hands. Here, like so much at Housie, was fruitful raw material for a psychiatrist.

Another tradition familiar to readers of *Tom Brown's Schooldays* was kneeling by one's bed at night to say one's prayers, a compulsory routine in the junior dormitory and, I think, voluntary but still occasionally observed among the seniors. Even the most unpopular individual was supposed to be free from assault while so employed, and I can recall one of the regular bullies protesting when another kicked a boy while he was on his knees. Undeterred, the attacker repeated the offence and I can still hear the sickening thud as his foot connected with the base of his victim's spine, the agonised shudder this boy gave and the bully's triumphant cry of 'Got him!' Once I was myself kicked in the same spot and remember it as uniquely painful.

This incident apart – and who knows what lasting physical damage such assaults did, not merely to me but to others? – I realise that it was less any specific act of brutality I found intolerable as the consistently hostile nature of the world around me. One could never feel secure. At any moment a remark, or silence, an action, or failure to join in some activity, possibly the persecution of another boy, would prompt the derision of a noisily critical claque.

Mostly I was the victim of group bullying rather than singled out for particular attack, suffering most not from my own year, or even older boys, but from succeeding intakes who, though younger than me, overtook me in growth and resented the fact that, in theory, I enjoyed greater seniority and status than them. I cannot recall any particularly serious blows, but have many memories of being pushed about, tripped up, having my heels trodden on, and similar minor assaults, trivial in themselves but cumulatively oppressive. A favourite form of bullying from which, like others, I often suffered, was being forced by one boy into apparently insulting another. The victim would be forced to contradict some absurd statement made by a second, who would then ask in anger, 'Are you calling me a liar?' I can recall on many occasions seeing one or more boys, thus taunted, at the centre of a hostile circle, being violently pushed from one side to another, only to be thrust back again as in some bizarre dance.

Bullying took many forms. Occasionally one boy would seem to take a particular dislike to another and almost claim a monopoly of the right to make his life miserable. I suffered in this way for much of one term, for no reason that I could ever discover, until my persecution by this particular boy, a couple of years older than me, became so blatant that even Noel noticed it and, with surprising subtlety, intervened. What sanctions he used I never discovered, but the boy concerned suddenly became almost embarrassingly helpful. Later, by an odd twist of fate, as I shall describe in the next chapter, where I call him Denver, I could probably have got him expelled. I stayed silent, however, and his death has since evened out whatever scores remained.

Often, in my experience, bullying was subtler than the name suggests and I, and no doubt others, was often the victim of what I will call 'bullying by proxy'. Interestingly enough, that prince among sadists, the Marquis de Sade, mentions this somewhere, as the most sophisticated form of his particular perversion. To plunge a poor peasant into despair by murdering his child was, the evil nobleman thought, but a poor substitute for the pleasure to be gained by then falsifying the evidence so that the bereaved parent is hanged for the crime. Such, on a milder scale, was 'bullying by proxy'. I can recall an atlas being hidden to get me into trouble with a master who never concealed his dislike for me; paint being thrown over my clothes during art class to make the next coat-cleaning session a nightmare; games clothes being removed from my peg, to make me late on the playing field. (This particular ploy misfired. Since I was invariably one of the last to be picked I got there before my absence was noticed.) Far more dangerous, and requiring a fair degree of effort, was the carving of my name in the lining of one of the urinals in the school lavatories. This was a serious, as outside-the-house, offence, meriting a major beating, and I can remember my quandary when I discovered the inscription. Who would believe my explanation if I was caught trying to scrape it off with my penknife? Happily, for reasons already indicated, the 'school bogs' were unpopular and I was undetected.

It must have been via one of my fellow Newburians, with none of whom I ever became friends – we all, as I have said, preferred to keep our two lives separate – that some of my persecutors in Peele A discovered that even by Housey standards my family were very badly off and this discovery prompted the most unpleasant non-violent episode I had to endure. Some boys for various reasons were not taken out even for one afternoon a term and occasionally others invited one of these unfortunates to join them during a parent's visit. I had absolutely no desire to have any other boy with me on this precious occasion and knew that my father's funds could not possibly stretch to entertaining two of us. I suspect, as it was, he got home with barely a coin in his pocket. I was thus deeply embarrassed when three different boys were told by another that I planned to invite them out with me on the coming Whole Holiday and all thanked me warmly. Whether they really believed the story or were part of the plot to distress me I never discovered, but eventually I confided my dilemma in a sympathetic senior, and the would-be guests were told the truth, which probably came as no surprise to them for I suffered no dire consequences.

The supposed convention, even at Tom Brown's Rugby, that bullies never insulted their victims' parents was certainly not honoured at Christ's Hospital. I never heard any offensive remarks about mine, but I can recall them directed at others, particularly the boy I have mentioned earlier guilty of bed-wetting, which, it was crudely suggested, was due to some inherited factor. At Tom Brown's Rugby, or Harry Wharton's Greyfriars, every 'decent fellow' in the dorm would have leapt from his bed to thrash the cads responsible. But Christ's Hospital, as I had already discovered, was not Greyfriars. The boy concerned, like the rest of us, stayed silent, reasoning perhaps, as we did, that it was better that parents, being absent, should be the target of the bullies' wit than themselves.

On the whole Housie was remarkably free of snobbery related to parental profession or income and I can recall only one occasion when I felt painfully conscious of our poverty. This was after the boy 'Denver' mentioned earlier as having a down on me, had flung my face flannel out of a window after dark, when I could not retrieve it, and by the time I could do so, it had vanished. I was upset at having to write to my parents to ask for a new flannel and even more upset by my father's response: 'Boys ought not to throw your things out of windows.' How right he was, but how was I to protect them?

The incident now seems trivial, but on such things did one's happiness rest at eleven or twelve and the worst assault I suffered now seems almost comic, though it did not feel so at the time. On the last afternoon of term, a kind of licensed saturnalia as I have described, two or three boys, uncertain how to dispose of their chewing gum, called me to them and then rubbed it into my scalp. The gum set solid and proved extraordinarily difficult to remove, until a small crowd had gathered round me in the downstairs washroom trying, with a combination of hot water and nail scissors, to dissolve or cut away the offending grey lump, now firmly embedded between hair and skull. This crude surgery left me with a large bare patch on the top of my head, which caught the eye of matron who told the junior housemaster. He managed to identify the culprits without involving me, so successfully that both thanked me for not having given them away. They duly went home next day, bearing their stripes and I my unwanted and far more visible tonsure. My parents were inclined to make a joke of it whereupon I burst into tears, less for my indignity than for the gulf revealed once again between my experience of school and their perception of it.

The worst bullying occurred in the senior dormitory and affected the 'junior seniors', the 13 and 14 year olds who, having ruled the roost in the junior dormitory, had now become new boys again. I have always felt grateful to Noel for deferring my promotion to the senior dormitory for a year, and the most memorable misbehaviour I witnessed there seems in retrospect more a prank than an assault, though it did not appear so at the time, when harmless mischief could so easily take an ugly turn. On this occasion I recall lying awake, afraid to stir for fear of attracting attention, while a group of older boys toured the dormitory looking for anyone sleeping with a hand outside the bedclothes. If this were suddenly to be immersed in water, one of the group claimed, the sleeper would involuntarily wet the bed. A boy with extended hand was found, a basin filled with water was brought to his bedside and his hand plunged in it, but the only result, to the loudly voiced disappointment of the experimenters, was to cause him to wake up.

Very different were the experiences of a close friend who became a senior a year ahead of me when the worst of a bad intake were in their final year. He later described to me some of the outrages he had witnessed, which left the vast majority of boys as disgusted as he was, but as he remarked, 'You kept quiet, glad it was someone else who'd been picked on.' A common practice in other houses, I later learned, was 'stuffing someone's head down the loo and flushing it', but Peele A had its own variation, that of boys lining up to urinate in turn on the imprisoned victim. This boy did not dare to 'sneak' to authority but during the next holiday did reveal what had happened to his mother, who duly informed Noel. *His* dormitory patrols, as I shall describe later, were dedicated to hunting, ineffectually, for evidence of sexual misconduct, to which we turned a tolerant eye; two boys amusing themselves could not be bullying anyone else and were likely to emerge relaxed from the experience. Our housemaster now, however, conducted a major enquiry, ending no doubt in 'a jolly good whacking', but he managed to conceal his sources and though my informant for long afterwards lived in fear of being unmasked, he never was.

Just as in the German concentration camps people were often killed for wholly trivial reasons, so as Christ's Hospital cruelty was often inflicted capriciously, and not inspired by malice, though the results were no less painful. One victim, whom I will call Craig, suffered from 'Craig's Christmas Cracker', a name repeated by his torturers with shrieks of laughter as he endured it almost nightly. The 'cracker' consisted of being rolled tightly in his bedclothes. His hair and feet, projecting at either end, were then vigorously and simultaneously tugged, and finally the 'cracker' 'exploded', with both groups of boys flinging off the blankets and brutally pummelling the boy inside them.

Another version of this particular torture was practised a little further along the Avenue, in Middleton B, as an Old Blue who entered it on the same term as I joined Peele A, recalls:

33: Inside the library, date unknown, a posed but not misleading picture

34: Boy scientist. At work in my 'laboratory', the bathroom, in the holidays, c.1941

35: A typical dayroom, date unknown, but less crowded than in my day. Note the lockers on the left and house trophies on the right

36: Dinner Parade at Horsham, c.1938

37: The band about to play us into dinner

38: A house about to enter the Dining Hall. Marching was a constant feature of life at Horsham

39: Big side with the Music School in the background, c.1937, a striking contrast to the cramped conditions of Newgate Street

40: CH at war, 1941. Playing fields in front of the tuckshop have been ploughed up to grow crops

41: The sandbagged school office, June 1941, with my brother and myself in the foreground

42: The Old Science School, where I made a false start as a science specialist

43: The Library, where I found my real vocation, with 'The Garden' in the foreground and Dominions Library on the right

44: The former History Grecians' room, photographed, like the two buildings shown above, in 2000

> I cannot think now how I submitted to such a torture, but I was 'bedpoled'...To 'bedpole' a victim, he was forced to lie on the bed and the boys put full weight on each end of the pole [normally used to tidy our blankets and pillows] and gradually rolled it up the entire body, except the head, starting at the toes. Memory of the crunching pain on the shins has remained with me...My glasses were in their metal case in my pocket but between the pole and my right thigh. The case was flattened and the glasses broken inside...I managed without glasses for many years after this.

This was not, however, the only form of mass bullying to which this boy was subjected:

> Worse than being 'bedpoled' was to be trapped in the bath by a duck-board with two boys sitting on it. The bath was then filled to the brim. I remember only being able to breathe by positioning my nose between two slats. This was made even more difficult by having fingers poked into my nose. This particular experience was frightening and is difficult to erase from the memory.

A Peele A friend witnessed the same process but with an extra dimension of sadism added; the bath was filled alternately with very cold water until the victim was shivering as well as half drowned, then drained and refilled with very hot water until he was crying out with the pain of being scalded. As my informant remarked, when next he read of this practice it was in an account of a war crimes trial of concentration camp guards, a comparison which speaks for itself.

Of what happened in other houses I knew at the time very little, but one custom we were spared in my house, the licensed bullying of the initiation ceremony, supposed to put newcomers in their proper, suitably humble place.[*] One Old Blue, who entered via the supposedly gentler route of the Prep, recalls that 'New Squits Tortures' were a recognised part of its life. One involved the older boys sitting on either side of the boot room on the lockers while 'the new squits had to pass the length of the room in a hall of kicks'. Robin Hull has described with medical precision his very first night in Prep B in 1941:

> A senior boy decided to give one of the new boys an enema. The naked victim was bent over the bath where his buttocks were separated while soapy water was poured into an anus in tight spasm...Fortunately authority

---

[*] For example, the housemaster in *The Guinea Pig*, released in 1948, defends the indignities inflicted on the hero on these grounds. In recent years, however, some regimental initiation ceremonies for recruits have resulted in courts-martial and heavy sentences.

appeared and the victim was released before awkward questions were asked.[3]

The boy given this crude introduction to Christ's Hospital life had, it seemed to this nine-year-old observer, watching with 'fascination tinged with fear...apparently been enjoying the experience' – a far more dangerous reaction, the layman may feel, than terror and revulsion.

Arrival in a senior house might also involve some unpleasant experiences, but the worst I heard of was the new boys being forced to strip – an ordeal in itself for those new to boarding school – and then being imprisoned one by one in the cupboard in the lav end while basins of water were poured on top of them. This could conceivably be defended, but there was no excuse for the brutality so widely practised later on, often by the very boys supposed to prevent it. These are the recollections of one boy who, in 1936, moved up from the Prep to what was then called a senior house:

> [My house] was run by the monitors and we hardly ever saw the housemaster or his deputy. I remember some very decent kindly monitors, but the ones with a vicious or sadistic streak in them had a free rein.
>
> Prep in the evening was often a painful misery. Certain monitors would patrol the junior tables and forbid anyone to lift their eyes from the page or to move their head. Any movement was greeted with a heavy book crashing down on the offending head. It was a strain to stay in one position for so long and was of no help to the process of learning, but provided some fun for the monitors concerned.

This was the Horsham version of the 'owling' common at Newgate Street, while a correspondent to *The Blue* recalled that when he arrived in Middleton B in 1943 'bacon slicing, a sharp vertical blow with the edge of the hand on another boy's bottom when he was in pyjamas or games clothes was in vogue.' 'Radiator grilling' was also practised, a modern version of the 'roasting' in front of an open fire to which fags were subjected in Dr Arnold's Rugby, as *Tom Brown's Schooldays* describes.[4]

The war had to some extent re-created the situation which had existed in London of unsuitable and inadequately supervised monitors, for the grecians, though no longer living separate lives, were now liable to removal by call-up at the age of 18. Many of these wartime monitors were quite clearly unsuited for their responsibilities; a contemporary in Maine A recalls one in his 'pretty tough' house who 'was reputed to prick offenders' names on their bottoms with a pair of dividers'.

Usually, as I have mentioned, a poor accent was regarded as a source of amusement rather than persecution. An exception, however, was one unfortunate in Maine A who came from working-class Hackney, and whose rendering of his own name, which I have altered, attracted the attention of three notorious bullies, as a friend of his remembers:

> The gruesome trio would fix him in the bootroom.
>   'What's your name, boy?'
>   'Myer'.
> Fotch.
>   'What a little pig. Your name is Mayer. What's your name, boy?'
> Eventually, after one or two slips, poor Mayer would get it more or less right.

Some boys may have suffered lasting ill effects from their maltreatment at school. Today blows to the face are strictly outlawed in the classroom, at least of state schools, but for most of its history, 'fotching' was a Housey tradition. One Middleton B Old Blue, quoted earlier, can still recall the facial 'smarting' and 'loud ringing in the ears' which followed a well-delivered fotch. 'I suspect that some boys suffered ear trouble from this.' His own particular problem related to another organ. 'I had some difficulty breathing through my nose and as a consequence often had to have my mouth slightly open. I received many chastisements for not being able to obey the command "Take that silly grin off your face!"' Far worse was the fate of a contemporary with a speech impediment, whose 'life was made hell by...teasing. I remember being sorry for him as he sat whimpering, seated in a hand bowl with his feet dangling down after having had his private parts rather vigorously burnished with shoe blacking.'

Sometimes the line between bullying and legitimate schoolboy self-expression seems hard to draw. What should one make, for example, of the Maine A boy addicted to roller-skating, who, through cajolery and coercion, persuaded seven of his housemates to lie on their back on the asphalt behind the house while he approached them at speed and then leapt across the whole group? One participant at least, who used to position himself, prudently, in the middle bears the would-be stuntman no resentment.

I must confess to smiling, though the victim was a friend of mine, when the boy known by his initial, 'C', had a basin of water tipped over him while his assailant sang from a familiar hymn:

> For nearer and nearer draws the time
> The time that shall surely be,
> When the earth shall be filled
> With the glory of God
> As the waters cover the sea.

This was more what at Greyfriars would have been called a jape than true bullying, motivated by sadism, or at least a desire to cause discomfort, and its prevalence at Christ's Hospital was an ever present and disagreeable feature of my time there. It was the accepted wisdom that things would get better as one got older, but even as one of the *crème de la crème* of Housey society in my last term, a 'Button grecian', my name whispered in awe to new boys by their nursemaids, I still suffered occasional persecution. I recall my newly-acquired, and, in wartime, irreplaceable bicycle being vandalised from sheer malice by a boy resentful of my standing in the school. He had, I think, hoped to gain some prestige by this act of defiance, which left me puzzled as to how to punish it. In the end, unwilling to beat him, and making allowances for his having owned up, I opted for leniency and a couple of 'Post Offices'.

I left school physically unharmed but there were other less visible scars. For seven years I had lived in a deeply uncongenial atmosphere, in which, almost until my last term, I might at any minute be struck, or rudely interrogated, or have my property stolen or damaged. So often had I heard that scornful comment, even if no physical attack followed, 'Look what Longmate's doing', or 'Did you know that Longmate...?' that I got into the habit of preparing a justification for my actions in advance. Today I can still hardly cross the road, or go upstairs, or choose a shirt to wear, without mustering the words to defend myself, sometimes aloud. It is not, I think, fanciful to suppose that a sensitive boy could be driven mad by a bad boarding school. Certainly I, who went to Housie self-confident and cheerful, if somewhat shy, left it self-conscious, unsure of myself, introverted and unhappy. Perhaps the price was worth paying to secure our great aim, a university scholarship. I remain uncertain. But what of the many who suffered without the compensating reward, who left after a miserable five or six years for some uncongenial job? As for myself, it is, I think, no accident that I still feel more at ease in the company of women than men and have never shared the prejudice against women doctors or dentists or lawyers held by so many of my generation, indeed I have always welcomed female professionals of all kinds. On the hidden, long term effects of my unhappy schooldays I would not dispute the diagnosis of the woman counsellor to whom I described them while being treated for some troublesome phobias late in life. 'If you ask me,' she said with admirable directness, 'it's all the fault of that bloody school.'

---

[1] *A Book of Christ's Hospital Slang*
[2] Hull pp.101, pp.138-9 & pp.146-7
[3] Hull p.43
[4] *Tom Brown's Schooldays* Chapter VIII

37

NOT WORTH THE CANDLE

'If you're still tempted, just remember, the game's not worth the candle.'

Headmaster of Christ's Hospital addressing senior boys, c. 1941

Our ignorance of sex was well illustrated by an incident which occurred when I was, I suppose, aged around twelve. Some pious boy had acquired a religious booklet supposed to be used before confession, which listed the various sins which might be on one's conscience. We rapidly disposed of stealing, lying and blasphemy, but, one boy then asked, contemplating the next offence listed, 'What on earth is adultery?' We remained bemused until an older boy helpfully commented: 'Don't worry. You haven't committed it yet!' with which we had to remain content.

Sex education was easily disposed of. Before confirmation one was summoned to see the chaplain who, clearly embarrassed, asked 'Has anyone ever talked to you about sex?' I knew from other boys that this question would be asked and gave the expected answer: 'Oh yes, sir, my parents told me about it before I came here.' This was a lie, as I suspect the Rev WC Johns, a thoroughly nice man, realised, but we then, with great relief on both sides, dropped the subject. Back in Peele A, when we compared notes, it was agreed that I had done the right thing; another candidate, who replied, 'I picked things up from other boys' was felt to have let the side down.

The history of non-education in sex is long and discreditable. The clerical author of *Eric or Little by Little,* published in 1858, and a classic in its day, inveighs so obscurely against what he describes as 'a part of my subject inconceivably painful' that one never actually discovers the nature of 'the deep, intolerable, unfathomable flood of moral turpitude and iniquity' on which Eric is swept away.[1] Even the most determined searcher after something salacious in this famous work must have been puzzled by the mysterious statement: 'Kibroth-Hathaavah! Many and many a young Englishman has perished there!', this oddly named place being in fact, though the author later fails to reveal this, the site in the book of *Numbers* where those guilty of the sin of lust are buried. By 1891 the school physician of Rugby was denouncing the provision of beer at bedtime as liable to encourage 'a vice which is as infectious as the measles'[2] and Housie responded, as I have mentioned, by banning not merely alcohol but all food at bedtime. Private citizens were no better than schoolmasters and doctors. In 1912 Rudyard Kipling wrote to his 13-year-old son, who had just gone away to Wellington, to stress the importance of 'keeping clear of any chap who is even suspected of beastliness' and 'swine of that type...Whatever their merits may be in the athletic line they are at heart only sweeps and scum.'[3] I was by no means inclined to idolise boys who were good at games, but the advice which my father sent me, around my fifteenth birthday, when I sought enlightenment after a scandal in the house, to be described in a moment, was equally baffling. 'If any boy ever mentions anything in connection with yourself, pay no attention and at once inform your housemaster,' a suggestion I failed to follow.

Only one master, I believe, attempted anything like formal sex education. This was CF Kirby, a lifelong bachelor, some of whose eccentricities I have already described. Kirby taught human biology, as he did everything else, in a robust, uncompromising fashion, his technique being to order a boy to strip and stand naked on a bench while he drew attention to relevant parts of his anatomy. I am grateful I was not exposed to such a lesson and, even when a science specialist, the nearest I came to learning about human reproduction was observing a primitive amoeba-like organism, paramecium, which reproduces sexlessly by splitting in half. I have not found this knowledge helpful in later life.

Robin Hull, who has written by far the frankest account of the sexual side of life at Christ's Hospital at this period, had, as a member of the newly founded Young Farmers Club other opportunities for enlightenment. The Club had acquired two nanny-goats and 'the goats, to produce milk, had to be mated...This led Hull to a long walk to find a billy-goat to do the honours. This occasion was the only real piece of heterosexual sex education Robin received at Christ's Hospital.'[*] In the event I learned about the facts of life from two sources, both unofficial. One term a number of senior boys in Peele A took it upon themselves to relieve their juniors' ignorance. How they had acquired their own knowledge I have no idea, but they divided the rest of the house who had reached the age of puberty up into small groups whom they addressed in readily intelligible down-to-earth terms. My old friend, Bob Pitman, whose pupil I became, approached his task in not merely a conscientious but an enthusiastic spirit, creating in me the anticipation of a normal and pleasant experience rather than, as the school's attitude had implied, a sinful and disgusting one. The immediate concern of the self-appointed sex-educators was to ensure that a boy suffering his first wet dream

---

[*] Professor Hull (p.197) adds: 'The experience, though extremely interesting, left the boy with lingering doubts about the reputed pleasure of copulation if it were always so malodorous.'

would not, as *had* happened, go along to matron to report that he was suffering from some appalling disease. Pitman – he was later for a time a schoolmaster – took me through the whole subject in a straightforward fashion. He was, however, shocked, when anxious to seem receptive, I asked if the term 'homosexual' came from the Latin 'homo' for man. 'No, no,' he replied, 'it's from the Greek *homos*, meaning "the same"', a lesson I have not forgotten.

Noel was unaware of this useful exercise in progress in his house and would no doubt have objected to it had he known about it. As it was we went around in the smug consciousness that we were better informed than the members of other houses, which in any other context would have delighted him. There were also opportunities for private study, both theoretical and practical. The war here, too, had brought a vast improvement, with more explicit references to sexual matters than in the prudish past. The newspapers now carried stories about rape and illegitimacy, and, later in the war, advertisements warning of the dangers of venereal disease, prompting boys to trade what information they had – often grotesquely inaccurate – with each other. In my final year someone introduced into the school an admirable book written for just such an audience as us, *That Youth May Know*, while the History Grecians were uniquely fortunate in having a master who openly discussed such questions as contraception and abortion. It then emerged that one of our group of 17 and 18 year olds thought both to be illegal, a natural assumption when harmless (if repellently sentimental) books like Marie Stopes's *Married Love* and Eustace Chesser's far superior *Love without Fear* were still being prosecuted as obscene. None of us had, of course, ever seen a condom though some boys from London talked knowingly of seedy shops in the Charing Cross Road where a mysterious item called Durex, which I at first assumed to be a chemical, was to be bought; outside London you apparently had to practise abstinence. Somehow the phrase 'French letter' got into circulation and we used it eagerly as likely in some obscure way to be offensive to our housemaster, but it was not until the barber, a great source of worldly knowledge, was applied to that we learned what it meant. In spite of all the efforts to keep us in the dark, the knowledge that we all possessed sexual instincts which could be pleasurably indulged in could not be hidden for ever. The basic principle on which school discipline rested, as I have stressed already, was the segregation of boys from different houses and when scandals did come to light it was the inter-house aspect which raised them from a minor internal matter to a major expulsion-meriting crime. Merely to be caught meeting a boy from another house without permission merited a beating, the assumption being that something immoral had either occurred or been contemplated, and thus sodomy, often imaginary, provided the excuse for actual sadism.

When serious relationships, involving physical penetration, did come to light the tradition was said to be that, assuming the two partners were not equally culpable the 'active' one was expelled, the 'passive' one, ie his catamite, merely thrashed. I can remember only one or two cases where, for such reasons, a boy was ordered not to return at the end of a holiday, or, as I shall describe, formally expelled in mid-term, and there was perhaps safety in numbers for I can recall no expulsions after the discovery of a school-wide network of sexual contacts. This affair was considered so serious that the headmaster himself took charge of the investigation, visiting each house in turn. One winter 'lock-up' the house was subjected to a furious bout of 'scavenging' and by a more than usually strict 'coat-inspection', as if the cleanliness of our surroundings and clothes would somehow convince 'Oily' of our mental and physical purity. In due course the Head arrived, to be ensconced in Noel's study, to which one by one Peele A boys who had been named during earlier visitations to other houses were summoned to be interrogated. We looked with a mixture of sympathy and admiration, but certainly not with disapproval, on those called out and I cannot recall any being expelled; we were, it should be remembered, the last house in the Avenue and perhaps by this time HLO Flecker was tiring of the role of Grand Inquisitor. I have speculated since as to whether he relished his task, as clearly some masters did, or found it a necessary, if disagreeable, duty. I incline to the latter conclusion, but being questioned by him must have been a terrifying experience for there always lurked below the urbane surface the threat of a volcanic eruption of temper, which I heard (from the far end of a school corridor) occur on at least one occasion. One boy who was questioned in Noel's study, but survived, later described the scene, with Noel standing deferentially by, for once silent, while the Head filled in a large chart, somewhat resembling, my informant remembered, a football pools form covered by an elaborate permutation, a new mark being added as each new relationship came to light. There was a good deal of cross-checking of earlier information, on the lines of 'But A says he saw you there with B and C, whom you've already admitted knowing', and it would have been an exceptionally brave or resourceful offender who managed to get away with anything less than the full truth.

On some occasions the Head certainly tempered justice with mercy. I recorded in *First Bloom* being told by a fellow science specialist, while we were tidying up after an experiment, how a relationship with a smaller boy in his house had been discovered and that 'he would probably be expelled in about ten minutes time'. He was still there, however, in our next lesson, and quoted to me the headmaster's actual words. 'Well, -----, you have been rather a fool, haven't you? You can start with a clean sheet now and you've got brains so you should be able to forget all about it, which is what we'd all better do, isn't it?'

Had this boy, then aged about 16, shown less academic promise the result, I suspect, might have been different. I can recall another boy, not, I think, regarded as grecian material, being called out of class one morning to see the headmaster and returning ten minutes later to pack his books. There was, he explained to the master in charge, no point in his finishing the lesson. 'I'm leaving now, sir.' We received no further explanation and wondered how he got home, for we assumed his uniform would be stripped from him before he left.

Only once in my time was there a public expulsion, almost as terrifying, though less brutal, than the 'flogging out' of a boy who had twice run away described by Charles Lamb.[*] The offender's crime on this occasion had not been primarily sexual, though some of those involved may have used for sexual purposes the inter-house network which now came to light. The affair began dramatically when the acting house-captain, the normal incumbent being absent on, I think, a Home Guard course, burst into the dayroom after attending a school monitors' meeting, to declare in mid-prep: 'No one is to leave this room without my personal permission!' While we were thus incarcerated an enormously thorough search was undertaken with every possible hiding place being explored. Not merely were the often inspected lockers and settles minutely scrutinised, and the odd corners of the house where half-made model aircraft and butterfly collecting bottles tended to accumulate, but every locked case was opened up and emptied out and even the tuck cupboard, bare – this must have been 1942 or 1943 – as it was. Nothing was found and only later did I discover that this investigation had been set off by the realisation that some hand grenades and detonators were missing from the Home Guard armoury. The trail had revealed, in some way I never discovered, the existence of a kind of Hellfire Club among older boys from a number of houses, who, like its original members, met underground, in this case in one of the mysterious chambers which opened off the Tube. (How they assembled, since the Tube was now blocked off with sandbags, remained a mystery.) Here, apparently they had smoked, drunk cider and, we assumed, had as much of an orgy as they could with no women available. This aspect had, however, assumed minor significance compared to the theft of the explosives and, another heinous crime, the use by the conspirators of the inter-house telephone network installed along the Tube for use in air raids only.

The affair, which had begun so strikingly, ended in an even more memorable fashion. We were all assembled in Big School to hear a speech from the headmaster, a rare event in itself, and he recounted the facts I have given above, ending with a denunciation of the culprit, whom I will call Baverstock. I can still recapture the moment when the Head declaimed, 'Baverstock stand forth!' and a boy of about 16 whom I barely knew shuffled uneasily out of his seat and stood in the central aisle of Big School where 800 pairs of eyes were fixed upon him. HLOF, pointing at the shrinking figure in our midst, went on to say that he had been the ringleader in the recent theft and that the stolen detonators might easily have exploded if some small boy or master's child had found one, treated it as a plaything and blown his hand off. There was a pause, then the headmaster announced, 'Baverstock, you are expelled!' The disgraced boy

---

[*] See Chapter 14 above.

walked slowly out of Big School, with our now pitying glances directed to him as he passed each row of seats, until the great doors at the end swung shut behind him and he disappeared out of our lives, 'struck off the foundation'.[*]

On this occasion the sexual element was merely peripheral to the chief offence, but when the Head did deal publicly with this alone he was more relaxed and genial, adopting a man of the world approach. There had, said Flecker, been a rash of 'sentimental friendships' in which big boys became attached to small ones. This was entirely understandable in our all male society and he was not suggesting that such relationships always went too far, but they could easily do so and were bad for both parties. The selected juniors became swollen-headed, while pursuing them distracted their admirers from their real business, to help run the school and to prepare for their next exam. He had up to now been tolerant of such cases but henceforward, even if innocent, he would assume they were not and punish the offenders accordingly. 'If you're still tempted,' he summed up, 'just remember the game's not worth the candle.'

Curiously, when, ten years later in the Lent Term of 1952, the Head came to confront publicly the other problem then common in public schools, what the courts used to call 'gross indecency', between boys of the same age, he handled it far more clumsily. One Old Blue, a History Grecian like myself, still vividly remembers every detail:

> Whispers, hints, rumours began to circulate about nefarious goings-on...A group of boys (four/six/eight?) had been caught in the act...Investigations were under way, retribution was at hand, expulsions were imminent...Then the startling rumours came. We were all to assemble in Big School...As people filed in, the nervous chatter gave way to an ominous silence...From the platform the Headmaster looked down...with one of his famous stares...and he launched into a very angry series of pronouncements... He gave no lurid details...but he made it clear that there had been a great evil in our midst. He had to extirpate it immediately...The acts were disgusting, dirty, dangerous...a sin, he proclaimed, against the Holy Ghost.

The invocation of the deity was too much for this boy, a self-confessed atheist, who gave an involuntary smile, leading to HLO Flecker angrily declaring 'A very senior boy is not taking this seriously' and to the offender being subsequently summoned to see him. The culprit, bravely taking the initiative, aware that his Oxford scholarship was already secure, explained that he had not smiled in derision but because he thought that to speak of 'a so-called sin against the Holy Ghost was grotesque' and might distress those who, unlike

---

[*] Robin Hull p.141 gives further details in a letter dated 18 July 1943, describing events 'some time ago'. His recollection was that four grenades were 'found under a tool shed' after the police had been called in and that two boys were expelled.

himself, still believed in God. It was equally 'cruel and deeply unfair' to threaten 'to expel boys' for what in a segregated boarding school with 'no sex education, no girls, no outlet for natural teenage energies' was predictable and 'basically harmless' behaviour.

He expected a furious reaction but found himself treated by the Head to a reasoned argument instead:

> I had seen him silent before, often seething with rage, but never flummoxed. I think he recognised straight away that I...had given the subject considerable thought...He could not accept my analysis, he said. Self-discipline in sexual matters was essential at all ages...Homosexual activity of any kind was a sin...Moreover he, as a headmaster, *in loco parentis*, had a special responsibility...to the boys entrusted to his care...He congratulated me on my scholastic success and hoped I would appreciate the benefits I had received at Christ's Hospital. We parted, after twenty minutes, on equable if not amicable terms.

To return to 1941, I think the Head's remarks had some effect. 'The love that dares not speak its name' was not thereafter silent but it became a whisper rather than a shout and the school certainly avoided the kind of posturing (and probably simulated) homosexuality that I later encountered at Oxford and in the broadcasting world. Occasionally over my last two years at school I heard a confession from a contemporary of his admiration for some fresh-faced new boy or junior, and we frequently spoke of 'having a pash on' someone, those notorious for attracting such attention, often in the form of 'pash-notes', being known as 'pash-boys'. Occasionally a love poem, supposedly to a girl but in fact addressed to a particular boy, would be published in *The Outlook*. (One, I believe actually spelt out his name in the initial letters of each line, but still went undetected.) Inevitably we fell in love with other boys; how could we not, as normal adolescents with no girls around? A late developer, as I have already mentioned, I must have been around 16 when I first really became aware of sex and it hit me hard. I cannot recall ever writing poems or love letters to other boys but, reading *First Bloom* again, I am embarrassed to read page after page devoted to my romantic feelings for boys whom I cannot now even identify. Not one of those for whom I cherished such impulses, or the smaller number with whom I had any sort of physical contact, turned out what I would still regard as 'queer' and everyone of whom I have kept track subsequently became happily married.

The public schools have often been accused of turning out generations of homosexuals and sado-masochists, but while the latter charge may have some justification the former seems to me unjust. It is now, I think, generally accepted that those who suffer from sexual inversion are born in this condition, though upbringing and environment may encourage an innate disposition to prefer one's own sex. The aggressively manly atmosphere of Housie gave no encouragement to the self-consciously effete or aesthetic type of boy. This was the sort of self-indulgence with which rich boys at more famous schools might amuse themselves; we were too busy with the more important business of making our way in the world. I must, in my seven years there, have seen hundreds of boys at close quarters and in my last years at school prepared detailed character studies of a dozen or more of those I knew best as a preliminary to writing *First Bloom,* but even with the wisdom of hindsight, I cannot identify one as truly homosexual.

There was undoubtedly a good deal of illicit sex at Housie, both physical and, more commonly, emotional and it may well have taken some boys a year or two after leaving school to realise their sexual orientation but all the contemporaries with whom I have kept in touch have displayed total, and sometimes exuberant, normality.

If *Tom Brown's Schooldays* provides a yardstick against which to measure bullying at Housie the comparable study in relation to sex is Alec Waugh's *Public School Life*, published in 1922, a sequel to his autobiographical novel, *The Loom of Youth*, first published in 1917, which encouraged me to write *First Bloom*. Sherborne during the first world war seems to have had much in common with Christ's Hospital in the second, though there were some obvious differences. Waugh refers, for instance, to boys carelessly placing incriminating notes in the pockets of waistcoats left 'in the matron's room to have a button sewn on them',[4] a hazard we escaped, lacking waistcoats and having to sew on our own buttons, though, as at Sherborne, the risk existed of letters being dropped 'in the cloisters'. Waugh also mentions boys walking arm in arm,[5] which would not have gone down well at Christ's Hospital, but in many ways the situation was the same. He recalls one new boy writing innocently home to say that 'a rather decent chap in his house had been nearly sacked for "smut". "Is this," he asked, "anything serious?"'[6] My letter to my father after the dormitory scandal I shall describe in a moment was equally naive. The parents of Christ's Hospital boys, lacking experience of public school themselves, were ill equipped to offer advice. I can remember the mother of a close friend asking me, shortly after I had left school, 'But what is it that homosexuals actually do?'

Her ignorance was by no means unusual. I recall a Peele A friend whose mother happily let him go on holiday alone with a bachelor uncle. When he returned early, after this relation had attempted to assault him, his mother was more incredulous than outraged. Even my mother, whose life, in a farming community and on a council estate, had been far less sheltered, knew nothing of homosexuals. When I innocently told her during one holiday that we had a new junior housemaster who came to sit on the smallest boys' beds after lights out, she repeated the story to another mother as proof of what a caring school I was attending. When I got back for the next term, however, the good-natured new master had already left, without explanation.

The dismissed man was, I now believe, unlucky to be reported for many masters notorious throughout the school for their over affectionate disposition remained for years. HLO Flecker, as public schoolboy, master and headmaster, had clearly come to regard such behaviour by members of staff as more acceptable than the expressions of adolescent sexuality on the part of the boys. His attitude is strikingly revealed in a story told me by a close friend who, while house-captain of Peele A, learned from a distressed small boy in the house that a junior housemaster in another house had attempted to fondle him. Our own housemaster, when told, reacted in his honest, uncomplicated way. 'What a horrible man!' he exclaimed, insisting that the Head must be told. HLO Flecker, however, adopted a far more worldly attitude. 'It isn't,' he remarked, 'as if he'd taken the boy's trousers down and had him. He merely let his hands wander where he shouldn't.' The offender stayed on the staff – it was, admittedly, wartime when replacing him would have been difficult – but was presumably reprimanded and was henceforward either reformed or more discreet.

In my time the term 'child abuse' had hardly been invented and not even the most sophisticated of us would have known what a paedophile was, though several of the staff hardly bothered to conceal their inclinations. It must in fairness be said that the very youngest boys were probably unaware of what was going on, and if a kindly arm round the shoulder or gentle hand on the knee proved only the prelude to a full-scale embrace or avuncular kiss the line between affection and indecency, especially for a nine or ten year old, missing his home, was hard to draw. The offenders were often admirable teachers and humane individuals, in contrast to the notorious beaters mentioned earlier. Given the choice most boys would have opted for an unwanted cuddle rather than a ferocious beating and I know of no boy who has been harmed by such experiences and several who survived them to emerge entirely normal.

But a problem there undoubtedly was. One friend suffered, at around the age of 14, from the wholly unwelcome embraces of an unmarried master, a lifelong bachelor, well known for such behaviour and only escaped more serious attentions by fleeing from the culprit's study. Three or four more masters regularly behaved in a way that would now be considered, at the very least, highly suspect. In one case, which occurred after I left and under a less tolerant headmaster, a senior housemaster, and long-standing bachelor, was actually caught *in flagrante delicto* with one of his own boys. He was an excellent teacher, a good-natured individual and – perhaps his strongest defence of all – an Old Blue, but was, very properly, dismissed on the spot and never taught again, though he ultimately received a generous, and highly selective, obituary in *The Blue*.

Noel Sergent, in his decent conventional way – he was, it may be recalled, happily married, despite his alleged infidelity – did his best to maintain the moral tone of his house, keeping a close eye on boys he suspected of pairing off for immoral purposes – 'Noel,' we would say, 'has formed one of his theories about them'. Because I displayed a lamentable lack of interest in house games, my housemaster clearly assumed that I must also be retarded in other ways, indeed I came, as I have said, late to adolescence. When, finally, I did begin to grow rapidly, I can recall his almost incredulous remark: 'Say, old Longmate, you're becoming quite a good-looking fellow!' This was perhaps intended as a veiled warning, but his assumption that I was still sexually naive was now to stand me in good stead. I must, I think, only just have entered the senior dormitory when I found myself occupying a bed between two boys rather older than me, whom I will call Darwin and Noakes. Darwin was an exceptionally good-looking young man who had at one time bullied me and then become my protector, as I have described earlier; Noakes was a charismatic figure, a natural games player, with a jolly extrovert disposition, highly sexed. (A friend who later found himself in the Infirmary between Noakes and another boy had a similar experience to the one I am about to describe and, deeply embarrassed, would protest: 'I say, you do know I'm still awake?')

We were at one end of the dormitory and, in the grey dimness after lights out, it became Noakes's regular custom to leave his bed, creep past the end of mine, and climb into Darwin's. Unhappily, the lovers fell out. Darwin complained too audibly that he was being forced to continue the relationship against his will, in effect suffering a nightly rape, and somehow news of the affair reached Noel's ears. This time, since the relationship was in every sense in house the Head was not involved but Noel treated it with great solemnity. The senior dormitory were assembled in the dayroom to be told, what most of us already knew, that, in Noel's words, 'Noakes has been visiting Darwin in his bed'. Darwin might have been forced to submit, said Noel, though he sounded a little sceptical, but even if he had not, the physical relationship was a serious crime. 'You can,' he warned us, 'get two years in prison for such tricks.'

In the investigation which followed, I was, to the general surprise, the one person not asked to give evidence. By sheer good fortune I had mentioned the scandal in a letter home, since it made an interesting titbit in an otherwise dull report on the week's events. My father responded with a letter of which a Victorian parent might have been proud. 'I thank God, my son,' he wrote, 'that you are not part of this horrible mess,' and went on, not before time, since I must by now have been 14 or 15 to attempt to instruct me in the facts of life. He did so in such a vague manner, omitting all the essentials, that, but for Pitman's helpful session a term or so earlier, I should have been more bewildered than ever. Luckily he also wrote to Noel, suggesting he might like to supplement this belated lesson with some face to face remarks. Noel failed to take the hint but assumed that I must be both innocent and ignorant, a state in which he was happy to leave me. Noakes survived; he was, after all, a great asset on the playing field. Darwin survived; he was, after all, assumed to be more sinned against than sinning. The main result was that Noel redoubled his efforts to stamp out any sexual activity in his house, though with little success. Every technique was tried, from collecting written depositions, to vigilante style patrols. Once, I recall, we were all required to write a detailed account of where, and with whom, we had spent the preceding Saturday evening and Sunday afternoon. The nominal purpose was to identify boys seen smoking on a local farm but the resulting documents were eagerly scrutinised by Noel for clues about unsuitable friendships or possible assignations in suspect places. The real danger, however, lay in the dormitory and Noel began to appear a little while after lights-out, having given possible offenders time to settle down together, before patrolling the blacked-out room with a torch, which he focused in turn on each pillow. Once – and this was typical of how he so often managed to get things wrong – he stopped his patrol a yard or two short of the one bed which did, we all knew, contain two boys. When he left the dormitory we all heaved a sigh of relief and the visiting boy hastily returned to his own bed, amorous intentions abandoned.

I witnessed a similarly hairbreadth escape involving a monitor, when another two boys were quite blatantly sharing a bath at one end of the 'lav end' while the rest of us were still washing. While they were happily splashing about one on top of the other, the door opened, leaving just time for one of the pair to leap out and hide behind the screen which stretched half across the room, like the partition which divided off the WC. By extraordinary chance the monitor chose to carry on a long conversation with the boy in the bath from just beyond the screen, to which the bather, though somewhat uneasily and tersely, replied. Eventually, after what seemed an age to all of us, the monitor withdrew and the boy who had been hiding, and was now shivering, leapt back into the bath with a fervent oath of relief.

The extensive literature on boys' boarding schools, some examples of which I have already quoted, suggests that what happened at Housie between the boys was no worse, and no better, than occurred elsewhere. A few boys engaged in actual intercourse – at least four or five in Peele A, to my certain knowledge, and this was probably no different from other houses; a much larger number sought relief through mutual arrangements with other boys, usually in the same age group; and perhaps a majority, including some of those in the categories already mentioned, formed what the head had called a 'sentimental friendship' with another boy, usually, though not invariably, younger than themselves. Alec Waugh claimed that 'the greater part of active immorality in schools takes place between 15 and 16' and this was probably also true of Housie in my day.[7] If we were denied all sex education we were also kept clear of the ludicrous stories still circulating, or being actively encouraged, in other schools. One school novel, perhaps *The Loom of Youth*, contains a scene in which a conscientious house-captain tells the members of one dormitory to forget the rumours that 'cogging' as it was called there, led to blindness, impotence –

though we would not have known what that was – or insanity.* Robin Hull mentions a housemaster who 'to counter the rumours of dire consequences' sportingly assured his boys that 'it was quite safe and he even did it himself', but this must have been after my time for I cannot recall hearing of this brave confession, which surely spread through the school.[8]

In marked contrast to the army, sex was little discussed at school. There was a general recognition, I suspect, that we all had the same needs and the less said about how they were satisfied the better. The monitors, as the oldest boys, were probably those most plagued by adolescent desire, and, often culpable themselves, were prepared to turn a blind eye when, for instance, two boys might be seen suspiciously often emerging together from the 'new bogs' with their row of adjoining cubicles opening on to a sheltered corridor. Once a monitor and his partner, who occupied the only cubicle in the senior dormitory, overslept, so the younger boy had to emerge after the morning 'Get up!' call and walk the length of the large room to knowing looks, but no word of this escapade reached Noel's ears. Only once indeed can I remember our housemaster getting things right in his perpetual watch for indecency. One boy, whom I will call Hobart, a non-academic youth who left early, was notorious among us for his obsession with sex, which mostly took the form of seizing every possible opportunity to undress and stand about exposing himself. Once he attempted to attract the attention of Noel's maid while naked by the crude device of firing at her with his catapult, using missiles – this was later part of the charge against him – made from lead torn from the window flashings. This novel form of courtship proved unrewarding and ended in the offender being beaten. When he left, defying the Headmaster's rule that nothing unfavourable could be written on a final report, Noel added to the misleading tributes paid by his colleagues, his own verdict, 'This boy is sexually perverted.' Hobart simply tore the document up and when I next saw his name it was (a little oddly in all the circumstances) in the school Roll of Honour, as he had been called up and killed.

Noel, as I have mentioned, devoted much effort to trying to keep us out of suspect places like the shrubberies which the original landscape architect had so thoughtlessly created, but other places of assignation took their place, especially in the winter. The Tube, smelling of damp games clothes and, in the war, of sandbags, was not the most romantic of locations, and gave a new meaning to the concept of love forced underground, but was readily accessible from every block. One boy in my house became notorious for his mating cry, based on our German-inspired slang, of 'Ins Tube!', uttered to a prospective partner. Outside the house, the school pavilion and the tunnel beneath the organ

---

* On the history of so many schools' obsession with this subject and its incidence among 15-16 year olds, see Jonathan Gathorne-Hardy, *The Public School Phenomenon*, pp.88-92.

in Big School were often left unlocked and could be used for assignations with a partner from another house. Another useful venue was the biology laboratory used for training by the Air Training Corps, left open so keen cadets could study the aircraft recognition posters on the walls. Ardent adolescents were far from deterred by the silhouettes of enemy bombers and fighters all round them, but the dead snakes and other specimens in glass cases that lined the benches were said to be even more offputting.

About most such encounters precious little romance existed. The circumstances of school dictated a separation between the physical aspects of desire, which prompted relationships between contemporaries, and the emotional stirrings of adolescence, which led to the type of sentimental friendships, often, though not invariably, between boys of different ages, against which the headmaster had warned in the talk previously quoted.

I was, as mentioned earlier, a late developer in this area and hardly bothered by the impulses which so many of those around me seemed to find disturbing. Once a boy offered me a shilling [5p] to go into the Tube with him but I declined; his nickname, 'Pimp', suggests I was not the only person he approached. Looking back I feel that sex ought to have bulked larger in my life than it did. The prudishness which I felt on reaching Housie never really left me and I still wince at finding myself on a nudist beach or having to walk though a male changing room. Long after leaving school I heard from a colleague who had been a Prisoner of War in Germany in his early twenties that during all his years of captivity the absence of sex had barely bothered him or most of his fellow prisoners; what haunted their thoughts was food. I confess that I am far more conscious of being hungry at Housie than of being sexually frustrated and now wonder if there was not something in the implicit public school notion that what was ignored long enough would go away.

If a boarding school at this time failed to promote proper instruction in sex, and only the crudest experience of its practice, what it supplied in abundance was sentimental education. The late AL Rowse, himself homosexual, wrote in his autobiography, *A Cornish Childhood*, which appeared in 1942, 'that public-school boys by their end of their time are ten years ahead of us day-school boys in sophistication, knowledge of the world, of human beings. Before they are thrown out upon the world in all seriousness, they have already had a pretty good apprenticeship in the torrid conditions of boarding-school life; a good many of them have already had a considerable (and useful) experience in the ways of the human heart, before they come to deal, more seriously, with women.'[9]

I was instantly reminded of my schooldays when I first read Max Beerbohm's *Zuleika Dobson*, published in 1911, which describes how a young woman of such devastating beauty arrives in Oxford that all the undergraduates lose their hearts to her and ultimately drown themselves *en masse* from unrequited love. This last tragedy apart, Peele A towards the end of my time there acquired its own Zuleika, an extremely pretty dark-haired boy with a perfect complexion, as charming and well-spoken as he was attractive. Soon so many boys were seeking him out that my friend Pitman, by then house-captain, called a special meeting of the senior boys to discuss the problem. Henderson, as I'll call him, was, Pitman complained, 'being pursued' on all sides, not surprisingly, perhaps, as it had become his habit to greet new acquaintance with the artless invitation 'Would you like a kiss?' Typically, with a real scandal to get his teeth into, Noel Sergent was unaware of what was happening but Henderson came to no harm as we all agreed to a self-denying ordinance not to encourage his provocative behaviour. This policy worked. The amorous 16 and 17 year olds who had formerly competed for the new boy's attention now turned their gaze back to the traditional objects for admiration, the trebles in the choir, who paraded before the rest of the school as they made their way out of Chapel. The boy himself settled down happily to a conventional school career and when, several years later, our paths briefly crossed, he seemed a pleasantly balanced, still very attractive, young man, enjoying a normal career.

It was to be many years before Christ's Hospital, or indeed other schools, came to grips with this delicate subject. One Old Blue arriving about the time I left remembers how sex education was still regarded as the chaplain's special province, but half of one divinity lesson was now devoted to it. Even more bravely, a drawing was displayed of the naked male body, with which they were already familiar, but not the female, of which they remained wholly ignorant.

Long before I left school I realised that, despite some close friendships and occasionally being attracted to other boys, such attachments were for me a mere interlude, a read-through, barely even a dress rehearsal, for the real performance, which must clearly involve the opposite sex. On the last page of *First Bloom*, aged 18 and still with no real knowledge of girls, I wrote, with the cheerful confidence of adolescence, 'If so much can be derived from so short a time with a chosen friend, how much more is likely...when I come...to that perfect woman whom I am confident lies waiting for me.' This expectation proved somewhat over optimistic. But here at least Housie had left no lasting scar. Within a year or so, serving as a 19-year-old soldier in a country that seemed to be populated by attractive young women, I found that my attitude to the opposite sex, if still inhibited by my seven segregated years, was unquestionably, indeed troublesomely, normal.

[1] Gathorne-Hardy p.85
[2] *The Waterdrinkers* p.132
[3] Laski p.130
[4] Waugh *Life* p.150
[5] Waugh *Life* p.148
[6] Waugh *Life* p.134
[7] Waugh *Life* p.136
[8] Hull p.96
[9] Rowse p.181

38

SUSSEX BY THE SEA

*And the law prevents us journeying
To Sussex by the sea.*

The author's first published poem,
The Outlook, *July 1941*

The Summer Term of 1941 saw a major extension of the war. On the day that Germany invaded Russia, Sunday 22 June 1941, the Debating Society was meeting in the Dominions Library and here, surrounded by reminders of our imperial past, we were able to hear the prime minister's speech on a radio brought in for the occasion. Admiring Russia and left-wing views in general became respectable overnight, but already a massive shift in public opinion was under way as wartime experience showed the necessity of centralised planning and 'Fair Shares'. The success of anti-government candidates in by-elections indicated the silent revolution now in progress. I had, as I have described, been an unwavering supporter of the Labour Party since the age of nine. I was now 15-and-a-half and the rest of the country was beginning to catch up with me. My own family was typical. My father, who had suffered all the misery of pre-war unemployment, and my mother, now able, thanks to rationing, to feed her family decently, both shared my opinions. So did my elder sister, exposed to the stern reality of working-class life in the raw in a munitions factory, and, I suspected, my brother, suffering, as an ordinary aircraftsman, from the petty tyrannies and antiquated class structure of Service life. The war, I recognised, had first to be won, largely by people like us who had benefitted precious little from peacetime, but then, I was confident, would come a General Election and the overdue reckoning with the Conservatives. Later, reading the diaries for this period of comfortably-off people moaning about the loss of their cooks and their cars I am amazed at the gulf between them and us.[*] Cars and cooks were

---

[*] See, for instance the wartime diaries of the journalist Charles Graves, who escaped being called up but was highly indignant when his cook left to join the Women's Land Army. The library copy of the wartime reminiscences of the romantic novelist Ursula Bloom which I read had been sarcastically endorsed by one reader: 'A lovely war for some!', a sentiment I have often echoed.

unknown in Camp Close and to the vast majority of families everywhere else. 1941, with the acceptance – even the idolisation – of Russia and the positive popularity of rationing, was, I believe, the turning point. Henceforward those who talked of returning to the supposedly idyllic pre-war world were out of touch with the national mood.

Christ's Hospital remained, as always, a paradox, a school which drew on the working and lower-middle classes for its pupils but was, in every sense, innately conservative. It was also more ready to preach patriotism and sacrifice than to practise them. When, on 1 June 1941, clothes rationing was, quite unexpectedly, introduced, the school was given a unique opportunity to shed its silliest tradition, the retention of a uniform appallingly extravagant in terms of both material and labour, and to silence the critics by the then unanswerable argument that it was in the national interest. The opportunity was ignored. It was to be another year before, and then only for the very youngest, the ancient uniform began to be abandoned in favour of rational dress, and for most of the school it remained in use throughout the war.[1] The result of clothes rationing was indeed to increase our dependence on the school to an extent unknown since it had drawn its intake from the streets. All our clothing coupons were appropriated, with only a tiny number returned to enable us to buy such necessities as handkerchiefs.

We then faced the prospect of having to wear Housey clothes during the holidays, something no one had done since the nineteenth century, when it had ceased to be compulsory – proof enough that the uniform was not, as was often claimed, popular among those forced to endure it. All our parents must, therefore, like mine, have been exceptionally generous with their own coupons in providing us with normal outfits, and exceptionally resourceful in recycling worn-out items. I still regret the governors' decision. Here was the second great opportunity, the first having been at the time of the move from London in 1902, to abandon this costly, wasteful and impractical incubus, at a time when it would have attracted little attention and, if noticed at all, would have been praised as a patriotic sacrifice. As it was, part of the school were now dressed like normal twentieth century schoolboys while most of us continued, as I have written elsewhere, to look as if we were expecting the Spanish Armada.

Some reduction in wear and tear on our Housey clothes did, however, result from the increasing amount of time we spent in uniform – Home Guard, JTC, which had now replaced the old OTC, or ATC, of which I shall say more later. Between January and July 1941 the JTC held no fewer than three Field Days and it was clear that one tradition at least had survived from the old OTC years: the weather was, more often than not, appalling. *The Blue* for June, and, later, July 1941, recorded these experiences:

> On Tuesday, March 25th, we held our first Field Day of the year. The day dawned cloudy, and as we made our way to Denne Park, fighting as we

went, the storm broke. From then on it rained unceasingly, and having made up our minds that we were going to get wet we did...

After a month of dry weather Field Day brought us rain. Once again we fought our way to Denne Park where we continued the programme we had begun on our previous visit. Occasionally towards the end of the day, the rain ceased and we saw the sun. It would be impossible to pass the lunch without comment; few of us saw the heap of anhydrous fragments of meat-pie crumbled in our very hands to a thick paste without some pang of despair. The watercress, however, was in its element.[2]

The third exercise proved more enjoyable:

Our last Field Day took place on Friday, July 4th...The weather was excellent. Denne Park looked a little different since our last visit. Luxuriant bracken had sprung up making new and extensive cover. At lunchtime nothing could have been more welcome than the van which brought the drinking water. After lunch we fought. It was a bloody battle and some of us lived through three lives that afternoon; the field was littered with our corpses.[3]

I had not yet escaped from what, in *First Bloom*, I still called, as did everyone else, the OTC, and the account I wrote of these events three years later adds some enlivening detail to these official accounts:

The OTC, having begun to take the war more seriously, celebrated its growing importance with two Field Days, instead of the customary one...A certain damp morning found James crawling along the bracken of a nearby park. It was cold, and the rain descended with monotonous regularity, to add to the prevailing gloom and depression of the troops. At intervals a flag would be waved, causing a depressed and bored umpire to announce that Number Three Platoon's machine-gun had now annihilated Number One platoon, or that Number Two Platoon were now laying down a barrage of covering fire. Visibly cheered, for casualties meant a welcome break in the advance, half of the platoon dropped back to the shelter of the trees and speculated on the chance of 'old Jennings' ever venturing into the rain to inspect the condition of his men for himself.

In spite of their cynicism he strode up at last, and, with a voice more fruity in timbre than ever, clicked his cane on his muddy boots and announced, as if news of the interruption would be unwelcome to his men, 'Lunch!' The troops, grimy, wet and sweating, repaired toward the lorry bearing the lunch, and expressed the usual disgust at the cheese, bread, watercress and cake provided for their refreshment.

After lunch the attack continued. There were long detours, occasional shouts and, when the fog lifted for a moment, bursts of firing which indicated boredom rather than the presence of the enemy. They charged at last and were greeted with realistic shouts of 'Don't shoot!' by the vanquished, who saw fingers trembling on the trigger and had no desire to receive blank cartridges in their faces. The lunch van had brought their greatcoats and the sun, as if to spite them, had emerged when the long detour preliminary to the attack was at its height, so the body of troops who marched back to Middlestone were bathed in their own sweat as plentifully as they were bedewed with the rains of heaven. They trudged along singing the ditty made immortal by generations of public school cadets . . .

Old King Cole was a merry old soul, and a merry old soul was he,
He called for his pipe, and he called for his bowl, and he called for his privates three . . .

The song wound out its weary length, through the whole hierarchy of ranks, each verse ending with a patriotic burst of

There's none so fair
As can compare
With the Middlestone OTC.

But in spite of this assurance, in the following term the newly formed ATC received into its ranks a great number of disillusioned infantry.

This was a period when the reputation of the British army did not stand high. The formation of the Air Training Corps at last gave non-military-minded boys like myself an alternative to the OTC, though the government at first only 'recognised', ie provided a grant for, entrants to the ATC, as to the new JTC, aged 15 and upwards; the Housey OTC had press-ganged its victims into their peaked caps and puttees at 13-and-a-half. Nevertheless there was about the new organisation a real sense of volunteering, whatever one's motives, and, having positively opted for it, we felt some sense of superiority to the mere cannon-fodder forcibly enrolled in the JTC which, by some process I never understood, continued to take in boys at the younger age.

The ATC first appears in *The Blue* in June 1941:

No 679 (Christ's Hospital) Flight was formed last February and now has a strength of about sixty cadets.[4]

My twin sister took her School Certificate that summer and her cookery 'practical' reflected wartime shortages; she was required to make a 'cabbage pie' which was not a success: even my kind-hearted mother confessed that she was hard put not to laugh aloud at this sad travesty of a dish – her own pastry was always superb. I, meanwhile, was under less academic pressure, for it was the custom at Housie for boys of grecian potential to sit the School Certificate exam a year later than at most schools, the theory being that we should take it in our stride and not be distracted from our real aim, to capture a university scholarship in two years' time. Having chosen, for reasons explained earlier, to specialise in science I found in the laboratory my escape from the misery of daily life in the house where I still displayed an embarrassing inferiority at games to boys much younger than me. It was rapidly clear, however, that of the three science subjects the only one where I had any chance of success was chemistry. Biology I liked well enough, though handicapped by a total inability to draw; my representation of a dissected cockroach, one disgusted master told me, would have disgraced a five year old. Physics I could not cope with at all. One master told me in a kindly way that the 'water equivalent' I had calculated for a metal beaker would have been more appropriate to the boiler of a locomotive. The head of the department, 'Kappa' Sills, of whom I have already written, conscientiously drilled into me a number of useful propositions such as Newton's Laws of Motion and Ohm's Law, which I can still recite. Nevertheless, when set to calculate with an instrument called a Post Office Box where a failure in a circuit had occurred, I failed miserably, interested in electricity though I was. This procedure, we were told, was used to work out where a cable serving a town had developed a fault; so far as I was concerned the community, it was clear, would have to remain in darkness. After I had achieved the lowest mark on record in an end of term exam, one out of 50, it was wisely decided that I should not sit the Physics papers for School Certificate, with 'Kappa' charitably noting on my report, 'Physics is not his subject'.

My subjects, it was becoming increasingly plain, were English and history and I was fortunate in being taught both throughout my time at Housie, apart from a single year, by masters whom I both respected and liked. For English I returned to Roy Macklin and I can still reconstruct many of his lessons from my surviving exercise books. He combined, like all good English teachers, a proper concern for the basics of spelling, grammar and such essential arts as précis writing, with encouragement for more imaginative and creative work. His comment on my first précis for him, in the Michaelmas Term of 1940, could have applied to almost every subsequent piece of work I wrote: 'Much too long, though you have got everything in and expressed it well.' The war by no means dominated our lessons. For prep on the night of 7 November 1940, when London suffered one of its then almost nightly heavy raids, from 193 enemy bombers, and the RAF sent 63 aircraft, far less effectively, to attack Essen,[5] we were required to write a Gothic horror story on the lines of *The Castle of Otranto*. My composition, *The Alchemist of Monavero*, was commended as

'An ingenious idea' and rated 'Good', but Roy Macklin sternly highlighted in red pencil every minor fault. 'Much money', I was told, should have been 'great wealth' and there was no excuse for omitting the apostrophe in 'servants rooms'.

Admirable training for a future journalist was provided by our next prep, which required us to describe an aerial battle 'in "matter of fact" style by a BBC observer who was on the spot' as well as 'in the romantic style as it seemed to an author watching from the garden'. 'You have,' I was told, 'caught the idea.'

Meanwhile we were receiving a good, solid grounding in the English classics, now so often neglected. Macklin was surprisingly tolerant of my arrogant judgement on 'The Letters of John Keats', which I described as 'a collection of pompous trivialities'. 'You have,' he conceded, 'thought about it and come to an honest conclusion. I'll tell you why I don't quite agree.' He was, however, unequivocally hard on my 'Comparison of Dickens and Thackerary'. *Vanity Fair* I was too young to appreciate, while my heart warmed to the exposure of Dotheboys Hall and the pre-Victorian workhouse in *Nicholas Nickleby* and *Oliver Twist*, prompting the conclusion: 'Dickens is both a writer and reformer. Thackeray is neither', a verdict I now blush to read.

Looking back at this formative year in my education, from 14 and a half to 15 and a half, what strikes me is that it was the fact-based work which regularly earned the poorest marks, while essays on more abstract subjects were almost invariably praised. Macklin was, rightly as I now realise, very hard on my adolescent tendency to show off. 'It is your idea that you are a critic,' he wrote after I had mauled some established writer in a review. 'I am rather afraid you may be right.' By contrast an essay on 'Fun', which raised the interesting question as to why 'most people would get more enjoyment from...breaking a window than from carefully mending one' – a proposition I would no longer, as a house-owner, support – earned me one of the highest marks I ever received. The essay reveals, incidentally, how innocent were the ambitions of a boy of my age at that time, not extending beyond enjoying 'a cooling bottle of lemonade and some chocolate' with 'fruit of all kinds and oranges in particular'. Macklin considered this artless confession 'a spontaneous and thoroughly successful piece of writing' and I was evidently still in favour on 15 May 1941 when I sat down in the Peele A dayroom to write a *Now*, a detailed account of what was happening at a particular moment on a single day. Five days before, the blitz had ended with the last great attack on London; the Germans had just driven the last British troops out of Greece; the first great round-up of Jews was under way in Paris and, that Thursday night 101 British aircraft were delivering another ineffective raid, this time against Hanover. Meanwhile I was happily back in the late eighteenth century, doing my best to imitate the style of Leigh Hunt, my favourite among the

'Housey school' of writers since I had discovered that he had been considered too radical and disreputable to have a house named after him:

> Now the house is being ransacked for that mislaid umbrella and the passages are damp with the water the mat has not removed. Now only the most hardy foliage stays upright and the flowers are bent with the force of the pelting rain...Now the washerwoman bemoans the downpour that prevents her clothes from drying and the schoolmaster becomes short tempered with his form...Now the ducks who quacked with delight at the first few drops are becoming tired of the steady downpour and the rain still hisses down on the rising river...Now is a bowl of warm punch an irresistible attraction and your scribe can no longer resist its temptation and must needs conclude his 'Now'.

This Macklin considered 'Very good' while another essay, later that term, 'Recollections', already cited, received the ultimate accolade: 'Excellent'. History, meanwhile, I found somewhat less rewarding, since that year we were studying the eighteenth century, which did not greatly appeal to me, though I had again a first class teacher, the amiable, lively-minded, 'Warny B', already described, who in June 1941 was ordained, becoming the Rev Michael Warneford-Brown. I can remember only a single, inadvertently humorous, line, from his teaching; 'Robert Walpole drank like a fish and was called to the Bar.' For one lesson we were taught by the master in charge of the history grecians, the Hon. DS Roberts, known throughout the school, from his kindly manner, as 'Daddy' Roberts. DSR, as I later came to know him, was, I now realise, 'talent-spotting' for recruits to his speciality. This was, I think, the first time I ever spoke to him and, most fortunately, I caught his eye by comparing the allegedly subversive *North Briton*, prosecuted by the government in 1763, with the Communist *Daily Worker*, recently, in January 1941, suppressed for opposition to the war. I was also struck by his reaction when a boy caused some laughter by referring to a sailing ship 'steaming up and down'. DSR brushed aside the anachronism: 'Don't worry. It's a good word!' Here was a true teacher in action. A bullying pedant like Blam or Macnutt would have seized on the trivial error, not encouraged the enthusiasm which prompted it.

In July 1941 I had the satisfaction of seeing a piece of my work in print for the first time in the annual school literary magazine, *The Outlook*, founded 20 years before but destined to succumb shortly afterwards to the paper shortage. It must have been inspired by a visit to Worthing with my mother on a day out:

> The beach is barricaded with upright iron posts,
> The emptying town protected from the grey invading hosts;
> Great concrete blocks are standing, in grimly silent lines,
> And where, before, the deck-chairs stood, lie rows of deadly mines.

No gaily coloured dresses parade along the shore,
Even the ice-cream stalls are now, alas!, no more.
The pier re-echoes dully to the tramp of booted feet,
The band pavilion's empty where the trippers used to meet.
There is no noisy laughter to float upon the air.
The promenade, once crowded, is now completely bare,
And now no boisterous welcome is awaiting you or me.
And the law prevents us journeying to Sussex by the Sea.

Although the same issue of *The Outlook* carried an article by my friend Pitman, on ghosts, none of the other contributors have since achieved any literary fame, and I cannot recall my sonnet attracting much attention. We were more conscious of the reports in *The Blue* of the military career of boys we had known and that term's issue contained an extract from a letter from my old hero and former house-captain, JCD Lawrance, who had left the Colonial Service on the outbreak of war to be commissioned in the army:

> I am serving with a Mountain Battery – an Indian Army Unit. I find the language and customs very strange and have never before had to do with mules...Our only grumble is the elusiveness of the enemy...I have seen more in the way of game than Italians so far.[6]

By now I was old enough to attend the meetings of the Debating Society and, having forced myself to my feet, can recall the enormous satisfaction I felt on realising I had the audience's attention. The incident was important to my development, not merely giving me a liking for public speaking, but also vastly increasing my self-confidence. It was a gratifying change to find myself applauded, instead, as so often happened in the house, jeered at, and it also brought me once again to DSR's attention, as he often presided at debates.

What also stands out in my mind that year, far less creditably, are German lessons, which for my form were entrusted to a young and inexperienced master physically unfit for military service. This was his war work and I recall with shame how little appreciation we showed of his undertaking a job for which he clearly had little aptitude. Eventually this much tormented man hurried out with vast relief at the end of one lesson to leave us to face the wrath of the formidable Head of German, who revealed that during the last two periods we had spent with Mr Weston, as I will call him, he had been listening to the uproar from the adjoining classroom. 'Jem' made us all feel thoroughly ashamed of ourselves, before ordering us to fetch water and dusters to 'Clean up that insulting remark on the wall!' – an inked-in inscription referring to 'Weedy Weston'.

By the end of the summer term of 1941 I had been five years in the house and, with most boys now leaving before their eighteenth birthday, was approaching the time when I might reasonably expect to become a monitor. Being a monitor transformed one's daily life. A monitor had a small table of his own, which he could surround with books and prints of his choice, could dispense punishments instead of receiving them and, above all, was largely free of the rigid timetable which ruled ordinary boys' lives; he could even stay up after 9pm and enjoy the luxury of a 'brew up' on the study fire of the house-captain or his deputy. A monitor was also exempt from trades and such chores as bed-making and cleaning his own shoes, these services being provided by a 'swab', a word in use since at least 1860. The swab was the Housey equivalent of a fag, but it was a voluntary and paid post – the usual rate was about five shillings [25p] a term – with many advantages. A swab was excused trades, had a ready-made excuse for such misdemeanours as being late for prep, as he was probably running an errand for his swab-master or giving his buttons a fresh polish before Corps parade – and was to some extent protected by him from punishment and injustice. I had been a swab myself, serving a boy of whom I can recall nothing except his name, Green. I remember feeling gratified when he said I had been the best swab he had ever had, though I have never heard of him since.

The agreeable prospect of becoming a monitor in a year's time was suddenly put in jeopardy by an unforeseen attempt by our housemaster to achieve that rapport with his boys which had always eluded him. With, in the summer of 1941, three boys due to leave, Noel, instead of appointing the three most senior non-monitors to succeed them, suddenly decided to have what was in effect, though not in name, an election, ordering us all to write on a 'ballot paper' the names of the three boys in order of preference, whom we would like to see fill the vacancies.

Noel did not, as might have been reasonable, accept the results as a useful guide but simply appointed in that order the three boys who had come top of the poll, a decision with far-reaching consequences, for the boy with most votes became in due course house-captain, the first holder of the office with whom I felt nothing in common. In *First Bloom* I called him 'Johns'. He was, as his election showed, popular, a strong, noisy, cheerful extrovert, good at games, often surrounded by an admiring circle of boys like himself. Meanwhile the boy who was pushed into second place, whom I named 'Marchant', was a much quieter, more serious-minded, type who had joined the house at the same time as me and become a friend. Whether anyone voted for me I do not know, but once Noel announced the election I realised my chances of becoming a monitor in the near future were doomed. In *First Bloom* I recorded the results of Noel's excursion into democracy:

> Like other reformers, he had omitted to temper his zeal with discretion and had elevated the boy who secured most votes to the senior vacancy, irrespective of the consequences. The juniors, with their usual capacity for

hero-worship, had accepted him as a fit object for it and since Mr Breton [ie Noel Sergent] had not realised that even in a democracy the very young are not given votes at all, much less equal power with the experienced members, juniors of eleven and twelve had largely contributed to the overwhelming success of Johns at 'the polls'...It was an experiment doomed to failure from the outset. Marchant, who had grown into a quietly responsible youth, felt himself to some extent slighted, and the other rejected candidates, whose seniority gave them a great deal of importance in the house, were equally resentful.

Although the nightly air raids on London had finished in May, the risk remained that they might be resumed and at the end of the Summer Term 1941 an appeal was made for hospitality during the holidays for boys from areas still considered particularly vulnerable. For once I felt grateful that my home was so small that there could be no question of us squeezing anyone else into it, indeed it was already full to overflowing.

The war was increasingly involving us all. The photographic business of which my father was in theory manager but in practice for most of the war the sole employee was kept fully stretched. Though the traditional 'D and P' business had largely dried up because of the shortage of film, his services were in constant demand to take regimental groups and, that old standby, weddings; the war was a great time for getting married before the bridegroom went overseas.

He also 'did his bit' in other ways. After the great fire raids of December 1940 a national scheme for fire watching had been introduced and my father was asked to become organiser for our estate. He was a natural choice, just as my mother had been as representative of the Hospital Fund, for there still clung to us something of our former middle-class status. My father took his duties very seriously and drew up a rota of all those required to turn out when the siren sounded and duly put it up on a placard in the central archway of the entrance to the estate, though almost at once it became a target for stones. He persisted, however, and he and I both conscientiously turned out whenever there was an air raid warning, though this was no sacrifice for me, as I was not working next day.

We were also asked to take charge of the keys to the surface shelters which had been erected on the green in the middle of Camp Close. I am now doubtful how necessary these were, for Newbury was a reception area for evacuees, officially classed as unlikely to be attacked. Nevertheless these brick shelters had been built and had apparently suffered from vandals, though never, I think, as certainly happened in some places, used by illicit lovers. Not merely were the entrances under observation from 84 backyards but, in our highly moral community, 'carrying on', at least on one's own doorstep, would, I believe, have been universally disapproved of. The council sternly threatened any family found damaging a shelter with the loss of their house, though I do not believe this condign punishment was ever inflicted. It was, during the holidays, my duty to unlock and lock the doors when the Alert or All Clear sounded, a task I was only too glad to undertake. I cannot remember anyone actually using this shelter, but its existence enabled us to scrap the home-made dug-out on our allotment constructed, as I have described, back in 1939.

Even if there were no cosy get-togethers in the shelter, the war was proving a great leveller. Acquaintances who lived in semi-detached houses in 'ordinary' roads, then the height of my social ambition, could no longer buy new curtains or saucepans when they needed them, all such goods being either rationed, subject to some sort of official control, or unobtainable. Thanks to our pre-war poverty and wartime shortages I grew up almost unaware that it had ever been, or would at some time in the future be, possible to walk into a shop and purchase any item one required. I assumed that 'the table' or 'the cupboard' or even 'the teapot' once acquired was there for life. This was how the poor had always lived; now, although they started with larger stocks of household equipment and clothes, the more comfortably-off were in much the same situation. Families like ours, used to making every scrap of food go as far as it could, and to developing all the shifts and substitutes resulting from poverty, were indeed better placed to cope with wartime conditions than more prosperous households. My mother's sweetness of disposition and readiness to help others, and her refusal to give herself airs even though she had clearly 'come down in the world', made her a universal favourite with tradesmen and shop assistants who now enjoyed unprecedented power. 'I have a friend at court,' my mother would say proudly as she unpacked some scarce item from her basket and I believe the war years, when she had at last a regular income and we all visibly depended on her, must have been, despite her fears for our safety, among the happiest of her married life.

It was, I believe, during the summer holidays of 1941 that the first bombs fell on Newbury. I was far more excited than frightened to hear the sudden explosions, like heavy thuds, in the town – the bombs had fallen harmlessly on a large open space, Northcroft, behind the main street – around teatime one afternoon, followed by the sight of the aircraft responsible, which I immediately identified as a Heinkel 111. (It was surprisingly low and the neighbour, mentioned earlier, suspected of illegal poaching, lamented that he had not had his shotgun handy.) This was my second, and last, sighting of a manned enemy aircraft during the war – flying-bombs were a different matter – and my reaction was that of a bird-watcher 'collecting' a rare species. As an aircraft spotter, I felt even more satisfaction, I remember, at seeing my first Westland Whirlwind, indeed not one but twelve in formation. (I was right to feel privileged, for the type proved a failure and was rapidly withdrawn from service.)

The contribution to the war effort which my family was now making was typical of that of millions of others. My twin sister was, like me, still at school, though soon to leave and join the Ministry of Labour, en route to the WRNS. My elder sister volunteered that year, 1941, for work in a factory, because, she admitted to me, she hated the idea of being called up into the services and having to leave my mother. She was somewhat embarrassed, on going to the Ministry of Labour office with a friend, she confessed to me, to be told by the clerk behind the desk: 'You're a pair of really patriotic girls!' Conscription for women had not yet begun. Although the other three of us were to serve, respectively, in the RAF, army and 'Wrens', Freda had, I think, the toughest war. For much of the year she was up before daylight and faced a long walk down into the town to catch the works bus to a newly opened factory at Theale, 13 miles [21km] away, returning home by the same route 12 hours later. Periodically she was 'on nights' which meant sleeping uneasily while the rest of the estate went about its sometimes noisy business and missing out on the evening dances in the Corn Exchange or visits to one of the town's three cinemas which made up most of her social life. Private parties, which bulk so large in the wartime recollections of so many young women, were virtually unknown in our circle and I cannot recall any of us attending more than two or three until the time I left home for good. Freda's work was physically hard, far harder than Peggy or Gordon or I were to face in our service careers once our initial training was over, and I can recall seeing her hands and arms covered in an unsightly rash. This was caused by the oil which lubricated the machines on which, day after day, or night after night, in a deafeningly noisy workshop, she repetitively drilled and shaped torpedo or Sten gun components. At least once she was also 'off sick' from the injuries inflicted by metal fragments on her hands. By now, too, her fiancé was in the RAF, as a ground-based photographer, an admirable job from my point of view since he would occasionally bring me illicit copies of the silhouettes of new aircraft still on the secret list. For fear of getting him into trouble I never dared show these to anyone, but hugged the knowledge proudly to myself. He regularly cycled all the way from the base where he was stationed, Harwell, some 15 miles [24km] away, to spend a few hours with her, before returning at the last minute, to avoid being put on a charge for lateness, a phrase I now heard for the first time. Harwell was at this time, I believe, an Operational Training Unit where crews all too often suffered fatal accidents. My future brother-in-law often talked about 'kites', such as 'Wimpeys' (ie Wellingtons) and later 'Lancs' (ie Lancasters) but I cannot remember that he ever mentioned the heavy casualties suffered by air crew during the final stages of their training and nothing he said discouraged my intention, should the war last long enough, to join the RAF. Later in the war he was posted to the Far East and my sister's only contact with him was via his frequent letters, or flimsy Airgraphs, which once a week or so dropped or fluttered through the letter box.

By that time my brother Gordon had already been several years overseas, sailing, as he later told me, from Liverpool en route for Egypt, Iraq and ultimately Italy. With his strange diet, mentioned earlier, which caused him to reject all vegetables, except fried potatoes, and all meat, except, I think, bacon and sausages, he must have found life in the Forces singularly difficult, and, unlike me, he had had no experience of communal living or even of being away from home. Nor can his dominant interest, Anglo-Catholicism, have been widely shared in most barrack rooms or air force offices. Nevertheless in his weekly letter home, to which my mother replied with equal regularity, he never complained. I recall learning from him of the existence of racism, for his troopship made the long voyage round the Cape of Good Hope, the Mediterranean being closed, and he went ashore in South Africa, to be shocked by the 'Whites only' and 'No blacks' signs on public buildings. I think he may, at least in retrospect, have enjoyed this break in a life spent otherwise, from 15 to 65, in essentially the same job in the same town. He delighted in Italy, which before the war we would never have contemplated visiting, discovering an aptitude for the language and an enthusiasm for opera and pasta, both also outside our experience.

For my elder sister there were no compensating benefits, apart from being able to live at home, from her daily servitude in the factory. Not till after the war, when collecting other women's reminiscences for *How We Lived Then*, did I begin to appreciate the culture shock which having to spend one's working life in such an environment must have provided for a girl from a decent, if always poor, home, where moral standards were high and obscenity unknown. Only much later did I realise how in a factory, just as at school or in the army, the loud-mouthed and the foul-mouthed tended to impose their standards on those from gentler backgrounds. The daily transition from the comparatively restrained atmosphere of Camp Close to a world where women not much older than her boasted of their drunken and sexual adventures must have provided a constant trial for my sister, but she never let it affect her cheerfulness and her work.

My sister's life at the factory brought one unforeseen bonus. She became friendly with a girl of her own age from a similarly modest but respectable background – her father was a building worker – who was living in a hostel away from home and hating it. A little later in the war Sadie came to live with us though how we managed to fit six adults into the available space I cannot recall. My sister's friend was soon another member of the family and, with two young women aged around 20 in the house I rapidly became familiar with the mysteries of female make-up, the weekly ritual of hair-washing and such occasional oddities – much enjoyed by me as an observer – as facial mud-packs. Thanks to Freda and Sadie I heard the popular songs of the time, on the wireless or on our old wind-up gramophone, another aspect of wartime life of which our restricted life at school had left me deprived. Above all, unlike so many of my school contemporaries, I grew up by no means in awe of the female sex, but with what has, I hope, proved to be a relaxed and appreciative attitude towards them.

---

[1] Mar-Apr 1942 p.42
[2] Jun 1941 p.134
[3] Jul 1941 p.177
[4] Jun 1941 p.136
[5] Collier p.495 & Middlesbrook p.102.
[6] Jun 1941 p.153

39

HOUSIE VERSUS HITLER

Partly owing to enemy action and partly to clothes rationing and national economy, 1st XI colour blazers are no longer obtainable.

The Blue, *November-December 1941*

The school year which began in mid-September 1941 marked the start of another bleak period in the nation's history. Defeat remained unthinkable but victory was a distant dream and as the nation further tightened its belt and women everywhere took over men's work a profound change took place in our all-male world. 'We welcomed to the staff this term...' began the usual entry in *The Blue* for November-December 1941, then went on to list only one man and five women, three of them 'Miss'. They had a mixed reception, as one who arrived two years later, when the first hostility might have been expected to have declined, has recorded:

> The masters who were too old for military service, mostly bachelors, and some past retirement age...did not take kindly to the idea of women on the staff...We were not admitted to the masters' common room until after 7pm, and then only via the kitchen entrance...Younger masters, ineligible for military service...were in fact a great deal more welcoming...We were kindly welcomed by married housemasters and their wives...The Headmaster at that time was a remote figure for those of us who came from girls' schools, where headmistresses had a much closer contact with both staff and pupils...The boys for the most part were very ready to accept us and were a pleasure to teach. They often called us 'Sir'...We were known as 'form masters' and 'junior housemasters'.

This 24 year old, fresh from the much more relaxed atmosphere of a girls' school, had mixed reactions to her new environment:

> CH was an excellent school for intelligent boys on scholarship who would not otherwise have had access to a school of such high academic standards...But little interest was shown by the masters (with a few notable

exceptions) in the boys who were 'presented', unless they were good at games. The arrival of women on the staff brought a new element of interest in these boys...We also brought a civilising influence. We used to invite boys to our studies for tea, and to let them talk in a relaxed atmosphere. I had a collection of classical records and several of the boys in Peele B used to come and listen to them...We introduced dancing classes to the music of Victor Silvester, which we hoped might help the boys to be more at ease in the company of girls.

The dancing classes were, alas, after my time, but one member of Peele B has testified in *The Blue* to the 'civilising efforts' of the woman just quoted, though her immediate superior, Macnutt, was 'openly and unprofessionally disparaging' about these new colleagues. They were indeed a mixed bunch. The one I got to know best in the classroom was a former don with whom I got on well enough on a one-to-one basis but she was, I suspect, too intellectual for us and must have had a hard time from less academic classes. Our lives were also enlivened by a sad and soulful Central European who taught Modern Languages and was liable to respond to poor work or misbehaviour by bursting into tears. A third was involved in a spectacular scandal which ended in her being sent to prison for theft. (This was probably the same woman whom the Old Blue quoted earlier recalls as 'a preposterous creature...a female Münchhausen', denounced by a colleague as 'a shocking little liar'.)[1]

I cannot recall any special instructions as to how we were to behave towards these strange new recruits to the staff but the same observer is now full of contrition for his behaviour. 'On one occasion the class I was in spent the whole lesson looking at poor Brenda six inches [15cm] to the left of her face and she simply didn't know what to make of it. If they were the odds we were the sods.'[2]

To our eyes almost any female under 40 would have appeared beautiful but the new 'masters' included several exceptionally attractive young women in their twenties. The victim of the 'staring' episode just described had the older boys, as well as all but the most misogynist members of staff, at her feet. One particularly scruffy middle-aged master, the very caricature of a dissolute roué, his uncared for clothes permanently covered in cigarette ash, followed her about with dog-like devotion, and each fresh sighting of the two together was eagerly discussed, but we concluded, I am sure correctly, that he had no success.

In Peele A we still had a male junior housemaster, Fred Haslehust, but as he had his own house the vacant study and bedroom were occupied by one of the women staff, Miss DE (Elizabeth) Harvie, who taught science. I shall say more of her later.

Even the Headmaster was not immune to the charms of this disturbing new presence in the school. One woman 'master' invited to visit HLO Flecker at his West Country retreat during the holidays found that not merely was she expected to spend most of her time working in the garden – a common complaint by visitors of both sexes – but that, when Mrs Flecker was out of sight, she also had to evade her host's affectionate attentions. Though not pressed to the point of harassment they proved alarming and embarrassing none the less.[*]

Meanwhile the war was taking its toll of our former schoolmates. That December of 1941 *The Blue* announced the compilation of a Roll of Service covering all Old Blues now in the forces and recorded a sad statistic, destined to grow much larger:

> Twenty-six, possibly thirty, Old Blues, have given their lives in this fight for freedom...Christ's Hospital has just cause to be proud of her sons. Many have achieved lasting fame for their gallantry and superb courage, while all have shown fearless devotion to duty whenever they have been called upon to face the enemy.

For the dedicated games-player the war was now bringing cataclysmic changes. *The Blue* recorded two that had occurred the previous term:

> On the advice of the Medical Officer it was decided to cut down swimming this year, with the result that crawl classes had to be given up entirely. This may seriously affect the standard of our swimming in the near future.

In the first world war it had been a spectacular defeat at rugger which had prompted a re-examination of the school regime. What caused Dr Friend's concern this time is not on record, but it was probably an anxiety about the general stress and fatigue imposed by wartime conditions. Clearly the situation was serious for now even cricket was being affected by the war:

> Partly owing to enemy action and partly to clothes rationing and national economy, 1st XI colour blazers are no longer obtainable. If any Old Blue feels he can spare any of his old colours it would be a greatly appreciated kindness if he would give, lend or sell them to the school.[3]

Noel had duly appointed as monitors the three victors in the previous term's popularity contest and in order of the votes cast for them, but the house-captain, happily, was still selected on merit. This was JC (John) Turner, later a much-loved GP on the South Coast,[4] now dead, and the judgement I recorded of

---

[*] HLOF here invites comparison with the late Lord Reith, a famous moralist in public but in later years notorious for his attentions to young women, and wandering hands, in private. We had at the time no inkling of the Head's double standards and it was, of course, only against homosexuality that he campaigned at school.

him in *First Bloom*, where I called him Matthews, remains unaffected by my post-school acquaintance with him:

> It was doubtful if, but for the war...Matthews would have occupied the post, but as circumstances had called him to it, he filled it with a genial refusal to take offence, and usually an equally charming indolence. His profusely freckled face, ginger hair, and almost invariable smile, made him extremely popular. He was not too bad at games to be an embarrassment to the house, nor yet so good as to awaken hero worship among the juniors or jealousy among the seniors.

Turner had an engaging habit of remarking that he was 'Just off to enjoy the weed' as he disappeared for a quiet smoke and he did his best to make my increasingly anomalous position as the 'oldest inhabitant' of the house who was not a monitor as tolerable as it could be. He raised no objection when, along with other non-athletic boys, I opted for the thoroughly un-martial, but patriotic, activity of leaf-gathering whenever I could instead of games, the leaves being used for compost for vegetables. Here was another way in which the war had helped to make games-besotted Housie a little more humane. Leaf-gathering was, alas, confined to only a few weeks of a single term but I looked forward to this autumnal activity, which I described in *First Bloom*:

> On many afternoons James, armed with a rake, would muse and rake leaves beneath the scant-leafed branches of the limes in the Avenue or in one of the coppices to be found all over the estate. The task of organising the work was given, for no reason except his reluctance to remove the smile from his face and answer 'No' to a request, to Mr Templemore [ie Michael Warneford-Brown], and he became a familiar figure, pedalling furiously on his bicycle, in a brightly striped jersey and shorts, with perhaps a rake in one hand.
>
> Leaf-gathering afternoons marked the beginning of Conway's emancipation. He was frequently assigned to the work owing to his incompetence at rugger and, as the same process occurred in other houses, he soon began to meet others more akin to his temperament than his games-worshipping contemporaries in Blake...Often an afternoon passed pleasantly in a discussion of the causes of the war, or the absurdities of compulsory games. The conversation rarely flagged, in spite of the frequent eruptions of Mr Templemore – for no lesser word sufficed to do them justice – his neck free of clerical collar and open to the winds, with leaves lodged in his flowing hair, causing him to look more than ever as if he had just been dragged through a thicket himself.

The Lent Term of 1942 brought another monitorial vacancy and, though this time there was no election, I was again passed over, in favour of a boy who had joined the house after me. With the one exception of the boy I have already mentioned, all the monitors treated me with great consideration, but it was still humiliating, at 16, to have to seek permission from boys younger than, and hitherto, junior to me, to visit the dormitory or leave the dayroom during lock-up. The Lent Term of 1942 brought the usual relay sports and, as much in the house's interests as my own, John Turner decided that instead of taking part I should immortalise the occasion in verse. I can still recall the opening, scene-setting line:

> A fair green field, beneath a smiling sun

and the closing one, red being of course the Peele A colour:

> We see the victor's jersey. It is red!

It must have been, I think, in the following term that, as the most literary member of the top table in the dayroom, I was asked to write the Peele A entry for the regular House Notes feature in *The Blue*. I failed to mention, regarding it as of no importance, that we had won the relay sports or some similar competition, which John Turner thought was a great joke. Outside the house, apart from leaf-gathering, my most pleasurable activity was attending the Debating Society, where I again caught the eye of David Roberts and also Miss Harvie. I recall her predicting that I would end up as the Society's Secretary, the first time any sort of school office had ever been suggested as within my grasp. In one debate, early in 1942, David Roberts, seconded by Pitman, carried a motion in favour of co-education by 93 to 29.[5] In hidebound Christ's Hospital this was a remarkable result, reflecting, I have no doubt, the favourable impact that the arrival of women like Miss Harvie had made on all but the most bigoted.

In the best 'Love the Brotherhood' tradition, the Christ's Hospital Club had begun, in January 1941, to organise the sending of food parcels to Old Blue prisoners of war, an existence for which, I reflected, they must have felt well prepared by their schooldays. A letter from one beneficiary, printed in *The Blue* that spring of 1942, hinted at this truth:

> Thanks for yours, it brought with it not only memories of Housie, but also of English village greens in summer, both very welcome when one wilts behind barbed wire; not that my memories of Housie are all happy. I'm afraid I shall never look back when in my dotage to say that my schooldays were the happiest in my life – they weren't…However, the good fellowship amongst Old Blues afterwards makes me look back upon those years in a kinder light. There are two Old Blues here with me…One…runs our canteen

here and runs it very well...no doubt the fact that he is an Old Blue helps him greatly...I find the fact that I am helps me to endure this tedious time.[6]

Thanks to food rationing our diet continued to improve, though the school tended to treat the regulations in its own, lordly, way. After 'Controlled Distribution' of milk[*] was introduced in November 1941 we were given printed slips of paper to take home and hand to the milkman, instructing him he was now to supply us as well as our families for the duration of the holiday – documents which, the Newbury Office of the Ministry of Food indignantly complained, had no legal validity whatever. Happily the amiable Mr Ratcliffe managed to add the odd half pint [275ml] to our family entitlement or we should all have gone short. In July 1942 the introduction of sweet rationing hit us harder. This time, I think, we were given our own 'Personal Points', as the coupons were known, for the holidays, but in term were issued with vouchers for the permitted amount, cashable only at the shop. One enterprising, and unpatriotic, boy in Middleton A discovered an unsuspected skill as a forger, managing to produce, with Indian ink, a mapping pen and the thin paper blank margin of the *Daily Telegraph* – no other was of the right quality – an acceptable substitute for the official coupons. This 'ensured his niche in the society of the House and protected him against bulllying'.[7] Meanwhile the school's draconian solution to maintaining the uniform – appropriating almost all our clothing coupons, as described earlier – had proved inadequate to maintain our Tudor appearance. *The Blue* for March-April 1942 carried, for the diehards, appalling news:

> It is understood that supplies of the traditional Housey dress are to be cut down yet further and that it is likely that at least a part of the school will be seen in modern clothes before the war is much older.[8]

The change came in fact in the following September when, for the first time in 400 years, boys joining the school were fitted out in grey shorts and sports coats, though the rest of us were dressed as before. The heavens failed to fall, even at the incongruous sight of modern dress and Housey uniform appearing together at Dinner Parade, though the change must have made those traditional punishments 'Post Offices' and 'Triangles' much less demanding.

The campaign for war savings became an important feature of wartime life from 1941 onwards, with three major short-term drives[**] to maintain and stimulate interest, 'Salute the Soldier', 'Wings for Victory' and 'Warships

---

[*] 'Controlled Distribution' allowed a retailer to distribute surplus supplies to registered customers once the minimum, guaranteed, ration had been provided. See *How We Lived Then* for details of this and other aspects of wartime life.

[**] See Chapter 31, *Hit Back with National Savings*, in *How We Lived Then*.

Week', all highly successful. The June-July issue of *The Blue* described how the school in 1942 made its own contribution to Warships Week, supposed to raise money through savings certificates and bonds to buy vessels for the navy:

> At Housie we held a fete in Big School, a dozen side-shows, including a skittle alley, a rifle range, a modified form of coconut-shy and other such games of skill and chance. At one side-show we were invited to guess the subjects of photographs of members of the staff taken many years ago; this was irreverently called the Rogues' Gallery. Another most popular stall was under the Tuckshop management.
>
> Noises of a kind never before heard within Big School echoed among the roof-carvings; dance music from the gramophone, the rattle of pennies, delighted shouts when a winner was acclaimed, and strange cries of the Fair.[9]

I remember best an ingenious device rigged up by boys who were clearly better at physics than I was, whereby on pressing a switch an electric circuit was broken and a 'bomb' descended on its target. The occasion provided a most welcome break, and occupied a Saturday afternoon that would otherwise have been devoted to cricket. Another interest was provided by the increasingly important salvage drive, which also occasionally replaced games with more useful exertions. I can remember us being sent off one afternoon to scour the countryside and my delight at finding, along with another boy, a large pile of cans deposited by a local farmer at the corner of a wood. He raised no objection to our removing them, remarking 'There should be enough there for a couple of Spitfires', but another team were even more successful than us and staggered wearily on to the asphalt behind the house dragging a handcart laden with what appeared to be several old ploughs. Our enthusiasm had, however, outrun the authorities' capacity to profit by it. The material we had assembled was left behind the house, a growing source of embarrassment, and when eventually removed, got no further, I believe, than the school incinerator, housed beside one of those mysterious buildings just outside the school perimeter which were strictly out of bounds to us. I have wondered since if some enterprising boys had already discovered this and simply contributed to the collection items already sent for destruction there, now re-cycled.

As I have described, Christ's Hospital had always employed its pupils to do much of the work undertaken elsewhere by paid employees, and the loss of domestic staff to war work led to an extension of this practice. Some groups of boys were sent to help with the washing up, a not unwelcome duty since, it was whispered, there were still a few females employed in the Kitchens. Much less popular were the dusting and cleaning now added to the regular scavenging rounds in the houses. The general feeling was that this was one job too many and, with neither aprons nor proper equipment provided, the main result was even more frequent and frenzied coat-cleaning.

Closed communities are notoriously prone to suffer from sudden enthusiasms or even mild collective madness. In the camp in Italy described in one of the best POW books, *The Cage*,[*][10] the inmates of one hut would pretend every night that it then put to sea, with shouted commands based on the Hornblower stories, and similar fantasies flourished at Christ's Hospital. I recall how one term a curious semi-secret society grew up and – sufficient reason for the authorities to distrust it – even spread between the houses. Suddenly nearly every boy who counted for anything claimed to belong to the Order of Lushus (*sic*) Foos, and some even to have attained the highest rank, that of Pukka Foo. There were, I believe, admission ceremonies, but it was the society's recognition sign which proved fatal, for every member was required to inscribe the words 'Lushus Foos' on the underside of his bands and lift them up in salute when he met a fellow member. Its secrets stood no chance against the protests of matrons over the ink-stained linen reaching them and I recall the result: a notice, highly puzzling to visiting parents, which appeared on the house notice board: 'The state of Lushus Foodom is hereby abandoned.'

Even stranger was the absurd story that was circulated concerning one perfectly normal and pleasant young master, PR Haynes, who was given the nickname of 'Hydrogen' Haynes. Boys solemnly assured each other that he was lighter than air and that he required lead in his trouser turn-ups to prevent his floating off into the stratosphere. Some asserted that, when rashly wearing games clothes, he had been seen clinging desperately to his bicycle handlebars, legs above his head. Even the most trivial incident was sufficient, in our restricted world, to put such legends into circulation. I remember one rugger match in which at half-time the visiting referee, presumably needing the exercise, bent his knees and crouched down on the ground. The watching school preferred to find a different explanation and the fixture was known for the rest of term as 'that match where the ref peed on the pitch.'

Housie had always, as I have mentioned, had an exceptional collection of school slang and this special vocabulary was by no means static. In my day the prevalence of German as our preferred foreign language was reflected in a constant use of the German word in place of its English alternative. *Schön*, meaning 'good' or 'beautiful' was employed by all age groups, and I recall someone referring to a state of bliss as 'a day of national *Schönheit*'. *Dankeschön* was used between us instead of 'Thank you very much', to the astonishment of local residents, thanked in this way after giving directions. Briefer lived was the usage 'foot', which does not appear in *A Book of Housey Slang* but in my time was for a term or two used to describe a foolish person,

---

[*] Published 1949. The author, Dan Billany, escaped when Italy surrendered, but his fate remains a mystery.

as in 'He behaved like a perfect foot!' Also in vogue, in imitation of a master famous for saying, 'Yes, by which I mean No', were such variants as 'Black, by which I mean white,' and 'Quick, by which I mean slow.' A phrase used by a visiting lecturer, 'Mr X, who is himself a scientist...' started a similar fashion, with more and more absurd versions of this simple relative clause. Thus one boy would say 'Jones, who is himself a drainpipe...' and be answered by another: 'Smith, who is himself an alligator...' Proper names too, might be given a new meaning. For some reason that of President Roosevelt's personal representative in London came to fascinate us. 'Averill Harriman!' could be used alone as an oath or a form of incantation, or be employed, no doubt unjustly, as a yardstick of derogatory behaviour or appearance: 'He behaved', or 'looked', 'like an absolute Averill Harriman'.

Just as it is the moderately well educated who like to lend an air of profundity to their conversation by a ready use of proverbs so it was the less academic boys who seemed most eager to enrich our conversation with some new word or phrase. Lacking access to a wireless we were, of course, unable to draw on the catchphrases from comedians like Tommy Handley then heard in every factory and office.[*] Sometimes a boy would become well known simply for putting some unfamiliar expression into everyday circulation, like one whom in *First Bloom* I called Brown, though in this case the phrase had been used by Shakespeare to describe an enraged cuckold, when Housie was still young:

> Brown [was] a jolly and charming person whose work inside the school was the study of modern languages and, outside it, the extension of the school vocabulary...Conway remembered seeing a row of normally sedate and stolid seniors sitting on the end of the table reserved for their use in the dayroom and chanting with a fervour of almost religious ecstasy the latest of Brown's treasured expressions:
>
> > 'He was horn mad! He was horn mad!
> > He was, he was, he was, he was, he was HORN MAD!'

---

[*] See *How We Lived Then* chapter 35.

[1] Mar 1997 p.69
[2] Mar 1997 p.68
[3] Dec 1941 pp.36, 12 & 2
[4] Jun 1991 p.140
[5] Mar-Apr 1942 pp.42-3
[6] Mar-Apr 1942 p.60
[7] Hull p.114
[8] Mar-Apr 1942 p.42
[9] Jun-Jul 1942 p.85
[10] Dan Billany and David Dowie, *The Cage*, Longmans, 1949

EFFICIENT SERVICE

During his membership of the Air Training Corps he has fulfilled the necessary conditions as to efficient service.

Air Training Corps Certificate of Proficiency, June 1942

In September 1941, when I began my sixth year at Christ's Hospital, no end to the war seemed in sight. My sixteenth birthday was a mere three months away and it now seemed all too likely that I should have to join one of the Services myself. As to which I should choose I felt little doubt. The navy had never appealed to me and I had seen more than enough of what belonging to the army involved in the OTC. It was the RAF, first in the Battle of Britain, since then in the bomber offensive, which seemed to offer the hope of victory. The Air Training Corps had come on the scene at just the right moment, for me as for countless other boys, and at Housie, despite the entrenched position of the now renamed OTC, it made rapid progress, as *The Blue* for June 1941 testified:

> No 679 (Christ's Hospital) was formed last February and now has a strength of about sixty cadets. No uniforms have yet arrived, but parades are held three times a week for the study of navigation, signalling, engines and aircraft recognition. Mr [AL] Creed has kindly allowed his laboratory to be used as an ATC room and copies of the *Aeroplane*, photographs and silhouettes of planes are exhibited there. The following commissions in the RAFVR (Training Branch) were granted in April: Acting Flying Officer (on probation) Mr CWS Averill; Acting Flying Officer (on probation) Dr G Van Praagh, Mr AL Creed.

These first officers were among the best-liked members of the staff and the ATC was to be a major source of interest to me for the rest of my school career. Others shared my feeling. By December the Housie contingent already totalled 71 and the strength of the JTC, noted *The Blue*, was falling as 'a number of boys leave the Junior Training Corps in their sixteenth year to join the ATC.'[1]

EFFICIENT SERVICE

In the unacknowledged contest for public recognition the RAF was also currently winning hands down. In August 1941 the semi-dramatised documentary *Target for Tonight* using shy, well-spoken but real air-crew in the story of an imaginary raid, had proved on its release an immediate success, and on my return to school I was positively proud to put on ATC uniform. Drill, which so obsessed the JTC, was kept to a minimum and ATC parades dealt with subjects in which I was actually interested. I had already mastered the Morse Code, the subject of our first instructional session, and the rest of the syllabus was a schoolboy's dream, like learning how automatic weapons, from pistols to machine-guns, functioned. Thanks to the excellent tuition of our new Commanding Officer, an engineer, I gained for the first time in my life some glimmering of how the internal combustion engine worked while aeronautics proved equally fascinating. I rejoiced, as essentially a non-scientist, to find I could understand the meaning of 'thrust', 'lift' and 'drag' and, no mathematician either, by the end of my time in the ATC I was instructing younger recruits in 'calculations', the practical arithmetic we were required to master. Geography at Housie had always been regarded as something of a non-subject, a reaction encouraged in my case by personal antipathy between the head of the department, TK Mortimer Booth, and myself, though why he so obviously disliked me I never discovered. Now I became enthusiastic not merely about maps in general but about such hitherto despised facts as the identity of a nation's chief ports and principal exports. Suddenly Hamburg, Bremen, Essen and the rest of the RAF's regular targets became relevant to our lives and to know the difference between the River Elbe and the River Main became of more than academic importance.

Our navigation instructor was my chemistry master, 'VP', an excellent, and good-natured, teacher. Thanks to him I can still recite the rules for obtaining a compass course free of 'variation', caused by geographical causes which distort the correct, magnetic, bearing, and 'deviation', due to local causes like the magnetism surrounding the instrument. 'MATE' – 'Magnetic to True, add East', and 'CAME' – 'Compass to Magnetic, add East' – in my view beat the JTC's favourite fire-order mnemonic, 'DRINK', hollow.

My interest in flying spiralled over into my school work. Later I remember my admired history-master, DSR, reading to us from the short stories of HE Bates, published under the pseudonym of 'Flying Officer X', of which the first volume appeared in 1942.* It had, however, not yet been published when, in the Michaelmas Term of 1941, I wrote my own short story about the bomber

---

* ie *The Greatest People in the World*, followed in 1943 by *How Sleep the Brave*. A vast success, they ultimately sold 2 million copies and are famous in publishing history for the resulting dispute over the author's royalties, described in his autobiography (1969-72). After the war he became even better known from the television adaptation of *The Darling Buds of May*, published in book form in 1958.

offensive, based on a stay in the school Infirmary. I later came to dislike the genre but this solitary example, *The Quality of Mercy*, seems worth quoting at some length – about half the original – as an illustration of how deeply the regular reports on Bomber Command's exploits affected one air-minded 15 year old even before the assault on Germany had really got under way:

> He lay silent with the white sheets falling loosely around his shoulders. The white mask of bandages which encircled his head merged into the white of the pillow on which his head lay unmoving. The light that had crept round the blinds at midday was now self-consciously retreating, as though it, too, had to make ready for the night. The pale green of the walls and the brown solidity of the fittings of the room, breathed an air of peace.
>
> The man in the bed lay motionless, staring into space, through the dull mist that obscured his eyes, which stood out as dark pools of life in the enswathing white of the bandages. It was becoming dark now, he thought, and miles away his friends would be already alone and isolated in the dark expanse of sky, all except himself, who lay here useless, who could do nothing to help them. Perhaps they might be going to Italy tonight, he reflected, Naples, perhaps, or Turin.
>
> 'You should be glad you are out of it,' he said to himself, 'not worrying over them,' but the thought persisted. How well he remembered that last flight! Every detail of it seemed stamped on his brain, only to be removed by time. It had been Cologne that night and they had been the first to reach the city. There had been no stars to help them and he remembered the terrible moment of doubt when he thought he had made a mistake in his plotting and that they were lost, with only enemy country beneath them. He had disregarded his doubts then and he had been right to do so. He would try to do the same now. Sleep was what he needed, sleep to make him strong to go back to his companions. 'Tired nature's sweet restorer' – he remembered learning that at school, or was he thinking of another of those advertisements for Horlicks?[*] No, it was Shakespeare, of course. Had he learnt any other passages, anything to keep his mind away from flying? What about *The Merchant of Venice*? But that reminded him of Italy; he must not stop to think about it, something about 'the quality of mercy', well, he hadn't had much of that, not since he had seen his wife lying dead under the ruins of their home. But he must try and forget, and go to sleep, sleep which he had dreaded on those long outward journeys but which he was eagerly seeking now. Anything to make him forget the world outside. He was thinking of Shakespeare a moment ago, yes – *The Merchant of Venice*. 'The quality of mercy is not strained', but what came next? In a flash he remembered:

---

[*] The makers of this bedtime drink ran for many years an advertising campaign claiming that Horlicks made sleep more valuable by preventing 'night starvation'.

'It droppeth like the gentle rain from heaven.'
Shakespeare should have been in an aeroplane with a thunderstorm going on outside and only the cold, cheerless slopes of the Alps beneath. He might have thought twice about the 'gentle rain' then. More solid things dropped from heaven nowadays than rain, he thought cynically, bombs for instance, but perhaps they didn't come from heaven; nor did rain for that matter...He realised suddenly that the sleep he desired was at last upon him. He let it spread itself round him like a luxurious garment and its thick warm folds draped themselves around him.

But though he was asleep his mind was still restless. He was in his bomb-aimer's position in the nose of the machine and already his fingers were adjusting the instruments of the aiming mechanism. He had made the correct allowance for height, wind speed and all the other factors, and now was watching the earth so far below slip silently past. The target was coming near now – he must get a direct hit this time – he sought the button which would release the bombs and caressed it lovingly. The picture of his wife's body rose before his eyes. He would avenge her just by the pressure of his thumb on this little knob.

With the swift, deft ease born of practice he pressed it hard, but instead of releasing it he kept his thumb tight on the button. He would show them, he would repay them for the wrecked home...

The opening of the door woke him. With a great effort he roused himself and found the agitated figure of the night nurse beside the bed. Understanding came to him in a flash as he saw that his thumb was on the bell-push, which he had been told to press if he required anything in the night. The nurse understood too, and, moving aside the blind, pointed out towards the sky, already tinted a pale red with the first hints of dawn. A distant droning could be heard, faintly and softly, not the sound of an enemy, but the gentle, self-satisfied hum of engines that had done a good night's work and knew it.

'They are coming back now,' she said, 'You can sleep content for they have avenged you.' She turned and left the room with the determined yet kindly air that accompanies those who spend their lives attending the sick.

The man in the bed realised that he was once more alone with his thoughts...but they were no longer gloomy, for the comforting drone of the home-coming aeroplanes was growing louder. Soon he would be back with them, with his head in a flying helmet instead of bandages and a bomb-release switch not a bell-push by his side. As the dawn crept confidently round the blind his black thoughts disappeared before a new light of hope. He would build a new life on the old one's ruins and would build it rejoicing, happy in the knowledge that the dark days were behind him. The droning of the aeroplanes became louder still. They were almost overhead now and he realised with something of a shock, that he was happy. He remembered mocking Shakespeare's words and felt ashamed of himself for what he had believed then. Into his now peaceful mind there came a picture of the nurse, thoughtful and tender...He re-arranged the pillows as he re-arranged his mind and let his head sink back among them, content.

Michael Warneford-Brown gave me an 'alpha-beta' for this piece of imaginative writing, which owed more to *Target for Tonight* than to the reality of air-crew life. Only much later did I learn that the bomb-aimer, by then distinct from the navigator, rarely even saw the target, much less actually hit it. Had we, or the nation, realised how little Bomber Command was at this stage of the war accomplishing, and at what appalling cost, no doubt we should have approached ATC training in the same unenthusiastic spirit as our khaki-clad contemporaries went on JTC parade. Meanwhile, as *The Blue* recorded in December 1941, the ATC was clearly making progress:

> Uniforms for all but a few have been issued...Equipment continues to arrive in small quantities; we have a few navigating instruments and a lot of wire, and we still believe that some Morse keys and buzzers will arrive one day. Meanwhile, the number of aeroplane photographs and silhouettes in Mr Creed's laboratory increases almost weekly. By the end of term, we hope to have visited a neighbouring aerodrome, to which the flight is now affiliated.[2]

Among the equipment we did receive was a rubber dinghy, as used by 'ditched' air-crew, and I was deeply impressed, and comforted, at seeing how rapidly it inflated itself during a demonstration in the school swimming bath. (Seeing the boy who acted the part of a shot-down airman floundering about in the chilly water before he clambered on board was not quite so reassuring.) A little later I watched a parachute being opened on the ground, delighted to see how rapidly the pilot chute sprang open and caused the main canopy to unfold. That we might one day owe our lives to such a device seemed at that time more exciting than frightening.

The parachute lesson was at the 'neighbouring aerodrome' of Gatwick, then a small, almost somnolent, RAF station, where I spent a most enjoyable day. We were delighted by seeing some of the first Mustangs – this must have been well into 1942 or 1943 – then in use by the RAF; later they saved the American daylight offensive from destruction, providing escorts for the supposedly self-defending but highly vulnerable Flying Fortresses of the 8th US Air Force. We had our first encounter with an RAF NCO, who chased us out of a hut in which we were happily studying the silhouettes of some still secret types of aircraft – thanks to my sister's friend, Leslie, I had already, as mentioned earlier, acquired my own copies – and, much more significant, our first flight. Somewhat to my alarm we were not issued with parachutes and carried no dinghy in case we strayed out to sea, but were seated, without seat-belts, on benches along the sides of the ancient twin-engined biplane, which we easily identified as a De Havilland Dominie. It was not a turbulent flight but it left me feeling distinctly queasy and I was relieved to get back to earth without being sick. Nor was I much cheered when a former member of the ATC returned to tell us how he had been grounded for good after, as he put it, 'having littered the fields of East Anglia' from above.

I suspect that a similarly weak stomach might have disqualified me from flying, the RAF taking a sterner view of this malady than the navy did of sea-sickness, and I discovered around the same time another potentially serious physical defect though I managed to conceal it. Reading Morse by ear presented no difficulty but taking messages by signal lamp I found impossible, since the eye retained each message long after it should have 'digested' it and received another. This was, I imagine, like my poor night vision, an indication that my eyes were abnormally slow at adapting to changing circumstances and I have read since of other people suffering from the same condition. At the time, however, I supposed I must be uniquely disabled, since I knew the Morse alphabet perfectly, and I remember a wretched afternoon on the Quarter Mile trying to read the Aldis lamp signals sent from a distant operator which, instead of forming distinct dots and dashes, arrived as an almost continuous blur.

The ATC scored another success in its unacknowledged rivalry with the JTC in the summer of 1942, when the latter was forced to lower its recruitment age and also began (as the ATC already did) to provide uniforms resembling those of its parent service. *The Blue* for June-July 1942 told the story:

> As the War Office decided that the age of enrolment in the JT corps should be lowered from 15 to 14, our recruits, who in the past have not been officially recognised by the War Office, are now counted as full members of the contingent, thus raising our numbers to 330. We are busy fitting them out with uniforms which, for smaller boys, will consist of battle dress, of which we are to have a free issue in the future when old uniforms have to be replaced.[3]

The ATC, like the old OTC, had its periodic exercises, but they were a more gentlemanly affair than the former Field Days. Small teams, representing the crew of a single aircraft, were sent out to follow a specified route, known only to the 'navigator', by compass and map-reading – 'dead reckoning' as the services, rather ominously, called it. In charge was the 'pilot', responsible for seeing that we crossed roads safely, while the 'gunners' and 'bomb-aimer' kept a look-out for the 'fighters' trying to intercept us at various points, and were required to gather up information on the various places we passed. It was a little like *Swallows and Amazons* on dry land and I recall being commended for being able at our 'de-briefing' at the end of the afternoon to draw a somewhat crude sketch of an oddly shaped bridge we had passed. ('I already know what it looks like, so I can just recognise it,' our CO told me, a little grudgingly.) On another occasion we carried out a 'raid' on a German city from the safety of a science laboratory. The RAF was far more generous with equipment than the army had ever been to the OTC and we eagerly took possession of the type of charts and calculators recently used on real operations. Meanwhile the 'radio operator' passed on to us changes in wind strength and direction which forced us to alter course in mid-flight. It was all thoroughly enjoyable, though I suspected even then that this warm, well-lit classroom in mid-afternoon was not quite the same as the chilly and cramped crew compartments of a Halifax or Lancaster heading under fire for Berlin or Essen.

Unlike JTC Field Days, no one was ever 'killed' on our exercises, and I remember another that summer which earned immortality in *The Blue*, for June-July 1942:

> Some were curious to know why a dozen cadets were pushing a perambulator about the Estate, halting periodically to stare at blinking lights on the Chapel and Big School roofs. However, the exercise was quite good practice in following a compass course, after making the usual corrections, from instructions received in morse from Aldis lamps.[4]

I well remember this exercise, because one of our party had somehow secreted a block of iron which threw the compass off course whenever he approached it, so we were in danger of ending up where we had started off, after a curiously zigzag 'flight' across Big Side. 'VP' was, understandably, furious, but I now realise it was a most useful demonstration of how a local magnetic field could upset a compass reading and hence the need to allow for 'deviation'.

By this time Bomber Command was, unknown to us and the general public, increasingly relying on radio devices to find its targets, but among the traditional methods of finding one's position still being taught was astro-navigation. Before taking a sight on a star one had first to identify it and this brought a further enrichment to our lives in the shape of astronomy classes, necessarily conducted after dark, with boys from other houses. Noel consented to us joining them with reluctance but could hardly refuse; once again the war was helping to liberate us.

Handling a sextant, I rapidly discovered, was not nearly so easy as I had supposed and I began to wonder if in fact I was cut out to be a navigator, but about joining the RAF I had no doubts. The headlines in the papers might have been designed to encourage our interest in flying. The spectacular daylight raid on Augsburg by a dozen Lancasters on 17 April 1942 was a true *Boy's Own Paper* operation, inspiring to adults as well as schoolboys. In May 1942 came the first Thousand Bomber Raid, on Cologne, which also captured the national imagination and gave a great boost to morale, although we now know that, like the others which followed it, it had little lasting impact on the German economy. In October 1942, another successful semi-documentary feature film, *Coastal Command*, was released and, we were most unusually, taken, or rather marched, into Horsham to see it. In May 1943 came the epic raid by the Dambusters, which again thrilled the nation to a somewhat unjustified degree so far as its long term consequences were concerned. It was only when I saw the film *The Dambusters*, released in 1954, and later still, when I interviewed some of those involved for a BBC programme, that I realised the real significance of this aptly named raid, *Operation Chastise*.* Surprisingly, Noel failed to make the raid the occasion for one of his little homilies, for the whole attack had been initiated and made possible by a former member of Peele A, but, as an ex-poilu, our housemaster rarely drew attention to the RAF's achievements.

From a surviving Certificate of Service, I find that I joined the ATC on 16 September 1941 and by the time I left it in December 1943 had attended 237 parades, my 'general conduct' being assessed at the highest level, as 'Very Good', and my proficiency as 'Superior', the next grade down. Our CO had described me as 'A good keen cadet who should do well', in other words qualify to join a Bomber Command air crew. This judgement was clearly based on my having, on 3 July 1942, passed my Certificate of Proficiency, Part I, the ATC equivalent of the JTC's Certificate A. I still remember this occasion, the peak of my, as it turned out, non-flying career. I passed the more academic subjects, including navigation, easily, but only just scraped through on drill, thanks to narrowly escaping an appalling muddle when ordered to carry out the complicated parade ground manoeuvre, which I believe the RAF itself had scrapped, called 'Forming Squad'. One had, I recall, not merely to issue the necessary commands, which was easy enough, but also act as the key figure of 'marker' on whom the whole operation pivoted, and who, if he hesitated, could leave the ranks embarrassingly tangled.

Somehow, however, I survived and this modest success boosted my self-confidence. I knew perfectly well, if my housemaster and so many of my housemates did not, that this was far more important than being good at games. I still feel grateful to the ATC. It gave me some slight status, as a Leading Cadet, the rank which my new Certificate had earned me, it protected me from the tedium of the rival 'Corps', and it generated an interest in all things aeronautical which years later bore fruit in a radio programme, *The Bombers*, for which I interviewed one of the real dambusters, and a subsequent book of the same name.

Curiously, I failed to draw the obvious deduction from the preponderance of RAF names in the Roll of Honour read in chapel, and in the list of casualties which appeared a little later in *The Blue*. The bomber offensive really got into its stride after March 1942 and of nine recently killed Old Blues listed in the next issue in June-July, the army accounted for one, the navy for two, and the

---

* See radio script of *The Bombers* and the book of the same name, Chapter 18.

RAF, or more precisely, the RAFVR, ie wartime recruits who had chosen to fly, for the remaining six. The next *Blue*, for November to December, recorded that a further 16 Old Blues had died, of whom nine were airmen, four were soldiers, and one each had served with the Royal Navy, the Royal Marines and Merchant Navy.[5] The RAF remained a uniquely dangerous service. The term after I left another boy whom I had known well was killed 'on active service', the usual formula for a training accident, which accounted for 15% of Bomber Command fatalities.[6] His brother, another Peele A Old Blue and pilot, was already dead, killed while serving as an instructor after, near miraculously, surviving 43 operations; the normal life expectancy was 14.

Almost more shocking than the death of boys I had known was the realisation that masters were also vulnerable. Soon after I had joined the ATC a former Prep master returned to tell us of his experiences while training with the RAF in Canada. He gave us such useful advice as not to volunteer for washing-up duties on the ship taking one there and confessed that, though he had finally got his 'wings', he still found landing difficult. Don't be disappointed, he counselled us, if you can't get into fighters; they are only for the most exceptional, natural fliers. Soon afterwards we learned that he was flying photo-reconnaissance missions over the enemy coast. By July 1942 he was dead.[7*] Long afterwards, when I spoke to an audience of sixth-formers far too young to remember the war, I remember one teacher recalling how he and five school friends had volunteered for the RAF on the same day and he was the only one to survive.

Curiously, although the news bulletins reported day by day the number of aircraft which had failed to return from the previous night's raid, and the figures mounted as the RAF grew more powerful, I cannot recall anyone ever remarking on how choosing to fly loaded the dice against you. I can remember a boy who had been in my house describing to the ATC his experiences in the Fleet Air Arm. The worse job, he explained, was that of 'batman' who directed the pilots when landing on an aircraft carrier. Inevitably accidents occurred and they left the 'batman' feeling responsible for the victim's death. This admission surprised me. I had not remembered this young man as a sensitive boy, concerned with what happened to others. I still had no desire to join up but remained convinced that the RAF was the best of the options available. In fact I was, as I shall describe, to end up in the army, due less to choice than chance.

---

* This was HC (Claud) McComas, whom *The Blue* truthfully described as 'a person to whom everyone of whatever age was instinctively attracted...never happier on his short leaves than when he returned to his old job in the classroom and in the house'. Robin Hull confirms that 'Comi' was 'loved to the point of idolatry by all the boys who knew him' in the Prep and even by those who only met him on these brief visits. (Hull pp.61 & 82)

[1] Nov-Dec 1941 p.21
[2] Nov-Dec 1941 p.21
[3] Jun-Jul 1942 p.84
[4] Jun-Jul 1942 p.84
[5] Jun-Jul 1942 p.92 & Nov-Dec 1942 p.24
[6] Mar-Apr 1944 pp.55-6
[7] Nov-Dec 1942 p.3

41

SATISFYING THE EXAMINERS

This is to certify that Norman Richard Longmate...was awarded the School Certificate of the Oxford and Cambridge Schools Examination Board.

Text of School Certificate, July 1942

'In this world nothing can be said to be certain,' wrote Benjamin Franklin in 1789, when life was more than usually uncertain, 'except death and taxes.' During the war, for schoolboys in their mid-teens, 'call up and examinations' might have been substituted. Of far more importance to me than the distant prospect of victory, when the school year began in September 1941, was the immediate challenge of School Certificate the following July.

'School Cert.' was the great goal to which grammar and public school education was directed, whether it provided the basic qualification with which one left at 15 or 16, or was the first hurdle to be leapt on the path to university. At a time when the vast majority of children left the 'council' schools at the age of 14, Christ's Hospital did a notable job of coaxing and prodding boys of similar background through this important test. By the grecians, however, or more specifically the 'probationary deputy grecians', who elsewhere would have formed the lower sixth, School Certificate was supposed to be taken in their stride. As mentioned earlier, we took the examination a year later than other schools, with no provision for re-sitting it, and it was far more important to us than 'Higher Cert.', the forerunner of 'Advanced Level', taken two years later. For us this was mere academic decoration since our goal was not a place at some provincial university, perhaps financed by a state scholarship, but an open award at Oxford or Cambridge, which did not require 'Higher' for admission. What they did demand, however, was 'Matric. Exemption', ie a sufficiently high standard in School Certificate to free one of the obligation to take a separate matriculation examination, to qualify for university entrance. This was more difficult than it sounded since one had simultaneously to obtain a credit, the second of the three possible grades, in five specified subjects: English, mathematics, a modern language, a classical language, and one other subject, the range at this time being far more restricted than it has since become.

In my case the great bugbear was Latin. My father, not understanding the subtleties of the Oxford and Cambridge admission system, bravely sought an interview with the headmaster, without consulting me, to ask, even more bravely, if his son ought not to be concentrating on more useful subjects than 'all this Latin and Greek'. I did not, in fact, know a word of the latter and my father's plea must have sounded the most appalling heresy to such a dedicated classical scholar as 'Oily' Flecker. Nevertheless he treated my father with such courtesy that my father came away not merely convinced of the value of Latin but much impressed by 'Oily' himself.

The Headmaster's nickname, incidentally, we attributed to the perpetual sheen on his swarthy, almost semitic skin. In fact it derived from his first sermon to the school, after his arrival in 1930, when he had observed 'The school is a rusty machine, and I am the oil that has been sent to lubricate it.' He attracted no other nicknames or jokes, though after the release in 1943 of a popular film *My Friend Flicka*, 'My friend Flecker' briefly became a catchphrase.

The task of teaching what was essentially a remedial class of boys with no aptitude for Latin but whose careers depended on obtaining a credit in it in School Cert. was entrusted to the fearsome DS Macnutt, of whom I have already written at length. He tackled it conscientiously, not to say ferociously. He made no attempt to engage our interest in the subject, but, very properly, set himself the objective of implanting in our memories sufficient grammar and vocabulary to carry us past the vital 40% mark in the coming examination. Later I discovered how the use of Latin had been regarded in earlier ages as the mark of an educated man. I failed to appreciate that, in that small ground floor room where the unlatinate few assembled for a double period every Saturday morning, we were heirs to a great tradition and keeping alight the flame of civilisation in a world again threatened by barbarians. I can, on the contrary, still remember the moment of terror each week when Macnutt would sit beside each of us in turn to see the results of the test he had just given us on the previous evening's prep. This consisted of ten questions, each involving the translation into Latin of some sentence designed to demonstrate our mastery of, or failure to master, such arcane mysteries as the imperfect subjunctive, the ablative absolute and, most dreaded of all, the gerund and gerundive. Any score below seven invited reproof and extra work. Once, almost by chance, I got all ten right and was rewarded, for the only time in my school career, with a commendatory word from Macnutt. On every other occasion when our paths crossed, inside the classroom or out, his manner was grim and hostile. The reason, I suspect now, was the reputation I had for being clever, based solely on my aptitude for English. 'You're not like these others,' he told me once, while checking my marking of that week's test, 'You could do it if you wanted to.'

This was untrue. I did want to, quite desperately, if only to escape from his classroom, but Latin, as later French, I found impenetrably difficult.

These occasions stand out in my memory because they were the only lessons in the whole of my schooldays – apart from the idiotic raffia work of distant memory – which I truly dreaded. I can remember the growing sense of oppression each Friday night as I flogged my brain to retain the lists of words or grammatical variants set for us to learn by heart, and how I particularly loathed deponent verbs, a permanent linguistic trap with their active meaning and passive form, a standing disproof of the assertion that Latin is a logical language. Worse still was the steadily mounting sense of fear as the first period on Saturday morning approached and my relief when, as often happened, chapel practice for the Sunday services overran so that school started late.

Macnutt was, as many other Old Blues who sat in his classroom have testified, an outstanding teacher, with a genuine love of his subject and it was probably as disagreeable for him to be teaching us as for us to be sitting at his feet. The atmosphere in the classroom was full of foreboding, so threatening that I recall one boy being too terrified to admit that due to short sight he could not see the blackboard. His first test paper revealed results so appalling that the truth was discovered and his desk was thrust ignominiously forward to the front of the classroom, where, directly under Macnutt's eye, he sat almost rigid with fear. Only occasionally did I glimpse the pleasure that so many of my contemporaries seemed to find in the classics, though it is significant how many, having thereby reached Oxford or Cambridge, then changed to other subjects. I enjoyed being taught about Roman life, which was done, as Macnutt candidly admitted, not to increase our appreciation of Latin but because being able to reply, in English, to questions on the composition of the senate or the meaning of 'dictator' could earn us the few extra marks needed to take us from the 'pass' to 'credit' category, a 'pass' for our purposes meaning failure. For similar reasons we were also taught to scan Latin poetry and I looked forward to having to divide up the lines with vertical strokes into such unfamiliar metric forms as dactyls and spondees, this being the first time I had realised that rhythm might be as valid in defining verse as rhyme.* The Romans, we were told, were particularly fond of enshrining some significant thought in a poetic couplet or quatrain, though it was not Macnutt who quoted to us an admirable example, using Latin style scansion, in English, attributed to a pre Noel Sergent Hall Warden:

> Boys when they come into hall,
> Wipe their knives on the edge of the table.

---

* For those who lacked such instruction I should perhaps add that a dactyl is a metrical 'foot' consisting of an unstressed syllable followed by two stressed. A spondee consists of two syllables, both stressed.

> Monitors please take note
> And send the offenders to me.

For us to fail to master Latin would have been a double rebuff to Macnutt, since in addition to his teaching, which, in drilling into us the essentials of the language, was first class, we had the benefit of the Latin textbook and accompanying grammar he had produced in collaboration with the headmaster. This replaced the classic, unbelievably old-fashioned, work known to generations of schoolboys, *Kennedy's Shorter Latin Primer*, a title which had proved irresistible so that almost every copy had had ingenious variants inked in on top of it, such as 'Kennedy's way of eating prime beef'. Macnutt confided to us that it was the inadequacy of such works which had led him to undertake his own. What earthly use, he reasonably asked, was it to teach the average pupil, as Kennedy did, the Latin for 'bell-wether'? He had, he also explained, wanted to engage the reader's attention with humour, lacking though this was in his own classroom. Hence to illustrate the use of the word *ut*, 'in order that', the reader of Flecker/Macnutt was set to translate 'We went out into the garden in order to eat worms.' Even bolder was the printing of words in different colours according to gender, to implant this painlessly in the pupil's memory, black nouns being masculine, red feminine and green neuter. It never worked with me – I would remember the word and its gender and then try to see it in the proper colour – and Macnutt himself admitted it would be useless with the colour blind, of whose existence the Forces' selection tests were currently making the public more aware. Perhaps for this reason, and because colour must have added enormously to the cost of production, Flecker/Macnutt never displaced the notorious Joseph Kennedy, but he deserves credit for an imaginative innovation.

Macnutt gave excellent advice on examination technique, aware that we needed every mark we could get. He advised us to tear the examination paper in half, so that while working on the hardest part, the translation of an English passage into Latin, we could have before us the words and constructions printed on the other side in the much easier 'Unseen', the Latin text to be rendered into English. It was from him, too, that I discovered how authors were paid, for one morning he came into class in an unwontedly jovial mood, having, he explained, just received a royalty cheque for sales of the very book we were then studying.

Looking back on those cheerless, sometimes terrifying, Saturday mornings and on my encounters with this talented but unpleasant schoolmaster I remember the verdict of the Head of the Women's Voluntary Service on their wartime work: 'It was not nice but it was necessary.' Happily the rest of my work that year was both. Much of my time was spent in the laboratory, the school Alphabetical List describing me as 'psd', ie 'Probationary Science Deputy Grecian', and as I was not attempting biology in School Cert., and was obviously incompetent to take physics, I was able to concentrate on, and enjoy, chemistry. We had an outstanding teacher, already described, 'VP', amiable as well as efficient, and I was deeply impressed when he lectured us on 'The scientific method', which I have found a useful mental discipline since, and related illuminating anecdotes about the history of science. What I liked best was 'qualitative analysis' when we tried to identify some unnamed substance, but I was already beginning to suspect that science was not really my forte. Physics was less rewarding, but I at least learned, unlike the vast majority of my school at that time, to wire up a plug – useless though this skill was in our gaslit home – and years later, while working in the Electricity Supply Industry, amid electrical engineers, felt grateful for the grounding I had received.

Other subjects posed no problem. I had no fears about English Language or Literature or in maths., since our target was only a credit in the 'elementary' paper, I could keep my end up. Divinity we had now, I think, dropped, and were certainly not taking in the examination – a pity, I now feel, as I would have liked to have confounded the ludicrous Quick with a high mark – but I recall working hard at German, taught by that amiable 're-tread' 'Feeston Ho', ie A Featherstonehaugh, whose arrival I have already described. He soon realised, I believe, that we ought comfortably to achieve the modest credit we needed and obligingly allowed us to develop our vocabulary in the areas which interested us most. The war had made German a subject of obvious practical use – more so than French, since who would want to communicate with our defeated and despised allies? Addressing our enemies in suitable terms was different. I happily mastered such phrases as *'Hände hoch!'* ('Hands up!') and *'Übergeben Sie mir ihre Waffen!'* ('Hand over your weapons!'), invaluable should I, as was all too likely in 1941, encounter *Ein Fallschirmjäger*, ie paratrooper. Later, as a military historian, I was to find the German for 'rifle', 'hand grenade' and 'trench mortar' far more useful than the terms for 'wizard', 'secret charm' and the like which featured in the poetic legends regularly read to us. As an end of term treat we sang German songs, which reflected a world of smiling walkers in *Lederhosen*. Apart from *Röslein auf der Heiden* ('Little rose in the hedgerow'), we particularly enjoyed *Die Wandlung ist der Müller's Lust* ('Rambling is the miller's delight') since this gave us the chance to substitute for the proper words of the chorus, 'Holla hi!' Holla ho!', our own version: 'Holla hi! Feeston Ho!' We also learned to read, and attempted for light relief to write, Gothic script, now discarded even in Germany. The printed version, then commonplace, we were expected to take in our stride.

Before the war I had only met one American, who had, imaginatively, been sent to us under some form of scholarship scheme, though no one went back in exchange. George Cunningham who, I have since learned, came from Phillips Academy in Andover, Massachusetts, was an admirable ambassador for his country. He made no complaint about our primitive living conditions and ridiculous uniform, though it always seemed bizarre to hear an American accent issuing from a throat housed in Tudor style bands. He managed to enforce discipline as a monitor without punishments and left us all with an admiration of the United States and its language, enriching our vocabulary with such phrases as 'Going to the john'. He was reported to have told the master, DS Roberts, to whose care he was entrusted, as the most open-minded member of the staff, that he wished 'to get a load of old Aristotle', having apparently 'mastered old Plato' previously.[1] He was duly found some suitable text which, it was reported, 'kept him happy' and his year with us ended all too soon.

Now, on 7 December 1941, a week before my sixteenth birthday, the United States was at last drawn into the war on our side. By a happy chance the foreign history paper of the School Certificate syllabus that year covered American history from 1814 to 1870 and we were being prepared for it by an admirable teacher, ACW ('Teddy') Edwards, a long serving and universally loved Housey 'character'. Like all good history teachers he recognised that the basis of all study and discussion was a solid bedrock of facts. We did not waste time on imagining what it would have been like to be a slave in the South, or serve as a soldier in the Union army, but mastered instead such essentials as the main powers of the American president and the advantages which each side enjoyed in the Civil War. I was fascinated by American history and learned by heart the whole of the Gettysburg address. Later this interest was to encourage me to write *The GIs*, sub-titled, *The Americans in Britain 1942-1945*, and, closely linked to the slavery question, *The Hungry Mills, The Story of the Lancashire Cotton Famine*. I felt then, as I feel still, a far greater affinity with our 'cousins' across the Atlantic than with the aliens who do not even speak our language, across the Channel, a reaction shared by many of my contemporaries. For countries like Norway and Holland, bravely resisting German occupation, we felt unstinted admiration, for the Germans a certain grudging respect, but for the French, so long our enemies and so recently our worse than useless allies, we had no time at all.

I remember with distaste only one of Teddy Edwards's lessons, when, most untypically – it was perhaps the end of term – we read round the class a play about Abraham Lincoln. My American accent reduced the whole class to laughter, underlining the lesson already learned at house concerts that I should never make an actor.

The year 1942 was not merely the turning point of the war but also, I believe in retrospect, the decisive period in that great seismic process of change in public opinion which I have already mentioned, the results of which were to become evident in the General Election three years later. The great landmark, an unmistakable sign pointing to the coming welfare state, was the publication in December 1942 of the Beveridge Report, a blueprint for the post-war welfare state, but even before then the new tendency to question long established assumptions had affected Housie. Hitherto the task of keeping us in touch with the world outside had been entrusted to The 1930 Society, consisting of senior boys, which organised three or four lectures a term from outside speakers. I still remember one by Dingle Foot, a Liberal MP, and Parliamentary Secretary to the Ministry of Economic Warfare, who spoke excellently on his department's work and the necessity of central planning. The school now began actively to encourage the discussion of current affairs, as *The Blue* for the Summer of 1942 recorded:

> At the end of the Lent Term a number of Study Groups were formed. Their object is to increase knowledge of present difficulties so that we may be better able to help in the work of reconstruction. Ten groups have been formed, each consisting of eight or nine senior boys and a master, and they usually meet once a week. Three groups are studying education, three the problems of India, and four post-war reconstruction...Numerous books and pamphlets have been bought, and as we are affiliated to the Council for Education in World Citizenship we are able to call on first-class speakers to come and address us.[2]

I enthusiastically held forth in one of the Education groups, advocating an educational system which was in most respects as unlike that prevailing at Housie as possible, and later moved on to Political Creeds, where we each chose some particular party's policy to espouse. Apart from the obvious expanding of mental horizons such discussion achieved, the Study Groups struck another blow at the school's obsession with keeping boys from separate houses apart. They gave me an excuse to be out of the house after Lights Out, often in the company of Pitman, whose views were then even more radical than mine, and together, feeling a little like anarchists in Tsarist Russia, we crept from Peele A – Noel could not actually prevent his boys belonging to this school organisation but he would allow no meetings under 'his' roof – to harangue our schoolfellows on the need for social revolution, beginning with the abolition of the public schools.

Curiously, the Debating Society, which should have flourished at a time of intellectual ferment in the nation, had fallen on hard times. *The Blue*, in April 1942, expressed the hope that it 'will in a year or two recapture some of its former glory', but of this there was little sign. That summer Pitman, who did not share my views on the United States, successfully opposed the motion 'That we welcome the influence of America on this country', which was lost by 26 to 21, while, much to my disgust, the motion 'That the Nazi rather the German is responsible for this war' was carried by 46 to 36.[3] (I must here pay a tribute to my *bête noire,* Macnutt, who led the opposition.) The Debating Society was later to founder in stormier waters, as I will describe in due course.

Meanwhile, the war dragged on. *The Blue* for April 1942 provided a uniquely Housey perspective on a great national disaster, recording, belatedly, a Founder's Day dinner in Singapore the previous October. By the time we read of it the participants must have been dead or in captivity, for the great fortress had fallen on 15 February. I cannot recall that we were particularly horrified by this disaster – the Far East seemed a long way away and our Old Blue visitors came from nearer home – but I do recall the laugh which went up in a geography lesson when we read in a textbook that pre-war fortification work had made Singapore impregnable. We felt, however, like everyone else, humiliated by the famous 'Channel dash' on 11 February, when the *Scharnhorst* and *Gneisenau* escaped from Brest and made their way up-Channel in defiance of all the navy's efforts to stop them. Those of us who had opted to join the ATC smugly congratulated ourselves on our choice as the RAF alone appeared to be winning its battles, as the attack on Augsburg and the first Thousand Bomber Raid, already mentioned, seemed to confirm. On land, however, it seemed to be left to the Russians to ensure that the Germans did not have things all their own way. We eagerly studied the tiny maps in the newspapers recording the Russian advances and bandied about such strange names as Omsk, Kharkov and Dnepropetrovsk.

Noel Sergent's morale boosting talks had grown noticeably less frequent following the Fall of France, but in April 1942 he once again interrupted prep to give us 'some really excellent news', the escape from captivity of a former French army commander, General Henri Giraud, 'a splendid chap' who would rapidly transform the allies' fortunes. We were, rightly as it proved, unimpressed.

Our English History paper in School Certificate covered the nineteenth century, later a period of special interest to me, and from my surviving exercise books I find that we tackled all the basic questions which have exercised generations of historians: "'Peel betrayed his party.' What does this statement imply?" "Estimate the influence of Lord Palmerston on the history of his time." "Which do you think the greater statesman, Gladstone or Disraeli?" I warmed, as so many children had done, to Lord John Russell and his fight for the Reform Bill, to Palmerston's contemptuous dismissal of foreign tyrants, and to Gladstone's championship of the poor. Peel and the Corn Laws were later to provide me with the theme of a book, *The Breadstealers*, and I was not put off from enjoying history lessons by the unfortunate circumstance that we were taught that year by a geography specialist, TK Mortimer Booth. His deficiencies were largely made good by an excellent textbook, by GW Southgate, which not merely adopted a properly factual approach but contained useful summaries which I copied out into a notebook and memorised whenever I had a spare moment.

If history that year was mainly hard work, English was fun, for we were taught by the Rev. Michael Warneford-Brown, whom I have already described. My exercise book for Michaelmas Term 1941 reveals the width of the syllabus we covered and the mixture of encouragement and admonition so often provided by the best teachers. A conventional essay on 'My Home Town' – 'On the whole I really enjoyed this Dickensian effort, but watch the length of your sentences and do not let your style become over-rich' – was followed by 'Detection', when we were required to offer possible explanations for an apparently simple situation: 'A man is seen to come out of a shop and run along the street. A few minutes later a bomb explodes in the shop.' This earned me an alpha minus and the heart-warming comment 'A very good prep indeed'. One of Warny-B's imaginative ideas was to set us to speak, without prior warning or time for preparation, on some theme contrary to our actual opinions. I was required to produce, on the spot, 'A Defence of Capitalism' and, having heard Noel's predictable views on the deficiencies of the pre-war Labour governments, did so with a fluency that in retrospect appalled me and earned warm commendation. Our English master also delighted in setting us controversial subjects for our essays, among them 'Blood Sports', 'Capital Punishment' and, far more daring, 'Compulsory Games' and 'The school OTC'. The subject which really aroused my eloquence was 'Co-education':

> We realise now how wrong the dark rooms and endless punishments of the last century were. The time will come when we shall realise, too, how wrong this unnatural, illogical, iniquitous segregation has been. The stumbling blocks of superstition, tradition, ignorance must give way to a new era of truth, beauty and enlightenment.

From this I deduce that, approaching my sixteenth birthday, I had become aware of girls.

In contrast to this recent discovery of sex, at least in the abstract, my political opinions had been formed long before. I had been a socialist as long as I could remember and my last essay that term, entitled 'Christmas 1941', struck a chord, I am sure, with my warm-hearted, charitably-minded master. I had, as I have described earlier, known what it felt like to be poor at Christmas and I now warmly commended an East End vicar's appeal 'for money, boots, clothing, Christmas fare for the unfortunate destitute people of the bombed areas'.

> Christmas 1941 has left behind the otiose days of peace...We are apt to neglect to think in peacetime of all the labour that has gone into producing our Christmas dinner...It is only in the last year we have had this thought forced upon us...It is a real sacrifice to surrender one's own coupons to give food to a poor family, or clothing to a friend.

Along with such impeccable sentiments, however, went a somewhat gloomy view of the future:

> We shall certainly have to fight and not heed the wounds, toil with little rest, and, in a rationed world, give *and* count the cost.

This, with the year which followed it, was the intellectual watershed of my time at school, the justification for all the shortcomings and miseries of Housey life which I have described elsewhere. From a surviving list of 'Books Read, Sept – Dec 1941' I can see how my interests were expanding, and how I was still prone to criticise, with adolescent arrogance, rather than praise. *Pride and Prejudice* I merely found 'quite interesting', *Decline and Fall* 'after an excellent and promising beginning...tailed off into mediocrity', though, I noted with relish, 'the whole school staff ended in prison, mental home or murdered'. I failed to respond to Hemingway, finding *A Farewell to Arms* 'vaguely disquieting, with stress on the unpleasantness of war', an oddly unperceptive comment, though realism closer to home was more acceptable. 'The descriptions of the slums in the mining areas would alone make this book worth reading', I wrote of *Unfinished Journey*, 'the autobiography of...a Welsh miner, author, political agitator', his name unrecorded by me. I had already developed what has proved a lifelong distaste for historical fiction, rejecting DK Broster's *The Gleam in the North*, about the Jacobites, as 'very boring'. I thought the start of *Cold Comfort Farm*, in which I have delighted since, 'very jerky and the end very disappointing', while I damned *Diary of a Nobody,* now one of my favourite books, with faint praise as 'Quite amusing'. I read a lot on education, under the influence of the Study Group on that subject – 'A few pages explaining away the myth of classics training the mind for all subjects met with my wholehearted approval', I noted of one collection of essays, perhaps after a more than usually traumatic Saturday morning session with Macnutt – but the book which made the most impact on me I am still surprised to have found in the school library, *Moscow has a Plan*. I returned to it again and again and can still picture its black covers and strikingly simple layout. I understood even then its Marxist purpose but still responded to it as its authors had intended:

> This is the translation of a Russian child's textbook. It is not just propaganda, however, but an exceedingly good attempt to vindicate the five year plan. It left me ready to hoist the red flag on the nearest building.

If my enthusiasm for politics, and certainly far Left politics, has now waned, this was the period when I discovered a life long source of pleasure, reading poetry. Rupert Brooke, I recorded around my sixteenth birthday, 'is without doubt my favourite poet, *The Dead* being the finest of all his poems.' Robert Bridges I rated lower, though 'certain poems, notably *London Snow*, I liked very much'. The Sitwells, however, earned a stern judgement, which time has vindicated. 'I made no attempt to discriminate between the various members of the family in my reading and I formed the possibly rash opinion that I disliked them all intensely.'

Private reading apart, this was also the year I became mature enough to discover in English literature a source of enjoyment as well as examination marks. We were, I think, a talented and lively minded class not dragged down by the pernicious nonsense of 'mixed-ability' and 'non-streaming' from which later generations have suffered. Warneford-Brown encouraged the voicing of independent opinions and, I remember, called my bluff when I suggested that we could not really appreciate Shakespeare without acting him. I now believe I was entirely wrong and particularly dislike attempts to update the plays by decking out the cast in modern dress or, even worse, equipping them with motor-cycles or machine-guns. Better by far, in my view, to leave them to be enjoyed in private as literature, so the stage can be devoted, as in Shakespeare's own day, to newly-written works. (By an odd irony, had we performed *Julius Caesar* in our ordinary school uniforms it would, in Tudor terms, have been a 'modern dress' version.) I described in *First Bloom* the resulting performance, to which I contributed an Elizabethan style Prologue. It ended 'Look not upon the players but the play', which was, as this account makes clear, good advice:

> The form learned the parts assigned to them without much diligence and declaimed it with imaginative fervour. On the morning on which the scenes were at last to be portrayed, the Lower Sixth did its best to obtain convincing items of dress or equipment to add relish to its acting. The players as a whole mumbled away at their lines, and immediately they left the stage accused each other of being painfully inaudible, in voices which were themselves painfully distinct, and indeed only came to life when Caesar was hurled on to the floor from the chair in which he sat enthroned with a vigour reminiscent of the original murder. Amidst his bruises and indignant protests he could hardly gasp out '*Et tu Brute!*' in a tone that was far from forgiving. The sensation of the performance was provided, however, by the appearance of Headley, the Cockney member of Blake, whose accent had now disappeared except in moments of extreme excitement, or when he wished to infuriate some precise speaking master. He had procured an immense stage sword that would have taxed a guardsman's strength to raise, and strapped it to his waist. When in the scene in Brutus's orchard of the conspirators' meeting the line was reached that was the cue for his speech there was a long pause, in which he was seen to be wrestling with this weapon. Eventually he dragged it forth with both hands and waved it toward the roof of Big School, announcing in dubious tones:
>
> 'Here, where I point my sword, the sun arises!'
>
> The shout of laughter which greeted this gallant effort was considered by the Lower Sixth to be sufficient compensation for the drudgery of rehearsals.

Our 'set books' for School Certificate were *The Tempest* and *The Prologue* to Chaucer's *Canterbury Tales*. Here it was impossible to bluff one's way through, since one was being tested on detailed knowledge and understanding of the text, and I soon decided it would be helpful to learn most of both works by heart. Other boys reached the same conclusion and we were soon quoting from both in our everyday conversational exchanges. 'Look, he is winding up the watch of his wit. By and by it will strike!'[4] we would declaim as another boy paused for a retort, and we greeted the signs of adolescence on each other's faces with unkind references, based on Chaucer's 'sompnour', or pack-driver, to 'The knobbes sittyng on his cheekes'.[5]

Reading *The Tempest* in class was almost as enjoyable as performing *Julius Caesar*, again thanks to the distinctly non-Housey accent of the boy I have already mentioned:

> The class had developed an affection for the first scene of the play owing to the opportunities it presented for seaman-like bellowing and Headley's 'Here master! What cheer?', with the last two words pronounced in the derivative Cockney fashion, was audible a corridor's length away.

We also seized any opportunity *The Prologue* provided for laughs. I also noted how one boy's not-quite-impertinent response to being asked by the Rev. Warneford Brown to name his favourite character among the pilgrims, was to look pointedly at our form-master's dog-collar and chant, spacing the final word out to scan as in the original, 'A good man was there of re-lig-i-on'. I described, though I cannot now recall, a scene during an afternoon on the Farm, when a group chanted, in a good imitation of Warny-B's slightly falsetto voice, the opening sequence of *The Prologue*, beginning with the famous line

'When that Aprillë with his schowrës swootë…'

while another boy 'conducted' us, flourishing an onion as baton like Dr Lang in his most extravagant mood. The 'concert' ended, I recorded, 'When someone called "Gaff's coming!"' – ie 'Gaff' Seed, who supervised our labours – 'and with a look of concentration on their faces they bent back to their work'.

Both *The Tempest* and *The Prologue* were to become familiar friends; I can still quote extensively from them today. I carried copies with me everywhere, along with my history notes from Southgate, and was indignant, on seeing the former at the Shakespeare Memorial Theatre in 1994, at the liberties the company took with the play. (The 'business' the director had added included a comic character flourishing a ventriloquist's dummy and another apparently urinating on stage.) It delighted me to stay, in the same year, in a house on the Pilgrim's Way in Chilham near Canterbury. Chaucer must have passed the very church that stood opposite and perhaps drunk, as I did, in the nearby pub which had occupied the same site in the fourteenth century.

Looking back, I am glad I was compelled to master these two very different works so thoroughly. The systematic study of this one play provided a far better understanding of Shakespeare than a superficial reading of the whole of the rest of his work and the demands of the examination accustomed us to seeking out the meaning of any difficult phrase or allusion and not simply skipping over it. Chaucer provided different insights. *The Prologue* left me with no desire for further linguistic research, but it was obviously valuable to be compelled to master what was almost a different language and to learn how English literature had begun. The set books, in fact, prevented this subject being a 'soft option' and though we grumbled at the time at Chaucer's obscurity we were, I believe, in the end enriched by encountering it.

Apart from our set books, we seem to have spent a great deal of time that year on Charles Dickens, for whom I conceived a dislike which, as already mentioned, has lasted a lifetime. I can recall being asked to comment on the 'storm scene' from *David Copperfield* and to rewrite in my own words some of the Fagin scenes from *Oliver Twist*, but I enjoyed neither experience, and I remember with vast distaste an appalling anthology called *The Wellers*, of supposedly humorous extracts from *Pickwick Papers*. Later in life I was to find solid grounds for what at the age of 16 was an instinctive dismissal of this innately Victorian novelist. He was, I discovered, although a journalist by background, useless as a historical source even on his own times, with inflated over-writing taking the place of dispassionate description or solid fact. I took pride when writing about the workhouse not to quote from *Oliver Twist*, or, when describing nineteenth century elections, not to draw on the famous Eatanswill passage in *Pickwick Papers*.

Thackeray was much more to my taste. Warneford-Brown aroused our interest by reading to us first the famous scene in *Vanity Fair* in which Becky Sharp throws out of the carriage window the presentation dictionary given to her on leaving school. I remember wondering if I would be brave enough to treat my leaving Bible similarly. (I wasn't.)

Everyone at that time was required to obtain a pass, or for those aspiring to 'matric exemption' a credit, in English Language, and though we were expected to achieve this without difficulty we were, more by way of light relief than for examination purposes, duly drilled in some of what HW Fowler in his *Dictionary of Modern English Usage*, to which we were now introduced, describes as 'Technical Terms'. Today one hears horror stories of undergraduates incapable of identifying an adverb, much less, as we were expected to do, distinguishing between a simile and a metaphor – inventing the latter was a frequent exercise – or providing examples of onomatopoeia. I am still impressed by people who can instantly identify an example of oxymoron – an apparently contradictory expression, as 'falsely true' – synedoche – using the part to represent the whole, as in 'the kettle boils' – and zeugma, where one word carries two meanings, as in 'She went home in a flood of tears and a sedan chair.' Precise grammar was taken for granted – not for us today's sloppy practice of confusing the present and imperfect subjunctive and writing 'may' where 'might' would be correct – and spelling mistakes rigorously corrected. Miss House's daily tests at junior school proved their worth, though I developed a blind spot over 'separate'. My mother, after I had written 'seperately' in a letter home sent me a reply in the summer of 1942 in which the word appeared, correctly spelt, half a dozen times; I have never got it wrong since.

After our year of preparation it was almost a relief, on a warm and sunny morning in July 1942, to enter Big School to see the desks spread out at well-spaced intervals, each bearing on it a blank exercise book for our answers and a printed paper at which we dare not even glance before receiving the order 'Turn over!' School Cert. had already brought us one benefit; we were allowed to wear cricketing flannels and blazers instead of being handicapped by our normal, excessively hot and heavy outfits. I had always been a good examinee and the following week passed quickly. I can remember best the German paper, and the solemnity, as if our very lives depended on listening carefully, with which 'Jem' Massen read out three times, at varying speed, the German story we then had to render back in that language in our own words. I also recall my session with the elderly clergyman sent by the examining Board to test our knowledge of the spoken language. He was so kindly and encouraging that I found myself for once almost fluent and, when I hesitated over a word, he obligingly translated it for me. Latin was, as I had anticipated, a nightmare, but I collected every possible mark on the non-language parts of the paper. The chemistry practical, about which I had felt confident, proved unexpectedly difficult. Having gone through all the standard procedures I still could not identify the substance set before us for qualitative analysis and finally confessed defeat, recording that it seemed to have the characteristics of both an acid and an alkali. This was a sensible comment. It was in fact an ammonium salt. In a final despairing attempt to name it I was tempted to taste it, but remembered the story of a former candidate who had, he believed, been asked to identify citric acid, and removed the unlabelled specimen at the end of the exam to make, as he supposed, some lemonade for his friends. Happily the chemical was missed and a notice given out in Dining Hall that the seemingly innocuous crystals consisted of highly poisonous oxalic acid.

The results of the German oral examination were given to us almost at once. I can still remember Feeston Ho's incredulous tones as he read out my mark, 24 out of 30, but he warmly congratulated me and it seemed a good omen. Another encouraging portent, which I believe also dates from this period, was the result of the Lamb Essay Prize competition.[6] Lamb was always regarded by the school with particular affection – more so than Coleridge, a greater writer, for whom no commemorative poetry prize existed – and in 1875, the centenary of his birth, the governors had instituted an annual contest for a silver medal to be won by the best essay on a subject not known beforehand. Thanks to the war, the medal was no longer being awarded, but the competition continued and in 1942 the subject was 'Unselfishness', about which my Peele A friends later joked that no one could have known less than me. I was clearly on form that day for Roy Macklin later told me I had won the prize by a handsome margin, and that, although we used a pseudonym on our papers, he had immediately recognised my inelegant handwriting. It was typical of Housie that it kept up the tradition while telling us nothing of its origins. I did not know then that the prize had in the past been won by both Edmund Blunden and Keith Douglas, nor that another winner, the writer, Middleton Murry, had described the medal, by an outstanding Victorian designer, as 'a beautiful thing'.[7] My name, I recall, was not even recorded in *The Blue*, in which, as I have mentioned, I made barely a single appearance in 22 terms, and I had to be content with a promissory note for post-war book tokens.

I had hardly taken my last School Certificate paper when I virtually collapsed, just as after the Special Place exam six year earlier. This time the nominal cause was sunstroke contracted when I was tending lettuces behind the New Science School after opting for 'gardening' in preference to games. The truth was, as in 1936, I had worked myself to a standstill and lacked my normal physical resilience.

At any other time I would have been delighted to retreat to the 'sicker' but now my confinement, though comfortable enough, in a single ward with curtains permanently drawn, was highly unwelcome. As mentioned earlier, it was not possible to choose history at the normal 'options' selection time, but after School Certificate a few boys showing promise on the Arts side, but not committed to more 'respectable' subjects like classics, were selected by the head of history to take a special examination to transfer to the small group of History Grecians. I was eager to take the exam. and swotted up dates from my School Cert. notebooks, until these were, I believe, confiscated by the nurses, who instructed me to seek lighter reading in the Infirmary library. This had the happy result of enabling me to discover the Hornblower novels, of which I have ever since been a great admirer, for their historical accuracy no less than for their narrative quality.

The imaginary Hornblower had, I later discovered, a tenuous connection with Christ's Hospital.[8] In *Mr Midshipman Hornblower*, not published until 1950, he referred to himself as having been a grecian and thereby acquired his knowledge of mathematics. Enquiry by the Headmaster in the following year, however, led to Hornblower's creator, CS Forester, revealing that he envisaged his hero as having received 'a good grammar school education at some market town somewhere on the Hants and Berks borders', a location which might well fit Newbury. The maths and the 'grecian' term, suggested Forester, might have been picked up from his Old Blue schoolmaster. The author himself, he explained, had narrowly missed attending Christ's Hospital for he had won a scholarship there early in the century only to be disqualified by the size of his father's income.

Agreeable though my week away from the house had been, I was dismayed on returning to it to find that I had missed the vital examination which could have transferred me from science to history. My disappointment was made worse by the repellent Mortimer Booth, who sneered at me 'So you've come back now it's all over', as though I had been malingering instead of desperate to take this further test. Fortunately the master most concerned had more understanding. He had never taught me, but decided purely on the basis of the little he had seen of me and having read my Lamb Essay – he had, he told me, much admired it – that history would suit me as a subject. The vital conversation took place, I well remember, in one corner of the Quad, on a July afternoon as I was literally running back to Peele A for some futile sporting occasion, and I stopped reluctantly. DSR, as his pupils came to call him, intercepted me. The Science School, he managed to convey, would raise no objection if I decided to abandon chemistry and he would be happy to accept me as a historian. I cannot remember that Noel, although I was one of 'his' boys, was even consulted. Here, I now realise, was a defining moment of my life, settling its whole future direction.

---

[1] Jul 1988 p.130
[2] Jun-Jul 1942 p.83
[3] Jun-Jul 1942 p.83
[4] *The Tempest* II, I, line 12
[5] *The Prologue* line 633
[6] Morpurgo p.64 & p.67
[7] Morpurgo p.67
[8] Apr 1951 p.88

42

TEACHER EXTRAORDINARY

Historian and teacher extraordinary.

Inscription proposed for memorial to David Roberts, recalling 1942-43.

If 1942 was an important year in my intellectual development, in personal relationships, ie contact with the opposite sex, I was still woefully immature. During the summer holidays of 1942 a girl of about my own age, 16-and-a-half, came to stay with us from the north country manse to which her father, a nonconformist minister, had moved from Newbury. She was a pleasant, amiable person who fitted immediately into our little group, endured without complaint our cramped living conditions and seemed indeed to have a soft spot for me. I must, I now realise, have been a sad disappointment to her. Once, on a walk on the fringes of Greenham Common, I remember we sat in a churchyard while I plaited straws in her hair, but I failed, as I am sure she expected, even to attempt to kiss her, and when I inadvertently glimpsed a letter she was writing to a friend, read her verdict on me: 'Jim is shy'. I gained some kudos at school, however, by boasting of my 'girl friend' at home, especially when she wrote to me, letters as chaste and innocent as herself, though after a year or so the correspondence died away. What I now remember best of Margaret was that she accepted my mother's offer of cheese with her apple pie. I gladly saw some of our meagre ration sacrificed to this strange combination, my first realisation of the North/South divide.

It was, I think, in this same holiday that I got to know another girl, through two of my male contemporaries at the local grammar school. They told her, which was true, that I had greatly admired her while she was literally on display, dressing a window in a local clothes' shop. Eventually a meeting was arranged and one Sunday afternoon, I went for a cycle ride with her, at the end of which she invited me home for tea. Churlishly, I now feel, I declined; conversation with their daughter having, thanks to my gaucherie, flowed so stiffly I could not face trying to talk to her parents, who would, I anticipated, expect me to display some signs of my supposed 'braininess'.

In mid-September I returned to the girl-less world of Christ's Hospital, now no longer wholly male. That term Peele A acquired its first woman 'junior housemaster', Elizabeth (officially Miss DE, and known to us as 'Hearty' from her window-opening tendencies) Harvie, who had hitherto, as mentioned earlier, merely been a resident in the block. She was by no means the most physically attractive of the women staff and her subject, chemistry, was one I had rejected but she was the first educated woman with whom I had talked on something like equal terms and I formed a warm, though wholly unsentimental, attachment to her.[*]

We all, especially the youngest boys, whom she visibly befriended, liked and respected her and, to everyone's surprise she got on well with Noel. He had, perhaps, a Gallic susceptibility to women for which we never gave him credit.

By some curious quirk of school demography, Peele A that year contained only 17 boys in the Lower School, ie the Little Erasmus and below, out of 52, so that the youngest must have felt more than usually lost. Miss Harvie's study soon became open house to them, and the rest of us she treated with brisk common sense. I had always been a champion of co-education, as I have described, because it would introduce us to that mysterious species, girls. Now I realised it had an even greater advantage: it would involve contact with adult women as well.

I had still met no girls of similar interests to mine and this term, foolishly as I later felt, inadvertently rejected the chance to do so. Following on its introduction of Study Groups, already described, under the auspices of the Council for Education in World Citizenship, the opportunity occurred to send a representative to an inter-school conference organised by the Council in the forthcoming Christmas holiday. A sympathetic master suggested that I should attend, hinting that funds might be found to pay my fees, but, unhappily, the detailed arrangements were entrusted to Kappa Sills. I eagerly knocked on his study door to be met by silence and when I finally opened it, planning to leave a message, found he was there and had chosen not to say 'Come in!' He now sent me out to enter again, a procedure which, approaching 17, I found humiliating, and I ungratefully declined the proffered place. It was a mistake. A friend who attended a later conference found it thoroughly enjoyable and reported that the delegates, radically minded teenagers like us, included some of that strange but fascinating species, girls.

During the school year which began in September 1942 the war situation changed dramatically although I have no recollection of my response to any of the important events responsible. We must have been cheered by the attack at El Alamein on 23 October and the subsequent victory, the real turning-point in

---

[*] After the war Miss Harvie left teaching to become a Children's Officer, eventually in charge of her county's Children's Department; I was gratified to receive a fan letter about one of my books from her. She has since died.

the land war, which caused the church bells to be rung. The American landings in North Africa followed in November, and I am sure the German occupation of 'unoccupied France' immediately afterwards must have brought Noel into the dayroom to protest at the perfidy of the hated 'Boche'. I can, however, recall the upsurge of spirits after the German surrender at Stalingrad, on 31 January 1943. We did not know then that during this period the navy achieved its greatest triumph when, in May 1943, Admiral Karl Dönitz suspended U-Boat operations against Atlantic convoys, conceding defeat in the Battle of the Atlantic. Like the country as a whole we tended to take the navy's vital but unspectacular role almost for granted, and often its greatest successes, as on this occasion, could not be publicised. The headlines that month, as so often, were captured by the RAF, with the 'Dambusters' raid, as already described.

But this school year I had far more urgent preoccupations than the war. My first act in September 1942 on returning to school had been to check my School Certificate results. I had obtained the top 'Very Good' grade, in four subjects – we called this 'A Distinction' – English Literature, English Language, German and History. In the remaining three, Mathematics, Chemistry and Latin, I had 'Credits'. I was thus safely through the great test of 'Matric. Exemption', though it had been a close-run thing: in Latin I had received only 43%; the required minimum was 40%. This achievement was entirely due to Macnutt's teaching but he responded ungraciously to his, and my, triumph. 'So you just scraped through,' he told me sourly, as though I had got the lowest mark I could to spite him.

'School Cert.' confirmed how right I had been to abandon science, for with a mere credit in both maths and chemistry my prospect of an 'Open Schol.' at Cambridge, the natural destination for Housey scientists, was negligible. The best I might have achieved had I continued with chemistry would have been early departure from school and perhaps a career, once contemplated for me by my father, as a pharmacist. By contrast, I was the only one of the little group selected to specialise in history to achieve a distinction in that subject, and now found myself the only boy in the School List described as 'HD', or 'History Deputy Grecian'.

Although the phrase 'The Two Cultures' had not yet been coined I was conscious that the whole direction of my life had changed, as I walked past my former school 'home', the Old Science School, permanently surrounded by a smell of chemicals, along the ground floor corridor of the Modern Language Block, and entered the small, book-lined, History Grecians' room tucked into the far corner. Here we worked privately, but most of our time was spent in the School Library and it was a favourite joke to warn boys against making a noise as they entered it, 'Or you may disturb the History Grecians reading their novels.'

With School Certificate safely behind us and our status as future grecians firmly established the whole nature of our education changed. Normally this was also when, if he had not achieved this already, a boy became a monitor, making his daily life infinitely more agreeable, though, as I shall describe, this failed to happen in my case. The staff tended to treat us as almost adult and though our time was mainly devoted to our particular subject, we continued to have a few periods a week outside it, including in my case German, French, which I now began with a conspicuous lack of success, Latin, and English..

Other languages have never been my forte but English was, as always, a source of pleasure, especially as I again found myself under that prince of English teachers, Roy Macklin, who, since it was not possible to specialise in his subject, made the most of teaching the grecians and deps, ie deputy grecians, from other departments. He was one of that small nucleus of outstanding teachers who enriched the lives of many generations of boys, for, having taken a first at Oxford, he spent his whole career at Christ's Hospital until leaving to become head of a teacher training college. I later met him there, while myself working in educational broadcasting, and decided the move had been a mistake; being a schoolmaster and, in a minor way, a rebel had suited him better than being an administrator. Macklin was renowned at CH, to quote a tribute in *The Blue*, 'for his brightly coloured...green, maroon or mustard corduroy or velvet sports jackets, with matching shirts and gaily coloured ties.'[1] In my first year he had given me much needed encouragement and now he attempted, no less valuably, to cut me down to size. Once, in an anti-American moment, I referred to '*The Star Spangled Banner* being not without a gratuitous addition of blots.' My teacher was not amused. 'Ugh!' was his marginal comment and at the end of my essay he admonished me: 'You can write very well. When you find yourself sounding like a fifth-rate journalist stop!' Poetry, above all Shakespeare, was his real love and under his guidance we discussed the merits of the classic nineteenth century writers. Only one, Browning, failed to give me pleasure, but I was bored, as I still am, by such arid eighteenth century authors as Pope, for whom poetry was, I felt, primarily an intellectual exercise, enabling them to display their classical erudition, which they expected their readers to share. This was a reasonable assumption, but inevitably deprived them of the timeless, universal appeal which truly great poets like Byron and Shelley achieved. *The Rape of the Lock*, the title of which had aroused our adolescent expectations, seemed to me, as did the rest of Pope's work, sad, mechanistic stuff, enlivened only by an occasional memorable line. I extended the same condemnation to John Dryden, who had died in 1700, 44 years before Pope, whose dreary unreadability (even his titles, like *Absalom and Achitophel,* were boring) contrasted so strikingly with the real poets, like Sir John Suckling (who had died in 1642), Robert Herrick (1674) and Andrew Marvell (1678) writing in the same century. One of Roy Macklin's great legacies to me was to make me realise that without true feeling there was no inspiration. The poets I disliked might be able to place the syllables and stresses in their work as neatly as in a set of Latin verses but their work lacked vitality. Far from constructing their own terms of reference (though I had not yet come across the phrase) they relied on their readers' knowledge of the classics to provide such frames for them. Clearly the personalities of the men who had taught me played their part. Everything classical I came to associate with the grey, pompous and pedantic Macnutt, everything innovative and romantic with the colourful, lively and imaginative Macklin. As yet I had hardly looked at a single picture or piece of sculpture but I subsequently came to believe that the Christian religion, though occasionally a source of inspiration, had overall had a similarly stultifying effect on the visual arts. It had encouraged artists who should have been recording the world and people around them to spend their time turning our yet another *Annunciation*, sometimes – always a particular source of annoyance to me – with cherubs or angels floating about in the background; fantasy I still found unacceptable even when it claimed a divine origin.

Thus in this intellectually fruitful year, begun when I was approaching my seventeenth birthday, I came to form a theory, however crude, of aesthetics, and to acquire what I would then, in late adolescence, have been embarrassed to describe as an awareness of beauty. I had as yet had barely any contact with painting and none at all with sculpture; my introduction to the enjoyment of art came essentially through the written word, but already I had realised that it was possible to admire the ingenuity and technical accomplishment of a work without liking it and that it was liking which really mattered. Art, I later read somewhere, was to be enjoyed like being in love. This was a condition of which I had as yet no experience but I instantly recognised the statement as true.

This realisation was encouraged by the poets I have already mentioned, along with others I now began to read from John Donne to Rupert Brooke and AE Housman. Love was their favourite subject but its enlivening, humanising influence seemed to spread through all their work. Herrick's *Litany to the Holy Spirit* still consoled me 50 years later when I was lying awake in the small hours after a major operation, and, after a similar time lapse, I found AE Housman's *Shot? so quick, so clean an ending* helpful in comforting a friend distressed by a colleague's suicide. 'Of course such poetry is a form of therapy,' one practising poet, George MacBeth, told me many years later when I discussed with him the work he was seeking as BBC Poetry Producer, 'But why not?'

A by-product of our reading, due partly to our ignorance, was that we came to assume that love must involve the opposite sex; there could have been no more powerful lobby than Donne, Marvell and the rest for the superior attractions of women. When we did come across a same-sex romance we were unaware of the fact. I had no idea that Housman had a more than poetic interest in the young men who seemed so often in his poems to be destined for an early grave and WH Auden's classic 'Lay your sleeping head, my love,' we assumed in our innocence to be addressed to a woman. Shakespeare's Sonnet number

126, which begins 'Oh thou, my lovely boy...' was harder to dismiss and was sometimes quoted by someone in the throes of a 'pash' on an attractive junior, but I cannot recall that this ever prompted a discussion on the nature of Shakespeare's sexuality. Similarly all the great eighteenth and nineteenth century novels to which we were introduced invariably revolved round man-woman relationships.

The message of the classics was more confused. The classical specialists liked to tell the rest of us of the tolerance of homosexuality in classical times, but knowing no Greek and only elementary Latin, I had to take what they said on trust. Catullus demanded his 'thousand kisses' from an unquestionably feminine, if by our standards unfortunately named, Lesbia, while Ovid, though I only discovered his *Ars Amoris (The Art of Love)* after leaving school was even more explicit, and no less normal. I did read in translation, however, Helen Waddell's *Medieval Latin Lyrics* and here, too, there was no hint of inversion. Although some homosexual activity, as I have indicated earlier, undoubtedly went on it was not, at the grecian level at least, boasted about or even shamefacedly admitted. Bob Pitman, still a great influence on me, was indeed what would now be called a homophobe. 'What were the Greeks,' he remarked to me once, 'but a group of dirty old queers?' Later, on a national newspaper, he delighted in denouncing what he labelled 'the lilac establishment', who on every issue argued what was then called 'the trendy' case and would now be labelled 'politically correct'. Thus in this decisive year I absorbed the belief that those sexually orientated towards their own sex were more to be pitied than admired, though I certainly saw no reason, as the law did, why they should be punished.

Pitman was now house-captain of Peele A, but was, disastrously, given no chance to make me a monitor, as was his right, and mine, since Noel insisted the three vacancies should go to those who had headed the poll in his 'election' the previous terms. I was thus given the next most senior post in the house, that of trades-monitor, an appalling job, the worse I have ever occupied, where one had far more burdensome duties than any of the six 'real' monitors, with no compensating privileges. Absurdly, considering my age and the fact that, thanks to the war, I had less than the normal time to get my vital scholarship, I had to ask Noel each evening for permission to work after 9pm when the rest of the seniors went to bed. He refused to give me permanent leave to stay up for an hour like the monitors, mainly younger than me, so night after night I had to waste precious minutes hanging about outside his door to await his return from one of his ineffective immorality-seeking tours of the dormitories. Occasionally, when a monitor was away for some reason, I was temporarily promoted to fill the vacant place, though it was difficult to exercise proper authority over boys whose status I normally shared. I suffered particularly at the hands of three or four loutish boys in their last year who resented my position in the school and made my job of dispenser of trades and occasional stand-in monitor as unpleasant as they could. Lacking any privacy to work, even my own small table such as the monitors enjoyed, I realised once again how the great weakness of Housie, the poor living conditions, cancelled out much of the advantage which the excellent teaching provided.

Apart from Pitman (and my closeness to our house-captain made me more unacceptable to the final year dullards) I had two close friends in the house, specialising respectively in Maths and Classics and destined to follow, after Cambridge, very different careers, as a missionary in East Africa and a Civil Servant – ultimately an under-secretary – in Whitehall. The former was notably virtuous, the latter as sophisticated as one could be at 16 or 17. We grandiosely called ourselves the Post-Socratic Debating Society and talked together constantly about books, the services in chapel, the abilities of the various masters, general questions of philosophy and politics, even – the future missionary abstaining – the relative physical charms of the women now joining the staff. Justifying Charles Lamb's remark about Housey boys making 'friends for life' I kept in touch with both, intermittently, though the Civil Servant, Christopher Herzig, is now dead.

So, too, alas, is my then house-captain, Robert Pitman.* This was indeed his year. That term he won an open exhibition in classics at Oxford, and combined two offices rarely held by the same person, President of the Debating Society and Captain of Athletics. *The Blue* recorded the contribution 'to the general mirth' at a summer forestry camp, made by 'Pitman's flute', and noted, after a reference to such wartime activities as 'collecting books and magazines for the Merchant Navy', that 'We have also, under RP Pitman's organisation, collected and dispatched for the war effort over 1,000 lbs of conkers';[2] what these were needed for I cannot recall. In the following term Bob's triumphs continued. 'RP Pitman made a great hit' in a performance of *HMS Pinafore*, *The Blue* confirmed, while his final appearance on a Housey stage, in the leading part in *Love from a Stranger*, the Peele A house play, was also, in the next issue, singled out for praise.[3]

Although, like so many grecians, he immediately abandoned them on reaching university, the fact that my former nursemaid was specialising in the classics made me feel that there must be more to Latin than I had so far realised, a view encouraged by having that year a master who clearly enjoyed teaching the language. AH Buck, universally known as 'Buckie', was an Old Blue who had come back to Housie with a classics degree to spend the rest of his working life as a schoolmaster there. He had been at school, and remained throughout his life, a close friend of Edmund Blunden, a volume of their correspondence being published posthumously in 1996.[4] Buckie had a real feeling for English as well as Latin; I can recall his delight when someone

---

* His obituary appeared in *The Times* of 14 February 1969, reprinted in *The Blue*, Lent Term 1969, pp.192-5.

suggested 'castaway' as the best translation for the Latin *naufragus*, as it comes with the same hint of contempt as the original passage. A lifelong bachelor, whose own inclinations were all too clearly, and in the end somewhat disastrously, not towards women, this talented, if flawed, schoolmaster had a penchant for mildly improper double entendres, which delighted us less for their coarseness than for acknowledging that we were near-adults. I can recall his translating *natu dubius*, meaning 'of doubtful birth', as 'a bit of a bastard' and he delighted another class with a proposed inscription for the tombstone of 'John Longbottom, who died aged 15 years': *Ars longa, vita brevis.*[*] He claimed, too, to have seen a classic schoolboy howler, whereby the famous tag *Timeo Danaos et dona ferentes* had been rendered as 'I fear the Greeks even when they bring their girl friends', 'Donah' in Victorian slang having meant a female companion.[5]

For the school as a whole the main event of that term was the visit from the President of Christ's Hospital, the Duke of Gloucester, in October, who addressed us from the Warden's desk in Dining Hall at the end of dinner. I had expected an impressive flow of eloquence from the king's brother, despite George VI's crippling stutter, and was astonished at his embarrassing, tongue-tied performance, still the worst speech I have heard in my whole life. I could understand now why the suggestion made in the vote of confidence debate in the House of Commons the previous July that the Duke should be made Commander-in-Chief had caused the critics' case to founder in incredulous laughter.[6] It was no wonder, I decided, that Churchill had survived this, the only attempt to overthrow him during the war, by 476 to 25, though 40 other MPs had deliberately abstained from voting. What made the Michaelmas Term of 1942 of unique importance to me was meeting the man whom I admired then and have come to idolise since. Often it is claimed that a single, gifted and sympathetic teacher, encountered at the right moment, has transformed an individual's whole life. This was emphatically true in my case. Without the Honourable David Roberts – 'DSR' to his senior pupils, 'Daddy Roberts', in recognition of his kindly manner, to the rest of the school – I would, I suspect, never have reached university, never have become a writer, never have enjoyed the range of intellectual interests and experiences I have been fortunate enough to discover. Here was the heart of my 'shaping season', the time when Christ's Hospital did what it was designed to do, to take someone of impoverished background and modest prospects and made him heir to a whole new world. The credit lies, of course, less with the school, of which he was a wholly untypical servant, than with the man himself, but it must in fairness be admitted that it had appointed him and left him to develop his private genius for teaching. Time, as this book bears abundant witness, has not dimmed my recollections of

---

[*] The English version of this text was carved over the entrance to the Music School: 'The life so short, the art so long to learn.'

the school's enormous shortcomings, some innate in the institution itself, some easily overcome. But if anything could compensate for my years of misery and frustration it was this final year of intellectual flowering and accomplishment.

When I first met David Roberts he was 41 and at the height of his powers. Ill health, luckily for us, had kept him out of the forces, though he served, as incompetently as I was soon to do, in the Home Guard. For the next year I was to see him for long periods almost every day, often alone, but I can still vividly remember my introduction to the History Grecians as we assembled at the start of the Michaelmas Term. There were only nine of us and we knew we were privileged – privileged to be specialising in history and, as the five of us who had just joined the form hardly yet realised, to have a master with a reputation for being both kindly and eccentric. The four 'full grecians', a year ahead of us, included a boy who was already a school celebrity, for having torn up his 'fair copy' book after his last lesson with Macnutt and dropped it in the wastepaper basket, declaiming 'As a gesture, sir!' Of the four just starting out with me on this new school career I knew nothing; all we had in common was that no one else wanted us.

Although the first and second year history grecians were often taught as separate groups, or individually, we occasionally came together in the library for a joint session, as at the start of the Michaelmas Term, an occasion I described in *First Bloom*, where I altered 'Roberts' to 'Williams':

The history specialists were gathered round the fireplace at the end of the room, in the usual attitude of a class at the beginning of a new term. But there was in their pose a certain something, a trace of proprietary interest in the building, a certain poise and confidence in their own significance, which no other group of Sixth Formers possessed...

The reason for this self-confidence was not only that the history specialists were universally and traditionally accepted as *poseurs*, the recognised intellectuals of the school...but, much more, the possession of the most remarkable master at Middlestone. Mr Williams never failed to attract notice. There was something in the shape of his head, in the quality of his walk, which refused to allow anyone to ignore him. At a closer inspection, the perpetual twinkle in his eye, and his hearty guffaw, for the word 'laugh' cannot adequately describe it, deepened the conviction that this was no ordinary man. The school as a whole viewed Williams with amusement, the older masters with suspicion, but of the history sixth's attitude there could be no doubt – they loved him...All who ever came to know him soon wished above all else to obtain his praise. He never lost his temper, or wrote painfully cold and neat comments beside an unbalanced passage in an essay, yet his forms never misbehaved and his pupils made strenuous efforts to write English that pleased him...His wit was never cynical nor childish, yet he had a reputation for putting the most nervous third-former at his ease in a few minutes and of setting the most pompous historian laughing at himself in no longer a time. James came later to realise that Williams hardly took even himself seriously and that his delightful air of utter indifference to his surroundings and of detachment from his colleagues was deceptive and served to provide a protective cover for a superb teacher and serious thinker...

On this morning he rolled – for his progress though slow was not conventional enough to be called a walk – and beamed benignly at his waiting pupils. He was still smiling benignly when they were all seated round the large table in the centre of the floor and he began to go round the circle with his questions about the value of the holidays just past.

The first youth addressed murmured modestly: 'Well, I went to a Fabian Summer School, hitch-hiked to the Lake District and read *Tom Brown's Schooldays*.'

'Ha!' bellowed Williams...'*Tom Brown's Schooldays*!' He started to talk, very quickly, about the book. 'Arnold of Rugby – great man. Read his life story? Well, you ought to! *Rugby Chapel*? Well, if you've read that you ought to read *Clifton Chapel*. Have you read it? Give you a good laugh! Terrible poem!' In a derisive voice, apparently intended to mimic the tones in which Henry Newbolt might have declaimed his masterpiece, he launched into, 'Here is the chapel! Here my son...', but one of the older boys had whispered audibly in the ripened tones of Major Jennings [ie Harrap] of the Middlestone OTC, 'Here my son!' and the whole table roared with laughter. Williams, with the deceptive twinkle more prominent than ever in his eye, remarked in tones of surprise, 'Well, I didn't think Newbolt was as funny as all that,' and passed on to subject the next student to a torrent of questions.

Eventually he came to James, who stumbled through a long catalogue of second-rate novels and mentioned at the end, 'Oh, and that Trevelyan you gave me to study.'

'Ah, Trevelyan!' exclaimed Williams, 'Great man that. Do you know that his second name is "Macaulay" after another historian? What was Macaulay's second name?' he fired suddenly at one of the third years, who had evidently witnessed this catechism before and whose gaze was now fixed on his fingernails...The youth was silent, then 'Babington!' he said suddenly, with an air of courteous protest at being troubled.

Williams guffawed cheerfully. Any small incident of this kind always served to amuse him.

'If you did that to the dons at Exeter [ie Exeter College, Oxford] I don't wonder they gave you a scholarship! That's it,' he continued to James, 'Babington. But because he talked so much and wrote so much they said that TBM stood for "Thomas Bablington Macaulay". You must meet Macaulay!' he added, for Williams always ordered one to meet an author, exactly as if he were waiting outside in the quadrangle

With School Certificate behind us, the whole nature of our education seemed to have changed overnight. The mere acquisition of facts from a single textbook and their orderly regurgitation was no longer enough. Now we were given an essay subject and reading list, required to do our own research and compare sources, advance and justify our own conclusions and submit the resulting essay to DSR's searching scrutiny, followed by vigorous discussion, often on a one-to-one basis. I recorded my response to this experience in *First Bloom*:

> The conventional atmosphere of the science specialists, whose conversation had seemed, in the previous year, to be far from subdued, seemed church-like compared to that of the History Sixth. Member after member of it interrupted Willliams to disagree on different points, either with a languid, 'I don't think that I quite agree, sir,' to, from the most excitable, a vigorous, 'No! No!' Far from objecting to such interruptions, Williams seemed to welcome them and broke off what he himself was saying to conduct a vigorous argument with his questioner. Indeed that was the secret of his teaching method. He never lectured, but, rather, conducted a debate, only intervening, as a good chairman, when the points raised became irrelevant and the speeches merely humorous or dull.
>
> He conducted his history classes rather as he contributed to school debates…His entry into the debating room…seemed to enliven the atmosphere like a blast of cold air. When he rose to his feet, with the inevitable little bounce, a stir of anticipation always passed through the house.
>
> 'This motion, sir,' he would begin, waving a podgy and contemptuous finger at the blushing face of the honourable proposer, 'is both mischievous and misguided! Mischievous and misguided!', he would repeat firmly, rolling the words with complacent satisfaction off his tongue, and the whole house would repeat them after him, as if they contained the whole essence of wisdom.

DSR was, I now feel, remarkably indulgent over the first work I did for him, which showed little of the qualities which had led him to select me as one of his pupils. Re-reading with embarrassment those early essays I have wondered why they were so bad. In 1993, while writing this book, I was astonished to be given an explanation by another ex-History Grecian, an ex-MP who had contributed an admiring obituary of DSR to a national newspaper. 'You used to be aggressive and enjoy putting people's backs up,' this candid contemporary told me, happily adding: 'You've mellowed.' I suspect that both statements were true. Though of normal height I was, in Housey terms, distinctly 'small', a non-games player who had not succeeded in carving out a real place for himself in any other area of school life. It is traditionally the 'little man' who is the most combative. I did not think of myself in such a way, and was already confident that the world outside would provide a more sympathetic environment than Housie, but I probably compensated for being despised, if not actually pushed around, in my basically philistine house by being over-assertive in class and on paper, and verbally demolishing poets, politicians and historians who could not hit back. A more sensitive housemaster might have restored my self respect, but Noel regarded me with suspicion as not contributing to 'house-spirit' and, the ultimate offence, of making friends outside Peele A. I can recognise now that I needed encouragement in the house and cutting down to size in the classroom. The former I never received; the latter was achieved by the joint efforts of Roy Macklin, already mentioned, and in his good-natured way, by David Roberts, who successfully implanted in me what every historian requires, a degree of humility in confronting the past and the work of previous historians.

This very necessary chipping away at my conceit began with the very first paragraph of my very first essay for him. The subject was 'The essential characteristics of the Eleventh and Twelfth Century Village'. 'All that happens is the result of history,' I began pretentiously, feeling that I ought in some way to mark the start of my new career. 'This is a rather hackneyed platitude but it is none the less worth quoting.' DSR's response was discouraging. 'Blaa!' he wrote deflatingly in the margin. Nor was he impressed by my supposedly colourful second paragraph, which I now cringe to read. 'Eight centuries ago, before the cinema had dawned on a world thirsting for effortless amusement, and the scarlet facade of Woolworth's stores had made every High Street hideous, most of the population of England lived in villages.' This attracted a large question mark from my new form-master, who added a variety of sceptical comments as I rambled on for twelve pages. His final comment, when I wrote, 'To sum up all that I have said, sometimes with an excessive prodigality of words...' was even more hurtful: 'Agreed!' 'You'll have to cut this down,' he added. '50% could go.'

By the following month we were answering such questions as 'What Purpose did the Craft Guilds serve in Twelfth Century Town Society?' and 'On What Lines was Village Life changing in the Thirteenth and Early Fourteenth Centuries and how far were these changes influenced by the Black Death?' By November I was writing on 'St Bernard and St Francis' and had learned to get to grips with the subject at the very start. 'The difference between St Bernard and St Francis,' I wrote, 'is more than the difference between a monk and a friar. It is the difference between two men.' I was also writing much more concisely. DSR's reactions reflected my progress. More than one point or quotation attracted 'Good' in the margin and his verdict at the end was: 'I like this. It's interesting and in places well put.'

The period we were studying, the Middle Ages, is not one that has attracted me since but had the great virtue of giving us a firm foundation for reading about later centuries and of interlocking the various factors which shape any society: its physical environment, economic development, powerful personalities and, of outstanding importance in this period, religion. I decided early on that time spent in looking for a philosophy of history would be better devoted to research into a specific subject and that it was as fallacious to suppose that outstanding individuals alone – 'Heroes' as Carlyle labelled them – could affect the course of events over the long term as to subscribe to the Marxist heresy of trying to squeeze every change into a materialist, economic framework. My Anglo-Catholic upbringing had made me well able to appreciate what present day students probably find difficult, the overwhelming importance of the medieval church, but I soon came to distrust the school of 'Catholic historians' with their distorted view of events and their refusal to believe that any non-Catholic could be impartial.

One of the first books we were encouraged to read outside our immediate subject was by a Roman Catholic priest: *'What are Saints?'*, a good example of how our work in history was used as a jumping off point for widening our minds in a more general way. We were also from the beginning encouraged to get back wherever possible to the original sources, not merely reading about the spread of monasticism but studying the actual *Rule of St Benedict*, later adopted by many other religious orders. I have made extensive quotation from primary material and eye-witnesses a feature of my own subsequent writing, although I learned early on how often the latter can disagree. I was shocked to read two different accounts of the Battle of Hastings, one of which even questioned its name and referred to it as Senlac. DSR was always ready to listen to any theory, provided it was based on fact; about inadequately researched essays he was scathing. It was from him I learned too, in this immensely fruitful term, that our knowledge and interpretation of the past were always changing and that one needed to keep up to date, just as scientists did. I now discovered the existence of the *English Historical Review*, and was set to assess an article in it, concluding, with a revival of my old arrogance, 'It is good, but not very good.' DSR would have none of this. 'It is *very* good,' he assured me and I was set to re-read the work I had thus dismissed and try again, this time being rewarded by a characteristic comment: 'Much better. There is some meat in this.'

Another early lesson, which I hardly needed, was that mere quantity of factual information, essential though this was, was no excuse for poor presentation. DSR was not, I think, sorry to see us having to wrestle with some badly written books as an awful warning of what to avoid. The facts, logically set out, came first, as we were never allowed to forget, but style, too, was important to the historian. 'Listen for the ring in the sentence,' he would urge us as he read out an example of good writing, perhaps from Gibbon or Macaulay, or, very occasionally, from one of our own essays, including mine. He was hard on verbal infelicities and over-elaborate or imprecise images were sternly discouraged. 'It takes time and trouble to be a master of metaphor,' he commented reproachfully when I referred to the castles of feudalism darkening the medieval landscape, while a reference to Pope Gregory VII making his famous declaration, '"I have loved righteousness" as he lay dying in...Salerno while much of Rome was in ruins' was endorsed discouragingly: 'A bit rich'. Nevertheless DSR's final verdict on my essay was encouraging. 'It has some shape...This is both interesting and considered, but not considered quite far enough. See Tellenboch.' It was typical of DSR to follow criticism with practical advice though who Tellenboch was I cannot now recall.

I was always puzzled by DSR's 'Honourable' for he was the least pretentious of men and the only member of the staff at CH to have a title. Occasionally he referred to his family background, as when he mentioned them taking a house in London for the season during his childhood, which made me conscious of the vast gulf between his world and mine. Only later did I discover the basic facts about him and, since he received only a short tribute from another appreciative ex-pupil, in *The Times*, not a full scale obituary, I shall note them here.[7]

David Stowell Roberts was the second son, born in 1900, of a successful Liberal MP, John Herbert Roberts, a politician of some standing in his day. First elected, for West Denbighshire, in 1892, he rose to be chairman of the Welsh Parliamentary Liberal Party at a time when both the Welsh and the Liberals were still a force to be reckoned with at Westminster. JH Roberts was duly rewarded with a baronetcy, in 1908, at the peak of the party's power, and a peerage, in 1918, the year of its eclipse, when he became first Baron Clwyd ['Cloo-id'] and thereby made his younger son 'the Honourable'. He lived until 1951.

DSR must have talked to his colleagues of his early years for one of them was able to quote his recollections in an obituary in *The Blue*. 'His...childhood with his two brothers in that lonely mansion on the Welsh hillside above Abergele must have been strange; "growing up among nurses and governesses, house-keepers and housemaids, gardeners, coachmen and grooms, remote from other children inevitably we were different." His most Celtic qualities, his fluent talk and vivid imagination perhaps nurtured by that Welsh nurse who told him tales.'[8] As he grew up he was subjected to frequent contact with more highly educated and sophisticated 'adults who came to call – the Liberal politicians and Welsh ministers on his father, the artists and musicians on his mother, and the temperance workers on both.'

The young DSR suffered badly from ill-health, with three bouts of pneumonia before he was 16, and was sent to the most bracing of English counties, Norfolk, to be educated, at Gresham's School, Holt, which had a reputation for offering a more tolerant and eccentric regime than other public schools. From here he went on to read history at Trinity College, Cambridge, taking only a 'third' – proof enough that academic class is not an infallible indicator of ability. He arrived at Housie to teach in the Prep before, unusually, moving up to the main school, where he found his real metier.

I still find his acceptance of, and by, Christ's Hospital, surprising. He was no sportsman, although he played golf, and his interests, as a painter in water colours and art collector, were shared by few other masters. Yet the praises heaped upon him by his colleagues when he died, tragically early, at the age of 55, in 1956, have the ring of sincerity as well as truth – qualities rarely in evidence in obituaries in *The Blue*. I can only endorse what one master, whom I disliked and who never concealed his dislike of me, wrote of him: 'The central theme of his life [was] his burning passion for history and for making boys fall in love with history.' The Headmaster himself, to whom every other subject always came a second best to the classics, acknowledged his subordinate's unique talents. 'His genius as a teacher lay largely in his capacity to pose questions which throw a boy past his books, his secondhand ideas, his preconceived opinion, back to his ultimate resources of thought and belief...I used to protest sometimes at his taking on boys whose minds (as revealed in my Great Erasmus Latin set) were at best pedestrian. David calmly overruled me and more often than not he proved to be right.' Another master recalled that over the 24 years in which DSR had charge of the History Grecians he saw 72 boys win open awards at Oxford and Cambridge, and that 'the DSR tradition...will be remembered by ex-pupils for the rest of the century; not least by those who were "rescued" after failing in some other Department', a prediction which this book helps to fulfil.

Forty years after his untimely death, I still regard David Roberts as by far the most important influence in my life apart from my mother and still regret that he did not live to see me become a published historian, as he had predicted. All that I could do by way of repayment was, in 1966, to dedicate my first serious historical work to his memory, and, to campaign, with some other Old Blues, for a permanent memorial to him. I had hoped for that ultimate Christ's Hospital accolade, a stone tablet in the Cloisters, and had, devised with another of his beneficiaries, what seemed the appropriate inscription, 'Historian and teacher extraordinary', but we were obliged to settle for an, in my view, inadequate substitute, a picture by an Old Blue with a small commemorative plaque. The principle, however, had been accepted and it is pleasing to record that almost a hundred former pupils and colleagues contributed and that, on the day of its unveiling, in 1978, a large table was covered by books written by those he had taught. A memorial sermon was preached at a special service in Chapel by one ex-History Grecian who had become a bishop. It was, sadly, unworthy of its subject, who was barely mentioned, and its pedestrian phrases, inapt references and rambling construction would certainly, I reflected, have had him reaching for his marking pencil.

Far more fitting were the comments of another former History Grecian, later an academic, author and publisher, Professor JE Morpurgo, who has since written a history of Housie. David Roberts, he told the audience at the Founder's Day dinner in 1979, was 'the finest teacher that CH or any other school or educational institution has seen in this century, a man who taught much more than history and the mentor who...has "fixed the destinies of my life"'. Here is one judgement by an eminent, pro-CH, Old Blue which I can wholeheartedly endorse.[9]

---

[1] Dec 1988 p.215
[2] Nov-Dec 1942 p.8 & p.2
[3] Mar-Apr 1943 p.45 & Jun-Jul 1943 p.72
[4] Carol K. Rothkopf and Barry Webb (eds.), *More than a Brother, Correspondence between Edmund Blunden and Hector Buck, 1917-1967*, Sexton Press, London W12, 1996
[5] 1987 p.123
[6] Taylor p.554
[7] *The Times* 23 May 1956 p.15
[8] Sep 1956 pp.131-7 for this and later quotations.
[9] Dec 1979 p.231

43

SUNDAY MORNING SOLDIER

In the years when our country was in mortal danger...gave generously of his time and powers to make himself ready for her defence by force of arms.

Letter of appreciation from the king to members of the Home Guard, not received by the author for his service in the Christ's Hospital Company

On my seventeenth birthday, 15 December 1942, I found myself in the Home Guard, but almost as soon as I had attended my first parade term was over. We were not expected to take our uniform or weapons home, it being considered that the Germans would not be so unsporting as to invade during the holidays. My principal present that Christmas was *The Collected Poems of Rupert Brooke*, which I had requested, though with my call-up now only a year away I found his verses about dying for one's country less and less appealing and, as I plunged deeper into my teens, the poems about girls increasingly attractive. In January 1943 I again helped behind the scenes at France Belk's pantomime, this year, *Red Riding Hood*. The producer was, very deservedly, much praised in the town for her ingenuity in overcoming the effects of clothes rationing, in force now for the past 18 months, and if the result was an excess of flimsy garments largely made of materials like curtain net requiring few, or no, coupons, there was no complaint from me. Like new clothes, young men were now in short supply, and two of my male friends from the local grammar school played leading roles as comedians, so that we were able to spend many agreeable if frustrating minutes in the wings discussing the relative merits of the young women in the chorus.

It was all, like the script, which contained not a single double entendre or coarse expression, exceedingly innocent. The utmost limit of our ambition was to kiss someone we admired – the ambiguous term 'fancied' had not yet come into use – and we were more bemused than aroused by the display of female flesh on stage or glimpsed through the doorway of the women's dressing room. The pantomime was a glamorous oasis in our drab wartime lives, just as it had been in our poverty-crippled years before the war.

In spite of the unsettling effect of the pantomime I returned to school without reluctance aware that every day was precious if I was to get my scholarship before the guillotine of the call-up descended. On top of my all important work and my burdensome duties as trades monitor, with the usual time-wasting daily appearances on the playing fields, though the Lent Term, being devoted to athletics, was relatively endurable, I now had an additional commitment.

As mentioned earlier, I had been inducted into the Home Guard on my seventeenth birthday. The method of my recruitment into what was after all, part of the Armed Forces still seems to me highly irregular, if not downright illegal. I was, I seem to recall, simply instructed to report to the school office, not to be offered 'many happy returns' but to be informed I was now a member of this part-time army. I had never volunteered; I had not, as was my right as a citizen, been informed that I was a 'directed man', as conscripts were called; I never received any document informing me that the nation required my services, nor – far more important – an identity card confirming that I was a soldier, of a kind, and entitled not to be shot out of hand if captured. Such subtleties did not trouble Christ's Hospital which, in its high-handed way, simply enrolled any boys who reached the minimum age without consulting them. Had I been asked I would, I think, have agreed to serve on condition that I was given the normal privileges of a boy of my age. As it was, I resented then, and am indignant still, that the school should have not merely have allowed but required me to roam the countryside with a loaded weapon in my hands while not considering me responsible enough to enter the dormitory to change into my uniform without a monitor's approval, or stay up after 9 pm, even to go on guard, without seeking the permission of my housemaster. By a nice irony he was exactly the same humble rank as me. Here Private Sergent and Private Longmate were, in theory, equal.

I have been grateful ever since for my year of service in the Home Guard since it enabled me to take an insider's view when writing *The Real Dad's Army*, then the only post-war history of our force, though I was unable to do justice to that unique unit, the Christ's Hospital Company of the 3rd Sussex (Horsham) Battalion. I did eventually get a somewhat grudging certificate of service from my commanding officer, but when, while writing my book, I asked to see the school archives on the subject, astonishingly, for an institution so obsessed with its past, learned that none had been preserved. I still suspect that the Housey Home Guard had a dubious legal basis. No doubt its foundation, in May 1940, was prompted by sheer patriotism, but by the time I enrolled it was serving a secondary, unacknowledged, purpose, of keeping senior boys occupied and providing yet another source of discipline in our already over-disciplined lives.

I can find no reference to the Christ's Hospital Company, nor even the Horsham Battalion, in any of the Home Guard histories I have consulted, though many other units, in contrast to Housie, kept a detailed record of their activities. 1942, the year I joined, was described by the historian of one Cambridgeshire unit as 'the flowering time for the Home Guard. Numbers were high, training had worked a remarkable transformation, weapons were now adequate to defence commitments and the spirit of the men was excellent'.[1] I saw little sign of any of this when, on the very evening of my seventeenth birthday, I made my unimpressive debut as one of the nation's unpaid defenders, clad in a borrowed uniform and steel helmet, both far too large for me. Looking more like the member of a comedy team than a soldier I duly paraded at the school office with three or four other boys to sleep on the floor. Our task was not merely to repel the Germans if, improbably, they were suddenly to appear in West Sussex, but to rouse the school in the event of the imminent danger signal being given by the detachment posted, if the siren sounded, on the Chapel tower. For such duties we received a small subsistence allowance of two or three shillings [10-15p] and I was later one of the small purchasing party sent into Horsham to buy the solid, almost meatless, meat pies and sausage rolls supposed to sustain us while on guard. Both cash and food provided a useful supplement to what we normally received and the war supplied once again a means of escaped from the stifling confinement of the ring fence.

Further compensation for this extra demand on one's time was the opportunity to talk to boys from other houses and, as even Housey recognised that we could not be in two places at once, members of the Home Guard were excused the Sunday morning service in chapel, since non-attendance at parade was a criminal offence. The principle of compulsory chapel was retained however, with evensong, and the normal Monday to Saturday services.

On Sunday mornings I now found myself doing yet more drill on the asphalt behind the houses or crawling across the playing fields chanting the words of some current military mantra, like the infantryman's guide to survival when fired upon: 'Down, crawl, observe, fire.'

I formed the view then, and my subsequent research as a historian of the Home Guard confirmed, that the organisation was by this time unnecessary, except where its members could be employed in actual operations, to relieve coastal or anti-aircraft artillerymen.[2] The public suspected, and the government knew from its ULTRA intelligence, that the Germans had long ago abandoned all thoughts of invasion and had they – the excuse for keeping the force in being – attempted coastal raids to disrupt allied preparations for D Day they could easily have been repulsed by the armies assembled for the coming invasion. The millions of men in the Home Guard, all by now playing some active part in the war effort or awaiting call-up, would have been better employed in being encouraged to relax in their leisure hours, or enjoy their last year of freedom. However, as I was to discover again as a full-time soldier, having got a man into uniform no government was going readily to let him go again.

Here the philosophy of Christ's Hospital was wholly at one with that of the nation's rulers. In December 1941 all 16 year olds had been required to register as the supposed prelude to *voluntary* participation in a youth organisation, though Housie had, very typically, got in ahead of the authorities and forced boys from 13 onwards to undergo military training even long before the war. I had, as already mentioned, joined the former OTC and then the Air Training Corps, membership of neither organisation being legally compulsory though required by Christ's Hospital and schools like it. I was, I felt, 'doing my bit' and indeed, as I have mentioned, enjoying being trained as a future airman. To be, in effect, also drafted back into the infantry was unwelcome, the more so as, in the very months that I was forced back into khaki, new regulations were introduced laying down that henceforwards Arts students would be conscripted as soon as they became 18 whether they had secured a university place or not.[3] No deferment would be granted to allow a second attempt or to take Higher Certificate, which offered the chance to return to further education at a later date.

In view of the sacrifices others were making it was not perhaps unreasonable to close down the Arts courses at universities as, in effect, the government had already done, but to cut short the school career of sixth formers, thereby perhaps denying them the chance to go to university at all, was far harsher. In view of the tiny numbers involved and the fact that they would not evade conscription, merely postpone their call up for a term or two, this has always seemed to me one of Ernest Bevin's least defensible decisions as Minister of Labour and National Service. The effects in my own case, thanks to the Housey practice of taking School Certificate a year later than elsewhere, and the chance that my birthday fell in mid-December, so that I would be in an earlier call-up group than someone born a fortnight later, were likely to be calamitous. This knowledge overhung my final terms at school, and made me begrudge the time I had to waste on military training which I believed then, and now know, to have been futile and unnecessary. This was all the more true because the army preferred to train its recruits from scratch, regarding the Home Guard, as I shall describe, more as a joke than an ally.

In 1943, however, I had no opportunity, as unwilling private, Home Guard, or perfectly content leading cadet, Air Training Corps, to offer my opinion on such matters, and I did not foresee that, as a civilian military historian, I would one day have the chance to discuss them with the Home Guard's founder, the former Sir Anthony Eden, by then Lord Avon, as well as with generals and Air Chief Marshals, a belated victory for the pen over the sword. In fact, though I resented it at the time, my service in the Home Guard, which covered precisely one year, was to have lasting consequences for me, arousing my interest in the whole subject of invasions, and invasion attempts, affecting the British Isles. As the last two-volume history of this subject before mine appeared in 1876[4] it seems likely that my *Defending the Island, from Caesar to the Armada* (1989) and *Island Fortress, The Defence of Great Britain 1603-1945* (1991), may hold the field for some time to come. All my research, incidentally, confirmed that in every age the regular forces have been highly sceptical of the value of assistance from the part-timers. When, years later, I asked the author of the official history, *The Defence of the United Kingdom*, this question, he told me candidly that he believed that if an invasion had occurred, the regular forces would have required the Home Guard to keep out of their way while they repulsed the enemy.*

My time in the Home Guard was not, however, wasted, since it gave me a first-hand, worm's eye view, of the organisation, such as few historians can have enjoyed. This was an advantage I shared with one of my heroes, Edward Gibbon, like me a most un-military minded, reluctant warrior. Gibbon was, in 1760, called out as part of the Hampshire Militia, to help defend South-East England against a threatened, but in fact imaginary, enemy landing. He admitted candidly in his *Autobiography*, a book I came to admire, that he did not enjoy his 'bloodless and inglorious campaigns' but acknowledged that 'The captain of the Hampshire Grenadiers...has not been useless to the historian of the Roman Empire.'[5]

The Home Guard was notorious for the proliferation of strange units as pigeon fanciers, train enthusiasts and small boat owners tried to maintain their hobbies under the pretence of serving some military purpose. Few companies, however, can have been stranger than that provided by Christ's Hospital. It would, as I have mentioned, only have been up to full strength in term-time; the Headmaster, most conveniently, but not unreasonably – he had served on the Western Front in the first world war – was appointed commanding officer. Some of the more self-assertive masters were also given commissions or made NCOs. The remaining masters and estate staff were segregated into one platoon, the boys made up two others, so there was no danger, even in the heat of battle, of a boy being able to give an order to a master. Noel Sergent, despite his front-line experience in France, was said, uniquely, to have failed his proficiency test and to have threatened to resign, while this was still possible, after being required to take orders from the school Estate Agent.

The Home Guard has often been praised for the supposed comradeship existing between all ranks, but this was not much in evidence at Christ's Hospital, where their new commissions gave already self-important members of staff new opportunities for being unpleasant. I can recall the pompous, cane-addicted LM Carey, strutting about during an exercise with his swagger-stick under his arm, and reproving me when I delivered a supposedly urgent message in the middle of a battle for not saluting him, although bullets were supposed to be flying all around and I was reporting that we were about to be overrun. He was, I felt, itching to deliver his favourite punishment, but happily, the army, more civilised than Housie, had long since banned the beating of subordinates.

Carey clearly found it impossible to forget the usual classroom relationship and was equally unimpressed when my friend Peter Scroggs, playing the part of

---

* See the script of *The Weekend Warriors*.

a German in a small raiding detachment, enterprisingly hid on the roof of a building below which the defending officers were conferring and lobbed over a lump of mud, calling out: 'That's a grenade! You're all dead!' The response was 'Don't be ridiculous, Scroggs!' Boys, it was clear, were not allowed to kill members of staff, even on the battlefield.

'Oily' himself made only rare appearances that I witnessed and his new rank of major left us unimpressed. What could possibly be grander than being Headmaster of Christ's Hospital? My only personal contact came when he asked me what I would do next after we had supposedly been engaged in a brisk battle which had left a field near the Post Office littered with our casualties. Remembering stories of heroic Old Blues and the ever present obligation to 'Love the Brotherhood', I said I would go back to recover the wounded. 'No, no,' our commanding officer told me, 'You must leave them where they are and withdraw.'

Good natured masters tended to become even more approachable when in uniform and being on duty with Roy Macklin was a particular pleasure. It was in his company that I was involved in the only incident of all my years at Christ's Hospital that is likely to be remembered and which lived up to the fictional world of Greyfriars, though *The Magnet* had, sadly, been killed off in May 1940. On one warm, sunlit evening in the summer term of 1943 my Home Guard section was engaged in Fire Guard practice and specifically in dealing with a supposed incendiary bomb on the chapel roof. At ground level was a large, wheeled, tank, resembling a dustbin, with a protruding crossbeam worked by hand to operate the pump, an appliance now seen only in museums. The exercise involved pumping water up from the ground level via a thin hosepipe to the top of the Chapel towers, where it was used to fill a series of buckets supplying a stirrup pump on the roof.

I was with Macklin and another boy who was in charge of filling the buckets on the tower. When the first was overflowing, instead of tipping it down the nearest drain, he emptied it over the adjoining parapet into the headmaster's garden. We had no idea anyone was there, but there came a cry of sheer surprise, followed by a barely articulate scream of 'Who did that?' Peeping over the edge, we saw the headmaster standing beside the garden chair where he had been peacefully reading, dripping water from his white summer jacket and – the only time in my life I have witnessed such a spectacle – literally dancing with rage. We prudently made no answer to his question but crouched down behind the parapet, choking with suppressed laughter. The exercise was abandoned and while the Head was indoors changing we crept back to ground level and made ourselves scarce. To drench simultaneously one's Headmaster and CO was not an achievement that could be kept dark long but by the time the culprit's identity was known – he was in fact one of Flecker's own privileged pupils, a classical grecian – the Head had decided to treat the whole affair as a joke.

Service in the Home Guard confirmed what I already knew, that I had virtually no night vision, though the school chose to ignore this potentially crippling, indeed dangerous, handicap. I recall an exercise on the Quarter Mile when someone was sent out to make a noise by striking a rifle on his steel helmet, the rest of us then being required to walk towards it. Having reached the supposed location of the 'enemy' we had to stop, our commander then coming round to see how near to him we had actually been. I invariably set off confidently enough but soon wandered off, sometimes until I was out of earshot of the order 'Stay where you are!' My comrades would then have to send out a new patrol in search of me, as I blundered into the wastes of the distant Bird Sanctuary or found myself pinned against the fence beside the railway. On one after-dark exercise I was blamed for our position being overrun when the 'enemy' burst upon us with triumphant shouts from only a few yards away. Had I, as a negligent sentry, been threatened with shooting – though even Housey did not contemplate such measures – it would have done no good. I simply could not see in the dark and a diet of carrots, the supposed wartime specific for this condition, would have made no difference.

'Black-out blindness' it was possible to live with, even in the army, where guards were usually static, but it was only later that I began to suffer from a much more troublesome phobia. In case they may be of help to others who have suffered from the same defect – it is said in some degree to affect around 10% of the population – I record my experiences here.

I must have been around 15-and-a-half when we were assembled in Big School to be enrolled in the Fire Guard, set up nationally a few months earlier after the great fire raids of December 1940. Most unusually, since the school normally favoured a 'You, you and you!' approach to volunteering, boys who knew themselves to dislike heights were told to leave. Confronting the question for the first time, I felt a sudden nausea at the thought of scaling the roofs of the adjoining buildings, just as I had when given the chance years earlier to climb the Water Tower, and was among the large number of boys who left. Our departure created no problems. To many others the chance to play the fireman was a dream come true and the Fire Parties needed were oversubscribed.

Curiously, during the intervening 18 months before I joined the Home Guard, the condition apparently disappeared and here it was simply assumed we would, when called on, walk along the narrow paths between the tiles and the low walls, barely knee height, which bordered them, on the roof of the Dining Hall, Chapel and other blocks. I cannot remember this troubling me, nor the ascent of the Chapel towers, scene of the fire-bucket incident described earlier. With greater insight into the condition I can recognise that the decisive factor is not so much distance from the ground as its accessibility. I suspect that other sufferers will confirm that what arouses the worst anxiety is being separated from a potentially crippling or fatal drop only by a barrier, whether fence or wall, it would be possible to climb. The essence of the irrational fear one feels is a compulsion to get over the very obstruction that keeps one safe, presumably as the easiest way to end the phobia that torments one.

What later investigation suggests revived dormant acrophobia, and added to it what I have named pontophobia, the fear of crossing bridges, was an exercise one morning after school. We were required to climb up on to the flat roof projecting from the side of one of the three storey house blocks, in fact, I believe, Coleridge B, with a sandbag over one shoulder, to deal with an imaginary incendiary bomb. To get there we had to use the turntable ladder which was the pride of the school fire brigade, a wobbling, wooden affair operated by turning handles at its base. I have repeatedly since recalled – or even, conceivably, imagined – being left on the small oblong of roof with not even the lowest ridge round its edges to prevent me sliding, or jumping, off. Oddly, I have no recollection of feeling particularly frightened at the time, though I can remember the sense of insecurity I felt climbing up and down the wobbling ladder. This incident seems the likeliest source of the severe phobia which surfaced much later in my life and has resisted the combined efforts of several experts, using different techniques, to dislodge. The eminent psychiatrist I consulted after the condition had become intrusively troublesome described it as a 'long-standing and deep-seated phobia' but could not identify the cause. Nor indeed could the psychologist and counsellor to whom he referred me and whom I saw regularly in parallel over a long period. The account which I gave week by week of my schooldays, however, to which they listened with a mixture of horror and incredulity, has proved a most useful preparation for writing the present book.

Acrophobia has become in recent years a progressively more inconvenient complaint, as glass-sided, external lifts, unenclosed internal escalators, and high-rise buildings of all kinds become more common. It is perhaps naive to expect the architectural profession, openly contemptuous of criticism from those who have to look at or use the buildings it creates, to consider the needs of this minority, large though it is. Fear of heights has, however, made me far more sympathetic to the irrational anxieties of others, which are far more widespread than is commonly supposed. I can recall how, as an authority on invasions, I had to refuse to be interviewed for television on the very edge of the white cliffs of Dover. Afterwards members of the filming crew came up to me privately, one after another, to confess to the similar, though different, phobias, from dread of snakes to fear of flying, which had caused problems in *their* working lives.

To return to the Home Guard, our fire-watching duties were essentially a sideline, subsidiary to our real task, of playing our part in the defence of West Sussex. By the time I joined it, the original conception of the Home Guard's role had changed. Back in 1940 it had been too ill-organised, poorly trained and badly equipped to do more than look out for parachutists and man hastily improvised defence works, the strategy being for small units to slow down the German advance and stop enemy forces roaming the countryside at will, by contesting every road junction and river crossing, with the Christ's Hospital company protecting the newly strengthened banks of the River Arun. By late 1942 the original temporary barriers of wood and sandbags, like those around Newbury which I have already described, had largely been replaced by pillboxes and roadblocks of brick and concrete, but meanwhile the war situation had changed. It was now a question of *us* invading *them* and, with the country full of regular, well-armed troops the need for a part-time amateur army was highly doubtful. The generals had now, however, found a new role for it. The former idea of strongpoints and obstacles was contemptuously dismissed as mere 'passive defence'. Roadblocks would, it was explained, merely delay our own forces advancing to eject the enemy, and the solid cube of concrete which had once obstructed the road on the main bridge leading into Horsham, forcing traffic to crawl past it in a single lane, had now been disdainfully pushed aside and lay piteously at an angle, marooned in the mud of the River Arun. Instead, we were told, coils of wire would be spread at the last minute to entangle the leading enemy tank, which would thereby itself form the road block to halt those behind. We would then surge forward from our ambush – one of the fashionable words of the time – and annihilate the immobilised invaders.

This neat explanation left me somewhat unconvinced. What use would the original roadblock have been anyway, I wondered, if it could so easily be pushed aside? And what heroes were going to ensure the enemy tank obligingly enmeshed its tracks in coils of wire which, incidentally, we have not been trained to use and did not appear in our stores? (The answer 'Us' did not much cheer me.) Along, however, with such minor changes in tactics went a whole new strategy. The new scenario no longer envisaged the Home Guard having to deal with small raiding parties but becoming part of a much larger force engaged in a full-scale encounter battle. The belief now, we were told, was that the Germans might try to disrupt the preparations for D Day by a massive landing, by air or sea or both combined.[6] We would therefore combine with other battalions to form a comparable defending force.

I was even then not impressed by this explanation. If the Germans had not been able to land in force in 1940 they were certainly not going to be able to do so in 1943 and any small marauding parties that did get ashore could easily be dealt with by the army. As for airborne attack, the skies over Britain were no longer safe even for individual enemy bombers, let alone a fleet of lumbering troop carriers. If by mischance a handful of parachutists did land safely the old style Home Guard platoons, scattered about the countryside, were far better equipped to respond than a painfully assembled division. The truth was that the government, not brave enough to stand down the Home Guard, which the army had never really welcomed, had to find some justification for keeping it in existence.

None of this was clear to us in 'F' company, 3rd Sussex Battalion, as we spent every Sunday morning, and at least one evening a week, preparing for a battle we never expected to fight. Many of the Sunday sessions took place on the playing fields or on the asphalt behind the houses, making them appear, as the school seemed to regard them, as an extension of compulsory games. The most boring occupations were arms drill and ordinary foot drill, of which we had already had our fill in the old OTC and indeed in the routine school parades several times a day. The most interesting type of training was battle-drill, the great Home Guard preoccupation of the period. This was designed to teach elementary tactics, which most of us had already mastered in the Corps, but must have been useful to those new to the military arts. A small group would take up their position on one of the rugger pitches while another detachment was sent to attack the enemy in the flank. Meanwhile the rest of the attacking unit stayed under cover, supposedly giving support, until the commander shouted 'Cease covering fire!' Simultaneously the outflanking group were supposed to reveal themselves, rise to their feet, and charge forward with fixed bayonets or grenades. This manoeuvre at least reduced the risk that one would be shot by one's own side, and was, to my mind, a pleasanter use of a rugger pitch than that to which it was usually put.

By now the Home Guard was well armed and its training well organised. I am astonished how much we packed into that year, including some skills that were omitted from my full-time basic training in the army. One weekday afternoon was spent in constructing barbed wire barriers like those so often seen in World War I films, a disagreeable job even wearing the heavy reinforced gloves which wiring parties had no doubt used in Flanders. Another afternoon was devoted to checking and cleaning hand grenades. This involved testing the firing mechanism, a spring propelled bolt held in place by a pin, after fitting and then removing the detonator, which resembled a short piece of chalk. If, absent mindedly, one had not taken it out first, the result was bound to be disastrous. As a poor performer with a cricket ball I was relieved not to be required to throw a grenade. When I did have to do so, in the army, I found there were others far worse than me, who barely lobbed the missile out of the firing trench; perhaps those miserable hours in the nets at school had achieved something after all. I feared the worst when I found that Blam, incongruously transformed into a Home Guard officer, was to supervise our first firing practice, but he proved far more suited to this than to teaching classics. The range was sited in a narrow ravine in a piece of wasteland near the Doctor's Lake, known as 'The Lag', already mentioned, the haunt of boys seeking a quiet place to smoke. Luckily then I had not read the witty description by one Home Guard of a 'typical Home Guard weapon' as 'One that was dangerous to the enemy and, to a greater degree, to the operator'[7] nor *The Ballad of the Sten*, written soon afterwards by one of my fellow History Grecians. This, clearly based on the Lag, recounted how a group of Home Guard thus armed descended into 'a deep dark glen', never to be seen alive again.

The Sten Gun was a weapon much praised, for its cheapness and simplicity, by those who had never fired it, but already had a reputation for blowing off the little finger of the left hand if one held the barrel too close to the slot through which the spent cartridges were ejected. I was so determined to avoid this fate that I hardly looked at the target and was astonished to be commended by Blam for having managed to fire single shots while the control knob was in the 'Automatic' position, apparently the test of a skilled operator. Later, again under Blam's direction, I attempted at the former OTC indoor range to fire a 0.22 rifle but even at the short range involved, a mere 30 yards [27.4m] or so, the target was a blur to me. Blam, in a remarkably kindly way, sympathised, supposing my poor performance to be due to sheer nervousness. In fact soon afterwards, when, aged about 17-and-a-half, I began to wear glasses, all was changed. Others whose short sight was discovered, like mine, almost by chance, will have experienced the same blessed relief of suddenly finding that objects which had been vague and shapeless now acquired line and definition. I was never, as it turned out, required to shoot at anyone in earnest but was gratified after joining the army to find myself labelled a first-class shot with a .303 rifle. With a Bren I remained merely second-class, though this has proved no handicap since.

The Home Guard, in spite of the number of elderly bespectacled warriors in its ranks, made no provision for defective sight, indeed mine was discovered by an observant master who had noticed me peering close up at a book. I recall asking the lecturer after a session on anti-gas precautions how people like myself – by then I was equipped with solid-sided hornrims – could

45: Christ's Hospital before the addition of the grecians' houses.
The Arts Centre is on the right, the Sports Centre in the background to the left

46: St John's church, Newbury,
after bombing, 1943

47: My brother in server's robes, date unknown

48: With my father, date unknown, but probably c.1938 or 1939

50: My elder sister enjoying a break from her war factory, 1943

51: My twin sister in WRNS uniform, c.1944

52: My holiday friends, Harold and Gerald, 1943

53: With my twin sister and friend Keith, 1943

49: With my brother before he went overseas, 1941

54: Peele A, 1937

55: The Avenue, 1937, seen from Peele

56: Peele A house photograph, 1940-41

Back row: Second from right, my friend C Herzig

Fourth row: Extreme left, myself, far right my friend WG Silk

Third row: Far right, my friend B Harris

Second row: Third from left, RP Pitman, fourth – JC Turner, fifth – NJT Bailey (house-captain), then JNB Sergent, F Haslehust and the Peele matron

Note the Royal Mathematical School badge on the shoulder of the boy on the right of the front row

57: On Sharpenhurst on my eighteenth birthday. Note the large buttons, cutaway collar and turned back cuffs of my grecian's coat

58: Schoolboy into soldier. My shoulder flash indicates I was on the strength of SHAEF

59: Outside Peele on my eighteenth birthday, 1943

60: In the same spot, 29th February 2000

simultaneously wear a respirator and fire a rifle, since the spectacle side pieces would prevent the rubber mask fitting securely against the cheeks. He replied that one would have a choice, of blundering about short-sightedly or of being gassed. The army, more sensibly, had solved the problem, I later discovered, by issuing 'gas mask glasses', unflattering but tough, with circular lenses and a flat, metal sided, frame. I still have mine, as a souvenir of my undistinguished military career.

While the army was adopting the far more practical short, meat-skewer type of bayonet, the Home Guard had acquired its discarded, carving-knife version, but 'going in with the bayonet', the final stage of the attack as taught in battle-drill sessions, never made much appeal to me. Being the object of such an assault appealed even less. I remember one peaceful morning in which our instructor, Sergeant Usher, took on the role of a German storm trooper, and charged towards me with rifle and fixed bayonet. We were, for some reason, supposed to be unarmed ourselves, so could not engage in the stylish parrying and thrusting, like old style duellists, shown in the newsreels depicting army training. The recommended response was to step to one side, thrust out a foot to trip up the attacker and then grasp the bayonet firmly with both hands to throw him off balance. Happily the bayonet during this exercise was still in its scabbard so I duly seized it, but, inhibited by his superior rank, failed to throw him to the ground. I had a strong suspicion that I would have had little more success had the good sergeant been a real German, for I made a poor showing in unarmed combat lessons, for which an instructor came from Horsham; it would clearly not have been good for discipline to have boys hurling masters to the ground or inflicting on them the other recommended injuries. These included trying to blind one's assailant with one's finger nails, bringing a knee up sharply into his groin 'to damage his matrimonial prospects', as it was delicately put, and, as a last resort, spitting in his face to put him off. Spitting at a German was perhaps something I might have managed, but the few private experiments I made suggested that expectoration, at least on the scale required, was not as easy as it sounded.

A curious consequence of the master/pupil division in 'F' Company was that most of the unit was not allowed to train with its most powerful weapons, and even denied knowledge of their existence, a policy which could have had disastrous consequences on the battlefield. I can recall being puzzled when I saw Roy Macklin, as unconvincing a soldier as I was, apparently burying something in the bank of a road leading to Tower Hill, just outside the school gates, an area well known to me from house runs. Only long after the war, when writing *The Real Dad's Army*, did I realise he was installing a 'Fougasse' or oil-drum trap, designed to project a jet of flame at any enemy tank approaching up this narrow road. It was only then, too, that I learned the name of the curious stove-pipe like object, mounted on a four legged frame, which the masters' platoon could be seen man-handling one Sunday morning on a rugger pitch. As mere boys we were not allowed near this 'masters' toy', in fact a Northover Projector, designed to hurl glass bottles full of phosphorous at the enemy.[8] (My later research, incidentally, removed any resentment I had felt at being kept in the dark; the Northover, another 'typical Home Guard weapon', was notoriously liable to envelop its operators in flames if the bottles burst prematurely.)

To a similar category belonged the 'sticky bombs' which we, as boys, were also not allowed to use, and I only learned of their existence as a member of a working party required to transport a load of them from the school armoury to a Nissen hut built just outside the grounds. Again, it was only as a historian, not as a Home Guard, that I discovered what they were – glass containers containing an explosive mixture which was supposed to cling to a tank and go off on impact. That afternoon it was impressed upon us that the objects we loaded on to a hand cart and then trundled up the path from the Post Office and across the Avenue to the open spaces of Three Mile Ash, would explode if dropped. I do not know if this was true, but we made that journey very gingerly.

My year in the Home Guard included one major exercise, held during the summer term and lasting a whole weekend ie, since proper priorities still had to be preserved, from the time when cricket finished on Saturday afternoon. The intervening night we spent 'in the field', in the case of my section on the floor of the cricket pavilion, which had its own lavatories, so no digging of latrines was required. (This was less to spare us this experience than to prevent damage to the sacred turf of Big Side.) Next morning we were ordered to help locate and round up a detachment of enemy parachutists, played, not very convincingly, by the masters' platoon. Overweight, balding and elderly, they bore little resemblance to the tough looking storm troops who appeared on the 'Know your enemy' posters, and, with their forage caps pulled down over their ears, they looked even less intimidating than we did in our steel helmets. I later took part in a somewhat similar exercise in the army but this was, in a curious way more convincing and more fun. I remember a pleasant march through the Sussex countryside on a glorious summer Sunday morning, ending around midday, when we found ourselves advancing into a local wood, charged with the duty of flushing out the last, obstinate, well concealed remnants of the invading force.

It was in some respects inferior to a pre-war Field Day, for then we had had blank cartridges to simulate small-arms fire. Now we merely had fire crackers tied to our rifles. Our sergeant, otherwise undistinguished for his school achievements, like so many who excelled in the Corps and Home Guard, divided us into pairs labelled 'No 1 Section' 'No 2 Section' and so on, and ordered us forward in turn from bush to bush, while the rest of the platoon, in the best battle-drill tradition, provided covering fire. In addition to exploding their fire-crackers, some hurled thunderflashes, clay-encased fireworks simulating grenades, which burst with a gratifying crack. The result was never in much doubt, for it would clearly not have done for the 'Germans' to have routed us, and they surrendered with gratifying alacrity; a thunderflash fragment could have inflicted an unpleasant wound on an unprotected head. We were then, for the only occasion in my year in the Home Guard, rewarded with a hot meal, prepared by the ladies of the estate, on a field cooker. Their inexperience showed; the food was burnt.

A few months later, in December 1944, the Home Guard was stood down, and the king sent a letter to former members. 'In the years when our country was in mortal danger,' wrote his Majesty, '. . . gave generously of his time and powers to make himself ready for her defence by force of arms and with his life if need be.' I never received this sign of the royal gratitude, but the army did, in its distinctive way, recognise the existence of this auxiliary service. I recall the sergeant, soon after I had started my basic training, entering the barrack room, to ask those who had served in the Home Guard to identify themselves. I had learned enough of the military mind not to be the first to come forward and so missed the privilege given to another former Home Guard of cleaning the sergeant's boots.

---

[1] *The Real Dad's Army* p.96
[2] See *The Real Dad's Army*, pp.112-14.
[3] *How We Lived Then*, p.208
[4] By HM Hozier. See *Defending the Island*, p.504
[5] Quoted in *Island Fortress* p.176 & vii
[6] *The Real Dad's Army* p.102
[7] *The Real Dad's Army* p.63
[8] *The Real Dad's Army* pp.79-82

BEING EDUCATED

On the whole I have enjoyed being educated.

Essay by the Author, What have twelve years of education done for me?, c. *January 1943*

With the start of the Lent Term of 1943 the tempo and intensity of my schoolwork speeded up. DSR had decided that I should make the first of my two possible attempts at gaining a scholarship that autumn and I still have the plan he set out for me: 'First go in Sept. Oxford. Hertford, New College Group'. With only two terms to cover what was normally two years' work he sensibly ruled out trying to cover the whole medieval period. '3 questions out of 6 or 8', he wrote firmly, listing the seven subjects I needed to study to attempt this essential minimum in the European History paper: 'Charlemagne, Viking Invasions, "Feudal" Europe, The Recovery of the Church and the Papacy, Monastic Reform, The Rise of Normandy (Normans in Sicily), Crusades, Mohammedan Power'. A similar programme covered English History, from 1066 to 1215. Week by week I was thoroughly drilled in these chosen topics and, re-reading now DSR's marginal comments on my essays, I can see that he felt little concern about my ability to master the facts but was concerned at my journalistic tendency to over-simplify complex issues and to sacrifice scholarly qualifications in favour of a striking phrase. The dons who would be marking my papers, he hinted, would be looking for objectivity and balance, even a degree of dullness, not for literary fireworks. 'Arguable point', he wrote against the simple assertion with which I began one essay, 'Between 1073 and 1085 the medieval Papacy reached its high water mark,' but 'Yes' against the more restrained statement, 'The discussion hinges on the exact meaning of the words "righteousness" and "iniquity"', which had appeared in the question I was answering. 'Why?' and sceptical disclaimers such as 'Not on your basis' appeared later, but I was encouraged by his final judgement: 'It has some shape', modified by a typical reservation: 'Style – is it too rich?'

DSR once described me as 'One of the most prejudiced individuals in the world,' a judgement which, at 17, I heard with pride, especially as he added 'Don't lose the bias.' Strong views were, he always stressed, acceptable, even welcome, provided one was able to justify them in argument. Every one-to-one session with DSR forced the pupil to be on his intellectual mettle. A slighting reference to Victorian architecture, for instance, would prompt a demand to explain what was wrong with it, until you had made an adequate case, or revealed your ignorance.

Almost as important to our future as the paper on English and European History were the two others required by every group of colleges, the General Paper and the Essay. (We would also have to face others in Latin and a Modern Language, but about these there was little DSR could do.) In preparing us for the General Paper DSR was in his element. Some questions were likely to be history related and on 24 February 1943, for example, I found myself attempting to answer 'How far is it safe to use the word "medieval" as a term of abuse?' and to discuss the provocative assertion: 'Anyone who attempts to define the Renaissance is an ass'. We were also, with the aim of enabling us to demonstrate the breadth of our interests, for the first time introduced to the visual arts, which Housie had hitherto ignored. I now discovered a love of fine paintings which had me at 17 collecting small colour reproductions and, later in life, was to see me visiting professional galleries and amateur exhibitions to buy whatever originals I could afford. I was also vastly gratified to be thanked in my sixties by someone I had last seen in my late teens for passing on to her a similar enthusiasm. The ultimate credit was DSR's. The school had, as I have described, a fine set of Brangwyn murals as well as one outstanding painting – the 'shark' picture I have already mentioned – but no attempt had been made to use these to develop our interest in art. We were never taken to look at such pictures as could still be seen in wartime London, which I found perfectly possible a few months after leaving school. Painting was, I now believe, subconsciously seen – unlike literature or music – as somehow subversive of the Housey spirit, a challenge to the essentially philistine ethos which prevailed. It strikes me now how rarely we were invited into the married masters' houses and, when we were, how little there was in them to delight the eye. I only discovered from his obituary that DSR himself had dabbled in watercolours, but it was under his roof that I first remember seeing a picture hung to give pleasure, rather than as part of the furniture, and what was more, a modern original, indeed it was only then that I realised that it was actually possible to buy the work of a living artist.

The school library did, however, possess many of the excellent Phaidon series of large books devoted to famous artists, with full-colour plates; to buy some of these for myself became one of my first pleasures when I began to earn money. That January I was set the exercise of writing about a picture of my own choice, selecting Raphael's *Portrait of a Young Man*, which I still admire. This was, as I wrote, the first time I had ever really looked closely at a picture and I wrote a thousand words of detailed analysis, concluding, 'It is indeed a work of genius.' For DSR such a conclusion was merely the start of a debate, not its end. 'What makes a good picture as opposed to a good photo?' was his reaction, and he urged me on to further research. 'Compare Sargent, Eva and Betty Wertheimer', which I duly did.

Like most people new to looking at painting, I developed an enthusiasm for the impressionists and post-impressionists; the mere names implied entry into the arcane world of art criticism. That June I wrote a further study of a Phaidon reproduction: '"The Drawbridge" (Spring 1888) by Van Gogh as a Work of Art.' This was a more ambitious essay which tried to distinguish between art and skill and compared 'The Drawbridge' to Picasso's 'Woman in a Red Armchair'. I preferred the former but acknowledged that though the latter 'calls for very hard consideration, it is probably unfair to say that for this reason Picasso is an inferior artist to Van Gogh...Their intentions are different, just as Auden would hardly claim to be trying to do the same thing as Keats.' Here was the very essence of a General Paper answer, showing that I was familiar with modern poetry as well as modern painting, and the balanced comment indicated how much I had developed intellectually in a mere four months. DSR clearly felt this, too. 'I like this,' he commented on my conclusion, 'It's interesting and it's honest.'

From my surviving 'General Notes 1942-3' notebook I can reconstruct many of the lessons of that period, so crucial to my future prospects. As always, like any good teacher, DSR worked from concrete examples and factual information towards studying the concepts behind them – the reverse of modern teaching techniques which expect children to run intellectually before they can walk. There are painstaking notes about major painters with their dates and brief summaries, as, on Botticelli, 'Madonnas, unreal and forced expressions, pleasant colouring, but poor Venus in "The Birth of Venus"'. Some of these I now read with embarrassment, but they served their purpose of implanting basic facts in my mind. Of lasting value were the books we were advised to read to give us some terms of aesthetic reference, like Clive Bell's *Art* (1914), Roger Fry's *Vision and Design* (1920) and Eric Gill's *Autobiography* (1940). I find juxtaposed in my notebook such statements as Gill's 'Art is skill' and Fry's 'Art is the creation of significant form', while from some unrecorded source I transcribed another sentiment, 'The beginning of all aesthetic judgement...is emotion' and its corollary: 'The artist must know what he is about, and what he is about must be...the translation into material form of something that he felt in a spasm of ecstasy.'

Eric Gill's insistence that there was not an unbridgeable gulf between the artist and the craftsman, though in one the pursuit of beauty was the sole aim and in the other it was ancillary to a practical purpose, struck me with the force of a revelation and it was only half a century later that I attended an exhibition of Gill's work and saw the full range of his accomplishments. About the same time I read a biography of him which revealed what an appalling individual he was, combining fervent Roman Catholicism with promiscuity and incest.* Had we known this at the time it would no doubt have prompted a DSR-led discussion on the extent to which an artist's character was relevant to an assessment of his work. While I was writing about Van Gogh's 'Drawbridge' another of our group was composing his essay on 'A pair of shoes considered as a work of art'. I recall being astonished to realise that a printing type-face, an armchair or even humbler object, like a knife or a lamp shade, might possess aesthetic quality as well as being useful.

As with painting, no master had yet, I think, ever suggested to us that architecture was worthy of study, but as early as January 1943 I find that I answered 'architecture' to a question 'Which art of the Middle Ages interests you most?', on the naive if honest grounds that it was the one I knew least about, and by the following month we were writing essays on 'The Architecture of Christ's Hospital':

> The houses are, on the whole, tolerable pieces of architecture. Especially where ivy has assisted the mellowing influence of time and weather, they seem…from the front both dignified and stately, being externally neither antiquated nor outstandingly modern and functionalist. The architects of the school were inspired with a pleasant sense of symmetry and the blocks are divided into two opposite and similar parts. The dignity of the front entrance (enforced by the school rule which says so decidedly it is not to be used by any boy, whatever his status) is greatly enhanced where a pleasant front garden exists.

About the backs of the houses I was less enthusiastic:

> The rear of the block is in all cases a deplorable failure. A dingy patch of tarmac and gravel, possibly ornamented with scrap iron heaps or dustbins, opening on to an equally dreary road on the far side of which are ugly fives courts, is the prospect which greets the visitor. It is a general criticism of the school to say that while almost invariably pleasant from the front, the back view of the buildings is, to say the least, a rather shabby one.

I suggested that 'the vacant space be partially filled by the erection of two new rooms for each house' to remedy some of the worst inadequacies of the living accommodation, about which I was severe:

> There exists within the house a deplorable lack of space. The washing facilities are grossly inadequate, as anyone who has seen as many as 20 people waiting to wash after some cold, wet or muddy outdoor activity will

---

* See Fiona MacCarthy *Eric Gill*.

appreciate. Possibly the fact that the swimming baths were once cowsheds influenced the architects...The dayroom provides yet further evidence of the parsimony or poverty of the architects or governing board. While adequate as a room for noisy recreation, it has been made to serve as common room, prep room, reading room, writing room, library and now [ie since the provision of soup in the evenings] even dining room. It could...serve any of these functions tolerably well, but it cannot serve them all at once. The solution...is to erect at least two new rooms behind the block, leaving the dayroom for lovers of noise, ping-pong, billiards. One of these rooms would be for hobbies, such as wireless or aeroplane making, and the second room for reading, writing and quiet.

I am gratified to note that DSR disputed only one of my critical comments, on the general lack of soundproofing, so that 'all that is said in the changing rooms is painfully audible...in the junior housemaster's study'. Was not such inadvertent eavesdropping, he suggested, part of a housemaster's duties? He was remarkably indulgent about the rest of this comprehensive survey, pleased, I think, that I had obeyed his instructions to *look* at the whole school with a fresh eye and to apply the twin tests of appearance and practicality to every part of it. I am somewhat embarrassed, however, by the arrogance underlying so many of my judgements. The chapel I dismissed, unfairly I now think, as 'a revolting building inside and out. The exterior is an undignified red colour while stupid little turrets are stuck on its corners.' The Old Science School was dismissed as 'internally...rather muddled...Certain laboratories...are badly lit and generally gloomy inside.' Big School, I patronisingly observed, was 'externally quite sound, though there are the usual excrescences in the shape of turrets'. The Kitchens, I concluded, 'whilst possibly efficient for their purpose are an offence to the eye'. As for the Works, 'the unpleasant suspicions one has on hearing the name are amply justified.'

I am pleased to find, since criticism is so much easier than praise, that I did like some buildings. 'The Library...is well designed. Externally it is admirable and internally is also good...The New Science School is also a commendable architectural achievement. The New Quadrangle is a most successful piece of planning, probably because it is so much more recent than the rest of the school.' In retrospect what I find encouraging, since today 'new' and 'modern' almost invariably mean 'worse', is that in 1943 it was the later buildings, added in the twenties and early thirties, which aroused my enthusiasm, like the classrooms and theatre built behind the original residential block of the Prep:

The Preparatory School buildings are the most modern part of the school and...while possessing all the grace of a well designed building are...those best suited to their purpose. What I have seen of it is enough to make me praise it for its modernity...without loss of beauty, and its smoothness of line and air of healthy, well-lighted comfort. If boys who leave the preparatory school buildings are old enough to consider such matters, they must be disappointed by the classrooms of the main school.

Among the authors to whom DSR had introduced us as preparation for this exercise – and my study of Housie in 1943 ran to 2500 words covering 16 pages – was the humorist and architectural cartoonist Osbert Lancaster. His influence is clearly to be traced in one section of my essay, which DSR endorsed 'Hurray!' and read approvingly to my classmates:

> Passing up the Avenue, which is a well planned feature of the school, my eye lights next on the Headmaster's house. This is an extraordinary piece of architecture, possessing certain of the characteristics of Pont-Street Dutch, Tudor, pseudish, and Gothic-revival styles. Possibly Mr Lancaster, with his customary wit, would refer to it as 'pedagogic transitional' or 'head-magisterial baroque'. I, who am less ambitious, merely remark that is 'queer' externally, while unknown to me internally.

Looking at buildings, like visiting picture galleries, was to remain an abiding interest which I owe, like so much else, to David Roberts, and I find that, under his influence, I even ended up taking a rosy view of the future of the school, which earlier in my career I would have been happy to see demolished:

> My general conclusion at the end of this survey is that though the school has many faults, architecturally, it might be very much worse. Ambitious town-planners hope to build garden-cities in place of the dreary dwellings which cover vast areas of our industrial areas today. I hope that by means of the improvements I have suggested Christ's Hospital may become a garden-school. If the ex-playing fields on which at present crops are grown, can, after the war, be converted into shady gardens for the service of the whole community, and many of the dingy and haphazard parts of the grounds...can be likewise altered, this dream may well be realised.

Like the reconstruction of British cities, plans for the re-shaping of the educational system were very much in the news in 1943 and the following year saw the passage of a major Education Act remembered by the name of its chief author, RA (later Lord) Butler. The whole subject had already been discussed by the Study Group to which I belonged and DSR, as part of his policy of introducing us to new ideas, now encouraged us to read the work of such pioneers, or revolutionaries, as AS Neill and the American Homer Lane. Unhappy as I had been, and, out of the classroom still was, at Housie, I eagerly explored every alternative to what was, despite the school's unique entrance system, in many respects a traditional public school. I soon decided, however, that Neill's assertion that 'There are no problem children, only problem parents' was an over-simplification, worth saying, to promote thought, but intrinsically unsound. I realised even at 17 that Neill's doctrine of total freedom, both inside and outside the classroom, though conceivably helpful to a disturbed minority, would, for the vast majority, be a recipe for disaster. I was much more taken with other educational innovations we now heard of for the first time, like the Dalton System, whereby children were encouraged to select their own subjects and decide their own rate of progress, and I became a great enthusiast for continuing education for those who had missed their chance at the proper time. We bandied about names like Dartington Hall, residential establishments which catered for adults without formal qualifications, and the Cambridgeshire Village Colleges, then bringing part-time further education to the countryside. (These were the educational equivalent to the 'Peckham Experiment', another name then constantly on progressive lips, whereby health care was being provided for a whole community in South East London through a single, free, centre.) The ideas which seemed so exciting then are now commonplace, given concrete form in institutions like the Open University and the National Health Service, but co-education is still far from universal. In 1943, however, it seemed to sum up the changes of which I, at least, dreamed. With the new post-war world ahead, everything seemed possible. I remember reading that Bible of the Labour movement, RH Tawney's *Equality*, published in 1931, and eagerly discussing the then popular proposal for retaining the public schools but undermining their class basis by increasing the number of free places, an idea later given respectable, almost official, status in the Fleming Report published in 1944. I did not then foresee that education would be a continuing thread throughout my life, both professionally, through involvement with schools television and radio, and personally, through being married to one schoolmistress and father to another, but I felt already that change in this area was fundamental to the new society I wished to see created.

The essay in which I set down my thoughts on 'Present Discontents in Education', in November 1942, was less judicial than it might have been a few months later, but even longer than my *magnum opus* on the school's architecture, running to 4,200 words, as substantial as a chapter in an average book. What now surprises me, however, is not its sheer bulk but the amount of research involved. I had, I find, mastered the difference between 'Part II' education authorities, responsible for both secondary and elementary schools, and 'Part III', only controlling the latter, and established the academic background of all the Presidents of the Board of Education, discovering that 'of 19 Presidents to date only one came from an elementary school and he remained only a few months'. Of the seven since 1931 'three went to Clifton, Upppingham and Marlborough respectively, the other four to Eton and Oxford'. There were, though I failed to make the point, no Old Blues among them.

I can still read this essay, the most solid piece of work I was to complete until my first book several years later, without embarrassment, indeed it to some extent anticipated the recommendations of the Butler Act and has to a considerable extent been adopted as national policy. It began in the best General Paper tradition with a quotation from Matthew Arnold, which would, I hope, lead the reader to deduce that I knew that he was not merely a poet but a school inspector and son of the great reformer of the public schools, Thomas Arnold.

'A system founded on inequality,' said Matthew Arnold, 'is against nature and in the long run breaks down.' Our educational system is an extraordinary compromise between equality and inequality, with the latter in preponderance.

I went on to support the selection at the age of ten or eleven, based on a written examination to test knowledge, an interview to assess personality, and an intelligence test to provide an objective indication of potential, even suggesting the use of school records to identify bad examinees and a further transfer at 14, though I took no account of the practical difficulties, for those who slipped though the net. Bolder than RA Butler, and, of course, uninhibited by the cost involved, I urged the extension of the period of education at both ends, with kindergartens available from the age of three – another fruit of our extensive reading, this time about the Froebel system of nursery education – and a school-leaving age of around 17, with the option from 16 of part-time attendance. I urged that 'all schools...should be placed on a national register' and 'have to submit to inspection by government authorities', as has indeed happened since, and, less defensibly, I now feel, gave short shrift to the odd, untrained eccentric who provided the backbone of so many private schools and even managed to get on the staff at Housie. 'It need hardly be said that...unqualified teachers would not be allowed in any school.' I cheerfully proposed the abolition of the independent schools – 'The private and public schools, run for profit very largely, would take their place in the unified organisation' – and brushed aside the problem of church schools, that rock of conviction or bigotry on which so many education Bills had foundered:

As for that terror of political agents and politicians, 'The Roman Catholic vote', I should try to disregard it. I do not believe that countless children's futures should be jeopardised for the sake of a handful of Papists.

The universal state system which I wished to see imposed was based, as the Butler Act subsequently proposed, though it left the independent and church schools in existence, on three separate educational streams. The first led, via the selective grammar school, to an unchanged School Certificate and either to university or to leaving school at any age from 17 to 19. The second, 'a greatly improved elementary school' would lead to leaving school at 16 or 17. The third, the technical schools envisaged but, unhappily, never created by the Butler Act, were designed to take from the elementary school or grammar school at 14 children with a marked, but non-academic aptitude, to provide specialist training as a preliminary to a variety of apprenticeships at both the 'craft' and 'student' level, around the age of 17.

DSR took all this in good part apart from my dismissal of what I described as 'those blasphemously named educational exiles, the Church schools', commenting that 'There are two sides to this question' and adding a derisive question mark to my assertion that 'my conclusions were reached after considerable thought'. What strikes me, however, on re-reading this massive essay, is how little 'the Christ's Hospital solution' to the nation's educational needs appealed to me and how my conclusions reflected the mental climate of the time. My essay was written only a week or two before the publication of the Beveridge Report at a time when every by-election reflected the country's desire for radical change. It represents a fair statement not merely of my political opinions but, I suspect, of those of millions of others at this time:

> Finally, all this reorganisation will be useless if there is not a corresponding improvement of conditions in other branches of our life. Free milk is only a poor substitute for proper feeding at home...The finest school buildings will be of little value if their occupants spend their nights huddled with several other people into some dark and filthy room of a slum. Nothing can be so discouraging for a child as to see his father doing nothing, not because he wants to but because society has nothing for him to do...Such an example will not inspire the child to work hard. It is to be hoped that the Means Test and other social abominations, described with such bitter poignancy by Walter Greenwood in *His Worship the Mayor, Love on the Dole* and *The Secret Kingdom,* will never again make justice a mockery in this country. Towns must be replanned, too; for some children their only experience of a river is some evil smelling, dye-poisoned, dark and filthy stream bearing with it the offal and refuse of all the paths it passes in some grimy, despairing, smoke-choked industrial city. Such a child is hardly likely to appreciate Milton's description of the Severn in *Comus,* with its lovely beginning
>> Sabrina fair, listen where thou art sitting
>> Under the glassy, cool, translucent wave.[1]

DSR's reaction to my evocation of life in an industrial town, no doubt inspired by photographs in that highly influential magazine of the time *Picture Post*, was unkind: 'Too smelly'. He left my peroration unchallenged, however, and did not accuse me of the heinous fault of 'dragging in' the references to Walter

Greenwood and Milton, designed to demonstrate how widely I had read. Perhaps he was disarmed by my flattering reference to his profession. After five days of work by the artists and builders to create a suitable environment, I wrote, 'on the sixth day the teacher, the only real essential of an educational system, takes over', and it was thanks to his efforts that 'on the seventh day we may rest content with our labours'. At all events he did not discourage what now seems to me to have been an almost obsessive interest in education and around the same time set me a question which was almost an invitation to self-indulgence: 'What have 12 years of education done for me?'

The result has proved useful in writing the present book, giving as it does my response to Housie *at the time*. Most evaluations of a Christ's Hospital career have been attempted years later from the standpoint of maturity. Looking at this early essay in autobiography I am impressed by the degree of insight it reveals, while distressed by the occasional signs of priggishness. There are passages which would have won the warm approval of the most conventional Victorian teacher:

> In the 12 years during which I have been at school I have come to realise the value of out-of-school work. It is obvious that a valuable lesson has been learned, for in times of difficulty the man who is prepared to do just the little extra that the law does not demand of him will save a business or a nation.

About School Certificate, constantly amended since 1943, and always, in my view, for the worse, I was as enthusiastic as the most old-fashioned examiner could have wished:

> While preparing for this examination I was, naturally, one of its harshest critics. Now with it safely behind me, I am quite as eloquent in its defence and, I think, with more justification. First, it provided a very powerful incentive to work; second, it made inevitable a certain amount of self-imposed work; third, it provided me with some experience of an examination, which...will be of great value later on; finally, despite a great deal of 'cramming', some of what I learned, from the set books in particular, will remain fixed in my mind.

About the institution which had affected me most I had no doubts:

> Much of this essay was written in the library and it is, I think, fitting that the story of what my education has meant to me should be written there, for the last three of these 12 years have taught me its value. The library possesses an air of culture, an indefinable but all important atmosphere of learning, which I have discovered nowhere else...Often I have gone into the library

intending to work or read some fixed book and often I have just wandered round the shelves 'browsing'.

I was equally clear about the worst feature of Housey life and all the frustrations and humiliations of the preceding six years now found expression in what was less a balanced judgement than a propagandist diatribe:

> The criticism frequently levelled, that the public school exaggerates the importance of physical education and makes the athlete a greater hero than the intellectual is justified...It may seem heresy to the advocates of compulsory games, to those who would turn out a race physically superb but devoid of intelligence, to those who would rather that their sons at the university obtained their Blue for cricket or rugger or rowing than that they should obtain a good degree, to all those who consider Grace a superman and Shakespeare 'just another writer', to those to whom 'Play the game!' is a sacred exhortation and 'not cricket' a lasting condemnation, to those whom the public schools have turned out who have become governors of the outposts of the Empire and have spread cricketing metaphor and contempt of Britain over many corners of the globe. The government of these last has been distinguished only for its incompetence, its complete failure to understand the native; of this the disastrous campaign in Malaya, when the population would not come to our aid, is the best example.

Much of this was, I now recognise, unfair, though I still stand by my conclusion:

> From this impassioned cloud of words my heresy emerges: that the task of games is to keep the schoolboy active and healthy enough to do his schoolwork; that they have never been and never will be an end in themselves; that the public school, now assailed on all sides, would gain a new lease of life for itself by throwing this ballast of games tradition overboard; that games cannot justify their existence by the plea that they provide 'team spirit'...and their chief use in many schools at the moment is to keep the pupils occupied...If a school such as this cannot really think of anything better to do with its pupils on five or six afternoons a week...the public school is doomed and justly so.

The response of several masters to such sentiments would have been outrage and a complaint to my housemaster. DSR contented himself with such marginal comments as 'Unfair?' 'Very phoney' and the final condemnation 'TBM', which, as I have described, stood for 'Thomas Bablington Macaulay'. He left unchallenged my analysis of the benefits I attributed to having come to Housie:

First, come the non-scholastic achievements. By being away from home I think I have probably acquired more self-reliance than if I had gone to a day school. I have received some experience of life in a small community, where it is difficult if not impossible to get away from the 50 other boys with whom you are herded for periods of three months at a time...Though this existence may have made me more sociable, I am inclined to think it has acted more in the other direction, to make me retreat into myself or the make-believe world of books.

I rather doubt if I have become more tolerant during my time here...Certainly I have become more ready to accept other people's peculiarities, but that is...merely toleration enforced by the circumstances, and not a great change of attitude. Possibly I have become broader-minded, but that is a dangerous phrase. I would rather have definite views of my own and be called a bigot than none at all.

I summed up with what seems in the circumstances a remarkably mild conclusion:

On the whole I have enjoyed being educated, though I do not know that if suddenly faced again with the choice of school I should reply so glibly [as I had in 1936] 'CH of course!'

Even more than its predecessor, this was a year of intellectual enrichment, by far the most formative of my life. Economics was not then taught at Housie, but I find page after page of well organised notes enunciating such basic principles as 'Wealth is made up, not of things, but of economic values attaching to things', and similarly succinct summaries define socialism and communism. Pacifism had never attracted me, but in that Lent Term of 1943 I wrote a review of a powerful anti-war novel, Richard Aldington's *Death of a Hero*, first published in 1929 at the peak of the 'Peace at any price' period. DSR's strictures on over-stating one's case were clearly having some effect. I find that I substituted for my initial verdict 'This is a great book' the distinctly feebler 'This is a book worth writing and reviewing.' I could not resist, however, the temptation to quote in full sentences which had appealed to me, like Aldington's somewhat absurd suggestion; 'We should turn churches into temples to Venus and set up a statue to Havelock Ellis,' another writer I had just discovered. It now seems strange to have been reading in the middle of the Second World War so many books prompted by the First. I read about the same time AP Herbert's moving novel about a man shot for cowardice, *The Secret Battle* (1919), and Beverley Nichols's hysterical *Cry Havoc!*, published in 1933, a denunciation of arms-dealers, who were labelled, in just the type of phrase that had once appealed to me, 'Merchants of Death'. Beverley Nichols, though his *Twenty-Five* (1926) was the first book to put in my mind writing an autobiography restricted to the early years of one's life, seemed to me unbalanced. He was later to be briefly a passionate advocate of the highly suspect Oxford Group. I held no brief for international capitalism but had too much sense to blame it for Hitler and it might, I had reluctantly realised, sometimes be necessary to fight. '*Cry Havoc!*, with its morbid, purposeless, revelling in the horror of war seems mean and contemptible.' 'Unfair' cried DSR in the margin, but for once I was right and he was wrong.

    I learned much that year from Roy Macklin, with whom we seem to have spent a lot of time, English being regarded as useful for the General Paper which all of us, whatever our subjects, would have soon to sit. Here we could largely choose our own syllabus and, at the suggestion of Bob Pitman, who, for the only time in my school career was in the same class as me, we studied 'The Housey school', that 'golden generation' of writers of whom Christ's Hospital was so proud. We were also instructed to seek out and study some writer new to us. I selected TS Eliot, then regarded as the last word in modernism, and it must I think have been somewhat to my parents' bewilderment, if they dipped into one of my chosen presents at Christmas 1942, that I asked for his *Later Poems*, followed four months later by his *Poems 1909-1925*, which I bought for myself. (Even the somewhat cramped wartime volume cost 3s 6d [17.5p], an appreciable sum when my whole term's pocket money was only 15s [75p]; the council had not increased it as I grew older.) I can recall – indeed have recorded in my exercise books at the time – my mixed reaction to Eliot, combining delight and irritation, delight at such accessible works as *The Love Song of J. Alfred Prufrock* and striking lines like 'April is the cruellest month' which begins *The Waste Land*, and irritation at the incomprehensible foreign names and words which appear later in the same poem. Eliot's provision of explanatory notes to his own lines in my eyes compounded the original offence, a view time has not changed, though it now seems they were added to pad out the original text to a more publishable length.

    Roy Macklin was still stalwartly trying to improve my style and refine my judgement. When I began an essay on the promising, if un-Housie like, subject of 'Women' with the sentence 'The first duty of a woman was once to be ornamental' he dismissed this opening as 'Vague and unhistorical', a cruel thrust at a History Grecian, while when I referred to 'the Victorian twilight' he demanded: 'Why this figure of speech?' Overall my essay rated a beta – another sign of our progress was that we were now marked, as at the universities, with letters from the Greek alphabet – but his final judgement was, as always, balanced and no doubt well deserved:

> Good in many ways. Vigorous, at times sweeping, but generally interesting. You still say things because you like the sound of them, or even (Notice this!) because you have heard them said elsewhere.

Housie, as I have already mentioned, attached great importance to letter-writing, but I find it surprising even so that in July 1943, when I was 17-and-a-half and my classmates all around the same age, that we were still being drilled in this elementary discipline. Macklin clearly took it very seriously. I find that, in his eyes, I wrote a 'quite good' letter to the Clerk of the Horsham Magistrates Court, explaining my inability to attend when charged with a cycling offence, though the experience did not bring me much benefit for when I had to send such a letter in real life, as an undergraduate, I was still fined the sizeable sum of 30 shillings (£1.50). He thought my effort merely 'fair' when I wrote a letter to an imaginary doctor to enquire about my mother's health, and positively 'ponderous' when approaching my vicar for a testimonial. An apology for failing to attend a party – 'I was called suddenly to an interview in London and in the haste of my departure I must confess that my engagement for the afternoon quite slipped my mind' – which merited the same criticism, was considered 'Fairly good' but marked only 'Beta minus', a poor performance for a Lamb Essay prize winner. The truth was I regarded such exercises as beneath my dignity and a diversion from more interesting work.

For in our English lessons that year, General Paper material or not, there was much to enjoy. We earnestly attempted, and abandoned, as Macklin himself confessed he had done, *Paradise Lost*. We read, inevitably, Jane Austen. 'Good. Shows feeling,' was Macklin's response to my subsequent essay, from him the highest praise. We read Virginia Woolf, not merely her novels, to which I failed to warm, but her collections of feminist essays, *A Room of One's Own*, published in 1929, which has since been regarded as a milestone on the progress towards women's rights, and *Three Guineas*, these being used to introduce a discussion on the status of women. We also read James Joyce's *Portrait of the Artist as a Young Man*, but not *Ulysses*, which had become notorious following its publication in Paris in 1921, and was still unobtainable, as a 'dirty book', though Macklin consoled us by telling us it was largely impenetrable and that its successor, *Finnegan's Wake*, was even worse. (He was, I confirmed a few years later, absolutely right.) We must have read some Hardy for we certainly consulted Lord David Cecil's classic *Hardy the Novelist*, published that year, though, curiously, I can find in my notes no reference to Trollope, who has given me even more pleasure over the years.

Looking back I am amazed at how much, considering the demands of the Home Guard, my duties in the house, and, always and inevitably, games I managed to read between my seventeenth and eighteenth birthdays, and most of it between January and July 1943. In April I began to keep a book labelled 'Quotations', no doubt with a view to memorising them for the General Paper to be sat in September, setting out on the inside of the cover one of DSR's favourite maxims, taken from CP Scott – DSR was a natural *Manchester Guardian* reader – 'Facts are sacred, comment is free' – and one I had found for myself, taken from the medieval theologian Peter Abelard: 'We are led to enquire, by enquiry we perceive the truth.' Whether the extracts which I thought worth recording lived up these high sentiments seems less certain, but the sources reveal the range of my reading and the width of my interests. From the then popular novelist Eric Linklater I borrowed an aphorism attributed to Lenin: 'Work was my autobiography' and an observation I now find somewhat puzzling: 'Marx didn't say that a man must change his mind every time he changes his shirt.' In addition to Linklater I read other undemanding novelists – Howard Spring, Clemence Dane, Henry Williamson and – a major enthusiasm of mine at one time – Doreen Wallace, a Somerville graduate who wrote somewhat soil-bound, rather than earthy, novels about Suffolk. I make less apology for having enjoyed another 'country' writer, Mary Webb and, a particular favourite ever since, Rose Macaulay. I also, like any other progressive minded schoolboy, read a good deal of HG Wells, though I had no interest in what would now be called science fiction, and preferred such 'straight' novels as *Ann Veronica* (1909) and *Joan and Peter* (1918). I now find his books hard going but at the time the feeling that he was on the right, ie progressive, side, made me blind to their defects and from one of them I noted the sentence: 'The fear of the undergraduate is the beginning of fame.' I am still not quite sure what it means but, hoping at that time soon to be an undergraduate, decided it merited preserving.

Very much of the period were the numerous quotations I took from the writings of Professor CEM Joad, then enjoying a great vogue as resident philosopher of the BBC's radio *Brains Trust,* and I now discovered one of the joys familiar to every keen reader of how one book leads on to another. From Eliot's poetry I moved to his *Idea of a Christian society* (1940), and that curious novel by 'Baron Corvo' (ie FW Rolfe), *Hadrian the Seventh*, published in 1904, led on to AJA Symons's *The Quest for Corvo*, which appeared exactly 30 years later.

DSR encouraged us to read books about the writing of history as well as factual textbooks and it was due to him that I discovered what has since become a favourite text, Herbert (later Sir Herbert) Butterfield's *The Whig Interpretation of History*, published in 1931. Butterfield's thesis was that it was important to view events from the standpoint of their time and not, like Victorian historians, only praise rulers who brought their societies closer to their own ideal, that of a Liberal-minded, constitutional democracy. I did not respond as intended, deciding that in fact this was an admirable test to apply. I was also much taken with a famous dictum of Lord Acton, Professor of Modern History at Cambridge around the turn of the century, who had told his students not to be afraid to make moral judgements but – I may have altered the precise words slightly – 'Always apply the test you would use in your own lives.' Here was a doctrine that immediately appealed to me, the historian as avenger, righting posthumously the wrongs of earlier ages.

A moral issue much debated at the time, to which I shall refer again, was how the Germans should be treated after the war. In 1943 we had yet to suffer the totally indiscriminate and pointless bombardment by the flying-bombs and rockets of 1944-45, and the horrifying discovery in the liberated extermination camps of how this supposedly civilised race had set out to destroy another. I had never subscribed to the 'pity the poor Germans' theory fashionable in some quarters and thought it more than a coincidence that my father should have had to serve in one war against them and my generation in another. I therefore read with warm approval the autobiography of the historian EL Woodward, published in 1942, and was much taken with his profound anti-German feeling, based not on the ephemeral chauvinism of wartime but on a deep knowledge of German history and of his own observations in Germany before 1914. When he predicted that 'Within a decade...the Germans will try once again the plan which succeeded so well during the interval between the two wars...to "organise sympathy"' I fervently agreed.

My distrust of the Germans led to my only real disagreement with Roy Macklin. He was highly critical of my enthusiasm for Lord Vansittart's *Black Record*, which had caused a sensation on its first appearance in 1941 for its denunciation of Germany as 'the butcher-bird of Europe'. Vansittart had cited authorities from Roman times onward in support of his case but Macklin dismissed it as unsound and unhistorical and argued that the Germans could not be held to blame for their past. I disagreed then and disagree still.

---

[1] 'A Mask presented at Ludlow Castle' 1634

45

SCHOLARSHIP

For an English Essay: Scholarship.

Oxford University scholarship examination paper, September 1943

The summer term of 1943 was, as I well realised, crucial to my school career for it was the last before the Oxford scholarship exam in September on which my whole future depended. It was also to prove one of the most miserable. My friend and champion Bob Pitman had left at the end of the previous term to attend a university short course, and he was succeeded by the only house-captain of my seven years in Peele A with whom I did not get on. A keen sportsman, and popular extrovert, he had come top of the poll in Noel's experiment in democracy, which, incidentally, he had not repeated, a year before. Noel accepted his recommendation to appoint to the monitorial vacancy, which was clearly mine by right of seniority in the school and house, another boy, junior to me, whom I had always disliked. It was clear from the start that, despite working for a scholarship and serving in the Home Guard I could expect no concessions from the new regime. I found myself sentenced by our new house-captain for some no doubt trivial offence – it cannot have been serious for I was always law-abiding – to half an hour's 'rolling'. Normally this was undertaken by several boys, as a summer term variant on the usual 'Post Offices' etc, but I had to perform it alone. So I trudged up and down between the shafts like an animal, not so much wearied as humiliated, helping to maintain a cricket pitch on which, too senior for a junior team and too incompetent for a senior one, I was most unlikely ever to play. Pulling a roller, I later discovered, had been a punishment inflicted, sometimes until the victim died, in the German concentration camps.[*] I bitterly resented the experience then and resent it still, believing that in no other school in the country could a boy of my age and in my situation have been subjected to such treatment. Here

---

[*] A survivor described witnessing such a scene in *The Road to Auschwitz*, broadcast in June 1993 on Radio 4.

was Christ's Hospital, in its obsessive passion for punishment and its readiness to treat a 17-and-a-half year old like a naughty small child, at its very worst.

My real crime, of course, was not being good at games, although, thanks to the war, that great liberator, I was, along with other non-games players, on some games afternoons able to escape to help on local farms. No transport was provided – we were, after all, merely helping the war effort, not going to play a match against another school – but I was able to seize the opportunity thanks to Miss Harvie, who generously lent me her bicycle. At first I felt somewhat embarrassed at riding a woman's machine but I soon looked forward to afternoons of cycling through the surrounding countryside to undertake work which though heavy, for the Sussex clay was unrelenting and clung to the games clothes and rugger boots we wore, was at least useful. The farmer for whom we principally worked seemed to welcome us almost as much for our company as our labour and often joined in our conversation as we hacked away at his weeds or lifted his potatoes. Far from being the old-fashioned Tory I had expected he turned out to hold radical, if not revolutionary, views with a deep distrust of the government and indeed of all authority. I realised then, as I have confirmed since, that the alleged Conservatism, at least in the political sense, of all those who live in rural areas is a myth, though no doubt true of the comfortably-off minority. Farm work brought other benefits, since we actually received a small payment for it, which, along with some unspent Home Guard subsistence, meant that for the first time I had a few shillings to supplement my minuscule pocket money from Newbury Council.

Most of my time in the classroom that term was spent in receiving tuition. I still have an essay, dated 5 May 1943, answering the question 'Why did the Normans ultimately fail in Sicily and succeed in England?' dotted with observations on both content and style. The very first sentence was criticised on the latter ground because I had used the words 'main' and 'remain' in close conjunction, and later passages were sidelined with such comments as 'You don't develop the geographical situation' or 'Is this to the point?' The following day my efforts to consider the proposition 'In William the Conqueror, William II and Henry I can be seen the Norman at his best and worst' produced a flurry of marginal notes and later that month an essay on the Crusades was endorsed: 'Not a bad discussion, but you are quite unscrupulous in your treatment of the papacy'. Knowledge, balance, presentation, all three were demanded and DSR was no doubt trying to turn out good historians as well as get us into Oxford or Cambridge. I am still struck by how hard I worked that summer, writing a whole essay on some new subject nearly every day, often packed with fact and of substantial length. A typical question, 'In what ways did Henry II restore strong government between 1154 and 1170?' yielded six close-packed pages, which DSR described as 'In general a good account, well put except for some VVH expressions'. 'VVH', a typical DSR abbreviation, stood for 'Very very horrid', an instance being where I had written 'Henry made a move towards that date'. Inadequate research was dealt with with equal sternness. Another essay on Henry II provoked a long quotation from a book I should have consulted and a characteristic question such as all too few historians ask themselves often enough: 'Legal Reforms of Henry II. *What were* they?'

Thanks to my miserable situation in Peele A, neither monitor nor normal subordinate, subject to a housemaster and house-captain with whom I felt nothing in common, my self-confidence reached a low ebb in the second half of that summer term and plunged still further as the result of our termly exam in history, a dress rehearsal for the 'real thing', set by an outside examiner. I was mortified to attract more criticism than any of my four fellow candidates, especially for my General Paper, on which I was relying for extra marks to make up for any failings, caused by my truncated course, in my history papers. I had, I realised, made a mistake when asked to write of a favourite novelist in choosing a somewhat minor figure, Francis Brett Young, author of such works as *My Brother Jonathan* (1928) and *Dr Bradley Remembers* (1935). I knew his work better than that of more substantial writers such as Hardy, but it was a tactical misjudgement none the less and DSR having sung the praises beforehand of the man who had judged me so severely I became depressed about my prospects. Nor did I enjoy the work which filled the last few weeks of term, devoted to medieval German history, using a textbook written by a man of vast learning but a total lack of ability to express himself. It was perhaps no bad thing to be reminded that history could be written so badly that one had to wrestle with the text to extract every fact, and DSR did his best to present the subject in lively terms, drawing attention to the disagreements between the historians concerned, some German and some English, with, to add further piquancy, different interpretations from the 'Oxford men' and the 'Cambridge men'. History as controversy was very much to my taste, but encouraged my natural tendency towards diffuseness. 'Seven and a half pages,' commented DSR at the end of what now seems an interminable essay on medieval Germany. 'Do you need it all?'

Apart from the regular departure of older boys for the forces the war affected us little that summer, and Double Summer Time made even the black-out more acceptable. There was one major fund-raising effort, as *The Blue* reported:

> On May 19th Big School was again full of the clamour of the fair as money poured in in aid of the Red Cross...A total of over £64 was counted. A short programme of songs, dances and recitations was given by children of the estate in Mr Codd's garden on June 19th. £5 was raised in aid of the Horsham 'Wings for Victory' Week.[1]

The *Notes and News* feature set out other sacrifices now being demanded. 'Owing to insufficient supplies of petrol, each house has been made responsible for the mowing of the lawns fronting their own block...At the beginning of term it was decided not to use the hard court, owing to the wear and tear caused to gym-shoes.'

Tennis had never rated very high among school activities, but more alarming was the war's effect on Speech Day. 'The break in tradition of ceremony and programme was very noticeable...We missed the governors' procession...and the few words we have come to expect from the Lord Major.' We had our own explanation of why this distinguished visitor had to leave early, blaming not wartime necessity but a weak bladder. Even so we had done better than our sister Blues at Hertford, where the Lord Major and Sheriffs failed to turn up at all. There were also echoes of the war in the formation of a Young Farmers Club, already mentioned, which was soon breeding rabbits and poultry, though these never reached the tables of Dining Hall, and the news that the ATC had reached a new peak of membership, 75. 'We have,' the squadron's chronicler reported, 'been issued with a .303 Browning Machine-gun and have had a bomb sight on loan,' while an Old Blue wing-commander had returned to talk about 'his exploits as a fighter-pilot in Malta and elsewhere'.

Just before the end of term I filled in my entry form for the scholarship exam in the group of colleges holding its examination in September, opting for Worcester as my first choice and Exeter as my second, to avoid competing with anyone else from Housie. I welcomed the choice of Worcester College, where Bob Pitman had just gained his classics exhibition, or minor scholarship, and accepted DSR's advice that, after only a year's preparation, it would be over ambitious to attempt the most academically prestigious college, Balliol. I later wrote a somewhat romantic account in *First Bloom* of the last night of that summer term, when I watched the sun set over Sharpenhurst – 'Brackenhurst' in the novel – with a close friend. 'Behind them,' I wrote, 'the last glow died over Brackenhurst, and the deepening twilight spread wraith-like over Sussex.' I added, at the start of the next chapter, 'It often seemed to James...that the sun which set on Middlestone on that July evening, rose next on Oxford.'

This was a simplification, for a period of intensely hard work lay between the two events, as, after two weeks of idleness, I devoted every moment to intensive revision. In our small, all-purpose sitting room there was barely room to spread out my books and it was impossible to remain undisturbed for long, but my father, so far as he could, put the studio over his shop at my disposal, trying to arrange appointments with customers for the afternoon. Occasionally he was forced to make one in the morning and I would then gather up the weighty volumes of the *Cambridge Medieval History* and move downstairs to the shop until the photographic session was over.

Mostly, however, I was left alone to my books and, such was my absorption in them, that I was hardly aware of the young women who shared the behind-the-shop facilities from the ladies' hairdressers next door. A more serious threat to my concentration was the school having issued an edict, in its lordly fashion, that all senior boys were to devote their holidays to helping on the land, happily without making the arrangements for us. Conscious that I was already, in the Home Guard, ATC and in farm work, doing at least as much as any other 17 year old to help win the war, and that the chance to enter Oxford would not come again, I simply ignored the order. As a precaution, I created a fictitious account of having helped to bring in the harvest, complete with the name of the nearest farmer, but the subject was never raised.

DSR had advised me to spend the afternoons in the fresh air and, my brother being now in the Middle East, I was able to use his bicycle to visit country churches, then invariably open and almost always empty. It was an ideal recreation, for apart from military vehicles, usually American, the roads were almost deserted, while the churches I inspected, often Norman or Early English, helped to keep alive my interest in both medieval history and architecture.

To ensure that during these weeks my power of self-expression did not grow rusty, DSR had instructed me to write to him at his home in Wales every few days, generously giving up his own free time to reply fully, and sometimes critically, to every letter. I have no record of what I wrote but I have kept his answers. 'Dear Longmate', he wrote on 3 August 1943 – I did not become 'Dear Norman' until after I had left – 'I did enjoy your letter and I do prefer your epistolary style!', no doubt a back-handed reference to some over-written essay. He went on to take me to task for an admittedly ridiculous comparison I had made between William the Conqueror and a former Borstal Boy whose autobiography he had encouraged me to read. Later he described how he had 'bristled' at the treatment of education in the recently published White Paper, *Reconstruction in Education*, the forerunner of the Butler Act. He went on to list, having dismissed a Stella Benson novel he had just read, 'the many more interesting books lying about the house', which included two much praised titles of that period, Eve Curie's *Journey Amongst Warriors* and the French resistance novel *Le Silence de la Mer*. His next letter, on 11 August, included a helpful quotation from EM Forster and praise of Max Beerbohm's *Zuleika Dobson*. I never came to share DSR's admiration for the rest of Beerbohm's work, but I was intrigued to learn that his own tutor at Trinity had known Beerbohm well, a glimpse into the academic world far removed from Camp Close and the shop in Northbrook Street. I had recently read Alec Waugh's public school novel, *The Loom of Youth*, published in 1917, and DSR now admitted that he had been 'very excited about it' when he read it and, in another of those behind-the-scenes glimpses I so much enjoyed, revealed that the original of one of the characters at the imaginary Fernhurst, a particularly tough member of staff was, as I have mentioned earlier, the father of a somewhat similar master at Housie. 'I wonder if this war will produce anything like it,' mused DSR. 'On the whole I doubt it.' I did not tell him that I was already planning a similar work on Housie and had a notebook full of character sketches for the purpose.

That same letter contained an extract from one of James Elroy Flecker's poems, *The Painter's Mistress*, later a favourite of my own, and a helpful, quotable, comment from the critic and poet Humbert Wolfe, who 'said that JEF's muse had dropped him halfway up Parnassus', a fair assessment in my judgement and eminently useful for the General Paper. At the very end came a reference to the purpose of our correspondence. 'I heard from Scroggs', a fellow historian, in the group ahead of me, who had recently tried for Cambridge. 'He says there were fifteen in for three awards at Sidney [ie Sidney Sussex College], that he thought he might have done worse but was a bit sapped in confidence by the competent appearance of his rivals. Don't you worry about appearances.' My future friend Peter Scroggs's judgement proved sound. He was one of the successful candidates and later we were to work together on a television history series to which his former Cambridge tutor, now Master of the college, was adviser.

The writer Vita Sackville-West is now best known for her eccentric personal relationships but in 1943 was still being judged on her work. I find that DSR shared my high opinion of her novels, *The Edwardians* (1930) and *All Passion Spent* (1931), while I had greatly enjoyed her long poem, *The Land*, published in 1926 and then enjoying a new vogue as part of the wartime enthusiasm for all things rural. In the same letter he gave a rare description of his life in Wales, clearly very different from mine in Newbury. 'From our drawing room window I can see Rhuddlan Castle,' he wrote, going on to recount how as a child he had thought Edward I vastly inferior in importance to his own father, who was, as I have described, a Liberal MP. 'An enormous tablet let into the wall of a minute cottage' near the family home, announced that 'Here Edward I held his Parliament'. John Herbert Roberts, first Baron Clwyd, by contrast and more impressively, had 'legislated in St Stephen's, Westminster, under Big Ben'.

DSR's next letter, on 30 August, urged me to 'bully' the Newbury Public Library into buying a life of the archaeologist Arthur Evans, *Time and Chance*, but this was one piece of advice I did not take, archaeology never having made any appeal to me. I can enjoy now the irony of his quoting to me the discovery of 'Piltdown man', not far from Horsham, as proof of its importance, a classic find now discredited as a fake.

The General Paper was not forgotten. I was urged to find out more about Augustus John, whom DSR clearly admired, Romilly John's *Seventh Child* being recommended for 'vivid glimpses' of her father, and William Rothenstein's *Men and Letters*. There was also a mention of *Horizon*, the great literary magazine of the time, which it would clearly do me no harm to mention.

Much of this letter, with my rendezvous at Oxford only a week or so away, was devoted to last-minute advice:

> Go up with your tongue in your cheek, enjoy yourself, write naturally but be careful about letting your pen get control and like Hopkins [a reference now

lost on me] who thought he could not have made a greater mess of things, you may be surprised. But in any case I am not worrying; if you want to get to Oxford after the war there should be no great difficulty in getting you there if all these enlightened ideas of the new Education Bill go through. So don't get het up...Take your time. Three answers will see you through if they're interesting enough and don't plunge into any of the papers...Good luck...Don't forget:
1. 'History is a fickle jade.' (Herbert Butterfield, *Whig Interpretation of History*)
2. 'There are some historians who would make a hero of James I and geld Charles II.' (Horace Walpole)

Knowing how little money my family had to spare, I asked DSR's advice on the minimum needed for my brief stay in Oxford. 'I should think £3 would do,' he replied, 'but, if you can, take £5 and bring back the change.' He added one final, encouraging anecdote. The great historian HWC Davis, when facing the same challenge as myself, DSR reminded me, had said '"Well, I shan't see this place again, so I had better make the most of it while I'm here." But he did.'

Oxford was only 26 miles [42km] from Newbury and one afternoon my father and I went over to it on the bus and, for the first time, I saw the college to which I was applying and then walked the route to University College (Univ.) where all the candidates for the 'New College group' were to sit the scholarship exam. My father, I am sure, enjoyed the excursion, feeling that in ensuring that I could at least find my way around the city he was giving me some practical help and we walked through Christ Church Meadow in the sunshine, watching the cadets on university short courses under training. (One unmilitary-minded young man, to the delight of the bystanders, simply forgot his Bren Gun and had to be reminded by their helpful shouts to come back for it.)

I also, if *First Bloom* is to be trusted – I cannot now recall this reconnaissance – made a private visit by bicycle 'on a glorious day of late summer, with the wind as fresh as the earth, with the leaves stirring, and the sun adding colour to the scene'. My hero, James, apparently stopped at Abingdon to visit its fine, ancient church and to say a prayer for his success in the forthcoming trial, then 'swept along between the green covered hedges towards the city he was so shortly to storm'. There was a good deal of Jude the Obscure about my attitude at this time, though Oxford in the summer of 1943 was far from looking its best. Many buildings, like the Examination Schools in 'the High', as I learned to call it, had been requisitioned, along with parts of many of the colleges, including Worcester, while 'Air Raid Shelter' signs defaced the ancient stonework, and intrusive metal water tanks, labelled 'SWS', for 'Static Water Supply', were erected on the centuries' old lawns of the quadrangles. I ignored these imperfections and wandered about looking on the buildings, river, and open spaces, with all the naive rapture of a medieval scholar. Not for nothing had I recently read Helen Waddell's *The Wandering Scholars* (1927), another book which was soon to stand me in good stead.

Along with Housie, Oxford was to be the dominant influence in my life and in *First Bloom* I set down a detailed account of the impression it made upon my barely-fictionalised 17-year-old hero:

> So deep sunk was he in his meditations that the final turning came upon him unexpectedly. The road divided, to Boars Hill one way, to Oxford the other. He took the right fork and a few minutes later was riding past Christ Church, up St Aldates towards Carfax...Leaving the long grey front of Shelley's college [ie University] on his right, he rode down the High, 'the loveliest street in the world', as it has been called, and, having looked at Magdalen Tower to satisfy his curiosity as to why it should have come to represent for so many writers the essence of Oxford, he turned back the way he had come, along Longwall to the University Parks, where he ate his lunch, past the squat ugliness of Keble. He remembered as he looked at that gloomy monument to nineteenth century piety and munificence a remark of Williams about it: 'I don't put historians in for Keble. It was built for nonconformist parsons and was designed externally to mortify the spirit and internally to mortify the flesh!'

Although this remark has the authentic Roberts' ring he cannot have been unaware that Keble was a monument to the Oxford Movement, not nonconformity, and in the next round of scholarship examinations, he *did* put another of us in for Keble, where this pioneer duly won a scholarship. At the time, however, I rejoiced in the 'Oxfordness' of jokes at that college's expense. More positively, I was excited to be sitting my own exam in 'Univ', once home to Shelley, though I honoured him more as a rebel – the Rev Quick would have found him a tougher nut to crack than me, and Noel would, I am sure, have considered his attitude to house games distinctly unsatisfactory – than as a poet.

My account of leaving Oxford that afternoon is in the same vein as the description of my arrival, and would no doubt, had he ever seen it, have called forth some caustic comment about over-writing from Roy Macklin:

> He rode back along Keble Road to St Giles and then down again to Carfax. All the clocks in the world seemed to be striking three as he passed across St Aldates Bridge. A few moments later he paused on the hill that leads to the Abingdon road and looked back upon the most ancient of English university cities, now radiant in the August sun. He knew too few of the colleges to be able to identify the various spires and domes that were thrust against the sky, for the 'City of Spires' appeared at that moment to justify its name.

The beauty of the scene made his eyes glisten as he turned back to the road, murmuring as he went the words of Lionel Johnson's 'Oxford':[2]

> Over the four long years, and unknown powers
> Call to us, going forth upon our way;
> Ah! Turn we, and look back upon the towers,
> That rose about our lives and cheered the day...
> Think of her so! The wonderful, the fair,
> The immemorial and the ever young:
> The city, sweet with our forefathers' care;
> The city, where the Muses all have sung.
> Ill times may be; she hath no thought of time;
> She reigns beside the waters yet in pride.
> Rude voices cry; but in her ears the chime
> Of full, sad bells brings back her old springtide.

These lines, when I first read them, and especially the reference to 'ill times', for what could be more ill than a war? seemed to speak to me personally, like the sentence about Oxford by Max Beerbohm I treasured and often repeated mantra-like to myself: 'The mere sight of the name written, or sound of it spoken, is fraught for me with the most actual magic.'

My actual arrival a fortnight later was something of an anti-climax, but I enormously enjoyed having two rooms to myself and being waited on at meals in what then seemed to be the over-decorated hall of Worcester; it has indeed been much improved since. I was, happily not forced, as I had come from home, to wear Housey clothes and I do not think that by either dress – clothes rationing had been a great leveller – or accent, I betrayed that I came from a much humbler background than my rivals. It was pleasing to find that among those who had heard of it Christ's Hospital seemed to enjoy some grudging respect. I became quite friendly with one boy, from a provincial grammar school, who told me he had come to Oxford 'for a holiday more than anything else', and he was not, I think, among the successful candidates. He did, however, much impress me by his passion for the works of Oscar Wilde and if his reference to that author's homosexuality had some hidden significance I failed to respond to it.

Although we all did our best to treat each other with adult courtesy, we were well aware that we were rivals, for there were sixteen entrants competing for four awards, two of them open scholarships, the other two exhibitions, of somewhat lesser value and status but also providing a guaranteed place in the college. I had faced far worse odds in the Special Place examination seven years before and, as always, responded to the challenge of the occasion. DSR's strategy of teaching very thoroughly a limited range of subjects proved sound. I managed to find three questions, in both the English and European History papers, I could answer adequately, but could not even have attempted a fourth.

I felt I had done disappointingly in the General Paper and even worse in the Latin and German 'unseens', but came into my own on the final morning, when, according to *First Bloom*, I slipped away to visit the Shelley Memorial, a few yards away from the hall of 'Univ', while waiting for its doors to open:

> The exquisite cold white marble figure, lying as if the waves had lifted it up on to the black background of its pedestal, caught in its curves all the agony and beauty of Shelley's life and Shelley's poetry. Here was the poet returned to the place which had proved itself narrow and bigoted and had hurled him forth in ignominy. Here he whom the world had reviled, mocked and persecuted had, at last, as is the way with those whose only crime is their genius, outlived his tormentors, and lay in peace, honoured for all time and by all the world. The authorities who had allowed so wonderful a monument to be erected...had perhaps desired to remove that blot from their history, to make atonement on behalf of the university to the poet whose life had ended, so characteristically, in the stormy waters of a distant sea...the Ariel against whom so many Calibans had battled so long and, at the last, in vain.

This reminder of Shelley's triumph seemed to me a good omen and, as *First Bloom* records, sent my hero into the examination room in a suitably confident mood:

> James looked across the hall at the small oil painting of the poet that was one of the greatest treasures of the college and then, suddenly realising that this was the last paper...he glanced down at the sheet before him. His eye took in the words: 'For an English Essay – Scholarship'. No subject could have been chosen which was more perfectly in keeping with his mood and his knowledge. He began eagerly to make a note of points, and then with two and a half hours still before him, began to write...
>
> He wrote of Peter Abelard, the pattern of all scholarship...He extolled the virtues of a life devoted solely to the acquisition of knowledge materially worthless and he saw in casting light where before there had been darkness the justification of a life of undistinguished diligence. The Twelfth Century Renaissance was described with all the fervour he could command...'In this century', he wrote, 'there came into being the institution which was to prove the greatest legacy of the Middle Ages to Europe – the Universities. For reasons far to seek, hundreds of young men from all over Europe were moving towards a handful of intellectual Meccas – to Rheims, to Chartres, to Orleans, to Bologna, to Paris, to Oxford. Students crowded into the lecture room during the day, begged or borrowed money for their fees, and perhaps after a noisy brawl at a nearby tavern, would still stay up half the night copying manuscripts, for to a student greedy for knowledge any book was a feast of many tasting foods. To add to the itinerant populace of

Europe, the friars, and brigands, and merchants, there sprang into birth a new class – the wandering scholars.'

James tried to show the continuity of tradition between the wandering students and teachers of the twelfth century and the scholars of the twentieth. He quoted with approval the precept of Abelard: 'We ought in all things to have recourse to reason, for the voice of reason is the voice of God!', and, a little later, 'A doctrine is not to be believed because God has said it, but because we are convinced by reason that it is so!' Finally, after a cautious reference to the other side of medieval thought, typified by Aquinas and Anselm, he came to the last sentence of the essay and wrote of 'The never to be forgotten cry: "Turpe nescire!" – "Shameful to be ignorant!"'

He handed in his paper as twelve o'clock was striking and walked out into the High feeling that at last he had brought forth the best that was in him.

Looking back I can realise that it was no bad thing to have sung the praises of the academic life to men who had themselves opted for it, and managed to remain in it when so many other college Fellows had abandoned it, for the forces or Whitehall. The history don who subsequently interviewed me had never in his life, so far as I am aware, written as much as a single article for a single learned journal and he was not perhaps displeased to find himself ranked with Abelard and Aquinas. I had, however, no such thought at the time and felt I acquitted myself badly, as indeed I have done at interviews throughout my life. He began by remarking on my unusual surname and its derivation, a question I ought to have anticipated but was unable to answer, and I was hardly more articulate when asked about my favourite poets, on which I should have been eloquent. Before leaving Oxford, however, walking in the beautiful gardens of Worcester, still well maintained despite the war, I had something of a revelation, feeling so much in tune with the place that I felt I must surely return to it. Someone in a ground floor room was playing a tune I could recognise, *Jesu, Joy of Man's Desiring,* and like the statue of Shelley, this seemed a good omen. It was specifically Worcester, not merely Oxford, for which I now longed. I had seen enough of Univ, to regard it as infinitely less attractive, and my official second choice, Exeter, also made no appeal.

If *First Bloom* can be believed I spent my next Saturday afternoon searching out the works of Oscar Wilde in the secondhand bookshop in Newbury which had become my favourite retreat during the holidays. The owner, an amiable, quiet, seemingly bookish man, knew, I suspect, less about most of the authors who formed his stock than I did, but kindly urged me never to think I must buy something merely because I had spent hours in his shop. Regularly I would collect a heap of possible purchases and then reduce this to a level which matched my current financial resources. On this occasion, according again to *First Bloom*, I toyed with, and indeed subsequently acquired, an Oxford edition of Shelley, a 'Temple' edition of Shakespeare's *Sonnets*, small enough for the pocket of my sports coat – another disadvantage of our ludicrous uniform was that it would not accommodate a normal-size book – Alec Waugh's *Public School Life*, a non-fictional sequel to *The Loom of Youth*, quoted earlier, and Thomas de Quincey's *Confessions of an Opium Eater*. This last, which fails to live up to the promise of its title, attracted me because de Quincey had been at Worcester, a college otherwise largely lacking in famous literary alumni.*

What I was seeking on this occasion, however, was Oscar Wilde, inconveniently placed 'just below the ceiling', as my *alter ego* observed, before succumbing to one of the enthusiasms to which he was prone:

> And so, at the top of a ladder in a secondhand bookshop, straining his eyes to read the titles, he discovered *De Profundis*. It was a battered copy, on which the gold print had long since faded into the now dirty-grey binding, as though to accompany its once glittering author into dark obscurity. He read it through the same evening and when he returned to school a few days later the sheer beauty of some of the phrases continued to spring fresh from his memory and caused something to swell in his throat. 'Where there is sorrow there is holy ground.' 'Winter days so full of sunlight that they will cheat the crocus into squandering its gold before its time,' up to the sublime splendour of its conclusion: 'She will cleanse me in great waters and with bitter herbs make me whole.'

This edition contained no indication that it was incomplete. The full text, since published, gives a very different picture of Wilde, as small-minded and vindictive, but at that time he seemed to me, like Shelley, a victim of society's prejudice and envy and I later bought, and admired, the rest of Wilde's work.

This was a good time to be building up a library. I rarely bought new books, then often appallingly produced thanks to the strict 'War Economy Standards' and relatively expensive; the still new Penguin paperbacks contained more modern authors than the classics I was seeking. Hardback secondhand books, however, in 1943 were far cheaper and more plentiful than now and the pre-war publishing trade had excelled in producing hundreds of worthwhile titles in cheap but serviceable editions, which had gravitated to the secondhand shelves and become even cheaper. My particular favourites were the little dark blue World's Classics, so robustly bound that, as my shelves still confirm, they would stand up to years of hard wear, and small enough to carry everywhere. I

---

* To forestall the wrath of other Worcester men I must add that its predecessor, Gloucester Hall, did produce the poet Richard Lovelace (1618-1658), author of nine entries in *The Oxford Book of Seventeenth Century Verse*. The best known, *Going to the Warres*, ends with the famous lines
>> I could not love thee, Deare, so much
>> Loved I not honour more.

also delighted in Jonathan Cape's 'Travellers' Library', which cost only a fraction of their original 3s 6d [17.5p] by the time they were available secondhand. The same firm's 'Florin Books' I also regularly picked up for well below their original 2s [10p]. The accepted leader, and pioneer, in this field, Dent's Everyman Library, cost only 1s [5p] per volume new, but I found the close packed type and meagre margins off-putting.

Book buying has often been described as an addiction and it was one to which I now fell victim. My parents took in good part my filling up every spare corner with my recent purchases and displayed a polite interest in them. It was in August 1943, though I did not discover it till later, that *An English Library* was published, sub-titled 'An Annotated List of 1300 Classics', with, to commend it still further, a Foreword by Edmund Blunden. The Introduction, by a London chief librarian, described it as 'an attempt to provide a bibliography listing every work written in English which by common consent is termed a classic', in response to 'the urge of young men and women to seek a fuller understanding of the civilisation they are called upon to fight for and respect'. I identified immediately with this target audience and dreamed of acquiring every book mentioned. This aim I subsequently abandoned, after finding some of the titles listed extremely boring; others that I did buy still remain unread. *An English Library* became, however, a significant influence on my book buying, an easy yardstick to apply, though books by living authors were excluded, to distinguish the truly significant from the merely meretricious. So, no doubt taking *De Profundis* with me, I went back to school, still uncertain if I had reached Oxford, but now desperate to return there if I could.

---

[1] Jun-Jul 1943 p.69
[2] *The Minstrelsy of Isis* p.92

46

NEVER FORGET

I charge you never to forget the benefits you have received in this place.

Headmaster to boys leaving Christ's Hospital, 16 December 1943

In mid-September 1943 I went back to school, regretting, as would have seemed inconceivable a little earlier, that this was to be my last term. This reaction grew even stronger on my arrival for this was to prove by far the most pleasant of my 22 terms at Housie and I was bitterly aware that my school career was to be cut short just as it had become truly enjoyable. Almost simultaneously I joined the two school elites, the house monitors, who had a degree of freedom denied to everyone else, and that even older superior caste, the grecians, of whom I will say more in a moment.

My appointment as a monitor was absurdly overdue and when, in my eighth year at Housie, approaching 18, I finally achieved it this must have been a school record, though not one recorded in *The Blue*. It meant that at last, as should have happened two years, or at the very latest one year, before, I could stay up late, enter the dormitory or leave the dayroom during lock-up without permission, and had the services of a 'swab', the Housey version, as mentioned earlier, of a fag. I was fortunate in mine, a delightful, willing small boy and was able, as tradition demanded, to act as his champion when he was threatened with a beating for some minor misdemeanour. A close friendship often developed between master and servant and was sometimes the subject of house gossip, but much though I liked my swab, it was certainly groundless in our case. I was, I find from *First Bloom*, mildly troubled by sexual desire that term. Its expression took the form of talking about homosexuality a good deal. We tended to note eagerly any mention of it in public-school novels like *The Loom of Youth*, and I find listed among the books I read that term a novel about Shrewsbury, *David Blaize*, by EF Benson, which had been innocently recommended to me by my mother, who still retained a romantic view of the public schools. This, published in 1915, touched on, rather than explored, the hero's relationship with an older boy. I also read Henry Williamson's *Dandelion Days* (1922), and the early volumes of Compton Mackenzie's *The*

Four Winds of Love, a six novel sequence published from 1937 to 1945, though to what extent any of these featured homosexual feelings I cannot recall. I read somewhat frenziedly that term, expecting to be engulfed a few months later in illiteracy and philistinism, especially the serious works I anticipated it would then be hard to come by. Among them Walter Pater's *The Renaissance* (1926), which deeply impressed me, and such religious classics as St Augustine's *Confessions* (c.397) and St Thomas à Kempis's *Imitation of Christ* (1418). For light relief I turned back to poetry and that term worked my way through Rupert Brooke, TS Eliot, John Keats, Ezra Pound and Francis Thompson, determined to acquire as much intellectual baggage as I could before being incarcerated in a barrack room.

I also recognised that, on being called up, I would again be back on the very bottom rung of a rigidly hierarchical ladder, just as at Housey I was comfortably ensconced near the top. Noel's reluctance to make me a monitor, as a punishment for being no good at games, for in seven years I had not blotted my copybook in any other way, was now shown to have been ill-founded. I positively enjoyed supervising the games of small boys instead of performing incompetently with the big ones and, since I could readily identify with those who were new and frightened, was, I believe, for the first time in my long Peele A career, popular with at least this, the least important, part of the house. On many afternoons I took groups of juniors on runs into the countryside or organised games of 'Release' in the coppice behind the house and never was anyone more conscientious about seeing that the smallest boys were not overlooked when teams were picked, or left behind as the faster runners forged ahead.

What had also transformed my life, however, was my academic success. Term had hardly begun when a telegram arrived from home 'You are elected to Worcester College', followed by a letter from the then provost, which I still possess:

> You have been elected to an Open Exhibition and I hope that you will have a happy and profitable course here. I shall be glad to hear when you think that you will be able to come into residence...
>
> I understand from the examiners that you very nearly failed to get an exhibition because of the extreme weakness of your Latin and French and you ought to try to make some gain in these languages before you come up.

I forbore to point out that I had not even taken a paper in French and was unlikely to make much gain in Latin, since I was once again under the charge of the incompetent 'Blam'. As for the date of my entry into residence, I was tempted to reply that I only wished I knew. But these were minor irritations compared to the overwhelming fact of my success. I had made it, I reflected, as I had so rashly predicted back in 1936, and all the miseries of the past seven years, if not blotted out, were to some extent justified. For me the Housey system had worked after all, carrying me from council house to Oxford, in spite of my being manifestly not boarding school material and the unforeseen complications introduced by the war.

I proudly bore my telegram to DSR; it was, as I was well aware, more his triumph than mine. My father wrote him a letter of thanks, to which, to my gratification, he replied, disclaiming the credit for my success and attributing it to my 'grit and determination'. These were always qualities he valued. I remember his remarking to me as I struggled to reconcile the contradictory accounts of two historians, 'You're worth taking trouble over. You're a fighter!' Somewhat small mindedly I did not tell Noel the news, though even at Housie, where such achievements were commonplace, a 'schol' or exhibition still reflected some glory on the winner's house. He had, I reasoned, done nothing to help me and I left him to ask me in my next French lesson to confirm what he had already learned in the masters' common room. Macnutt failed to congratulate me, like other old adversaries on the staff, though the admirable Teddy Edwards made a special journey to Peele A to do so.

One pleasing consequence of my success was the encouragement it gave to the other four boys in my history set, since they could reasonably expect to manage in four or five terms what I had accomplished in three. I will note here that all four duly reached Oxford, two with full scholarships, one with an exhibition, and one via a University Short Course, a solution not open to me. Three later entered the teaching profession, where one became a headmaster, and another a senior Education Officer. The fourth joined the insurance industry. None, apart from me, became a historian.

With my scholarship secured I automatically became a 'first-parting grecian' ie someone in his final year, destined for the university, the very top rank of the Housey hierarchy. Being 17 I also qualified for my 'buttons', the outward sign of one's eminent status. I recall reporting to the Wardrobe to be fitted with the imposing new coat with its cutaway collar, turned back velvet cuffs and imposing row of large buttons down the front, recalling how I had put on my first Housey uniform as a quaking new boy seven years earlier almost to the day.

Now everything was changed, except my increasingly anomalous position in Peele A. As one of only about a dozen 'first-partings' I enjoyed the privilege of eating my breakfast and tea on 'the dais', the High Table at one end of Dining Hall occupied, at dinner time, by the Headmaster. In school terms, I now outranked my own house-captain though in Peele A I was still his subordinate, as he did not fail to remind me. I recall his coming up to the dais one breakfast time to upbraid me for some alleged neglect of duty – probably failing to turn reluctant boys out of bed the moment the rising bell went – in front of my fellow grecians, though they were more embarrassed than impressed. I was also now permitted to own a bicycle, and by dint of advertising and perseverance, my father managed to obtain one, though they were extremely scarce at this stage of the war. I rode this proudly down the Avenue and, even more proudly, walked along the path immediately in front of the houses, the use of which was restricted to masters and 'first-partings', so that my own house-captain could look from his study window to see me exercising a right denied to him.

Another custom from which I benefitted was that of Q Shot, the termly allowance given to button grecians in London, as I have mentioned earlier, to finance their private teas or, according to some accounts, a superior quality of beer. Typically this was never explained to us, nor were we told whether this welcome largesse should be correctly known as 'Q Shop', presumably derived from Quartermasters Shop, or as 'Q Shot' (or Shott), meaning 'payment'. I received, I think £1.5s [£1.25], double my normal term's pocket money, and probably spent it on books. By the time Robin Hull obtained his 'buttons', in 1949, the amount had risen to £2.5s [£2.25] which was openly described, and treated, as 'beer money'.[1] By 1973, with the opening of the Grecians' Club, which I mention later, it even became legitimate to spend it for this purpose and on the school premises.

With such privileges as Q Shot went a traditional duty, which I came to enjoy, that of saying grace at dinner in Dining Hall. I looked forward to my turn to mount the ancient pulpit facing the vast Verrio painting and waiting for the Hall Warden to silence the noise of nearly nine hundred boys and a dozen or so masters, before declaiming the sonorous words delivered on such occasions for several hundred years:

> Give us thankful hearts, O Lord God, for the table which Thou has spread for us. Bless Thy good creatures to our use and us to Thy service, for Jesus Christ His sake.

The 'Amen' was rarely said with much conviction, as the assembled school contemplated the meagre 'good creatures' spread out before them, but the response to the closing grace, as they prepared to leave the hall, was often more hearty, though my own feeling was that it went on a bit:

> Blessed Lord, we yield Thee hearty praise and thanksgiving for our founder and benefactors, by whose charitable benevolence Thou has refreshed our bodies at this time. So season and refresh our souls with Thy heavenly spirit that we may live to Thy honour and glory. Protect Thy church, the king and all the royal family. And preserve us in peace and truth through Christ our saviour, Amen.[2]

Taking my turn at reading the lessons on weekday mornings in chapel, another obligation of the first-parting grecians, was less enjoyable. In Dining Hall, speaking from an elevated position in the centre of one side, I had never found any difficulty in making my voice carry. In Chapel, at one end of a long, narrow building – how right I had been to criticise it in my essay a few months earlier, I felt – it was a different matter. It was difficult, unless one spoke very loudly, to make oneself heard; even the clergy addressed us from the centre of the building. But, far worse, one had to sit beside the Headmaster in his long, ornate pew facing down towards the altar. The Head was known to slam his book shut in disgust, and even rumoured to hurl it on the floor, if the reader mispronounced some Biblical name or stressed the wrong word, but though this never happened to me I found my week on chapel duty very unnerving.

Another not wholly welcome result of my new status was that I was now invited to an occasional supper and play-reading on Sunday evenings in the Headmaster's house, the first time I had set foot in it since going, as a timorous new boy, to tea with Mrs Flecker back in 1936. Eating a meal with 'Oily' was an intimidating experience, and, though I greatly respected and admired him, I cannot pretend we ever developed any sort of rapport. I also remember as more frightening than enjoyable the occasion when we read *The Corn is Green* after supper. I made a very poor attempt at a Welsh accent, and wondered if the Head's failure to respond to his cue was an expression of his disapproval, but as the silence lengthened we realised he had fallen asleep. What seemed an endless silence followed until his wife, with what we considered amazing temerity, prodded him awake.

As a monitor I now regularly read 'Duty' in the evenings, another task I always enjoyed. The choice of prayers and readings, provided one ended up with the Prayer Book grace, was left to the monitor and, after consulting Miss Harvie – Noel, I knew, would have objected – I managed to insert some fresh material in place of the usual hackneyed passages from the New, or, far worse since they so often lent themselves to mockery, the Old Testament. I doubt now whether the ten and eleven year olds among my 'congregation' received more spiritual benefit from the extract I chose from TS Eliot's *The Journey of the Magi* than they would have done from the *Book of Genesis* or *Joshua* but at the time it seemed the very stuff of revolution.

Miss Harvie also took in good part my attempt to use Duty to further the progressive cause. I had discovered in *The English Hymnal* a hymn, No 563, containing positively revolutionary sentiments, though the author had no doubt had in mind – in words which curiously anticipated those of Sir Oswald Mosley at a famous Fascist rally in 1934[*] – a country's readiness to embrace Christianity rather than any earthly political cause:

Once to every man and nation

---

[*] A key passage from Mosley's address – 'Once in the life of every nation comes the moment of decision, the moment of destiny' – is often heard on television when film extracts are shown of his meeting at Olympia on 7 June 1934.

> Come the moment to decide
> In the strife of truth with falsehood
> For the good or evil side...
> Then to side with truth is noble,
> Ere her cause bring fame and profit,
> And 'tis prosperous to be just...
> Though the cause of evil prosper,
> Yet 'tis truth alone is strong;
> Though her portion be the scaffold,
> And upon the throne be wrong.

There were echoes here of *The Red Flag*'s

> Come dungeon dark or gallows grim

which I might perhaps have quoted had I had the text and it was indeed the difficulty of finding such classic sources which later encouraged me to compile my first book, *A Socialist Anthology*.

Like the nation as a whole, Christ's Hospital seems at this time, thanks to the successes of the Russian armies and the general desire for a new beginning after the war, to have been moving to the left. In the previous January a motion to the effect 'That this house believes a Communist government for this country to be wholly undesirable'[3] had been defeated by 27 to 20, the opposition being led by my friends Bob Pitman and Ivan Yates, both future political journalists and Labour candidates. Now, in the Michaelmas Term, recruits to the staff included a delightfully outspoken young man, presumably medically unfit, though he had no problems with discipline. (I omit his name in case his opinions have changed.) He was a striking contrast to the school 'Old Guard' and I was shocked when he cynically remarked that the arrival of US soldiers had put Anglo-American relations back half a century. I did not agree then, and agreed even less after serving in an Anglo-American unit later, but the thought remained and was another influence in prompting me to write a book on the subject, *The GIs*.

The war, while stimulating political debate, had stifled its normal consequences, thanks to the electoral truce, which allowed the party which already held any seat to nominate its next MP with the other main parties allowing him an uncontested election. Challenging the coalition government was therefore left to independents, usually on the left, and in 1942 the Common Wealth Party (*not*, it must be stressed, the Commonwealth Party) was founded, at first to support such candidates, then to put up its own. About Common Wealth, which had the support, among others, of the author JB Priestley, whose broadcast *Postscripts* back in 1940 were almost the founding charter of the movement for a new society after the war, there was always a near revivalist spirit. In April 1943 it won its first seat, in a rural constituency in Cheshire which the Labour Party had not even contested in the past, on a programme which included the nationalisation of agriculture.* As a post-war historian wrote: 'CW, in by-election after by-election represented the refined essence of "Beveridgism" – the revolutionary zeal, the millenarian dream, the unselfishness.'[4] All these made a deep appeal to me as an idealistic, even naive, 17 year old. I warmly endorsed the new party's basic tenets of Common Ownership, ie nationalisation, and public access to large privately owned estates, a cause still not wholly won, its championship of Vital Democracy, which covered proportional representation in elections and joint consultation between management and workers in industry, and Morality in Politics, which is self-explanatory, though recently, ie before the 1997 general election, somewhat neglected. Later I was to work for a nationalised industry and see joint consultation in action. I was deeply impressed by the fact that the Common Wealth Party's first leader, Sir Richard Acland, a renegade baronet and landowner, had handed over his own estate to the National Trust. He was obviously an individual of high principle, comparable to Sir Stafford Cripps in the Labour Party, and I constantly repeated to myself his favourite slogan: 'What is morally wrong cannot be politically right.'

In a minor way I did my bit to prepare the way for the coming General Election. One of the legacies of my father's failed business was a small printing set, designed to print shop notices and price lists, and I set by hand Acland's inspiring sentence, adding the address of Common Wealth headquarters as a source of further information. I prepared scores of leaflets, on patriotically small slips of paper, and left them in rural telephone boxes alongside the instruction about pressing Button B to retrieve your twopence after an unconnected call. During my cycle rides to country churches, described earlier, I added a few copies to the postcards and parish magazines invariably on offer at a table by the entrance, comforting my conscience by the reflection that Sir Richard was a Christian Socialist.

The Common Wealth Party served for me, as for others who felt disenfranchised by the electoral truce, a valuable purpose. I argued its cause in school debates and in private discussions and corresponded with its headquarters, in Gower Street, after I had become a member; there was nothing in the School Rules forbidding one to join a political party. There was even, I recall, some suggestion of my writing a pamphlet to persuade like-minded schoolboys to follow my lead, though this never materialised and by the time I was able to take an active part in politics Common Wealth had, for most practical purposes, become an adjunct to the Labour Party.

I talked a good deal that term to Miss Harvie, whose opinions were, I now feel certain, close to my own. Among the matters we discussed was the house

---

* On this by-election, and Common Wealth generally, see Calder pp.546-50.

library, for which, as, I think, fourth monitor, I was now responsible. This was the sole source of recreational reading for the younger boys, who were not allowed to use the school library, and an important one for the rest of the house for more recent books, especially novels. One of my pleasantest recollections of that term is spending an afternoon in the excellent bookshop in Horsham, which, owing to our virtual confinement within the ring fence, I had hardly ever visited before. Although books, naturally, came far further down the priority spending list for house funds than cricket stumps or rugger balls, I had managed to obtain a few pounds to replace some of the most battered and tattered volumes and thought I had better consult Miss Harvie before buying AJ Cronin's *The Stars Look Down*, published in 1935, which contained, by the standards of the time, some distinctly explicit material. Noel, I was sure, had not read it but would certainly have banned it. 'Hearty' Harvie took just the sensible line I had expected. Censorship, she thought, would do more harm than good. Anyone old enough to read the book would not be corrupted by it and if they did 'turn back to look again at the juicy bits', this was surely natural enough. 'Perhaps,' she suggested, 'you should go through it first and write on the flyleaf, "Turn to pages 17, 93, and 201."' I did not follow this advice, but Cronin's bestseller joined our little stock of modern novels without, to my knowledge, inflicting any further harm on the house morals.

That term I held my first, and only, school post, that of secretary of the Debating Society and this proved even less onerous than I expected, for I had hardly taken over when it was suppressed. This was no fault of mine, except in so far as I spoke on the losing side in what proved to be the last debate of the war, though even the record of it was censored and did not appear in *The Blue*. It was only in the Lent Term of 1996 that it at last printed the facts, quoting from a letter written on 14 November 1943, by a Peele B contemporary of mine to his mother. I remember the debate, on the motion that 'A free Germany with equality of opportunity is the best guarantee of world peace after the war'. My already deep anti-German beliefs were made even sharper by the realisation that thanks to Germany my school career was being cut irreplaceably short just when I was beginning to enjoy it. I gladly led the opposition and can still recall the closing words of my peroration, that if the views expressed in the motion prevailed 'generations of men not yet conceived will be sacrificed on that same altar of the German lust for power'. Noel was, surprisingly, not present at the debate but, when the 'treat Germany leniently' party won, addressed the house after Duty on the folly of such beliefs and ended by saying 'I am very glad that a member of my house opposed the motion and, I believe, spoke very well in so doing.' This was the only public compliment I ever received from my housemaster, but he was not the only person to be disgusted by the result, which was attributed largely to the intervention of an Austrian woman on the staff who bravely stood up to champion her countrymen. The letter mentioned above records what followed:

Yesterday I heard the whole story from Mr Macnutt...Some boy had written to his Governor and happened to tell him about the debate. The Governor was a fiery old Tory and wrote a vehement letter to the headmaster saying he was disgusted, and was the school going to the dogs and everyone turning pro-Nazi?, or words to that effect. The headmaster thought this was a big fuss over nothing, but he looked into the Society, found that now Mr Roberts was the only master on the committee and...other masters couldn't find time to go to debates. He saw Mr Macnutt and various others and asked them...if they would go often so as to get the Society on a new footing, but they refused. So, presumably to avoid any further rows from Governors or the like, he reluctantly suspended the Society. It seems pretty disgraceful, doesn't it, in a country where free speech is one of the few real freedoms now?[5]

I now faced the question of what service I wished, or more precisely, had to, join. The great aim of boys in my situation was to be accepted for a University Short Course, which offered not merely six months at Oxford or Cambridge, combined with not too demanding military training as an officer cadet, but a further term or so at school, until one's course started. It also, a most important bonus for those who had not obtained their 'schol', provided a back-door into the university, for on joining a Short Course one formally 'matriculated', ie was admitted to the university, and given a place in a college, to which one could almost count on returning after the war.

My first choice of the three services was the RAF, but, thanks to my poor sight, only recently discovered, acceptance for air crew, and thus a probable commission, was ruled out. A visiting RAF officer whom I consulted – 'His heart was set on air crew,' my ATC CO told him, which was somewhat overstating my motives – gave the succinct advice; 'Learn Jap'. There was indeed a demand by all three services for Japanese speakers and this was what my friend Pitman became, contriving to get a university short course without a commission and ending the war a sergeant-major in the Far East. Once in the RAF I might, I suspect, have found my way to some reasonably congenial posting, but, when consulted, both Macnutt and 'Jem' Massen, who had taught me German, advised, fairly enough, that I had no aptitude for languages. Historians, sadly, were not in demand. Thus, determined not to join the Navy, unable to get into the RAF with any hope of becoming an officer, I opted, when that autumn I registered for call-up, for the army, as this seemed to offer the only hope, although a slim one, of a few months at university and a commission.

How slim that hope was became evident when that autumn I was summoned to London to what the Head – I had to get my exeat from Noel counter-signed by him – called 'The War House'. I had not been in London since the day my father had taken me there for that earlier 'call-up' as a Housey boy, seven years before, since when it had become bomb-battered and shabby. Fearful of getting lost on the bus or tube – not perhaps the best of reasons for one aiming to become a leader of men – I walked from Victoria to the unimpressive room in the Horse Guards Building in Whitehall, and faced first an intelligence test, which presented no problem, then the interviewing panel. Only three Corps were on offer, the infantry, which I had absolutely no desire to join, the Royal Electrical and Mechanical Engineers, for which I had even less aptitude than for learning Japanese, and the Royal Artillery, my somewhat reluctant first choice. (I had hoped the Intelligence Corps or something unmartial like the Royal Army Service Corps might be open to me, but was disappointed.) I was first questioned about my knowledge of science and, thanks to HD Sills' teaching was complimented on how much I had remembered. The second part of the interview, directed to assessing my officer-like qualities, also began encouragingly, but rapidly deteriorated. 'House monitor' sounded all right but my failure to have captained any team except the house third eleven, about which I kept quiet, told against me, and my only school office, secretary of the Debating Society, suggested, I felt, the officers' mess equivalent of a barrack-room lawyer.

There came finally some general questions. What did I want to do after leaving university?, I was asked. 'Explorer', or 'Colonial Administrator' might have struck the right note, but my honest answer, that I hoped to become a don, aroused no enthusiasm. Finally came the equivalent of that famous first world war question about a German raping one's sister: Was I eager to go and kill Germans? This took me by surprise and, after an embarrassing pause, I replied diffidently that I was not burning with such a desire but had no moral objection to what was, at this moment in history, necessary.

I was not surprised to learn soon afterwards that I had been turned down. 'You've backed the wrong horse,' 'Oily' told me, not unsympathetically, after summoning me to see him. There was now, he said, nothing for it but call-up as an ordinary soldier since I could not now choose, as I would have preferred, to enter the RAF as an aircraftsman. He offered to do what he could, via a contact at 'The War House', to get me assigned to the type of job I was least likely to find unpleasant, though whether he did so, and his intervention had any effect on my military career, I never discovered.

The Ministry of Labour machine now ground out its remorseless way. I was summoned to a medical board in Brighton, which at least meant a day away from school, though to be allowed to wear ordinary clothes I had to have my exeat suitably endorsed by both Noel, who was somewhat reluctant, and the Head, who was courtesy itself. I still feel grateful that I did not have to move round the inspection room looking rather like a Victorian pugilist with knee-buttoned breeches and yellow socks below my bare waist.

The panel of civilian doctors carried out their inspection in a dingy hall in a back street, and one was required to move from one partioned-off area to the next. I was, I think, the only 'grammar school' boy seen that afternoon and one doctor, having learned that I was going on to university, took me under his wing, introducing me to the next medical man with a brief summary of my educational record, as though this were a social encounter. It was with mixed feelings, after all those years of being despised for my non-athleticism, that I learned that Housey's insistence on games and PT had left me in the top category, A1, and thus fit for front-line service in a fighting unit.

Soon afterwards I was summoned to a selection interview, again in Brighton. This time Noel insisted I must wear Housey clothes, which made an already disagreeable occasion profoundly embarrassing, for the young working men who shared the waiting room with me were clearly puzzled by the contrast between my accent and my uniform, which they assumed to belong to an orphanage. The army officer who interviewed me was much less sympathetic than the two I had met at the Horse Guards, who had clearly regarded me as in some degree one of themselves. He was shocked that I did not know in what regiment my father had served in the first world war, and seemed to think I was to blame for his having transferred at the first opportunity to the Royal Flying Corps. It was with relish rather than regret, though I had told him this was the very last type of unit I wished to join, that he remarked; 'You're young and you're fit. The infantry is the obvious thing,' words that, remembering all I had read of the trenches in the first world war, fell on my ears like a death sentence.

Briefly, another alternative seemed to present itself. That November Ernest Bevin broadcast an appeal to boys approaching call-up to volunteer instead to go down the mines. He addressed himself particularly to those at grammar and public schools and the school, which had never so far as I knew yet sent an Old Blue into the pits, made arrangements for us to listen to his speech. DSR urged us to search our consciences as to whether to respond, and I was indeed tempted, partly because I felt nowhere could be worse than an infantry barrack room, but also because this seemed a unique opportunity to find out at first hand about the group who seemed to epitomise the Labour Party and the trade union movement. It soon became clear, however, that the enlistment process was already too far advanced to be reversed, indeed on joining up I found that Bevin's broadcast had had the very reverse effect from what he had intended, causing some boys from mining areas to volunteer for the army to avoid any risk of being sent down the pits. From a friend who did become a 'Bevin Boy' I later heard enough to be profoundly grateful I had opted to become a soldier, not a miner.

Academically this was for me a wasted term. Had I been at a day school I would probably have spent it in discovering alcohol and girls, but at Housie neither was available and, facing an indefinite future in the army, I felt little incentive to learn. DSR, very properly, spent most of his time with the boys still to take their scholarships. He had decided, wrongly I now feel, that I try and cover the remaining three centuries of the Middle Ages superficially, to reach a convenient point at which to abandon my studies, but the result was to leave me remembering nothing of this period. In my essays for this term I find little of the old liveliness, though I must still have indulged occasionally in unacceptable generalisations for I find, in an essay on 12 October 1943 contrasting the views of two historians on 'The Origins of the House of Commons', a marginal 'No!' and 'I disagree violently.' About my non-history work, with no General Paper to prepare for, there was also an unreal quality. With only the army ahead such questions as 'How far should the arts of painting and sculpture be subsidised by the state?' or a discussion of the proposition that 'Punishment should not fit the crime but the mentality of the criminal', now seemed irrelevant. DSR's comments remained encouraging as well as critical. 'This shows insight into the problem and is very well expressed,' ran one. 'Ideas good, but logical connections between them are poorly constructed,' went another. But who, I thought, would care on the barrack square or in the slit-trench that lay ahead?

I did only one useful piece of work that term, after I had happened to remark to DSR after re-reading Chaucer's *Prologue* 'I wonder where the Wife of Bath got her wool?' He urged me to find out, a useful, if elementary, exercise in historical research, though I have now forgotten the answer.

Occasionally, for the only time in my Housey career, I was taught by a woman. It was not a great success. She was smartly turned out, not unattractive, highly intellectual – she was, I think, a Cambridge don who had taken up school teaching as her war work – but she lacked DSR's liveliness as a teacher and we never established a rapport. The truth was I felt resentful of my situation. In contrast to the uplifting axioms I had formerly inscribed as epigraphs in my history exercise books I find in that term's 'History Notes' the somewhat cynical, as well as hackneyed, tag: 'A scholar is a man who knows more and more about less and less.'

The red letter days remained those when I was taught by DSR. With no need to boost my self-confidence before I faced the examiners he clearly felt free to be more severe on my work than in the past and his final exhortation on the last page of my final exercise book pulled no punches and reiterated the very same complaints about my style and approach he had first made a year earlier:

> One gets the impression that you have not had a clear scheme of argument in your mind before starting off. Your sentences are not sufficiently well linked together, nor do paragraphs follow well. You seem to think that a few dogmatic assertions can stand by themselves without any argument to support them.

I took comfort from the comment he added to soften the blow: 'Parts of your writing are very good', and a conversation that followed. He would, he said, be happy to see me become a don and a professional historian: 'It wouldn't suit everyone, but I think it would suit you.' Failing this, he suggested, I ought to look towards a career in one of the industries which I was so keen to see nationalised. 'They'll need able managers,' he said encouragingly, 'and you're a man of some ability.' This was the only career guidance I received at school, which was reasonable enough. The school had got us to Oxford or Cambridge: now it was up to us.

I wrote my last essay for DSR on 14 December 1943, the day before my eighteenth birthday. Its subject was highly appropriate, 'The function of the historian' and I can still read the closing words with approval:

> 'The past is not dead, but sleepeth.' It is the function of the historian to rouse it gently so that it may speak with all men.

DSR endorsed this: 'Good ending'. It seemed an apt verdict on my whole, otherwise unhappy and unimpressive, Christ's Hospital career.

The last weekend of term seemed to arrive all too soon. The carol service on the last Sunday of the Michaelmas Term had always been my favourite chapel occasion, and in 1943 my father came down for the weekend to attend it. This was the one occasion on which I felt close to him. My obvious dislike of the school of which he had had such high hopes must have been a disappointment to him and the only comments he had received hitherto on my progress from the Newbury Education Committee had been, as I have mentioned earlier, complaints of my poor handwriting and that I was not 'settling in'. My award at Oxford, the first, I think, for a West Gifts boy from Newbury, had brought no congratulations to him or me, merely an announcement that it was hoped soon to have a vacancy for another Newbury nominee.

I was glad, therefore, that this visit went so well. We walked into Horsham, I remember, where my father took great delight in taking me out to lunch in the main hotel, since demolished, where we enjoyed a conventional roast dinner; the days when the greatest conceivable treat was scrambled egg were, thanks to the wartime improvement in our diet, long past. On the way back, with obvious satisfaction, he gave me a pound, a substantial part of his week's wages, to enable me to make my swab a handsome leaving present. He seemed almost more distressed than I was that instead of going on to Oxford I was having to join the army and, I later learned from my mother, was apprehensive about what might happen to me in it, his own memories of service life being far from nostalgic. His annoyance on my behalf contributed to his deep contempt for the Conservative party which had failed to prevent the war and then come close to losing it. He also, as I did, loathed the Germans. I can recall him, normally the kindest of men, sharing the then widespread view that only mass sterilisation of the whole German race could guarantee peace for the future.

A few days later came the end of term, though this time I could not share in the general euphoria. Housie always stage-managed big events superbly and the Leaving Service in chapel had been refined over the centuries into an event liable to bring tears to the eyes of the most senior or cynical. 'Leaving Housie,' wrote one contemporary of mine, 'is a small death and participation in the lugubrious hymns, solemn charges and distribution of Bibles...is rather like attending one's own funeral as a spectator.'[6]

I cannot recall anyone remaining unmoved by this polished ritual, the climax of which came as the *Nunc Dimittis* was sung and the boys who were leaving slipped one by one out of their pews and followed the headmaster as he made his slow, dignified way up the central aisle to the chancel, in front of which stood a table piled with Bibles and Prayer Books. Inside each was entered the name of the recipient and the imposing inscription: 'The Gift of the Governors of Christ's Hospital'; here was the foundation's final present to its sons, supposed to keep their feet on the path of righteousness now that its daily *recta disciplina* was removed.

I remember as I walked towards the altar hearing one small boy in another house, whom I did not know, say my name aloud, perhaps pleased to be able to identify at least one grecian. Recognition at last!, I felt. I then joined the end of the two ranks of boys facing the Head, who read out our full names, the only time this happened in our whole school career, after which each boy walked up to receive his Bible. By tradition the most senior came last. I was therefore standing alone when I heard him say 'Norman Longmate' and having accepted a Bible and Prayer Book, returned to join my fellow leavers. We stood in two ranks, deeply impressed, while the Head delivered 'the charge' given to generations of leavers:

> I charge you never to forget the great benefits you have received in this place and, according to your means, to do all that you can to enable others to enjoy the same advantage. And remember that you carry with you, wherever you go, the good name of Christ's Hospital.[7]

The silence during this ceremony was remarkable and it was not unknown to see those addressed sobbing as they walked back to their places. I was not far off tears myself, but felt that such a display would disgrace my 'buttons', and got back to my seat dry-eyed, to join in the hymn that was sung as the leavers made their way back to their places between the long pews filled with their schoolmates. It was not a specifically Christ's Hospital composition, having been written by a Dean of Durham and set to a suitably mournful tune based on a thirteenth century original,[8] but I found it unbearably poignant. Here once again was something that Housie got entirely right:

> Lord, Thou has brought us to our journey's end;

Once more to Thee our evening prayers ascend:
Once more we stand to praise Thee for the past;
Grant prayer and praise be honest at the last.

For all the joys which Thou hast deigned to share
For all the pains which Thou hast helped to bear,
For all our friends, in life and death the same,
We thank Thee, Lord, and praise Thy glorious name.

If from Thy paths, by chastening undismayed,
If from Thy gifts ungrateful, we have strayed,
If in Thy house our prayers were faint and few,
Forgive, O Lord, and build our hearts anew.

If we have learnt to feel our neighbour's need,
To fight for truth in thought and word and deed,
If these be lessons which the years have taught,
Then 'stablish, Lord, what Thou in us has wrought.

The Leaving Service ended with a special blessing, urging us to 'render to no man evil for evil' and 'to support the weak', as well as that familiar Housey injunction to 'Love the Brotherhood'. I was sufficiently moved by it to forget the resolution I had made years before to have nothing more to do with the school once I had left and to write off that very evening for membership of the Old Blues' organisation, the Christ's Hospital Club. Already I realised that the memory of those seven formative years could never be cast off.

Leavers were, on the last night, even allowed to visit other houses, but there was only one person to whom I wished to say a proper goodbye and I made my way down the blacked-out Avenue to David Roberts' home, where I spent the whole evening. What we talked of I cannot recall, though I think we touched on women and marriage. We had never discussed this subject before, but it looms large in my account of that last night in *First Bloom*:

He stared into the darkness to where behind Brackenhurst the first radiance of the rising moon was to be seen. He thought of what was past, of what was to come, of Oxford...of the black gulf of military service that lay ahead...Books, he thought, remain. Poetry...painting...great words, great art, and the comfort and consolation to be drawn from a knowledge of the past. But they are surely the stuff for old minds...but little things to carry with one in the long adventure of life. And love...If so much can be derived from so short a time with a chosen friend, how much more is likely to lie waiting for me...when I come into that wider life at whose threshold I now stand to that perfect woman whom I am confident lies waiting for

> me...Surely life, when this wartime episode is finished, can prove indeed to be full of colour and sweetness...
>
> As James returned to Blake the moon that had for so long hidden behind the slopes of Brackenhurst rose, as if to mark the end of James's schooldays, rose as if to welcome him into manhood.

Leavers were supposed to be back in their houses by 10.30 pm. When I arrived some time after that my house-captain, for the last time, reproved me, commenting on my lateness. I realised with joy that I was now beyond the reach of his dislike and slept as soundly as on my first night in Peele A.

Next morning, for the only time, I simultaneously defied both a wartime appeal to patriotism and a school rule and filled my bath to the brim, in defiance of the 'Plimsoll line' painted round it at five inches [13 cm] above the base. Here was one feature of Housie, its hot water system, I should miss. Then I put on the civilian clothes I had somehow acquired, feeling an unexpected twinge of regret as I laid down my blue coat, shapeless shirt, impractical bands and yellow stockings for the last time. The heavy Housey shoes I retained, having no others.

The other objects I carried away were all books: a copy of *The Collected Poems of James Elroy Flecker*, given me by DSR; Helen Waddell's *Peter Abelard*, from one of my two close friends in Peele A, and from the other, the future missionary, a small pocket-sized khaki-bound edition of the Bible. My leaving Bible, we agreed, was too bulky to accompany me onto the battlefield.

Coleridge had written a poem on 'Quitting School for College' which recorded how he had done so 'with as great a pang' as he had left home during his 'weeping childhood', and other Old Blues had obviously found the transition equally traumatic. The future diplomat Edward Thornton, who had left in 1785, had contributed five pompous stanzas 'On going to the university from the hospital':

> Long blest within these hospitable walls,
> In which benevolence has raised her throne...
> I go obedient to the stronger calls
> Of wisdom, her delightful path to tread.[9]

I might have said the same, except that it was not wisdom but the army which called and to a far from delightful path. I identified more with my contemporary Keith Douglas, who in *On Leaving School* in 1938, wrote of how

> it is awkward
> Realizing happiness seems just to have started
> And now we must leave it.

My feelings were, however, best expressed by a poet I had never much cared for, Milton, for I find as epigraph to the closing section of *First Bloom* some highly pertinent lines from *Paradise Lost*, strange though it seemed to think of Housie in such terms:

> Thus with the year
> Seasons return; but not to me returns
> Day, or the sweet approach of even or morn,
> Or sight of vernal bloom, or summer's rose...
> But cloud instead, and ever-during dark
> Surrounds me, from the cheerful ways of men
> Cut off, and, for the book of knowledge fair
> Presented with a universal blank.[10]

---

[1] Hull pp.108-9
[2] *CH Book* p.368
[3] Mar-Apr 1943 p.39
[4] Calder p.547
[5] Jul 1996 p.173
[6] Dec 1986 p.258
[7] Jul 1993 p.136
[8] CH *Supplement* No 51 pp.36-7
[9] *CH Book* p.151
[10] *Paradise Lost* Book III, line 40

PART IV

LIFE AFTER HOUSIE

*'Is there life after Housie?...
I am still trying to make up my mind.'*

**Old Blue contemporary of the author
writing in** The Blue, *December 1986*

47

DEEMED TO HAVE ENLISTED

'You are now deemed to have enlisted.'

Ministry of Labour official to the author, 28 December 1943

Christmas 1943 was the most unhappy I had spent since those dark and distant pre-war days when my father was unemployed and I fear my gloom must have cast something of a shadow over the rest of the family. I heard my father grumbling privately to my mother about my depressing demeanour and lack of gratitude and my mother, in her saintly way, urging him to say nothing to me since this was such a miserable time. A few men in Camp Close faced with being called up were said to have thrown the unwelcome documents on the fire and denied receiving them, though no doubt the army caught up with them eventually. So it did with the one resident on the estate who, to my knowledge, deserted. I would not have dreamed of doing either and was indeed perfectly willing to do my bit, but did resent not being allowed to complete my last year at school, with reason as it turned out. Some of my contemporaries managed to serve as little as a year, half of that on a university short course, less than would have been required under the post-war National Service Acts. By ill-chance, however, I belonged to the relatively few who neither qualified for deferment nor early release and had I known that I faced nearly four years in khaki, most of it after the war was over, I would have felt even more disgruntled than I did.

My last school report – as a grecian I did not get a special Leaving Report, it being assumed we could now make our own way in the world – seemed curiously irrelevant to my situation. I can remember only two entries. DSR had written warmly of me, concluding: 'I look forward to seeing him get a "first" at Oxford.' Blamire Brown's last words on my prospects as a Latinist, were 'He is handicapped by his inability to express himself in English.' This was one fault never laid at my door before or since. I can only imagine that Blam, in his prematurely senile way, had confused me with someone else.

Among my Christmas mail were my call-up papers, requiring me to report at Reading on 28 December, less than a fortnight after I had reached my eighteenth birthday. I duly made my way there, the start of my usual return journey to school, only to find that this was a mere formality, the twentieth century equivalent of 'taking the king's shilling'. An extremely surly, middle-aged official, clearly enjoying the opportunity to bully younger men, was notably unhelpful in setting out the various military careers open to me, a choice supposed to have been settled at my earlier interview in Brighton. Given the choice of infantry, Royal Artillery and Royal Army Service Corps I opted for the latter, as the least military sounding, a fortunate decision, for, as I found, despite the elaborate selection tests every recruit took during his basic training, one's initial preference tended to be what counted.

Reflecting how fortunate it was that I had not, as others had no doubt done, given up job and lodgings when summoned by a false alarm, I went home again, with mixed feelings, aware the evil day of actually joining-up had merely been postponed. I remembered, too, that earlier day when I had come ingloriously back from Reading after failing to go back to school on time. One of the most wretched periods of my life followed. I felt unable to look for a job, so had no income, and could not enjoy my enforced leisure. I made a half-hearted attempt to do some research into the 'Newbury martyrs', executed by Queen Mary for their protestant opinions, but the local library lacked the books I needed and my heart was not in it. I idled the days away, often wandering aimlessly by the canal in the dreary January days, feeling a curious affinity with my father, who had once similarly walked there when he, too, was unemployed, penniless and saw nothing but misery ahead.

If France Belk produced a pantomime that year I was barely aware of it, though I would have had ample time to cultivate members of the cast, and incredible as it would once have seemed I felt sad not to be returning to school in mid-January. However at least the end of my time in limbo was in sight for soon after the 'enlistment' fiasco I received my call-up papers in earnest, requiring me to report at the other end of the country, Lanarkshire, on Wednesday 2 February 1944. Members of the Home Guard were ordered to bring their uniform with them and, nothing of this having been said at school, I wrote to my old CO for guidance. The Headmaster's reply was terse to the point of rudeness: 'You should have taken your uniform with you. If you need it come and collect it. Let Fielder [the quartermaster] know when you are coming.' That was all: no good wishes for my coming career in the army or regret at my premature departure from Housie. As an example of the 'ancient house's' care for its departed sons it was not impressive.

My next contact with the school came some weeks later when, as a new recruit, I was enjoying a mid-morning break in a training session, lying on a Scottish hillside from which the snow had only recently vanished. Seeing the Horsham postmark on the envelope I had saved up a letter I had received that morning to read at leisure, anticipating that it would contain details of a local Old Blue offering hospitality to those stationed nearby, or perhaps a morale-boosting book token. I soon learned differently. My correspondent was the Lady Superintendent, 'the Hag', and she wasted no words on good wishes or even normal courtesy. Had I been a pantry-boy who had made off with the school's spoons I could not have been addressed more peremptorily. She had, she said, learned that I had literally walked off with my school shoes, which remained its property, and I should return them at once. The school's policy of appropriating all our clothing coupons had, of course, left me no option. Was a leaver, I wondered, expected to re-enter the outside world barefoot as so many newcomers in its early days had joined it? I wrote as cold a reply as I could that evening in the NAAFI promising to return the shoes at the first opportunity, amused once again at the gulf between that noble sentiment 'Love the brotherhood' and the chill reality.

Later still came a copy of *The Blue* recording my departure in the Peele A House Notes. As the 'oldest inhabitant' of the house, now serving his country, I had expected a modest 'obituary' but found my name merely listed as a leaver with two other, much younger, boys, one of whom had achieved an eminence of his own, for he was still a new boy, having succeeded where others had failed, in persuading his parents to let him leave after his first term.

That same issue of *The Blue*, as well as recording the death on active service, in the RAF, or in captivity in the Far East, of several members of my former house, also contained an intriguing idea:

> Some amusing stories are told of Old Blues being for weeks in the same mess, the same camp or the same office without recognising one another...It has been suggested that Old Blues should occasionally whistle or hum a few bars of the Votum, which, if heard by another Housey man, would lead to instant recognition.[1]

I never put this to the test and recognised all too readily the one Old Blue – the same individual who had years before competed with me in the Newbury 'Special Place' exam – I did encounter. But I was well aware, though at that time I felt little desire to claim the title, that I was an Old Blue for ever.

Others have reached the same conclusion. 'Is there life after Housie?' asked one of my contemporaries in *The Blue* in 1986, 38 years after he had left Barnes B. 'I am still trying to make up my mind.'[2] Proof of his uncertainty was provided by the reminiscences he contributed to the magazine around that time, on which I have drawn heavily in earlier chapters. My own immediate response was, as I have described, to begin the autobiographical novel which has proved invaluable in writing the present book. It has been said that one of the hallmarks of the Old Blue is an obsessive desire to talk about his schooldays and this I believe to be true. 'It sounds as though it all happened only yesterday,' I can remember one observer remarking after listening to another Old Blue and myself indulging in recollections of our years at Horsham, and I have sometimes given a public pledge on joining a group or dinner table not to mention Christ's Hospital, only to break it at the first mention of games or education or food. Few topics do not seem in some way to lead back to Housie – the foundation has marked, or scarred, us for life.

Meanwhile in that bleak Scottish field, conscious that I was better fed, no worse housed and less subject to perpetual games and niggling discipline than I had been at school, I put that final uncaring letter in the pocket of my battle-dress, the last I was to receive from my old school until it began to send me appeals for money. A landmark, I realised, had been passed. Camp Close, with its poverty but prevailing warmth, Christ's Hospital with its occasional riches and perpetual privations lay behind me, having made me, for good or ill, what I was. The shaping season was over. Real life lay ahead. Meanwhile there was a war to be won.

---

[1] Mar-Apr 1944 p.49
[2] Dec 1986 p.258

48

A FRIGHTFUL BANG

A frightful bang woke me in the night.

Diary of Peele A boy, 29 June 1944

Having spent the first four years of the war at school I was, sadly, not there to witness its closing stages. While I was preparing for my new career as an Army clerk the fields and roads around Christ's Hospital, as throughout the south of England, were displaying signs of the approaching invasion of Europe. The units stationed near the school were Canadian, destined for 'Juno' beach in the centre of the British assault area, and they were extremely popular with those boys who, no doubt illicitly, ventured near their camps during Sunday afternoon walks to return laden with chocolate and 'candy'.[1] The climax of the Canadians' presence came with an inspection in the school grounds of this part of his forces by the future Field-Marshal (later Viscount) Montgomery. He was then a great popular hero and the boys were, to their disgust and no doubt to his, strictly forbidden to approach him for his autograph; one who did was warmly welcomed. 'Monty' was a less impressive figure in the flesh than in newspaper photographs. To one schoolboy observer he seemed disappointingly small in stature, while another felt that the Commander-in-Chief of 21 Army Group appeared 'scruffy in his black tank beret decorated with various badges and his ill-fitting battle-dress...He never looked like a real general at all.' The school's own sergeant-major, a stickler for correctness in such matters, loudly voiced his disapproval of the then general's turn-out to the members of the school JTC lined up, for no very good reason, since *they* were not about to be committed to battle on the beaches, behind the Canadians in the Quad. His schoolmates presented, this witness felt, a 'somewhat anachronistic appearance' with their 'out-of-date weapons' but all was redeemed by their commander, Blamire Brown, who, as I have suggested earlier, was more suited to the military than to the pedagogic life. 'Immaculately turned out in his cavalry twill, highly polished Sam Browne belt and boots and his regulation peaked cap' Blam easily outshone Montgomery.

A curiously ill-timed prank occurred at this period, since described by a member of Middleton A. There a group of Signals enthusiasts set up a home-made wireless transmitter on the fire escape outside the senior dormitory, and, identifying itself as Radio Anti-Kappa, a nickname I have explained earlier, 'broadcast clandestinely to the whole school in strange schoolboy humour and Housey vernacular'. This being largely German-based the transmissions, when picked up outside the school, caused some concern to the authorities 'and much interrogation ensued', those responsible being fortunate to escape serious consequences.[2]

The approach of D Day brought the Housey Home Guard its finest hours. In a night exercise it humiliated a Canadian battalion, arriving undetected after 'an approach march of several miles, the last part at the crawl...within easy watching distance of the battalion HQ.' At first light, recalls one proud participant, 'we went in like a posse of Red Indians just as the colonel was served with his breakfast. They did not know what had hit them and we felt it wise to keep moving before they really got angry. Later that day there was an official visit to the school to congratulate us on our fieldcraft.' [3]

Soon afterwards the School Home Guard unit was warned to be ready 'to provide sentries on the South Coast during the first seven nights of June'[4], as one boy naively revealed in a letter to his mother on 21 May. 'This...,' he admitted later, 'practically told the world when to expect D Day', but luckily the mother had more security sense than her son and the secret remained undisclosed. As it was, groups of boys, equipped for once with live ammunition, were sent to fend off any German attempt to disrupt the embarkation process. Some actually spent the night of 5/6 June 'in a slit trench...on the beach at Angmering near Worthing', the nearest to action the Christ's Hospital company ever came.[5] Another member of it recalls waiting the summons to arms in a requisitioned bungalow behind the shore and looking out in amazement at the vast armadas of aircraft passing overhead, all making for France.

The Home Guard had hardly returned to their classrooms when the flying-bombs began, the offensive starting in earnest on the night of Thursday 15 June.* Although the main line of attack lay over Kent, Sussex was not far behind and eventually 880 of the missiles crashed within its borders, while many others flew over it en route to the real target, London. The Chapel tower, from which we had once watched for incendiary bombs, again provided a perfect vantage point and the Home Guard just quoted recalls seeing his first ever V-1 buzzing purposefully across the sky above the eastern Avenue heading north-east. Like Kent, Sussex suffered far more from flying-bombs shot down on to it by the defences than those which simply fell short of their target and it

---

* On this whole subject see my book *The Doodlebugs*. It includes no reference to the incident described here which did not merit a special mention in the official records.

was one such 'success' which ended the school's long immunity from damage. According to *The Blue* 'a little before 5 am on Thursday June 29th a flying-bomb, shot down by a zealous night-fighter, crashed into the trees' between the Infirmary and the back of the houses on the eastern side of the Avenue.[6] An account of what followed, previously unpublished, was written at the time by a Peele A friend, then in his last term before call-up:

> A frightful bang woke me (and not me only) in the night, but the Tube was a certain amount of comfort to me and soon I was asleep again. The next thing I remember was A. waking me and saying 'Home Guard's got to muster!' Once conscious I proceeded upstairs and to don my HG uniform, wearing my first year chevron [recording twelve months' service] for the first time. Then we learn that we had to muster on the 'Sicker' mile [ie the road behind the Infirmary] because the bang had apparently been a PP [Pilotless Plane] exploded in the air by fighters above our Sanatorium, just missing the Sicker...
>
> Suitably clad for guarding, L. and I set out on bikes shortly after 7am. L. was determined to go via the Post Office and Doctor's House. By the [Home] Farm, glass was over the road and when we entered the road end of the Sicker mile we saw the mess. The row of eight lock-up garages was shattered and six cars belonging to masters etc were damaged beyond repair. Several trees had been blasted free of leaves and branches...Leaves covered everything, as in autumn, though the trees were still in their prime. The night's Home Guard picket were guarding all approaches and three policemen were strolling about. San B's roof had collapsed and San A was none too happy. We talked with one policeman and he said, 'Anyhow, it's a blessing there's been no life lost.' The Sicker had several broken windows, but it blared the[radio] news at us, as always, from the wards. Then at the back of Maine, which was also bereft of some windows, we met our party with Blam, looking very tired and unwashed, but amiable...
>
> We had come to relieve those who had been on duty since 4.30 or 5.30 am. L. and I were posted with R. near the Sanatorium and all we had to do was to prevent unofficial people from coming near, ie we just waited about. The Head came to view the mess with Blam and was not delighted. I just stood and enjoyed contemplating the day (my eighteenth birthday) [and] the sky. About 8.15 I was relieved by 'Sweat' [a Peele A boy] who stayed all morning to stand about and sweep up glass and miss school. I went for breakfast with a few others...then returned to Peele A to wash, open post and go to school one period late.

The school had got off remarkably lightly; if the missile had not exploded in the air but had come down 100 yards or so further south the whole Maine block would have been demolished with, almost certainly, heavy casualties. As it was only one person was cut by flying glass but her injuries were officially 'minor' and she was able to carry on with her work. The whole incident was in fact clearly more stimulating than frightening, at last giving the Home Guard and the ARP services a taste of action. Beside Blam, made unwontedly cheerful by it, 'Bonzo' Averill, as Chief Warden, was soon happily directing salvage operations, aided by the engineering grecians.[7] The wrecked building had been used as a storehouse and it was the smell those involved remembered best, from the carbolic disinfectant which impregnated the boots of those who cleared up the broken bottles in the infirmary 'shaken off the dispensary walls by the explosion'.[8]

Although the Home Guard had apparently been safe underground when the V-1 landed, the rest of the school had been sound asleep in their dormitories, until awakened by the explosion and, in some houses, by the sound of broken windows tinkling on to the floor.[9] The wire netting over the frames, installed, as I have described, back in 1939, worked perfectly and no one was as much as scratched, though one boy in Maine A, nearest to the explosion, became hysterical, a lapse he was probably not allowed to forget.

This incident, which could so easily have caused a major disaster, ended any disposition to take 'the doodlebugs' lightly. The rigid discipline the school had for so long imposed upon its pupils and even their archaic uniform now came into their own. One Old Blue remembers the evacuation drill in chapel when V-1 activity was reported. 'Houses at both west and east ends make a rapid but orderly exit and disperse, while those in the middle dive under the pews with their Housey coats over their heads.' Only the most junior years, in 'civvies' because of clothes rationing, lacked such portable protection. The siren, since flying-bombs often arrived unheralded at any hour of the day or night, singly or in convoys, was an unreliable guide, but the school bell could now be rung to signal imminent danger – in 1940 it had been silenced as bells were then reserved for warning of invasion. Best of all were one's own ears, for the missile was immensely noisy and the engine cut out about twelve seconds before it dived to earth and exploded. As everywhere else, it was soon realised there was little danger so long as you could still hear the machine.

One boy was deeply humiliated when his mother, from Yorkshire, 'flung herself under some conveniently handy bushes' when a flying-bomb appeared over Big Side during a cricket match while the 'more sophisticated and world weary' players and other spectators ignored it. Later he was told 'She's a real funk – like you', an insult that had to be avenged in blood.[10]

At times, when the unwanted visitors overhead seemed particularly persistent and frequent, the school spent part of the night in the Tube, as during the Blitz, but mostly life went on almost as normal. Apart from its time in chapel the boys were at greatest risk when assembled in the Dining Hall but here a new routine was rapidly evolved. Noel Sergent, as Hall Warden, would give four sharp blows with his gavel when an approaching flying-bomb was reported, whereupon the boys dived under the heavy tables, until a further knock announced that the danger was past.

For Christ's Hospital, as for the whole country, the last winter of the war was a trying, cheerless, seemingly endless time, with only the standing down of the Home Guard in November, an event considered of too little importance to be recorded in *The Blue*, to give promise of approaching victory. The melancholy list of Old Blues killed or wounded in action grew steadily longer. (By the end of the war the Roll of Honour of those killed was to reach 175, a grievous loss, but happily less than the 368 of World War One.)[11] By late 1944 nearly 2000 Old Blues, of whom I was one, were in the forces, but already there were signs of the approach of peace. A committee, it was recorded, had been set up to consider what form the school's war memorial should take.[12] By early 1945 the first master serving in the army had been released to return to teaching.[13]

With the end of the fighting in sight and a return to 'real soldiering' in prospect the JTC had once again been able to hold a camp in the summer of 1944, though the numbers were lower than pre-war. Meanwhile the steady erosion of older boys due to the call-up continued, with only future scientists, doctors and engineers able to complete their school education.

The news that the war in Europe was over, sadly mishandled though the announcement was,[*] reached Christ's Hospital during prep., when the school bell, one who heard it remembers, 'started to go on and on and on.'[14] Here was a message even more welcome than 'No PT' or the end of a lesson. 'Everyone got up from the tables, flung down books...and started to pour outside into the Avenue...shouting with jubilation "The war is over! The war is over!"...We never did return to prep....[but] broke up into a series of informal, anarchical parties which went on...until midnight.' Boys of all levels of seniority actually walked on the sacred path and lawns normally reserved for the feet of first-parting grecians but for once neither house-masters nor monitors intervened. 'That evening', recorded *The Blue*, 'we spent chiefly in spontaneous outbursts of exuberant joy, which took various forms, ranging from hurtling over the asphalt on considerably overloaded bicycles to adorning King Edward with garments he would never have worn of his own accord.'[15] My old housemaster was said to have demonstrated his newly acquired dual nationality by parading with a Union Jack over one shoulder and a tricolour over the other, while singing the *Marseillaise*.

The following day, VE Day itself, was a holiday, with the rising bell sounding later than usual, a thanksgiving service in chapel, a band concert in the quad and a bonfire, formed of 'a condemned rick', on Sharpenhurst, the traditional site for such celebrations. 'Most of the most prominent members of the late unlamented Nazi Party were present,' *The Blue* reported of the guys,

---

[*] See my *When We Won the War* p.55.

'though a casual observer might not have recognised them...An atmosphere of general fun and games prevailed, punctuated by intermittent bursts of song...Another rick was fired...[which] threatened to set fire to Eastlands copse but, much to the disappointment of certain elements, that catastrophe was avoided. After the bugles', playing the *Last Post*, ' had sounded and a well deserved cheer had been raised for the Headmaster, we joined hands for *Auld Lang Syne*.'[16] It was a most un-Housey like scene, repeated in a milder form on the following day, 'a three-quarter holiday' when *I do like to be beside the Seaside* was, unprecedentedly, played on the Big School organ. Even more appreciated was the 'two-course supper' served on VE Day itself and the short-lived improvement in the food that followed. 'I think at one time,' records an Old Blue, writing in 1986, 'we even had egg and chips.'[17] That autumn, for the first time since 1938, St Matthew's Day was celebrated with a march through the City. Christ's Hospital, having survived the second world war, as it had the first – just as it had survived the Reformation, the Civil War, the Great Plague, the Great Fire, the Glorious Revolution and the Gordon Riots – was getting back to normal.

---

[1] Mar 1986 p.127
[2] Hull p.176
[3] Jul 1995 p.145
[4] Mar 1996 p.67
[5] Jul 1995 p.145
[6] Nov-Dec 1944 p.2
[7] Nov-Dec 1944 p.2
[8] Dec 1992 p.216
[9] Jun 1991 p.129
[10] Mar 1986 p.126
[11] Sep 1960 p.133
[12] Nov-Dec 1944 p.18
[13] Mar-Apr 1945 p.35
[14] Mar 1986 p.128
[15] Jun-Jul 1945 p.72
[16] Jun-Jul 1945 p.73
[17] Mar 1986 p.128

49

A BETTER AND A HAPPIER PLACE

CH is a better and a happier place to live in than it was when I left it.

Old Blue and former master, January 1969

Christ's Hospital was slow to respond to the vast changes in society and the educational world which followed the end of the war. The regime altered little in those first post-war years and by 1950 even the new boys were back in the traditional uniform.[1] An outstanding education was still being provided for the few destined for Oxford and Cambridge, especially those fortunate enough to join the History Grecians, where my hero, DS Roberts, was joined as assistant, and after his death succeeded as Head of History, by a man soon regarded with the same devoted, near idolatrous, affection, Michael (MT) Cherniavsky. 'Cherney', had a most unlikely background to be teaching at Christ's Hospital, being born in Argentina, of a Ukrainian Jewish father and rich Venezuelan mother, and having, as a Pacifist, served in the Pioneer Corps during the war. He had hardly arrived at Housie, in 1948, before being denounced by a matron as a Russian spy, and outraged many of his colleagues by abolishing beating in 1953, when he became a senior housemaster.[*] In 1956, during the Suez crisis, his telegram to the Leader of the Opposition 'Pull no punches tomorrow, Eden must go', 'caused a furore in the Common Room which almost ended in fisticuffs'.[2] When Cherniavsky left, to join a Canadian university, in 1966, the History Grecians were described as 'a privileged sect...expected to imbue their contemporaries with political and social awareness, with an appreciation of our cultural heritage'.[3] They benefitted especially from 'Cherney's journeys to the historical cities of Normandy, Anjou, Burgundy and elsewhere, where sightseeing was supplemented by a rich diet of food and drink', though I would have disagreed with his dictum, during the first post-war visit to France he led in 1949, 'I would prefer a good Romanesque church to a good steak.' I met him

---

[*] His obituary in *The Blue* is incorrect. Cherniavsky was not junior housemaster in Barnes B, but moved there as senior housemaster in 1953, having been junior housemaster in Lamb A.

only once, at a post-retirement lunch in his honour, but was delighted to read in his obituary in the *Daily Telegraph* that 'His more conservative colleagues were alarmed at the way he quietly encouraged his pupils to question some of the school's traditions.'[4]

One of these, as I have made clear, was the lack of amenities taken for granted elsewhere. 'At last we have a house wireless!' rejoiced the Peele A House Notes in *The Blue* in the summer of 1948;[5] it had been paid for in memory of the boy whose nursemaid I had been, who had died in an accident soon after leaving. Far more significant was the next step towards a more civilised environment, the provision in 1954 of a 'Quiet Room', as I had suggested in my essay on the school back in 1943. The school authorities had been pushed into action by an enlightened master and the enterprise cost a mere £350. 'Those who wish to work or read in peace now do so,' the House Notes recorded, 'leaving the dayroom free for more noisy pastimes.'[6] This long overdue facility, regarded as an experiment, confined as it happened, to my old house, unleashed an avalanche of improvement, for 'The Headmaster brought down a group from the Council of Almoners to inspect the new arrangements', leading to the creation of 'a committee...to make plans that would not only include more studies and a quiet room but also more accommodation for masters, as a result of more members of staff being married.'[7]

Progress thereafter was slow. This was partly because the new Treasurer, Barnes Wallis, whose authority, especially in technical matters, was unchallengeable, insisted that he was 'building for the future'[8] but also, as the then Headmaster acknowledged when the blueprint for the first round of improvements was finally unveiled, 'The winds of change seem rude and almost sacrilegious when they blow upon an institution so intimately loved by so many as Housie.'[9]

What had made drastic reform unavoidable was the announcement by the Ministry of Education in May 1946 that university grants would not in future be confined to the small handful who won a scholarship or exhibition but would be awarded to all those 'likely to complete a university course with credit'.[10] Good results in Higher Certificate, soon to be replaced by 'Advanced Level' passes in the General Certificate of Education, would henceforward almost automatically enable those achieving them to go on to university, or some other form of Higher Education, with finance being provided by the local authority. In the next few years new universities, and courses in new subjects, multiplied and Higher Education of some kind became the norm for a wide range of school leavers instead of the exception.

Hitherto Christ's Hospital, academically at least, had catered admirably for the very able, especially in a few subjects, adequately for the routinely competent, discharged at 15 or 16 with School Certificate passes they might not have obtained elsewhere, hardly at all for the middle category of those who in other local authority or independent schools entered the sixth form for two years to leave at 17 or 18 for employment or professional training. Now this neglected group, rapidly growing in numbers, began to be encouraged to stay on at Housie. The arrival in 1953 of a new Headmaster, CME (George) Seaman, accelerated the acceptance of the new situation. Seaman was both an Old Blue and, like his immediate predecessor, a classicist, but he was far more receptive to the spirit of the times than his predecessors. According to that shrewd observer, Michael Cherniavsky, on the staff from 1948 to 1966, the new Head, who himself served to 1970, 'gave to boys of merely respectable academic ability the same opportunity of pursuing an "A" level programme as they would have had at any other good secondary school.'[11]

This new group, at first known by the quaint nickname of 'Joggers Deps' – Deputy Grecians specialising in the hitherto despised geography, or below the university scholarship level, in History and other subjects – rapidly grew in numbers. The sacred 'Discharge Regulations' which had laid down that no one could stay on beyond 17 unless likely to get a scholarship to Oxford or Cambridge, were given 'increasingly liberal interpretation' and finally scrapped, 'easily the most important innovation', in Cherniavsky's opinion, 'of the Seaman years'.[12]

An immediate consequence of these developments was an increase in the number of older boys, who took up more room, required more space for their books and possessions and were much affected by the liberated spirit of the times. To this even Christ's Hospital, in its rural fastness, could not remain immune, as the Senior Grecian's oration on Speech Day in 1960 reluctantly acknowledged:

> The Christ's Hospital boy is no longer so ready to accept as undiluted wisdom the counsel of his elders...Some boys are slow to recognise the restrictions of a boarding school...In spite of our blue habits...we remain children of our age....Juniors are no longer regarded by older boys as either servants or as objects beneath recognition...The school must in some respects adapt itself to the needs and changes of the times.[13]

For Christ's Hospital this was in itself a revolutionary sentiment and it found its expression in a long article in *The Blue* in September 1962 headed simply DEVELOPMENT, assumed to be written by the Headmaster. The 'sixth form' of grecians and deputy grecians, requiring smaller classes and hence more classrooms and masters, he pointed out, now numbered 250, while some houses contained twenty boys aged 16 and upwards instead of three. 'The present House buildings make little concession to their needs,' admitted the writer. 'For them privacy is not a mere luxury; yet the dayroom offers almost none.' Meanwhile younger boys were being exposed to 'the attitudes – often critical and sometimes bored and disillusioned, of their elders, and were not receiving' – here was an echo of the old Housie – 'proper training...to be clean, to be punctual, to be obedient...In continuing to keep together in one House, and for much of the time in one dayroom, boys of twelve and boys of seventeen, we are failing to provide what is desirable for either.'[14]

The solution proposed was radical, the division of the school by age, with six houses, from the Prep to Barnes, catering for boys aged up to about 13-and-a-half, where 'the dayroom will be the principal living place', but supplemented by 'a reading...and a hobbies room'.[15] The senior houses, from Lamb to Peele, occupied by boys from around 14 upwards, would have 'an entirely different character...in which life is not so implacably public', being provided with six additional studies, four of them shared, and, for all other boys, a 'toyce' in the existing dayroom, a small private area with a desk and shelves above. There would also be a 'brew room' where boys could provide their own snacks and hot drinks, new changing rooms and better lavatories. The proposed extension was to be built, just as I had suggested in my 1943 essay, at the rear of the houses, creating behind each block an enclosed courtyard and garden.

The programme of reforms even extended to the sacred area of sport. 'Games are the staple' of 'out-of-school activities' it was asserted, and 'Rugby football is...of all games the one most suitable to hold the interest and suit the capabilities of a large number of boys,' but better provision was needed for fives and tennis and less emphasis should be given to cricket. 'There is little value for boys of 17 in afternoon after long afternoon of compulsory and incompetent cricket; and a fair-minded observer might well think that this does more harm than good.'

The proposed reforms would mean a major change in the composition of the school. Entry via the Prep was to be abolished. The youngest boys would now arrive, as I had done, around the age of ten-and-a half, but would enter a junior house, moving on to a senior three years later. They would not, however, be transferred en bloc. At present, it was acknowledged, although 'unhappy, perhaps an odd man out', a boy 'is imprisoned for too long in a pattern of relationships...fixed when he was no more than twelve. A fresh start would be a clean wind of hope.'[16]

The reorganisation made possible the remedying of an old injustice. 'We shall,' the Senior Grecian announced in his oration on Speech Day, 1965, 'lose the Prep, but shall gain Leigh Hunt, to complete the trinity of Golden Age authors.' The official name, could, however be shortened to Hunt 'on the touch-line' – hard though it is to picture the essayist, or come to that, Lamb and Coleridge, venturing on to the rugger pitch.[17]

The separation of juniors from seniors meant the end of the Housey version of fagging, swabbing, and the Senior Grecian did not exaggerate when he declared in June 1965, 'In September, My Lord Major, the school will be entering upon a new era.'[18] Three months later, on Founder's Day, in October, with the improvements now well under way, the Headmaster was already claiming: 'We have escaped from the almost slum conditions of the old changing rooms and lavatories. We have also, I am convinced, the promise of an ampler life.'[19]

The same issue of *The Blue*, in January 1966, bore out his words. 'Amazing things are happening inside the Houses', it reported, recording the provision of new library books, 'three works of art' in one of the Quiet Rooms and, most amazing of all, that 'Peele A have now concluded their fourth term without a house punishment system'.[20]

Almost as revolutionary, and equally overdue, was the abandonment of the old, obsessive attempts to keep boys from different houses apart. 'School activities have become the norm', *The Blue* revealed in January 1966, explaining that the junior houses were being assigned to games and other recreations on an age rather than house basis. Boys in the senior houses could now choose from a number of permitted activities on Friday afternoon instead of being required to parade with the Combined Cadet Force.[21] As early as January 1959 a few unwilling conscripts had escaped to join the Public Service Corps, created to 'do something constructive for the community' such as creosoting the bicycle sheds or removing fallen trees.[22] One commentator in *The Blue* sourly dismissed it as 'a bolshey [sic] or pacifist let-out' but its numbers grew after the Ministry of Defence had ordered a major cut in the CCF, enabling it, as the observer just quoted commented, 'to throw out some of the worst elements'.[23] (The RAF Section, successor to the ATC, evidently contained, as in my day, people who actually wanted to belong to it; it retained 60 members, while the previously much larger Army Section shrank to 100.) The re-named Public Service Group had risen to 50, and 'become less of an institution employing the unemployable and more of a body doing a useful job'.

The Duke of Edinburgh's Award scheme also offered another non-military occupation, while membership of the Scouts was no longer discouraged, and a force of Community Service Volunteers helped at an old people's home and at a School for Spastics, whose pupils were 'always pleased to see the "boys with the yellow socks"'. In 1970 Field Day still continued, but, by a nice irony, since this was after all what battles were all about, the Community Service Volunteers spent it 'sorting out charred X-ray records in the mortuary of Horsham Hospital'.[24]

The Debating Society had been resurrected after its wartime suppression and the slightly suspect Study Groups of my time had been joined by many hobby clubs, devoted, among much else, to aero-modelling and agriculture, archaeology and astronomy, music and literature, films and politics, at last exploiting the opportunity a boarding school offered to bring boys of common interests together.[25]

Not everyone welcomed the modernisation programme. 'The old style house had its faults, like the naval gunroom,' conceded one Old Blue who had left in 1924, in *The Blue* in 1968, 'but like that institution it bred a type of man with much to commend him; could it be that the new system will turn out a race of self-centred prigs?'[26] Many, however, who experienced the supposedly liberal regime of this period would question whether things had really changed. One, at Housie from 1964 to 1972, recalled the school as resembling at that time, 'a totalitarian state, with no appeal and no justice' and had still not shaken off the effects 20 years later: 'Things come back to haunt you.'[27] An unidentified new boy, who arrived in 1965, made the same point more succinctly. 'After being at Christ's Hospital for two months,' he was heard to remark, 'I can now see why Coleridge smoked opium.'[28]

If much was left to do, however, improvement had undoubtedly occurred as the testimony of that most 'anti' of Old Blues, Keith Vaughan, confirms. 'In 1964, his biographer discovered, 'he revisited "Housey" (*sic*) and found that, while the Brangwyns and the distinctive uniforms...were just the same, the ethos of the school had changed beyond recognition. The good manners, openness, and seeming happiness of the boys astonished him.'[29] One master, in a farewell letter to *The Blue* in 1968 recalling his years as a boy in Barnes B from 1947 to 1955, and on the staff since 1963, was in no doubt. 'CH,' he wrote, 'is a better and a happier place to live than when I left it 13 years ago.'[*30]

The great reorganisation was accompanied by other changes. 'He found it necessary,' *The Blue* recorded in Seaman's obituary, 'to start with a cleansing of the Augean stables,' an intriguing allusion never explained.[31] Only from another reference at the same time can one deduce that he was also responsible for at least the beginning of the end for another Housey tradition. Soon after the new Head's arrival, in 1955, it was explained, a mother arrived on his doorstep with her son, a senior boy who 'had run home after receiving a beating for producing some totally inadequate prep'. She had brought him back, 'in high dudgeon' at his treatment. HLO Flecker would have rejected such parental interference. His successor, however, privately told the offending housemaster, 'Well, maybe you were a little over hasty.'[32] During the succeeding years, with no public announcement, the right to inflict corporal punishment was removed first from monitors, then from masters. A later Headmaster, Richard (RC) Poulton (1987-1996), told me that after taking over he had come across a long disused cane and had immediately sent it to its proper home, the School Museum.**

A number of changes had already taken place in the school's religious life designed to make the services more accessible to a wider age range. Separate Sunday morning services for juniors and seniors had been introduced, voluntary house prayers had replaced the compulsory Duty each evening and communion

---

* He later rejoined the staff, from 1972 until his retirement in 1996 and subsequently told me he had enjoyed his time at CH even as a boy.

** Beating has been banned in state schools in the UK since 1987 and in fee-paying ones since 1998. (*Daily Telegraph* 24 September 1998.)

services had regularly been held in the dayrooms. In 1950, for no very obvious reason, the *Christ's Hospital Supplement* and *English Hymnal*, which had given me so much satisfaction, had been replaced by the *Public School Hymnbook*. Other changes were to come later, with the introduction, in 1973, of *Hymns for Church and School*, a new and expanded *Psalter*, and the arrival of candles, carried in procession, and vestments. (The Brangwyns, happily, remained unchanged, but were now too uncontroversial to merit a second glance.) [33]

It was George Seaman who bravely undertook the most dramatic innovation, the ending for seniors of compulsory weekly attendance at Chapel, which he himself described as 'the most painful decision of his life'.[34] *The Blue* remains infuriatingly discreet about the background, but that it was pressure from below – this was the end of the 'Swinging Sixties' – which produced this then sensational change seems clear from the sermon Seaman delivered in July 1969. 'You have,' he told his mainly teenage audience, 'been deafened by the clamour of a grievance...So we must try a new way.' The juniors still had to attend Chapel every Sunday, but the seniors were allowed to stay away, except on the first and last Sundays of term, the minimum acceptable to maintain the school's claim to be a 'religious foundation' as past benefactors had assumed. 'This is a liberation for us all,' the Head told the school, 'for the few hostile and the many indifferent...You will hardly be able now to think of Chapel as belonging to the same order of things as Dinner Parade.'[35]

The consensus of opinion among those who worked under both seems to be that while George Seaman reformed the existing school it was his successor who transformed and humanised it. Dr David (DH) Newsome (1970-79) was not an Old Blue or a classicist but a historian. Educated at Rossall, he had previously been Head of History at Wellington – to which after leaving CH he returned as Headmaster – and senior tutor of his former Cambridge college. He was recognised from the moment of his arrival 'as a man for action and change'[36] and himself concluded that the school he took over in 1970 was infected by 'a somewhat stifling element, a claustrophobic atmosphere', demanding a 'relaxation process'. The first major sign of the new, long overdue enlightenment, came in 1973. 'On Sunday morning, July 8th...' recorded *The Blue*, 'as noon struck, the first half-pint was poured in the Grecians' Club.' This was housed in comfortable, purpose-built, centrally placed premises and here, amazingly to older Old Blues, beer and cider, though not spirits, were served. Equally remarkably, so greatly had the composition of the school changed, no fewer than 160 boys, being aged over 17, qualified for membership.[37] There was, however, one notable reminder of the Christ's Hospital tradition, at once economical and past-preserving. 'The front panelling of the bar,' *The Blue* recorded later, 'has been made from the old London table tops.'[38]

The Grecians Club, Dr Newsome believed, had 'enabled a boy to be the 17 year old he is', and, even more remarkably, had 'brought boys of different Houses together'.[39] His other great legacy, equally significant of the new spirit now prevailing, was the large new Arts Centre, opened in September 1974 in splendid new buildings on the edge of Big Side. The fruits of an appeal launched in 1971, to be mentioned later, the Centre included a number of new classrooms catering for the new or expanded specialisms of history, geography and economics, a modernised and enlarged Music School, an ingenious, strikingly modern, 200 seat auditorium for small scale productions, the Octagon, and, at its heart, a brand new theatre, internally not unlike Shakespeare's Globe, which could accommodate an audience of 600.[40] In a leaflet distributed to Old Blues, the new Head reassured them that the Drama Centre, housed within the Arts Centre, would not be 'a training school for future professional actors' nor 'pander to long-haired aesthetes' but would enrich the teaching of English, assist in curing 'adolescent self-consciousness and gaucheness' and provide a brand new sort of safety valve, a place where boys could 'let off steam in a new way'. The Appeal which financed the new facilities had been planned before his arrival but it was David Newsome who decided that 'a theatre was...much more necessary than a sports centre', a decision which led, he confessed later, on leaving, 'to alienation in some quarters'.[41] He remained unrepentant. 'The Arts Centre,' he claimed then, 'has been a real civilising influence. The boy who is fed up, who feels down, has only to cross the Avenue into the Theatre and he is in a new world; an exciting, a contemporary...escape from institutionalism.'[42]

The Appeal which financed the Arts Centre was merely the latest of a long series. I cannot recall any pre-war solicitation of funds but rising prices and a largely static income had created a new situation. On Founder's Day, 23 October, 1952, an Old Blues Thank-Offering Fund was launched, 'in the belief', a later letter explained, 'that Old Blues of both sexes would desire to mark a great occasion,' ie the fourth hundredth anniversary of the school's foundation, 'by acknowledging their gratitude to Christ's Hospital, and by coming to its aid in its hour of financial need'.[43] Every place now cost £223 a year instead of £117, as in 1939, but as HLO Flecker pointed out, 'unlike other public schools, Christ's Hospital cannot raise fees if it is to remain true to the objects of its foundation'.[44]

'The Thank-Offering appeal,' one master told me later, 'went off like a damp squib.' Those old friends of Christ's Hospital, 'the banks, insurance companies, financial institutions and larger business house in the City of London',[45] gave generously to the general Quatercentenary Appeal within which the Thank-Offering fund was subsumed, but individual Old Blues remained reluctant to put their hands in their own rather than their companies' pockets. 'Probably some 3,000 Old Blues' – including ex-Hertford girls – had, the letter of May 1955 complained, lost touch with their old school, while of the 5,000 contacted more than half (around 2,750) had not responded. [46]

It was charitably suggested that many potential donors were embarrassed to give only a small sum but the true explanation probably lay elsewhere. 'All training in our day had that one objective in mind...to win a university scholarship,' wrote one correspondent to *The Blue* in May 1954, still resentful of the fact 19 years after his premature departure from school. 'I wonder whether there is any correlation between the majority whose needs (if I am right) were not fully recognised and that other majority who have not so far responded to the recent appeal?' [47]

In 1962, an appeal was launched to finance the rebuilding required for the major reorganisation described earlier, but 18 months later a Progress Report recorded 'No less than 66% of Old Blues had not contributed.'[48] Six years later, in 1970, the President of the Christ's Hospital Club expressed astonishment that 'Very nearly half of the Old Blues presumed to be living appear to take no interest in their old School...It is doubtful, surely, that there are so many Old Blues who have no wish to have anything to do with the foundation.'[49] Subsequent events suggest, however, that he was mistaken. In February 1971 the then Treasurer announced the launching of a new Development Appeal with a target of £500,000 to finance the Arts Centre and other new buildings already described, as well as 'an indoor Sports Centre'. By June the Treasurer was professing himself 'disappointed' that the number contributing had been 'far fewer than we expected'. 'We must not fail Christ's Hospital,' he wrote, prompting me, and no doubt others, to reflect how in so many ways it had failed us.[50] Three months later the Appeal Director complained that an approach to 3,000 potential donors had resulted in 'only 900 subscribers'.[51]

This Appeal made use of small private house meetings to contact possible contributors. I attended one, having warned the host of my ambivalent feelings, which I found that others present shared. I expressed my sympathy to one of the professional fund-raisers involved, who told me disapprovingly 'Old Blues are the meanest lot of people I've ever had to deal with.' Not so, I told him. The school was now reaping the reward of the years when little was done academically for the majority of boys, while the few, like me, for whom the system had worked were likely for other reasons to recall their schooldays with horror. His most promising strategy, I suggested, was to forget any appeal to alumni nostalgia and to stress that every penny raised would help to make Christ's Hospital different from the place we had known.

In recent years fund-raising, less for specific objectives than to subsidise the school's regular income, has been a continuous process under the name of the Christ's Hospital Partnership, which unites parents, Old Blues and sympathisers including the City livery companies. Thus the Worshipful Company of Ironmongers paid for the purchase of a milling machine for the

Craft, Design and Technology Department,[52] successor to the humble Manual School of my day, and the Worshipful Company of Weavers financed the sewing machines used in a textile course in the same Department.[53]

The Partnership's activities are recorded in a newsletter, formerly *Link*, now *Housey*. Here, one can read of a woman giving away the family silver, ie selling a pair of silver candlesticks, for the school's benefit, and of boys raising money by 'carol singing', 'chopping wood' and even 'busking in Horsham'.[54] Did this hero, I wondered, still have to salute masters who passed him? As for the precocious punter who generously donated the £15 he had 'made on the Grand National' this would in my day have earned him a beating rather than public commendation.[55]

The money raised by the Partnership goes into an Annual Fund from which allocations are made to particular projects. In 1997, this consisted of further boarding house improvements including the 'redecoration of study bedrooms' and – a real breach with the past – 'the replacement of metal frame beds and purchase of new furnishings, curtains and carpets'.[56]

In seeking to attract support Housey suffered from a unique, self-inflicted, disadvantage, that those Old Blues who duly 'got on' in the world thereby disqualified themselves from sending their own sons or daughters there. This nettle, too, was grasped, in 1978, when the Council of Almoners decided that it was 'no longer correct totally to exclude children from higher income groups, and, in particular, children of Old Blues.' Henceforward 'up to 45 places for boys and 15 places for girls, in each year' were to 'be awarded on the results of competitive examinations' with 'preference...given to the children or grandchildren of Old Blues', without any income limit. The parents of the successful candidates would be charged according to their income up to the full annual cost, then put at £1,760 for a boy and £1,647 for a girl.[57]

Admitting children not in financial need marked a major step away from the traditional rules, though it had been argued as long ago as Coleridge's time that the school benefited from an admixture of entrants from better-off backgrounds. The new affluence, which had forced the change, was, however, accompanied by another increasing phenomenon of recent decades, marital break-up.

By 1989 a majority, 55%, of those admitted to Christ's Hospital came from 'incomplete families', usually with a single parent, and by 1991 the proportion was still 48%. 'We have found more and more disciplinary problems arising from instability', the then Headmaster admitted that year, predicting that raising the parental income limit from £23,500 in 1991 to £36,000, twice the national average income, in 1992, would 'create a bedrock of normality' and 'a balanced pupil community' by allowing in the children of Service officers and other professionals.[58] By 1998 the cut-off point, above which no reduction in fees was given, had reached £50,000, though one could, under the revised regulations, still send one's child there, even above that level, if he or she could secure a place as a New Foundationer, ie as a wholly unsubsidised pupil.

These changes have altered the character of the school less than might have been expected. In 1997/8 the full fees had reached £11,125, for either sex, but only nine parents were paying them, and 35% were being charged nothing at all.[59] The worst off also had their children's travel expenses paid and for everyone, however well-off, the uniform was free. Fees, though clearly important, form in fact only a relatively small part of the school's income, amounting in 1997/8 to £1,310,000, or 14.37% of the total running costs.

A curious feature of Christ's Hospital, basically unchanged since the earliest days, is that one can acquire the right to 'present', ie send a child there, though he or she has to pass a qualifying examination and the gift is technically an 'unqualified donation', with the would-be governor requiring the approval of the Council of Almoners. There are currently around 600 Donation Governors.[60] The minimum qualifying contribution is, from September 1999, £13,067 for an Old Blue, £16,331 for others, which entitles one to present a single child for his or her school career. These amounts can be reduced by making them tax effective, so that the net cost to an Old Blue becomes £10,060. The figure for a 'corporate donor' such as a company, is £39,195, and a few long-standing benefactors, like some City livery companies or Guy's Hospital, 'own' several presentations and can refill each place as its occupant leaves.[61] Of the 802 pupils in the school in October 1997, 484 of them boys and 318 girls, 193 boys and 130 girls had been 'presented', and 291 boys and 175 girls belonged to the 'competition categories', the balance being 'non-foundationers' with parents employed by the school.[62] All children now have to sit an entry examination but parents are advised to 'try and get a presentation' unless they feel their 'child is well above average in every way'.[63]

For anyone who remembers how eagerly the great prize of a place at Christ's Hospital was once sought it seems strange that the school now has to attract candidates for entrance. Special visits are arranged for primary school head teachers and – that old source of 'respectable' recruits – clergy, Open Days are held twice a year for potential parents to inspect the school and a continuous 'Raising Awareness' campaign tries to increase knowledge of the school through glossy but informative promotional literature and other activities. ('Please tell your friends and relatives. Offers from volunteers willing to distribute leaflets...are most welcome.')[64] There are even advertisements in the press, showing a smiling group of boys and girls in Housey uniform, with the caption 'These children will have an exceptional start in life...so could yours.'[65] The selection process, very sensibly, now involves a two-day stay at the school, which also enables them to demonstrate their prowess in sport, art and music.[66] One who remarked 'It's just like a holiday camp' must surely have been disillusioned later, but in September 1997 of 351 who 'experienced Housey at first hand' 126 were accepted, ie 36%.

Hostility for political reasons to independent education has led to a reduction in the number of entrants under the government's Assisted Places Scheme, now being phased out, and to far fewer competing for the 179 scholarships once offered by the London boroughs and the former London County Council. 'A majority of grecians had entered the school by this route,' recalled the school's historian, Professor Morpurgo, who was among them. 'The LCC provided an incomparable reservoir of talent.'[67] West Gifts were less affected, though here, too, the number of candidates, and successful scholars, dropped away from an average of 90 to an all time low of 19 in 1984.[68] Some local councillors and education officers in the three boroughs which benefit are indifferent, or opposed, to the scheme, but Newbury has remained notably loyal. On 29 October 1958 a plaque in memory of the Wests was unveiled in St Nicholas church by Barnes Wallis who admitted that 'the need for pure charity is passing away' but urged that 'it would be in the national interest...if the finest children were sent to CH'.[69] In October 1986 a party of grecians visited the town, touring a local electronics business, typical of the town's main new industry, and lunched in what was now 'The Old Town Hall' where I had tremblingly faced the examiners 50 years earlier.[70] In 1995 a memorial to the Wests was unveiled in the Cloisters at Christ's Hospital, a few yards from that of my old Newbury headmaster, GF Pyke.[71] In 1997 the largest group of West Gifts scholars, 24 of the total of 54 – early in the century it was 90 – came from Newbury and each Christmas the mayor continues to distribute largesse to them, though the modest shilling of my day has now risen to £1.[72]

Even if less eagerly sought after than formerly, a West Gifts place is still a major benefit to a parent, for in contrast to parents of presented children, who contribute on a sliding scale related to their income, no one, however rich, has to pay more than 50% of the true cost of a West Gifts place. The charity can well afford to be generous. Its assets in 1997 were £11.42 million, up £1.5 million on the previous year,[73] though, sadly, there seems little prospect of its surplus funds being divided among past scholars, and the 600 Wests pensioners, distant elderly kinsmen with no Christ's Hospital connection, receive only a meagre £130 a year.[74]

'I can't feel nostalgic about the school,' one of my contemporaries with whom I have revisited it told me, 'because it is no longer the place I remember.' Here, in my opinion, is cause for rejoicing and nowhere more than in an area where in our day it fell woefully short, the food. A dramatic improvement is said to have followed the arrival of a new Lady Superintendent in 1954. 'Notice-boards in the Dining Hall,' *The Blue* reported almost incredulously, on her departure 20 years later, 'advertised the fare for the week ahead and gathered around them appreciative groups of boys' eagerly anticipating 'not so much the turkey or the strawberries...as the imaginative variety of the ordinary meals, week in, week out.'[75] In 1968 came an even more remarkable change. The huge old tables, brought, like so much else, from Newgate Street were replaced by smaller ones, seating a mere 14 people, and food was now carried in on heated trolleys and served on a 'family system' at each table, largely ending the former tyranny of 'trades'. The food was now hot and the whole atmosphere improved, with, as one observer noted, 'hardly any standing up during the meal and...shouting up and down the table.'

Another significant change was the replacement in 1968 of the impractical bowls by normal, if substantial, cups and saucers. 'Let's have our kiff bowls back!' pleaded one reactionary, but these unhappy mementos of a rougher past had gone for ever, as out of date as the wooden platters they had replaced, or the crested chamber pots left behind in Newgate Street.[76] In September 1969, following the appointment of contract caterers, another concession was made to the changing times. 'Vegetarians', the Clerk reported in *The Blue*, 'are now catered for at separate tables.'

Changing the diet has proved far easier than improving the living conditions. If the years have vindicated the wisdom of buying a site far larger than the school then seemed to need, they have certainly not endorsed the policy of economising on the boys' houses adopted in 1902. No real improvement took place until the reorganisation in 1966 and the four individual studies per senior house, then provided, were inadequate both in size and number, though more have been added since and other changes are planned. A more modest reform, which affected even the most junior and which I would greatly have valued, was the installation, in 1969, 'of a an individual bedside lamp...for every boy in the school. Bedtime,' it was claimed, 'is now a much quieter and more civilised affair...The ceiling lights go out at the usual times, but the boys are allowed about half-an-hour's private reading.'[77]

When, back in 1943, I had argued in an essay in favour of co-education, I had had little expectation that this would ever be introduced at Christ's Hospital. But in 1980, faced with a rising deficit and the crippling cost of maintaining two separate establishments, the Council of Almoners took the heroic decision to merge them, explaining in a letter to Old Blues that, 'though its deliberations arose from financial considerations...the Council believe that...boys and girls would, on balance, benefit from being educated together'.[78] The process took five years and involved a cut of 300 in the number of boys to accommodate the same number of girls at Horsham. The sacrifice of Hertford – 'the oldest girls' school in the country', as its prospectus boasted – saved the joint foundation.[79] The £3,100,000 raised by the sale of the site to a supermarket financed the move and the consequential alterations at Horsham. These involved, one of the architects revealed, a preliminary 'debate on the dimensions of the average girl which...was never definitely settled, even by the Headmaster'.[80]

I visited Christ's Hospital, Hertford, for the first and only time, on the saddest day in its long history, Wednesday 11 September 1985, when the last items of furniture and equipment were being disposed of in a 'Final Sale by Auction'. As I made my way from the nearby station through the quiet market town to the encircling wall and through the ancient gateway, topped since the school's arrival in 1776 by statues of pupils in uniform, I felt that at last I had discovered the fictional Greyfriars of my childhood. This impression remained as I explored the central Square of dormitory blocks and main buildings, and made my way to the playing fields, all conveniently close together, giving the whole school a kindlier, cosier feel than the cheerless expanse of Horsham. In one room the uniforms from dark blue undergarments to the smart and sensible 'blue pinafore dresses...Harris tweed coats, raincoats and blazers' were being auctioned off.[81] On a blackboard in a now deserted classroom, was chalked the single poignant word 'Goodbye'.

The Merger, as it was known, was accomplished with remarkable smoothness, the reunited Christ's Hospital assembling on the first day of term, 13 September, in 1985, under an Old Blue Headmaster, John (JT) Hansford, with experience of co-education.[82] In contrast to their treatment during the war, women now became full members of the former Masters (now Staff) Common Room, while the boys, as *The Blue* described, made the newcomers welcome from the first. 'The atmosphere around the school was generally very sociable, somewhat akin to that of a good holiday camp...and some people, naturally, got a little more friendly.'[83] On Founder's Day 1985 the President, the Duke of Gloucester, unveiled a commemorative plaque, recording the reuniting of the two schools. Symbolically, perhaps, the original foundation stone had to be lowered to make room for it.

The girls' houses catered for all ages, with 'study/cubicles for the seniors on the second floor', while the juniors occupied small dormitories and worked at 'toyces' in the former dayroom. The scrapping of the urinals made possible the provision of 'a fully equipped laundry room...which even the boys may envy' and the ancient lockers disappeared 'to free the old bootroom for ironing boards'.[84] The inadequate buildings opened in 1902, however, and, no doubt, lack of funds, left the resulting accommodation less impressive than it sounded. I was dismayed at the tiny bare cubicles occupied by the seniors, which I saw soon after the merger, for they were markedly inferior to the elegantly furnished and comfortable bed-sitting rooms I had recently seen in another girls' boarding school. Another member of our party, a local government official, was even more shocked by the overcrowded, barely furnished, dormitories occupied by the junior girls. 'If I were here on duty,' she told us loudly, 'I would have to have this place closed down.'

The physical appearance of Christ's Hospital suffered sadly in the great storm which ravaged much of England in the early hours of Friday 16 October 1987. Clearing up the 240 trees 'blown down or hurt beyond recovery' made my wartime leaf-gathering seem a very minor achievement. 'The Avenue and Quarter Mile,' it was recorded, 'have been virtually destroyed.'[85] I read with wry satisfaction that 'the roofs of the swimming pool and gymnasium were blown off,' reflecting, as I recalled my many miserable hours in both, 'It's an ill wind...'

In fact plans were already in hand to replace the former cowsheds which had housed these amenities with an impressive new Sports Centre, occupying a 'total floor area almost the size of the quadrangle, containing six squash courts, a weights room, a 25m [80ft] swimming pool and two indoor pitches suitable...for badminton, tennis, hockey and football'.[86] It also, I discovered, on somewhat reluctantly visiting it, included a number of 'social' areas where groups of chairs and tables and machines serving hot and soft drinks, positively encouraged lingering to chat, making it the younger boys' equivalent of the Grecians' Club. The Sports Centre, like the Arts Centre, was also available for use by people from outside the school, and when opened in the Michaelmas term 1990, it formed the last major addition to the fabric of the school.[87]

The process of improvement in both the living and recreational facilities has in recent years been continuous, and unavoidable. 'The school of which you were so proud...even twenty years ago, would if it tried to exist today in exactly the same form be closed down by law within weeks,' Richard Poulton told the Founder's Day audience in 1994, and 'the press would be gathered at the main gate to expose the iniquities of the institution.'[88]

In the summer of 1999 a special edition of *Housey* was devoted to the grandiosely named New Master Plan for the coming century. This was designed 'after almost a hundred years of piecemeal additions' which had seen twice the amount of building envisaged by the original architect, to equip the school to cope both with 'current needs and...change and development in the next century'.

This message was underlined in an accompanying article by the Headmaster:

Despite the Barnes Wallis extensions and the conversion of many open dormitories, the houses today still have to accommodate the same number of children as the designers were happy to pack in a hundred years ago, despite the huge changes in parental expectation and the demands of the social services. Sheer lack of space in the houses has held back many desirable social, academic and recreational improvements.

The additions proposed cover almost every aspect of the school's life and reflect the transformation which has occurred in both the syllabus and the attitude to 'the children' since the original move to Horsham. A whole new Arts Quadrangle is planned, adjoining the present Main Quad and absorbing the former Car Park, with enhanced space and facilities for Design and Technology, for drama and music, including 'electronic music', for 'specialist language laboratories' and – perhaps most important of all – for 'private study' in the library, with the Dominions Library returning 'to its original use as a debating and recital place'. The visual arts, so neglected in my time, will be encouraged with 'covered routes and open verandas for making and displaying sculpture' and the motor car, almost unknown when the Avenue was built, is being so far as possible excluded, with 'a newly defined drop off point marking the beginning of the major pedestrian route through the school'.

One of the architects responsible is an Old Blue who arrived in Peele B in 1945, soon after I had left its neighbour. He had no doubt, as he recalled his reactions on returning to the school in 1998, that he was building for a very different place:

> The change from the almost monastic life at school in the middle of the century is remarkable. Everywhere one met a sense of enjoyment, with open relationships between staff and boys and girls.

As for the physical differences, he was, as I had been in my 1943 essay, quoted earlier, highly critical of the backs of the houses. 'Whereas the asphalts were the social core of our lives, they are becoming,' he complained, 'a large parking lot and buildings of indeterminate architectural parentage have been tacked on to the boarding houses.'

His approach, which he defined as one of 'creative continuity', is designed to impress anyone new to the school as soon as he arrives:

> We want the visitor to be met immediately by the marvellous romantic skyline before parking beneath the great old oak trees and walking past the new Common Room and Reception building through a sequence of spaces of changing character and scale, with contrasts of light and shade.

An enlarged Museum will be sited in the reception area, 'allowing', as *Housey* explained, 'school and visitors to engage with the history of the Foundation'. (Here is one move I regret. The Infirmary, for reasons I have indicated earlier, seems a wholly appropriate home for the Museum.) This reminder of earlier times is, however, merely a prelude to 'seeing the achievements of the modern school in parallel' via what might be called the 'Christ's Hospital trail' through the connecting network of paths and cloisters now planned.

While, as I have made clear, the governing body has often lagged behind the times, once the need for change has been accepted it has shown a striking readiness, when it does act, to do so radically. Nowhere has Christ's Hospital fallen further behind in the past than in the quality of accommodation in the houses, especially for the older boys and girls. Here, too, the Master Plan firmly grasps the nettle of improvement. The school's traditional elite, the grecians, are to be removed to two new custom-built buildings, one at either end of the Quarter Mile, at last giving them the comfort and privacy appropriate to their age and status, as the Headmaster himself has explained:

In the residence each house will occupy a tight-knit, self-contained 'pod' much influenced by an Oxbridge college staircase, with some social space at the heart of each unit of eight to ten rooms. The residences will cater for both boys and girls, with each gender in separate staircases or wings. At the heart of each residence is a superb common room...The design will encourage a positive, calm and civilised life style which has not always been easy to achieve within the hurly burly of the conventional house.

The removal of the grecians to separate accommodation will not, it is hoped, lead to the sharp division between them and the rest of the school which had such unhappy consequences in Newgate Street. This more mature minority, though living elsewhere, 'will,' in the Headmaster's words, 'retain a strong sense of identity and practical involvement with their house playing leadership roles, marching with it at lunch parade and feeling a full part of it through all their seven years.'[89] At the same time 'all age houses will be possible for boys', as has been the case with the girls since the Mergers, so the division into senior and junior boys' houses will disappear. It is also planned to raise the total number of pupils in the school to 850, still many fewer than before the Merger, but a major increase on the current total of just over 800.

The full Development Plan is expected to take ten years to complete and 'to bring the school's standards of accommodation for living and learning fully up to date' – an echo of the 'lodging and learning' first mentioned in 1552 – will cost £59 million, a formidable sum even for a wealthy foundation with assets of £224 million. Of this it is hoped that Old Blues will contribute £5 million through 'The 100 Years On Appeal', it being a century since the original move to Horsham. 'We can count on a very positive response from Old Blues,' the Clerk, Treasurer and Headmaster assured them in a note about the appeal circulated in October 1999.[90] Certainly the fund-raising is being approached in a highly professional way, with Old Blues being assigned to Decades, according to their time at the school, with a personal approach from an eminent and enthusiastic Old Blue of the appropriate period.[*]

Anyone who has observed the gulf between the professed intentions of modern architects and the often dismal reality of the resulting buildings may view some of the claims made in the Master Plan with a degree of scepticism. Nevertheless its aims, and boldness, cannot be faulted and it is undoubtedly a major landmark in the school's history. The occupation of the grecians' houses,

---

[*] My letter, from a Donation Governor, not known to me, who had left in 1939, was dated 6 October 1999. His task, he revealed, was to contact 'the boys of the Old Brigade' who had left 'prior to 1945'. There were, he revealed, '600 members of this Old Guard' who had joined the CH Club and 'thus their loyalty to CH cannot seriously be questioned'. To this appeal, a later letter, in December 1999, reported, 'Over 100 people have replied of which 70% have given financial contributions.'

and subsequent improvement in the existing houses, will provide a fitting start to the new millennium and the new century, the sixth into which Christ's Hospital has survived.

While in my day physical discomfort and incessant regimentation were regarded as a necessary, indeed desirable, part of the Christ's Hospital experience, the aim now is clearly to make the school as comfortable and civilised a place as funds permit, but there remain some notable exceptions to this policy. The most obvious example is the continuance of marching, with the girls now swinging their arms and stamping their feet in imitation of the boys. The Headmaster who presided over the Merger suggested that 'the marching and parades were to be regarded as...reminders of the traditions and history of Christ's Hospital, rather than just an expression of military discipline',[91] but I can recall a woman visitor laughing aloud at this outmoded spectacle and remarking how glad she was she had not exposed her son to such treatment.

Even worse, however, the third and best opportunity of the century to cast off that badge of a long departed past, the traditional uniform, has been thrown away. A board at the entrance to Christ's Hospital proudly proclaims 'The Bluecoat School', but for many years the uniform had become unfamiliar, even in London. As long ago as 1970 one boy taking part in the St Matthew's Day visit to the Mansion house described how 'we heard derisive comments like "What are those penguins doing?" and "Not another party from the Vatican?"'[92] The misconception that Christ's Hospital, that fiercely Anglican establishment, was a Roman Catholic seminary was even more widespread abroad. For the first post-war visit to France participants 'had been expressly asked to wear Housey uniform', but one who entered 'a demonstrably low joint near the cathedral' in Rouen was greeted by the proprietor 'with an explosive "Mon Dieu, un prêtre!"'[93] When the then senior grecian was invited to represent the school at the canonization service for Edmund Campion, supposedly an Old Blue, in Rome in 1970 he found himself addressed as 'Padre' while the mere sight of 'the uniform gave rise to people crossing themselves...I was even asked to hear a confession.'[94]

In the 40 years from 1945 to 1985 only trivial modifications were made to the traditional uniform. The introduction of 'a new and more comfortable light shoe' – though the old one was the least objectionable item of the previous outfit – merited mention in the Senior Grecian's Speech Day oration in 1969,[95] but the replacement of the old, inconvenient bands by a pre-fastened buttoned pair, in the following year, went unrecorded by *The Blue* until 20 years later.[*][96] It did report in 1971 the promise of better fitting breeches, 'measured for length as well as girth'. 1971 brought another, far more important, concession. Public

---

[*] See *The Blue*, March 1991 pp.60-61 for an informative account of changes in the uniform, prompted by a critical account of it in Alexander Davidson, *Blazers, Badges and Boaters* (Scope, 1990), a work I have not consulted.

display of the uniform had been since the sixteenth century its most valuable form of advertisement, but henceforward, it was announced, boys would no longer be required to wear 'Full Housey', ie the Bluecoat and yellow stockings, 'at the beginning and end of term', a concession later extended to Leave Days.[97]

If the full uniform is rarely worn outside the school, it is also frequently discarded within it. 'Half Housey', unknown in my time, is often the required dress, essentially 'shirtsleeve order' without the cumbrous Bluecoat, which to my eye seems to combine unsightliness with impracticality.

Instead, however, of the boys being given a redesigned uniform at the time of the Merger, it was the girls who lost their sensible uniform, resembling that of other schoolgirls, and were instead decked out in a ludicrous travesty of the boys' outfit, an ensemble never before worn by either sex in any century. I found it hard to believe my eyes when I first saw it or, rather, them, for the girls have two uniforms. For everyday purposes they dress, externally at least, like the boys, but with a short black skirt instead of breeches below the Bluecoat. For Speech Day, performing in public in the Band, and comparable occasions, they put on a more elaborate uniform, of short black jacket, long black skirt, boys' style girdle, and lace jabot. In a belated concession to femininity and common sense girls in the Upper Fourth and above (ie aged around 14 upwards) are allowed to substitute grey stockings for the unsightly and heavy yellow ones, another Housey 'trademark'.[98]

'Meat drincke and cloths, lodging and learning', it was to supply these to 'poore men's children' that Christ's Hospital was founded and 'learning' was interpreted from the first as enabling the brightest boys, whatever their background, to gain scholarships at Oxford or Cambridge.[99] This policy was, as I have described, much in evidence in my day and it continued for long afterwards, while the educational world changed. In 1966-7 grecians won a record number of such awards, 23; the former average had been 12. By 1980-81, however, the total had dwindled to a miserable three. 'Christ's Hospital was founded not simply to sustain the destitute and in need but to provide them with opportunities for advancement otherwise inaccessible,' the Old Blue Headmaster of the time, Derek (LG) Baker (1979-1985) reminded the Founder's Day audience in October 1981, admitting that he 'had not been happy with things academic' on taking over.[100] Others were similarly concerned. 'A school has higher priorities than the grooming of its most talented pupils for the Oxbridge scholarship stakes,' wrote the former Head of History, Michael Cherniavsky, quoted earlier, in 1982. 'All the same...the decline has been too great. As long as colleges continue to award entrance scholarships and exhibitions, CH should be winning its proper share.'[101]

Ten years later the trend had not been reversed. 'I am amazed,' wrote one who had left in 1956, 'at only four Old Blues going on to Oxbridge last year. Frankly those four, and the A level and GCSE results, hardly match the results produced at my daughter's comprehensive school, of similar size...If CH is not to give a better education than the public sector...there seems little point in being there at all.'[102] An Old Blue of the post-war generation – he had left in 1974 – while professing his concern 'at the apparent academic decline of the school', also widened the area of debate. Not only had Housey, he complained in 1982, secured a mere four places at the ancient universities, with not a single award, but 'the First Fifteen won only two of its 13 matches...Are there reasons for concern at CH?'[103]

A further complication has been introduced by the emergence in recent years of League Tables for schools, based on A level and, to a lesser extent, GCSE results. Much scepticism has been expressed about their value. 'Is it right?' asked Richard Poulton, Headmaster from 1987 to 1996, in *The Blue* in 1992, 'to compare, via one facet only, the multi-faceted jewels which are the best schools?' The true test, he suggested was 'added value', relating final achievement to the standard achieved on entry, and an assessment of 'the stability, the creativity, the integrity, the spirituality, the vitality of its leavers *ten years after they have left school*'.[104]

These are valid points. Most Christ's Hospital pupils, by definition, come from a less privileged background than those of other independent schools and are not solely selected on their academic ability. As for the other qualities mentioned, it is impossible to quantify such indefinables and Christ's Hospital has, however unfairly, to accept being measured by the same yardstick as everyone else.

Where, by this admittedly limited, test does Christ's Hospital currently stand? A list of 'Top Independent Schools' published in August 1999 and based on the recent A level results of schools entering more than 45 candidates placed it near the bottom of the First Division, at No 150 out of the 299 schools listed, a long way behind its old rival Manchester Grammar, which emerged at No 11 of the 20 schools making up the so-called Premier League.[105] A survey confined to 'The Top 200 Independent Schools in London and the South East' showed Christ's Hospital at No 74.[106] In 1998 the comparable national placing had been appreciably lower, at No 202 out of 312 and the regional one much lower, at No 74 of 200.[107] (The figures in 1997 had been 138 of 302 nationally, 68 of the 200 'Top Independent Schools' in London and the South-East.[108]) A comparison of pupils gaining five or more passes at grades 'A' to 'C' in the GCSE examinations, the nearest equivalent to the 'Matric Exemption' provided by the School Certificate of my time, left my old school at No 137 of 200 independent schools in London and the South-East in 1999, compared to 108 in 1998 and 126 in 1997.[109]

What of the Higher Education to which A levels now usually lead? An analysis in *The Blue* of those leaving in the summer of 1994 showed that 81 were going on to follow 70 different courses at 42 different institutions, some seeking qualifications in subjects such as Sports Studies and Hotel Management – useful, no doubt, but unlikely to produce a future Lamb or

Coleridge. A mere four pupils were going on to Oxford or Cambridge, with not a scholarship among them.[110]

In spite of such profound, but invisible, changes, Christ's Hospital is still recognisably the school I attended. The station, from which I made my way so reluctantly each term, still stands, though the last steam train chugged through it in 1964, the Guildford line, on which I travelled, closed in 1965, and the station itself, reduced in size, was demoted in 1972 to an unmanned Halt, with no porter left to deter would-be runaways.[111] The new community expected by the railway company to grow up nearby never did develop but now, a century later, a residential estate has been erected on the site of the former Home Farm under the evocative name of Bluecoat Pond. This was advertised as ideal for Old Blues 'seeking a retirement home in a unique setting', but I doubt if I shall be applying.

Just outside the ring fence the Post Office, to which we had to run as a punishment, still stands, though now a private house. The path still crosses the playing fields towards the Quadrangle and the Avenue, with its new-planted trees. In the distance, beyond the surviving Tuckshop, and the new but now mellowed Grecians Club and Sports Centre one can see the large red-brick pile of the Infirmary. Now far larger than needed, much of it has, since 1994, been converted into the school museum, and a single-bed Ward, like the one in which I recovered from sunstroke and so nearly missed becoming a historian, is now itself an exhibit.[112]

My old house, for all its Quiet Room and studies, remains to my eyes a cheerless place, where my spirits sink on entering. The history faculty, however, much expanded and complete with computers (the school acquired its first in 1977) now has a whole set of brand new classrooms, close to the splendid Arts Centre.[113] The woman teacher I encountered there had, understandably, never heard of the great DSR, but the Library, that constant source of consolation, where he presided, seems miraculously unaltered. So, too, does that other place of refuge, the Chapel, where I end my long, rarely nostalgic and often painful journey into the past, and at a specific moment, evensong on Thursday 23 October 1997. This was Founder's Day, the first I had ever attended, and a very special one, commemorating the laying of the Foundation stone of the Horsham buildings exactly a hundred years earlier.

It was surprising enough to find a woman priest, the Assistant Chaplain, leading the final prayers, but even more astonishing, after listening to the expected tribute to Edward VI, to hear her final words, which, I later learned, had been approved by the Headmaster:

Merciful Father, as we give thanks for the opportunities and pleasures of our own time at Christ's Hospital, remembering with joy those of our companions whom we loved, and those who by their good examples inspired and encouraged us, we also pray for those for whom school was not so rewarding – those who were lonely or unregarded, those for whom games or lessons were a trial, and those who felt a sense of failure. Graciously heal those who were hurt by their school experiences, help them to realise their gifts and know themselves beloved and cherished by you. For Jesus' sake. Amen.[114]

Here at last, I felt, was that public acknowledgement of imperfection, even guilt, which I needed to make my peace with that strange, unique institution where I had been so unhappy, but which had at the same time given me so much. Clearly others had felt the same uncomfortable mixture of resentment and gratitude, like one future Donation Governor who, to my knowledge, had been shamefully bullied and another, after my time, who actually ran away. I certainly felt no inclination to pay for anyone else to go there but I could now, I decided, come to terms with those seven years of my past which had haunted me for so long. I felt, at last and for the first time, no compunction about singing *Praise the Lord for our Foundation* and a little later, suitably fortified, or with sensibilities blunted, by champagne and Christ's Hospital claret, drinking a toast to the 445 year old Religious, Royal and Ancient Foundation.

---

[1] Apr 1950 p.78
[2] Dec 1992 p.232
[3] Sep 1966 p.194
[4] Quoted by *The Blue*, Dec 1992 p.232
[5] Jun-Jul 1948 p.132
[6] Jan 1955 p.5
[7] Jun 1992 p.149
[8] Jun 1992 op cit
[9] Sep 1962 p.144
[10] Dec 1982 p.13
[11] Dec 1982 pp.13-14
[12] Dec 1982 op cit
[13] Sep 1960 pp.129-30
[14] Sep 1962 pp.142-52
[15] Sep 1962 pp.144-50 & 172-73
[16] Sep 1962 op cit
[17] Sep 1965 p.162
[18] Sep 1965 op cit
[19] Jan 1966 p.2
[20] Jan 1966 p.8-9
[21] Jan 1966 p.29
[22] Jan 1959 p.2
[23] Jan 1966 p.29-31

[24] May 1970 pp.171-72
[25] Jan 1966 pp.32-37 & Jan 1970 pp.46-7
[26] Jan 1968 p.82
[27] Mar 1998 p.72
[28] Jan 1966 p.62
[29] Yorke p.33
[30] Jan 1969 p.50
[31] Mar 1975 p.2
[32] Mar 1975 p.11
[33] Apr 1950 p.78 & Feb 1973 p.4
[34] Mar 1975 p.4
[35] Sep 1969 pp.206-12
[36] Jul 1979 pp.61-2
[37] Nov 1973 p. 176 & pp.195-96
[38] Mar 1974 p.2
[39] Jul 1979 p.64
[40] CH Development Programme 1971-72. First Annual Report.
[41] Jul 1979 pp.63-4
[42] Jul 1979 pp.63-4
[43] Old Blues Thank-offering letter, May 1955
[44] HLOF letter Apr 1953
[45] May 1954 p.126
[46] Old Blues Thank-offering letter, op cit
[47] May 1954 p.137
[48] *The Building Fund* leaflet, nd but c.1964
[49] Sep 1970 p.285
[50] Letter from Sir Eric Riches, 1 June 1971
[51] Letter from Patrick Harrison, Sep 1971
[52] *Link,* July 1991, p.1
[53] *Housey,* Autumn 1997, p.4
[54] *Link,* July 1991
[55] *Link*, July 1991
[56] CH Annual fund 1997 leaflet
[57] Nov 1977 p.197
[58] *Daily Telegraph.* 2 Sep 1991
[59] Annual Report 1997 & 'Your Questions Answered' leaflet nd
[60] Annual Report 1997 p.43
[61] Information from the Partnership Office
[62] 'Number of Children' document 1 Oct 1997
[63] 'Registration and Information Form' c 1997
[64] *Housey*, Spring 1998 p.4
[65] *Evening Standard* 25 Sep 1998
[66] 'Registration Form' op cit
[67] Morpurgo p.125
[68] Annual Report 1997 p.40
[69] Jan 1959 pp.61-2

[70] Mar 1987 p.30
[71] Dec 1995 p.226
[72] Mar 1990 p.55
[73] Annual Report op cit p.28
[74] Annual Report op cit p.44
[75] Nov 1973 pp.241-2
[76] Jan 1969 pp.2-3
[77] Jan 1969 pp.4-5
[78] Letter of 16 April 1980
[79] 'CH Girls' School Hertford' nd but c.1980
[80] Dec 1983 p.12
[81] Hertford prospectus op cit
[82] Mar 1986 p.81 & Mar 1987 p.7
[83] Mar 1986 pp.75-6
[84] Dec 1983 pp.11-12
[85] Mar 1988 pp.6-13 & 47
[86] Mar 1988 p.47
[87] Mar 1991 pp.12-13
[88] Mar 1995 p.60
[89] *Housey* special edition Spring/Summer 1999
[90] Christ's Hospital, The 100 Years On Appeal. Undated circular, c.October 1999.
[91] Mar 1987 p.7
[92] Feb 1971 p.15
[93] Dec 1992 p.216
[94] Feb 1971 p.20
[95] Sep 1969 p.236
[96] Mar 1991 p.60
[97] Feb 1971 pp.61
[98] Information from CH
[99] CH Book p.9
[100] Mar 1982 p.119
[101] Dec 1982 pp.13-14
[102] Mar 1992 p.62
[103] Dec 1992 p.218
[104] Jun 1992 p.137
[105] *Daily Telegraph*, 28 Aug 1999
[106] *Evening Standard*, 27 Aug 1999
[107] *Daily Telegraph,* 29 Aug 1998 & *Evening Standard*, 22 Aug 1998
[108] *Daily Telegraph,* 23 Aug 1997 & *Evening Standard*, 22 Aug 1997
[109] *Evening Standard*, 3 Sep 1999, 4 Sep 1998 & 29 Aug 1997
[110] Dec 1994 p.170
[111] Dec 1983 pp.54-5 & Feb 1973 pp.5 & 74
[112] Mar 1995 pp.9-12
[113] Jul 1977 p.62
[114] 'Script for Evensong' 23 Oct 1997

50

AUTHOR RETIRED

The Worcester College Record *confirms that...Norman Longmate...now regards himself as 'author retired'.*

The Blue, *July 1993*

This book really ends with my leaving school but the reader may perhaps ask what use I have made of the education described. I remained in the army until September 1947 and in the following month went, belatedly, up to Oxford, aged almost 22, to read modern history. I duly took my degree in June 1950 but just missed the 'first' predicted by my former history master and by my tutors. I had, however, done sufficiently well to remain at Oxford for two years as a research student, but the resulting thesis failed to lead to a second degree and by the summer of 1952 I saw little hope of the academic career I had once contemplated.

In September 1952 I started my first job, as leader-writer on the London *Evening Standard*. This proved short-lived and I subsequently moved to the *Daily Mirror* as a feature-writer, a post I held from 1953 to 1956. I ultimately came to find working for a tabloid newspaper, even one whose politics I shared, unsatisfying and I realised I needed a more intellectually demanding position, with an administrative element. In 1956 I successfully applied for a post in the Central Electricity Authority, later the Electricity Council, thereby fulfilling my history master's second forecast, that I might help to run a nationalised industry.

Around the same time that I changed careers I was adopted as prospective Labour candidate for my home town, Newbury, then a safe Conservative seat, the necessary first step to Westminster. Disastrously for me, this was the period when the unilateralist nuclear disarmers were taking over the Labour Party and I was neither prepared to support them, nor waste my energies on a futile internal struggle. I rapidly resigned as a prospective candidate and by the time the Labour Party had returned to sanity and again become electable I had lost all interest in a political career.

My work with the Electricity Council brought me into contact with an Old Blue contemporary who had become a producer with BBC Schools Television.

He commissioned from me a trial script which was well received, and this led to further script-writing and ultimately to an invitation to apply for a post as producer of a new History and Current Affairs series in Schools Radio. The pay was derisory, involving a serious drop in income, but I had always admired the BBC and felt the opportunity to join it might not recur. I soon realised, however, that it was both more journalistic than I wanted and insufficiently demanding, with far less responsibility than I had been used to, and after only 18 months I applied for a post in the BBC's central 'Civil Service', the Secretariat, which resembled a government minister's private office. Though still, as so often in the BBC, ill-paid, the work involved constant contact with the BBC's senior management and Board of Governors and acquaintance (though at a subordinate level) with its policy making. It was, at least in the beginning, consistently interesting.

Ever since leaving Oxford I had been what the Inland Revenue described as 'a two job person', my second occupation being that of a freelance author, journalist and broadcaster. My first book, *A Socialist Anthology*, had been published in 1953, my second *Oxford Triumphant*, describing university life, in 1954, and, excluding some minor books related to the Electricity Supply Industry, my third, *Death Won't Wash*, the first of five crime stories featuring the same detective, in 1957. (I included 'Death' in all the titles to distinguish them from any 'straight' novels I might later write, but these have failed to materialise.)

Once settled into a basically 'nine to five, Monday to Friday' administrative post at the BBC I returned to my first love, history, as an 'all day Saturday' writer. My first social history, *King Cholera*, was published in 1966. My old school friend, Robert Pitman, was by now literary editor of a Sunday newspaper and he mentioned the book to an Old Blue publisher, who immediately commissioned it. Bob Pitman himself later gave it an enthusiastic review, as did numerous other newspapers and I was, as a result, approached by a different publisher with a suggestion for another book. I turned down the idea but he readily accepted my alternative, a detailed account of everyday life during the second world war, based on the reminiscences of ordinary civilians. The result, *How We Lived Then*, was published in 1971. The book was widely and favourably reviewed, serialised in a popular newspaper, and rapidly went into paperback. Thereafter I found no difficulty in obtaining commissions for books in either of my chosen fields, Victorian social history and the civilian side of the second world war.

In September 1983, after 20 years in the BBC, I took early retirement and began work on a major, two-volume book I had long contemplated, a history of all the invasions, and attempted invasions, of the British Isles, entitled *Defending the Island*. As the last serious study of this subject had appeared in 1876, there was a gap to be filled and I saw this as being my most useful and permanent contribution to British history. I was therefore disappointed when the first volume, published in January 1989, attracted very little notice, while the second, in September 1991 was almost totally ignored by the serious newspapers. Although both volumes went into paperback and still earn me a small Public Lending Right payment each year, the lack of reviews was discouraging and I decided not to undertake such a project again.

Having informed my college magazine, when asked for personal news, that I regarded myself as 'author retired' I was surprised to find this statement reprinted in *The Blue* with the addition: 'We shall see'. Perhaps the editor was right to be sceptical. Does an autobiography count? I am uncertain. At all events, should any publisher, Old Blue or non-Blue, wish to coax me from my self-imposed silence, or to commission a sequel to the present book, I am ready to listen.

A NOTE ON SOURCES

GENERAL

For background information on various aspects of the period covered I principally consulted:

BRIGGS, Asa, *The History of Broadcasting in the United Kingdom*, Vols. I-III, Oxford University Press, 1961, 1965 and 1970
COLLIER, Basil, *The Defence of the United Kingdom,* Her Majesty's Stationery Office, 1957
MIDDLEBROOK, Martin and EVERITT, Chris, *The Bomber Command War Diaries 1939-1945*, Viking, 1985, Penguin, 1990
MITCHELL, BR and DEANE, Phyllis, *Abstract of British Historical Statistics,* Cambridge University Press, 1962
MOWAT, Charles Loch, *Britain Between the Wars 1918-1940*, Methuen, 1955
TAYLOR, AJP, *English History 1914-1945*, Clarendon Press, Oxford, 1965

The main reference books I used were *Who's Who, Who Was Who* and *The Dictionary of National Biography,* with *Chamber's Dictionary* (1993 edition) for stylistic guidance. I also made considerable use of:

Chronicle of the 20th Century, Longman, 1988
Everyman's Dictionary of Literary Biography, Pan Books, 1972
Halliwell's Film Guide, 10th edition, HarperCollins, 1994
The Concise Oxford Dictionary of English Literature, 2nd edition, Oxford University Press, 1970
The Oxford Dictionary of the Christian Church, OUP, 1958
The Oxford Dictionary of Quotations, OUP, 2nd edition, 1958, and 4th edition, revised, 1996
Palmer, Alan and Veronica, *A Dictionary of Historical Quotations*, Paladin Books, 1985
The Oxford Dictionary of Music, OUP, 2nd edition, 1994
Ward, AC, *Longman Companion to Twentieth Century Literature*, 1970

PART I   BERKSHIRE BOY

The place of publication is Newbury, Berks, unless otherwise stated.

ADAMS, Richard, *The Day Gone By. An Autobiography,* Hutchinson, London, 1990

ALLAN, Stewart (ed), *Whereof that Town hath Great Need. A Brief History of Saint Bartholomew's Grammar School, Newbury,* The *Newburian,* 1972

ANSPACH, The Margravine of, *Memoirs, by Herself,* 2 vols, London 1826

BOOKER, Joan, *A Newbury Childhood,* Berkshire County Library, 1982

BOSWELL, James, *The Life of Samuel Johnson, Ll. D.,* 2 vols, Dent, London, Everyman's Library, 1946

BOWDEN, Puffy, *Wincanton, Pleasant Town in the Vale,* Privately printed for the Author, 6 Rushayes, Wincanton 1985

CANNON, Paul, *A Directory of Photographers: Newbury and District 1854-1945,* Newbury District Museum, 1991 (pamphlet)

CARSWELL, George, *The Descent on England,* Barrie and Rockcliff, London, 1969

COBBETT, William, *Rural Rides,* 2 vols, 1853, Dent, London, Everyman's Library edition, 1912

GARLICK, VFM, *The Newbury Scrap Book,* Published by the author 1983

GIBBS, Robert L, *History of St John's Church, Newbury,* Published by the author, 6 Wendan Road, Newbury, 1983

GRAY, Edward Whitaker, *The History and Antiquities of Newbury and its Environs,* Simpkin Marshall, London 1839

HADCOCK, R. Neville & MILLSON, Cecilia, *The Story of Newbury,* Countryside Books, 1979 enlarged edition, 1990

HOPSON, Sue, *Newbury, A Photographic Record 1850-1935,* Countryside Books, 1983

LUKENS, John, *The Sanger Story,* Hodder, London, 1956

MILLSON, Cecilia and others, *'The City', Newbury,* Littlefield Publishing, 35 Bartlemy Road, Newbury, for Newbury Field Club, 1992

MONEY, Walter, *History of Newbury* Originally published in 1887 as *History of the Ancient Town and Borough of Newbury,* re-published as *A Popular History of Newbury,* by WJ Blackett, 1905, and as *A History of Newbury,* with Introduction by Helen M Purvis, Newbury Bookshop, 11 Oxford Street, Newbury, 1972

NEWTON, REI, *St Nicholas School, Newbury, 1859-1959. A Centenary Souvenir* (Typescript) *St Nicholas School, Newbury, 1859* (pamphlet). In fact a guide to the school for the year 1983-4.

PHILPOTT, Bryan, *The Bombing of Newbury* (pamphlet), Pegasus Publications, 2 Cheviot Close, Newbury, 1989

PURVIS, Helen, *Talking about Newbury. A Brief History* (pamphlet), MD Weideli, 1988

'An Elder Resident', *A Little Bit of Wash Common* (pamphlet), Publisher not stated, 1995

RIGHTON, J, *Newbury and Neighbourhood,* Lovell Baines Print, Woolton Hill, Newbury, First published 1900, Second edition 1981

SANGER, George, *Seventy Years a Showman*, Dent, London, 1925

SMITH, E. Sharwood, *The Faith of a Schoolmaster*, Methuen, London, 1935

STOKES, Penelope, *'...No Apology is Needed'. The Story of the Newbury Weekly News 1867-1992,* Blacket Turner, 1992

SWEETMAN, George, *The History of Wincanton, Somerset, from the Earliest Times to the Year 1903,* Henry Williams, London, George Sweetman, Wincanton, June 1903

TOLMAN, Susan, *Newbury. History and Guide*, Alan Sutton Publishing, Stroud, Glos, 1994

WHITE, William (ed), *History, Gazeteer and Directory of Lincolnshire, 1856,* Reprinted by Kelley and Co, New York, 1969

On Holton I made use of the Local History pack in Wincanton Library, especially the extract from *Bragg's Directory* for 1840. On both Holton and Wincanton I consulted *Kelly's Directory* for Somerset for various dates from 1860 to 1910.

On my father's brief visit to Richmond I have consulted:

Kelly's Directory Richmond for 1907 and 1908, The *Richmond District Directory* for 1906, 1907, and 1908, The *Richmond Parish Magazine* for July and August 1907 and the *Richmond Herald* for 3 August 1907.

The dates of the quotations from the *Reading Gazette* appear in the text. On my father's career in Newbury I made use of:

Blacket's Street Directory, Newbury for 1930-33 inclusive, *Cosburn's Illustrated Directory* (the forerunner to Kelly's) for 1910 and 1912 to 1917 inclusive, *Kelly's Directory, Newbury* for 1930, 1931 and 1933 and *Kelly's Directory of Berks and Hants,* 1931. The *Newbury Weekly News* has been used extensively; the relevant dates appear in the text. My father's obituary was published on 26 July 1951.

On the pantomime see the *Newbury Weekly News*, especially for 2 January 1936 and 7 January 1937. On the great High School scandal see *John Bull* for 16 April 1932.

> PART II   THAT REMARKABLE SCHOOL
> PART III   BLUECOAT BOY
> PART IV   LIFE AFTER HOUSIE

My principal source has been *The Blue*, published at Christ's Hospital, Horsham, West Sussex. I have consulted every issue from July 1936 to December 1999, especially the historical material and personal reminiscences in the Old Blue section. To save space I have given only abbreviated references, eg Jun 1991 p.40. The date is that of publication, on the first right hand inside page, *not* that of the period described, eg 'Lent Term 1991', printed on the cover. I have omitted the Volume and Number details, eg, for June 1991, Volume CXIX Number 2. Where a source is not indicated the material or quotation comes from a private informant, whom I undertook not to identify in the text. All the other published books and other items I have consulted or mentioned are listed below. The place of publication is London unless otherwise indicated.

When a different version of a text published elsewhere appears in *The Christ's Hospital Book* I have usually quoted the latter. I have normally given the publication details of the edition of a book I consulted, which is not necessarily the earliest or the most recent version. Except, however, in the case of reference books there is likely to be no significant difference in the text.

ALLAN, GAT, *Christ's Hospital*, Blackie, 1937

ATKINSON, Gerald (ed), *A Book of Housey Slang*, Christ's Hospital Enterprises, 1994

BENNETT, Eric, and BLUNDEN, Edmund (eds), *The Christ's Hospital Book*, Hamish Hamilton, 1952

BLUNDEN, Edmund and others, *The Country Around Christ's Hospital* (pamphlet), Christ's Hospital Natural History Society, 1934

CARTER, Philip Youngman, *All I Did Was This,* Sexton Press, 1982

CHAPMAN, Hester, *The Last Tudor King*, Cape, 1961

COLERIDGE See HOLMES

COX, Homersham the Younger, *Who's Who in Kent, Surrey and Sussex, 1911,* Horace Cox, 1911

HOLMES, Richard, *Coleridge. Early Visions.* Hodder and Stoughton, 1989
- - *Coleridge. Darker Reflections,* HarperCollins, 1998

HULL, Robin, *A Schoolboy's War. Memories of Christ's Hospital during World War II,* Limited Edition Press, 633 Liverpool Road, Southport, 1994

HUNT, James Leigh, *Selected Essays*, Everyman, 1929

LAMB, Charles, 'Recollections of Christ's Hospital', Lamb's original essay on his old school, and 'Christ's Hospital Five-and-Thirty Years Ago', his subsequent, more critical account are in *The Complete Works of Charles Lamb in Prose and Verse*, Chatto and Windus, 1912. The second, but not the first, is in *The Essays of Elia and The Last Essays of Elia*, OUP, World's Classics, 1901

LASKI, Marghanita, *From Palm to Pine. Rudyard Kipling Abroad and at Home,* Sidgwick and Jackson, 1912

MORPURGO, JE, *Barnes Wallis* [Cited as Morpurgo: *Wallis*], Longman, 1972, Penguin, 1973 (The edition I quote.)
- - *Christ's Hospital* (A revised edition of GAT Allan's book) [Cited as Morpurgo], Town and County Books, 1984

MURRY, John Middleton, *Between Two Worlds. An Autobiography*, Cape, 1935

PLUMLEY, NM (ed), *Christ's Hospital in Photographs,* Christ's Hospital, 1985

SEAMAN, CME, *Christ's Hospital, The Last Years in London,* Ian Allan, 1977

WATTERS, Reginald (ed), *The Fortunate Blue-Coat Boy* (A new edition of the version published in 1789 under the title 'An Orphanotrophian'), Christ's Hospital, 1987

WOODWARD, EL, *The Age of Reform 1815-1870,* OUP, Oxford, 1938

YORKE, Malcolm, *Keith Vaughan. His Life and Work,* Constable, 1990

Other Christ's Hospital Publications Consulted

Christ's Hospital. A Short History (pamphlet), Christ's Hospital nd, in fact 1993

Christ's Hospital Girls School, Hertford (pamphlet). No place of publication, nd but c.1980

Christ's Hospital Founder's Day, Thursday 23 October 1987, Programme

Christ's Hospital, Annual Report and Accounts, 1996, 1997, 1998

Christ's Hospital Psalter (for use in Christ's Hospital chapel.) 1931

Supplementary Hymns (for use in Christ's Hospital chapel.) 1933

Christ's Hospital, Horsham Prospectus, untitled, nd but c.1980. Since revised and reissued.

Link, The Christ's Hospital Partnership Letter, 1990-93

Housey. The Christ's Hospital Newsletter, 1994 and continuing

Who's Blue, 1997, The Directory of Former Pupils of Christ's Hospital, Christ's Hospital Enterprises, 1998

Who's Blue Supplement, 1999, Christ's Hospital Enterprises, 1999

On West Gifts I principally used the document *The Charities of John and Frances West,* August 1991, prepared by Christ's Hospital.

I have also consulted numerous leaflets, Appeals letters and other minor publications, too numerous to be listed and often undated.

On freemen of the City, see *The Livery Companies of the City of London* (pamphlet), Corporation of London, 1997

I referred to the *Annual Register* for 1864 to 1868 inclusive on the Schools Inquiry Commission, though there are no specific references to Christ's Hospital, and the 1877 edition on the William Gibbs suicide and its aftermath.

Other Books Mentioned

ALCOTT, Louisa May, *Something to Do,* Ward Lock, 1873
ANSTEY, F [pseudonym], *Vice Versa,* Smith, Elder, 1882
ARNOLD, Matthew, *The Poems of Matthew Arnold 1840-67,* OUP, 1926
AUSTEN, Jane, *Pride and Prejudice,* 1813
BATES, Herbert Ernest, *The Greatest People in the World and Other Stories, by Flying Officer 'X',* Jonathan Cape, 1942
BAZELEY, Elsie Theodora, *Homer Lane and the Little Commonwealth,* Allen & Unwin, 1928
BEERBOHM, Max, *Zuleika Dobson,* Heinemann, 1911
BELL, Arthur Clive Heward, *Art,* Chatto & Windus, 1914
BENEDICT, Saint, *The Rule of St Benedict, c.545.* Most of the text can be found in *Documents of the Christian Church,* ed. Henry Bettenson, OUP, World's Classics, 1943
BENSON, Edward Frederick, *David Blaize,* Hodder & Stoughton, 1916
BETJEMAN, John, *Collected Poems,* John Murray, 1962
BILLANY, Dan and DOWIE, David, *The Cage,* Longmans, 1949
BLOOM, Ursula, *The Log of No Lady,* Chapman & Hall, 1940
BRIDGE, TC, *With Beatty in Jutland,* Collins, 1930
BRIDGES, Robert, *The Shorter Poems,* Clarendon Press, Oxford, 1931
BROOKE, Rupert, *The Complete Poems*, Sidgwick & Jackson, 1942
BROSTER, Dorothy Kathleen, *The Gleam in the North*, Heinemann, 1927
BRULLER, Jean: See VERCORS and CONNOLLY
BUTCHER, JS, *Greyfriars School. A Prospectus,* Cassell, 1965. See also: *The Magnet*
BUTTERFIELD, (Sir) Herbert, *The Whig Interpretation of History,* 1931, Bell, 1950
CALDER, Angus, *The People's War. Britain 1939-45,* Cape, 1969
CARROLL, Lewis (pseud.), *Alice in Wonderland* ie *Alice's Adventures in Wonderland,* 1865 and *Through the Looking Glass and What Alice Found There,* 1871

CHESSER, Eustace, *Love without Fear*, Signet Books, New York, 1949
CONNOLLY, Cyril, *Put Out the Light*, Macmillan, 1944 (Trans. from VERCORS, *Le Silence de la mer* (1943)
CORVO, BARON (pseud.), *Hadrian the Seventh*, Chatto & Windus, 1904
CURIE, Eve, *Journey among Warriors*, Heinemann, 1943
DASHWOOD, Edmée Elizabeth Monica: see DELAFIELD
DELAFIELD, EM (pseud.), *The Diary of a Provincial Lady*, Macmillan, 1930
DE QUINCEY, Thomas, *Confessions of an Opium Eater,* 1821, Ward Lock, The World Library, nd
DICKENS, Charles, *The Posthumous Papers of the Pickwick Club*, 1837
- - *Nicholas Nickleby*, 1838-9
- - *Oliver Twist*, 1837-8
DODGSON, Charles: see CARROLL
DOYLE, (Sir) Arthur Conan, *Sherlock Holmes. The Complete Long Stories,* John Murray, 1929
- - *The Complete Short Stories,* John Murray, 1931
DUNN, George E (ed.) *A Gilbert and Sullivan Dictionary,* Allen & Unwin, 1936
See also: GILBERT
ELIOT, Thomas Stearns, *The Idea of a Christian Society,* Faber, 1939
- - *Later Poems,* Faber, 1941
- - *Poems 1909-25*, Faber, 1942
FARRAR, Frederick William, *Eric or Little by Little*, 1858, Hamish Hamilton, 1972
FAULKNER, J Meade, *Moonfleet,* Edward Arnold, 1898
FEARON, Daniel Robert, *School Inspection,* 1876
FIRTH, JB (ed), *The Minstrelsy of Isis,* Chapman & Hall, 1908
FLECKER, HLO and MACNUTT, DS, *Complete Latin Course,* Book III, Longman, 1939
- - *Concise Latin Grammar*, Book IV, Longman, 1939
FLECKER, James Elroy, *Collected Poems,* Secker & Warburg, 1942
FLYING OFFICER 'X': See BATES
FORESTER, Cecil Scott, *Captain Hornblower, RN,* Michael Joseph, 1939
Consisting of: *The Happy Return,* 1938, *Flying Colours,* 1938, *A Ship of the Line,* 1938
FOWLER, Henry Watson, *A Dictionary of Modern English Usage*, Clarendon Press, Oxford, 1944

FRIEND, Dr Gerald Edward, *The Schoolboy. His Nutrition, Physical Development and Health*, Heffer, Cambridge, 1935
FRY, Roger Elliott, *Vision and Design,* Chatto & Windus, 1920
GATHORNE-HARDY, Jonathan, *The Public School Phenomenon,* Hodder, 1977
GIBBONS, Stella, *Cold Comfort Farm,* 1932, Penguin, 1938
GILBERT, (Sir) William Schwenk and SULLIVAN, (Sir) Arthur, *The Complete Plays of Gilbert and Sullivan,* Modern Library, New York c. 1947. See also: DUNN
GILL, Arthur Eric Rowton, *Autobiography,* Cape, 1940
GRAVES, Charles Patrick Ranke, *Londoner's Life,* Hutchinson, 1942
GREEN, Daniel, *Bunter by Appointment,* Hodder, 1987
GREENWOOD, Walter, *Love on the Dole,* Cape, 1933
- - *The Secret Kingdom*, Cape, 1938
- - *His Worship the Mayor*, Cape, 1943
GRIERSON, (Sir) Herbert and BULLOUGH, G (eds.), *The Oxford Book of Seventeenth Century Verse*, Clarendon Press, Oxford, 1934
GRIMM, JL and WH, *Grimm's Fairy Tales,* 1812-22
GROSSMITH, George and Weedon, *Diary of a Nobody,* JW Arrowsmith, Bristol, 1892, Penguin 1975
GUTHRIE, Thomas Anstey: See ANSTEY
HARDY, Thomas, *The Mayor of Casterbridge,* 1886
HENTY, George Alfred, *Out in the Pampas,* 1868
HERBERT, (Sir) Alan P, *The Secret Battle,* Methuen, 1919
HERRICK, Robert, *Poems,* 1648, Blackie, 1904
HOLTBY, Winifred, *South Riding,* Collins, 1936
HOUSMAN, Alfred Edward, *Collected Poems,* Cape, 1932
HUGHES, Thomas, *Tom Brown's Schooldays* (Originally published under pseud: 'An Old Boy'), 1857
HUNT, James Leigh, *Selected Essays,* Dent, 1828-55, Everyman's Library, 1929
IL'IN, M (Pseud. For LL'YA YAKOVLEVICH MARSHAK), *Moscow has a Plan. A Soviet Primer.* (Trans: CS Counts and NP Lodge), Cape, 1931
JOHN, Romilly, *Seventh Child. A Retrospect,* Heinemann, 1932
JONES, Jack, of Rhondda, *Unfinished Journey,* Hamish Hamilton, 1937
JOYCE, James, *Portrait of the Artist as a Young Man,* 1916
- - *Ulysses,* 1921

- - *Finnegan's Wake,* 1939

KEMPIS, Thomas A, *The Imitation of Christ,* c. 1418 in *The Consolation of Philosophy*, Modern Library, New York, 1943

KENNEDY, Benjamin Hall, *The Shorter Latin Primer,* Longman, 1931. Revised version of *Public School Latin Primer,* 1866

KIPLING, Rudyard, *The Jungle Books,* 1894-5
- - *Stalky and Co,* 1899

LANCASTER, (Sir) Osbert, *Pillar to Post*, John Murray, 1938

LANE, Homer, *Talks to Parents and Teachers*, Allen & Unwin, 1928. See also: BAZELEY

MACCARTHY, Fiona, *Eric Gill,* Faber, 1985

MACKENZIE, Compton, *The Four Winds of Love* (6 vols.), Rich & Cowan, 1937-45, Chatto & Windus, 1949

MACNUTT: See FLECKER

MAGNET, The. *The Magnet* was originally published by the Amalgamated Press weekly from 15 February 1908 to 18 May 1940. Facsimile reprints have been published by the Howard Baker Press since c.1969

MARLOW, Joyce, *The Uncrowned Queen of Ireland. The Life of 'Kitty' O'Shea,* Weidenfeld & Niclolson, 1975

MARSHALL, Bruce, *George Brown's Schooldays*, Constable, 1946

MARTINDALE, Cyril Charlie, *What are Saints? Fifteen Chapters in Sanctity,* Sheed and Ward, 1932

MILTON, John, *The English Poems of John Milton*, OUP, World's Classics, 1913

NEILL, Alexander Sutherland, *That Dreadful School,* Herbert Jenkins, 1937

NEWBOLT, (Sir) Henry, *Collected Poems 1897-1907*, Nelson, 1910

NICHOLS, Beverley, *Twenty-Five,* 1926, Penguin, 1936
- - *Cry Havoc!,* Cape, 1933

OFFICIAL PUBLICATIONS, *The Protection of Your Home against Air Raids,* (pamphlet), Her Majesty's Stationery Office, 1938

ORWELL, George (pseud.), *Collected Essays* (3 vols.), Penguin, 1970. The Essay *Boys Weeklies* is in Vol I pp.504-540

PATER, Walter Horatio, *The Renaissance,* Macmillan Pocket Edition, 1924

PEARSON, Angela, *The Whipping Club*, Ophelia Press, Paris, 1958

RANSOME, Arthur, *Swallows and Amazons,* Cape, 1930
- - *Winter Holiday*, Cape, 1933
- - *Pigeon Post,* Cape, 1936

-- *Secret Water*, Cape, 1939
-- *Great Northern?*, Cape 1947
READ, Miss (pseud.) *Village School*, Michael Joseph, 1955
  --(Numerous titles about 'Fairacre' and 'Thrush Green'.)
RINTELEN, Franz von, *The Dark Invader*, Lovat Dickson, 1933, Penguin, 1936
ROLFE, Frederick William: See CORVO
ROTHENSTEIN, (Sir) William, *Men and Memories*, Faber, 1934
ROWSE, AL, *A Cornish Childhood*, Cape, 1942
SACKVILLE-WEST, Vita (ie Victoria Mary Sackville West), *The Land*, Heinemann, 1926
  --*The Edwardians*, L & V Woolf, 1930
  -- *All Passion Spent*, L & V Woolf, 1931
SAINT, Dora Jessie: See: READ
SELLER, Walter Carruthers and YEATMAN, Robert Julian, *1066 and All That*, Methuen, 1930
SEWELL, Anna, *Black Beauty*, Jarrold & Sons, 1877
SHOOSMITH, Frederick H, *That Youth May Know. Sex Knowledge for Adolescents*, Harrap, 1935
SMITH, F Seymour, *An English Library*, National Book Council, 1943
SOUTHGATE, George W, *A Political History of Great Britain, 1783-1914*, Dent & Sons, 1940
STEVENSON, Robert Louis, *Treasure Island*, 1893
STOPES, Marie, *Married Love*, Putnam, 1940
STOWE, Harriet Beecher, *Uncle Tom's Cabin*, 1852, Signet Books, New English Library, 1966
SWIFT, Jonathan, *Gulliver's Travels*, 1726. OUP, 1919.
SYMONS, Alphonse Albert Jones, *The Quest for Corvo*, Cassell, 1934
TAWNEY, Richard Henry, *Equality*, Allen & Unwin, 1931
TENNYSON, Alfred (Lord), *Poems of Tennyson 1829-1868*, OUP, 1926
THACKERAY, Thomas Makepeace, *Vanity Fair*, 1848
THIRKELL, Angela: Numerous titles, not named individually in the text, 1932-52
THOMPSON, Flora, *Lark Rise to Candleford*, 1945, OUP, World's Classics, 1954
TROLLOPE, Anthony, *The Warden*, 1855
  -- *The Last Chronicle of Barset*, 1867

VANSITTART, Robert G (Lord), *Black Record,* Hamish Hamilton, 1941
VERCORS (pseud) *Le Silence de la Mer*, 1943. See also: CONNOLLY
WADDELL, Helen Jane, *The Wandering Scholars,* Constable, 1927
- - *Medieval Latin Lyrics,* Constable, 1929
- - *Peter Abelard,* Constable, 1935
WAUGH, Alec, *The Loom of Youth,* Grant Richards, 1917
- - *Public School Life,* Collins, 1922
WAUGH, Evelyn, *Decline and Fall,* Chapman and Hall, 1928
WEST, Victoria Mary Sackville: See SACKVILLE-WEST
WHEELER-BENNETT, (Sir) John W, *King George VI. His Life and Reign*, Macmillan, 1958
WILDE, Oscar, *Dr Profundis,* Original version Methuen, 1905. First complete version, Methuen, 1949
WILLIAMSON, Henry, *Dandelion Days,* 1922
WODEHOUSE, (Sir) Pelham Grenville, *The Great Sermon Handicap* in *The Inimitable Jeeves*, Hodder & Stoughton, 1933
WOODTHORPE, RC, *The Public School Murder,* Nicholson, 1932, Penguin, 1940
WOODWARD, (Sir) Ernest Llewellyn, *Short Journey (Autobiography)*, Faber, 1942
WOOLF, Virginia, *A Room of One's Own*, L & V Woolf, 1929
- - *Three Guineas*, Hogarth Press, 1938
YOUNG, Francis Brett, *My Brother Jonathan*, Heinemann, 1928
- - *Dr Bradley Remembers,* Heinemann, 1935

BOOKS BY NORMAN LONGMATE

MISCELLANEOUS

A SOCIALIST ANTHOLOGY (Edited, with Introduction)	Phoenix House, 1953
OXFORD TRIUMPHANT	Phoenix House, 1954
WRITING FOR THE BBC (Edited, with Introduction)	BBC Publications, 1966, 8th edition 1988

DETECTIVE STORIES

DEATH WON'T WASH	Cassell, 1957
A HEAD FOR DEATH	Cassell, 1958
STRIP DEATH NAKED	Cassell, 1959 Garland Publishing New York, 1983
VOTE FOR DEATH	Cassell, 1960
DEATH IN OFFICE	Robert Hale, 1961

CAREER BOOKS FOR BOYS

KEITH IN ELECTRICITY (a novel)	Chatto & Windus, 1961
ELECTRICITY SUPPLY	Sunday Times, 1961
ELECTRICITY AS A CAREER	Batsford, 1964

GENERAL SOCIAL HISTORY

KING CHOLERA, The Biography of a Disease	Hamish Hamilton, 1966
THE WATERDRINKERS, A History of Temperance	Hamish Hamilton, 1968
ALIVE AND WELL, Medicine and Public Health, 1830 to the Present Day	Penguin Education, 1970
THE WORKHOUSE	Temple Smith, 1974
MILESTONES IN WORKING CLASS HISTORY	BBC Publications, 1975
THE HUNGRY MILLS, The Story of the Lancashire Cotton Famine, 1861-5	Temple Smith, 1974
THE BREADSTEALERS, The Fight against the Corn Laws 1838-46	Temple Smith, 1984 St Martin's Press, New York, 1984

HISTORY OF THE SECOND WORLD WAR

HOW WE LIVED THEN, A History of Everyday Life during the Second World War	Hutchinson, 1971 Arrow Books (paperback), 1973
IF BRITAIN HAD FALLEN	BBC Publications and Hutchinson, 1972 Stein and Day New York, 1974 Arrow Books (paperback), 1975
THE GIs, The Americans in Britain 1942-1945	Hutchinson, 1975

AIR RAID,
The Bombing of Coventry, 1940

Hutchinson, 1976
Arrow Books
(paperback), 1978

David McKay
New York, 1978

WHEN WE WON THE WAR,
The Story of Victory in Europe, 1945

Hutchinson, 1977

THE DOODLEBUGS,
The Story of the Flying Bombs

Hutchinson, 1981
Arrow Books
(paperback), 1986

HITLER'S ROCKETS, The Story of the V-2s

Hutchinson, 1982

THE BOMBERS, The RAF Offensive against Germany

Hutchinson, 1983
Arrow Books
(paperback) 1988

THE HOME FRONT, An Anthology of Personal Experience 1938-1945 (Edited with a Preface)

Chatto & Windus, 1986

GENERAL MILITARY HISTORY

DEFENDING THE ISLAND,
From Caesar to the Armada

Hutchinson, 1989
Grafton Books
(paperback), 1990

ISLAND FORTRESS,
The Defence of Great Britain, 1603-1945

Hutchinson, 1991
Grafton Books
(paperback), 1993

CONTRIBUTOR TO

Jim Orford and Judith Harmwin, *Alcohol and the Family* Chapter on 'Alcohol and the Family in History'   Croom Helm, 1982

Jimmy Perry and David Croft, *Dad's Army* Historical Postscript 'The Army that never Fought a Battle'   Elm Tree Books, 1975

The Illustrated London News. Great Events of the 20th Century   Automobile Association, 1989

The Times Atlas of the Second World War   Times Books, 1989

SCRIPTS BY THE AUTHOR MENTIONED IN THE TEXT

BBC RADIO 4

The Night the Germans didn't Come. Transmitted 7 September 1971.
Bestseller. The First Book in the Universe. James Boswell's *Life of Samuel Johnson.* Transmitted 8 September 1974
The Weekend Warriors. Transmitted 19 November 1974.
Bestseller. The Little Book that Caused a War. (ie *Uncle Tom's Cabin.*) Transmitted 29 March 1978.
The Bombers. Transmitted 5 April 1978.
Good Old Greyfriars. Transmitted 22 September 1981.

YORKSHIRE TELEVISION

The episodes of the series *How We Used to Live* referred to, for which the author acted as historical adviser, were transmitted over the ITV network at various dates from Autumn 1975 to Spring 1988. The accompanying books were published at various dates from 1975 to 1981 by Macdonald Educational and from 1985 to 1987 by A & C Black Ltd.

INDEX

See 'Christ's Hospital' for entries related to the school.
See 'Newbury' for places and organisations in the town.
Individuals and businesses are listed separately, under entries of their own.

Abdication Crisis *see* Edward VIII
Abuse, Child 76 *see also* Christ's Hospital: bullying, corporal punishment, violence; Paedophilia; Sadism
Accents 346–7
Accountant, proposed career as 151, 358
Acton, Lord 576
Actors, Old Blue 306–7
Adams, Richard 98, 101, 253
Advertising 158, 219
Africa 6, 281
Africa, South 196, 494
Aircraft 343, 492–3, 510–11
Air Raids 364, 372, 373, 376, 389, 391–2, 394–5, 398, 487, 491–2
Aldershot Tattoo 88
Aldington, Richard 573
Alice in Wonderland 138, 328
Allan, GAT 249, 271, 330
Allen, Keith xii, 146, 291, 380–1, 389
Allingham, Margery 215,
Amberley (Sussex) 320
Americans *see* United States
Ammonia 147
Amusement Arcade 365
Andrews, Kathleeen ('Andy') 44

Andrews, WL 359
Arithmetic 143, 151
Armistead, HWC 347
Arnold, Matthew 569
Arnold, (Dr) Thomas 204
Art 219
Asia 307
Askey, Arthur 351
Attendance, School 113, 150, 157 *see also* Truancy
Attlee, (Lord) Clement 363
Aubourn (Lincolnshire) 2
Averill, CWS 246, 506
Avon, Lord *see* Eden

Bailiffs 51
Baker, Derek (LG) 639
Barnes, Thomas 169–70
Bates, HE 507
Bath (city) 21
Batteries (electric) 99, 82, 349
BBC 30, 107, 130, 252, 257, 316, 345, 346, 350, 354, 359 (& fn), 646
Beaven, PR 444
Beaverbrook, Lord 305
Bedford School 88
Beerbohm, Max 582, 586
Belk Society 140
Belk, France 134–41, 394, 548
Belk, Lorna 135–6
Belk, WR (Jack) 134, 136, 138
Bell, George (Bishop) 408–9

INDEX

Bell, George (Headmaster) 187–9
Berkshire 143, 148 *see also* Newbury
Betjeman, John 96, 219
Beveridge Report 521, 570
Bevin, Ernest 99, 551
Bible 161, 606
Blackberrying 101
Blackout 354, 375–6
Blamire Brown, C 199, 344–5, 558, 611, 615
Blandfords, Newbury 370
Blankets, inadequacy of 100, 289
Blitz *see* Air Raids
Blundells (school) 189
Blunden, Edmund 169, 216, 250, 252–3, 261,
Bombers, The 206, 409fn, 513
Bonfire Night 124, 191–2, 279–80
Boswell, James 102
Bournemouth 108, 149
Boyer, James 170, 172
Bradfield 159
Bradshaw, Captain 42
Brangwyn, Sir Frank 416
Brighton (Sussex) 207, 320, 364–5, 600
'Brother T' 76
Brown, Wilfrid 251
Browne, Charles E 203
Bruges (Belgium) 416
Bué, Henri 207
Buck AH 345, 538–9
Burleigh, DH 451
Burns, Alderman 47
Burt, Cyril 199
Butterfield, (Sir) Herbert 576
Butterfield, William 110

Cadbury's 158–9
Cadd, Horace 39, 55
Cambridge 114, 174, 187, 352, 359, 385, 445, 546
Cambridge, Duke of 183–4, 187, 192
Camp Close 64–6, 83, 89, 92, 93, 98, 122, 123, 124, 160, 491
Camp Hopsons (Newbury) 83–4, 161
Canada & Canadians xii, 3, 219, 615, 616
Candles 99, 349
Carden, Sir Freddie 28, 42, 57, 81, 137
Carey, Lionel M 426, 442, 552
Carnavon, Earl of 26, 28, 42, 81
Cars 100, 125, 134, 148, 207, 365
Carter, Philip Youngman 202, 211, 214, 217
Carter, Sydney 251, 294–5
Casual Ward *see* Workhouse, Newbury
Censorship (of plays and films) 140, 280
Ceylon (now Sri Lanka) 157, 281
Chalet School, The 327
Chamberlain, Neville 354–7, 363, 374
Charterhouse 183
Cheque book 56
Cheque 81
Cherniavsky, Michael T 621–5, 639
Chichester, Bishop of *see* Bell, George
Chocolate 95, 276 *see also* Cadbury's, Mars Bars
Choirboys 88
Christ, George 360
Christie, Agatha 88
Christmas 55, 80, 82, 86, 100, 119, 127 134, 139, 254, 289, 406

Christ's Hospital ix–xii
  academic standards 182, 639–41
  Air Training Corps 398, 485, 506–14, 581
  Architecture 197, 199, 228–9, 241–3, 565–7, 634–8, 641
  Arts Centre 628
  beds and bed-making 176, 197, 236, 238–9, 630
  Blue, The 187ff
  Bonfast 192, 284
  bullying 377–8, 454–66
  careers (future) of pupils 358–61
  Chapel 200, 334, 402–416, 550, 595, 626–7, 641
  Christian Union 410–11
  class sizes 246
  co-education 524, 633–6,
  cold baths 323, 443
  Community Service Volunteers 625
  corporal punishment 189, 201–3, 216, 422–30, 626
  curriculum 358
    Art School 206, 214–5, 218, 249–50 Divinity 413 English 378–9, 487–8, 523–4, 526, 535–7, 575 Geography 507, 523 German 246, 423, 489, 520 History 442, 521, 523, 534, 540–7 Latin 202, 246, 345, 353, 517–9, 536, 537 Manual School 203–4, 246 Metalwork 248, Science 203, 449, 486, 519–20 Woodwork 246–8, Printing 249
  Debating Society 220, 356, 378, 482, 500, 522, 598–9
  Dinner Parade *see* Parades

  discipline 190, 201, 216, 418–30
  drill (military) 178–9, 185, 189
  drill (punishment) 420–2
  expulsions 201, 471–2
  Farm, Science 242, 262–4, 385
  Field Day 320, 368–9, 483–4, 625
  fights 456
  film showings 280–2, 447
  fire brigade 187–8
  Fire Guard 553–5
  food 172, 175–8, 187, 203, 208–10, 216, 269, 270–9, 285, 330, 440–1, 632–3 wartime 395–8, 479, 484.
  footwear 208–9, 267, 613
  funding 183, 191, 628–33, 637 *see also* West Gifts
  girls' school 169, 184–5, 196, 210, 400, 581, 628, *see also* co-education
  Grecians 175, 186, 189, 199, 230, 245–6, 594–5, 627–8, 632, 636–9
  headmasters: *see* Baker, Bell, Flecker, Fyffe, Newsome, Poulton, Seaman, Upcott,
  health care: 204–5, 208, 210–11, 217, 329–41, 498 *see also* matrons, nose-blowing,
  Health Rules see health care
  hobbies & leisure 234–5, 266, 625
  holidays 188
  Horsham, move to 182, 188–93, 199
  House plays 300–7
  house system 198, 256–7, 432–3, 624–6
  hymns 221–2, 231, 405, 414
  JTC 450, 483
  lavatories 176, 235, 239–41, 279, 332, 376, 625
  Leaving Service 326, 605–6

Christ's Hospital cont.
Library 230, 525, 534, 540, 641 Dominions Library 220
matrons 199, 236
masters 198, 352, 399, 451–2, 552
see also Averill, Armistead, Beaven, Blamire Brown, Browne, Buck, Bué, Carey, Edwards, Featherstonehaugh, Hallows, Harrup, Haslehust, Haynes, Heywood, Hornsby, Hyde, Johns, Kelsey, Kent, Kirby, Lang, Macklin, Macnutt, Malins, Massen, Moore, Mortimer Booth, Parkin, Rider, Rigby, Roberts, Sergent, Sills, Tidmarsh, Usherwood, Waddams, Wallis, Warneford-Brown, Woodthorpe
Modern Literature Society 216
monitors 271, 443, 478, 490, 499–500, 537–8, 578, 591
Museum 636
music at 185, 218, 242, 250–2, 404–7
Newgate Street 165–193, 394
newspapers 283
nicknames 324, 451–2
nose-blowing 211, 238, 332–3
Old Blues 174, 628–33
Old Blues Day 320–1
OTC 215, 324, 343, 365–70, 381, 387, 391, 398, 483–5
Outlook, The 216, 218, 473, 482, 488–9
paintings 415–6
parades 238–9, 241, 258, 375, 638 Dinner Parade 185, 257, 627
parents 174, 176, 205, 253–5, 268–9, 279, 461, 503, 517
Peele A house 202, 217, 233–6, 256, 357
see also Sergent, Noel
prize-giving 325–6
Public Service Corps 625
Quiet Room 622
Royal Mathematical School 197, 229
St. Matthew's Day 176
Scouts 242, 391, 625
sex 467–480
sex education 446–7, 467–9
settles 300, 331, 420
sewing 267–8
Sharpenhurst 260–1
shoe-cleaning 267, 268
slang 192–3, 201, 207–8, 272–3, 278, 455, 503–4, 616
smoking 268, 335
social background of pupils 173, 183, 253–4, 288, 630–2
Speech Day 187–8, 233, 320–1, 581
sport: 258–9, 262, 265–6, 357, 624, 635 athletics, 187, 243, cricket 182, 186, 198, 243, 311–18, 498 gymnastics 259, football 182, 186, 198, 236, 244 rugger 243–4, 258, 264–5, 442–3, running 260–1, 285, steeplechase 298–9, swimming 187, 198, 318–9, 498
suicides 188–9, 295–6
swabs 490, 591, 624
Swizzling Sunday 283
Sundays at Newgate Street 177–8 *see also* CH: Chapel
theatrical productions 218, 300 *see also* House Plays
Trades 177, 257, 277
trunks 284
uniform 167, 171, 173, 178–9, 183–7, 192, 197, 229–233, 248, 265, 267–8, 324, 418, 483, 501, 593, 621, 638–1

Christ's Hospital cont.
violence 192, 201–3, 208, 284, 400,
washing 176, 197, 233
Whole Holiday 320, 386
women teachers 496–8, 500
World War I 209–211
World War II 330–1, 580–1
  air–raid shelter 376–7 blackout 375–6, Blitz, 391–2, 394 chapel 413, eight-day week 376 farming 579, 582 flying-bombs over 617–619 619 food 395–8 German plane 385–6, Home Guard 384–5, 387–8 Jokes 379 leaf-gathering 499 Phoney war 377 Old Blue casualties 392–3, 400–1, 498, 513–4, VE Day 619–20 *see also* Christ's Hospital: ATC, OTC; Prisoners of War
1930 Society 220, 343, 521
  see also Ghosts, Homosexuality, Swearing

Church of England 74, 110, 146 *see also* Christ's Hospital: Chapel; Newbury: Churches
Church Times 73
Cigarettes 81, 421
Cinema *see* Film
City of Benares 393
City of London *see* London
Class divide 15, 95–8, 72–3, 144fn, 160, 253, 482, 492
Clothes 83–4 *see also* CH: footwear, uniform
Coach (motor) 106, 149
Cobbett, William 27, 102
Cochran, Charles B 137
Cochrane, Rev WCM 404–5
Coffee 272
Coleridge, Samuel Taylor 169–173, 242, 412, 606, 626
Collins, Mr 149
Common Wealth party 597
Communists 76, 122, 596
Confirmation 407–9
Conscription 362–3, 611
Contraception 469
Cooper, Canon 146
Copyright 403
Cornwall 21, 103
Coronation (1937) 311
Coronation (1953) 104
Council for Education in World Citizenship 533
Council housing 85 *see also* Camp Close
Creed, AL 506
Crime 93, 144–5
Crime novels 215
Cunningham, George 520–1
Curwood, Mrs 118–20
Cycle shed 162
Cycling 371, 389, 466, 579, 593–4

Daily Express 124, 305
Daily Herald 215
Daily Sketch 357
Daily Worker 488
Dambusters, The 206, 513
Dancing 134 *see also* Belk, France
Dark Invader, The 435
Dartington Hall 249
Davies, AH 357, 364
Davis, Sir Colin 251
D Day 550, 557
Deadly Nightshade 107
Dean's, Newbury 84
Deaths 8, 93–4, 255, 446
Defending the Island 551
Defoe, Daniel 27
Delafield, EM 96
Denmark 383
Dental treatment 90–1, 340–1

Detective stories *see* Crime novels
Dickens, Charles 15, 58, 170, 357, 487, 528
Diptheria 94
Disability 444–5
Donnington Castle 291
Doodlebugs, The 616fn *see also* flying-bombs
Douglas, Keith 253
Drunkenness 93 *see also* Rokeby Arms
Dunkirk 386
Duraglit 366

Eden, Sir Anthony 551, 621
Education: elementary: *see* Newbury: Speenhamland School, St John's Infants School, St Nicholas School; private 45–6; secondary: *see* Christ's Hospital; Newbury: High School, St Bartholomew's; *see also* Attendance, Examinations; Longmate, Norman; Spelling, Streaming
Edward VIII 142, 220, 283
Edwards, ACW 199fn, 360, 521
Electricity 54, 68, 112, 125, 317, 343, 348–50
Ellis, Havelock 573
Empire, British 6
Empire Day 116
Evacuation 373–4, 378, 380
Evening Gazette (Reading) 149–50, 152, 157, 159, 161, 285
Examinations: Scholarship 114–5, 143, 147–9, 156–7, 162, School Certificate 486 516–531, 534, Higher Certificate 516, Oxford entrance 581–90

Fearon, Daniel Robert 181–2
Feathersthonehaugh, A 399–400
Film 33–4, 95, 100, 128, 138, 279–82, 371
Fireworks 123 *see also* Bonfire Night
Flecker, HLO 219–21, 304, 308, 358, 360, 387–8, 393, 404, 408, 470–3, 497–8, 517, 553, 612, 626, 628
Flying-bombs 616 *see also* Christ's Hospital: World War II
Food 84, 86, 99, 113–4, 348 *see also* CH: food
Foot, Dingle (MP) 522
Football 116, 160 *see also* CH: sport
Forester, CS 252
Formby, George 350
Fountain pen 87
Foxton, JHT 382, 400–1
France 147, 386–7, 447, 521 *see also* Sergent, Noel
Friend, Dr GA 271 *see also* CH, Health Care
Funerals *see* Death
Fyfe (Sir) William Hamilton 214–17, 219, 253

Games 104, 107–8, 286, 290 *see also* CH: sport
Gas, domestic 68, 99, 134
Gas masks 364, 373, 559
Gatwick 510
Geography 143, 151
George V, King 42, 142, 148
Germany 121, 147, 159, 302–3, 435–6, 577 *see also* World War II
Ghosts 340, 377
Gibbon, Edward 552
Gibbs, William 188–9

Girl Guides 347
GIs, The 523, 596
Glock, (Sir) William 251
Gloucester, Duke of 539
Gramophone 443, 494
Grimsby (Lincolnshire) 2, 5
Green, Daniel 274
Greene, Sir Hugh 252
Greenham Common 29, 35, 36, 100, 291, 380
Greyfriars School *see also Magnet, The* 145, 267, 274, 279, 294–5, 352, 381, 430, 437–8
Guinness 89

Haig Brown (Dr) 183
Hallows, MRD 451
Hansford, John T 331
Hardy, Thomas 13
Harley, T Rutherford 153
Harris, Bryan xii
Harvie, D Elizabeth 497, 500, 595
Haslehust, Fred 353–7, 362–3, 408, 444, 497
Hatten 324, 343, 382
Hay, Will 282
Haynes, PR 503
Head for Death, A 215
Health care 32, 55–6, 94, 334
  funding of 89–90, s*ee also* CH: health care; Dental Treatment; Vaccination
Hearts of Oak 117
Henty, GA 106
Herbert, AP (Sir Alan) 573
Herring, John 123, 150, 160
  Hertford, *see* Christ's Hospital girls school
Herzig, Christopher xii, 538
Highclere Castle 93 *see also* Carnavon, Earl of
Hitler 371–2 see also Germany, World War II

HMV 158
Holland 521
Holton (Somerset) 11–14, 20, 27 *see also* Wincanton
Home Guard, 42, 147, 384, 471, 548–61, 616
Homosexuality 469–80, 536–7, 586, 591
Honours Board 162
Hood, Miss 58–9
Horlicks 160
Hornsby, HR 432
Horris Hill Prep School 253
Horse–racing 103
Hospital Fund 89–90
House, Miss Fanny 142, 145, 158
Housing 85, 125 *see also* Longmate, Norman: homes
How We Lived Then 274, 374, 385, 397fn, 399fn, 494
How We Used to Live 13
Hungry Mills, The 521
Hull, Robin xii–xiii, 268, 275, 278, 296, 298, 319, 335, 407–8, 422, 424, 440, 456–7, 468, 472, 478
Hunt, Leigh 169–70, 487, 624
Hyde, 'Dido' 382, 399

Ice cream 81, 106, 276
If Britain Had Fallen 385
Ilness *see* Health care
In Which We Serve 338
Inch's (drapers) 83
India 157
Inoculation 210–1
Insurance man 85–6, 146
Irving, Richard 306
Island Fortress 117fn, 385, 551
Isle of Wight 347–8
Italy 124, 131, 494

Jack Hotel, Newbury 39, 55, 56, 80

Japan 149, 444, 599
Jews 355, 356, 407, 413, 489
John Bull 135
Johns, Rev WC 407–8, 467
Johnson, Dr Samuel 102
Journalism 174, 252, 359 *see also* Longmate, Norman
Journey's End 366
Just William 88, 107, 123
'Kappa' *see* Sills
Keats, John 487
Keble College, Oxford 72, 585
Keith, author's friend, *see* Allen
Kettering (Northamptonshire) 5, 6, 106, 107
Keys, Ivor 251, 323
Khula Krush 325
Kimber, Alderman Elsie 79
Kipling, Rudyard 328, 468
Kirby, Cecil F 449–51, 468
Kirk, Kenneth 72

Labour Party 142, 482 *see also* Longmate, Norman
Lamb, Charles 169–71, 173, 242, 274–5, 289, 340, 396
Lambert, Constance 216–7, 251,
Lambourn 103
Lang Dr CS 404–5
Lark Rise to Candleford 14
Lashley, Doris 84
Lavatory 99, 100, Lavatory paper 289
Lawrance, JCD 281, 285–6, 298, 314, 321–4, 326, 353, 382, 419, 458, 489
Leaney, TS 248
Levin, Bernard 251, 306, 359, 423
Lincolnshire, Longmate connection with 1–5
Lipscomb, Freda *see* Longmate, Freda

London 102, 156, 159, 227, 386, 392, 447, 563, 599–601
London, City of 159, 165ff, freemen of the City 168
London Symphony Orchestra 310
Longmate coat of arms 3–4
Longmate name, origin and history 2–3
Longmate, Ada 2
Longmate, Arthur Gordon 23, 36, 45–7, 57, 63, 68–70, 72–3, 79, 86, 100, 105, 158, 291–2, 347–9, 370, 372, 374, 380, 383, 389, 409–10, 482, 494
Longmate, Barak (d. 1793) 3
Longmate, Barak (d.1836) 3
Longmate, Elizabeth 2, 5
Longmate, Ernest, early life 2, 4–5, amateur dramatics 6, 39, 56, 139 marriage to Ellen Keep 6–8, marriage to Margaret Ellen Rowden 22–24, 56, service in first world war 36, fatherhood 36 work as photographer 27, 30, 35, 39–44, 52, 81, 347, 370–4, 380 financial difficulties 50–53, 56–7, 61–2, 79–82 in second world war 370, 373–4, 380, 482, 491 & NRL 161, 227, 279, 289, 292–3, 328, 409, 476, 517, 581, 584, 611 death 86, 93
Longmate, Freda Elsie xi, 7, 36, 45, 51, 55–7, 63, 71, 74, 83, 99, 105, 123, 125, 291, 347, 370, 372–4, 482, 493–4
Longmate, Frederick (d.1895) 2
Longmate, Frederick (d.1914) 1–2, 5
Longmate, Harriet 2
Longmate, Jack 2, 6

Longmate, James 3
Longmate, Leslie xii, 3
Longmate, Margaret Ellen,
  early life 9–15, 21, marriage 22–4 life in Newbury 27, 35, 46, 51, 54–6, 62, 70, 71, 73–4, 79–83, 86–90, 95, 99, 121, 139, 142, 147, 149, 158, 160, 269, 271, 288–90, 293, 350–1, 356, 373, 380, 383, 409–10, 482, 488, 492, 529, 611
  see also: Holton, Wincanton
Longmate, Mary 1
Longmate, Maud 2, 5, 6, 105–8, 356, 373

Longmate, Norman Richard
  46ff birth 46; infancy 47–9; homes 48, 53, 48–9, 53–55, 62–3, 63–8 *see also* Camp Close; church-going 73–4, 402–416; education: *see* Newbury: Speenhamland School, St John's School, St Nicholas School, & Christ's Hospital; wins scholarship 149–51; admission to CH 227–9, unhappiness at CH 292–5, runs away from CH 296–8, effect of bullying at school 457–60, 466, reading 327–8, 525, 573–6, 588–90, 591 career aspirations 151, 358, 380; & science 380–1, 486 juvenile authorship 377, 379, 486–8, 508–10 & poetry 325, 536 literary earnings 117, 159 career as journalist and critic 104–5, 117–8, 157fn, 356, 358, 645 at the Electricity Council 645, at the BBC 645–6 authorship, books 385, 513, 646–9 authorship, radio programmes 513 politics 96–7, 121–5, 362–4, 377, 482, 524, 570, 595–7 prospective Labour candidate 78, 162, 645 education in history 151, 344, 486, 488, 521, 531, 540–7, 579–80 education in English 486–8, 526–9 School Certificate 516–30, 534 Oxford entrance 581–90 interest in RAF 506–14, 599 Home Guard service 549–61 army service 266, 560–1, 599–600, 611–4 & girls 140–1, 480, 548 interest in art 563–5, views on education 567–73 on Asian culture 307, on nationalisation 68, on local government 68, marriage 7, daughter ix, 14, 568
  see also books and broadcasts, by title

Longmate, Peggy Ruth ix, 46–8, 52, 57, 63, 74, 78, 82, 84, 90, 105, 107–8, 119, 138, 150, 152, 157–8, 160, 290–1, 347, 351, 372, 374, 485–6, 493
Longmate, Proudl(e)y 1
Longmate, Rebekah 1
Loom of Youth, The 474
Lord of the Rings, The 138
Luckett, Miss 71
Luker, Esther 33, 135–6
Lysol antiseptic 90

MacDonald, Ramsay 121–22
Macklin, W Roy 283, 324–5, 429, 486–7, 535–6, 553, 559, 574–5, 577
Macnutt, Derrick S 426–30, 457, 517–9, 534, 536, 599
Magdalen College 88
Magee, Bryan 251
Magic lantern 95, 126

Magnet, The 69, 128–133, 153, 158, 264, 311, 324, 327, 553 *see also* Greyfriars
Maids *see* Servants
Maine, (Sir) Henry 242
Malins, EG 451
Marble Arch (London) 99
Marland, Michael 306
Marlborough (College) 182, 189, 220, 426
Marple, Miss 88
Mars Bars 276
Martin & Chillingworth garage (Newbury) 70, 148
Martin, Eric 5–6
Martin, Walter 5
Massen, JEM 423, 599
Masterman, Sir John 252
Merry Wives of Windsor, The 427
Middleton 242
Milk (free school) 114
Milkman 85, 99
Minstrel Boy, The 117
Money, Walter 26, 27
Montagu, Mrs Elizabeth 101–2
Montgomery, Field Marshal 615
Moonfleet 324
Moore, 'Plum' 202
Morpurgo, Prof JE 193, 546–7
Mortimer Booth, TK 507, 523, 531
Mothers' Union 89, 95, 149
Motor cycles 207
Munich Crisis 354–6
Murry, John Middleton 191 & fn, 192, 288–9

Newbury, (Berkshire) 25–36, Academy of Dance *see* Belk, France, Amateur Dramatic Society 46, Bookshop, second-hand 589–90, Churches: St John's 72–5, 111, St George's 75, St Nicholas 79, 145, 156 City Park 144 City, the 116 Conservative Club 124 Corn Exchange 26, 79, 88, 138, 140–2, 493 Corporation 63, 65, 68, 346 Council Education Committee 160, 285 District Hospital 89 Library xii, 30–1 Market Day 118 Mayor's Benevolent Fund 55 Mayor's Procession 289–90 Museum xii, 146–7 *Newbury Weekly News* xii, 34–6, 44, 109, 134–5, 137–8, 152, 156, 162, 388 Old Blues Association 155 Race Course 31, 80 Rotary Club 84 schools 33, 71 109–10 Girls' High School 33, 115, 151–2, 160, 290, St Bartholomew's Grammar School 115, 151–3, 290, St Johns Infants xii, 71–2, St Nicholas xii, 84, 95, 109–120, 143, 152, 161–2 Speenhamland 57–9 Skating Rink 42 Victoria Park 79, 147 *see also* Camp Close, Film, Greenham, Health, Jack Hotel, Martin & Chillingworth Garage, Newtown, Pantomime, Railways, Wash Common, World War I, World War II, Workhouses

News of the World 413
Newsome, Dr David H 627–8
Newtown Common 101
Newtown Hill 84, 94, 107, 113, 123, 150
Nichols, Beverley ix, 573–4
Night blindness 554
'Nitty Norah' 59

Nonconformists 110, 146, 365
Northampton 106
Norway 383, 521
Nurse Snowy 46

Observer 426, 429
O'Shea, Kitty 7–8
Oil 157
Opera (Gilbert & Sullivan) 308–9, 434
Opera glasses 87
Orwell, George 131
Oxford 72, 114, 151, 205, 245, 346, 352, 353, 359, 361, 366, 378, 385, 434, 473, 546, 574, 584–90, 599, 621, 639, 641

Paedophilia 319, 474–5
Palmer, Arthur Gray 47, 50
Pantomime 134–41, 290, 548
Parkin, CJW 302
Parnell, Kitty, see O'Shea
Parties 95
Pepys, Samuel 27, 322
Philpotts, Eden 302
Phobias 466, 554–5
Photography 370–1 *see also* Longmate, Ernest
Picture Post 570
Pitman, RP (Bob) xii, 232–3, 236, 238, 251, 280, 302, 303, 305, 357, 363, 407–8, 410, 420, 438, 476, 489, 500, 522, 537–8, 574, 578, 581, 599, 646
Pocket money 347, 351
Poets, Old Blue 252
Politics, British 32, 124–5 *see also* Longmate, Norman; World War II
Poor Law 60–2
Port wine 292, 445
Post Office 80
Poulton, Richard C 626
Poverty 50–7, 60–3, 81–5, 95, 120, 125–6, 147 *see also* Unemployment, Workhouses
Prewetts 330
Prison 171
Prisoners of War 500–1, 503
Public houses 156, 404 *see* Rokeby Arms, Swan Inn
Public School Life 474
Public School Murder, The 215
Puppets 310
Pyke, George Frederick 109, 112–3, 116–7, 143–5, 149–50, 156, 161–2, 276, 632
Pylon Poets 350

Quakers *see* Nonconformists
Queen Mary 158
Quick, Rev EK 412

Race 88, 281
Radio *see* Wireless
Radio Anti-Kappa 616
Radio Times 322
Railways 19, 102–4, 193, 343
Randall, Rev James 110
Ransome, Arthur 327–8, 380–1
Ratcliffe, Mr (Ratty) *see* Milkman
Rationing 380, 393, 396, 399, 482, 483, 492, 501
Rattenbury-Stonor case 144–5
Reading (Berkshire) 26, 70, 104, 145, 149, 156, 321, 328
Read, Miss 14
Real Dad's Army, The 385, 549, 559
Rent 84–5
Richards, Frank *see Magnet, The* & Greyfriars
Richmond (Surrey) 7–8
Rider, Arthur 246, 448,
Rifles 366
Rigby, Harold A 199, 206,

218, 249
Righton, JW 28, 39–40, 42
Ringwood (Hampshire) 8, 22, 27
Rintelen, Franz von 435–6
Roberts, Hon DS 382, 488–9, 500, 507, 521, 531, 539–47, 562–74, 576, 581–5, 611
Robeson, Paul 281
Rokeby Arms 63, 93, 292
Roman Catholic Church 74
Roman Catholics 413
Rose, John Septimus 154–5
Rotary Club *see* Newbury
Rowden, Henry 10, 11
Rowden, Margaret Ellen *see* Longmate, ME
Rowden, Tom 351–2
Rowse, AL 479
Royal Air Force 398, 400–1, 493, 506–7, 534 *see also* Aircraft; Air Raids; Christ's Hospital, ATC;
Royal Family 88, 177 *see also* Cambridge, Duke of, Gloucester, Duke of
Rugby School 200, 249, 467
Russia 482, 525

Sackville-West, Vita 583
Sadie (Crothall, née Lawrence) 494
Sadism 323, 424–30
Sanders of the River 6
Sandleford Priory 63, 281
Saving 85–6, 161
School Reports 162
School Uniform 160–1 *see also* Christ's Hospital: uniform
Schools: *see* Christ's Hospital; Newbury
Scotland 344
Scroggs, Peter xii, 305, 306, 308, 552–3, 583

Seaman, George (CME) 623, 626
Seed, R (Gaffer) 263–4, 331, 527
Sergent, Noel (Sam) 240, 242–4, 257, 271, 275, 283, 298, 302, 303, 328, 339, 345, 357, 364, 377, 379, 383, 386, 396, 400, 402, 408, 412, 420, 423–4, 433–441, 476, 480, 490–1, 513, 522–3, 549, 578, 595
Sergent, Mrs 264, 278–9,
Servants 51, 88, 267, 279, 478, 482
Sex 98, 144, 215, 217–8, 282, 323, 438–9, 491–2 *see also* Christ's Hospital: sex; Homosexuality; Sadism
Sharwood Smith, Edward 33
Shaw, (Sir) Eyre Massey 187–8
Shaw, George Bernard 307
Sherborne 474
Shortsightedness 559
Sills, Harold Darlington (Kappa) 432, 445–8, 486, 533
Silver Jubilee 121–3, 142
Silvester, Victor 350, 497
Skimmity ride 13
Slaughterhouse 43–4
Smollett, Tobias 191
Socialism 96, 215, 350
Sootybob Day 116
Southgate, GW 523
Spackman, Mrs 134, 292
Speen Halt 103
Speenhamland 57
Spelling 142–3
Stargroves 93 *see also* Carden, Freddie
Stenning, Rev E 72, 161
Stockcross 80
Stonor, George 144

Stoodley, John 79, 83, 157, 160
Strawberries 99
Streaming 115
Stretton, Tom C 340–1
Strip Death Naked 399
Study Groups 522
Swan Inn 101
Swearing 94, 98, 145, 351, 437–8
Sweetman, George 16–18, 20
Sweets 123, 501

Target for Tonight 507, 510
Tea 93, 99, 272, 292
Teachers *see*: Christ's Hospital: Masters
Television 305, 583
Temperance Movement 18, 93
Ten shilling note 99, 157
Thackeray, William Makepeace 487, 528
Thames Valley Bus Company 70
Thirkell, Angela 15
Thompson, Flora 14
Tidmarsh, Lionel W 423
Tom Brown's Schooldays 162, 357, 458–9, 461, 464
Toothpaste 161
Toys 82, 126–8 *see also* Games
Travers, Ben 304, 306
Treasure Island 69–70
Trek, The Great *see* CH: Horsham, move to
Trethowan, (Sir) Ian 345, 359–60
Tristam Shandy 191
Trolloppe, Anthony 15
Trowell, Brian 251
Truancy 113
Trunks 161 *see also* CH: trunks
Turner, John C 498–9

Tufnail, James 29, 30, 33–4, 42, 134, 158
Twickenham (Middlesex) 156
Typing 346 *see also* Spackman, Mrs

Unemployment 62, 78–80, 122, 125 *see also* Longmate, Ernest; Poverty
United States 10, 520–2, 596
University 551, 622 *see also* Cambridge; Oxford; Worcester College, Oxford
Upcott, Rev Dr AW 196, 200–1, 209, 211, 220, 416
Usher, Sergeant 259–60, 331–2, 420–2
Usherwood, Tom S 204

Vaccination 159–160 *see also* Innoculation
Vacuum cleaners 80
Vaughan, Keith 217–9, 626
Ventor *see* Isle of Wight
Verrio, Antonio painting 249
Vice Versa 201
Vickers (Aviation) 343

Waddams, LT 425
Wagner, FW 451
Wallis, (Sir) Barnes N 204–6, 208, 408, 632
Warneford-Brown, Rev Michael 378–9, 391, 488, 523
Warwick, Mr 100, 148–9
Wash Common, Newbury 95
Washing up 150, 502
Waterdrinkers, The 93, 270–1
Water supply 54, 107
Watership Down 101
Waugh, Alec 474, 582, 589
Weapons, toy 127–8, real 366–7
Webb, Aston 416

Weekend Warriors, The 552fn
West Gifts xii, 155, 156, 165, 183, 185, 227, 251, 632
Westerman, Percy 324
Westminster Choir School 378
Whisky 101
White, Rev LH 451
Whitehead, (Rev) Roger 304–5
Whittington, Dick 156, 290
Wilberforce, (Bishop) Samuel 72
Wilde, Oscar 586, 588
Wilding, Michael 306
Wincanton (Somerset) 11, 15–20, 27
Wine 334
Wireless 100, 128, 142, 158, 252, 266, 283, 343, 349–50, 374, 383, 386, 447, 494, 504, 616, 622
With Beatty in Jutland 69
Women: education 156, *see also* Luker, Esther employment 86–8, 123, employment in wartime 493–6, male courtesy to 436, rights 33, 575 in trousers 324 *see also* Newbury: Girls' High School; Christ's Hospital: women teachers
Woodthorpe, RC 215
Woodward, EL 577
Woolworths 126, 543
Worcester College, Oxford 581, 586, 588, 589
Workhouses: 178, 270, 422 Andover 13, 92 Newbury 17, 27, 33, 63, 92–3, 160, Wincanton 17–18
Workhouse, The 270
World War I 88, 147, 354, 435 in Newbury 35–6
World War II: drift to war 127, 147, 159, 343, 354–6, 362–4, 371–2 Phoney War 377, 380 in Newbury 96–7, 372–4, 380, 388–90, 394, 491–2 Savings 501–2 *see also* Air Raids; Blackout; Evacuation; Christ's Hospital: World War II; Gas Masks; Home Guard; Rationing; Women
Worthing (W Sussex) 320, 488, 616
Wristwatch 161–2
Wyatt, James 101
Wyllie, Dr 55, 56

Yates, Ivan 305, 306, 308, 363, 429
Yellow Sands see Philpotts, Eden
Young Farmers Club 581

Zuleika Dobson 479–80, 582